ART?

ART?

NO THING!

analogies between art, science and philosophy

Fré Ilgen

edited by
Megan Craig

PRO Foundation
Artists.Bookworks
2004

To Charles Biederman, Kenji Ekuan, Fons Elders,

Michael Kidner, Donald Kuspit and Dietrich Mahlow,

as I learned so much from them.

To my parents, to Pim and Anna, to Jacqueline for their neverending support.

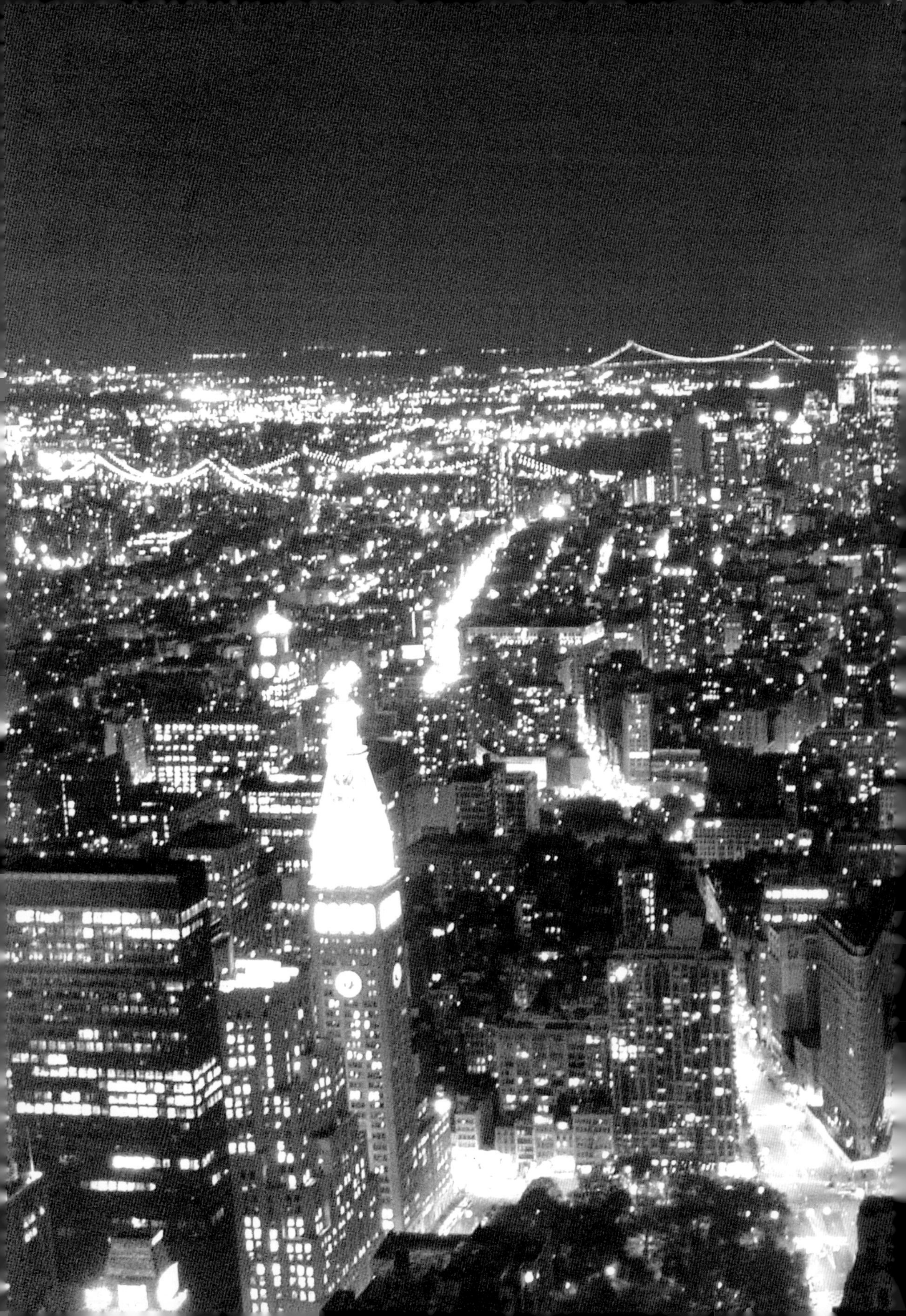

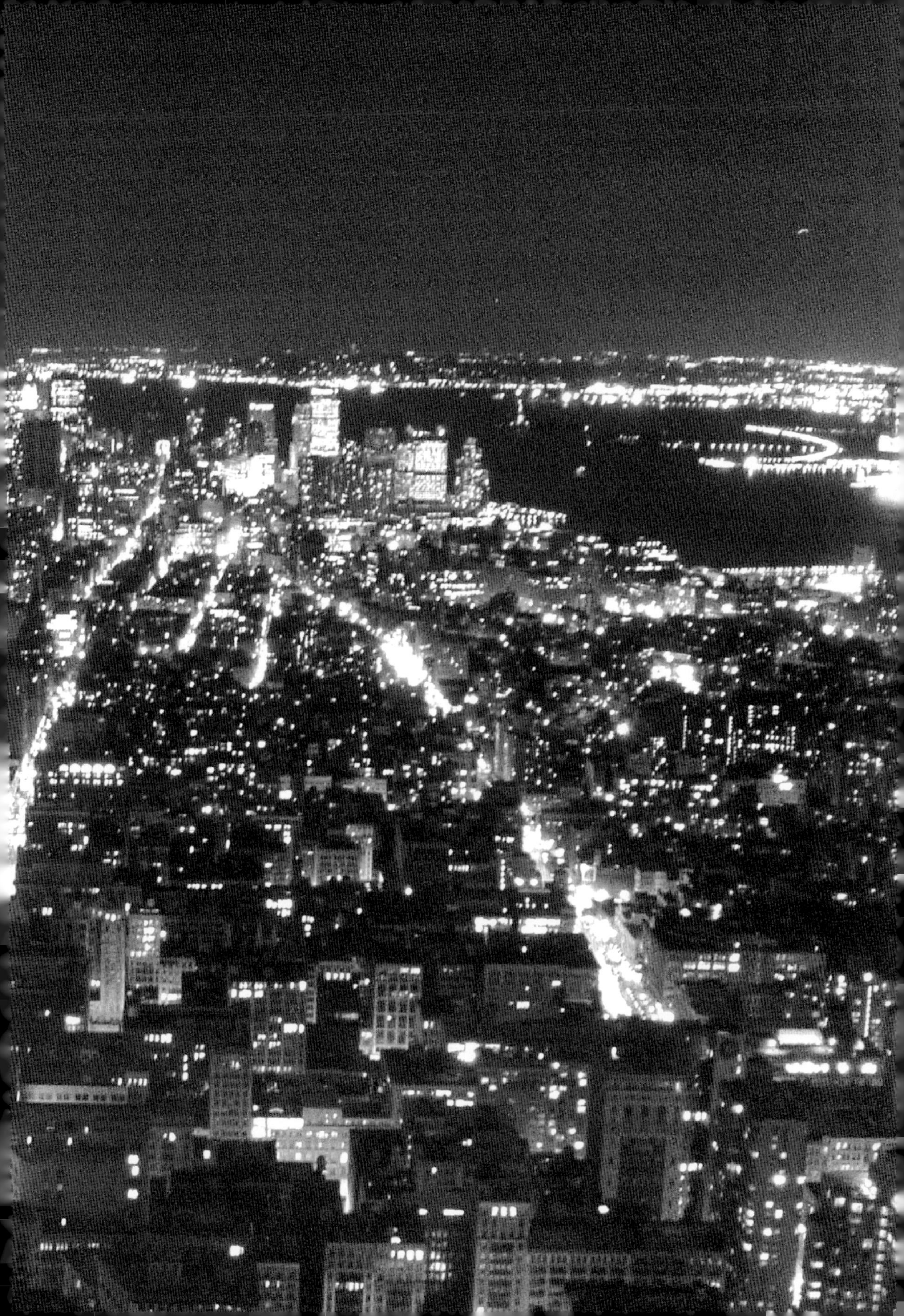

COLOPHON

Publisher
PRO Foundation, the Netherlands
www.ilgen.com/pro.htm

Distribution /ordering books
Artists.Bookworks
28 Freshfield Bank, Forest Row, East Sussex, England RH18 5HG
Phone/Fax +44 (0)1342 823568
www.bookworks.plus.com
info@artistsbookworks.co.uk
or through the publisher

Design
Fré Ilgen in co-operation with Studio SiMa, Leeuwarden, the Netherlands
Scans and photo editing Studio SiMa, Leeuwarden, the Netherlands

Description
Edition of 1000 copies
Paper 135 grs. MC silk, full colour pages 170 grs. MC silk
Type-set Garamond, MetaPlus
Printed in the Netherlands

Photography
The photo-credits are mentioned in the subscripts of the pictures.

Cover pictures
Front A Kirlian photo showing the disturbances of an electric field at a person's finger tips. The disturbances are caused by the electromagnetic emanation of the body. I understand this image as metaphor for our unavoidable and continuous immersion in our environment, our continous interaction with eternal "no thingness", which is the key issue in this book.
Back Fré Ilgen in front of his painting "A Bird That Whistled".

Special thanks the late Marion Kidner

Acknowledgement
For providing substantial information, photo's or introductions to some of the discussed artists, we thank: Lily Bafandi, Matthew Becker, Jürgen Blum, Linda Candy, Maxwell Davidson, Danese Gallery, Ernest Edmonds, Ulrich Fiedler Gallery, the late Vilém Flusser, Basil Hiley, Nancy Hoffman, David Juda, James Juszczyk, Neil Larsen, Jean-Pierre Maury, Arthur I. Miller, Heiner and Ulla Pietzsch, Patricia Railing, Max Protetch Gallery, Irving Sandler, the late Dr. István Schlégl and Aurel Scheibler Gallery.

ISBN 90 -9018543 -7

There is only one way that can lead you to understand life and reality: your own way.

Trusting your intuition, experience and theory helps you find your way.
Artists find their way through making works of art.

Painting, sculpting, etc. is their thinking on life and reality.
Theory and knowledge of other fields enhance the understanding of their own way.

The experience of art will enhance your intuition
and acknowledgement of life and reality as it is.

fré ilgen

ACKNOWLEDGEMENT

Artists in general do know what they are doing, but do not always have the knowledge, the ability or the means to communicate this to others. Unfortunately, too often, they keep their ideas to themselves. The importance of a dialogue, with the involvement of artists themselves, on the matters they are concerned with, is not to be underestimated. The many conversations I had and have with colleagues, scientists, philosophers, industrial designers, architects, art historians, art critics and art theorists have been and always will be precious to me. But I have also learned a lot from talking to art lovers, collectors and visitors of exhibitions who I meet thanks to the art dealers who represent my work. In great contradiction to a general understanding, I have experienced that for a serious artist it is just as important to walk around in the art market as it is to focus on working in the studio. The market is not merely the place to sell, but definitely also the place to meet and interact. Where else to learn about peoples' responses to your art or art in general? I feel very fortunate to have had in the past 15 years, and still have, lots of opportunities for good and very different dialogues in Europe, the USA and Asia. These dialogues are stimulated by asking myself again and again the maybe simple but still quite disturbing basic questions why? and whatfor? of art in general. This book is the logical result of my activities with the PRO Foundation that primarily took place from 1986-1993 - an intense period of publications, lectures, symposia, conferences and many, many exhibitions.[1]

I have to thank everyone who was involved in one way or another in these activities, including at some point some 150-200 artists from all over the world, many volunteers and communities, local authorities and press, who supported me and my work.

[1] See publications by the PRO Foundation in the list of literature. See §3. The PRO foundation is a non profit organization that I initiated and founded in 1986 together with Jacqueline Ilgen-Van Rooijen and Bert van Rooijen to research and make manifest the need for a re-newed international dialogue about the further development of constructivism. The foundation has initiated and (co)organized many international group exhibitions, symposia, conferences and publications, and stimulated contemporary constructive artists to get in touch more extensively. Today this organization occasionally acts as advisor and guest-curator for a variety of activities while it is not anymore focussed on constructivism but on the dialogue between art, philosophy and science in Europe, the USA and Asia.

NOTES ON THE STRUCTURE AND TRANSLATIONS

This book is divided into separate chapters following a progression I consider relevant and important. This means, however, that some chapters will be more dense or, to some readers, tougher to read than other chapters. Some are more philosophical, some deal with more complex issues offered by science, some others focus on specific developments in fine art.

Everywhere I refer to examples from art to illustrate the relevance of the discussed subjects for understanding the experience of art itself. The reader is kindly requested to read with patience, and whenever one comes across subjects that one does not consider of interest or that seem to delve too deeply into some subjects, one should read such a section as preparatory material for the rest of the discussion.

Basically, I consider chapter 8 to be a pivotal chapter, but simultaneously a subject that in my opinion one can only fully understand by having explored the subjects of the other chapters.

The reader will undoubtedly notice that the many footnotes fill a considerable part of the book. In my opinion, the main text is the tip of the virtual iceberg, while the footnotes allow the reader a glimpse of the size of the iceberg. The whole book will give a profound impression of an ocean of icebergs.
For instance, this book is also an attempt to explain how many aspects involved in the meaning of art are based on our humanity and not necessarely on one's own specific culture alone. Therefore, I have made some effort to explain the analogies and 'cross-fertilization' between Western and Eastern - Occidental and Oriental - cultures, while following the historical road of human thinking.

This explains why this book does not only attempt to explain my ideas but simultaneously has certain encyclopedic properties.

Whenever one finds a quotation in two languages, the English translation is often my own, and my responsibility. To allow the reader to check for him or herself I have mentioned the same quotation in the original language in a footnote.

I must thank especially Megan Craig and my wife Jacqueline for their expertise, hard work and patience with me to transform my manuscript into the publication that you have in your hands.

CONTENTS

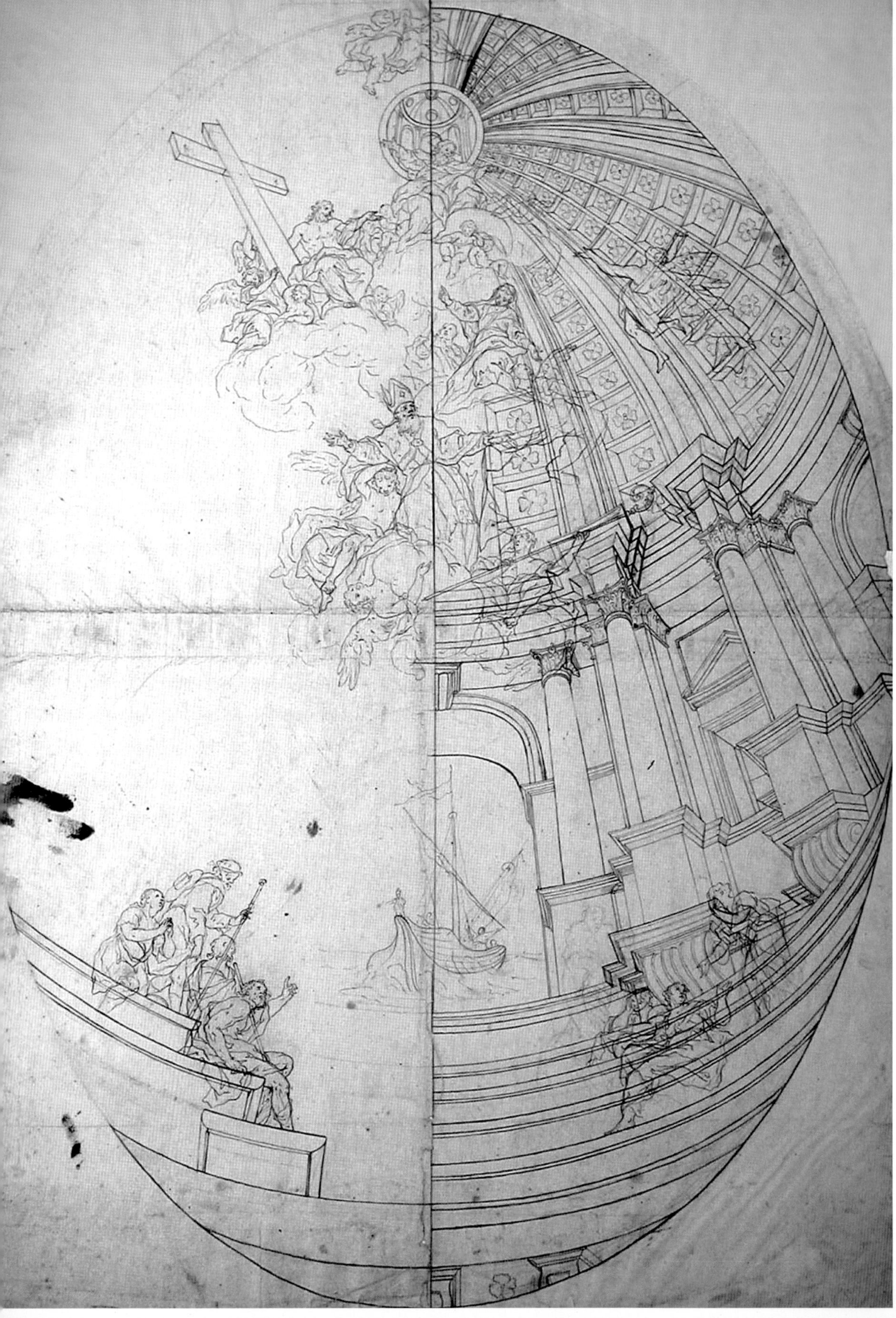

Why should we desire to become one with nature,
when we can never be separate from nature anyway?

fré ilgen

---

1. Joseph Keller (1775-1802)
Glorie des heiligen Nikolaus, ca 1780
Museum der Stadt Füssen

§1. INTRODUCTION

He who has science and art also has religion. Who does not have either should have religion. Johann Wolfgang Goethe[2]

Goethe quite probably refers here to the general meaning of religion as an understanding of a certain order with a hierarchy of all things in heaven and on earth. In religion, besides an intuited or more philosophical content, rituals, in which objects with special meanings are used to focus the belief that this is the true vision of reality, play an important role. Science is basically the search for an understanding of reality in which an empirical controllable process determines truth. Also visual objects (models, diagrams, simulations, etc.) play a growing role in focusing the attention on a rational vision of reality. And art? Art - comparable perhaps to philosophy - seems to fall in between religion and science. It is not precise, certainly not empirical. Nevertheless art is not completely without a fundamental structure.

But what is ART? Art is something one can appreciate or dislike at the first glance. Understanding your response to an artifact and why we seem to have a need for art is much more difficult. We will see that the real meaning cannot be found in the artwork as a thing, but in the response evoked by the artwork. The artwork is a catalyst. There are so many opinions about art. Most of the time these concern a general opinion that art is merely a luxury product or commodity, and, therefore, not essential in our lives. Most professional opinions concern explanations or preferences related to a particular style or trend. When written by an artist, essays on art seem to become a kind of semi-emotional statement (manifesto) explaining why one kind of art is better than another. This kind of writing seeks to prove the value of the personal position in history by putting somebody else down. Painting repeatedly has been declared dead in recent history, while it was considered the only real art in another period. Abstract art was deemed better than mimetic art and expressionistic gestures more human than geometry. The cliché war between fanatic (almost religious) believers of the mind against the believers of the emotion rages on, as if it ever would be possible to separate rational thinking from feelings! More recently, there is the trend that the 'new media', photography - video - computer generated art will make all other art media mere history. This compilation of essays is the result of my doubts about these black/white truths and the resulting need to approach art from a very different angle: a general necessity to understand our human existence through the experience of art.

For a long time I have been interested in the link between fine art - applied art - industrial design - architecture - urban design, with the ideal of improving the basic human living conditions through the improvement of the basic principles of the design of all parts of the human environment. As might be expected, I also had to find out that it is

---

2 "Wer Wissenschaft und Kunst besitzt, hat auch Religion. Wer jene beyden nicht besitzt, der habe Religion", see Otto Kraetz, "Goethe und die Naturwissenschaften" (Munich: Callwey Verlag 1998), p.187.

not so easy to have a clear idea about what kind of principles for design would actually bring such an improvement about. It led me into a much deeper search for the meaning and purpose of art and the more basic necessity for human made visualizations in our complex and eternal desire to understand our being as part of the world we live in. To understand wholeness.

This publication is the result of my own quest for some answers and from my frustration that there are hardly any books daring to present the analogies between art, science and philosophy at sufficient depth.[3] These are analogies that anyone can sense, but are hard to prove, or for many to believe. With a look into history together with our current state of knowledge we can more or less describe quite a few of these analogies. When you have read this book I can only hope that you will agree with me that there is sufficient reason to assume that many of these analogies are no mere coincidents. It must be emphasized that artists who are interested in scientific knowledge neither intend to be scientists in the strict sense of developing knowledge that helps save lives or that can put a person on the moon, nor do artists merely create illustrations of philosophical concepts. They are genuinely interested in science, philosophy, psychology, anthropology, religion, etc. for the enhancement of their own understanding of the broader meaning of art, their own art, the drive for creativity and the very reason of life itself. The initial impulse of artists to be interested in science and philosophy is caused by their intuition that scientists and philosophers explore reality in an approach that is different, though analogous, to their own.

In context to all references to artists' theories and their interest in science and philosophy in this book, I consider it very important that the reader will bear in mind that the actual thinking of artists virtually occurs 'in their hands' while creating works of art. Theory and knowledge obviously influence the artistic intuition, but in general should be considered essential considerations after the creation of a work of art and not before. Theory helps the artist to understand what he has done, not what he is going to create or has to create!

In these essays I try to make clear the necessity for art, devoid of style, group or other temporary phenomena. This necessity will become clear in the analogies between art and

[3] One can see in recent years a growing interest in these analogies, but for most symposia artists and scientists are invited who are well known and good in their fields, but have no particular interest in these analogies and, therefore, unfortunately, are not able to contribute anything meaningful to this discussion. However, good books are: Charles Biederman, "Art, Science, Reality" (Red Wing, MN: Biederman, 1988); Semir Zeki, "Inner Vision - An Exploration of Art and the Brain" (Oxford, New York: Oxford University Press, 1999); Thomas Vargish and Delo E. Mook, "Inside Modernism - Relativity Theory, Cubism, Narrative" (New Haven, CT: Yale University Press, 1999); Arthur I. Miller, "Einstein, Picasso - Space, Time and The Beauty That Causes Havoc" (New York: Basic Books Inc., 2001); Lyn Gamwell, "Exploring the Invisible - Art, Science, and the Spiritual"(New Jersey: Princeton University Press, 2002); Serge Lemoine, "Aux origines de l'abstraction" (Paris: Musée d'Orsay, Éditions de la Réunion des Musées Nationaux, 2003). There seems to be a tendency in modern art history to include in books on the pioneers of abstract art their interests in science - for instance, new books on Kandinsky, Kupka, Matjushin, Malevitch, Gabo, Gleizes, Boccioni, and Van Doesburg.

the different fields of science, philosophy and a variety of other fields (like religion). As such, this publication does not merely introduce another art theory, but attempts to help dissolve the rigid boundaries between disciplines.

I am convinced that it reflects a rather unintelligent denial of our own human history to allow oneself to only discuss these matters on a shallow level while ignoring deeper knowledge. It seems necessary to dig deeper, because though art still fulfills some function and importance in society, it risks slipping into an inessential game of trying to be temporarily popular and succesful. This danger must also not be exaggerated, because at other levels of the artworld than what becomes publicly visible, there are always a lot of other developments going on.

I have attempted not only to present certain views on art, but also to show the analogies and general connections between different sources of knowledge. You will also find many cross-references, overlapping information and even repetitions of information. This is not only unavoidable, but is done on purpose so that you can discover for yourself to what extent many important topics of everyday reality are interrelated or even equivalent when you dig just a bit deeper. Art history often discusses individual paintings or sculptures as isolated objects made of certain material and arranged in certain compositions in terms of handcraft and culture. Studying art history beyond this traditional limited frame allows us to understand that analogies between art, science and philosophy are not results of wishful thinking. That is also why in this publication I have attempted to deal more with the actual perceptual experience of an artwork and less with its material appearance (the thing-ness or 'das Ding an sich'). Of course there are artists who, similar to scientists, philosophers or religious pioneers, found truths about life by studying reality through a process of creating art without consciously being interested in science or philosophy. But there are also numerous artists who actually did and do have a profound interest in what additional information philosophy and science have to offer them. It is mainly on these artists this publication will focus.

How confusing a notion like 'reality' is. As we will find out, in the end we all are human beings who regardless of profession, age, race, culture, gender or time, try to understand what reality is. Therefore, there is sufficient reason to assume that a search for analogies in our different perceptions of reality is useful. The hypothesis of this publication is that art basically tries to help us deal with the very secret of life itself: that our being is a temporary and tiny part of one whole eternal process called nature. As a matter of fact - besides science and philosophy, maybe even religion - for our own sanity we desperately need art to deal with life. The drive for creativity, the desire for beauty and our capacity to experience the sublime, are not necessarely matters of free choice, but are to a certain degree influenced by very complex cosmological, biological and chemical processes.

Though I do not intend to define any new kind of simplistic stimulus-response theory, I suggest that, because of a process called synchronization, any actual 'free will' is impossible. Immediately connected to this idea is another important hypothesis in this book, which emerged from understanding the implications of synchronization: the meaning of art cannot be found within the framework of the artifact itself, but within the very interaction of the subject with the object. The appearance of the artwork (shapes, colours, proportions, contrasts) are important, not by themselves, but in their power as catalysts for the subject's experience. As we will see, the importance of this interaction is a straightforward link to the processes of nature itself. Art is definitely not reducible to an object nor to the properties of the material of the artwork. We find the actual meaning of art in the activity we call the experience of art. Art is therefore more than a thing or rather 'no thing'! I attempt to show that art in all its various forms plays a vital role in the acquisition of more insight into the coherance of reality and, as such, crucially contributes to a further understanding of wholeness in nature. Maybe it is too utopian, but I still hope this publication will be good enough to contribute to a deeper understanding of the essential value of art which is beyond any temporary political, art historical or commercial objective. I would be quite happy if this book is also understood as a call for more artists, scientists and philosophers to be openly interested in each others' fields.

I am certainly not able to offer you any hint of a final truth, but hope to stimulate your own thinking and a further dialogue from which I hope to learn more myself. The sheer complexity of the subject - with the necessary extensions into the various humanities - dawned on me during the initial years of my struggle to find the right clues while starting to combine and link the various perspectives of understanding reality and art. The following essays will take you on a quest through subjects that do not seem to have anything in common with art as you know it, but are necessary for understanding how deeply and profoundly art is embedded in the process of focussing our attention on reality, and is therefore a more important aspect of our human existence than is assumed when one tries to understand a work of art by trying to isolate it from everything.

I can only hope the reader will be patient with my attempt to put things together that seem to make sense. This is not necessarily a new theory, but still can offer enough means for understanding a new approach to art.

Fré Ilgen

§2. THE ESSENCE - EIDOS - NO THINGNESS

The moon in me looks up at the moon.
The moon that looks,
Looks back at herself.
Kanjiro Kawai, 1953[1]

I will start my argument for a new and hopefully better understanding of art by exploring the meaning of life itself. Throughout this publication it will become clear that to get a better idea of the meaning of life, we will need to acquire more knowledge about the fact that we are a part of the whole of nature.[2] This is a search for the ideal.[3] Because we do not exactly live isolated in our brains, many aspects of being human play important parts in understanding the motivation, methods and tools in this search. Therefore, I will deal with a variety of these aspects in different chapters. We will see that being is a process of doing and becoming. A notion that seems to cover the subject of this search can be found in the various interpretations of *essence* in general; or the Occidental concept of *eidos* and the Oriental concept of *no-thingness*.

This chapter tries to elaborate the meaning of these concepts, though it must be stated up front that there are no exact descriptions possible. Still, these are very suitable notions for showing how not just recently, but all through human history and in a great variety of cultures, similar ideas and concepts have emerged about the true properties of our world and the role of art in this understanding.[4]

2.1. THE EIDOS

Eidos is a Greek word, elaborated in the philosophy called 'eidosphilosophy'. Eidos is generally understood as the essence of being. I understand eidos as the essence of reality and the essence of nature as a whole, which we can perceive in our interaction with all things and therefore, in our interaction with artifacts or artworks as well. This means, essence is not described empirically and translated into a specifible elementary building unit or particle of nature, but the essence of nature is understood by approximation and in a holistic sense as the main property of reality. Because man is not an entity separated from nature, but submerged in the whole of nature we call reality, in my opinion it is no longer useful to discuss the existence of the soul of individual man. If there is some-

---

[1] Quoted in Yoshiko Uchida, "We do not work alone - the thoughts of Kanjiro Kawai", (Kyoto, Japan: Kawai Kanjiro House, Nissha Printing Company Ltd, first edition 1953, second edition 1973).

[2] Whenever in this publication 'nature' is mentioned, not merely a plant, tree or the landscape is meant, but the whole of nature including macro-nature (the universe) and micro-nature (the world of particles).

[3] The desire to search for the ideal will be discussed later more extensively.

[4] We will see how the confrontation or interaction between the self and the object plays a central role. Because the subject-object interaction has its own complex features this particular feature is extensively described in §7.

thing like a soul, one should consider the soul of (the whole of) nature of which we and all other phenomena in the world are small particles.

In this publication I will not explore the different understandings of the notion of soul as phenomenon, because it would lead to many theological concepts, religious implications and confusing yes-no discussions. Still you will repeatedly find descriptions of phenomena that may remind you of a soul. It is quite interesting and revealing, for instance, to understand how the concept of essence by early thinkers in Greece[5] and other cultures has been translated by later emerging religions, like Christianity, into the concept of soul and has occupied philosophy all through history. In science the concept of essence led to the search for the basic elements of all things and 'laws of nature'. Our current level of knowledge from the various fields of science, including theoretical physics, neurophysiology and astronomy, offers us several new incentives to improve our description of the eidos, aspects that will be discussed later in this publication. In art it led to the search for universal principles of composition, form and colour or to the concept that the essence is present in the material itself and the artist 'merely' has to release it by shaping and cutting. Artists touch the eidos in works of art when we experience them as great works of art. The discussion on the eidos is maybe one of the leading themes in human history and certainly still matters to our modern society. It will be clear that in my own opinion a re-newed interest in the eidos will offer art a further great future and supply a real content beyond any temporary, fashionable, superficial, political or merely entertaining meaning. From where does the notion of the eidos originate?

Plato assumed that in all cases in which we give the same name to a group of beings that are perceived or proclaimed as individuals (who also clearly have a lot in common) there exists a structure or entity independent from our perception or our understanding. This independent entity is immaterial, eternal, constant, perfect, and specifies a certain group. Plato called this the eidos or idea.[6] Later in Christian philosophy, 'idea' became equivalent to thought, state of consciousness,[7] or form,[8] and led to the emergence of the concept of the soul. Eidos is understood by Plato in a different manner than by Aristotle, although both saw it as the universal. Plato understood that eidos can only be found through thinking - the idea with mathematics as its tool. Aristotle

---

[5] Of course in even older cultures there have always been concepts that something essential is in everything, leading to belief in spirits or deities as present in natural or man-made objects or in natural phenomena. These concepts undoubtedly have emerged together with the emergence in history of human consciousness: being conscious means understanding somewhat that a self exists and that it has an interrelationship with its environment, therefore that other selves must exist and that some aspects must be valid for all selves.

[6] Described in J. Mansfeld, "Enige opmerkingen over 'mens' als idea en eidos in het Griekse denken" ("Some remarks on 'man' as idea and eidos in Greek thought"), published in Prof. Dr. G. Quispel, "De Hermetische Gnosis in de loop der eeuwen - Beschouwingen over de invloed van een Egyptische religie op de cultuur van het Westen "("The Hermeneutic Gnosis through the ages - Reflections on the influence of an Egyptian religion on Western culture") (Baarn: Tirion, 1992), p.176.

[7] See Carl Friedrich von Weizsäcker, "Zeit und Wissen" (München, Wien: Carl Hansen Verlag, 1992), p.68.

[8] Ibid., p.260. See §5. Form = latin for idea or Gestalt.

emphasized a sensory approach.[9] The ousia, the substance or particular universal property of an individual object, is what can exist independently and will always stay the same; Aristotle considered it to be the first and most important aspect of being. Everything else, like characteristics, circumstances, localization, etc. are not independent, but always related to the ousia. The ousia is basically the individual eidos, the form inherent to an individual being. Secondly, it is the name-giving property of a group of beings (like human being). Later, in Christian religion, the concept of a soul emerged that, to a certain degree, seems to be a religious translation of the Aristotelian eidos.[10]

Descartes distinguished between physical and spiritual substance. Spinoza defined God or nature as the highest, eternal and final substance. The mechanical scientific view on nature in the 19th century proposed energy and mass as essential properties of substance.[11] Scientist and philosopher Carl Friedrich von Weizsäcker explains how in the philosophies of Plato and Aristotle the eidos is linked to understanding the forces within a form.[12] These thoughts form quite a fascinating connection between early philosophy and modern scientific theories.

2.2 NO THINGNESS

In the old Hindu (and later Buddhist) culture of India the essence of being is the Universal Law, which is considered to be the Absolute and to be the highest ranking force, even higher than the gods. This should not be mistaken for a strict, precisely written law, but as a non-concrete order understood in very general and open terms. The highest principle is that which is free from precise qualifications.

---

[9] Ibid., p.102: "To Aristotle substance (ousia) means the individual thing exemplified by an eidos as the real thing (on). This is what Plato denies. To him, the idea is so much more a real being (ontos on) than the thing as perceived by our senses, as he acknowledges in his phenomenology." (orig.: "Für Aristoteles bezeichnet Substanz (ousia) das durch ein Eidos bestimmte Einzelding als das eigentlich Seiende (on). Eben dies leugnet Platon. Die Idee ist ihm so viel mehr wirklich Seiendes (ontos on) als das Sinnending, als sie, gemäß seiner Phänomenologie, erkennbar ist als dieses.")

[10] See J. Mansfeld, "Enige opmerkingen over 'mens' als idea en eidos in het Griekse denken", published in Prof. Dr. G. Quispel, "De Hermetische Gnosis in de loop der eeuwen - Beschouwingen over de invloed van een Egyptische religie op de cultuur van het Westen " (Baarn: Tirion, 1992), p.182. Lucius Annaeus Seneca (Cordoba ±5BC - Rome 65AD) was an influential Roman stoic philosopher and great writer, who mentions substance or ousia as 'essentia', which he exchanges for a broader interpretation of being -"to on, quod est" (same article by Mansfeld, p.184). The great religious thinker Thomas of Aquino founded many of his ideas on Aristotle's thoughts.

[11] The implications of new scientific theories on the object and on matter, etc. are extensively discussed in §7 and elsewhere.

[12] Carl Friedrich von Weizsäcker, "Zeit und Wissen", p.258: "Plato's philosophy is not, as is often thought, a duality of idea and appearance, but in the end it is a monism of moved shapes (Gestalten). Aristotle makes a different nuance. The thing as we perceive it by our senses is 'contracted' (con-cretum; the greek notion of synholon, meaning united with the whole) from the shape, called by him the eidos or morphe (form), and matter (hyle, literally meaning wood). The eidos is eternal, because it manifests itself in ever newer individual things." (orig.: "Platons Philosophie ist nicht, wie man oft meint, ein Dualismus von Idee und Erscheinung, sondern letztlich ein Monismus der bewegten Gestalten. Aristoteles nuanciert anders. Das Sinnending ist 'zusammengewachsen' (con-cretum; griechisch synholon, d.h. zum Ganzen geeint) aus Gestalt, von ihm Eidos oder Morphe (Form) genannt, und Stoff (hyle, was wörtlich Holz heißt). Das Eidos ist ewig, weil er sich in immer neuen Einzeldingen manifestiert."). It is interesting to note here, that in the Middle Ages the

The notion used is the eternal 'Atman'; the self regarded as identical to the Absolute, the Ultimate Ego. The Indians perceive a strong relationship between the self as part of the individual and reality as part of the ultimate self, the Universal Self - also referred to as the 'Brahman', True Self or the Universal Law.[13] The Universal Law itself never changes, while all existing things seem to change. By understanding that the Universal Self never changes, one can perceive that, in principle, life is static. Thus, being is considered more essential than becoming (a crucial difference with western thinking). Dharma means law or order but also 'things', because the law is substantial in all things. The Indians understand Dharma to be the reflection of the Universal Law that guides man to perform moral acts and to bring truth as a reflection of universal truth into the world. The emphasis on the universal results in perceiving all beings, all objects, and all phenomena as inseparately interrelated with each other, with their environments, and with the larger phenomena in nature. Thus the significance of the individual is almost neglected, and the difference between that which supports a substance and the substance itself is not clarified. The perception of particular beings as separated is understood to be an illusion.[14] Only the universal is considered real. The more something is individualized the less it shares in the essence of reality. This clearly implies that the

qualities of the material and craftmanship of artifacts were highly valued. This was a result of considering the most perfect object, made by using the most expensive materials (like gold, rare wood, gem-stones), to be a reference to how much greater and more perfect the realm of God Himself must be imagined. See Umberto Eco, "Art and Beauty in the Middle Ages", translated by Hugh Bredin (New Haven and London: Yale University Press, 1986 - orig. "Sviluppo dell'estetica medievale" in "Momenti e problemi di storia dell'estetica" vol.1, 1959). Besides, a group of early abstract artists in Russia, under the leadership of Vladimir Tatlin, were advocating that the truth in art would be in the application of the elementary properties of the chosen material itself. Thus they were strongly opposed to painting colour on a material as it would be a non-essential coating, misleading from the essence. See §3 On Constructivism. This opinion is reflected later in Clement Greenberg's art theory when he tried to promote the essential material powers of painting in American Expressionism of the 1950's. Today one still encounters further repetitions of the emphasis on the material used, as exemplified by the frequent references by artists to explore 'new media' or 'new materials'.

13 See Hajime Nakamura, "Ways of Thinking of Eastern Peoples - India, China, Tibet, Japan" (Hawaii: University of Hawai Press, 1964), p.61: "Because their method of thinking puts more stress on the underlying features or essence of the individual than on the particular surface qualities of the self, the Indians seem inclined to stress more the relational meaning of a thing than its fundamental uniqueness. According to the dominant way of thinking in India the nature of the individual or the particular is dependent on the universal through which the individual or the particular is supported and inferred." Nakamura's book is a very good explanation of the main features of the cultures of India, China, Tibet and Japan and discusses the relationships between philosophies and language. By overcoming the 'mine' (the ego-centric) - denying the importance of all things considered valuable to establish one's importance for life on earth - one can obtain the level of a Brahman, meaning becoming consciously one with the Universal Law; so, the objective of life is not a complete denial of 'self', but of 'mine'. It is a strengthening of the small reflection of the Universal Self that already is part of each self by getting rid of all individual ambitions.

14 See Swami Vivekananda, "JNana-Yoga"(Almora, India: Advaita Ashrama, Mayavati, 4th edition, 1930), p.243: "Illusion arises from illusion alone. There will be no illusion as soon as the truth is seen." The perception of concepts of illusion (for example: all beings exist completely separate from each other) are results from wrong pre-conditioned ways of looking. Swami Vivekananda (1863-1902), a very famous Indian teacher, lectured between about 1890-1900 in England (London) and the USA (New York, Chicago, California, etc). He also visited China and Japan. In the western world he became very well known after his speech at the International Religious Conference, September 27, 1893, Chicago (the same congress where a Zen-master

essence of life is to be found in the essence of nature as a whole and that all individual beings each contain a tiny part of this larger and universal essence.[15] In this context it makes sense that the ultimate beauty of art is seen as the self-unification with the Absolute. One does not seek a precise or concrete image - like one can find in most western art, but a more non-concrete image.

A very abstract notion used in Hindu and Buddhist philosophies comes from the Sanskriet 'Sunyata', literally meaning emptiness. It can best be described as the unshaped cloud of eternal energy of nature that is the foundation of the whole of micro- to macro-nature, meaning the level of the formless smallest particles to the formless entirety of the universe. In the original Hindu and Buddhist meaning this sunyata is not changing and static. It just is.

Through the publications of Swami Vivekananda's lectures many of the early pioneers of abstract art found an interest in Vedantic philosophy. For instance Kandinsky. Vivekananda wrote: "It is the Atman, beyond all, the Infinite, beyond the known, beyond the knowable; in and through That we see the universe. It is the only reality. It is this table; It is the audience before me; It is the wall; It is everything, minus the name and form."[16] And, quoting from ancient Vedantic texts: "In This world of many, he who sees the One, in this everchanging world, he who sees Him who never changes, as the Soul of his own soul, as his own Self, he is free, he is blessed, he has reached the goal."[17]

In my own interpretation this can be translated: the person who acknowledges the unity of everything in total 'no-thingness' - the totality of energies that as a whole does not change (the basics of the principle of the conservation of energy), though on a local level may fluctuate (a continous changing process of becoming and dissolving) - that person understands his or her own temporary existence to be immersed in this process - allowing the spiritual experience to feel free from a limited being, while not denying existence itself.[18]

The very beautiful paintings of Indian-American artist Natvar Bhavsar seem to be the perfect contemporary example of the Vedantic concept. These artworks are highly

---

introduced Zen-philosophy for the first time), appealing to all world religions to focus on their mutual analogies and not on their differences - thus to allow a (new) Universal Religion to evolve, contributing essentially to the well being of all people. His lectures were published in English and for instance - before 1920 - in Russian. Vivekananda often combined in his lectures Vedantic concepts with new theories in western science and philosophy of late 19th century; for instance referring to cell-theory, electromagnetic forces, space and time - still as separate entities, etc..

15 When we observe a meadow, all grass seems of equal colour and shape. Closer observation reveals the many individual differences between parts of the meadow and - at even closer range - between all the grass blades.

16 See Swami Vivekananda, "Jnana-Yoga", p.240.

17 Ibid. p.225. Vivekananda emphasizes that when the Advaitists, the Vedantic school of a non-dualistic approach, proclaim: "I worship my Self", not an egocentric perception is meant, but the deep experience or immersement of self as integral part of the universe (the universe is the the Infinite Self, that can only be found within us, in one's self, thus the connection).

18 Ibid., p.333: "When we have become free, we need not go mad and throw up society and rush off to die in the forest or the cave; we shall remain where we were, only we shall understand the whole thing. The same phenomena will remain, but with a new meaning."

coloured and very abstract. Their appealing beauty provide associations with frozen streams of light particles or pure unformed energy. Bhavsar's technique of pouring dry pigment onto canvasses also reflects the emphasis on the non-individual expression of nature. His works exemplify a strong simulation of motion that seem to refer more to a becoming than only to a being. One can also find this simulation of motion in many glorious statues in the Indian culture, exemplified by the dancing Shiva and Krishna-sculptures.

see picture 35

One can hypothesize that in India the starting point for defining the essence of reality was found in the transcendence of nature, while Greek philosophy started with the study of nature. Bhavsar's own reference to his concept of 'tuning' himself to the universe clearly acknowledges Vedantic philosophy, as stated by Vivekananda above. The following quote from Vivekananda seems to function very well as a description of the process simulated in the dynamic gas-clouds of Bhavsar's paintings (though no actual form exists in these):

> *"Different currents of air coming from different directions meet and at the meeting-point become united, and go on rotating; as they rotate they form a body of dust, drawing in bits of paper, straw, etc., at one place, only to drop them and go on to another, and so go on rotating, raising and forming bodies out of the materials which are before them. Even so the forces called* **prâna** *in Sanskrit, come together and form the body and the mind out of matter, and move on until the body falls down, when they raise other materials, to make another body, and when this falls, another rises, and thus the process goes on."*[19]

There are small differences between various Buddhist schools in the understanding of the concept of nothing, no-thingsness and 'sunyata' that range from absolute nihilism to the concept 'full of meaning'.[20] The notion 'no-thingness' led to an understanding of reality at two levels: the level of everyday life and the level of reality. The first was considered to be conventional reality (samvrti-sat), which is an illusionary reality (samvrti-satya), in which truth is but a relative truth - basically no truth, more a degree of ignorance. The second concerns the absolute and ultimate reality (paramartha-sat),

---

19 Ibid., p.249.

20 See Hajime Nakamura, "Ways of Thinking of Eastern Peoples - India, China, Tibet, Japan", p.590. For a discussion on the origin and understanding of the number zero - as equivalent to 'nothing', see Charles Seife, "Zero - The Biography of a Dangerous Idea" (New York: Penguin Books, 2000), p.73: "The Indian name for zero was *sunya*, meaning 'empty', which the Arabs turned into *sifr*. When some Western scholars described the new number to their colleagues, they turned *sifr* into a Latin-sounding word, yielding *zephirus*, which is the root of our word zero. Other Western mathematicians didn't change the word so heavily and called zero *cifra*, which became *cipher*. Zero was so important to the new set of numbers that people started calling all numbers ciphers, which gave the French their term *chiffre*, digit." It seems that it took so long for Western mathematicians to actually accept 'zero' as a concept, because they assumed the possibility of an empty nothing to conflict with their understanding of the supremacy of God (see the discussion on Leibniz's monadology in §7.2). A wrong interpretation of zero, caused by the described transformations of the original word - wrong, because an empty nothing is not implied in the original Indian concept!

involving the absolute truth (paramartha-satya), that cannot be expressed in verbal concepts or expressions belonging to the conventional level of everyday life.[21]

In the Chinese philosophies of Lao-Tse (also written as Lao-Tzu) and Chuang-Tzu, 'no-thingness' is called 'Wu' - something that can only be perceived and imagined by the wise.[22] 'Wu' is preferred by the Chinese to the Indian 'Dharma', while its meaning is equivalent. One may acquire the level of perceiving 'Wu' - the non-being or no-thingness - by adjusting to the 'great transformation': following one's natural impulses while trying to get rid of all conscious willing and acting, being free of (egocentric) ambitions, being modest and adjusting to all circumstances.[23] In my understanding, this is a valid definition and way of understanding 'intuition' - a subject I mention repeatedly in this book. Later it was added that the aim was to become totally unified with the 'path', the 'dao' (pronounced 'tao'), thus acquiring the elementary forces of nature - an attempt that could be supported by certain yoga-practices. Lao-Tse and Chuang-Tzu emphasize the harmonious unity of all phenomena despite continuously changing appearances. Tao is considered to be the eternal and steady but continuous fluctuating field of everything of which 'change' is the basic notion. Within Tao, 'qi' is the continuous and always changing stream of energy, the 'soup' in which all things, beings and phenomena, are immersed, emerge from and at some point dissolve back into, without any original source or starting point, without any underlying or hidden structure and without any hierarchy.[24] The only basic notion of reality that never changes is 'change' itself. Like an eternal river keeps flowing, a phenomenon may not change as a whole, although it

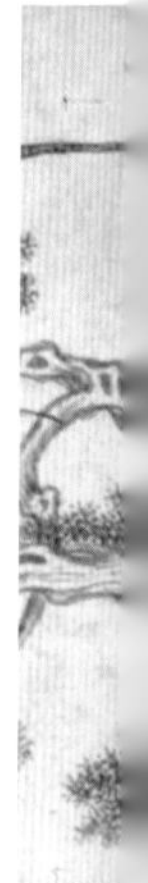

[21] See Jan Bor, Errit Petersma, "De Verbeelding van het Denken, Geïllustreerde geschiedenis van de westerse en oosterse filosofie" ("The Imagination of Thought, Illustrated history of western and eastern philosophy") (Uitgeverij Contact, 1997 - orig. 1995), p.82/83.

[22] Though there is no evidence he actually lived, it is said that the sage Lao-Tse was a royal archivist assumed to have lived in the 6th century BC. He promoted Taoism. 'Tao' - pronounced 'Dao'(= 'path' or 'field' in Chinese), is described in the book that is attributed to him and called "Dao De Jing" ("The Book of the Path and Virtue"). The earliest known copy of the "Dao De Jing" dates from about the 4th century BC. It is argued by some researchers that the "Dao De Jing" probably originally was a work in progress written and adjusted by various authors. This book introduces the concept of Tao and serves as a guide for human behaviour and experience, promoting the importance of cultivating simplicity, detachment, virtue, and of living in harmony with nature. Taoism originally was a philosophy that later became a religion, incorporating elements of Buddhism and Confucianism. See Stephen Little, Shawn Eichman, "Taoism and the Arts of China" (Chicago and Berkeley: The Arts Institute of Chicago, in association with University of California Press, 2000).

[23] One distinguishes the *wu* - forms in: *wuwei*, *wuzhi* and *wuyu*. See Roger T. Ames and David L. Hall, "Dao De Jing 'Making This Life Significant' - A Philosophical Translation", featuring the recently discovered bamboo texts (New York: Ballantine Books, 2003), p. 39 - 42: "... *wuwei*, often translated (unfortunately) as 'no action' or 'non-action', really involves the absence of any course of action that interferes with the particular focus (*de*) of those things contained within one's field of influence. Actions uncompromised by stored knowledge or ingrained habits are relatively unmediated: they are accomodating and spontaneous." "*Wuzhi*, often translated as 'no-knowledge', actually means the absence of a certain kind of knowledge that is dependent upon ontological presence: that is, the assumption that there is some unchanging reality behind appearance." On the above mentioned pages Ames and Hall propose that the best rendering of '*wuyu*' would be 'objectless desire', which they define as: "Desire, based upon a noncoercive relationship (*wuwei*) of it, is shaped not by the desire to own, to control, or to consume, but by the desire simply to celebrate and to enjoy. It is deference."

[24] Ibid., p.63: "Although the systematized and elaborate 'five phases' *yinyang wuxing* cosmology does not

changes continuously at a detailed level. The general immersion in this 'river' or 'soup' is understood as the universal and unifying truth underneath all cultures in the world, signaling analogies in moral principles and in religions. Like 'dharma' or 'wu', 'tao' is the eternal universal matrix that does not change. Only at a lower level can we perceive that men and all phenomena of our everyday world do change.[25]

A great example of 15th century Taoist art is the handscroll "Seven Junipers" by Wen Zhengming. An interesting example of Occidental art which evokes a similar experience in the viewer, while it never was intended to be Taoist, is a painting of the eternal tidal rhythms of the sea by the German artist Max Beckmann.

see picture 18

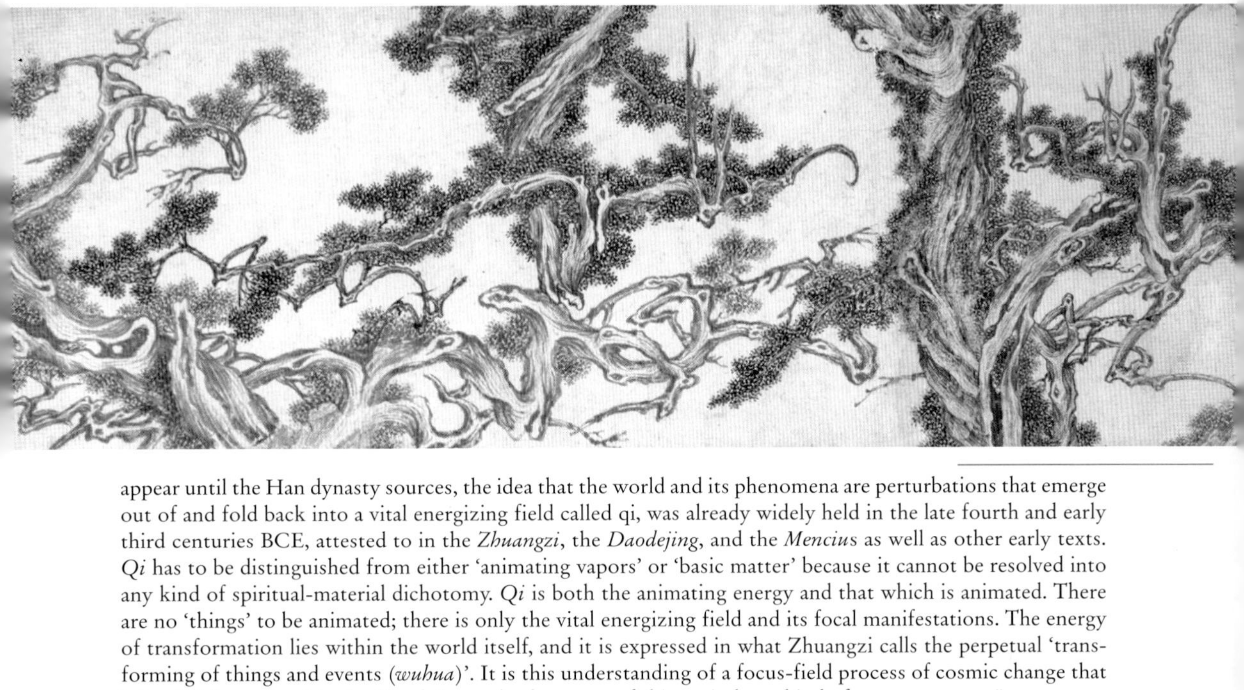

appear until the Han dynasty sources, the idea that the world and its phenomena are perturbations that emerge out of and fold back into a vital energizing field called qi, was already widely held in the late fourth and early third centuries BCE, attested to in the *Zhuangzi*, the *Daodejing*, and the *Mencius* as well as other early texts. *Qi* has to be distinguished from either 'animating vapors' or 'basic matter' because it cannot be resolved into any kind of spiritual-material dichotomy. *Qi* is both the animating energy and that which is animated. There are no 'things' to be animated; there is only the vital energizing field and its focal manifestations. The energy of transformation lies within the world itself, and it is expressed in what Zhuangzi calls the perpetual 'transforming of things and events (*wuhua*)'. It is this understanding of a focus-field process of cosmic change that is implicitly assumed in the *Daodejing* and other texts of this period as a kind of common sense."

25 Wu-Wai, 14th century, quoted in Hajime Nakamura, "Ways of Thinking of Eastern Peoples - India, China, Tibet, Japan", p.256: "Tao is not able to realize itself, but can be realized by man. Even though there are various ways to realize it, that tao itself, however, does not change through the ages. That which changes in time and place is not tao, but men and the world. The theory of one principle covers all (Confucius), the idea of non-creation (Lao-Tse), and the goal of nirvana (Sakyamuni), all point up the fact that different men taught the same truth." In the ideas of the Korean philosopher Choi Han-ki (1803-1879) one finds the concept of 'ki'- inspired by Chinese 'Ch'i', or 'qi', the breath of the universe, to be more or less a variant to the essence. Choi Han-ki quoted in Choi Min-Hong, "Comparative Philosophy - Western and Korean Philosophies Compared" (Seoul: Seong Moon Sa, edited by The Society of Korean Philosophy, 1980), p.19; "Before I was born there was only the Ki of formation. After I die my Ki returns to the state of Ki of Heaven and Earth. The Ki of Heaven and Earth is great and infinite. The Ki of formation exists only for a short time and then dissolves. The latter depends on the Ki of Heaven and earth and always returns to it." Another Korean philosopher, Choi Su-un (1824-1864), considers the self to contain part of the eternal being, thus to be understood as infinite, equal to the infinite universal entity, quite comparable to the mentioned Indian concepts. Choi Su-un speaks of the 'Boundless I'. On "Ch'i", see Michael Page, "The Power of Ch'i - An introduction

Another example in Oriental thought is exemplified in the Japanese culture.[26] Historian of religions, Joseph M. Kitagawa, discusses how the different phenomena in life might look different, but still share an inherent essential midpoint. The monk Kukai considered the sensing or acknowledgement of this midpoint to be important in the process of the creation of art and even suggests in the 'Shorai-mokuroku' that the Esoteric doctrines are only accessible through painting.[27] This seems very logical when we recall painting consists in making shapes or forms and briefly consider the interpretation of form in Japan. Form (in Japanese 'so') comes from the Sanskrit 'laksana' which has, as a Buddhist concept, a variety of meanings: external appearance, phenomenon (as

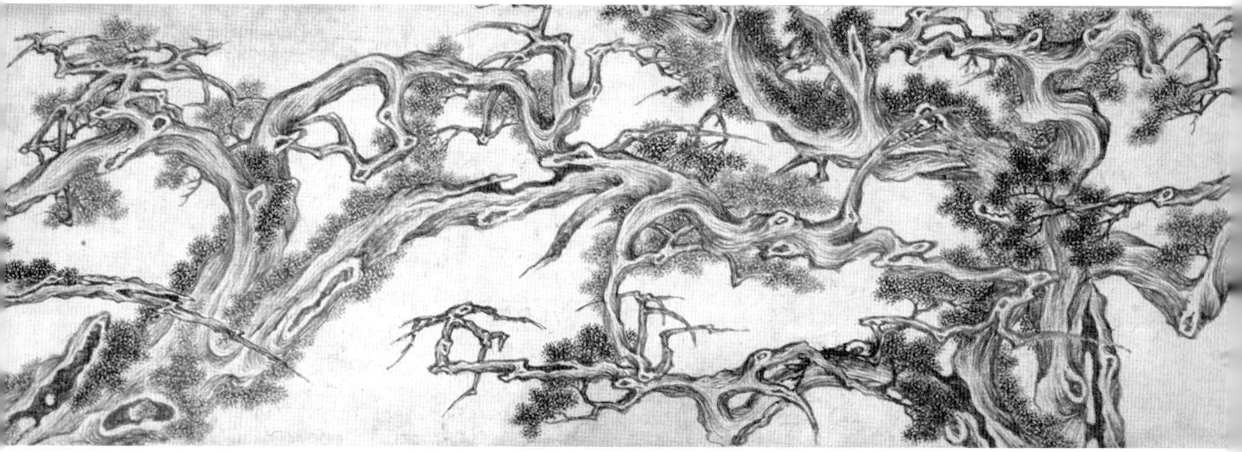

opposed to inner nature), mark, sign, characteristic, mutuality. This is slightly different from the ordinary and philosophical meaning of form, which is 'keiso'(= eidos), visible form or image ('kenso'). Every object, every being consists of its own matter ('koto').[28] To get to the core of the meaning of the koto of a thing one has more or less to accomplish the transformation of that particular koto into part of oneself (as we can experience

to Chinese mysticism and philosophy" (London: The Aquarian Press, 1988).

[26] Hajime Nakamura correctly pointed in his "Ways of Thinking of Eastern Peoples - India, China, Tibet, Japan", at the mere fact that in principle the cultures of for instance India, China, Tibet and Japan are so different, but also those of countries which are influenced by these like Korea, Indonesia, Mongolia, etc. that one hardly can speak of Oriental culture as such. Simultaneously one can critize the use of the notion Occidental or Western culture, German culture being quite different from French or American culture. Still, I imagine that as long as we are aware of these differences we can speak of Oriental and Occidental culture in very general terms.

[27] Kukai (774 - 835) was the founder of the monastic center of Shingon Buddhism at Mount Koya. See chapter 11. in Joseph M. Kitagawa, "On Understanding Japanese Religion" (Princeton University Press, 1987). Kukai quoted on p.199-200: "The various attitudes and mudras of the holy images all have their source in Buddha's love, and one may attain Buddhahood at sight of them. Thus the secrets of the sutras and commentaries can be depicted in art, and the essential truths of the esoteric teaching are all set forth therein ... Art is what reveals to us the state of perfection." See Yoshito S. Hakeda, "Kukai: Major Works" (New York: Columbia University Press, 1972).

[28] See Keiji Nishitani, "Religion and Nothingness" (Berkeley: University of California Press, 1982), p. 178-179.

when we are touched deeply by a work of art).

The doctrine in many religions that a god or gods are in all phenomena in nature also points towards the sensing of something of essence in all things. As in Buddhism, which originated in India and through China also came to countries like Korea and Japan, all things are trapped in the present existence but still possess the Buddha-nature, allowing them to become Buddha's in the future.[29] Japanese Zen-teacher Dogen emphasized that "... 'All-existence' is the Buddha-nature. One part of 'all-existence' whether sentient or not, is the Buddha-nature".[30] In an attempt to prevent one assuming Buddha to be a certain person, whose appearance, behaviour and way of life one merely needs to copy to

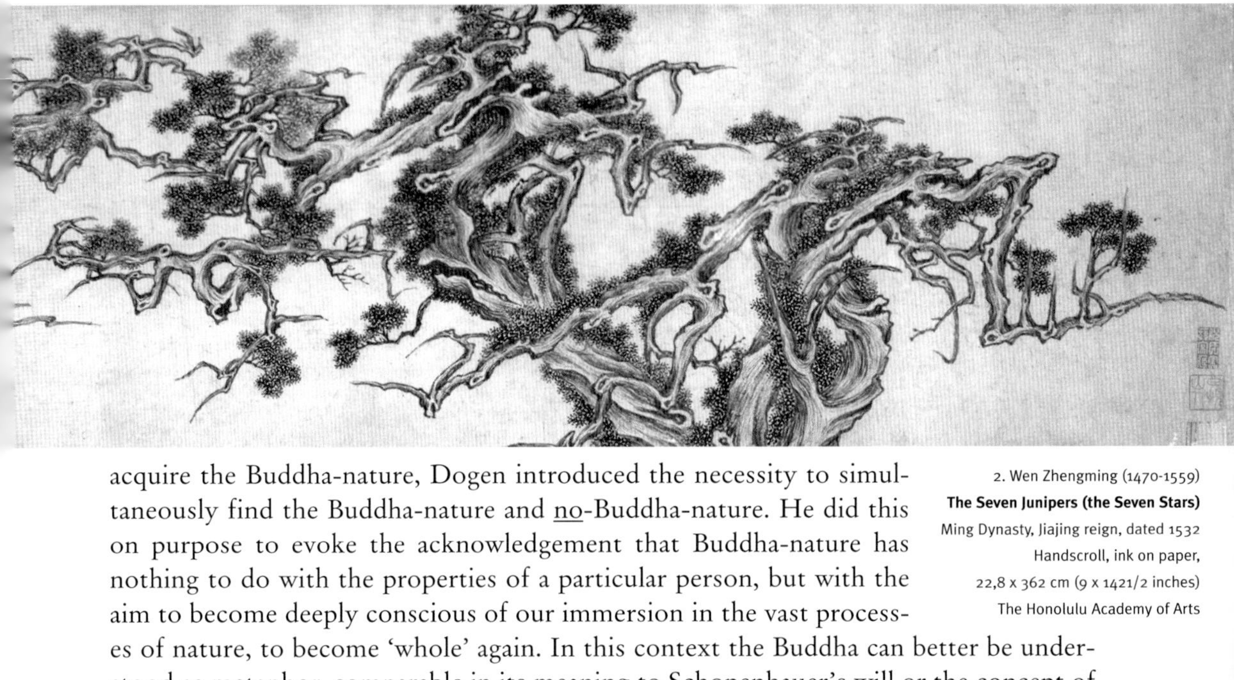

2. Wen Zhengming (1470-1559)
The Seven Junipers (the Seven Stars)
Ming Dynasty, Jiajing reign, dated 1532
Handscroll, ink on paper,
22,8 x 362 cm (9 x 1421/2 inches)
The Honolulu Academy of Arts

acquire the Buddha-nature, Dogen introduced the necessity to simultaneously find the Buddha-nature and no-Buddha-nature. He did this on purpose to evoke the acknowledgement that Buddha-nature has nothing to do with the properties of a particular person, but with the aim to become deeply conscious of our immersion in the vast processes of nature, to become 'whole' again. In this context the Buddha can better be understood as metaphor, comparable in its meaning to Schopenhauer's will or the concept of structure assumed to exist underneath the processes in nature.[31] The Buddha-nature in

[29]In the Nirvana Sutra one can read: "...all sentient beings have the Buddha-nature.", see Joseph M. Kitagawa, "On Understanding Japanese Religion", p.230.

[30] Ibid., p.230. Dogen (1200 - 1253), advocate of Soto-Zen and contemporary of Shinran (1173 - 1262). See §8, footnote 9. In this respect Dogen followed the interpretation of Tendai, which is different from the Chinese Buddhists, who (ibid., p.301) "... translated dharmata as the 'real aspects of all things', which refers to all aspects of all kinds of phenomena and which consists of two contradictory elements, i.e. 'all things' and 'the real aspect'. " Please, compare yourself this idea to the ideas of Plato and Aristotle to find the analogous way of understanding essence! For further reading about Dogen and the differences between his thinking and Shinran, see Masao Abe, "A Study of Dogen - His Philosophy and Religion" (Albany: State University of New York Press, 1992).

[31] The ideas of Schopenhauer are discussed later in this chapter.

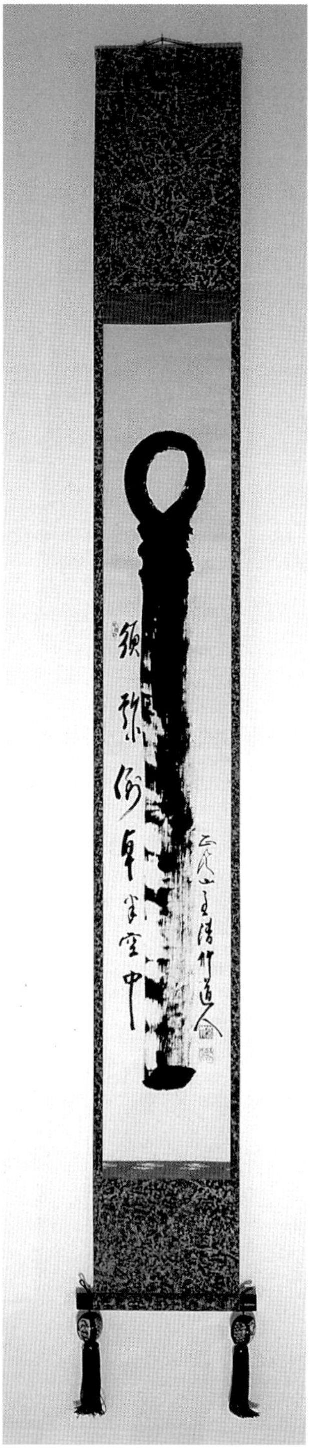

3. Kozuki Tesshu (1879-1937) **Rod**, Ink on paper, 198,5 x 22,5 cm (78 1/8 x 8 7/8 inches)

general means the latent capacity to understand and accept 'samsara', the conflict between birth-and-death, the contradiction between the finitude of everyday life with the infinite forces of eternal nature, as we can only 'see' by acquiring insight through knowledge and intuition.[32] Dogen understood the fluid aspect of impermanent being in itself to be the absolute state.[33] In my interpretation, this is a typically religious understanding all things possessing some universal meaning, having a certain essence that all things have in common, something we would today call the property of wholeness in all things.[34] It is rather important to understand that in Hindu, Greek and in for instance Buddhist philosophy a search for essence is different, but still related to, an interest in finding the essence of things in their material and form, topics so familair in art through all cultures and centuries. What is more characteristic in art than the handling of materials to capture some essence in a form? What is art but shaping material? What is the importance of a work of art but the interaction with what is shaped in material?

A powerful image that mirrors this in its immediacy is the staff or rod painting in Zen calligraphy.[35] These images consist of one powerful slam of ink on paper in one quick gesture resembling a stick. The expression of such a strong hit exemplifies the finding of truth - of enlightenment - as advocated in Zen: there is no gradual learning process, one is 'hit' by instantaneous insight - or not. One definitely can state the same about any good painting or sculpture.
Modern Zen philosopher Kitaro Nishida discusses the uniting force of nature - or force of wholeness - and the role of the artist:

"This uniting force, which defines the life of nature, is no notion artificially constructed by our thinking, but a fact evoked in our immediate perception. We study a flower that we love, an animal that is familiar to

32 The accomplishment of a mental state in which one is virtually liberated from the limitations of the cycle of samsara is what is called 'nirvana'.
33 Please, keep this in mind as it is remarkably analogous to the most modern theories in modern science, like Bohm/Hiley's notion of holomovement, that will be discussed later!
34 Dogen speaks about 'whole-being'.
35 Examples are by Hakuin (1685-1769), Shunso Shoju (1750-1839), Nakahara Nantenbo (1839-1925), Takedo Mokurai (b.1854) and Kozuki Tesshu (1879-1937). See for instance Audrey Yoshiko Seo, Stephan Addiss, "The Art of Twentieth Century Zen - Painting and Calligraphy by Japanese Masters" (Boston, London: Shambhala Press, 1998).

us, and immediately we sense the uniting something in its wholeness: the self of this thing, its noumenon. Artists are masters of this kind of intuition; with one glance they can get the complete reality of the thing in its wholeness. What they express is no superficial fact, but the unchangable noumenon hidden in the depth of things."[36]

Nishida not only refers to the capacity of artists to bring forward the essence of all reality in things, or that this essence is reflected in what we experience as beautiful and as such extends the idea Kukai already advocated centuries before, Nishida also connects this experience to the good in things.

"*Originally the phenomena do not know a difference between outside and inside. Subjective consciousness and the objective world of reality are one and the same phenomenon, only seen from different sides. In principle they form one and the same fact. One could say, that the world is constituted by the unity of the consciousness of the self, but also that the self is a small particularized system of reality. It is one of the fundamental principles of Buddhism,*[37] *that the self and the universe have the same root, yes, that they are directly identical. Thus we are able to sense in the soul of our self the infinite meanings of reality: in knowledge as infinite truth, in experience as infinite beauty and in the will the infinite good.*" [38]

Extending Nishida's ideas, philosopher Keji Nishitani has elaborated the Buddhist concept of sunyata in its meaning of nothingness.[39] He emphasized that nothingness has

---

[36] Kitaro Nishida (1870 - 1945) is the founder of the School of Kyoto, a major influence on the modern movement in Japanese philosophy. This quote is from Kitaro Nishida, "Über das Gute", translated by Peter Pörtner (Insel Verlag, 1990 - first edition 1989; Nishida's original "Zen no kenkyu" - "About the Good"- was published in 1911), p. 109: "Diese Einheitskraft, die das Leben der Natur ausmacht, ist kein von unserem Denken erkünstelter Begriff, vielmehr eine in unserer unmittelbaren Wahrnehmung aufscheinende Tatsache. Wir betrachten eine Blume, die wir lieben, ein Tier, das uns vertraut ist, und unmittelbar erfassen wir ein einheitliches Etwas in seiner Ganzheit: das Selbst dieses Dinges, sein Noumenon. Künstler sind Meister solcher Art Intuition; mit einem Blick erfassen sie die ganze Wirklichkeit des Dinges in ihrer Einheit. Was sie zum Ausdruck bringen, ist kein oberflächliche Tatsache, sondern das unwandelbare Noumenon, das in der Tiefe der Dinge verborgen ruht."

[37] See the first part of this chapter when some aspects of the culture in India are discussed; a major difference between original Buddhist philosophy from India and Nishida is that in India the Universal Law or Universal self is considered to be static while Nishida in the 20th century integrates the concept of dynamic change from modern science.

[38] Kitaro Nishida, "Über das Gute", translated by Peter Pörtner (Insel Verlag, 1990), p.184: "Ursprünglich kennen die Phänomenen keinen Unterschied zwischen innen und außen. Das subjektive Bewußtsein und die objektive Welt der Realität sind ein und dasselbe Phänomen, nur von verschiedenen Seiten gesehen. Konkret bilden sie eine einzige Tatsache. Man kann sagen, daß die Welt durch die Bewußtseinseinheit des Selbst konstituiert wird, aber auch, daß das Selbst ein kleines partikuläres System der Realität ist. Es gehört zu den fundamentalen Ideen des Buddhismus, daß das Selbst und das Universum dieselbe Wurzel haben, ja daß sie unmittelbar identisch sind. Daher können wir in der Seele unserer Selbst die unendlichen Bedeutungen der Realität empfinden: im Wissen als unendliche Wahrheit, im Fühlen als unendliche Schönheit und im Wollen als das unendliche Gute."

[39] Nishitani, student of Nishida, is generally considered to have furthered Nishida's ideas. See Taitetsu Unno,

nothing to do with the Occidental concept of nihilism. Nihilism implies a negative notion of hollow, mere black nothingness. Nothingness in Zen is a no-thingness, full of meaning. As discussed before, it is similar to the level of particles in micro nature or the level of the vacuum of the infinite universe in macro nature; levels at which both the particle world and the universe cannot be perceived as a particular formed thing, but as a formless whole, while still containing a lot. Each object, each being, in reality contains a particular part of this no-thingness. This is considered its 'true suchness' ('tathata')- one can say it is the connection and relationship to the essence of the whole of nature by which each object and each being is defined. The overruling whole of nature is more important than the individual features, because every individual is continuously influenced by the whole while never being able to become completely and only individualized. No object, no being can be put outside of the processes of nature as a whole - as already exemplified by our breathing process or need to absorb warmth from our environment.

In his modern Zen philosophy, Nishitani clearly tries to bridge Buddhist thinking with Occidental scientific theory when he defines sunyata as 'a field of force'.[40] Quite similar to theories in modern physics, he explains that to understand the 'explicate' appearance of objects and beings we need to understand their true basis on the level of no-thingness or of pure formless interconnections - or 'implicate order'.[41] Thus by 'seeing' through a process of thought - knowledge - understanding this implicate order of no-thingness, we can virtually return to and much better understand the explicate level of everyday perception. This is what is meant with 'the form of the formless'. All objects and beings that we perceive with our eyes as things with a form at a deeper level consist of no-thingness, having no form. This is an abstract vision we in the western world have accepted through particle physics. For Nishitani, actually and deeply understanding and experiencing eternal and infinite no-thingness/sunyata makes the infinite essence of nature a factual part of our finite life and allows us to live life as it actually is in its very essence, and not as victim of the birth-death fixation.[42]

Artworks that make this approach comprehensible are the great woodcuts by Swiss artist Franz Gertsch. His "Schwarzwasser" at first glance seems to merely depict a pond.

"The Religious Philosophy of Nishitani Keiji, Encounter with Emptiness" (Asian Humanities Press - an imprint of Jain Publishing Company, 1989).

40 Keiji Nishitani, "Religion and Nothingness" (Berkeley: California Press, 1982), p.159.

41 The notion of an Implicate Order is proposed by David Bohm, discussed in §4. Bohm introduced the notions of 'implicate' and 'explicate'. Very much related to Oriental philosophies, Bohm proposed an invisible structure underlying everyday reality, to which everything in micro and macro nature is connected. This structure he called the 'implicate order'. Everything around us consists of objects that have unfolded out of the implicate order to become 'explicate' in everyday reality, while they may be understood to be enfolded as part of the underlying (not perceptible) 'implicate' structure. See also §7.

42 A concept described by Nishida as 'the self-identity as absolute contradiction' ('zettai mujun no jiko doitsu'), see Kitaro Nishida, "Last Writings - Nothingness and the Religious Worldview" (Hawaii: University of Hawaii Press, 1987 - orig. 1946), p.29. It is a contradiction, because to become a self, naturally one desires to be separated from the rest (otherwise one stays merely a part of a universal whole), while this is never completely possible as we cannot get out of the whole of nature, we cannot step out of reality. It is also meant not to step out of reality, but to find the (true) self by acknowledging the immersion in larger reality - compare

Detail of picture 4

Certain specific properties of the artwork (both its image and its execution) transmit a sense of eternal quietness, incorporating change and the fluidity of time. A more precise view - a closer look - reveals the complete dissolution of the image in tiny dots. No-thingness underlying all phenomena of everyday indeed.

These are but a few concepts of 'no-thingness' to show the incredible analogy all through history between concepts from philosophies, religions and modern scientific theories and their impact on the evolution of modern art.[43]

2.3 LEIBNIZ, KANT, SCHOPENHAUER, HUSSERL, WHITEHEAD, DEWEY

Inspired by theories of Renaissance occultism, Gottfried Wilhem Leibniz[44] believed in the Platonic concept of the existence of an intelligible world of ideas from which the material world of created things has emerged. The understanding of the world in Renaissance philosophy was an animistic perception of the world as one harmonious whole, filled with

> "... *innumerable immaterial, vital souls created by God through a series of emanations.*"[45]
> "*The elaborate series of emanations described in the various neoplatonic, hermetic, and kabbalistic creation myths woven together in the rich fabric of Renaissance occultism served to explain how the one became the many or how spirit was gradually transformed into matter.*"[46]

Vivekananda earlier this chapter. It is a kind of psychological movement: by virtually reaching deep down inside one's self, one discovers the universal aspects of self beyond the restrictions of the desires of the ego-centric drive to merely get what is 'mine'. Thus, one in fact reaches out into the universe, then loops back into one's 'true' self.

43 Comparable concepts of 'no-thingness' are the kabbalistic 'Ein Sof' (the boundless or Infinite) and 'Ayin' (Mystical Nothingness). See Daniel C. Matt, "The Essential Kabbalah - The Heart of Jewish Mysticism" (San Francisco: Harper, 1994). There does exist also an incredible amount of all kinds of esoteric and 'New Age' interpretations, (Tarot, Osho-Zen, etc.). It is not my purpose to explore if and how these are variations on the major understandings as mentioned in my discussion of this subject.

44 Gottfried Wilhem Leibniz lived 1646-1716. For a very well researched book on the influence of Renaissance occult thought on Leibniz, see Allison P. Coudert, "Leibniz and the Kabbalah" - International Archives of the History of Ideas #142 (Kluwer Academic Publishers, 1995). One of Leibniz's major sources of information and influence was Francis Mercury van Helmont, who was very much involved in researching occult knowledge and was a well established alchemist. The frantic search of Renaissance alchemists for the way to make gold can be explained as a logical result of their excitement on discovering and combining chemical substances (contemporaries of Van Helmont and Leibniz were Boyle, Locke, Newton). It is Leibniz's genius that allowed him to filter true knowledge out of occult concepts and translate them into rational philosophies, contributing to the foundations of modern science. Important essays by Leibniz that are still available in print include Gottfried Wilhelm Leibniz, "Metaphysische Abhandlung" (in German+French; Hamburg: Felix Meiner Verlag, 1958, 1991, orig. "Discours Métaphysique", 1686) and Gottfried Wilhem Leibniz, "Monadologie", translated and edited by Hartmut Hecht (in German+French; Stuttgart: Philipp Reclam jun., 1998, orig.1714); see also Gottfried Wilhem Leibniz, "Fünf Schriften zur Logik und Metaphysik", translated and edited by Herbert Herring (in German; Stuttgart: Philipp Reclam jun., 1966, 1999).

45 See Allison P. Coudert, "Leibniz and the Kabbalah", p.7.

46 Ibid., p.8.

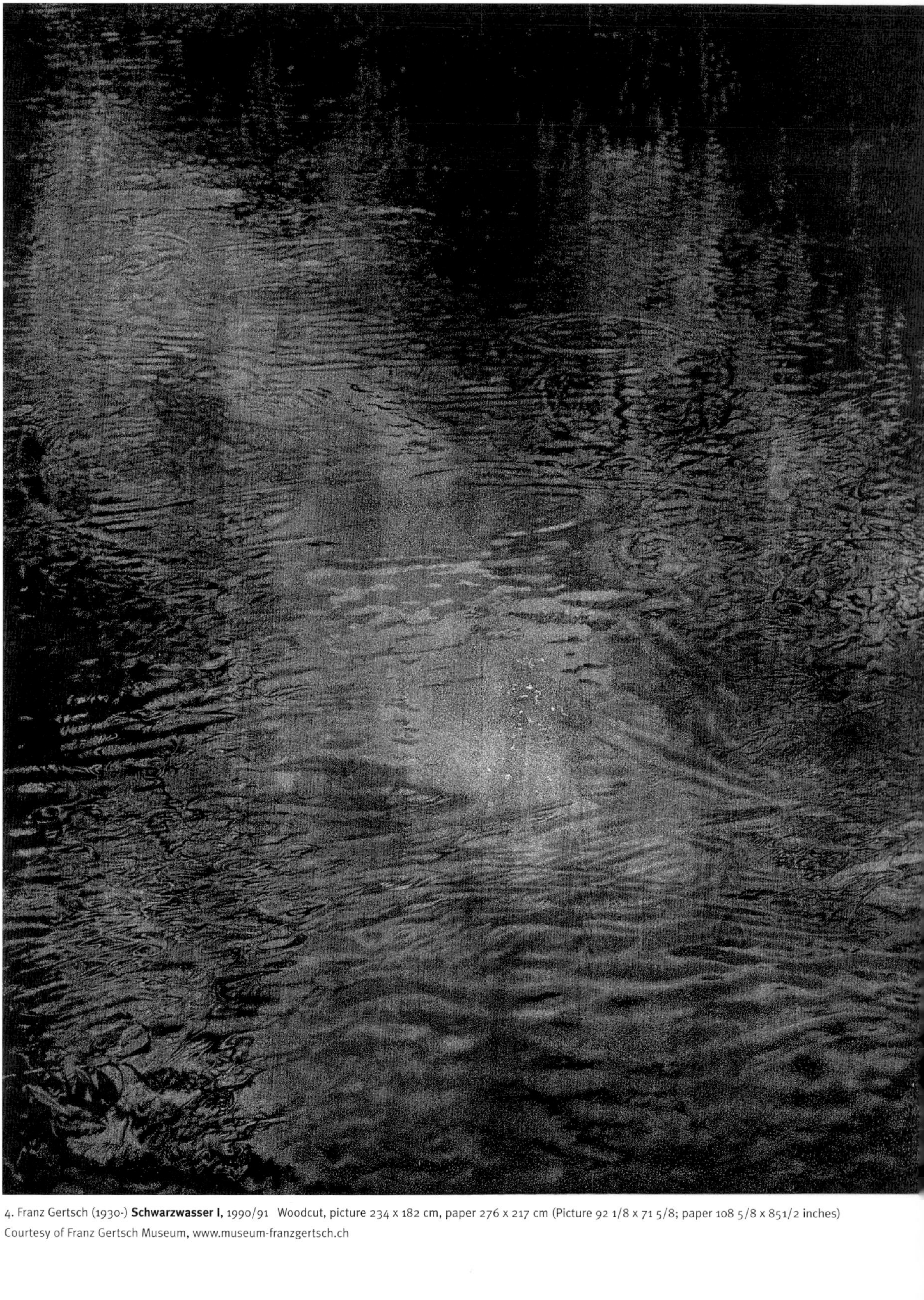

4. Franz Gertsch (1930-) **Schwarzwasser I**, 1990/91 Woodcut, picture 234 x 182 cm, paper 276 x 217 cm (Picture 92 1/8 x 71 5/8; paper 108 5/8 x 851/2 inches)
Courtesy of Franz Gertsch Museum, www.museum-franzgertsch.ch

Leibniz voiced the gradually emerging doubts of Europeans about the Church's explanation of the cohesive hierarchy of God, the world, mankind and the individual person. Quite logically, Leibniz and fellow thinkers tried to find descriptions for this interrelationship still within the ruling Christian doctrine.[47] Trying to understand this interrelationship will lead anybody to think about human perception and thought processes, including many aspects that are sensed and not easily rationalized, such as the power and meaning of signs or symbols. The correspondence between ideas and things led Leibniz to the notion that all knowledge can be reduced to a number of simple ideas that can be arranged logically and can be translated into simple signs. These signs would possess a character of their own. Our ability to combine these signs in our perception and thought allows us to understand complex propositions.[48] This also explains the interest of philosophers like Leibniz in numerology, as can be found in kabbalistic theories, in a kind of mystic mathematics or in number systems like the ancient Chinese I-Ching.[49] The emergence of such an interest in the impact and importance of the reduced symbol is important for our discussion, because it shows an early and serious attempt to find the eidos by accepting the importance of a non-verbal process of knowledge development using an abstract visualization (the reduced symbol) without depending only on a purely rational mathematical language, which involves a denial of the value of knowledge that cannot be translated into controllable mathematics.[50] A denial that began in the thinking of the very first European scientists is unfortunately still around today. It is a denial that ignores an important property of our processes of understanding reality.

Some time later, concepts like individual freedom gradually emerged and, because the Church started loosing its grip on free thought, could finally be openly discussed. European Enlightenment emerged, stating that one would become enlightened when one frees oneself from a dependency in one's thinking on the authority of someone else (a dependency which is one's own fault).[51] Enlightenment in this context means a progression towards free thinking for which no one but oneself is responsible. To that end, logical reasoning became the highest approach to knowledge, leading to ideas of control over reality and our fate.

---

47 That is also why they always had to balance between what they felt they should discuss and what was allowed by the Church to even think about. Some of them went too far in the eyes of the Inquisition and were executed. Van Helmont died in 1698 in a prison of the Inquisition. See also §7.2.

48 See Allison P. Coudert, "Leibniz and the Kabbalah", p.153.

49 Father Joachim Bouvert, a Jesuit priest who had been in China, saw Leibniz's study on Chinese language and culture "Novissimo sinica" (1697), and therefore, offered him a copy of the I-Ching. Thus Leibniz became the first European who tried to analyze and described the I-Ching.

50 As such, Leibniz was a step further than what for instance Galilei (1564-1642) had stated before. Galilei separated primary from secondary qualities; primary would concern mathematically describable qualities that, therefore, are preferred by scientific theory; secondary would concern qualities that cannot be described in mathematics, subjective entities like tendencies, <u>essences</u>, odors. See Arthur I. Miller, "Insights of Genius-Imagery and Creativity in Science and Art" (Cambridge Massachusetts, London: MIT Press, 2000 - orig. New York: Copernicus, 1996), p.106.

51 Philosophers of the Enlightenment in England were Locke, Berkeley and Hume, in Germany Herder, Lessing, Wolff, Kant and Mendelssohn, and in France Bayle, Diderot, Voltaire, Rousseau.

Continuing my brief discussion of a selection of philosophers to provide a sense of the historical development of thinking about reality, we now come to Immanuel Kant. Kant acknowledged that human beings are always tempted to fragment information one wishes to understand, but he emphasized we should first grasp a real picture of the whole of the subject as it is ('das Ding an sich') and only then try to see all parts in their mutual interrelationships. Kant believed in the logic of mathematical rules and the laws of nature, and he tried to superimpose the same logic on metaphysics. He distinguished between a priori knowledge - which exists independently of experience - and posteriori knowledge - which results from experience.[52]

Though an admirer of Kant, Arthur Schopenhauer developed a natural distrust of this rational conviction, based on seeing all the suffering in the world around him and not being able to understand the self in the assumed objective world of spatio-temporal, causal interacting objects.[53] Schopenhauer tried to come to terms with the observation that we are not in control over anything in our lives, but are at the mercy of a blind urge to exist and a belief that there are good reasons to exist as a human being. Schopenhauer did not acknowledge an individual will to exist by itself, but thought that the world (or, one can say, nature as a totality or the universe with everything in it) has a will and that this will defines everything in the world. The existence, the being of any object or living thing in the world, is a result of the drive of the will of nature.[54] This drive manifests itself as the individual will in each object or living being, pushing it into existence, if possible into organic existence - life - and always to a higher level.[55] Schopenhauer reasoned that the drive of this will is exemplified by the motives for any subsequent action. He assumed that the individual's inner essence must be the same as that of total nature and indentified this as the link between the microcosm and the macrocosm. He understood this 'will' as a more substantial part of our self than our intellect. He acknowledged the difficulty for individual man to understand this relationship and to find the essence while being part of material reality, which we perceive from inside our bodies.[56]

The combination of our material bodily selves with the universal immaterial essence of

---

[52] See further on this particular subject §7.

[53] Arthur Schopenhauer, 1788-1660. For an outstanding book on Schopenhauer, see Christopher Janaway, "The Cambridge Companion to Schopenhauer", (Cambridge University Press, 1999). Schopenhauers main publication was: Arthur Schopenhauer, "Die Welt als Wille und Vorstellung" part I+II ("The World as Will and Representation"; in German; Leipzig: Grossherzog Wilhelm Ernst Ausgabe, Insel Verlag, - orig. in 1836).

[54] To me this seems also a furthering of Leibniz's ideas, who understood a basic harmony between nature and the human mind and thought that the purpose of knowledge was to remember these archetypal ideas. Leibniz considered intuition to be the highest form of knowledge. See Allison P. Coudert, "Leibniz and the Kabbalah", p.152. Both Leibniz and Schopenhauer understand nature to have the 'will' that overrules everything and to which the individual mind is subject. The 'will' of nature and the general archetypes present in nature (archetypes are signs, symbols or stereotypes that are perceived the same by many individuals, therefore, they are caused by the processes of nature and not caused by processes/behaviour/preference of individuality). Leibniz considered intuition to be our individual capacity to perceive these archetypes. Schopenhauer's concept is based on this assumption, too, but in a more complex and detailed way.

[55] This belief in universal progress is typical for Schopenhauer's 'Zeitgeist' as exemplified for instance in Darwin's theories; this will be discussed later in this publication.

[56] Schopenhauer himself: "My body is the only object of which I know not merely the one side, that of the

nature leads to the complexity and conflicts between life and death that provoke our intellects and urge our knowledge further. It is so complex of course because the intellect itself is also basically defined by the will of nature. In this theory we do not will something because we believe it to be 'good', but the other way around; because something is willed, it is experienced as 'good'. Although the individual willing might be individually different, it still is driven by the eternal will of nature and thus our sense for what is 'good', 'truthful' or 'beautiful' can be understood as our motive for finding the essence of the will of nature. This quest illustrates the eternal process looping back and forth between our minds and the whole of nature. The driving force of this does not allow a status quo. This means: all our thoughts, perceptions and understandings must be endlessly adjusted. There is no universal truth, not one precise, linear and universal definition possible, only a very general universal understanding. Indeed, truth remains as non-definable as the Universal Law or sunyata in Hindu and Buddhist philosophies.

Schopenhauer understood aesthetic experience not only as going beyond what is possible by logical reasoning, but especially as offering a motive for finding what really is.[57] In the aesthetic experience we are offered ideas or forms constituting a timeless aspect of reality, offering the eidos. Art thus overcomes the limitation and worthlessness of our temporary being inside our bodies and allows us to look into timeless reality itself.[58] Although Schopenhauer's ideas are often interpreted as very pessimistic, I cannot agree. He attempts, as in Buddhism or Hinduism, to accept the restrictions and suffering of being in the world as we know it, while offering a kind of psychological salvation by showing a way to understand that this (our level of existence defined by birth/death) is not all but a short and tiny process of the eternal process of nature. His brilliant conclusion is that art offers this salvation by its capacity to attract and focus one's attention on the timeless essence of nature.

Art, by its aesthetic appearance, triggers one's perception to virtually find a connection to the essence of nature.[59] The self is lost by sheer absorption as a result of the high level

representation, but also the other, that is called 'will'. Thus instead of believing that I would better understand my own organization, and therefore my own knowing and willing, and my movements on motives, if only I could refer them to movement from causes through electricity, chemistry, and mechanism, I must, in so far as I am looking for philosophy and not etiology, first of all learn to understand from my own movement on motives the inner nature of the simplest and commonest movements of an inorganic body which I see ensuing on causes. I must recognize the inscrutable forces that manifest themselves in all the bodies of nature as identical in kind with what in me is the will, and as differing from it only in degree." quoted by Christopher Janaway, "Will and Nature", in Christopher Janaway, "The Cambridge Companion to Schopenhauer", p.145.

[57] Compare the idea of Kukai earlier in this chapter. One has found ample evidence that Schopenhauer knew a lot about Hindu philosophies, but not about Japanese philosophies. For a great essay on the Hindu sources known to Schopenhauer see Moira Nicholls, "The Influence of Eastern Thought on Schopenhauer's Doctrine of the Thing-in-Itself", in Christopher Janaway, "The Cambridge Companion to Schopenhauer", p.171-212. See 2.2, especially on Vivekananda.

[58] See Christopher Janaway, "The Cambridge Companion to Schopenhauer", p.9,10 and following.

[59] See Günter Zöller, "Schopenhauer on the Self", in Christopher Janaway, "The Cambridge Companion to Schopenhauer", p.36: "Schopenhauer locates the exclusive presence of Ideas to the intellect and the associated out-of-world experience of the self in the blissful states of the ultimate concentration on one thing - and

of concentration.[60] Again, the self is not absorbed in the composition, materials or colours of the artwork as such, but absorbed in the interaction with the artwork. If it should and could be defined, this absorption is located in between the artwork and the self. The artwork, which might be understood as objectification of the will, offers the 'motive' for this absorption. No wonder that Schopenhauer was also popular with artists. Later in the 19th century, when Cézanne started looking for his 'motive' in nature, we may connect this famous artist's statement to Schopenhauer. Cézanne, trying to paint the essence of reality, repeatedly said he was looking for his motive when he went out into the landscape. In response to what that motive should be he said:

"Everything we look at disperses and vanishes, doesn't it? Nature is always the same, and yet its appearance is always changing. It is our business as artists to convey the thrill of nature's permanence along with the elements and the appearances of all its changes. Painting must give us the flavour of nature's eternity."[61]

The interest of artists like Cézanne, but also the Impressionists and certainly the abstract artists following them, in studying movement and change in nature seems inspired by philosophies like Schopenhauer's, and particularly by his idea that 'real' reality is an eternal flow of everchanging forces within which all is interconnected and temporal objects and beings emerge as motives of the will of nature. Along quite similar lines, at the end of the 19th century, Swami Vivekananda combined Vedantic philosophies with late 19th century modern scientific theories and western philosophies - including some critical remarks on Schopenhauer. The publications of his lectures on the various yoga-schools had a reported influence on the thinking of early pioneers of abstract art.[62]

Vivekananda's clear ideas stimulated these artists to search beyond the world offered to one's individual sense to explore the essence of nature's whole. This becomes very clear in the following quote:

---

utter forgetfulness about anything else - that mark the production and reception of art. The focus here is not on the work of art as material object but on art as vehicle of Ideas. In aesthetic activity, be it of the contemplative or the productive sort, the self as subject of cognition loses track of everything else, the world as much as its own other self, which is inwardly its own self and outwardly its own body. Further, it could be said that the aesthetic self is lost in the contemplation of the Ideas to the point of forgetting itself entirely, of forgetting that it is a self and vanishing in the object contemplated - like the legendary Chinese artist who completed his painting by stepping into it and vanishing."

60 One can find exactly the same idea in modern Japanese Zen-philosophies like by Nishitani. See Keiji Nishitani, "Religion and Nothingness" (Berkeley: University of California Press, 1982), p.7 and following, on 'samadhi' - doubt or self-nullification.

61 See Joachim Gasquet, "Joachim Gasquet's Cézanne - A Memoir with Conversations", translated by Christopher Pemberton (London: Thames and Hudson Ltd, 1991), p.148. On the motive see p. 147-171, while on p.169 Cézanne is quoted to refer to Schopenhauer. See also Richard Shiff, "Cézanne and the End of Impressionism - A Study of the Theory, Technique, and Critical Evaluation of Modern Art" (Chicago: The University of Chicago Press, 1984) on the interest of artists and artcritics in Schopenhauer at the end of 19th century France. On the difference between 'motif' and 'motive' see chapter 8.2, footnote 33 - a crucial difference!

62 For instance Kandinsky, Franz Marc and other artists involved in the publication of the "Der Blaue Reiter

"Every item of creation is simply a composition: no one ever saw creation coming out of nothing. All that we know of creation is the combination of already existing things into new forms."[63]

At the start of the 20th century Edmund Husserl, an important philosopher and the founder of modern phenomenology wrote:

"The Eidos, the pure essence, can be exemplified intuitively in the data of experience, data of perception, memory, and so forth, but just as readily ***also in the mere data of fancy (Phantasie)****. Hence, with the aim of grasping an essence itself in its primordial form, we can set out from corresponding empirical intuitions,* ***but we can also set out just as well from non-empirical intuitions, intuitions that do not apprehend sensory experience, intuitions rather of a merely imaginative order."***[64]

He thus states that the essence cannot only be searched for by following a more or less empirical process, but also through a more non-empirical process - following one's imagination and intuitions. It seems rather likely to me that Husserl would include the artistic approach as a succesful process for finding eidos. This in my opinion, connects his ideas with those of Kukai and Schopenhauer, as earlier described, and also to quite a few of the abstract artists in the 20th century, as we will see.

In the 1920's, while discussing essence in relation to his philosophy of organism, the mathematician and philosopher Alfred North Whitehead distinguished between the real and the abstract essence.[65] In these thoughts Whitehead states that all objects or other phenomena or entities posses some properties that are universal. These properties he calls *abstract*. Correctly so, as they cannot be seen by merely looking at something, but only by a combination of looking, thinking and reasoning.[66] Besides, comparable to Aristotle, Whitehead says we can distinguish every entity by something it has in particular. This particularity forms the *real* essence. According to Whitehead, this is real, as the particularity of each entity allows us to distinguish one entity from the other.

Almanac" and the exhibitions organized to promote the ideas advocated in the book, but probably also had some influence on Malevitch and Matjushin.

63 See Swami Vivekananda, "Jnana-Yoga" (Almora, India: Advaita Ashrama, Mayavati, 4th edition, 1930), p.265. He clearly emphasizes that 'no-thingness' is not 'empty nothing'!

64 See Edmund Husserl, "Ideas - General Introduction to Pure Phenomenology" (Collier MacMillan Publishers, 1962 - orig. "Ideen einer reinen Phänomenologie und phänomenologischer Philosophie", 1913), p.50-51. Husserl defined phenomenology as a science of the Essential Being. He had quite some influence on young academicians in Germany and also on artists.

65 See Alfred North Whitehead, "Process and Reality" (Free Press, 1979 - org.1929), p.60: "Thus the real essence involves real objectifications of specified actual entities; the abstract essence is a complex eternal object. There is nothing self-contradictory in the thought of many actual entities with the same abstract essence; but there can be only one actual entity with the same real essence. For the real essence indicates 'where' the entity is, that is to say, its status in the real world; the abstract essence omits the particularity of the status."

66 Later in this publication you will see how important art plays a role in our reasoning process, comparable to how Kukai understood painting or how calligraphy is understood in Zen.

This is exemplified in the search for a combination of the universal and the individual in every entity in early abstract art, especially in early Constructivism or Mondrian's Neo-Plasticism. Entity is the equivalent of pictorial element in art. But, of course, composition in art is also an entity - an entity like 'wholeness'. Whitehead also clearly refers to the emerging idea that appearances in our reality are perceived separately, although they are connected at a deeper level, incorporating his contemporary understanding of space/time. As such, he foresaw David Bohm's Implicate Order and related theories like Chaos Theory, the Theory of Complexity, etc.[67] Whitehead's thoughts are also reflected in the search of artists in his time to fragment colours and shapes into abstract compositions that still present one clear whole. A contemporary of Whitehead, philosopher John Dewey, describes how already the Greek philosophers were aware of the difference between superficial beauty (easy or simple aesthetics) and real beauty in art evoked by the eternal essence.[68] Dewey explains how beauty and essence were still a unity in Greek thought but were separated by the concepts of duality in the Christian doctrine, like the separation between mind and body. Dewey quotes another thinker of his and Whitehead's time, Santayana:

"The nature of essence appears in nothing better than in the beautiful, when this is a positive presence to the spirit, and not a vague title conventionally bestowed. In a form felt to be beautiful an obvious complexity composes an obvious unity;..."

And (same page):

"The most material thing in as far as it is felt to be beautiful, is instantly immaterialized, raised above eternal personal relations, concentrated and deepened in its proper being, in a word sublimated into an essence".[69]

In my own opinion the moment we experience beauty in a work of art is the moment we perceive the eidos or essence of our reality. That beauty in a work of art makes the

[67] These theories will all be discussed later.

[68] See John Dewey, "Art As Experience", (New York: Perigee Books, 1980-orig. 1934), p.291,292. Dewey describes how Plotinus followed Plato's idea that in art one should desire excellence to become closer to the gods: "Proportion, symmetry, and harmonious adaptation of parts no more constitute the beauty of natural and artistic objects than does their sensuous charm. The beauty of these things is conferred upon them by the eternal essence or character that shines through them. The Creator of all things is the supreme artist by which is 'conferred upon the creatures' that which causes them to be beautiful. Plotinus thought it unworthy of absolute being to conceive it as personal. Christianity did not share this scruple, and, in its version of Neo-Platonism, beauty of nature and art were conceived to be manifestations within the limits of the perceptible world of the Spirit who is above nature and beyond perception." (emphasize mine). It is interesting to compare this to Dogen's interpretation of 'Shobo Genzo' or Buddha-nature discussed earlier this chapter.

[69] For both quotes, see John Dewey, "Art As Experience", p.292. Heidegger translates eidos or idea with 'Aussehen' (appearance). See Carl Friedrich von Weizsäcker, "Zeit und Wissen" (München, Wien: Carl Hansen Verlag, 1992), p.185: "The eidos is that what appears, said in a Heideggerian way, it is as it appears to be what it is."(orig.: "Das Eidos ist das, was sich zeigt, Heideggersch gesagt, was sich von ihm selbst her als das zeigt, was es ist.")

artwork as material thing immaterial (a 'no-thing'!) in our perception. This is the result of a process of concentration, which can be so intense that our selves become totally absorbed - or ultimately, an experience of the sublime.[70]

2.4 THE IMPRESSION

It seems quite interesting to offer a direct link to a well known development in art that changed our interpretation of nature in painting: Impressionism. Because the artists of Impressionism, like Monet, Pisarro, Renoir, Manet, Van Gogh, Sisley, etc. are well known, it should suffice to recall that an important feature of their painting was to present vague, non-concrete images of scenes and landscapes built with fragmented units of colour. After having read about and pondered the philosophies described earlier in this chapter, you might describe Impressionist painting as a way to approach reality as 'a form of the formless': seen from a certain distance we perceive clear images - seen from within one meter it looks like 'no-thing'.

What seems even more revealing is the original meaning and use of the word impression in the days of these artists. In an excellent book on Cézanne, art historian Richard Shiff explores some essential and less familiar information about the Impressionists. For instance, he discusses the ideas of Émile Littré, a positivist who studied new psychology in the second half of the 19th century. In 1860, Littré published a general statement on the problem of perception and knowledge of the external world. He emphasized the importance of the 'impression':

> *"Yes, there is something that is primordial, but it is neither the [internal] subject nor the [external] object, neither the self nor the non-self [non-moi]: it is the impression perceived [l'impression perçue]. A perceived impression does not in any sense constitute the idea of the subject or the object, it is only the element of these ideas [which develop] only when the external impression [i.e., physical resistance or contact] and the internal impression [i.e., pleasure or pain] are repeated a certain number of times."*[71]

Shiff explains that this means that from the impression both subjective knowledge of self as well as objective knowledge of the world emerge, and this exists before the distinction between the object and the subject. As I understand it, this description of 'l'impression' is very much equivalent to sensing the eidos - or sunyata. This discussion on the link between what we as individual selves see in the objective world with the experience of essence of the whole of nature is a major theme, because it may explain the role of art in our world. It also explains why experiences of 'beauty' and 'the good' are often

[70] See also §8.4 for a further discussion on beauty and the sublime.

[71] Richard Shiff, "Cézanne and the End of Impressionism - A Study of the Theory, Technique, and Critical Evaluation of Modern Art" (Chicago: The University of Chicago Press, 1984), p.19. Repetition, by the way, plays a crucial role in paintings techniques developed by "Impressionism", like Cézanne's modulations or Signacs' "Pointillism".

considered synonymous to experiencing art (as Nishida indeed already said).

Though he did not refer to 'l'impression' himself, it seems to me Von Weizsäcker could agree to my comparison of this notion to a sensing of the eidos. Especially when one constitutes 'perception of shapes' for 'l'impression'. Von Weizsäcker writes: "The notion 'art' explains the way of acknowledging the eidos: ... art is the perception of shapes through the creation of shapes."[72]

As was mentioned before in the discussion of some Oriental philosophies and Schopenhauer, I will repeatedly show in this publication how we can understand eidos or essence in relation to contemporary knowledge. Such a relationship is important for enhancing our ability to formulate a theory of wholeness, for which we have to start by understanding our immersion in reality; how we perceive and are related to the objects around us and how the creation of objects is quite important in this process. I will briefly discuss the development of this knowledge - a knowledge which has never been the sole right and mission of science alone, but also and simultaneously of philosophy, religion and art. This involves the essence of phenomena, of the universal, revealed to us through an individual objectified form and subjected to the interaction of our senses and thinking. That is how a work of art may function.

After initially formulating these texts, I found a remarkable thought by Nishida from 1915. After referring to Goethe, Max Raphael and Konrad Fiedler, he wrote:

> *"We say that science is ratiocinative and art intuitive, but science is also founded on a certain creative a priori element, and it is pure to the degree that the scientist becomes one with this element, becomes wholly absorbed in thought as the artist is wholly absorbed in visual perception. What corresponds to the artist's visual object in this case is the Idea, in Plato's sense, or the hypothesis 'that what is pure', which the Marburg philosophers identify as the foundation of science."*[73]

Nishida links the artistic to the scientific mission of finding essence. Contrary to the general interpretation, the essence cannot be found in the work of art as 'thing' itself, but in the interaction of the observer with the artwork in a process of focussing - of pure concentration and attention. Such pure attention creates a field of force engulfing at least the observer and the artwork. This effect is triggered by the artwork in the perception of the observer. Thus the actual working of a work of art happens as 'no - thing'. Since colours and materials are perceived by the waves of light they reflect and also by some emittance of electromagnetic waves, basically an artwork can be perceived as radiating a field of forces. The human observer also emits an electromagnetic field (and other waves, such as heatwaves). The existence of these emissions gives rise to much popularized but hypothetical non-sense, like theories on coloured auras and the like.

---

[72] Carl Friedrich von Weizsäcker, "Zeit und Wissen", p.259-260: "Der Terminus "Kunst" erklärt die Weise der Erkenntnis des Eidos: ... Kunst ist die Wahrnehmung von Gestalten durch die Schaffung von Gestalten."

[73] Kitaro Nishida, "Intuition and Reflection in Self-Consciousness" (New York: State University of New York Press, 1987 - orig. "Jikaku ni okeru chokkan to han sei", 1941), p.62.

However, the existence of such emissions cannot be denied and they do play a role in our perception. It is a process that allows us to sense a presence of a person or object in complete darkness. Without intending any 'New Age non-sense', one can assume it is a way we unconsciously and continuously scan outwards. The described interaction in perception can metaphorically be understood as a meeting and interacting of the two fields of forces: one emitted by the (art)object, the other emitted by ourselves. These fields are both, by definition, a combination of individual and universal forces.[74] After reading the other chapters in this publication (such as on the way our brain processes perception, in which the synchronization of rhythms plays a crucial role, as do rhythmic influences from outside the brain), hopefully it becomes clear that the existence and importance of these interacting fields of energies between the artwork and yourself is no weird theory, but quite a possibility. My hypothesis discards the idea that the essence can be found in the artwork itself as a property of the created object.

Unfortunately, in their quest to understand the meaning of art, art historians still seem to prefer traditional pictorial analysis above a possible different meaning based on a more profound understanding of our perception. Such an understanding has to include more complex aspects than the classic technique of standing in front of a painting, assuming to look at it in perfect isolation, and starting to analyze the composition, materials, etc.[75] This approach seems to be provoked by a wrong interpretation of statements by artists like Kandinsky. He wrote - clearly in the tradition of the Platonic and Aristotelian eidos-philosophy, and Hindu Vedantic philosophies: "... form is the external expression of the inner meaning ...".[76] Personal emotions of the artist obviously lead his or her choices while creating a work of art, but the strong analogies in composition, in dynamics, etc. in general between otherwise very different works of art suggest more than merely personal emotions. These properties of a work of art may give access to the essence of the world and life itself. New knowledge and theories that include the acknowledgement of projections outside our brains/bodies in the process of our thinking provide us with enough reasons to take the concept of interacting fields of force between observer and observed seriously.[77] Theories and ideas of artists like Kandinsky are very valuable, but should always be understood in immediate context to the time when they were developed. When explained differently, it is probably more correct to say that 'the inner meaning' is meant not merely as the personal emotions of the artist, but as a reflection of the deep meaning of nature that underlies all phenomena of everyday reality. With this interpretation, Kandinsky's quote assumes a very different content that is more related to our current information and thinking. This seems quite plausible when we recall the proven interest of Kandinsky in Vivekananda's lectures on Vedantic concepts.

---

74 This topic is discussed more extensively in §5 on the projective field, including the various artist's concepts, like by Frank Stella, Gotthard Graubner or my own.

75 Pictorial analysis is discussed later in this chapter.

76 Paul Overy, "Kandinsky - The language of the eye" (London: Elek Books Ltd, 1969), p.77.

77 See §5.

It seems that our acknowledgement of the relativity and limited duration of our lives fuels our desire for wholeness, to feel unified with the absolute and infinite power of reality, of nature as a whole. This desire seems to reflect the search for the eidos and seems to be a major source for art, science, philosophy and also for religion. Religion, here, is not meant as any specific institutionalized belief, but as the general human belief in a masterplan of nature designed in a certain cohesion of facts and intuitions.[78] That man slowly has become conscious of the fact that he is not the center of the universe makes a new understanding of our position in the cosmos even more desirable.[79]

"ART? No Thing!" concerns the essential, the combination of the universal and individual of nature offered to you as in-form-ation through your dialogue with what is presented to you in the individualized form of an artobject. Form is here understood as the manner in which an object appears to us. Appearance includes all the properties of size, colour, composition, material. Nature is not only landscape, but the whole from the macrocosm of the universe down to the microcosm of the smallest particles. The basic truth is that even when one lives in the back-room on the 17th floor of a building, one cannot escape being part of the overall processes of nature. In contrast to what we like to believe, in principle all phenomena, all processes of reality seem still to be interactive and logical processes, although not understood as earlier, simplistic interpretations of straightforward cause and effect - or stimulus and response - in behaviorist theory in psychology or the action-reaction theories in early physics. The level of complexity - that with all our modern knowledge we still can only know by approximation - of the infinite variety of interactions that influence every single one of these processes differently, allows these processes to appear to be unique - they appear to us to contain a large percentage of individuality and appear to suggest free will. This is so complex that one can safely state that there is no clearly definable difference between a next step in a highly complex logical process and a next step as result of individual choice; the individual choice we, in our culture, perceive as free will.

2.5 THE '8' AS METAPHOR

Metaphors are often useful to support the understanding of complex subjects. To that purpose I propose to use the sign '8' (also used on its side as symbol for infinity: ∞), as a metaphor for the processes that lead to understanding the eidos. When push and pull-forces occur around a static center one can imagine a set of circles around this center, like the ripples in a pond in which one has thrown a stone. But as in nature no center can be static - in the everchanging cosmos with its intricate interactions of gravitational

[78] Please, read the quote from Goethe at the start of §1 again!

[79] This I once discussed with the artist Michael Kidner, who considers this fact to be the reason why figurative art, that puts man in the center of the universe, is less 'realistic' than non-figurative art. Although this is a highly interesting hypothesis, we can never avoid that our own bodies are the starting point from all our activities and perceptions. Therefore, against all knowledge we will always put ourselves somewhat in the center of the universe. I agree with Michael, however, that it is our challenge to try to define our non-central position in nature without a denial of our individual selves.

forces no thing can actually stay in the same spot in space/time - these push and pull forces form a complex picture of three-dimensional shapes for which the '8' seems indeed to be the right metaphor.

The number 8 symbolizes a universal principle that you will encounter repeatedly in this publication: a seemingly infinite, oscillating and in itself returning movement. It symbolizes the combination of push and pull forces in nature which cause rhythm and change. In the terminology of The Spiritual Society, the '8' is called 'ogdoad' and is related to the Greek 'caduceus' and the mathematical symbol for infinity.[80] It is explained as the eternal and spiralling movement of cycles ... the regular breath of the Cosmos.[81] In the 17th century the German mystic Jakob Böhme sought to find the forces and conflicts that underlie human existence. He wrote: "The eternal center and the Birth of Life ... are everywhere. Trace a circle no larger than a dot, the whole birth of Eternal Nature is therein contained."[82] Maurice Tuchman describes how mystics as Böhme searched for the life-form that underlies everything. This life-form or 'Ur-Form' was considered to be the thyrsus or double ellipse.[83] This shape also brings to mind the endless Möbius-strip, although it does not necessarily show a real '8'- shape. This strip, named after August Möbius, who published its description in 1865, can be constructed by taking a long thin strip of paper and joining the narrow ends after giving the strip a half-twist. The artist/theorist Max Bill became famous for his Möbius-strip sculptures in stone, steel and gold, although he always claimed not to have known about Möbius. This can be quite true as it has happened frequently in history that artists have worked on certain form or composition-principles that show clear analogies to scientific discoveries, without knowing these discoveries.

---

[80] See Robert P. Welsh, "Sacred Geometry: French Symbolism and Early Abstraction", in Maurice Tuchman, "The Spiritual in Art: Abstract Painting 1890-1985" (New York: Abbeville Publishers, 1986) p.66. Ogdoad is a notion originally used in ancient Egypt; the "Ogdoas" was considered to be the 8th level, above the 7 planets, the heavenly level to which the souls of the dead rise. One could also rise to the 9th level, the "Enneas", and to a 10th level, the "Dekas", the level of the not procreated God (the agennètos) - the eternal who is One and Ten simultaneously; these concepts are discussed in the ancient manuscript "The Eighth and Ninth Level", in the Codex VI, found at Nag Hammadi together with the famous Dead Sea scrolls (see Prof. Dr. G. Quispel, "De Hermetische Gnosis in de loop der eeuwen - Beschouwingen over de invloed van een Egyptische religie op de cultuur van het Westen ", p.47). As such it seems the name 'ogdoad' reflects the function of the mentioned Spiritual Society to be an intermediate platform between the levels of everyday living and the higher, divine levels; without implying any spiritual contents, it seems that my proposal to use the "8" functions in a metaphoric sense as a comparable intermediary, only not referring to a divine higher level, but merely referring to the very soul of the whole of nature.

[81] Compare the remarks on Ch'i, beauty, chronobiology and the solar wind as will be discussed later. In 1694 Jakob Bernouli, the mathematician from Basel, Switzerland, gave the '8' the name 'Lemniscate'. His knowledge builds on Perseus (150 B.C.) and Giovanni Cassini (1625), who linked this movement to the orbits of the stars. See Dietmar Guderian, "Eine Lemniskate umschreibt Äußeres und Inneres erfahren", in "Lemniskatische Prozesse" (Weil am Rhein: Galerie Edition Stahlberger, Kunstverlag Gotha, 1995).

[82] See Maurice Tuchman, "Hidden Meanings in Abstract Art", in Maurice Tuchman, "The Spiritual in Art: Abstract Painting 1890-1985", p.19.

[83] In different cultures one can find images of two coiling snakes, possibly referring to the balancing of nature's forces. In Occidental culture we still can find this as the well known aesculape or caduceus symbol for medical services.

This has also often happened the other way around. On the cover of Scientific American issue October 1993 one finds a coloured picture of a still from a computer-generated film of a sphere being turned inside out (or 'inverted'), produced at the Geometry Center in Minneapolis, Minnesota, USA.[84] Now it becomes intriguing to look at the paintings by the sculptor Naum Gabo that show remarkable similarities. Especially Gabo's "Kinetic Oilpainting in four motions" from 1943 which is even in *exactly* the same colours as the afore-mentioned computer still (hues of orange-reds)![85] Gabo was a sculptor studying many properties of space with a keen interest in the analogies between art and science. At the start of his career he followed courses in medicine, physics and engineering. So, this could be more than merely chance. At the very least, Gabo can be considered to have had a highly intelligent intuition! The phenomenon of the endless Möbius-strip, which in principle is not exactly an '8' - shape, but nevertheless shows clear similarities as a spatial and endless form looping back into itself, was discussed at length by Douglas Hofstadter, popular in the 1980's.[86] His book was popular amongst scientists, mathematicians, philosophers and artists. This may not be surprising, as he discusses artificial intelligence while comparing the Möbius-strip to the mathematics of Gödel, the impossible figures in the art of M.C. Escher and the complex fuges of Bach. These ideas can be connected to discussions about the perception of art in direct relation to understanding the preferences of the artist for certain compositions. In 1900 the German writer and poet Rainer Maria Rilke, inspired by observing Rodin's sculptures, wrote:

> *"For sculpture another property is very important: that the artwork should end within itself. A 'looking from the image outwards' never happens as such, when the image of the specific meant figure could still be extended in front or in the same manner behind it, so that the perception of the shape (Gestalt) nevertheless stays inside the image and is separated from the observer as if by a non-conducting and airless space."*[87]

Clearly related to this idea, but more recent than Rilke, psychologist Rudolf Arnheim discusses in one of his books the confrontation of the artist with the center of the composition in his art. He writes: "A principal function of defined space is that it creates its

---

[84] See John Horgan, "Can Science Explain Consciousness?", Scientific American, July 1994, p.72-78. It is the scientific video proof of a topological theorem by William P. Thurston of the Mathematical Sciences Research Institute.

[85] See Herbert Read and Leslie Martin, "Naum Gabo - Bauten, Skulptur, Malerei, Zeichnungen, Grafik" (Neuchatel: Editions du Griffon, 1961 - orig. London: Lund Humphries, 1957), picture 129.

[86] Douglas Hofstadter, "Gödel, Escher, Bach: An Eternal Golden Braid" (New York: Basic Books Inc., 1979; in Dutch translated by Ronald Jonkers, published by Uitgeverij Contact, 1985).

[87] Rainer Maria Rilke, 17.Nov 1900, published in Rainer Maria Rilke, "Auguste Rodin" (Frankfurt am Main: Insel Verlag, 1984 - orig. 1955), p.115: "Für Plastik ist noch ein Umstand ungemein wichtig: daß das Kunstwerk in sich zu Ende gehe. Ein >Aus-dem-Bild-Herausschauen< ist insofern nie der Fall, als das Bild immer vor der betreffenden gemeinten Figur noch zu erweitern ist (Vordergrund) in demselben Maße wie hinter derselben, so daß der Blick der Gestalt immer noch im Bilde bleibt und vom Beschauer wie durch einen nicht leitenden luftleeren Raum getrennt ist."

own center." [88] As such, Arnheim describes how the artist is struggling with the concentric and eccentric push and pull forces at the center in the composition.[89] He supposes that the artist is more or less forced to circle or loop around the center. Although this is not an entirely false interpretation, I find Arnheim's typical Gestalt - psychological concept much too simplistic and too restricted. It is a good example of the danger of searching for the meaning of a work of art in pictorial analysis alone, expecting to find the meaning of a particular work of art by analyzing how the composition evolved as a result of a logical building process, while ignoring any other sources that could have influenced the preferences for creating such a composition.[90]

Likewise, it would be too limited to consider science to be only about exercising certain mathematical methods. Mathematics are applied to discuss a different problem (for instance, the orbit of the earth around the sun) instead of merely mathematics itself. Mathematics are the tools, not the objective. It is my conviction that in general we can find in many art - compositions the '8'-like oscillation of forces, because we instantaneously but unconsciously recognize in this composition the most fundamental property of nature, the eternal flow of energy, and the most decisive property of the reality in which we are immersed. If this were not so, somewhere through the century-old development of art someone would have come up with a different kind of composition that would have been interpreted as a more suitable solution. A tradition cannot just come out of nowhere, it is to a large extent a result of a natural desire. We do not find this '8'-like oscillation only in the artistic composition. It is also a good metaphor for the process of perception of looping back and forth as someone looks at an (art)object. Philosopher Henri Bergson clearly referred to this when he wrote in 1908 about the process of attentive perception, criticizing the general opinion that perception was merely a rectilinear process. Bergson believed perception was a cicuitous process, looping back and forth between the perceiver and the perceived.[91] Later in this publication we will see that this idea still is quite appropriate, as will be exemplified when we will look at some ideas about perception and some artist's statements, for instance by Frank Stella.

---

88 See Rudolf Arnheim, "The Power of the Center - A Study of Composition in the Visual Arts" (Berkeley: University of California Press, 1988), p.58.

89 Arnheim's concept pretty much seems to be based on the assumption by Heinrich Wölfflin, "Kunstgeschichtliche Grundbegriffe - Das Problem der Stilentwicklung in der neuen Kunst" (Basel/Stuttgart: Schwabe & Co Verlag, 13th edition, 1963 - orig. 1915) p.28: "Jedes Kunstwerk muß ein geschlossenes Ganzes sein, und es ist ein Mangel, wenn man findet, es sei nicht begrenzt." In English in "Principles of Art History - The Problem of the development of Style in Later Art", translated by M.D. Hottinger, (Dover Publications Inc., 1932), p.15: "Every work of art should be a finite whole, and it is a defect if we do not feel it is self-contained, ...". Quite similar to what Rilke stated, as mentioned above.

90 Later in this chapter we will see more about the problems of pictorial analysis.

91 See Henri Bergson, "Matter and Memory" (Zone Books, 1988 - orig. "Matière et mémoire", 1908 - first edition published in 1896), p.104: "We maintain, on the contrary, that reflective perception is a circuit, in which all elements, including the perceived object itself, hold each other in a state of mutual tension as in an electric circuit, so that no disturbance starting from the object can stop on its way and remain in the depths of the mind: it must always find its way back to the object from where it proceeds."

In aesthetic theory one studies our experience of the attraction to look at objects, which is quite relevant to our discussion on the eidos. The desire to understand eidos or essence stimulates our attention and curiosity, causing the experience of attraction. The property of objects that attracts our attention is not to be found as an existing 'material thing' or elementary particle in its construction, but as certain aspects of its appearance - composition, colour, shape - that seem to refer more or less to the fundamental *process* of nature's push and pull dynamics. This brings to mind the confrontation in science between the desire to understand nature as a huge and complex construction, but as construction nevertheless (discarding those non-empirical aspects that do not fit the concept of construction) and the desire to understand nature as the complex whole, accepting and including the immeasurable complexities that we see everyday around us. The first approach urges a search for the elementary particle. The second approach seeks the structure of the process of the whole.

How does art, as a medium of our perception, deal with this? Is not figurative art better equiped to inform us about actual reality? Or, is abstract art a more intelligent approach to what reality is actually about, and has it outdated figuration? What can we say about this non-sensical but still existing cliché battle in the artworld in context to our eternal search for understanding the eidos?[92] As is well known, in art one always refers to mimetic art, which represents nature as we see it, and to non-mimetic art, as that which refers to more abstract concepts of reality. Mimetic art focuses on the copying of parts of our immediate environment and tells stories as a form of visual literature. Non-mimetic art focuses more or less on the structure of processes, telling the story of reality in a way that cannot exactly be verbalized, but must be sensed at a deeper level.

Swiss aesthetical theorist and philosopher Professor Hans Heinz Holz describes how this notion of 'mimesis', as it is used in art theory, is wrong. Mimesis in fact means the copying of a process of action. Holz discusses Aristotle's understanding of our appreciation of painting, sculpture and poetry as not being something evoked by its similarity to reality or by its level of copying reality. Instead our appreciation is awakened by the spiritual act that makes us acknowledge the artwork in its accordance with the natural processes of reality, something Holz sees exemplified in the close interrelation between words and the magical-ritual function of dance.[93] In dance, the natural or mythical phenomena are presented through gesticulations to make their value for life in society accessible

---

92 The confrontation between figurative and abstract art as described here is indeed non-sense, that becomes clear when one for instance compares the dynamics of great Baroque paintings by Tiepolo or Rubens with early abstract painters like Delaunay or Kupka. The only difference is that the Baroque painters used shapes of painted persons and the abstract artists similar but abstract shapes. See §10 on the narrative!

93 Hans Heinz Holz, "Der ästhetische Gegenstand - Philosophische Theorie der bildenden Künste I" (Bielefeld: Aisthesis Verlag, 1996), page 145: "That mimesis in fact does not mean the copying of things, but of processes, so that its analysis by a syllogism can be made similar in meaning to the process of nature itself, can be retrieved from the narrow connection of the word to the magical-ritual function of dance." (orig: "Daß Mimesis nicht eigentlich die Nachahmung von Dingen, sondern von Prozessen meint, so daß ihr Nachvollzug durch einen Syllogismus als gleichbedeutend mit dem Naturvorgang selbst besetzt werden kann, ist aus der engen Bindung des Wortes an die magisch-rituelle Funktion des Tanzes zu entnehmen.")

(dancers, with the expressions of their bodies, hands, facial expressions, etc. provide access to some narrative on life, without actually using words). Besides, the aspect of repetition in ritual dance allows the evocation of the desirable or the avertion of the undesirable. In my opinion, dance offers a very good metaphor for the aspect of change in nature itself as well as for the functioning of art in our perception![94] That is also why the dance between chaos and order of the Hindu God Shiva is such a powerful image of change. In the dance the body is the center from which the arms and legs move through space in a kind of curved motions. The notion of dance as such, including the aspect of repetition, also can metaphorically be understood as a '8'-shaped process.[95]

2.6 SEMIOTICS, LINGUISTICS, THE SCIENCE OF ART

As a logical result of a growing need to study the real meaning of art, clearly related to the development of science and philosophy at the time[96] and falling in line with the tradition of the eidos-philosophy, at the end of the 19th century a diversity of theories emerged concerning a science of art (Kunstwissenschaft). Conrad Fiedler and Heinrich Wölfflin were important in these developments.[97]

This must not be confused with art-*theory*, which is a much older discipline, and has always been a part of general philosophy. The science of art focussed upon *the pictorial analysis*, which later grew into a conviction that it should merely concern a strictly formal analysis of the artwork - independent of context, theory, statement or emotion - studying our perception as if we are machines with mechanical eyes, ignoring many aspects of human perception. Its aim was a study of art itself devoid of all non-artistic considerations, in an attempt to offer an objective approach for discussing and analyzing art while avoiding a quality judgement.[98] In my opinion, this was a logical result of

---

94 The importance of the involvement of the actual human body in dance can be linked to the importance of the involvement of body-parts (mostly the hands) in the manipulating process we call the creative process of making art - see §5, where I discuss perception.

95 It might be interesting to refer to the old notations of choreography as developed by Raoul-Auger Feuillet, published in his "Chorégraphie, ou l'art de décrire la danse par caractères, figures et signes démonstratifs", 1700, which can be understood as the written transcription of movements. These notations show remarkable kinship to the attempts by early abstract artists to translate movements into painting a couple of centuries later! Because a lot of choreography deals with swirling movements on and around the center of a stage these notations are also interesting as they more or less reflect the '8' shaped movement. See Arnould Pierre, "Staging Movement", in Marla Prather, "Alexander Calder 1898-1976" (Washington: National Gallery of Art; New Haven: Yale University Press, 1998), p.334. Compare Calders own notations for his "Ballet in Four Parts" from 1934.

96 For instance the discussions in science on our natural need for geometry, the general foundations of geometry, the basics of light and colourperception, the emergence of phenomenology in philosophy, etc..

97 Both Fiedler and Wölfflin lived, lectured and published at the start of the 20th century. They influenced many art historians and early (abstract) artists in their own days and eversince.

98 Art historian Patricia Railing, "From Science to Systems of Art - On Russian Abstract Art and Language 1910-1920 and other essays", p.134-135: "... Fiedler shows that the artist's relationship to the world is of a particular kind, that through feeling and thinking he is seeking truth, and that therefore the artistic history of art must use intellectual principles that recognize and retain categories of analysis that are truly of art, if the history of art is to be about art itself."

trying to pin down the essence in a work of art and to provide the untrained some clues for understanding and appreciating this essence in a work of art.[99] Although the idea was pretty good, unfortunately, like with so many good ideas, in the end it erroniously led to only discussing one's perception of a work of art in terms of composition, craftmanship, material, etc. using standardized criteria instead of including and trusting the experiences evoked by one's personal and immediate encounter with the work of art - experiences that are more difficult to describe - if at all.[100] It seems to be one of man's largest problems in communication and acquiring knowledge that he needs notions or concepts to be able to discuss and understand phenomena, but as soon as such a notion or concept is proposed there are so many minds who approach the notion or concept in a sheer bureaucratic fashion and, therefore, miss its whole point and get lost in trivialities. Unfortunately this often leads to a discussion about the form of the concept, not about the content or intention. This clearly also happened with the great efforts of Fiedler and Wölfflin. The problem - also the reasons for wrong interpretations - of this concept is a double sided conflict: it can be helpful to focus entirely on the art as thing in an attempt to find its meaning, but simultaneously one can only find its proper meaning in its context - beyond its material thing-ness, in the experience of life itself, beyond the parameters of the history of art!

In 1915 linguist Ferdinand de Saussure published his theory that language was developed by man to communicate with another man. To that purpose language should be consistent and contain a strict order for words and sentences. The language thus consisted of *signs* that did refer to another reality: words referred to an object or a feeling.[101] That same year Heinrich Wölfflin, who had a more philosophical background, published his lectures on stylistic principles in art in Munich.[102] Wölfflin analyzed style

---

99 Was this an application of the aristotelian ousia as style in painting and sculpture perhaps? See at the start of this chapter.

100 It is an interesting phenomenon that always wherever, whenever, someone proposes an idea, concept or approach that is basically sound, succesful and new, later one always finds followers who, like good bureaucrats indeed, try to make all possible rules more precise, more restricting, often forgetting, ignoring or sometimes even opposing the original meaning, changing a helpful guidance into inflexible institutions. This happened to many religions, but also for instance to behaviorism in psychology, to pictorial analysis or to constructivism in art itself.

101 Ferdinand de Saussure, "Cours de linguistique générale", ("Course in General Linguistics"), 1915.

102 Heinrich Wölfflin, "Kunstgeschichtliche Grundbegriffe - Das Problem der Stilentwicklung in der neuen Kunst" ("Principles of Art History - The Problem of the Development of Style in Later Art"). Wölfflin lectured at Munich 1912-1924. His lectures were visited by artists like Kandinsky, Franz Marc, Hans Arp, Kurt Schwitters, Naum Gabo. See Railing, "Malevich and European and Russian Formalism", in magazine PRO-NR.9 (Dordrecht: PRO Foundation, 1993), p.41. Gabo probably studied with Wölfflin in the summer of 1913. He refers to private meetings with Wölfflin in an interview published in "Art in America" No.6-1966, see Christina Lodder, "Gabo in Russia and Germany 1890-1922: A Biographical Study", in Steven Nash and Jörn Merkert, "Naum Gabo - Sixty Years of Constructivism" (Prestel Verlag, 1987) p.49. Wölfflin understood "... art as elementary expression of human being and, therefore, as anthropological constant" (orig.: "Kunst als elementaren Ausdruck menschlichen Wesens und damit als anthropologische Konstante"), quoted in Hans Heinz Holz, "Strukturen der Darstellung - Philosophische Theorie der bildenden Künste II" (Bielefeld: Aisthesis Verlag, 1997), p.40. Hans Heinz Holz discusses how the ideas of sculptor Adolf von Hildebrand were important inspirations for Wölfflin. Hildebrand considered that art always concerned creation of space

characteristics based on the following polarities: 1) the development from the linear (the line of sight of the eye) through a devaluation of the linear to the painterly (mass); 2) the development from a two-dimensional plane into actual three-dimensional space; 3) the development from a closed form at rest (static) to the open form (in movement); 4) the development from a multiplicity of parts to a unity; 5) the absolute and the relative clarity of the mimetic object (composition, colour and form are not necessarily functioning purely to support the explication of the form, but have been given their own meaning).[103] Wölfflin thought style was strictly related to a particular worldview of the artist. This changes when his worldview changes. He was convinced that styles develope from simple to complex, from tectonic to non-tectonic, from closed to open, from linear to painterly forms, while the later forms could not exist without the earlier ones.[104] Wölfflin emphasized that the optical structures are only the lowest level, on which the levels of formal expression (concerning style)[105] are mounted, on top of which the level of real content is mounted. The 'Grundbegriffe'[106] only concern the optical constitutional conditions that allow the emergence of a variety in expression.[107] Once more it must be emphasized that there is nothing wrong with pictorial analysis - especially not in the way intended by Wölfflin. Pictorial analysis can definitely help one see how an artist simulated the complex dynamics that we perceive in our immediate perception of a particular painting. But, one should not leave it at that without including the more intuited meaning.

as a natural result of acknowledging that we are continuously surrounded by extending space. A sense for this space is created by the presentation of objects or by the spatial properties of objects. Space is exemplified by form and offers the medium for the co-existence of many individual things Hildebrand, in "Das Problem der Form in der bildenden Kunst", 1893, in Hans Heinz Holz, "Strukturen der Darstellung - Philosophische Theorie der bildenden Künste II", p.40-46: "The most elementary experience that we make in front of nature is that we are enclosed from all sides by a extending space. It is demanded from the painter, that he can embody this all enveloping space-experience in his painting." (orig.: "Die elementarste Erfahrung, die wir der Natur gegenüber machen, ist die, von einem allseitig sich ausdehnenden Raum umschlossen zu sein.Vom Maler ist zu verlangen, daß er diese alles übertonende Raumempfindung seinem Bilde als Wirkung einverleiben können."). It is highly interesting to compare this thought to the extended vision by Russian artist Matjushin, as will be discussed later.

103 See Heinrich Wölfflin, "Kunstgeschichtliche Grundbegriffe - Das Problem der Stilentwicklung in der neuen Kunst", p.27-29. Please, compare these polarities to the information on the point, the line, the plane later in this publication.

104 See Hans Heinz Holz, "Strukturen der Darstellung - Philosophische Theorie der bildenden Künste II", p.57. His emphasis on the process "from the simple to the complex" obviously falls into the tradition of believing in general progress in western thinking eversince the Enlightenment at the end of 18th century.

105 Style = characteristics according to time, culture and personality.

106 Heinrich Wölfflin, "Kunstgeschichtliche Grundbegriffe - Das Problem der Stilentwicklung in der neuen Kunst", p.5: "Die 'Grundbegriffe' sind hervorgegangen aus dem Bedürfnis, der kunsthistorischen Charakteristik eine festere Basis zu geben; nicht dem Werturteil - davon ist hier nicht die Rede - sondern der Stilcharakteristik." "Principles of Art History - The Problem of the Development of Style in Later Art", translated by Hottinger, p.VII: "The 'Principles' arose from the need of establishing on a firmer basis the classifications of art history: not the judgement of value - there is no question of that here - but the classification of style."

107 See Hans Heinz Holz, "Strukturen der Darstellung - Philosophische Theorie der bildenden Künste II", p.51.

Though both Fiedler and Wölfflin did not describe abstract art as examples for their theories, their own descriptions do sound like descriptions of abstract art.[108] They inspired, for example, Kandinsky, Malevitch, Gabo, Charles Biederman and later art critics like Herbert Read. The painter Malevitch, who extended his name as a theoretician in 1919 when he started working on his paper "On New Systems in Art/Statics and Speed", developed his educational 'Theoretical Charts'. These were a kind of pedagogic charts with pictorial analyses of very different kinds of art, formulating the history of art as a history of signs, clearly inspired by linguists as De Saussure and art scientists like Wölfflin. He wrote: "Through the analysis of colour and form in a work, we can cognise the mood of the experience of [the artist's] soul."[109]

Art historian Patricia Railing explains how Malevitch tried to analyze colour by selecting the consistent range of colours found in an artist's work. The analysis of form was achieved by the analysis of the line of the general order given to a work by the artist and by isolating the most characteristic line as a sign. Thus he found a linear, graphic sign that he understood as 'the additional element'. Malevitch wrote:

> *"Through its graphic delineation, the additional element is a formula or distinguishing sign that indicates the whole ordering and make-up of the painterly body, of its colouration and of the level of development of the culture concerned."*[110]

The actual shape of this curved additional element is also interesting since it comes quite close to the kind of oscillating composition I discuss as the '8'-shape of eidos (which I did not know at the time I became intrigued in the shape of the '8'!). To Malevitch, the additional element is the reference to the eidos that is buried in the art-work, comparable maybe to Dogen's Shobo Genzo or the Buddha-nature earlier described in this chapter.

In the same period, approximately between 1915-1920, in Western Europe new impulses for graphic design came from the industries and governments who needed new ways to communicate with the masses, while in Russia after 1917 such impulses were needed for propaganda purposes.[111] It should be of no surprise that this development went hand in hand with the emergence of advertising - psychology, which can be understood as a

---

[108] It might be interesting to note, that Wölfflin never applied his ideas to non-mimetic art, for instance on the paintings by Mondrian. See Hans Heinz Holz, "Strukturen der Darstellung - Philosophische Theorie der bildenden Künste II", p.52.

[109] See Railing, "Malevich said: "Art is Cognition", in Ernest Edmonds and Linda Candy, "Proceedings Second International Symposium 'Creativity and Cognition'" (Loughborough: Loughborough University of Technology, 1996); The quote is from Malevich, K., "Theoretical Charts" in "Malevich", edited by Catherine Cook, Art & Design Vol.5, No.5/6, 1989, p.37. For more information on this aspect of Malevitch's extensive knowledge, see Linda S. Boersma, "On Art, Art Analysis and Art Education: Theoretical Charts", in "Kazimir Malevich 1878-1935 (Amsterdam: Stedelijk Museum, 1989) p.206-222.

[110] See Railing, "Malevich said: "Art is Cognition", in Ernest Edmonds and Linda Candy, "Proceedings Second International Symposium 'Creativity and Cognition'", p.16.

[111] The emergence of commercial advertising and campaigns to promote the importance of hygiene, see also §3.

commercial application of the knowledge established by the 'Kunstwissenschaft' of Fiedler and Wölfflin in combination with the propositions of early semiotics. The links to avant-garde art and to the latest knowledge about signs in linguistics were logical and clear.[112] In my opinion, artists like Malevitch, Matjushin or Kandinsky seemed to have used the pictorial analysis to find the essence, the eidos, implying again there is in principle nothing wrong with the original implications of this method. Only through the following decades did the pictorial analysis in art criticism grow into a rigid fixation on the composition, the formal analysis of the chosen form and use of material, while ignoring questions about the *what* and *whatfor* of an artwork (its context or the ideas, circumstances and feelings of its creator).[113] This is also what has made the study of language extremely difficult.

The general agreement between semioticians about the clear meaning of a certain sign certainly does not mean that everyone understands this sign only in this way![114] The word 'cross' can mean to one person the symbol for Christ's suffering or salvation, to a second person it can mean the universal symbol for the sun, to a third person it means the cross-roads in life, to a fourth person it means the fundamentals of the horizontal and the vertical meeting, etc. Associations are often so complex and individually different that one can justifiably doubt if it is possible at all to build a theory around the meaning of signs. I can only hope that it is clear that the use of a sign as a metaphor - implying no strict meaning but a kind of field of meanings - like my use of the '8', is a different thing. In my opinion, it could still be interesting to study signs just as we find them, if we are capable of not being restrained by the explanation given by a particular culture and can acknowledge its more universal meaning. I believe only in such a way are we able to acquire access to the eidos and not to loose our way by confusing local explanations. The cross, for instance, is a powerful sign, but can only be studied without any described meaning. A sign has an a priori reason to exist, a verbalized meaning of a sign is attributed after the sign already exists and is, therefore, by definition an explanation that fits into a human-made doctrine and could miss the true meaning and original attraction to the sign completely. Attaching such cultural meaning to a sign gives it a kind of artificially projected eidos. The strong value of signs do exist of course, but mostly as illustration of a doctrine. But signs are not the complete story about the eidos.

The conviction that signs present the elementary truth has contributed quite substan-

112 Artists were involved in designing a general system for road-signs, like the German artists Karl Peter Röhrl, Werner Graeff and Walter Dexel. See Bernd Finkeldey, Kai-Uwe Hemken, Maria Müller, Rainer Stommer, "K.I. - Konstruktivistische Internationale 1922-1927 Utopien für eine Europäische Kultur" (Düsseldorf: Kunstsammlung Nordrhein-Westfalen; Stuttgart: Verlag Gerd Hatje, 1992) p.106+131.

113 An example is Rudolf Arnheim "The Power of the Center - A Study of Composition in the Visual Arts".

114 Semiotics is the study of signs resulting in a structural analysis of meaning. Signs can be words in a language - based on the phonetic expression (not on the grammar) - or visual signs in man made visualizations (for instance the cross) or even the meaning provided by the appearance, the form and colour, of an object (this is the reason why semiotics is considered important to industrial design). Important representatives of semiotics are Roman Jakobson and Charles W. Morris (who published "Foundation of the Theory of Signs", 1968). Semiotics has grown into a complex theory with its own highly specialized language.

tially to the wrong and regressive road of l'art concret, minimal art and its many dogmatic followings.[115] A very 'pure' sign would be absolutely objective and, therefore, communicate its universality immediately - and nothing else. As nothing in the world can be only universal this is quite impossible! Even the a priori meaning of signs is not strictly universal, which one may find when one tries to describe its universality, that is why the a priori meaning has to be more or less vague (more precise descriptions are for instance culturally influenced, therefore, not universal anymore).

One can find the acknowledgement of this fact in many philosophies and in Buddhist ideas, where always the individual and the universal are combined. Traditional pictorial analysis offers a means for understanding a work of art, but should never be the only access to art (and certainly not to the eidos!). It may never indoctrinate or lead the experience of the observer, as it leads to an unjustified mistrust of visual perception as such and the involved intuitions or feelings. This especially applies in German-speaking countries, where many still overvalue the 'Nachvollziehbarkeit' of art (the accessibility to retrace the process of creation of the work of art). Thus, in my opinion Kandinsky's pseudo-scientific approach in "Punkt und Linie zu Fläche" represents a wrong approach,

---

115 In art for a variety of reasons one can see a large leveling or equalizing on a simplistic aesthetic level, parallel to a general interest in easy entertainment. This is in contrast to the emergence of a new desire for more content and depth in combination with a plurality of styles, not only among artists, but also among art theorists. Holz, for instance, discusses the fierce critical remarks of Arnold Hauser on Wölfflins' fundamental notions as being much too limited (published in Arnold Hauser, "Philosophie der Kunstgeschichte", p.142, see Hans Heinz Holz, "Strukturen der Darstellung - Philosophische Theorie der bildenden Künste II", p.54-66). Holz himself summarizes how rule-setting leads to 'academism' and how out of 'academism' will grow a more complex new approach. Hans Heinz Holz, "Strukturen der Darstellung - Philosophische Theorie der bildenden Künste II", p.56: "In the confrontation with traditional patterns of order a desire for legitimation emerges, that is reflected in the invention and formulation of rules of space configuration - rules, that for their part are obtained from the 'objective' properties of space, defined for instance by the classification in the coordinates-grid; the fundamental notions of the classification, as were developed by Wölfflin, clearly show this origin. Once the limits of the rules are reached, it is exhausted within its possibilities in academism, thus a next phase of the search for visual expression becomes a transmission of simple rules of connections into complexity, approaching order in a seemingly disorder, to find new sensible relations, that formulate the till then unsaid." (orig: "In der Auseinandersetzung mit traditionellen Ordnungsmustern entsteht ein Legitimationsbedürfnis, das sich in der Erfindung und Formulierung von Regeln der Raumdarstellung niederschlägt - Regeln, die ihrerseits an den 'objektiven' Eigenschaften des Raumes, die zum Beispiel durch dessen Einteilung im Koordinatennetz bestimmt sind, gewonnen werden; die Grundbegriffe der Klassizität, die Wölfflin herausarbeitet, zeigen deutlich diesen Ursprung. Ist der Umkreis der Regeln einmal ausgeschritten, erschöpft sich das innerhalb ihrer Grenzen Mögliche im Akademismus, so wird eine nächste Phase der Suche nach visuellem Ausdruck eine Überführung der einfachen Beziehungsregeln in komplexe, der Ordnung in scheinbare Unordnung anstreben, um neue sinngebende Relationen zu erfinden, die bisher Ungesagtes formulieren."). This is exactly what happened in constructive art, in conceptual art and in more general and temporary fashionable tendencies like politically correct art, etc., and what will always happen in modern art. As soon as there is some success to a certain kind of art, definitions are written that are transformed into rules, finally leading to sheer artistic poverty and academism. But always new groups of artists emerge who revolt against such academism. This does not need to be in the tradition of modern avant-garde, meaning a destruction of what was considered mainstream art, but for instance by offering well crafted artworks of beauty and depth in contrast to easy jokes, cheap shocks or boring objectivism in art. The art-market in general, art institutions, the interest of a wide variety of art dealers, art-lovers and collectors, all can and do play an essential and positive role in this process, having the ability to stimulate such renewal.

still leading to so many false interpretations of a supposed hierarchy of pictorial means.[116] We definitely do not perceive first a point, then a line and, finally, a plane. This is a hierarchy resulting from the traditional belief that the drawing is the primary medium of visualization, which is based on a classical thinking out of the medium instead of out of perception itself!

This tradition stems from a very long debate on the philosophical, mathematical and theological implications of the point, the line, the plane.[117] We do perceive patches of colour (better: quanta of colour), allowing us, by sheer contrasts, to see borderlines and outlines on surfaces and objects, but still *no* lines or points as separate units in nature itself. Part of the confusion is that Kandinsky (and Malevitch[118]) used line as equivalent to form. Kandinsky's approach obviously has meaning, but it is an especially good example of how an idea of limited value through a process of pseudoscientific reasoning becomes a dogma, which by definition has nothing to do with the reality for which it was meant. When one studies the often highly coloured paintings from Kandinsky or Malevitch one can quite safely conclude that neither ever meant that the importance of the line should lead to artists using *only* black lines for representing truth![119]

Another example of a wrong pseudoscientific reasoning is the "l' Art Concret" manifesto from Van Doesburg and his co-signers in 1930. In its own time, it possessed a certain logic and certainly was important, but ever since it has been used and still is being used in a very wrong way. For instance the artist Van Doesburg declared that art is universal and that

"*... the work of art must be entirely conceived and formed by the mind before its execution. It must receive nothing from nature's given forms, or from sensuality, or sentimentality.*"[120]

This might indeed be a logical step after the development of the modern notion of the object from Kant's concept of the 'das Ding an sich'[121] and Schopenhauer's 'union of the individual and the universal' to a longing for finding the pure and universal, although

116 Wassily Kandinsky, "Point and Line to Plane" (Dover Publications Inc., 1979 - orig. "Punkt und Linie zu Fläche", 1926). Kandinsky also changed his opinion. He acknowledged that the artist has not to follow only strictly rationalized or pure logical ways of artmaking but the inner voice (intuition). See Wassily Kandinsky, "Betrachtungen über die abstrakte Kunst", 1930, in Max Bill, "Kandinsky - Essays über Kunst und Künstler" (Bern: Benteli Verlag, 1963 - orig 1955), p.147.

117 See §12.3 - discussing that it was not Kandinsky's original intention to be dogmatic, merely to offer an approach for education in graphic design (at the Bauhaus). Some recent ideas in neurophysiology suggest Kandinsky was still right, but not completely. See §5 The Projective Field.

118 See Railing, "Malevich said: "Art is Cognition", in Ernest Edmonds and Linda Candy, "Proceedings Second International Symposium 'Creativity and Cognition'", p.12.

119 In contrast, quite a few artists in the 1960's thought that only black and white lines and all white compositions were the 'essential'.

120 Van Doesburg together with his colleagues Carlsund, Hélion, Tutundjian and Wantz in April 1930, see Stephen Bann, "The Tradition of Constructivism" (Da Capo Press, 1990 - first edition 1974), p.193.

121 'The thing in-itself'.

this really is a repetition of Descartes' mistake to try to be able to think without influence from the senses.

Furthering Van Doesburg's concept, artist Max Bill saw possibilities for developing a way to make the creative process of art more objective. He promoted the 'mathematical approach' - not to be confused with the application of actual and exact mathematical formalism - but as conscious and logical implication of rhythms, relationships and laws defined by the artist.[122] The concept that art should be pre-thought before execution in combination with the emphasis on 'Nachvollziehbarkeit' (not even mentioning the influence on art by Wittgenstein and his ideas about a perfect language) has held geometrical art in an iron grip ever since. Especially in the late 1950's until the early 1980's many artists really saw this as an objective, almost scientific and undisputable approach for showing the pure eidos. The irony is that they still were (or are) stuck in a kind of Newtonian approach, although already since the late 1920's (Quantum Theory) in science a growing tendency emerged to no longer avoid or dismiss non-empirical aspects of reality perception.[123] After reading this essay it should have become clear that dogmatism in art is quite often related to dogmatism in other fields (for instance, in linguistics). Just as in linguistics one has become doubtful about signs and semiotics, just as in science one has become doubtful about linear laws of nature, just so pictorial analysis in art should not be limited to any formalistic method but involve also many more aspects of reality that do not fit in any method!

In 1996 I visited a Max Beckmann exhibition at the Soho Guggenheim Museum, New York. The walls were painted in a relatively strong Naples yellow that almost matched the yellow Beckmann often used in his paintings. The obvious result was that the brilliantly coloured Beckmanns did not seem as brilliant as they usually are. Although theoretically it was a sound idea to realize a clear link between the environment and the paintings, it was still a big mistake in the impact of the interaction of colours by the exhibition designer. One can only understand this consciously when one is not merely trying to approach the paintings by the traditional pictorial analysis which tries to isolate the painting as a product in one's vision. Even when you concentrate very hard, you cannot escape the influence of the environment on your perception. In this exhibition, while going from painting to painting, no visitor could escape the degrading impact of the yellow walls, though most people thought they were focussed only on the paintings themselves. A precise understanding of the composition of a work of art only tells you half the story. As was said before in this chapter, the real function of any composition

---

[122] Max Bill, catalogue text "Pevsner, Vantongerloo, Bill", 1949, in Annemarie Bucher, "Die Spirale - Eine Künstlerzeitschrift 1953-1964 (Aarau: Lars Müller Verlag, 1990), p.17: "The mathematical way of thinking in contemporary art is not mathematics itself, yes, it even hardly uses what one considers to be exact mathematics. Art concerns much more a creation of rhythms and relations, of laws that have an individual origin." (orig.: "Die mathematische Denkweise in der heutige Kunst ist nicht die Mathematik selbst, ja sie bedient sich vielleicht kaum dessen, was man unter exakter Mathematik versteht. Sie ist vielmehr eine Gestaltung von Rhythmen und Beziehungen, von Gesetzen, die individuellen Ursprung haben.").

[123] This will be discussed in §6 and §7.

in a work of art is that it triggers an interaction in the observer. That this is not a new idea, is exemplified by the following quote from the American philosopher John Dewey:

> *"The product of art - temple, painting, statue, poem - is not the work of art. The work takes place when a human being coöperates with the product so that the outcome is an experience that is enjoyed because of its liberating and ordered properties."*[124]

This interaction is indeed an *inter*-action, meaning involving an action coming from both sides. The action of the rebounding of the lightwaves evoking the colours, shapes and material of the composition of the artwork in combination with the action of the perception of the observer in his projective field.[125]

2.7 WHAT WE CONCLUDE AT THIS POINT

What can we indeed conclude at this point? The essence is a property of all phenomena that we can perceive, but it is not the only property of each phenomenon. Therefore, it is no use to try to isolate it in any empirical way. It is not possible to distill the essence in very precise terms. Nor is it possible to find any precise definitions or laws of universals. This is also true for the essence in art. The way to find the essence as reflected in, or better, evoked by artworks can clearly not be found by sheer simplistic pictorial analysis. One has to trust oneself to go deeper to the levels of our perception and understanding that are more or less 'beyond words'.

Our desire to find the essence of reality is a logical result of being conscious. As will be discussed properly in §5, we could never be conscious without any interaction with the world we live in. We only become self-conscious by reflecting upon this interaction, in which process projection of our thoughts into our environment and our motoric movements play important roles. As I discussed with several Oriental philosophies and Schopenhauer as examples, the concentration or focussing of our thoughts to the level of becoming fully absorbed and thus being able to venture beyond our individual personality is certainly a way to find the actual essence - eidos - sunyata, a level of concentration in which a certain material object as subject of concentration can be very helpful. The experience of the 'thing' leads to the acknowledgement of 'no thing'. Therefore, it becomes natural in this process to experience things, objects or phenomena as bearing meaning. It becomes logical to experience this meaning as essence - especially when we intuitively experience a similar meaning existing in more objects and phenomena. In this process of concentration, the projection of our own selves onto the objects perceived is unavoidable. The perception of the existence of the essence and the desire to understand, therefore, means nothing else then the desire to understand the self. When we do reach a level of understanding we indeed can state, "I see my self". Or, as Viveka-

124 See John Dewey, "Art As Experience", p.214.
125 See §5 "The Projective Field".

nanda said, this leads to the virtual experience of reality answering you: "Thou Art That!"
The key to appreciating the importance of art is to understand the reasons why art plays such an important role in this process - offering a road to the essence of the whole of nature in a different but still comparable way to science and philosophy. The essence in science might be described as the search for an empirical understanding of reality by finding the most elementary relationships at the micro-level of particles and the major forces at the macro-level of the universe. The location of our human perception lies in the middle between these micro- and macro infinities. That is the level where art tries to find and understand the eidos. Perhaps we can say: although science aims to find the eidos of objective nature, the experience of art aims to find the essence of comprehensible nature.

§3 ON CONSTRUCTIVISM

Representational or figurative art may be about literary illustration, certain aspects of relationships in society, the appearance of objects, persons or the landscape.[1] These can be with or without message, meant to educate, glorify, critisize, shock or entertain. Whatever their subject or objective, representational art always focusses on a part of reality. However, if one is interested in researching what art can contribute to a deeper understanding of reality - beyond the first impression of our immediate environment - and one is interested in how art can participate in the discussion of wholeness, then abstract art seems to be the medium. To get some idea of the importance of acknowledging the relationships between art, science and philosophy and building on the various traditions concerning the meaning of the essence of reality, it might be useful to discuss a tendency in 20th century abstract art that, from its very beginning, had clear links with science and philosophy: constructivism. It should be stated, though, that it is definitely not my opinion that constructive art offers the only access to the essence, nor that it is more important than any other form or direction in art! The narrative of which representational art is always 'accused' certainly can also focus one's attention on the essence of reality through the right use of composition, gesture, application of colours and forms, and the use of allegory - as in Impressionist or Baroque paintings. Besides, all abstract art also incorporates a narrative of some kind.[2]

Because of the extensive information that exists about the constructive tradition, information on all the magazines, groups and individual artists, I cannot really do justice to its rich history here. Hopefully the many footnotes will provide you with the right clues to find more substantial information.[3]

In this publication I will mainly discuss constructivism in art, not in science or psychology.[4] What is important is to understand that constructivism as a movement did not pop up out of nowhere, but was a logical result of the level and focal points of

---

[1] Mimetic art is not as clear a notion as is often considered. See the discussion on mimesis in §2.

[2] This obviously is no black/white truth. See §10 The Narrative of Being.

[3] Some of the aspects in the art and theory of constructivism will be discussed in other chapters more precisely, particularly in §6 Space/Time.

[4] In modern psychology constructivism is a general theoretical position which proposes that perception and perceptual experience are constructed out of - in the words of Gregory: "... volatile fragmentary scraps of information, for a part caught by the senses, for another part from memory-banks - that are itself constructions from bits and pieces out of the past." See A.S. Reber, "Woordenboek van de Psychologie" (Amsterdam: Uitgeverij Bert Bakker, 1994 - orig. "The Penguin Dictionary of Psychology", 1985), p.119. On Gregory, see R.L. Gregory, "Eye and Brain - the psychology of seeing" (World University Library, 1971 - orig. 1966). In this account, perceptual experience is not understood as merely a response to a stimulus, but as a construction of hypostasized cognitive and affective operations. In sociology, social-constructivism is the family name for all theoretical approaches that emphasize the social character of the human construction of meaning. Social construct<u>ion</u>ism is introduced by K.J. Gergen as a theoretical scientific approach of psychology and its field of enquiry. Gergen states that the phenomena studied by psychology are in fact historical and social constructions. More recently constructivism has been taken up by psychotherapy and is considered to be part of the postmodernist approach. This approach in modern constructivist or constructionist psychotherapy is based on the assumption that nobody makes his or her image of reality based on objective observation but as

knowledge in art, science and philosophy around the first two decades of the 20th century. Although the notion of construction is much older and the notion of constructing a painting was used by Kandinsky earlier,[5] it is generally believed that the word constructivism in art was first proposed by the Russian artist Vladimir Tatlin.[6] He is said to have been inspired by the three-dimensional developments from collages he saw in Picasso's studio in 1913.[7] Another Russian artist, Alexander Rodchenko, proposed the notion 'non-objectivism', using only a straightedge and compass to make drawings and sculptures.[8]

Constructivism, as it has been used by later generations of artists, is based on the assumption that the world around us is constructed according to some logic (consisting of elementary particles as building blocks and laws by which they are constructed). Our image of this world, reflected in art, should therefore also be constructed out of elementary parts and be based on pure logic. All non-logical aspects, all subjective elements, such as visual or optical illusion, should be avoided at all costs. Resulting from the desire to find the essence of reality in combination with the impulses provided by the new science of art, it was considered that art should only follow its own laws, not those of nature's appearance. Therefore, an objective approach comparable to the approach by a scientist or engineer should be adopted by the artists to explore the universal principles that constitute reality. This approach was the logical result of earlier theories and philosophies of universal laws, values and truths.[9] Artistically, it was the

---

a construction of subjective realities. See Barbara Held, "Constructivism in Psychotherapy: Truth and Consequences", in Paul R. Gross, Norman Levitt, Martin W. Lewis, "The Flight from Science and Reason" (New York, Annals of the New York Academy of Sciences, Volume 775, The New York Academy of Sciences, 1996). Held discusses the confusion and different interpretations in psychotherapy in terms of constructivism. It is interesting, in a sense, that the notion of constructivism also evokes very different interpretations in this field, similar to what happened 70 years earlier in art.

5 Wassily Kandinsky, "Concerning the Spiritual in Art" (Dover Publications Inc, 1979 - orig. "Über das Geistige in der Kunst", 1912) , p.57: "... I would remark that, in my opinion, we are fast approaching the time of reasoned and conscious composition, when the painter will be proud to declare his work constructive. This will be in contrast to the claim of the Impressionists, that they could explain nothing, that their art came upon them by inspiration. We have before us the age of conscious creation, and this new spirit in painting is going hand in hand with the spirit of thought towards an epoch of great spiritual leaders." Officially "Über das Geistige in der Kunst" is dated 1912, but actually was published Christmas 1911, while a Russian summary was published and distributed in Moscow a couple of days later, see Kunsthalle Tübingen, "Kandinsky - 'Die Welt Klingelt' - Hauptwerke as dem Centre Georges Pompidou Paris" (Cologne: DuMont Verlag, 1999), p.16. Kandinsky also wrote in "Über die Formfrage" ("On the Question of Form"), in Robert Motherwell, "The Documents of 20th Century Art: Der Blaue Reiter Almanac, edited by Wassily Kandinsky and Franz Marc ", edited by Claus Lankheit (New York: The Viking Press, 1974 - orig. 1912), p.186: "Later the reader can go on with the artist to objective reflections and scholarly analysis. Then he will find here that all the examples respond to the same inner call - composition; that they all restore the same inner basis - construction." The original German version is reprinted in Max Bill, "Kandinsky - Essays über Kunst und Kultur" (Bern: Benteli Verlag, 1963 - orig. 1955), p.46.

6 See Larissa Alekseevna Zhadova, "Tatlin" (London: Thames and Hudson, 1988).

7 Described by George Rickey, "Constructivism: Origins and Evolution", (New York: Georg Brazilier, 1967 - reprinted in the 1990's), p.17.

8 'Non-objectivism' can be understood as a consequence of the understanding that no solid matter exists, only particles in particular formations. Translated into art, early constructivists like Rodchenko understood this concept to mean that no objects should be depicted anymore, but abstract shapes and forms in a composition.

logical outcome of the process of art history.
Beginning with early rock paintings and engravings we can find all through human history an interest in geometric images.[10] In early cultures, like in the Hindu, Chinese, Egyptian, Babylonian, Greek and somewhat later in Islamic cultures, geometry in religion, art, philosophy and science played important roles. In the western world, Kant believed our interest in geometry resulted from our a priori intuition of the form of space. From the Enlightenment onwards artists gradually started to wonder what kind of reality art should represent. Schopenhauer and his contemporaries in the first half of the 19th century promoted the allegory as the subject, because it symbolizes something it does not show, thus making the hidden content more important than the presented image.[11] Schopenhauer also believed in the importance of well done architecture in manifesting the nature of light, which can have a wholesome effect on the mind. Impressionism[12] took the importance of the nature of light in painting much further. Pointillism[13] and Cézanne introduced the fragmentation of a painting in painted entities, like dots or similar brushstrokes put together into harmonic and rhythmic compositions. Nietzsche's philosophy was also widely studied by artists. He thought knowledge was fundamentally constructed, in a process based on our pragmatic need to find an order in our everyday experiences.[14]

In the 19th century there was a growing interest in geometry[15] and ideal compositions

---

[9] Compare the various philosophies and ideas as described in the previous chapter.

[10] It is assumed that the abstract rock-engravings and paintings found in South- and Northern Spain, Portugal, South France, Northern Italy, Corsica, Sardinia, Crete, Switzerland, Austria, Bulgaria, England, Scandinavia, Russia and the Canarian Islands, date from about 15.000 - 5000 BC. See for instance Felix R. Paturi, "Monumenten uit de Oertijd - Getuigen van de Prehistorie", translated by J.H. Esvelt (Deventer: Uitgeverij Ankh-Hermes, 1978, orig. "Zeugen der Vorzeit", Econ Verlag GmbH). On the British Islands, in Portugal, Spain and Switzerland one can find concentric circles scratched into rock (also in a great variety of other cultures in Africa, Asia and Australia). Famous places were scenes with animals and persons and geometric patterns are the caves in Altamira, Spain, and Lascaux, Dordogne, France. Also one has found objects decorated with geometric patterns or symbols. See for instance Carl Schuster and Edmund Carpenter, "Patterns That Connect - Social Symbolism in Ancient and Tribal Art"(New York: Harry N. Abrams, 1996).

[11] This seems quite comparable to oriental art in Zen, where the actual meaning cannot be - must not be - provided by the image shown, but must be evoked by the depicted scene or (calligraphic) symbol. The actual meaning is to be searched beyond the image shown, not within the image itself. In calligraphy this is the strongest: it is not about the words depicted, it is not even about the poem represented, but 'beyond' that, evoked by what one sees (the actual reason why a lot of Zen calligraphy is not actually readable, but barely recognizable as a poem).

[12] See the previous chapter on the meaning of 'l'impression'

[13] Pointillism is a way of painting by which the image is fragmented in little dots of pure (unmixed) paint. A mixing of colours is accomplished by combining dots of different colours close to each other in an optical effect known as the interaction of colour. Pointillism in particular is inspired by 19th century ideas about optics and light.

[14] Nietzsche considered that our sense for control provides us with the illusion that everything, including ourselves, is constant. This is a (superficial) construction of knowledge, because in fact everything, including ourselves, is changing continuouly while also being submitted to a continuous flux of events. Still, we cherish this illusion, because it allows the idea of being in control. See §7.3.

[15] In the 19th century Non-Euclidian geometry was discovered and the theories of visual perception by

based on certain series of numbers.[16] Henri Poincaré made a distinction between 'geometrical space' and 'representational space'. [17] Geometrical space, the more scientific domain, would be abstract, three dimensional and infinite, its properties everywhere the same. Representational space would be the domain of everyday reality and would include three spaces: the visual, tactile and motor space. It was only a matter of time until artists focused on a pure geometrical art with the ambition of finding a universal language in art, desiring to contribute to understanding 'real reality', comparable in importance to the contribution by science - meaning not *like* science, but *analogous* to science, through an artistic approach.

Since the late 19th century, exemplified and stimulated by the Arts and Crafts, Art Nouveau and Jugendstil movements, artists had been involved in dissolving the boundaries between fine arts and applied arts (continuing the approach of art, architecture and decoration design of earlier centuries, exemplified in the building of cathedrals). Ornamentation of buildings and furniture, utensils, embroidery, clothing, theater design, graphic design, were taken just as seriously as fine art painting and sculpture.[18]

The direct link the first generations of constructive artists saw between art - applied art/industrial design - architecture - urban design and everything in between (like graphic design, theater design) was enhanced by the opportunities for artists of the time. Due to certain political and economic developments, artists could earn a living in these applied fields and not so much in painting or sculpture.[19] In addition, it fired their idealist sentiments to contribute as artists to the dynamic process of socialization. Artistically, it was a natural and logical conclusion to think about the essential properties of shape, colour, form, and material - finding the essential in the work of art itself.[20] In general, constructivism in art meant the creation of abstract artworks in which the artist shows nothing more than the most fundamental construction. To show more would make the work of art unnecessarily ornamental, decorative, and not essential.

In science, constructivism means mathematics, which is considered the equivalent of

---

Johann Heinrich Pestalozzi had quite an impact on education. This is further discussed elsewhere in this publication. See for instance §12.

16 For instance, the Golden Section and the Fibonacci series. See Dénes Nagy, "Golden Section(ism): From Mathematics to the Theory of Art and Musicology", in "Symmetry: Culture and Science", Volume 8, Number 1, 1997 p.74 - 112 (Budapest, Hungary: ISIS Symmetry, 1997). Besides, there was a growing interest in Hindu, Indian Buddhist and occult philosophies which include many geometric- and number systems, diagrams, etc..

17 Published in 1902 in his well read bestseller "La Science et la Hypothèse". For an outstanding discussion on how and why it is clear many artists around 1905-1910 read or knew about these new scientific ideas about space, for instance through the explanations of the mathematician Princet, who frequently met artists like Picasso, Braque, Metzinger and others, see Arthur I.Miller, "Einstein, Picasso - Space, Time, and the Beauty That Causes Havoc" (New York: Basic Books, 2001).

18 See Peg Weiss, "Kandinsky in Munich - The Formative Jugendstil Years" (New Jersey: Princeton University Press, 1985).

19 As discussed later in this chapter, these developments include the emergence of industrial serial production, of commercial advertising and commercial fairs, of political propaganda, of international campaigns (for instance about hygiene), new ideas about social housing for people employed by the industries, etc. but also the emergence of traffic and the need for more uniformity in road-signs.

20 Clearly connected especially to the aristotelian concept of eidos: the ousia. See §2.

intuitionism founded by the Dutch mathematician L.E.J. Brouwer.[21] Brouwer considered mathematics a way of primary intuitive thinking independent of the general laws of logic and unseparably linked to the intellect itself. Mathematical activity consists of constructions and activities in the mind of the mathematician and as such is opposed to the pure formalistic opinion that mathematics is merely a formal manipulation of symbols existing for its own sake.[22] It is important to understand that the constructivist aspect of Euclidian geometry often refers to straightedge and compass constructions.[23] This obviously is related to constructivism in early abstract art.

When one hears of constructivism for the first time - or reads about the interpretations by Tatlin or Brouwer - it may seem that there is a clear understanding about its definition. As with so many directions in art, schools or groups, this is not so. But, then again, the same occurs in science, philosophy or politics.[24] When one studies the available

21 Luitzen Egbertus Jan Brouwer (1881-1966) published his ideas in 1912 in his "Intuitionism and Formalism", also translated into English, which received a wide audience. As early as 1907 he already had published his "Over de grondslagen der wiskunde" ("On the foundations of mathematics"). See Henk de Jager, Hendrik G. Matthes, M.H.J. Schoenmakers, "Het beeldende denken - Leven en werk van Matthieu Schoenmakers" (Baarn: Ambo, 1992). See Marvin Jay Greenberg, "Euclidian and Non-Euclidian Geometries - Development and History" (New York: W.H. Freeman and Company, third edition, 1994). See Jan Bor, Errit Petersma, Jelle Kingma, "De Verbeelding van het Denken - Geïllustreerde geschiedenis van de westerse en oosterse filosofie" (Amsterdam/Antwerpen: Uitgeverij Contact, 1997 - eerste druk 1995), p.338, 339.

22 Other *constructivist* mathematicians were Bishop, Beeson, and Stolzenberg. They insisted that a mathematical object can only exist when an effective method is found to construct this object with mathematics.

23 See Marvin Jay Greenberg, "Euclidian and Non-Euclidian Geometries - Development and History", p.49. Constructivism in early abstract art, for instance in Russian Constructivism and related groups like the Dutch "De Stijl", Polish "Blok" and "A.R.", Hungarian "MA", the "Hannover Abstracts", etc. See for example: Stephen Bann, "The Tradition of Constructivism" (Da Capo Press, 1990 - orig. 1974); Magdalena Dabrowski, "Contrasts of Form - Geometric Abstract Art 1910-1980" (New York: The Museum of Modern Art, 1985); Kai-Uwe Hemken, Reiner Stommer, "K.I. - Konstruktivistische Internationale Schöpferische Arbeitsgemeinschaft 1922-1927 - Utopien für eine Europäische Kultur" (Düsseldorf: Kunstsammlung Nordrhein-Westfalen; Stuttgart: Verlag Gerd Hatje, 1992); Hans Jaffé, "De Stijl: 1917-1931 Visions of Utopia" (Minneapolis: Walker Art Center, 19..); Andrei Nakov, "L'Avant-Garde Russe" (Fernand Hazan, 1984); Ad Petersen, "De Stijl", parts 1+2, the complete reprint (Amsterdam: Athenaeum, and Bert Bakker, Den Haag; Polak & Van Gennep, Amsterdam, 1968); Serge Lemoine, "Mondrian and De Stijl" (Art Data, 1987); Paul Overy, "De Stijl - Art.Architecture.Design" (London: Thames and Hudson, 2000 - orig.1991); Patricia Railing, "From Science to Systems of Art - On Russian Abstract Art and Language 1910-1920 and other essays" (Artists Bookworks, 1989) and "On Suprematism - 34 Drawings - K. Malevitch" (Artists Bookworks, 1990); George Rickey, "Constructivism - Origins and Evolution" (Georg Brazilier, 1967); Willy Rotzler, "Konstruktive Konzepte - Eine Geschichte der konstruktiven Kunst vom Kubismus bis heute" (Zürich: ABC Verlag, 1977); Irving Sandler, "Concepts in Construction: 1910-1980" (New York: Independent Curators Inc., 1982); Schirn Kunsthalle Frankfurt, "Die Grosse Utopie - Die Russische Avantgarde 1915-1932" (Frankfurt: Schirn Kunsthalle, 1992 - in English: "The Great Utopia", Guggenheim Museum NY); Sprengel Museum Hannover, "Internationale Avantgarde 1927-1935 - Die Abstrakten Hannover" (Hannover: Sprengel Museum, 1987); Ryszard Stanislawski, Christoph Brockhaus, "Europa-Europa - Das Jahrhundert der Avantgarde in Mittel- und Osteuropa" (Bonn: Kunst- und Ausstellungshalle der Bundesrepublik Deutschland, 1994); Maurice Tuchman, "The Spiritual in Art: Abstract Painting 1890-1985" (New York: Abbeville Publishers, 1986); Andrzej Turowski, "Konstruktywizm Polski - Proba Rekonstrukji Nurtu (1921-1934)" (Polska Akademia Nauk, Institut Sztuki, Ossolineum, 1981) and "Existe-t-il un Art de l'Europe de l'Est? Utopie & Ideologie"(Les Éditions de la Villette, 1986). See also the many books on the individual artists as some will be listed in the list of literature at the end of this book.

24 For instance, what was considered to be a socialist in most countries must today be called a 'social-democrat'.

information one finds quite easily that constructivism is a notion more or less related to a general concept for art, philosophy and science without a clear-cut definition. At the start of the twentieth century, thinking of reality as a construction was a generally discussed thought.

Lounatcharski, who after the Russian Revolution became Soviet-Russia's first commissar for propaganda and played a crucial role in involving early avant-garde artists to contribute to society, wrote already in 1908 about the new man as a construction.[25] He described construction in a way that was later taken up by the early constructivists: as total control over matter - over nature - involving all forces to accomplish a dynamic and effective artwork while searching to define and construct a new life. Another essay, published in 1913, pleads for the necessity of a universal science of organization, based on the assumption that the rules of organization that can be found in the cosmos should not be translated into absolute universal formulas, but into practical formulas that can be applied to better organize - construct - society.[26] El Lissitzky lists two groups who considered themselves constructivists.[27] But one must also mention Naum Gabo and his brother Antoine Pevsner who published "The Realistic Manifesto" in 1915.[28] Or, Alexei Gan and Alexander Rodchenko and the many simultaneous developments in other European countries like Hungarian artist, designer, theorist and important educator

Since the end of the Cold War mere socialist is understood to refer to the old communists!

25 Lounatcharski considered socialism to be the struggle of mankind with nature in an effort to submit nature to a complete sovereignity of logic. He understood the desire and hope of mankind to win this struggle to be a religion that, supported by a rightfully applied scientific socialism, would 'construct' the 'Übermensch', the improved or better man. Lounatcharski published these ideas in his essay "Religion and Socialism". His ideas clearly are built on Nietzsche's philosophy on the new man, to which we will come later. See Hubertus Gaßner, "Alexander Rodschenko - oder die Kunst, das Leben zu organisieren" (Frankfurt am Main: Fischer Taschenbuch Verlag GmbH, 1984), p.87. Lounatcharski's role is an outstanding example of how a politician can contribute to the history of art in a very important way - without prescribing what the artists should make. Without Lounatcharski we probably would have had no knowledge of the Russian avant-garde and its impact on all design - even today. His institute was called The People's Commissariat of Enlightenment, known as Narkompros, founded in 1918.

26 The essay mentioned is by A. Bogdanov, "Filosofija zivogo opyta"("The Philosophy of Living Experience"), see Hubertus Gaßner, "Alexander Rodschenko - oder die Kunst, das Leben zu organisieren", p.88. Gaßner, same page, quoting Bogdanov: "Such a universal science of organization is possible, as 'general methods and laws do exist, through which the different elements of the cosmos organize themselves into complexities. This thesis ...' - continues Bogdanov - '... allows the foundation of this new science - with which support human mankind can strictly organize its creative forces and its life in every sense...' " ("Eine solche universelle Organisationswissenschaft sei möglich, da 'allgemeine Methoden und Gesetzmäßigkeiten existieren, nach denen die verschiedenen Elementen des Weltalls sich zu Komplexen organisieren. Diese These..' - schreibt Bogdanov weiter - '... gibt das Fundament für jene neue Wissenschaft ab ... mit deren Hilfe die Menschheit ihre schöpferischen Kräfte, ihr Leben auf der ganze Linie wird planmäßig organisieren können...' "). Patricia Railing discusses the difficulties around the concept of constructivism even in its first years in Russia, see Railing, "PROUN: The Interchange Station of Suprematism and Constructivism", in The Structurist, issue 31/32, 1991-1992.

27 El Lissitzky in his famous lecture "New Russian Art" in 1922 in Hannover, Germany, presented in relation to an exhibition of his own art. He mentions the Obmokhu: the Stenberg brothers, Myedunyesky, Yoganson. And he mentions the Unovis: Syenkin, Chasnik, Klucis, Ermolayeva, Khidekel, Kogan, Noshov, and others led by Malevitch and El Lissitzky.

28 For an outstanding essay on the context, origin and impact of "The Realistic Manifesto" see Martin

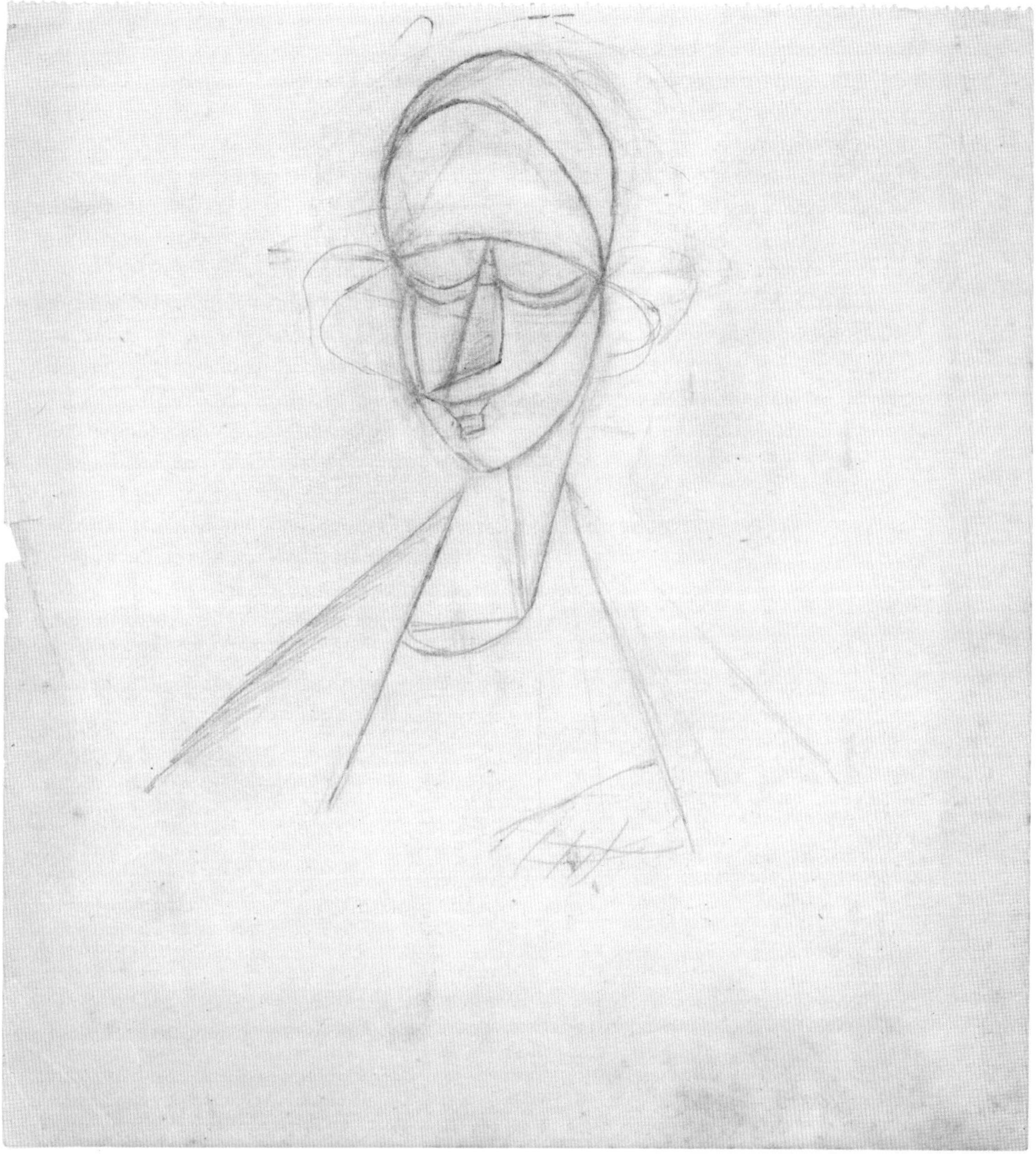

5. Naum Gabo (1890-1977) **Study for Head No.1**, 1915 Pencil on paper, 19 x 17 cm (71/2 x 63/4 inches), Collection Foundation for the New Arts FNA

This little drawing can be considered the start of Naum Gabo's artistic research to pioneer modern sculpture in which solid mass is opened up to the flow of space/time. Although Picasso, Balla, Boccioni and Tatlin experimented with three-dimensional translations of Cubist paintings, Gabo's heads went much further. To accomplish this, Gabo developed a 'reverse perspective', constructing his sculptures from cut-out planes. Together with Tatlin's amazing "Corner Counter Relief" of the same year, one may consider Gabo's drawing and resulting sculpture of historical value for all sculpture after 1915.

László Moholy-Nagy. Moholy-Nagy first became known in Hungary, before becoming one of the major professors at the Bauhaus in Germany. The Bauhaus, which theorized for a multi-disciplinary approach towards an improvement of our everyday environment and all the products in it, still sets the tone for all contemporary industrial design. Escaping fascism, Moholy-Nagy in the early 1930's moved to the USA where he first held influential courses on art and photography in New York before becoming one of the founding professors of The New Bauhaus at Chicago, which later was re-named the ITT School of Design that still exists today. In addition, there were many more simultaneous developments all through Europe in the 1920's and early 1930's.

An important general characteristic of constructivist art was an attempt to visualize the cosmic powers of nature; those powers that scientific knowledge and theories showed exist 'under' or 'behind' the visible reality of our existence. To be able to present this, the artists tried to show clear constructions as re-constructions of the motions of nature.[29] As such, many opted for clear and 'honest' visualizations, hoping to approach artistic problems in a kind of scientific way.[30] The result was that sculptors like Tatlin or Gabo wished to discard colour for its illusionary properties and preferred to use the properties of the material - like unpainted wood, steel or glass. Symmetry was not considered an important feature by these artists, although a kind of symmetry can be found in some paintings by Malevitch, Kliun or Gontcharova. The purest symmetry was used by Rodchenko (in a very nihilistic sense) when he painted his highly idealistic pure monochrome paintings in 1921 (one in red, one in yellow, one in blue), declaring that this showed painting in its elementary truth - as pigment on a canvas - without reference to any image, symbol or expression. The painting as object only exists as product of the producing subject (the artist). As the producer, however, does not manipulate the medium in any way - only shows it as it is - the object and the producing subject become one. The resulting unification lifts the barrier between man and object and, as such, realizes the unification of man with nature.[31] This would be the end of painting. This was a bold semi-political statement quite typical for that time, as painting was understood by many bolshevik artists as an academic, elitist metaphor for the bourgeoisie. It is also typical

---

Hammer and Christina Lodder, "Constructing Modernity - The Art & Career of Naum Gabo ", §3 (New Haven: Yale University Press, 1999).

[29] See §2, footnote 95 on the notations in choreography. See also §6 on "Space/Time".

[30] Please, recall also earlier this chapter the short reference to Poincaré's distinction between geometrical space and representational space. In those early days of 20th century, mathematics was considered to be the absolute language of science through which one must try to understand reality. It is interesting to understand that colour as phenomenon cannot be translated into mathematics, and would have no role in Poincaré's geometrical space. It would 'therefore' be of no real interest to a scientific view on reality. This makes it quite natural that some artists who desired to be as objective as scientists wished to disregard colour (like Picasso and Braque did around 1910 by limiting their colour-choice to browns and greys). Their huge mistake was obvious: whatever theory, we need to understand reality at 'eye-level', meaning that aspects of vision like colour cannot be ignored. It is interesting that colour was introduced as an important visual tool in scientific thinking when colour photography, but especially since computer-animations, diagrams and computer translations of all kinds of research have become standard.

[31] See Hubertus Gaßner, "Alexander Rodschenko - oder die Kunst, das Leben zu organisieren", p.46-48. A concept for at least a part inspired directly by the Vedantic philosophy of 'finding the True Self' beyond the

for the idealistic considerations in that era to be linked to ideas from Theosophy,[32] but also a result of very serious observations of artworks and of our interaction with a work of art.

Nevertheless, Rodchenko's statement does not hold, as an objective choice of colour is impossible: a red chosen by an artist is a subjective choice from the many reds that are available or can be mixed, just as the choice of the size of the canvas is a subjective one. Later we will see that the unification of artwork and subjective observer is a justified observation, but it is definitely not limited to monochrome painting, as it is more a property of attention and perception.[33] Painting in all its variations was never finished and never will be. Similarly, in the modern world the existence of the computer has not finished painting, sculpture or architecture.

The emergence of simultaneous interests of artists, architects and theorists in constructivism was not an opportunist response to incentives from the international art-market, as one might expect in today's world. In the 1920's or 1930's there still was virtually no art-market! The inspiration to take up constructivism came first from a commitment to contribute as artists to the improvement of our knowledge of reality - with the desire to be as important as scientists in this matter. The big impulses came however from politics and economics, which led artists to take up their responsibility to try to improve society by improving all design.[34] This was on one hand the result of the political changes in Europe: the communist revolution in Russia, the need for an international non-elitist society for all working-class people after the slaughter of World War I.[35] On the other hand, lots of excitement and inspiration to accomplish this new mission for artists came from modern science, especially from theoretical physics and astronomy. Although most artists will not have actually studied Poincaré, Minkowski, Bohr or Einstein, they picked up general ideas about space/time and translated their understanding into artistic concepts of a fourth dimension. Exceptions were some of

self as separate, egocentric entity, see §2.

[32] Theosophy was an approach initiated in 1875 by Helena Petrovna Blavatsky, considered to study and analyze all existing and accessible occult ideas, concepts and theories aiming for a spiritual way of life, based on the assumption that all knowledge has the same fundamental roots. See §8, footnote 38.

[33] Though in art all developments seem to be repeated once in so many years, it still is somehow ironic and typical for human history that first in the late 1950's and 1960's - mainly under influence of a superficial interest in Zen and sheer wrong interpretation of 'nothingness' as empty void (this concept became available to western artists through the publications of for instance D. Suzuki. See Heleen Westgeest, "Zen in the fifties - interaction between east and west" (Zwolle: Waanders Uitgevers, 1996))- one can still find many artists painting again only in dull monochromes, mistakingly believing that more than the monochrome surface would be too distracting.

[34] Every object in our environment has some effect on our perception of reality, and therefore, on our well-being. The artists researched how more consciously developed design could have a more positive effect. This coincided with the emergence of serious interests in hygiene as a social topic, particularly in working class households, inspiring artists to advocate clean, clear and non-elitist messages in their works. But this also coincided with the emergence of commercial graphics (advertisement) in the West and the need for new propaganda-tools in Russia after the revolution. This interest in typography also evoked further serious thinking about linguistics.

[35] The elite of the nobility and bourgeoisie were considered guilty for WW I, sacrificing working-class people by the thousands for their political games.

the pioneers of abstract art, like Naum Gabo,[36] Wassily Kandinsky, Frantisek Kupka, Michael Matjushin[37] and Kazimir Malevitch, who actually did study scientific knowledge - especially 19th century scientific concepts published by the American Hinton[38] or made available in Russia by the philosopher and mathematician Ouspensky.[39] The ideas of projective geometry became well known to Matjushin and Malevitch through the theories of Lobachevsky.[40]

El Lissitzky referred in one of his lectures to the space/time curvature of Einstein. Around 1919 El Lissitzky changed the Suprematist linear motion of his paintings (rectangles and squares virtually flying parallel in one direction) into compositions that clearly simulate a motion that is curved - often curling back into itself.[41] The abovementioned artists have all emphasized the importance of connecting art and science in a new synthesis. In my opinion, this explains why Kandinsky, for instance, developed an artistic translation and application of his ideas concerning the importance of the point, the line and the plane, exemplifying motion and dynamics similar to theories in the

---

36 Naum Gabo started studying medicine at the University of Munich in 1910. Martin Hammer and Christina Lodder describe in their outstanding "Constructing Modernity: The Art & Career of Naum Gabo" the reasons why around 1910 several Russian artists studied in Munich, Germany, who became key figures in the development of abstract art (Jews in Russia had very limited possibilities of studying at Russian academies and universities). Gabo also followed courses in organic chemistry, physiology, anatomy, dissection, histology (all his life he also took a serious interest in engineering) at the Technische Hochschule. After two years he stopped studying medicine and started following courses in civil engineering until the start of the First World War in 1914. During those years he also registered to study philosophy, following courses in logic, logic and cognition and Kant's "Critique of Pure Reason". See Christina Lodder, "Gabo in Russia and Germany 1890-1922: A Biographical Study", in Steven A. Nash, Jörn Merkert,"Naum Gabo - Sixty years of Constructivism" (Prestel Verlag, 1987), p.49. Gabo refered several times to his very early interest in the Theory of Relativity of Einstein, in his essay "The Constructive idea in art" of 1937, originally published in the artist's magazine "Circle", republished in Martin Hammer and Christina Lodder, "Gabo on Gabo - Texts and Interviews" (Artists Bookworks, 2000)", p.101. See also §6.3 on Gabo. Gabo also refers to other scientific theories like Maxwell's lines of force, see Martin Hammer and Christina Lodder, "Gabo on Gabo - Texts and Interviews", p.99. There are very good reasons to assume Gabo was keenly interested in the abstract three-dimensional constructions intended to be not artworks but mathematical models - see Hammer and Lodder, "Constructing Modernity: The Art & Career of Naum Gabo", §14 "Art and Science".

37 Matjushin was also an important pioneer in understanding the importance of the notion of growth in nature and as property of space/time. Kupka is still a bit underrated in comparison to Kandinsky, but was earlier involved in studying scientific concepts for instance of cells - he even worked some time in a biological laboratory when he got to Paris. Because Kandinsky, Matjushin and Kupka do not belong to the constructivists in a strict sense, they will be discussed elsewhere in this publication.

38 Translated into Russian around 1910.

39 See P.D. Ouspensky, "Tertium Organum - De derde canon van het denken - een sleutel tot de raadselen der wereld" (Servire Uitgevers bv, 1990 - orig, 1912, first published in 1922 in the USA) from 1912. Earlier, already in 1909, Ouspensky published his book "The Fourth Dimension" on abstract mathematical theories.

40 Lobachevsky was one of the inventors of Non-Euclidian geometry at the start of the 19th century. See §6.

41 One can often find an '8' shaped form in El Lissitzky's compositions. It is highly fascinating when one knows that in May 1919 there was a sun eclipse. Published observations of this eclipse described the event as proof of Einstein's concept of the bending of light rays. See Anthony Parton, "Mikhail Larionanov and the Russian Avant-Garde" (Princeton University Press, 1993), p.131. I so far have not found evidence that El Lissitzky refers to these observations, but the broad publications of these observations should have come to his attention. See Sophie Lissitzky-Kueppers, Herbert Read, "El Lissitzky - Life-Letters-Texts" (London: Thames and Hudson, 1992 - orig. Dresden: Verlag der Kunst, 1967).

modern physics of his day.[42] Around the turn of the 19th/20th century in philosophy and in science one of the hot debates was over our fascination with geometry.[43] Other Zeitgeist-related subjects included a further thinking about the Platonic 'idea' or essence, the principle of construction, the impact of various sensations on our perception, and the desire to find, define and applicate universal principles.[44]

For instance, in relation to sensation, the influences of certain colours on our physical well-being were explored, colours that occur in our environment. Obviously these subjects did not come out of the blue at the start of the 20th century, but are logical results of discussions in the 19th century - some discussions go even further back. Although it would take too long a detour to explain the relationships, or to prove what I say here, it should be sufficient for now to know that the debate over free will since the end of the 18th century and the start of the 19th century and later discussions on the object versus the subject led to ideas of a basic structure of nature as a whole,[45] to ideas about continuity, progress and the notions of space and of time, and ultimately led to ideas about the construction of reality. In the 19th century new theories of colour[46] and light emerged, but also discoveries like the principles of the conservation of energy and the discoveries of electromagnetism and of X-rays, by Röntgen. These clearly influenced the interests of scientists and philosophers, but also of artists around the turn of the 19th/20th century. As evidence of how subjects can be attributed to the spirit of the time, I would only like to mention that Maxwell's electromagnetism and new ideas about the properties of light, space and time obviously inspired scientists like Minkowski or Einstein, or a mystic like Ouspensky, but also coincided with an emerging interest in the occult.

Occultism includes theories about the relationships between self and universe, and the connection between everything through superstructures or supervised by higher beings. Serious interests in knowledge from ancient and oriental cultures became natural (a kind of late 19th century 'New Age', as we would call it today), leading to Theosophy, as initiated by Madame Blavatsky and later furthered by Rudolf Steiner into Anthroposophy.

---

42 See Wassily Kandinksy, "Point and Line to the Plane", translated by Howard Dearstyne and Hilla Rebay (New York: Dover Publications Inc, 1979 - orig. "Punkt und Linie zu Fläche", 1926). See §12.3.

43 The discussion on our fascination for geometry, both Euclidian and Non-Euclidian, is exemplified by the publications on this subject of Poincaré, Hússerl, Russell and also by Brouwer (although he dealt more with mathematics itself) - see at the start of this chapter - around the turn of the 19th-20th centuries. See also §8.

44 See §2 on the Platonian interpretation of essence as 'idea'. An example of the interest in universal concepts was the desire to define a universal religion, founded on the need to search for the analogies between all existing religions to thus help improve the various social aspects of humanity (proclaimed by Vivekananda, see §2). Another example is the desire to define a universal language, which was considered necessary for the fast development of global trade. And, an example in the general interest in universal concepts was the desire to find a universal concept for time, which was also meant to accomodate the emerging global trading (see §6).

45 This is exemplified in Schopenhauer's worldwill in philosophy and reflected later in the 19th century in Cézanne's search for a structure parallel to the structure of nature through painting in his typical style of 'modulations' or repetitions of certain interrelated quantities of paint. It is also reflected in Gestaltspychology, whose key-notion is to always see the whole.

46 For instance, by Goethe, Runge, Chevreul or Helmholtz.

In a different way, this occult interest included interests in electromagnetism, light and space/time.[47] Artists tried to combine the more scientific as well as the more occult approaches. In this sense, one could indeed understand art to be in between religion and science. To find the structure of nature and mirror the construction of reality, artists tried to search for the universal, filter it out and make it visible. To find the universal, they had serious interest in certain aspects of folk-art and in cultures other than their own.[48] Evidence of this can be found in the works of artists like Malevitch, Popova or Kandinsky, who clearly knew about Egyptian, Byzantine, Medieval, Hindu, Japanese or Islamic art.[49] Additionally, literature on Hindu- or Hebrew philosophies was translated into Russian before or around 1910.[50] It is also useful to remember the 18th and 19th century quest for the basic elements of nature; as exemplified by Goethe's search for the 'Urpflanze', by Haeckel's search for the 'Urform', or by Darwin's Evolution Theory.

47 All through this publication you will encounter 'space' and 'time' as separate notions, while at other moments 'space/time' as unseparable unity. The first understanding is meant more in a general context, the second understanding in the meaning expressed by scientific theories.

48 This interest in folk-art is especially reflected in the application of a certain choice or in the repetition of similar shapes (often geometric) and colours (often primaries) on every object and clothing. Kandinsky stated that his visit in 1889 to a village in the province of Vologda in the north of Russia, where everything of the house was decorated in a non-figurative folk-art style, felt like walking into an abstract painting. He has written himself that this inspired him to develop pure abstract painting. See Anthony Parton, "Mikhail Larionov and the Russian Avant-Garde" (Princeton University Press, 1993), p.96. See also Will Grohmann, "Wassily Kandinsky - Life and Work" (New York: Harry N. Abrams Inc., 1958), p.31: "Kandinsky had the impression of moving about inside of pictures - an experience of which he later became quite conscious when he invited the beholder to 'take a walk' in his pictures, and tried 'to compel him to forget himself, to dissolve himself in the picture'." See Nina Kandinsky, "Kandinsky und Ich - Mein Leben mit einem großen Künstler" (Munich: Knaur, 1999 - orig. Kindler Verlag, 1976), p.34,35. He found that the combination of a simplification of forms with strong colours dissolved objects and concluded that colour has its own affective powers independent of an object, clearly inspiring him for his great and absolute abstract "Compositions". See Magdalena Dabrowski, "Kandinsky Compositions" (New York: The Museum of Modern Art, 1995), p.16. See Peg Weiss, "Kandinsky and Old Russia - The Artist as Ethnographer and Shaman" (New Haven, CT: Yale University Press, 1995).

49 In summer 1910 there was a large exhibition on Islamic art in Munich where Kandinsky lived at the time. Dabrowski discusses how both Franz Marc and Kandinsky found this show spectacular, that particularly "... Kandinsky appreciated the technical virtuosity of the works and the great subtlety of line and 'primitive' quality of color, and especially the way the figures were at the same time 'modeled' and 'on the plane', thus avoiding the pitfalls of the pictures being purely ornamental." See Magdalena Dabrowski, "Kandinsky Compositions", p.29. Other artists, for instance, Matisse, visited this show. This show was in Paris a year later. From Popova, the contemporary of Malevitch, the Tretjakov Gallery in Moscow owns a study of an Islamic geometrical composition. In old 7th century Tantric illustrations one can find marvelous similarities to Malevitch's paintings of the famous black square or black circle.

50 Information available in Europe on Hindu and Buddhist philosophies dates from late 18th century, in which for instance Goethe is known to have been very interested. August Wilhelm von Humboldt (1765-1845) translated the Bhagavadgita into Latin. See Hajime Nakamura, "Ways of Thinking of Eastern Peoples - India, China, Tibet, Japan"(Hawai: University of Hawaii Press, 1964), p.144. As an example of a general interest in Hindu-philosophy at the end of the 19th century, it might be interesting to know that in the 1890's the Hindu-guru Swami Vivekananda toured the USA. Vivekananda's lectures were published and also translated into Russian already before 1910. In these lectures Swami Vivekananda discussed the interrelationships between East and West and how one can learn from the other without loosing one's own cultural identity. See §2.3, footnote 14. See: Patricia Railing: "From Systems to Science in Art - On Russian Abstract Art and

This will be more extensively discussed in §11.

Of great inspiration for the early pioneers of abstract art was the philosophy of Wilhelm Worringer.[51] He stated that style in art emerges as a result of a psychic need. Described in a very simplified way, figuration results from a happy pantheistic feeling of the relationship between self and the world, but (geometric) abstraction results from an inner need to come to terms with one's small self in relation to the phenomena of the larger world, the cosmos. Interests in other cultures, for which Worringer provided intellectual backing, give credence to the experience of visiting an anthropological exhibition and seeing so many analogies of (constructive) abstract art in the decorations of clothes, tapesties, ceramics, jewellery, utensils, etc. Be assured this oberservation is not merely your projection!

Obviously, the publications of new discoveries and theories in astronomy or of X-rays were sources of information to the early abstract artists.[52] Malevitch was fascinated by the evidence that, as humans on our little planet Earth, we are part of the universal motions, and developed his famous paintings of geometric shapes 'flying' past us as planets. This was the start of his Suprematism. The discovery of X-rays was exhibited to a large public, showing how they enable us to look through our bodies, showing the bones in one's hand or leg. To the kind of artists discussed here, X-rays proved that solid matter actually does not exist![53] It inspired artists from Cubism or Futurism to abandon painting solid shapes and instead to begin intersecting planes and shapes, giving the impression of transparency. Cubism and Futurism both tried to translate their understanding of the new scientific notion of space/time.[54]

The scientific interest in the basic nature of light also stimulated artists to take pho-

Language 1910-1920 and other essays". Several important early abstract artists like Chagall and his pupil El Lissitzky were Jews with a profound interest in their own Hebrew cultural heritage.

51 Published in Wilhelm Worringer, "Abstraction and Empathy", translated by Michael Bullock, with introduction by Hilton Kramer (Chicago: Elephant Paperbacks, 1997 - orig. "Abstraktion und Einfühlung", 1908). See §10, footnote 5. See §11. See Martin Hammer and Christina Lodder, "Constructing Modernity - The Art & Career of Naum Gabo" (New Haven: Yale University Press, 1999), p.24, on Worringer's ideas: "In the contrasting and equally valid tradition of abstraction, appearances are subordinate to geometric stylisation and spatial flattening, as apparent in the 'primitive' art of many cultures, Egyptian art, and in Byzantine, Asian and Medieval styles. Such artistic expressions stemmed psychologically from 'a great inner unrest inspired in man by the phenomena of the outside world'. For Worringer 'transcendental notions in a religious sense, and the urge towards abstraction in an artistic respect, are expressions of the same psychic disposition vis-à-vis the cosmos' ".

52 A very good example is the 1923 encyclopedia by the popular French publisher Larousse on astronomy, including many photographs of stars, nebulae, comets, explanations of star- and galaxy-structures and including an essay on Einstein's theories. See Alphonse Berget, "Le Ciel - Nouvelle Astronomie Pittoresque" (Paris: Libraire Larousse, 1923). For an outstanding description on proof of the influence of X-rays on abstract art, see Marlene Lauter and Beate Reese, "FormSchichten-Farbstrahlen, Aspekte russischer und osteuropäischer Kunst - Eine Ausstellung aus Anlaß des Jubiläums '100 Jahre Röntgenstrahlen' " (Würzburg: Städtische Galerie, 1995).

53 Please, remember the discussion on 'sunyata' in the previous chapter.

54 In Cubism, the looking at an object or a portrait from many different angles at the same time, as Cézanne already explored a bit in his still-life paintings. In Futurism, the simulation of dynamic motion by a repetition of the object or by repetition of its contours. A simulation of motion we know today from popular comics.

tography as an art of light very seriously. Inspired by Man Ray's photographic technology, artists like Moholy-Nagy developed fascinating abstract photograms. This technology was later also explored by American photography-pioneer Quigley.[55] Furthering earlier ideas and trying to come to grips with the confrontation between subject and object, partly as result of relatively new discussions about free will, the 19th century focussed on understanding the individual in the whole of nature, leading to a natural interest in universal principles for art with strong analogies to similar interests in Oriental and other cultures. To recognize similarities between constructivist art and illustrations from other cultures is, therefore, not merely coincidental![56] To say it in another way, how could one claim to be searching for universal principles if these principles are only Occidental?

Having come this far, it should be clear that the notion of constructivism is from the start not merely a painter's or sculptor's idea of a certain kind of composition. It is a much richer and clear example of the natural connection between artistic explorations and scientific knowledge. This connection became manifest against the backdrop of a specific cultural and political climate. The different aspects of the Zeitgeist, therefore, must always be taken into account when one tries to understand any development in history. The artists of constructivism hoped to become as fundamentally important as the scientist in establishing ideas about and knowledge of reality.[57] The direct link as seen by these first generations of constructive artists between art - applied design or industrial design - architecture - urban design and everything in between[58] basically has formed the accepted fundamental notion throughout the 20th century concerning the design of any object, product or environment that has shaped our societies.[59]

The early constructive artists' idealistic search for a complete renovation of society fueled dreams of a new world, a new man, and for some, a new order. These ideals were

---

[55] The interest in more mystical and even occult knowledge was enhanced by these theories concerning light and energy in science. These discussions seems to have triggered a more popular need for a translation into mystical properties of light and energy in the direct relation between the human body and the cosmic powers. This will be discussed in §14.

[56] This is a very good example why the observation of analogies can benefit the search for truth.

[57] In the new Russia after its revolution, there was of course every reason to have such ideal ambitions in such a new society. Unfortunately, history has taught that society was even more conservative and suppressive, forbidding abstract art on the grounds that it was not acceptable to the working-class and advocating social-realism instead. Still, for a couple of years, the Russian artists had the advantage of being officially acknowledged by the state and, therefore, they could do more than their contemporaries in the west. For artists like Van Doesburg in the west, who also had great ideas and visions, most ideas never got further than the planning phase - the 'Aubette' in Strassbourg, the Rietveld-Schröder House in Utrecht, the Bauhausproducts, some exhibition and stagedesigns and a lot of typographical works represent wonderful exceptions.

[58] Examples: graphic design or theater set-design. This development was stimulated by a fast growth in commissions for artists to make designs for advertisements, posters, murals, industrially produced products for the new mass consumer-markets, stage design and architecture for promotional political purposes, including promotional activities to enhance the public awareness on health issues.

[59] Important schools institutionalized these ideas, making their impact immense: for example, the German Bauhaus, the Russian vChutemas, both from 1919 till about 1933. Later the American New Bauhaus at Chicago and in the 1950's and 1960's the German Hochschule für Gestaltung Ulm (initiated by the Swiss artist/architect Max Bill).

idiosyncratically taken over by the national-socialists. Even worse, the fascist propaganda-machine used the knowledge of media-communication that was developed by constructivist artists; strong symbols in clearly designed graphics, powerful typography and dynamic photography illustrating concise messages without much text. It is somewhat ironic that the Nazis not only choose to copy the effective use of black and red for their propaganda and emblems from the constructivists, but even used a typical constructivist lay-out and typography for posters advertising the exhibition of 'Entartete Kunst'. After WWII, in the late 1940's and in the 1950's, one finds that the constructive artists generally retreated to their studios, focussing on painting and sculpture in a more classical sense. This was not only the result of the public mistrust of any art that they associated in appearance or statement to the new order of dictatorial fascism, but of course was also stimulated by a slowly emerging art-market. In that market, as a logical result of the post-war trauma, no geometric art, but rather personal and emotional tachistic or expressionistic art became dominant and the most sought after. As a result, many postwar constructivist artists had a hard time merely surviving. This was the same on both sides of what later became known as the Iron Curtain. Similarly to what went on in science, psychology and sociology (or linguistics), the constructivist artists from the 1950's and into the 1960's researched the notion of structure and structuralism.[60]

It is interesting to further explain the growing interest in a strict ordering of elements by referring to Quantum Mechanics, especially to Quantum Field Theory and a general interest in the notions of fields or nets as metaphors that explain all interactions and interconnections of events.[61] It is also interesting to consider structural chemistry, which stimulated the development of the DNA-structural model in 1956.[62] Simultaneously, the interests in structure were further enhanced by the new ideas in linguistics by Noam Chomsky. Chomsky stated that the structure of a language is more essential than its phonetics, revolting against Roman Jakobson's emphasis on phonetics.[63] In the 1960's Claude Lévy-Strauss followed in cultural anthropology with his structural anthropology, emphasizing the overall or underlying structure of a culture. In that period we can find in constructivist art many links to the Zeitgeist-related interest in structure, in units, cells, nets or grids.

For this generation of structuralist artists, the American artist Charles Biederman was a prime source.[64] Biederman focussed on the development of visualization through

60 See the discussion later on structure in §8.2. The interest of artists in structure ranged from artists like Charles Biederman, François Morellet to Jackson Pollock, Frank Stella, Michael Kidner, Brice Marden, Richard Purdy.

61 See §5.

62 This field was initiated by Linus C. Pauling's idea to structure the spatial arrangements of atoms in molecules and crystals and the interactions that bond substances, published in his "The Nature of the Chemical Bond" in 1939.

63 Jakobson, by the way, originally belonged to a group of artists, poets and early linguists called the 'Moscow Circle' in the time of early constructivist pioneering of graphic-design. Later he initiated the Prague School of Phonetics before going to the USA, where he acquired his international fame.

64 See Charles Biederman, "Art As The Evolution Of Visual Knowledge"(Red Wing, MN: Charles Biederman, 1948). See §4.

human history, and tried to better understand reality by translating natural light and the structure of nature at a deeper level into artworks. As the word 'evolution' used in the title of his major book already indicates, Biederman believes strongly in the general progress of knowledge and of mankind itself.

The artistic interest in structure is exemplified, for example, in the artists' magazines "Structure" and "The Structurist".[65] The interest of these artists in the notion of space/time was especially discussed in relation to the notion of growth and illustrated by following Van Doesburg's idea of a repetition of certain units or cells. This interest included the simulation of motion and naturally inspired artists to use actual motion in their sculptures, giving rise to kinetic art.[66] Examples of kinetic artists are the French artist Nicolas Schöffer, the late 1950's Russian group "Dvezhenye",[67] the Spanish group "Equipo57",[68] and the American and probably best known kinetic artists: Alexander Calder and George Rickey.

A different, but still familiar direction in constructive art was born just before the war in Switzerland: 'konkrete Kunst' (concrete art). It can be seen as the furthered version of Van Doesburg's Concrete Manifesto from 1931. A work of art was considered concrete when it did not refer to any natural object but itself. The main concrete artists were Max Bill and Richard Paul Lohse.[69] Their concept is still being followed by many artists

---

65 "Structure" was published in 1958-1964 by the Dutch artist Joost Baljeu. It included contributions by the artists Joost Baljeu, Kenneth and Mary Martin, Anthony Hill, Richard Paul Lohse, Charles Biederman, Peter Lowe and Jean Gorin. "The Structurist" has been published and edited since 1960 as bi-annual publication by Canadian artist Eli Bornstein, University of Saskatchewan, Saskatoon, Canada, and has included a rich variety of articles by artists, architects, art historians, etc.

66 It must be stated here, that the early constructivist pioneers already experimented with actual motion, especially Naum Gabo and Moholy-Nagy (Rodchenko, Klucsis and Kobro made suspended sculptures), but also one should recall Tatlin with his flying machine "Letatlin" or El Lissitzky with his moving stage-designs and exhibition-design projects. Maybe one could also mention Austrian Friedrich Kiesler with his fabulous revolving stage-design, which later led him to his utopian project for an 'endless house'. Most certainly the fabulous Alexander Calder with his exciting mobiles must be mentioned, although he does not really fit in the constructivist tradition and should be more linked to an Arp- or Miro-like interest in the organic. Also mentioned must be the fabulous early experiments with colour, sounds, and technologies of light, like those by the "Synchromists", the US artists Morgan Russell and Macdonald-Wright, and by Alexander Wallace Rimington with his colour-organ and Thomas Wilfred. See by Pascal Rousseau, "The Art of Light", in Éric de Chassey, "American Art 1908-1947 From Winslow Homer to Jackson Pollock" (New York: Harry N. Abrams Inc, 2001). See Gyorgy Kepes, "The Nature and Art of Motion"(London: Studio Vista, 1965). See Frank Popper "Origins and Development of Kinetic Art", translated by Stephen Bann (London: Studio Vista, 1968), p.94-95: in 1860 the word 'kinetic' (French: cinétique) was universally employed to describe phenomena connected with movement in physics and chemistry, in particular in the field of 'gas kinetics'. The meaning of the word 'kinetic' slightly changed several times, in 1920 was first used in connection to art (by Gabo and Pevsner) before around 1954 it became a commonly accepted art category. See also §6.

67 "Dvezhenye" means 'movement', founded in 1962 by Lew Nussberg, including Vladimir Akulinin, Boris Diodorov, Vladimir P. Galkin, Francisco Infante, Anatolij Krivcikov, Georgij I. Lopakov, Rimma, Sapgir-Janevskaja, Viktor V. Stepanov, Vladimir Scerbakov.

68 "Equipo 57", founded in 1957 including José Duarte, Angel Duarte, Augustin Ibarrola and Juan Serrano.

69 Others were Camille Graeser, Fritz Glarner, Hans Hinterreiter, Verena Loewensberg, Anton Stankowski, Kunstmuseum Winterthur, "Dreissig Jahre Schweiz Konstruktive Kunst 1915-45", with essays by Dr. Rudolf

in Europe, although most seem not to have studied the ideas and works of Lohse closely enough.

The modular and serial structures in Lohse's highly coloured paintings are much more complex than concrete artists generally seem to have noticed.[70] Lohse ordered and chose his colours so that they were virtually connected in a loop behind (or in front of) the canvas, allowing his paintings, strictly structured with squares, to evoke in the viewer an experience of the fluctuating 'breath of nature'. In my opinion, Lohse was a master at handling the duality of static-dynamic. This is based on a profound artistic knowledge of the interaction between a rational structure and sensitively chosen colours with our brains. His paintings exemplify a wholeness in which all parts are of equal value and depend on the interactions with all other parts. His works are fascinating, as he appeals to both rational and intuitive properties of our perception, while most concrete artists of later generations only use rational properties. In Switzerland the artists' magazine 'Spirale' was published 1953-1964, which furthered graphic design in relation to concrete art in particular.[71]

see picture 52

An exceptional development was initiated in Argentina in the 1940's. Inspired by South American artist Joaquin Torres-Garcia, who lived in Paris and was well known in Europe, the mathematical works of Belgian artist Vantongerloo, and especially by a visit and talks of Max Bill, in South America a branch of constructive artists emerged with very different features from its European relatives. South American constructive groups included 'Arte Concreto Invencion' and 'Arte Madi'.[72] The central figure was and still is artist Carmelo Arden Quin. The main interest of these groups was the implication of aspects of our perception in art. This led the Madi-group to break through the restricted orthogonal shape of a traditional canvas. Madi still exists today as an international movement, involving more artists from all over the world. Now artist Volf Roitman plays a central role and a Madi Museum exists in Dallas, Texas.[73]

These magazines, groups and ways of working went well into the 1960's. In general they all led to an interest in searching for an even more objective, more logical or rational and more scientific approach to art. Series of numbers, numbers resulting from

Koella, Dr. Ludmilla Vachtová (Winterthur: Kunstmuseum Winterthur, 1981).

70 See Willy Rotzler, "Konstruktive Konzepte - Eine Geschichte der konstruktiven Kunst vom Kubismus bis heute" (Zürich: ABC Verlag, 1977). See Joachim Albrecht, Rudi Fuchs, Hans Heinz Holz, Serge Lemoine, HansPeter Riese, Willy Rotzler, Ludmilla Vachtova, Richard Paul Lohse, "Richard Paul Lohse - Modulaire und serielle Ordnungen 1943-84" (Zürich: Waser Verlag, 1984). See Fondation Saner Studen, "Richard Paul Lohse - Die Konstruktion ist das Bild" (Studen: Fondation Saner, Richard Paul Lohse Stiftung, W. Gassmann AG Druck und Verlag, 1995). Hans Peter Riese, Friedrich W. Heckmanns, "Richard Paul Lohse, Zeichnungen 1935-1985" (Baden: LIT Verlag, 1986). For more books on Lohse, see www.lohse.ch .

71 See Annemarie Bucher, "Die Spirale - Eine Künstlerzeitschrift 1953-1964" (Aarau: Verlag Lars Müller, 1990). See §11, footnote 112.

72 Arte Concreto Invencion: Caraduje, Espinosa, Hlito, Prati, Nunez, Monaco, Werbin, Iommi, Molenberg, Maldonado, Contreras, Girola and Lozza. Arte Madi: Arden Quin, Kosice, Blaszko, Rothfuss, Laan, Steiner. See Miklos von Bartha, "Arte Concreto - Invencion - Arte Madi" (Basel: Edition Von Bartha, 1991). For contemporary Madi see the 2001 catalogue of exhibition in The Polk Museum of Art, Lakeland, FL, USA.

73 See www.madimuseum.org and www.volfroitman.com

throwing dice, or sets of 'objective' rules were used for making creative decisions and choices of composition. Most of the time colour was reduced to only black and whites. The moment the ultimate objective picture was thought to be found in compositions that did not have any pictorial elements or colours (which could still be regarded as personal preferences of the individual artist), painting and sculpture were reduced to almost nothing and (constructive) art came to a dead end (less than showing nothing is obviously a dead end).

Simultaneously the emphasis was on the pure non-illusionistic. The eye should see what the eye sees. This semi-scientific study by artists of perception led to interests in Optical Art, Minimal Art and Systems Art. Symmetry became an essential feature once more, because it supports the objective concept. The search for the ultimate objectivity in art is the equivalent to the search for the absolute balance between equal pictorial parts in an artwork. Therefore, symmetry was a natural choice. Accordingly, one can draw a line between these artistic efforts and democratic ideas in the politics of the 1960's.[74] These parallels are exemplified by a group like the French/German group 'GRAV'[75] and in France, England, Germany and the USA by the various important incentives for Optical Art.[76] In general one might recall this kind of art from the 1960's as Op-Art, not through works of art themselves, but through the highly commercial success and popular applications in fashion. In Germany, Italy, Belgium and the Netherlands similar initiatives for the pure objective came from groups like 'Zero', 'T' and 'Nul'.[77]

Especially in this art, pure symmetry (absolute mirror symmetry) became the prime tool for representing absolute zero-subjective art. In sculpture one should not forget Buckminster Fuller's pupil, Kenneth Snelson, with his magnificent constructions that exemplify a clear connection between art and engineering. Also in the 1960's, artists first began experimenting with finding structure with the aid of the computer.[78]

For a long time, American absolute objectivism in Minimal Art dominated international geometrical art.[79] The large sizes, the monumental features of the basic geometry,

[74] The ideal that everybody is the same and has the same rights making a symmetry of powers an appropriate symbol, because in symmetry there are no contrasts, no differences.

[75] GRAV = Groupe de Recherche de l'Art Visuel; founded 1960, including artists Garcia Rossi, Morellet, Sobrino, Stein, Yvaral, Julio Leparc. Also François Molnar, a researcher on visual perception, and professor at the Sorbonne University was involved in similar studies, as was his wife, the artist Vera Molnar. See, for instance, Dominique Szymusiak, "François Morellet - quelques systemes en hommage a Herbin" (Cateau-Cambrésis, F: Musée Matisse Le Cateau-Cambrésis, 2003).

[76] In France: Victor Vasarely, Yaacov Agam, Carlos Cruz-Diez, Yvaral, Jesus Rafael-Soto; in England: Michael Kidner, Jeffrey Steele, Bridget Riley in Germany: Ludwig Wilding. In the USA: Richard Anuskiewicz, Julian Stanczak. The high light of this movement was the exhibition "The Responsive Eye" at the Museum for Modern Art, New York, in 1965.

[77] Zero and Nul included artists like Heinz Mack, Otto Piene, Günter Ücker, Fontana, Manzoni, Peeters, Schoonhoven, Armando, Dekkers, Leblanc and many others. 'T' was founded 1959 and included Gianni Colombo, Giovanni Anceschi, Davide Boriani, Gabriele de Vecchi.

[78] Examples of early explorations with a computer are by Frieder Nake, Herbert W. Franke, Georg Nees, Gottfried Jäger, Vera Molnar, Peter Struycken, Ernest Edmonds, Manfred Mohr.

[79] The major American Minimal artists are: Donald Judd, Richard Serra, Frank Stella, Sol Lewitt, Carl André,

the omnipresence of this art on both sides of the ocean, and the bold definitive statements of Donald Judd made this possible. As such, Minimal Art became almost synonymous with the existence of the Cold War. In the atmosphere of that time, none of the involved artists dared to refer openly to early (Russian) constructivism. The preferences for pure symmetry, repetition of form and size, exemplifying the material in its own right, and using colour only in a functional way[80] were meant to purge any emotional content. It was a clear artistic analogy to the architectural concept of pre-fabricated building and to Functionalism in architecture. Within American art history, Minimal Art was the natural response of a younger generation of artists to the large and emotional paintings of the American expressionists,[81] a logical follow-up to Color-Field painting,[82] and a rational protest to the success of their contemporaries in Pop-Art.[83] An interesting feature was that simultaneously Minimal Art was also clearly related to Pop Art, because the artwork of the first also looked like it was the result of an industrial production process.

The success and the impact on the European artists by the American Minimalists can only be explained as part of the general glorification in those days of the USA as the major worldpower of democracy and as a result of the fast growing art-market in the USA. In a positive sense, the pure symmetry of the compositions can be understood as metaphors for the desire of the political movements in the 1960's for ultimate democracy. Also, analogies can be found with scientific ideas during that time. Ideas like David Bohm's Implicate Order[84] and a general interest in Oriental thought reflect the search for an order connecting everything at a deeper level, making everything of similar importance, making everybody the same. Only after the Cold War ended in the late 1980's did several of the Minimalists admit that they had been inspired by early European (Russian) artists.

Analogous again to the developments in science and to the general interest in society, at the end of the 1970's and into the 1980's some constructivist artists became doubtful about the dogmas of geometrical art and its reductionist approach and opened up to the concepts of Chaos Theory and the Theory of Complexity.[85] A growing unrest emerged,

Dan Flavin, Agnes Martin. See Jean-Pierre Maury, "The Revival and the New Orientations of the Constructivist Tendency", in PRO-NR.7 (Dordrecht: The PRO Foundation, Dec. 1990).

[80] This means an emphasis of the shape, not as something with its own meaning, which very clearly copies ideas of Rodchenko and Tatlin, without of course acknowledging this. Merely compare Carl André's simple rough wooden constructions with those by Rodchenko.

[81] Jackson Pollock, Franz Kline, Robert Motherwell, Adolph Gottlieb, Barnett Newman, Mark Rothko, Willem De Kooning, Helen Frankenthaler. See Irving Sandler, "The Triumph of American Painting - A History of Abstract Expressionism" (New York: Praeger Publishers Inc., 1970).

[82] Pioneers of Color Field painting are Mark Rothko, Clyfford Still and Barnett Newman. A pioneer of Color Field painting who used a more geometric language (inspired by his partly native-American background in combination with his interest in Mondrian) was Leon Polk Smith. Later Elsworth Kelly.

[83] Robert Indiana, Jasper Johns, Roy Lichtenstein, Andy Warhol, Robert Rauschenberg, James Rosenquist, Tom Wesselmann, etc.

[84] See §4 and §6.

[85] See §6.

and artists doubted whether construction as a notion could still reflect their knowledge of human perception without being too simplistic.

In an attempt to make this comprehensible, I will now briefly discuss a few artists. An artist like Frank Stella (never exactly a pure constructivist) understood these great changes in understanding reality through his own artistic development. From his early symmetric, pure objective, and straightedge - geometric paintings with stripes, through the phase of more dynamic geometric paintings in the 1970's known as the "Polish Village" series, he developed in the 1980's his fabulous dynamic and almost chaotic reliefs for the "Moby Dick" series to progress towards more complexity in the 1990's with his "Heinrich von Kleist" series.

see pictures 32, 64

Another important example of an artist who continuously offers new directives is Michael Kidner in England. He has been reading scientific literature for a long time - out of a personal interest in the process of reality and to search for a better understanding of what he was looking for as an artist. He is one of those exceptional artists who focusses on a never-ending artistic research for structure and complex order. Kidner is especially interested in units that are interrelated like life-cells, each with their own individual behaviour and still related in shape and purpose. He combines a highly rational approach with intuitive experiments and unusual combinations of materials. For instance, he makes a circle out of a thin fiber glass rod and attaches broad elastic bands differing in widths at certain rationally decided intervals along this circle, crossing the circle in a diagonal and symmetrical fashion. The result is often quite surprising, even to himself. The different tensions in the material, caused by the battle between the different widths of the elastic with the resistance of the fiberglass circle, make the perfectly-symmetrical flat circle jump into a three-dimensional and more complex shape - a kind of Möbius strip. The change from flat and perfect circle into its three-dimensional shape can be understood as a rapid process of breaking symmetry.

see pictures 30, 31

Kidner has been exploring the artistic implications of the highly abstract concept of Boolean nets using a kind of Penrose-tiling structure. He is currently exploring a kind of structure of geometric grid-units inspired by the general crystal properties of growth and mutual interactions of a virus - a kind of artistic research into artificial life. The form and shape of the individual structure-cell is decided by the interaction with its neighbours. Interactions that are pre-defined on a certain set or rules, which Kidner formulates based on his understanding of modern knowledge of bacteria and viruses. Kidner first follows the system almost as an observer, but in the end he always influences the results based on his artistic intuition for colour, form and composition.[86] Kidner is fascinated by the Penrose pentagonal tiling, because in his interpretation this pattern defines space

---

86 In a similar sense, the American artist Richard Purdy makes paintings based on a computer program he wrote himself inspired by the 'cellular automata' theory of Stephen Wolfram (called Wolfram-Sets). For more information, see www.gaugefield.net. Though different in concept, it is interesting to compare Kidner's "Crossroads" to Paul Dacey's "Lyra/Vega II", both reproduced in this book.

using five coordinates instead of the ususal four that define our sense of symmetry. The fifth coordinate allows unexpected directions in the process. Kidner recently has taken up the use of colour again, allowing his highly structured drawings and paintings to become quite exciting with new freshness.

Manfred Mohr, born in Germany and living in the USA, is one of the few artists using a computer who also knows how to program software.[87] He is especially fascinated by exploring the hypercube and distorting it through a certain sequence of actions in time. Earlier works showed parts of the hypercube growing and interlocking like a complex crystal. Mohr is further interested in studying a multi-dimensional motion projected - or flattened - onto a two-dimensional plane. His recent works have become so complex that one cannot read the picture anymore in the sense of still recognizing the turning and swirling motions of the hypercube. His fascinating new compositions show very complex simulations of a dynamic equilibrium in complex space/time.[88] Although highly abstract artworks mostly in black/whites, more recently also in colour, as translations of abstract explorations of space/time they match contemporary scientific diagrams explaining highly complex theories of space/time, which feature similar black lines connecting and disconnecting at certain points (compare the Feynman-diagrams).

see picture 36

Recently Mohr has developed a completely new software program with which he can set simulations of complex multi-dimensional rotations into motion, and is using colour to be able to explore this level of complexity. He then chooses certain stills of these animations to become paintings. He also presents this program in continuously moving and changing digital works on computer-screens.[89]

In the period of about 1986 - 1993 there was a certain revival of an international discussion about constructive art on a large scale, for a large part the result of a wide range of impulses by the PRO Foundation, founded in the Netherlands.[90] For obvious reasons, these activities could only be so succesful because there seemed to be a need for them. But this organization did not stand alone. Three magazines were published, the first two by other publishers: 'Constructivist Forum' in England,[91] 'MESURES - Art International' in Belgium[92] and 'PRO-pro art and architecture' in the Netherlands.[93] The artist group 'MESURES-A.I.' in Belgium was also very active in organizing exhibitions

87 See Marion Keiner, Thomas Kurtz, Mihai Nadin, "Manfred Mohr" (Zürich: Waser Verlag, Viviane Ehrli, 1994).

88 See §6.

89 See Peter Volkwein, "Manfred Mohr -space-color", (Ingolstadt: Museum für Konkrete Kunst Ingolstadt, 2001).

90 The PRO Foundation became so effective by focussing on publishing, exhibitions, interdisciplinary conferences (the 1st PRO-Conference Dordrecht'87, 2nd PRO-Conference Fulda'88, 3rd PRO-Conference Rotterdam/Vlissingen'89, 4th PRO-Conference Moscow'90) and symposia throughout Europe, involving not only artists, but also architects, art historians, urban designers, politicians, philosophers, and computer - scientists. Several of these events were visited by hundreds of participants, the majority of which were artists.

91 Nine issues were published (the last a double number) by the artists Nathan Cohen and Tim Johnson 1985-1989.

92 Six issues were published by the artists Marcel Baugniet, Jean Jacques Bauweraerts, Jo Delahaut, Jean-Pierre Husquinet, Jean-Pierre Maury, Victor Noël, Leon Wuidar 1988-1991.

93 Nine issues were published 1987-1993, accompanied with a series of PRO-Newsletters, that were occa-

and meetings.[94] An important overview of contemporary constructive art was the exhibition "Null-Dimension" realized in the German town Fulda in 1988, and including almost 200 artists from all over Europe, Asia and North America.[95] In Bonn, Germany, one can still find the Gesellschaft für Kunst und Gestaltung, existing longer than the above mentioned initiatives, hosting the largest archive on constructive and concrete art. In 1987 in Zürich, Switzerland, Swiss artist Gottfried Honegger established a foundation for constructive and concrete art, and in 1989 a similar organization was founded in Reutlingen, Germany.[96] A few years later Honegger founded another one, in Mouans-Sartoux, France. Other organizations and various museums specializing in constructive and concrete art popped up in the 1990s, initiating exhibitions or meetings on constructive art.[97]

One can find out for oneself that ideas of new generations are not always new or a next step in a supposed progress, but quite often repetitions of earlier accomplishments. So, too, in geometric and constructive art. The phenomenon of non-progression is probably similar to an academism in physics that still believes in the Newtonian reductionist and pure empirical approach.

Within art history the difference between constructive artists today and the early constructivist artists lies in their purpose, sensibility and the complexity of their work. The artworks have no particular political statement anymore. Complexity in form, colour, and visual illusion are no longer considered wrong.[98] The contemporary artists learned from the gradual developments of abstract art through the 20th century to handle shape, colour and composition more sensitively, using much more complex schemes. Continuous change has become the new paradigm.

As final remark on this subject I would like to add that constructivist art should not be labeled constructivist anymore, because our current knowledge of our perception of reality makes the concept of a construct in one's mind no longer feasible. Interactions

sionally published 1986-1999. The PRO Foundation continues to be active, but focuses more on subjects related to art, science and philosophy, and is not restricted anymore to constructive art.

94 For instance in the museums in Verviers and Antwerpen, in close collaboration with the PRO Foundation. Belgian painter Jean-Pierre Maury was the main initiator and impetus for these and other activities of "Mésures-A.I.".

95 A co-operative project by the Polish/German artist Jürgen Blum/Kwiatkovski, the Verein IDEA e.V. and the PRO Foundation. A catalogue was produced.

96 Initiated by the collector and architect Manfred Wandel and the art historian Dr. Gabriële Kübler.

97 In England, Spain, Germany, Austria and - more recently - in Calgary, Canada initiated at the university by artist and professor Ron Kostyniuk. In Germany currently a magazine "Konkret" is published by Galerie St. Johann, initiated by the artists Sigurd Rompza and Jo Enzweiler.

98 Recent research in neuroscience has found evidence for a large number of visual illusions experienced in direct perception (like a transcient motion after-effect) to be processed in certain parts of the brain, suggesting, in my opinion, that visual illusion is a part of our perception and cannot be discarded as wrong or misleading. See §5. It is interesting that as soon as 'illusion' is transformed into 'simulation'(this has happened by the emergence and acceptance of the computer-simulation as important tool to provide insight in complex problems) the notion seems to become acceptable to our culture. This is a nice example how technology (computing) can influence our ideas.

between our mind, our body and the phenomena of reality are more important than only the processes in our head. These interactions will be discussed throughout this publication. Also it will become clear throughout this publication that I believe that it would not be very intelligent to still try to limit one's pictorial vocabulary to Euclidian geometry. This has already been announced in the mixture of interests in geometry and the organic in abstract art through the 20th century, as Matjushin already advocated and was later exemplified by some constructive artists, such as Charles Biederman, Joost Baljeu, Michael Kidner, or by the artistic development of Frank Stella; in a younger generation by artists like Manfred Mohr, Jean-Piere Maury, Richard Purdy, and myself.

Today we should finally acknowledge that the importance of art must be found in the meaning of art itself and not in the superficial fights over style, like those between abstract, figurative, expressionist or other labeled schools, or the simplistic preferences for the 'mind' over the 'gut' (pure rationality versus pure feelings) or vice versa. This chapter has shown that the reasons for the developments in art have a deeper background than is assumed, still too often. The importance and development of constructive art can only be appreciated when one acknowledges the analogies between art and the developments in science, philosophy and society. The necessity of opening one's mind to see and acknowledge these analogies will become even more clear in the following chapters. The mutual interest of artists, philosophers and scientists in each others' fields has a long history and is the very basis on which a true understanding of the meaning of art is built.

§4 BIEDERMAN - BOHM

When the artist descends from metaphysical levels to the fields of the concrete causes of the realities of form, halfway he will meet the scientists, who - expecting to capture these causes and realities of form in their formulas - are ascending to the metaphysical levels.
Alexander Archipenko[1]

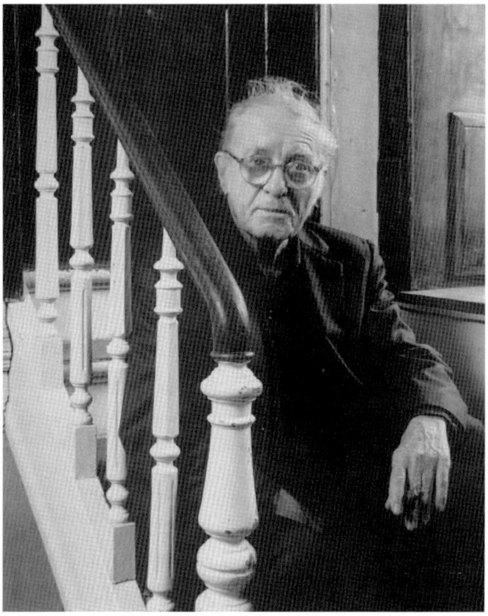

6. Charles Biederman (1906-)
On **Tour through Europe** organised by PRO Foundation
Picture taken in studio of Jean-Pierre Maury Bruxelles
Photo © Jean Dominique Burton 1988

As can be expected from what has been written so far, I understand the dialogue between artists, scientists and philosophers to be very important for any further understanding of the essence of reality or of the arts and sciences themselves. An extraordinary example was the classical dialogue between the artist Charles Biederman and the scientist David Bohm in the 1960's. It is as if Archipenko sensed such a dialogue would happen. Their dialogue took place in the form of a letter-correspondence. This is fascinating literature, as both of them also published texts, but clearly they are more relaxed in their personal letters where they force each other to make their various points comprehensible.[2]

The American artist and theorist Charles Biederman was born in 1906 in the USA and lives in Red Wing, Minnesota.[3] He published a series of books of which "Art as the Evolution of Visual Knowledge" is his magnus opus. It was the very first publication in which art history was rewritten from the perspective of continuities and discontinuities

[1] This quotation from Archipenko from the 1920's can be found written on the wall of the German Museum on Science and Technology, Munich, Germany: "Wenn der Künstler aus metaphysischen Sphären in die Bereiche der konkreten Ursachen und zu den Realitäten der Form herabsteigt, begegnet er auf halbem Wege den Wissenschaftlern, die sie in ihren Formeln einzufangen gedenken, sich in die metaphysischen Sphären begeben."

[2] The first part devoted to their correspondence was published in 1999 and I strongly recommend it for anybody interested in the dialogue between art and science. See Paavo Pylkkänen, "Bohm-Biederman Correspondence, David Bohm and Charles Biederman, Volume One: Creativity and Science" (London and New York: Routledge, 1999).

[3] For a good introduction to the life and development of Charles Biederman and his work - from Cézanne-like, surreal and cubist painting to biomorphic painting, sculpture, constructivist reliefs and his idiosyncratic reliefs, see the essays by Susan C. Larsen and Patricia McDonnell in Lyndel I. King, "Charles Biederman" (Minneapolis: the Frederick R. Weisman Museum, 1999 - a larger catalogue with the same essays published by the same museum in 2003). See www.charlesbiederman.net.

in the further development of visualization and not merely as a chronological order of styles and groups.[4] While living in his voluntary isolation in the country-side, far away from the art-world, Charles Biederman has always corresponded with scientists and artists.[5] Biederman's ideas have to be understood as a result of his acknowledgement of the analogous motivation of scientists and artists to understand reality and nature.

One must understand his thoughts about the content, aim and appearance of modern art in light of the principles of pictorial analysis, which was the generally accepted concept of the day during his artistic emergence (1925-1950).[6] Pictorial analysis is a method of analysing the features of a work of art to offer the observer a foothold for understanding what is perceived. For instance, nothing is said about the concept or content of the work of art, but composition and materials are precisely described. This approach, in combination with his conviction that progress in modern times should find its mirror in art, caused Biederman to conclude in the late 1940's that the traditional media (painting on a two-dimensional canvas, sculpting in a three-dimensional volume) would not be relevant anymore, and the artist should use new industrial materials like plastics and aluminum. Biederman considered the high relief to be the new medium, allowing complex compositions of artworks between the two-dimensional and the three-dimensional domains. One can find similar interests in industrial materials and the relief as the new medium replacing painting with quite a few other artists in the late 1920's - 1940's.[7]

Biederman is especially interested in a particular historical development of visualization caused by the gradual discovery of the importance of light-colour-space, as is evident in the progression through Rembrandt - Courbet - Turner - Cézanne - Monet - Mondrian. see picture 26
Simultaneously, this discovery of light-colour-space led to ideas about the structuring of colour patches in painting (especially by Cézanne) in a way that is understood to be parallel to the structuring of colours perceived in nature. These ideas emerged parallel

[4] Visualization to Biederman is the 'tool' of humans to understand reality. The kind of visualization and the way of visualizing one's perception of reality explains how one understands reality. See Charles Biederman, "Art as the Evolution of Visual Knowledge" (Red Wing, MN: Charles Biederman, 1948), p.26: "Art in its various forms constitutes the principal evidence of man's past efforts at visualization, and when studied in this way should produce data of inestimable value to many of the other sciences which deal directly or indirectly with the development of man's vision in relation to the phylogeny of the human nervous system."

[5] Biederman's correspondents have included Bart van der Leck, Georges Vantongerloo, Joost Baljeu, Jean Gorin, Anthony Hill, Joan Saugrain, and myself.

[6] See §2.6.

[7] In the early decades of the 20th century one can find the reflection of a general interest in the futuristic capacities of the machine in the works of a great variety of artists, not only the Futurists, but also in the works of individual artists like Léger, Itten, Gabo, Pevsner, Moholy-Nagy, Vantongerloo, Tutundjian, Domela, Gorin. Tutundjian is mainly known, because he signed the manifesto "l'Art Concret" in Paris, in 1930, together with Van Doesburg, Hélion, Carlsund, Wantz, Schwab. On the remarkable works by this Armenian artist, see Gladys C. Fabre, "Tutundjian" (Paris: Editions du Regard, 1994). The interest in the machine in art in the USA was expressed by the exhibition "The Machine Age" at the Museum of Modern Art New York 1934 (a show Biederman might quite well have visited). See Olivier Lugon, "The Machine Between Cult Object and Merchandise - Photography and the Industrial Aesthetic in the United States during the Interwar Years", in Éric de Chassey, "American Art - 1908-1947 From Winslow Homer to Jackson Pollock"(New York: Harry N. Abrams Inc, 2002 - orig. Éditions de la Réunion des musées nationaux, 2001).

to a developing desire to understand nature by means of scientifically controlled experiments (starting with the Greeks and their predecessors, continuing through Leonardo da Vinci and modern science). For Biederman's emerging philosophy, the semantic theories of Alfred Korzybski were also influential.[8] Furthermore, the theories of the mathematician and philosopher Alfred North Whitehead were extremely important to Biederman. At the focal point of Whitehead's philosophy of organism[9] is the metaphysical thought that there is only one reality and that there are no static elements or matter, only nets of events. Whitehead described a net as consisting of a coherent set of similar elements with strong interrelations between them. This idea is frequently discussed in physics at the end of the 1920's and beginning of the 1930's, when Whitehead's 'net' became identical with the physicist's use of 'field'.[10] Whitehead's philosophy emphasizes notions of process and system. These notions are reflected in his (Aristotelian) conviction that becoming determines being and that repetition is a transformative process, capable of engendering something new (which he called 'a novel immediacy').[11] Whitehead's philosophy is typical of the ongoing debate in science and philosophy about space/time, the arrow of time, the continuum, infinity, and is also related to the general interest in the organic, or the emerging interest in growth.[12] Growth, as metaphor for a time-based process, like the abstract notion of the fourth dimension, became a popular subject in abstract art.[13]

Translated into Biederman's reliefs, Whitehead's influence is reflected in the repetition of the same geometrical element under different circumstances, produced by applying different colours to rectangular elements of the same size or by changes of light (caused by placing elements at different angles). The result is that the same geometric forms appear unique, as they reflect different colours on each other and light reflects between them onto the surface of the coloured plane on which they are mounted (every change of light realizes 'a novel immediacy'). By colouring connecting parts differently, they seem to be disconnected and to move. The careful composition of a maximum of five different colours in one work leads to a dynamic and oscillating movement, combining centrifugal and centrepetal forces. The viewer's eye jumps between the different colour combinations, the reflection of the light on the coloured forms and the coloured plane, connecting and interrelating the parts into a dynamic whole. The size and contrasting

---

8 These ideas are published, for instance, in "Science and Sanity: An Introduction to Non-Aristotelian Systems and General Semantics", 1933. Korzybski was a Polish mathematician and philosopher. He developed general semantics and considered every new generation to double the knowledge of the previous one. Biederman attended in 1938 the first seminar Korzybski held at the General Semantics Institute, Chicago. Later he also published in Korzybski's magazine "Etc.".

9 See Alfred North Whitehead, "Process and Reality" (Free Press, 1979 - orig.1929).

10 For instance, Quantum Field Theory of 1928.

11 See Alfred North Whitehead, "Process and Reality", p.23: "That <u>how</u> an actual entity <u>becomes</u> constitutes <u>what</u> that actual entity is;... Its 'being' is constituted by its 'becoming'. This is the 'principle of process'."

12 As was mentioned in §3 and will be explored further in this publication.

13 The fourth dimension was already a subject of early abstract art, but was more commonly explored by artists in the 1950's. See §6.3.

colour of the plane creates the strong impression of a 'colour-space'.

This mirrors the physical way we actually perceive everything around us, as a certain clustering of colourquanta in colour-space. The individual pictorial elements in Biederman's work (the rectangles) have no meaning in themselves, but only in their non-local interconnection or composition. This connection results from a combination of our actual eye-perception, our knowledge and our intuition of nature. Comparable to Cézanne's paint-patches or 'modulations', Biederman seeks to create a whole out of a clustered group of coloured rectangles on a mono-coloured picture plane.[14]

Since the 1950's, Biederman's work has reflected Whitehead's philosophical interest in becoming, or growth, through the stacking of elements on top of each other, allowing these constructions to virtually grow into space. In a very abstract sense, Biederman's artworks could be understood as a complex and three-dimensional *net*. This kind of ordering of the same basic elements into compositions based on theories of growth and repetition was simultaneously explored by artists in England, France, Canada and the Netherlands in the 1950's, but without Biederman's emphasis on colour (with the exception of Richard Paul Lohse).[15] These other artists were clearly more dogmatic and more oriented towards a kind of mathematical logic than Biederman was.

According to Biederman, the artist does not copy what he perceives directly in nature, but translates it. In this process, Biederman emphasizes the importance of the immediate visual and mental perception (the 'eye-brain perception', a process that simultaneously incorporates both eye-sight and brain) of nature, and being able to see the structure of nature. This is related to Schopenhauer's theory of immediate perception and also to recent ideas in neurophysiology.[16] Obviously Biederman does not mean that by just staring at a landscape or a forest we will see its underlying structure. Rather, through a combination of thought and vision, one finds the eidos or essence of the whole of nature.[17] As he said at the 3rd PRO Conference '89: "One does not see simply because

[14] This aspect seems also to be related to Whitehead's philosophy, that speaks about the extensive continuum as a medium for understanding everything as one large whole, following the frequent interest in the continuum in mathematics and new ideas about space/time. See Alfred North Whitehead, "Process and Reality", p.67: "Thus the continuum is present in each actual entity, and each actual entity pervades the continuum." Whitehead fits into the tradition of the Veda's, Aristotle, Leibniz, Descartes, Kant, Schopenhauer and Hegel, but also his ideas can be related to some ideas of his contemporaries, like Croce in Italy or Nishida in Japan.

[15] In England by Anthony Hill, Victor Pasmore, Kenneth and Mary Martin. In France by Jean Gorin. In the Netherlands, following Theo van Doesburg's ideas on 'cells', by Joost Baljeu, Josef Ongenae, Carel Visser, André Volten, Siep van den Berg, Koos van Vlijmen, Constant. In a similar way in Switzerland artists like Richard Paul Lohse explored the idea of using units/cells in a repetitive structure simulating growth or progression. The net, or grid, was already explored by several of the early pioneers of abstract art, like Kupka, Kandinsky, Mondrian, Klee, and - a bit later - by Otto Freundlich, Hans Hinterreiter, M.C. Escher. In the 1960's the relief was also chosen as medium in Germany for instance by Klaus Staudt, Hartmut Böhm, Max H. Mahlmann, and Gudrun Piper. In Poland, for instance, by Henryk Stazewski. In Canada and the USA by followers of Charles Biederman like Eli Bornstein, Elisabeth Willmott, Charles Hess, Ron Kostyniuk, Jurije Strutynski.

[16] Discussed in §5 The Projective Field. See Semir Zeki, "Inner Vision - An exploration of Art and the Brain" (Oxford: Oxford University Press, 1999).

[17] It must be explained here that Biederman himself does not refer to the essence or the eidos, nor does he

one's eyes are open!"[18]

In contrast to most scientists, Biederman tries to combine an understanding of nature's underlying structure with the essential means through which we experience reality: light-colour-form. For however deep we may dig into nature, we still have to try to understand it at the level of reality where we find ourselves. This means, we cannot avoid projecting our ideas onto reality at a perceptable level using the media that appeal to our perception. Biederman is not merely interested in randomly-chosen nice pictures of nature, but combines a conscious looking at nature with our knowledge and our intuition of nature (our *real* eye-brain perception).[19]

Biederman has always understood the usefulness of the dialogue between the scientist and the artist. He wrote to the physicist David Bohm:

> *"When we come to the creative structural view of nature presented by art, in contrast to the atomic structural view presented by science, it cannot be shown with any instruments whatever, not even as the camera instrument can show the old structural view of nature as objects. The new vision of nature can only take place in the human un-aided eye."*[20]

The emphasis on eye-brain perception is not considered strange anymore since in modern neurophysiology the eye is understood as part of the brain - not as an organ separate from the brain - making the involvement of the eye, and therefore vision, in our process of understanding reality essential! It also emphasizes that looking outwards (scanning) from our body into the environment is an essential part of our thinking process. What happens in our immediate environment is relevant to our perception.[21] This process of seeking parallels between perception and the structure of nature is an evolutionary process, proceeding from the simple to the complex, and contradicting the Newtonian reductionist approach.[22] The continuous study of nature by actually looking

---

refer to any Oriental philosophies, nor to Schopenhauer (he does refer to Goethe). But he does speak about 'the structure of nature', 'the method of nature' and 'the depth process of nature'. See Charles Biederman, "The New Cézanne" (Red Wing, MN: Charles Biederman, 1958), p.13 + 70.

18 See Charles Biederman, "Art, Theology, Technology, Science", in PRO-NR.6 (Dordrecht: the PRO Foundation, 1990), p.11.

19 See my discussion of Edmund Husserl, §2.

20 Quoted from a letter by Charles Biederman to David Bohm, June 28, 1960, see Paavo Pylkkänen, "Bohm-Biederman Correspondence, David Bohm and Charles Biederman, Volume One: Creativity and Science", p.36.

21 See §5.

22 See Charles Biederman, "The New Cézanne", p.80: "Form, colour, space, composing, everything develops from the simple to the complex. The new art must germinate, grow logically like a seed sprouting out of the earth to ever increasing interchange between its forms and the surrounding space and light. For the laws of all life are growth, and growth is creation." The concept 'from the simple to the complex' is comparable to the opinion voiced around 1900 by the Dutch physicist Lorentz: towards more differentiation. In modern science, reductionism is understood as the method to first retrace and understand the fundamental properties of the molecules or whatever smallest entity one can find and from that level on to build up knowledge to levels of higher complexity, aiming in the end to 'climb back' to the complex level of everyday. See Edward O. Wilson, "Consilience - The Unity of Knowledge" (New York: Vintage Books, 1999 - orig. 1998). Wilson advocates the

at nature makes the involvement of light, and therefore, colour, an absolute necessity as a means of discerning structure. Biederman understood the relief to be the best medium for allowing light and colour to interact in a way that we see around us every day. He gradually developed his quite specific reliefs in the early 1940's, while researching a possible synthesis of his own thinking with the Russian Constructivists[23] and the Dutch De Stijl.[24]

When one studies Biederman's book "Art as the Evolution of Visual Knowledge", one must not forget that at the time he wrote this magnificent book, not a lot of information was available anywhere on the theories of Russian art. Nevertheless, in Paris in the 1930's, Russian artists like Naum Gabo and Antoine Pevsner, but also Piet Mondrian were around and influenced younger artists like César Domela and Jean Gorin. In the late 1930's Biederman stayed and worked in a studio in Paris, where he became acquainted with many artists. However, Biederman only discovered Gorin's reliefs after he had already returned to the USA.[25]

Biederman felt a strong kinship to Jean Gorin, the French pupil of Mondrian. He took up correspondence with Gorin. As Gorin did not know English and Biederman knew no French, both Biederman's and Gorin's letters were translated by Biederman's wife. Through the mail they established a close friendship. Although he had a hard time making a living himself, Biederman supported Gorin financially after the war for a couple of years.[26]

The scientist/philosopher David Bohm and Charles Biederman have acquired such a vast amount of knowledge in their search for truth during the 20th century that it is impossible to present a complete review of their ideas, theories and considerations. Here it is merely possible to describe the framework of their dialogue. Theirs has been the discussion of an open minded scientist and a thinking artist. Their dialogue, which took place from March 1960 until April 1969, in the form of typed letters, focused mainly on the perception of the structure of nature, including perception, consciousness and many related topics.[27] A short reflection on the position of Bohm and Biederman will

conviction that only through this understanding of a reductionist approach will we be able to both connect all fields of human interests (mainly bio-physics and genetics to ethics, religion, art and the other humanities) and understand our reality. For obvious reasons one may wonder if this can ever work, because there clearly is no garantee that in the future no smaller particles will be found - or other entities that cannot even be imagined as particle.

23 Especially Gabo, whom Biederman met on one occasion in the USA. On Gabo, see §3.

24 Especially Mondrian and Domela, who he met during his nine month stay in Paris from 1938-1939. See Michel Seuphor, "Piet Mondrian - Life and Work" (New York: Harry N. Abrams, Inc., 1956). See Jacques Meuris, "Mondrian" (Nouvelles Éditions Françaises, 1991). See Serge Lemoine, Bernadette Contensou, "Domela - 55 Ans D'Abstraction" (Paris: Éditions Paris Musées, SAMAM, Musée de Grenoble, 1987).

25 See Marianne Le Pommeré, "The Works of Jean Gorin" (Zürich: Waser Verlag, 1985).

26 In the 1950's, Biederman was only able to make models as he could not afford the material for actual reliefs, still he managed to send Gorin a small amount of dollars as support every month. This Biederman told me himself.

27 The original correspondence involves over 4000 letter-pages: 3300 Bohm's, 700 Biederman's.

prove their discussion to be a classical dialogue, a logical outcome of several streams of research connecting in the flow of history. This is also important, because without understanding Bohm and Biederman in concert, David Bohm's ideas could be misunderstood as just another abstract theory and Charles Biederman's works as just typical structuralist art works from the 1950's, denying both their actual and unique value.

From the beginning of history, it seems man has always been interested in understanding his position in the world by finding some relationship between himself and the things he perceives or understands to see in nature, searching for structure, for some order. This focus of interest on structure - or order - is reflected in almost all cultural visualizations through all centuries.[28] Besides, it is interesting to remember that being a physicist originally meant being a doctor, a medical man seeking to understand the processes of nature in order to understand the (physical) body better. There always seems to have been an interest in finding order by looking at nature through a combination of verbal formulations and visual means. The combination of geometry[29] and colour permeate many of the visual means of ordering and seem to be real universal media for understanding our position in the whole.[30] In the 1950's and 1960's structure was the keyword across several disciplines. It was, therefore, not surprising that the early 1960's saw a quantum scientist with a profound interest in the order of the whole, combined with a desire for a new world-view.[31] It is hardly surprising that there is an artist namely, Charles Biederman, re-discovering the combination of Cézanne's (and Monet's) method of actually looking at nature's light and colour with the search for an overall pattern or structure. A dialogue which could earlier have been comparably fruitful could have been developed between a Cézanne and a Poincaré if they had had the vision Bohm and Biederman had and a reason to get in touch, but they had not.

David Joseph Bohm was born in 1917 in Wilkes-Barre, Pennsylvania, USA.[32] He studied physics, graduated from Pennsylvania State College, and obtained his PhD in 1943 at the University of California at Berkeley under the supervision of J. Robert Oppenheimer. In 1946 he became an assistant professor at Princeton University. There he wrote his book, "Quantum Theory"(1951), the classical defense of the Copenhagen Interpretation of quantum mechanics. Bohm himself soon doubted the validity of this theory, because of its denial of the difference between the object and the subject, and he published his alternative not much later, in 1952. Connectedness between entities (as

---

[28] See for instance E.H. Gombrich, "The Sense of Order - A Study in the Psychology of Decorative Art" (Phaidon, second edition, 1984 - orig.1979).

[29] Geometry originally comes from the Greek words geos, meaning earth, and metron, meaning measure.

[30] You are kindly advised to visit any museum of anthropology or folk art and search for colourful geometric patterns.

[31] Bohm understood 'whole' as 'totality', <u>not</u> as 'everything'. The here meant new world-view was the result of the ethical debate in the 1950's after the two atom bombs on Japan. Einstein (with whom Bohm developed a friendship) said that the world was changed forever, but not our thinking and we would need a different world view for mankind to survive.

[32] David Bohm unfortunately died in 1992. His work has been continued by Basil Hiley. See §7.3.

between the observer and the observed) does not necessarily imply that there is no difference between them. Although we perceive entities to be separate in reality, they can still be connected at a deeper level.

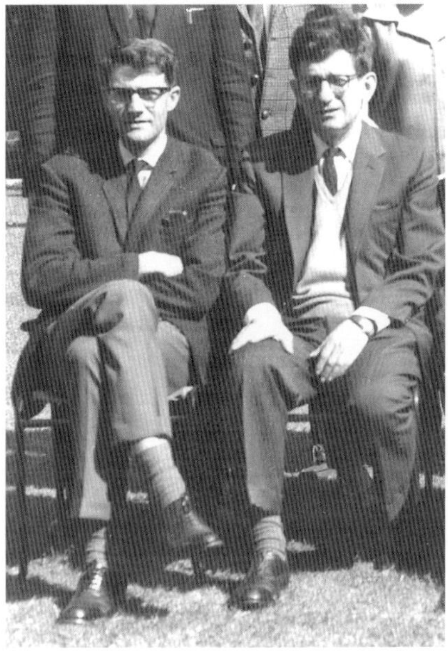

7. Basil Hiley and David Bohm, late 1960's
Courtesy of Prof. Basil Hiley
www.bbk.ac.uk/tpru

David Bohm became a victim of one of America's worst social nightmares during the Cold War: the McCarthy hunt for intellectuals thought guilty of un-american activities, and therefore thought to be sympathizers of communism. The McCarthy trials forced Bohm to move to the University of Sao Paulo in Brazil, then to The Technion in Israel,[33] before staying as Research Fellow at Bristol University (1957-1961) and finally settling in 1961 at Birkbeck College in London, where Basil Hiley became his collaborator. In 1959 he discovered and proved with his student, Yakir Aharonov, that Quantum Mechanics predicts that the movements of charged particles can be influenced by the presence of magnetic fields, even when those particles never enter the regions to which those fields are confined (this has become known as the Aharonov-Bohm effect). A related interest by researchers at Birkbeck College formed the reason for Bohm and Birkbeck College to be interested in each other. On his way to London, Bohm stayed for a while at the Niels Bohr Institute in Copenhagen. In the late 1950's David Bohm continued to be interested in philosophical approaches to understanding an order in nature. This interest was enhanced by his dialogue with the artist/theorist Charles Biederman and his friendship with the Indian philosopher and popular guru Krishnamurti, whom he first met in 1961. David Bohm was quite interested in philosophy and was familiar with the ideas of Kant and Schopenhauer, but he considered Whitehead especially important (as did Biederman) and Hegel's logic was his favorite.[34]

Bohm gradually developed his Theory of the Implicate Order and continued to search for a deeper Quantum Theory, writing several books.[35] In relation to the almost classically vague interpretation in Quantum Theory that a particle is a certain substance (a quantity) and a wave at the same time, which cannot be perceived in the same experiment (some experiments show the particle as wave, others as quantity), Bohm stated

[33] Here he finished writing "Causality in Chance and Modern Physics", published in 1957.
[34] Hegel: "Wissenschaft der Logik", 1812-1816. Hegel considers the philosophy of being and the philosophy of the being as objective logic and the philosophy of the idea as subjective logic.
[35] David Bohm, "Causality and Chance in Modern Physics" (London: Routledge and Kegan Paul, 1984 - orig.1957). David Bohm, David Peat, "Science, Order & Creativity" (London: Routledge, 1989 - orig.Bantam Books, 1987). David Bohm, "On Dialogue - David Bohm Seninars" (Ojai, California, 1990). David Bohm, Basil Hiley, "The Undivided Universe - An Ontological Interpretation of Quantum Theory" (London: Routledge, 1995 - orig.1993).

that the wave function is not merely a mathematical property, but a physical one. The wave functions move the particles around and guide them along their courses.[36] David Bohm understood all occurences to be interrelated with each other through an order that is not visible at the surface but underlies all events. This implicit order (Bohm: 'implicate') is a result of furthering Quantum(field) Theory to explain the objects around us as explicit (Bohm: 'explicate') forms of an underlying implicate (or enfolded) order.

This can also be understood by using the holographic picture as a metaphor. With the help of a laserlight, a holographic slide shows a three dimensional object. Every fragment (or broken part) of this slide will show the same object, but only from a certain angle. In the same way, in the implicate order every entity includes a reflection of the whole. This is very much linked to earlier thinkers and artists. Bohm was interested in the analogy between the ordering of pictorial elements in the paintings of Impressionism - determined by the relationship to the whole - and Quantum Theory. Like other scientists,[37] Bohm was interested in visualisation as a method for understanding a complex theory, although he prefered that one obtain an intuitive understanding or feeling for all complex behavior.

According to Basil Hiley, he and Bohm experimented in the 1960's with a kind of mathematical notation for the description of structural physics. But as mathematical notations are quite static and reality is not, they studied art for finding clues and analogies to their attempts to develop a better mathematics to describe process, activity or movement.[38] Their analysis of art provided Bohm and Hiley with several insights. In Bohm's theory another aspect is very important: the principle of *non-locality*.[39]

Non-locality emerged out of the discussions between Bohm and Hiley about Bohm's ontological interpretation of Quantum Mechanics. The principle of non-locality means that any entity will have some effect or influence on another entity somewhere else, although no direct connection is apparent. In my opinion, this is a different way of defining objectivity or autonomy, which seem to exist, but nevertheless are impossible in a strict sense (on a deeper level). Our unavoidable interrelationship with the rest of nature is exemplified by our breathing-process, the very process by which we live, which makes any autonomy from our ecological environment impossible.

Bohm's fear that science was ruled too much by mathematics urged him to be open to world views other than the scientific view. He did not subscribe to one particular worldview - as for instance Buddhism - but looked everywhere for helpful knowledge. Therefore, Bohm saw the utility of looking into concepts of Oriental thought, too. Obviously, one does not need to become a Hindu to acknowledge the value of Vedantic

---

[36] See §3.

[37] For instance Roger Penrose, as will be discussed later.

[38] In concepts of order and structure in works like from Cézanne, Gabo and Biederman. On Gabo, see Martin Hammer and Christina Lodder, "Constructing Modernity - The Art & Career of Naum Gabo" (New Haven: Yale University Press, 1999), p.379.

[39] See §6.

philosophy[40] or the metaphorical value of Shiva's dance between chaos and order for understanding nature's fundamental process of seeking symmetry (or harmony) and breaking symmetry simultaneously! This openness to and interest in various fields of knowledge outside science stimulated Bohm's interest in Charles Biederman.

The connection between Biederman and Bohm was stimulated by the English artist and mathematician Anthony Hill, who introduced Biederman to Bohm's book, "Causality and Chance in Modern Physics", after reading Biederman's article on determinism and indeterminism (Einstein versus Heisenberg) in the magazine "Etc.", edited by the semiotician Alfred Korzybski.

Both Bohm and Biederman were highly interested in understanding the structure of reality(including the notion of growth).[41] Both concluded that reductionism cannot be the right approach, because nothing can be studied in actual isolation. Such a study in isolation is impossible, because of the intricate interactions of the studied particles or other fundamental building blocks with other things (a result of the discussion of the the subject-object distinction). Biederman and Bohm also agreed that infinity is a process of change. They were each trying to understand the notions of determinism as opposed to free will- and whether both notions could exist.[42] Biederman and Bohm both understood and accepted that following pure rationalism alone (for instance in the form of pure mathematics) would not suffice.

The following is an example of their dialogue. Biederman describes the difference between the artist and the scientist thus:

"While the physicist pursues the creative process of nature, even to how nature began, the artist is working at the other end of this process, extending this creative process. The physicist wants to get at the beginning of nature, to the very birth of the atom. While the artist wants to continue with what that atomic world already manifests in its evolution. Think of the evolution of nature evolving new forms, that is, the new art is continuing the evolution of ***nature as*** *art."*[43]

Bohm responded by explaining that the physicist studies the origin of nature in order to also understand evolution. He responded to Biederman, "... there is no way to reduce the large scale to nothing but atoms..."[44] Bohm clearly was a physicist who advocated

40 See especially on Vivekananda, §2.2.

41 Bohm suggests all structure is the trace of process - a very interesting thought, obviously linked to modern ideas about space/time (see §6). See Paavo Pylkkänen, "Bohm-Biederman Correspondence, David Bohm and Charles Biederman, Volume One: Creativity and Science", p.88.

42 Biederman proposes the intriguing thought that free will is a fiction of the human mind and that instead creativity is much more interesting. To my interpretation creativity is looking for a virtual free choice within a (causal?) restriction of possibilities. For instance, with paint one cannot do everything, but still can be quite creative to do a lot of diverse things.

43 Letter by Biederman to Bohm of May 22, 1960. See Paavo Pylkkänen, "Bohm-Biederman Correspondence, David Bohm and Charles Biederman, Volume One: Creativity and Science", p.23.

44 Letter by Bohm to Biederman of June 6, 1960. Ibid. p.27.

the idea of trying to understand the whole of nature in all its complexity.[45]

The main difference of opinion was that Biederman kept emphasizing the importance of the eye-brain perception, the actual looking at nature while thinking, while David Bohm saw a primary role for consciousness (meaning, only thinking). It is not strange for a physicist to be interested in consciousness. For example both Poincaré and Einstein were interested in understanding consciousness, too. Bohm thought it was possible to find knowledge of the physical world within one's own body, as the body is part of nature and should naturally contain this knowledge. This is an idea very connected to Oriental philosophies and also the philosophy of David Hume, who believed sense-perception was accompanied by the perception of 'the withness of the body', which makes the body the starting point for one's knowledge of the surrounding world.[46]

In their letters, it is apparent that Bohm and Biederman tried hard to understand each other, as exemplified by this quotation from Bohm:

> *"Here, I would like to stress again that all art has as its object not so much the embodiment of the process of nature as the initiation of these processes in the viewer. As we both agree, art does not communicate, but rather, it helps to guide a creative process in the viewer. Structurist art should according to this notion, set up in the viewer a process which reveals, not a particular object, but rather, the general laws and possibilities of nature, the essential structure of reality. If it does this, then it will itself be a reality, and not just a copy of something else. For the essential character of reality is that it is constituted by such processess. Would you say this is a correct interpretation of your point of view?"*[47]

Biederman wrote back to Bohm a month later on the topic of chance in connection with Bohm's criticism of Niels Bohr:

> *"A nature with chance is just as repugnant as one of mechanistic determinism. The latter eliminates the essential quality of creation, the former reduces it to the absurd, to that creative irrationality seemingly implied by Bohr's "irrationality treat", p.91 your book."*[48]

---

45 This was a concept later furthered by scientists like Ilya Prigogene or the Santa Fé Institute, the main seat of the research on the Theory of Complexity (see §6).

46 David Hume lived 1711-1776. His concept "withness of the body" meant the presence and involvement of the body.

47 Letter by David Bohm to Charles Biederman, November 17, 1960. See Paavo Pylkkänen, "Bohm-Biederman Correspondence, David Bohm and Charles Biederman, Volume One: Creativity and Science", p.71. 'Structurist Art' is a term proposed by Biederman in his first published texts, later he discovered that many artists started using the term, while merely making geometrical structures - without references to nature, which prompted Biederman to start using the term 'the New Art' in stead of Structurist (or Structuralist).

48 Letter by Charles Biederman to David Bohm, December 28, 1960. Ibid., p.78.

Further, on causality and chance Biederman also wrote:

> *"What I feel, I don't mind admitting that it's instinctual, is a notion of causality remarkably altered by nature seen as purely creative process - not the atomic particles, but what is at the bottom of that structure, not the objects we perceive with our eyes, but what is at the bottom of that perception. A creative causality that rejects any form of mechanistic thinking equally with any notions of chance. A process where what appears as chance is but the subtle intricacies of creation, causality as a process of diverse orders of creative determination."*[49]

That Biederman is not a cliché believer of rationality, as is often expected of an artist working with geometry, is proved by the next quotation from his correspondence with David Bohm, in which he discusses his feelings and thoughts on nature:

> *"In speaking this way, I am not under the impression that I prove anything, that I am talking in a way that seems to utter trivialities, lacking what is needed for their serious consideration. So why talk like this at all? Because I feel that human feelings are the place where an ever greater degree of objectivity can be born. I think this has been true of all the great art and great scientific discoveries. Our feelings are our life-link with nature, as they are with other human beings. In this way I have found the direction that I believe leads to a genuine art of our times; in the same manner, I find the way to the development of that art. We live, but to fully live we must feel. And whatever we say about the structure of nature and human life must lead us to feel it, and to always seek to feel it deeper. Otherwise, it is like making love to an apparition."*[50]

It is known, for instance, that Einstein first 'saw' (meaning he 'felt') the solutions to his famous theories before proving them by a process of rationalization.[51] Bohm also emphasized that feeling - intuition - was essential.

The correspondence between Biederman and Bohm was abruptly ended by Biederman when Bohm - in Biedermans opinion - became overly involved in Oriental thought. This was quite a pity, as Occidental and Oriental thinking were always related, as you will find repeatedly stressed in this publication. Both Bohm and Krishnamurti were very much concerned with the black future the Cold War promised, and both concluded that the only possible solution could come from escaping the egocentric self within consciousness.[52] This is very similar to Schopenhauer's expectancy of life at the start of 19th century caused by all the suffering of famine and disease he saw around him, which one could only escape by escaping one's own will, for example through art, as artists like

[49] Letter by Biederman to Bohm December 28, 1960. Ibid., p.77.
[50] Ibid., p.78.
[51] See Arthur I. Miller, "Imagery in Scientific Thought - Creating 20th Century Physics" (MIT Press, 1987 - orig. 1984).
[52] To be distinguished from the 'true self'. See §2.2.

certain Impressionists and Cézanne tried.
Biederman wrote in his 1948 book, long before connectedness became the modern paradigm:

> *"There will be a sense of unity between the self and the non-self, yet distinctions between the two will be recognized. The world and self will be regarded as interrelated, but not as interchangeable processes; 'entities' will be distinguished, but not isolated."*[53]

This remark is comparable to Bohm's principle of 'implicate' order or to his ideas about perception as he expresses them in one of his letters to Biederman:

> *"Indeed, because there is no fundamental distinction between 'inner' and 'outer', there can be no basic distinction either between ordinary perception and understanding, although the functional mechanisms involved in both are very different. Nevertheless, one passes into the other, blending and merging in a whole process."* [54]

Since the Bohm-Biederman dialogue, these ideas have been furthered, as will be discussed later. Although everywhere one sees a growing understanding of the need for the multi-disciplinary approach, art's contribution is still too easily left out. Even if art is involved, it seems the aspect Biederman advocated is being avoided: to accept and, therefore, include the way nature appears to our eyes in our discussion about nature's deep and underlying connectedness.[55] A very different and certainly confusing problem is that art tendencies and trends have existed and do exist, which claim that the involved artworks are based on a scientific approach. This was something Bohm was critical about:

> *"... the essential point is that in creativity, a pre-given pattern is never what is relevant. Rather, it is an understanding of totality, in which something new emerges. So, it would be wrong for the scientist to impose the artistic pattern on his work, as for the artist to impose the mathematicians concept of space in his work, etc."* [56]

In fact, these kinds of artistic interpretations concern mere illustrations or models of scientific theories, and generally add nothing to the existing theory.[57] Sophisticated as this kind of art might be, art will only be able to contribute something substantial when

---

53 See Charles Biederman, "Art as the Evolution of Visual Knowledge" (Red Wing, MN: Charles Biederman, 1948), p.624.
54 Letter by Bohm to Biederman March 23, 1962. See Paavo Pylkkänen, "Bohm-Biederman Correspondence, David Bohm and Charles Biederman, Volume One: Creativity and Science", p. 203.
55 The justification for this idea you will find in the §5.
56 Letter by Bohm to Biederman March 17, 1962. See Paavo Pylkkänen, "Bohm-Biederman Correspondence, David Bohm and Charles Biederman, Volume One: Creativity and Science", p.184.
57 This was very apparent in the artistic interpretations of fractals of Chaos Theory, for instance, as in the paintings by Swiss artist/designer Karl Gerstner, who literally painted fractals. It was and is also quite clear in

it trusts the fundamental properties of it own field, and focuses on the possibilities of eye-brain perception. By doing so, art can actually add something of value to the discussion of reality. Art will add something different than science, but something that can nevertheless be added to the knowledge developed simultaneously by science. Not one field following the other, but cross-fertilization. Biederman himself wrote already in 1960 to Bohm:

> "*Why is it, however, that the quantum outlook upon nature, and for something drastic we have no equal, is so readily accepted while the structural view of nature as a creative process for art, is not readily accepted? The physicist has some marked advantages. These lead everyone to accept his innovations even though few care to comprehend them. Nature herself produces certain manifestations on the physicist's observational instruments that are above dispute, as such, aside from interpretations of them. So that to this day, even though no one has seen an atom, all accept the notion.*"[58]

Only when it is finally accepted that art and science offer a comparable and compatible combination of facts, abstract interpretations, and translations, will we be able to understand the full potential of a multi - disciplinary dialogue including art and science!

In their dialogue both Bohm and Biederman gradually trusted themselves to bring forward thoughts they probably felt uncomfortable mentioning in their official publications. The scientist - analogous to what Archipenko sensed - opening himself to non-scientific ideas. David Bohm, after discussing the analogies between art and science with Biederman, covering topics such as creativity, abstraction, understanding and the object-subject distinction, concludes that not only the artist can benefit from a better understanding of science, but:

> "*I think that in a similar way, the scientist must understand his own level of experience better, because: 1. All of his data finally come from perceptions and abstractions at this level. 2. His concepts and ways of thinking are subtly influenced by all of this experience. 3. So therefore, both in order to suggest new ideas and to see how he is being unconsciously conditioned by all of his experience, he should understand how the artist is seeing this level of experience. For example, a better understanding of art would give a scientist a new slant on space, connectedness, relationship, contingency and necessity, totality, etc.; ...*"[59]

Although the scientist should allow himself to know more about his own level of experience (after all a scientist and an artist are both human beings, who experience like any other human beings) an interest in the experience of eye-brain perception (meaning, not only how the eye and the brain work from a neurophysiological point, but also

many computer generated images made by academics (often mathematicians or computer-scientists) who consider their works 'art' when they have some colour and seem pleasing to the eye.

58 Letter by Charles Biederman to David Bohm, June 28, 1960. Ibid., p.36.

59 Letter by Bohm to Biederman March 17, 1962. Ibid., p. 184.

how we experience perception) in general is still not openly accepted in the scientific or academic world. Comparably, it often seems that artists better not speak out about their own theories and ideas too much, as the average art historian or art critic still prefers the artist to do his painting or sculpting in silence and leave the explanations and analyzing to them. This makes the Bohm - Biederman dialogue special, as both are facile with very vague, difficult to describe, but nevertheless highly interesting subjects, like their experiences of sensing wholeness. Biederman describes his experience such:

> *"Initially, I try to experience nature on a non-verbal level of perception, maintaining verbal silence within myself. This achieves the following results. I put aside all I know, i.e., my consciousness of vision at the time, so that I will not function, at least with the intruding deliberateness of consciousness, with a prejudiced vision. This then permits me to submit myself as much as possible to the experience of nature, each time anew. At such times I have the experience of totality, not as knowing that totality of nature, but because I have removed the barriers to being in it."*[60]

While describing his hard work to get a hold on the concept that there is no fundamental difference between 'outer' and 'inner' (discussed above) Bohm admits:

> *"... after some work, I occasionally got a sudden 'glimpse', in which one felt that reality is in a different dimension (as two views of an object in a stereoscope fuse to three dimensions). In this new set of dimensions, one saw that the inner and outer are basically one. However, this glimpse lasted for only a moment. I think that I saw why it didn't last. In this state of unity of 'inner' and 'outer', the new truth starts to operate."*[61]

David Bohm and Charles Biederman might not be the inventors of seeing structure and connectedness in nature, but they should be given credit for synthesizing knowledge from different disciplines and being early advocates of the necessary multidisciplinary approach. Theirs was a classical dialogue indeed. Biederman's unorthodox approach of seeing art as a medium for visual knowledge caught my attention immediately, although in the beginning I had great difficulties understanding it, indoctrinated as I was by my own background in general art history and modern European constructive art. Thus Biederman, especially, has clarified for me how art is not merely a temporal and perhaps even superfluous market product, but can actually contribute to our image and understanding of reality in the same way that science does - he inspired me to search for the essence of reality. Although I do not agree with many aspects of Biederman's often rigid

[60] Letter by Biederman to Bohm May 29, 1961. Ibid., p. 121. Having discussed things like this with Biederman myself, he showed me where he preferred to sit and open-up to nature. He had his chair on a quiet spot in the forest a little bit up hill behind his house.

[61] Letter by Bohm to Biederman March 23, 1962. Ibid., p. 204-205. To my interpretation both this statement by Bohm, and the previous one by Biederman, give reasons to refer here to the Oriental concept of pure enlightenment. See §2.

view of art, he still gave me a reason for being an artist who is not merely a producer of artifacts. In the same way, Bohm gave me hope that a real dialogue with scientists is possible and can be very helpful in understanding why we seem to need art and how art seems to function in our way of thinking and physical being.

In this chapter you have encountered ideas about the importance of 'eye-brain' perception. The next chapter will discuss perception in greater depth.

§5 THE PROJECTIVE FIELD

So quiet in the mountains.
Like a diver I meditate.
My breath.
Rhythmic sizzling of the blood in my ears.
The microscopic colour pallet of the Alps.
The unique radiating ultramarines, fluorescent reds, pinks and greens.
Far and near flow thro' my body.
It sets me free.
Fré Ilgen 1996

So far I have discussed general ideas about essence and the dialogue between art, science and philosophy. The importance of (eye-brain) perception in our process of understanding has been mentioned in the previous chapter. It is now time to try to understand more about perception, especially because our understanding of reality, including works of art, finds its meaning in the process of perception and nowhere else.

Our habit of explaining something in verbal language, meaning in spoken or written words, creates a significant problem when we try to discuss something visual - like fine art. The problem is that verbal language evolves in a linear way, but our understanding does not, as it is mixed with prejudices, associations, etc. This linear order of verbal language also makes it impossible to simultaneously describe simultaneous phenomena. For instance, if I tried to describe to you in exact words all the things I perceive through my senses right at this moment (including what music I am listening to) in combination with all the images I see in my mind while I write this sentence, I would have to write a very, very thick book. Still it would not become clear to you what I really perceive. Although language appears linear, it can still be interpreted in multiple ways.[1] To actually see information during a verbal argument certainly helps one understand it. This is also why communication between two persons is easier when they actually meet face to face than when they are limited to writing letters. Communicating essences is possible only by approximation. This can be accomplished by building on a mutual sensing of

[1] Words can have very different meanings as their understanding depends on the associations and knowledge of every different individual, making human communication as difficult as it is. This is the topic of study by the science of semiotics, the study of signs and their meanings. The writer and semioticist Umberto Eco pointed out, that the many different interpretation possibilities of the same words or texts - which for instance may change under influence of a change in trend or Zeitgeist - has led repeatedly to very different interpretations of Plato. For a very good book, that deals with the historical development and confusion about the search or desire for a perfect language, see Umberto Eco, "Die Suche nach der Vollkommenen Sprache", translated by Burkhart Kroeber (Munich: Verlag C.H. Beck, 1994). See also Umberto Eco, "Die Grenzen der Interpretation", translated by Günter Memmert (Munich, Vienna: Carl Hanser Verlag, 1992 - orig. "I limiti dell'interpretazione", Gruppo Editoriale Fabbri, Bompiani, Sonzogno, Etas S.p.A., Milan, 1990).

truth, as through poetry or by interacting with a work of art, but not by any empirical approach alone.

5.1. THE BRAIN

Our thinking - including our perception - is a flowing totality of complex and simultaneous processes. The current understanding of our brain is quite well developed, but still it is based mostly on theories. What is certain, though, is that the neural network of which our brain consists is extremely complex, especially because any activity in this microscopic network in the brain is interrelated with other activities in the rest of the body. Just consider, for instance, the influences of blood-pressure, sugar level, the hormone-production, temperature, hunger, fever, etc., on your thinking and feeling. Besides, there is enough evidence to show that all brain activities are also open to influences from outside the body. When we wish to understand the possible relation of art to our perception of reality, we need to understand some fundamentals about our perception and our thinking-process. Although in fact it is impossible to separate them, in general we can distinguish two major aspects of conscious being: the physiological process of perception being processed in our brain and the resulting psychological process of interpreting perception.

Let us first briefly explore what we now know about the brain. Our brain contains a very complex network of neurons, that can be imagined as very tiny wires with thin twigs along their lengths. It is estimated that there are about 100,000 neurons per mm^2 in our brain. These neurons continuously fire small quantities of electrochemical energy at pulsating frequencies along the wires of the network. When in the network sufficient concentrations of these energy-impulses emerge, thinking - processes become conscious (they become acknowledgable). It should be noted that researchers use the word 'consciousness' in many different ways. This is caused by the acceptance or denial of the importance of subjective experience. It seems quite likely that 'subjective' experience emerges from a 'physical' or, more precisely, bio-chemical process. In this process, not the individual neurons, but the coherence of the network of connections is essential. It is very important to understand that the brain cannot be studied as an autonomous or isolated entity. Brains do not only process new information or in-put entering the body through the senses, but are continuously on-line - are in continuous interaction - with all the other parts of the body. Therefore, brain processes are continuously open to influences from inside our body, but certainly also to influences from outside our body.

This is maybe better understood by referring to modern scientific evidence, but was already imagined much earlier by philosophers. Henri Bergson, who influenced artists like Kupka and Kandinsky, and also other philosophers like Whitehead and - in my opinion - Husserl, believed that the actual source for a deep understanding of reality could be found in immediate contact with the real, which one does not merely observe, but with which one is involved, or, even better - from which one cannot be separated. Bergson wrote as early as 1896:

"But is it possible to conceive the nervous system as living apart from the organism which nourishes it, from the atmosphere in which the organism breathes, from the earth which that atmosphere envelopes, from the sun round which the earth revolves? More generally, does not the fiction of an isolated material object imply a kind of absurdity, since this object borrows its physical properties from the relations which it maintains with all others, and owes each of its determinations, and, consequently, its very existence, to the place which it occupies in the universe as a whole? Let us no longer say, then, that our perceptions depend simply upon the molecular movements of the cerebral mass. We must say rather that they ***vary with*** *them, but that these movements themselves remain inseparably bound up with the rest of the material world."*[2]

Rhythm is the essential word in understanding the processes of our body and, therefore, of our brain and its influences. Rhythms can influence other rhythms when they occur in each other's vicinity. This is studied as *the principle of synchronization*.[3] In relation to the neural network, this implies that any incoming impulse on its path through the brain to the area where it will be processed will undoubtedly spark responses in many other neurons which have no direct relationship with this impulse. This could explain why we can have spontaneous thoughts or see images in our minds although there seems to be no reason for these to emerge in consciousness. The neurobiologists Francis Crick and Christof Koch have suggested that consciousness may arise from oscillations in the cerebral cortex that become synchronized at the moment neurons fire at a frequency of 40 times per second.[4] There are quite a few rhythmic phenomena that occur outside the brain and influence the functioning of the brain, considering phenomena that occur inside the body and some that occur outside the body. For instance, the rhythm of the heart varies during every twenty-four hours, differing its rhythms during the day and at night, affecting the pressure and flow of blood and all involved processes, including our brain processes. The importance of the cyclic behaviour of such physical rhythms is studied in chronobiology.[5]

Chronobiology researches rhythmic temporal patterns in biological phenomena and tries to build knowledge on the different cycles that occur in nature and thus in our bodies,

---

2 See Henri Bergson, "Matter and Memory", translated by N.M. Paul and W.S. Palmer (New York: Zone Books, 5th edition 1996 - orig. "Matière et mémoire", 1908), p.24+25. As modern evidence proves, Bergson's remark cannot be regarded as merely being related to ideas in certain occult or theosophic ideas that were fashionable at the end of the 19th century.

3 In February 1665 the Dutch physicist Christiaan Huygens, inventor of the pendule clock, discovered by chance the principle of synchronization. He was lying ill in his bed looking at two pendule clocks that were swinging in exactly the same rhythm. When he disrupted the rhythm of one of these clocks he discovered to his astonishment that after a certain lapse of time they swung again in absolute unision. Only after he hung them at a certain distance from each other did they not seem to influence each other anymore.

4 See John Horgan, "Can Science Explain Consciousness?", Scientific American July 1994, p.72-78. See Francis Crick, "The Astonishing Hypothesis - The scientific search for the soul" (London: Simon & Schuster, 1994), p.210.

5 The word chronobiology stems from the Greek word 'chronos', meaning time. The principle of chronobi-

with the aim to more effectively administer medication. Many of these patterns follow a kind of twenty-four hour pattern.[6] Scientist William J.M. Hrushesky writes:

> *"As de Mairan's work was the first to suggest, circadian rhythms are widely held to be endogenous or innate, to living systems, governed by shadowy physiological mechanisms known as biological clocks. Indeed, in the past two and a half century endogenous time-keeping rhythms have been demonstrated in yeasts and nucleated unicells and* ***at all levels of biological organization*** *- cell, tissue and organ - as well as in the human body as a whole.".*[7]

Hrushesky also points out the immense influence of these biological clocks on the ebb and flood of hormonal production in our body (affecting our emotions, which also affect our thinking) and that, for instance, the quantity of white bloodcells, necessary to our immune system, can vary as much as 50% in one single day! It can be safely stated that these circadian rhythms influence our thinking, our perception, and our whole behaviour. However, keep in mind that influencing is not the same as deciding. One can still have the impression of having free choice, but it should be clear that not every choice, preference or desire is a result of a process of actual free chosing!

Information, impressions, and experiences are processed in our brains and translated into quantities and frequencies of electrochemical energy. Frequencies are rhythmic patterns. Because of their rhythmic behavior, the principle of synchronization will cause that they can influence or be influenced by other quantities of energies that consist of related rhythmic frequencies. For instance, when we see something, this will lead to a new impulse entering from our eyes into our brain. This impulse consists of a new quantity of energy with a rhythmic behaviour. Inside the brain, this rhythmic quantity of energy will touch or collide with our memory, consisting also of small quantities of energy, present and 'stored' in the brain. At the moment of this 'collision' (better: the moment the rhythms connect) the principle of synchronization causes the frequency of the stored energy to become intensified or not. When this process leads to an intensification, the neurons will start to fire signals at a higher frequency and, described in a simplified manner, when the frequency is amplified enough, the stored information will start to play a role in our thinking in relation to this new information. In this process of amplification of a signal a phenomenon called 're-entry' plays an important role. When a wave of impulses enters the brain it will lead to the firing of a certain path of neurons in the brain, causing these impulses to be processed in various regions of the brain. This processing happens as these impulses are led by synchronization to follow multiple parallel paths, virtually circling or looping around the brain (re-entering), thus

ology was already discovered in 1729 by the French astronomer Jean-Jacques de Mairan while studying the opening and closing of flowers. See William J.M. Hrushesky, "Timing is Everything", The Sciences July/August 1994, p.32.

[6] This 24 hour pattern is named circadian rhythm, after the Latin word for day.

[7] See William J.M. Hrushesky, "Timing is Everything" (emphasis mine).

strengthening the impulses sufficiently to make them conscious.[8]

In 1990 Crick and Koch expressed their hope that the presence of synchronized oscillations in cortical structures might be indicative of the neuronal correlate of consciousness (NCC). In the meantime, their hope seems to have been confirmed. The complexity of this research is a result of the assumption that the neurons are packed so densely that a change in frequency of one neuron can influence the rhythm of many neighbouring neurons.[9] The principle of synchronization appears to be decisive in the perception of the objects around us. Synchronized neurons make us aware of the several attributes of a particular object, while asynchronous neurons make us aware of separated objects.[10] Besides, in our brain many processes evolve simultaneously.[11] This complexity and simultaneity make it impossible to actually separate our brain processes or to localize them exactly. Most modern brain-scans, therefore, show more or less vague localizations, or imprecise areas of the brain that are supposed to be specialized in a certain task, with no exact borderlines. The strict separation between incoming and outgoing impulses is doubtful, since it appears the impulses influence each other.

Additionally, the existence of external influences on the rhythms of these processes is plausible. In principle all phenomena of nature, like the familiar impact of a full moon or murky or sunny weather on our emotions, have everything to do with rhythmic patterns.[12] Serious researchers in neurophysiology and neuro-anatomy acknowledge that the level of complexity of the matter will require a very new approach to get closer to

---

[8] See Gerald M. Edelman and Giulio Tononi, "A Universe of Consciousness - How matter becomes Imagination" (New York: Basic Books, 2000) p.85: "It is important to emphasize that reentry is not feedback. Feedback occurs along a single fixed loop made of reciprocal connections using previous instructionally derived information for control and correction, such as an error signal. In contrast, reentry occurs in selectional systems across multiple parallel paths where information is not prespecified. Like feedback, however, reentry can be local (within a map) or global (among maps and whole regions)." Research on bees concerning their capacity for odor discrimination seems to be compatible with the idea that temporal synchronization is necessary for fine discriminations of sensory data, whether visual, somatosensory or olfactory. Research by Stopher, Bhagavan, Smith and Laurent, 1997. See Francis Crick and Christof Koch, "Is Neuronal Synchronization Necessary for Fine Sensory Discrimination?" (see www.phil.vt.edu/ASSC/engel/crickl.html).

[9] Compare Prigogene's concept of order-fluctuations and his and Stengers' reference to the principle of adaptive organization. See §7.6. See Gerald M. Edelman and Giulio Tononi, "A Universe of Consciousness - How matter becomes Imagination", p.47: "For example, from one day to the next, some synaptic connections in the same brain are likely not to remain exactly the same; certain cells will have retracted their processes, others will have extended new ones, and certain others will have died, all depending on the particular history of that brain. The individual variability that ensues is not just noise or error, but can affect the way we remember things and events."

[10] See Gerald M. Edelman and Giulio Tononi, "A Universe of Consciousness - How matter becomes Imagination", p.118: "Furthermore, the activity of neurons responding to different attributes of the same object was synchronous at the time scale of tens of milliseconds. This synchronous firing was observed not only in parallel across different streams, such as those for form, color, and motion, but hierarchically between lower and higher visual areas. However, the activity of neurons responding to different objects was asynchronous."

[11] This phenomenon is studied in cognitive science as PDP - Parallel Distributed Processing. See Howard Gardner, "The Mind's New Science - A History of the Cognitive Revolution" (New York: Basic Books, 1987).

[12] Rhythmic means repetitive in a sequence, it does not mean repetitive in the sense that this phenomenon

understanding all these aspects.

Mathematician, cognitive scientist and philosopher David J. Chalmers, who has specialized in artificial intelligence and the philosophy of the mind, compares it to the problem in the 19th century that the electromagnetic phenomena could not be explained with the principles known at that moment. To solve this dilemma scientists introduced the notion of electromagnetic charge as a new fundamental entity. Chalmers proposes to look for "... high-bridging laws, connecting physical processes to experience at an everyday level." He defines awareness as "... the process by which information in the brain is made globally available to motor processes such as speech and bodily action."[13] This seems to me to be a very adequate description for interacting with a work of art, insofar as this theory combines brain activity with some (other) physical activity, something that seems important to our learning process. We meet artworks at everyday eye-level with the goal of connecting physical processes (like the process of vision) with experience (like association).[14]

Based on experiments in modern neurobiology, there does not seem to be a different and autonomously operating cortical zone in the brain for seeing and another one for understanding what is seen. Instead, there seem to be several visual systems acting in parallel, which implies that the process of seeing and understanding cannot actually be separated. This is well researched and described by scientist Semir Zeki.[15] This is something we all can experience while looking at a work of art. It is beside the point that this does not mean that one instantaneously understands *all* aspects of the artwork at the moment one sets eyes on it. It merely suggests that by seeing the artwork there is a certain level of immediate understanding.[16]

always occurs in the same way - or same sequence - as it occured before. For instance, the rhythms of the seasons do exist, although every single year shows still a different picture. For further reading about the fundamental importance of rhythms inside and outside our bodies, see the book by German biochemical and molecular biological scientist Friedrich Cramer, "Symphonie des Lebendigen - Versuch einer allgemeinen Resonanztheorie" (Frankfurt, Leipzig: Insel Taschenbuch, 1998).

[13] Chalmers envisions awareness as objective and physical, which he understands to be the difference with consciousness. See David J. Chalmers, "The Puzzle of Conscious Experience", Scientific American December 1995, p.62-68. See also the discussion on talking to oneself in learning and conscious perception and my proposal for the concept of thought as process of self-argumentation, later in this chapter.

[14] Experience is by definition an aspect of memory, of past - association, and therefore, always refers to an event in the past.

[15] Semir Zeki is Professor of Neurobiology at the University of London. He is a Fellow of the Royal Society and a Member of the American Philosophical Society. Discussing research on the complexity of locating which parts of the visual brain are specialized in the perception of very different subjects (for instance, familiar faces and multi-coloured abstract compositions are not processed by the same part of the brain), Zeki writes, see Semir Zeki, "Inner Vision - An exploration of Art and the Brain" (Oxford: Oxford University Press, 1999), p.63: "Such studies establish beyond doubt the presence of functional specialisation in the human brain. They also suggest strongly that it is not with the primary visual cortex, area V1, alone that we see - the contribution of the surrounding areas is essential, and this is indeed what is found in patients in whom only the cortex surrounding V1 is damaged. We thus no longer think of two cortical zones, one for seeing and one for understanding what we see, but of several visual systems acting in parallel, the activity in each leading to both seeing and understanding a particular attribute of the visual scene."

[16] This seems to come quite close to Nishida's concept of immediate perception. See this chapter footnote 84.

A remarkable conclusion based on the research of neural activity that connects with art is that consciousness appears to need a continuous changing neural activity in the brain, which is spatially and temporally differentiated. The higher the level of complexity in the interacting groups of neurons becomes, the higher the chance for conscious experience.[17] This seems to me to provide evidence for the necessity for contrast and complexity in art, because the perception of contrast provokes a continuous jumping of the eye, and focus, thus causing a continuous changing neural activity. Or could it be the other way around? Is this feature of consciousness responsible for our preference of contrast and complexity in art?

5.2 A FEW EXAMPLES IN ART

After reading the above, it should hardly be surprising to find evidence of the relation between art and perception in the statements and theories of artists themselves. For instance, Russian artist and musician Michail Matjushin, after ten years of artistic research, in 1923 published his concept of 'SorVed',[18] connecting Occidental logic and rationality with Oriental illogical acknowledgement. Matjushin focussed on the extension of vision in a 360° radius, inspired by the principle of growth in cell-theory.[19] Accordingly, he promoted the importance of understanding our vision as not restricted to looking rectilinearly in front of us, but as an extension of perception (and thought) in a large radius all around us.[20] This seems compatible with philosopher Henri Bergson's understanding of the perception of an object as a non rectilinear process, but as "... a circuit, in which all elements, including the perceived object itself, hold each other in a state of mutual tension as in an electric circuit, ...".[21]

In the 1930's the Polish artist Wladyslaw Strzeminski began intensive studies under the title 'Teoria Widzenia'. This 'Theory of Vision' concerns an interpretation of the historical development of painting viewed from the perspective of visual experience. Strzeminski understood visual experience to be an evolutionary process, which

---

It also shows again that only trusting pictorial anaylysis to understand a work of art is just not enough.

[17] This is called the 'dynamic core hypothesis'. See Gerald M. Edelman and Giulio Tononi, "A Universe of Consciousness - How matter becomes Imagination", p.148. See also p.73 and p.74: "In the 1930's, psychologists discovered that when people gazed into a featureless field of vision (a Ganzfeld), all color would soon drain from the field of vision, after which visual experience itself would fade. It would appear that a sufficient number of variable and differentiated brain states must be continually available for conscious experience to arise and be sustained."

[18] 'Sorved' (or 'Zor-Ved') means 'Seeing and Knowing' or extended vision. See Alla Powelichina, "Michail Matjuschin - Die Welt als organisches Ganzes", in Heinrich Klotz, "Matjuschin und die Leningrader Avant-Garde" (Stuttgart-Munich: Oktogon Verlag, 1991), p.29. See Alla Povelikhina, "Matyushin's Anthropologism: The ZOR-VED System in the Perception of Nature", in Alla V. Povelikhina, "Organica - Organic. The Non-Objective World of Nature in the Russian Avant-Garde of the 20th Century" (Cologne: Galerie Gmurzynska, 2000), p.42. Notice, please, that the differences in spelling of Russian names, like of Matjushin, occurs when they appear in German or English and are just different interpretations from translating cyrillic writing into western writing.

[19] Cell-theory, in Matjushin's days, studied the simultaneous extension of cells in all directions.

[20] Compare also Hildebrand's ideas of 1893, mentioned in §2 footnote 102.

[21] See Henri Bergson, "Matter and Memory", p.104.

especially develops in times of social instability, but in stabile times occasionally may stagnate or even be impeded in times of a social change that can be perceived as regression (for instance, a time that becomes a return to a dictatorship).[22] The American artist and theorist Charles Biederman discusses a more or less comparable concept.[23] Biederman translates art's progress as visual knowledge as a slow process over long periods of history, translated into terms of continuities and discontinuities. Both Strzeminski and Biederman clearly believed visual knowledge could raise mankind to higher levels of evolution.[24]

I myself doubt this, although I agree that visual knowledge is essential for understanding reality. If there would be any progress - not in technology but in the general understanding of reality - it is in a new and slightly improved look at earlier established ideas and conclusions. Although man accomplished great things in medical knowledge or technology, for instance, unfortunately he does not succeed in improving himself much as a being. It is a different thing for an individual man to get to higher levels of consciously understanding his true self. Philosopher Nishitani, for instance, discusses how between the individual self (of which we have the illusion that it is independent) and the structure underlying everything in nature (eternal 'no-thingness' or 'sunyata') in the middle one may find the true self in its real selfness.[25] We may find the real meaning of our selves not by understanding our bodies and brains as autonomous, but as part of the larger processes of nature while simultaneously remaining individual. The notion of the middle appeals to me because one can say that in the middle, between our thinking (the process inside our brains) and nature (outside our bodies), we use objects - like art - to understand the whole of reality including our own individual selves. Our need for objects to be able to find access to certain information about reality (information that is materialized in a perceptable form), seems to be confirmed by psychological research.[26] Information here means that which makes us understand what the object is,

---

22 Strzeminski's 'Teoria Widzenia' means 'Theory of Vision'. See Lise-Lotte Blom, "Katarzyna Kobro's and Wladyslaw Strzeminski's Conception of Art", in Franciska Clausen, "Tre Pionérer for Polsk Avant-Garde/ Three Pioneers of Polish Avant-Garde" (Helsinki: Fyns Kunstmuseum, 1985), p.33.

23 See Charles Biederman, "Art As The Evolution of Visual Knowledge" (Red Wing, MN. Charles Biederman, 1948), p.26: "Art in its various forms constitutes the principal evidence of man's past efforts at visualization, and when studied in this way should produce data of inestimable value to many of the other sciences which deal directly or indirectly with the development of man's vision in relation to the phylogeny of the human nervous system." This book made quite an impression on several generations of artists and art historians. See §4.

24 Biederman's belief in progress quite probably is based upon Korzybski's idea that a new generation will double the knowledge of the previous generation - see §4, footnote 8. It would be interesting to know if Strzeminksi also was familiar with Korzybski's ideas, which could be the case. Like Korzybski, Strzeminski was Polish.

25 See §2.2.

26 Chalmers (mentioned earlier this chapter) offers reasons to connect his ideas about consciousness and awareness to the functioning of art, referring to the abstract notion of information as proposed in Information Theory. See David J. Chalmers, "The Puzzle of Conscious Experience", Scientific American December 1995, p.62-68: "We can also find information embodied in conscious experience. The pattern of color patches in a

for what reason or purpose the object exists, supporting our understanding of our world and ourselves. The reader will hopefully understand why I propose the hypothesis that the objective information is embedded in the material thing-ness of the artwork, while the experiential information is evoked by the appearance of the artwork and emerges in our immediate interaction with the work of art (because this information finally exists in the interaction, it emerges 'in the middle' between oneself and the material object, thus, it virtually emerges as no-thingness). I hope this will become more clear at the end of this publication.

5.3. ON ILLUSION

Another way of putting the above is to say that our perception cannot be separated from our thinking. Just try to think without the involvement of new sensory input. Impossible! Even when you close your eyes you still perceive changes of light. When you shut your ears, you perceive the rushing of your blood. Even if you are able to completely shut your ears and eyes, your thinking will still be affected by your touch (for example by sensing your body touching an object or the floor as you stand, lean, sit or lie down) or by sensing the changes of temperature in the space you occupy. You may also feel any slight change of draft in the air. Philosophers like René Descartes tried to concentrate on thinking alone - aiming to find pure thought, isolated in the head. Descartes first concluded, that the senses should be mistrusted, because they could be fooled (as if the rational mind could not be fooled by itself).[27] Descartes of course had to discover that a conversation with oneself is only possible by using the metaphors, images and symbols that we use for communication, but which he wanted to avoid. In short: Descartes' question and experiment merely prove the importance of sensory perception for our thinking and that thinking and perception cannot be separated. It is interesting to note here that philosophers like Descartes were convinced that they needed to find truth by avoiding all things illusory (things that cannot be considered to be real). This meant, for instance, avoiding illusion in perception because this (like visual illusion)

---

visual field, for example, can be seen as analogous to that of the pixels covering a display screen. Intriguingly, it turns out that we find the same information states embedded in conscious experience and in underlying physical experience in the brain. The three-dimensional encoding of color spaces, for example, suggests that the information state in a color experience corresponds directly to an information state in the brain. We might even regard the two states as distinct aspects of a single information state, which is simultaneously embodied in both physical processing and conscious experience. A natural hypothesis ensues. Perhaps information, or at least some information, has two basic aspects: a physical one and an experiential one." This seems compatible with studies on how the blind draw, which shows that vision and touch are closely linked. See John M. Kennedy, "How the Blind Draw", Scientific American January 1997, p.60-65. Information Theory was defined by Shannon in the 1940's. Information is a set of separate states with a basic structure of similarities and differences between them.

[27] See Dalia Judovitz, "Derrida and Descartes: Economizing Thought", in Hugh J. Silverman, "Derrida and Deconstruction" (New York and London: Routledge, 1989), p.46: "He proposes to close his eyes, shut his ears, suspend his senses, efface from his thoughts all images of corporeal things (but since this is impossible, esteem them as vain and false) and thus 'holding converse only with myself and considering my own nature' he tries to reach a better knowledge of himself."

fools the senses and, therefore, would not be real.[28]

Modern art has struggled a long time with illusion. It has, so far, been a history of acceptance and denial. Optical illusion in abstract art was understood as something impure, and therefore, something that should be avoided at all costs. Wladyslaw Strzeminski, already mentioned, is an example of this mentality in the first half of the 20th century. With his concept, 'Unizm', he aimed to create a painting without any illusion (without the illusion of depth, for instance). Like all other serious artists, he had to admit at a certain point that optical illusion cannot be avoided. It is interesting to note here that contemporary computer technology, with its capacity for creating visual simulations, has changed this debate overnight.[29] When we do not describe a painting that involves perspective as one that contains an illusion of space, but as one containing a simulation of space, then it somehow seems to become acceptable to everyone! Art seems to be far ahead of most philosophy and science in accepting illusion as a fact of our perception of reality, which seems to be confirmed by neurobiology.

In contemporary neurobiology the process of perception in our brain is considered to be very similar to the process of creating art. Neurobiology perceives the different processes of the brain involved in perception to work in parallel, but at different speeds. Basically, each brain-cell involved in our visual system has a receptive field, meaning it involves a part of the visual scene. Distinguished are three main features: a position, a shape and a specificity.[30] Experiments have shown that there are differences in tens of milliseconds between the perception of colour, form and motion. Colour is perceived first, then form and then motion. Neurobiologist Semir Zeki:

> *"In broader terms, the brain does not, over brief periods of time, seem to be capable of binding together what happens in real time; in stead it binds the results of its own processing systems and therefore misbinds in terms of real time."*[31]

Neurobiology shows that our brain is not just a passive administrator and processor of external physical reality, but, because of its parallel processes, takes an active role itself in generating our visual image according to its own processes.[32]

In summary, after a perceived object is fragmented by these different processes of perception, these fragmented properties are all processed in different specialized parts of the brain before being put together again to become the whole object as it appears in our

[28] Please, remember Vivekananda saying, "Illusion arises from illusion alone. There will be no illusion as soon as truth is seen." See §2.2, footnote 14. See Matthew Luckiesh, "Visual Illusions - Their Causes, Characteristics and Applications", introduction by William H. Ittelson (NewYork: Dover Publications, Inc., 1965 - orig. 1922). A book read by artists like Charles Biederman.

[29] For instance, CAD or Virtual Reality-programs.

[30] See Semir Zeki, "Inner Vision - An exploration of Art and the Brain", p.102.

[31] Ibid., p.66, p.67.

[32] Ibid., p.67: "They (these experiments, ed.) provide compelling evidence to show that different processing systems take different times to reach their end-points, which is the perception of the relevant attribute. This in turn suggests that the processing systems are also perceptual systems, thus allowing us to think of several

visual awareness (the so-called binding-problem). It seems fascinating that this perception's basic process of fragmenting at different speeds and binding together is nothing else than a process of simulation itself, and very comparable to making art. What else is art than choosing fragmented pictorial parts and putting them together - binding them together - in a whole which we call a composition?[33]

Semir Zeki makes a good point by showing that the creative process is very similar to the functioning of the brain. In my opinion, he shows why we perceive optical illusions or simulations in art as quite natural: the brain's physical functioning does not make an exact representation of reality a feasible option. Instead, the brain introduces simulation, which necessarely includes aspects of illusion.[34] In art, one can find evidence for illusions or simulations of depth, motion or energy formed by using contrasts, rhythms and repetitions of colour, form and line.[35] Thanks to scientists like Crick and Koch, Chalmers, Edelman and Tononi and especially Zeki, we know these are not merely artistic inventions, but necessary results of some conscious or unconscious intuitions artists have about how the brain and perception function.[36]

In this light, it is fascinating to re-read what some artists have stated on this subject. Kandinsky, for instance, was very inspired by what he understood of the modern theory of atoms (he was shocked to learn that even atoms can disintegrate under impact of radioactive rays) and the evidence of X-rays proving the non-existence of solid matter. As a result, he tried to create paintings with suspended non-material forms. In his opinion, this could be accomplished by applying contradictory illusions of space to create a virtual plane in front of the actual plane of the canvas.[37] He called this the ideal plane. When one takes time to visually consume a good Kandinsky painting, one can observe

parallel processing-perceptual systems." And: "Since we perceive two attributes, say colour and motion, at separate times, it follows not only that there are separate consciousnesses, each a correlate of activity in one of the independent processing-perceptual systems, but that these different consciousnesses are also asynchronous with respect to each other."

33 Fragmented pictorial parts can be brushstrokes, bits and pieces of material, parts of a sculpture, patches of colour, geometrical forms, dots of pigment, drawn lines, etc., etc..

34 The formal meaning of 'illusion' is (the seeing of) something that does not exist, something as different from reality, a false idea or belief, or, a state of mind in which one is deceived in this way. The formal meaning of 'simulation' is a pretence, an imitation. This means that the distinction between illusion and simulation is that the first misleads one's perception while the second supports our actual perception. The confusing issue, discussed in the main text, is that many illusions do occur as simulation of reality within our brain, comparable to how illusion and simulation often can be exchanged in art.

35 The simulation of motion - like in a work of art - is entirely created by the brain in the area indicated with V5. See Semir Zeki, "Inner Vision - An exploration of Art and the Brain", p.163.

36 See §3.

37 See Wassily Kandinsky, "Concerning The Spiritual in Art", translated by M.T.H. Sadler (New York: Dover Publications Inc., 1977- reprint from English orig. "The Art of Spiritual Harmony", 1914) p.44: "The thinness or thickness of a line, the placing of the form on the surface, the overlaying of one form on another may be quoted as examples of artistic means that may be employed. Similar possibilities are offered by colour which, when rightly used, can advance or retreat, and can make of the picture a living thing, and so achieve an artistic expansion of space. The combination of both means of extension in harmony or concord is one of the richest and most powerful elements in purely artistic composition." See §10, footnote 9.

how true his statement was. The small and tiny shapes start to float towards the observer as the painting comes alive, showing deep space and space reaching out towards the observer.[38] Kandinsky's paintings show how important visual illusion - simulation - is to our perception.

Although I suspected it, I was still quite pleased to find a text by the American artist Frank Stella also emphasizing the necessity of illusion in art. In an exciting article, Stella discusses whether illusionism and abstraction will ever come together.[39] He describes how well the magnificent illusionistic magic of the very large Baroque ceiling and dome paintings worked and how the development of the tableau - the portable canvas - brought with it a very different kind of perception. A painting on canvas is portable, therefore, not as large as a whole ceiling or dome painting, and can be taken in at a glance. Because compositions on tableaus or canvasses can be seen in one glance, one can see pictorial space immediately (the space that we perceive by focussing our attention on a work of art). This led to an academic tradition of avoiding letting the frame function as a 'window-pane' and instead seeing the picture-surface as it 'really and honestly' is: flat and two-dimensional. Any pictorial illusionism should be avoided. Stella correctly points out that this, however, is merely an academic and incorrect way of reasoning, because our perception of reality does not mean standing here and looking at a flat surface over there. Perception demands the great sense of depth in which we are engulfed by the right pictorial illusion. He concludes that this feature makes art look real.

Reading a novel can only offer a good experience of reality when one is able to look beyond the mere two-dimensional flat surface of the book and beyond the abstract shapes of the printed letters. Just as it takes some basic experience in reading to be able to have this experience with a novel it takes some basic experience to experience the deep sense of reality in artworks. Just enough basic experience allows the right pictorial illusionism in a work of art to evoke in one's perception a deep sense of continuous streaming space/time, comparable to the experience of standing in a landscape being engulfed completely.

In my own opinion - the focus on the handcraft of painting and the focus on the act of painting as phenomenon has undermined the essential value of painting as experience, causing painting in modern times to come to a virtual standstill. In other words, although painting is one way to search for the essence of the whole of nature, it became a search for the essence of the material itself. The desire to find the essence by looking for the essential of the selected material and medium led to the same mistake made by the Newtonian tradition in science: one cannot expect to find the essence of the whole by focussing on an essence that is but a tiny part and that cannot even be isolated from the whole. Comparably, mathematics is a very useful medium for calculating the orbit of a satellite around the moon, but cannot explain our experience of the moon.

---

[38] This is an impression one can also get from a computer-monitor that runs a 3-D programme.

[39] See Frank Stella, "Grimm's Ecstasy", 1991, in Bonny Clearwater, "Frank Stella at two thousand: Changing the rules" (North Miami, FL: Museum of Contemporary Art, 2000), p.57-69.

Just as traditional pictorial analysis[40] makes us forget the more intuitive or overall aspects of our perception that are important properties of our appreciation of a work of art, Stella argues that we desperately need to re-discover the importance of 'succesful pictorial illusionism' in art.[41] Illusionism in a picture allows the observer to be completely engulfed by and absorbed in the composition of forms and colours that are simulated to fly in front of, on and behind the actual two-dimensional pictorial space, creating a feeling of being engulfed and mirroring our actual and unavoidable immersion in everyday reality. This means that abstraction must use the same pictorial space as figuration did ever since Baroque art. This is a big shock to most abstract artists, but to me it is quite logical.

Like Stella, I came to an obvious conclusion: we all live in the world we call our reality. What we produce or create emerges in this reality. Therefore, every kind of art can only be from this reality and only exist in this reality. This means that art can only be realistic. The common self-created pit-fall to define bureaucratic formulations or rules for rules' sake makes it so important to always return to seeing how reality actually is, to look at nature anew! Thus, abstraction and figuration are not as widely apart as they are often believed to be, and Stella is correct when he states:

"However, if we look at illusionism in a larger way I think it's possible to have succesful, even 'real' painting without getting hung up on the necessities of representational illusionism. I imagine that the goal for painting is to create a 'habitable illusion' for the subjects of painting."

"The habitable illusion is really pictorial space that is expansive rather than restrictive, space that is more easily understood in terms of normal vision than in terms of artistic vision. It is pictorial space that takes into account a fuller range of our visual perceptual abilities, for example, our unforced ability as we work at our desk, say, to look out the window, take in a painting by Mondrian on the wall, and still read our own reflected facial grimace on the polished chrome lamp face immediately in front of us. Normal vision actually has a greater knack than we give it credit for in terms of handling sensations of what might be called multi dimensional space. Sitting at our desk, penning a note, we

[40] See §2.6.

[41] See Frank Stella, "Grimm's Ecstasy", p.65: "Not only did the evolutionary success of the tableau obscure the success of the great illusionistic inventions of the past, it helped create the monster of selfdefining, reductionist abstraction that threatens illusionism itself. If we accept the idea that art is and must be an illusion, manifest or less an illusionistic object, it's not hard to see that the end of art is in sight." And, referring to the fight of twentieth century abstract art to avoid any illusion of depth in painting (compare the discussion on Strzeminski): "We all are familiar with the mechanical stresses pictorial space has had to endure in the twentieth century. We are aware of the confrontation of pictorial illusionism by abstraction." Stella continues: "But these efforts can't seem to make up for the loss of recessional depth, the one absolute and necessary element for succesful pictorial illusionism."

[42] See Frank Stella, "Grimm's Ecstasy", p.65, 66. The idea that abstraction would not deal with reality while figuration does, is very probably a result of the Occidental (Christian?) belief that man is above, and therefore, separate from nature.

ticked off about eight dimensions - three out the window, at least two from the Mondrian on the wall, and three plus in our reflection from the luxor lamp. We see a lot all the time without worrying about it. Only when we get wound up trying to translate normal vision into artistic vision do we seem to get into trouble. We get tangled up by trying to frame what we see and confused to fit it into the boxes marked X, Y, and Z."[42]

One can argue about Stella's eight dimensions. Nevertheless, he clearly makes the point that we experience so many visual illusions in the complex dynamics of our everyday perception that the supposed problems of illusion that arise when we discuss the translation of this perception onto a two-dimensional picture are only academic and not very essential.[43] Stella argues further in this article that much of so-called 'pure painting' has ignored another essential feature of reality: change. Because this subject will be discussed in §6, it should be sufficient here to mention that change in painting is also an aspect that cannot actually be shown, but can be simulated very strongly, as the early pioneers of abstract art did - and also major Baroque painters like Rubens, Tintoretto, Tiepolo or late Baroque painters like Joseph Keller. Stella advocates the idea that painting should come as close to normal vision as possible - in contrast to so-called artistic vision which is more academic than real:

see pictures 1, 13, 14

"*What the best art does, consciously or otherwise, is to never lose its connection to immediate, everyday, ever-present perceptions. It has the knack of staying in touch by absorbing and dissolving spatial incongruities. When you get the talking artist with the black cat on his head in focus, just reach out and pat the cat. Now you are in touch with pictorial experience.*"[44]

It is also my own experience that works of art that offer multiple layers of illusions of depth and motion - which are especially powerful when they combine painting with sculpture - virtually arrest the observer and do not let go easily. This impact cannot be disregarded as entertainment, because entertainment art only holds one's attention in a short flash - like all entertainment in modern society.

5.4 EXTENSION

Considering how complex our conscious perception is, it is not suprising that enough evidence has been found that suggests we perceive more than we are conscious of. This makes distinguishing between true perception and a false perception influenced by illusion

[43] See Frank Stella, "Melrose Avenue", 1995, in Bonny Clearwater, "Frank Stella at two thousand: Changing the rules", p.83: "Without the necessary illusionistic ingredients, it is impossible to have the striking physical opticality that has made art-making such a profound and satisfying activity. Without the optical sensation that only illusionistically informed painting can provide, literalist art making is, by and large, visually dull." In this article Stella calls for "the grand synthesis of illusionism and literalism." See §10.

[44] See Frank Stella, "Grimm's Ecstasy", p.68. Stella in this article refers to the greatness of the dome-painting, "Martyrdom of Four Saints", by Correggio in Parma.

even more complex. One example of this complexity is the phenomenon of blindsight. Blindsight occurs when patients with brain-damage in the primary visual cortex V1 (the striate cortex) still can localize an object in their immediate vicinity with a certain accuracy without seeing it consciously. In fact, they deny perceiving it. The patient thus does perceive something, but without consciousness.[45] Francis Crick refers to research showing that the cones in the eye are actually actively involved, and that the blindsight phenomenon is not an illusionary perception or a trick of the mind. In spite of the brain-damage, some connections in the brain seem to be strong enough to still realize a motor-output.[46] A phenomenon that appears related is 'sublimal perception': perception without awareness, caused by impulses that are too short and too weak or too noisy to be consciously preceived, but are strong enough to trigger a behavioral response.[47]

Recent research on how people who are born blind draw has shown that they are quite capable of translating touch into drawing.[48] The interesting thing is that blind people make linear drawings of the outlines of objects and faces very much like sighted people do. It is even more interesting that they have a similar understanding of the simulation of depth and motion in linear drawing to sighted people. Although such research undoubtedly is valuable, I am hesitant to categorize this as a similar phenomenon to blindsight. One reason is that blind people's concept of reality is also influenced by verbal communication with sighted people.

While discussing art and perception, I was explaining the phenomenon of blindsight to the artist Manfred Mohr. Manfred Mohr instantly responded that that is exactly what artists do: making visible what we all see, but do not consciously see.[49] The question could thus be posed: are artists more conscious of their unconscious blindsight than other people? Blindsight can be widely interpreted as being able to point at a consciously unseen object. Perhaps blindsight can be understood as the perception of the essence of reality, which artists point to through their works without being actually aware of this perception. In light of the general opinion that artists are able to express not only their own individual feelings, but also more general human feelings, it might be said that artists are specially qualified by talent and training to stimulate and enhance the

---

[45] This is very different from the psychological concept of denial. Research has been done on this phenomenon by psychologist Larry Weiskrantz. See Larry Weiskrantz, "Blindsight - A Case Study and Implications", Oxford University Press 1986. See Francis Crick, "The Astonishing Hypothesis - The scientific search for the soul" (London: Simon & Schuster, 1994), p.172-173.

[46] The person that is blindsighted still seems to be able to point at the unconsciously seen object.

[47] See Gerald M. Edelman and Giulio Tononi, "A Universe of Consciousness - How matter becomes Imagination", p.67.

[48] See John M. Kennedy, "How the Blind Draw", Scientific American January 1997, p.60-65: "How the Blind Draw - Blind and sighted people use many of the same devices in sketching their surroundings, suggesting that vision and touch are closely linked."

[49] At the symposium "Creativity and Cognition 2", Loughborough University. See Ernest E.A. Edmonds and Linda Candy, "Proceedings of the Second International Symposium 'Creativity and Cognition' " (Loughborough: LUTCHI Research Center, Department of Computer Studies, 1996). This observation has

recollection of our immersion in nature as a whole.[50] We lost the recollection of this immersion somewhere on our road to modern civilization, but it is still stored in the material memory of our bodies.

When we understand the importance of such an interpretation of art and see that phenomena like blindsight and sublimal perception support the existence of such an interpretation, it make us understand that our thinking is not merely a process restricted to the electrochemical processes in our brains - inside our heads. The processing and storing of an experience takes place inside the body, but is interrelated so much to the things around us (consciously and unconsciously) that it is irrelevant to disconnect our immediate environment from our thinking. We continuously scan the immediate environment with our senses. Our thinking can only evolve through a continuous interaction with the things around us. We even need objects outside ourselves to enhance our thinking by focussing our attention. This continuous interaction between inside and outside makes our conscious being and our functioning possible. It has a double connotation. On one side, the field around us offers continuous input, allowing us to find points of reference and vectors in a space, which we need to be able to act and proceed through this space. On the other side, it underscores the importance of considering our output into that space - like works of art.

5.5 ON THINKING AND GEOMETRY

The fascination with geometry has a lot to do with an everyday need to orientate in space: imagining straight lines and other geometric shapes helps us judge distances, speed, movements, danger.[51] Therefore, it is quite natural to find in all cultures in our world some interest in geometry. In addition, modern neurobiology shows the way the brain scans the world for essentials leads to a preference for geometry: geometry in general is processed with less effort, hence faster than for instance organic or amorphic shapes.[52] Experiments have proven how abstract compositions activate a smaller part of our brain than representative or figurative art.[53]

Geometry plays an essential role in our understanding of the whole. The ability to understand the whole of events in everyday life can also be understood as a property of space.[54] As an example for the discussions about geometry in the 19th century, influential and popular scientist Hermann von Helmholtz wrote:

earlier been stated by Paul Overy. See later this chapter, footnote 67.

50 Philosopher Henri Bergson tried to analyze perception and memory. He stated that "... perception and recollection, always interpenetrate each other, are always exchanging something of their substance as by a process of endosmosis." He continues, "... if recollection is regarded as a weakened perception, perception must be regarded as a stronger recollection." See Henri Bergson, "Matter and Memory", p.67.

51 See §8.

52 See Semir Zeki, "Inner Vision - An exploration of Art and the Brain", Chapter 12 "Mondrian, Malevitch and the neurophysiology of oriented lines."

53 Ibid., p.207.

54 Remember: geos = earth and metron = measure.

"1. The axions of geometry, taken by themselves out of all connection with mechanical propositions, represent ***no relations of real things****. When thus isolated, if we regard them with Kant as forms of intuition transcendentally given, they constitute a form into which any empirical content whatever will fit, and which therefore does not in any way limit or determine beforehand the nature of the content. This is true, however, not only of Euclid's axions, but also of the axions of spherical and pseudospherical geometry. 2. As soon as certain principles of mechanics are conjoined with the axions of geometry, we obtain a system of proportions which has real import, and which can be verified or overturned by empirical observations, just as it can be inferred from experience. If such a system were to be taken as a transcendental form of intuition and thought, there must be assumed* ***a pre-established harmony between form and reality****."*[55]

Somewhat later, in 1917, philosopher Kitaro Nishida wrote on geometry:

"Kant would reject this attempt to found the continuity of lines and numerical series on the relationship between the universal and the particular, pointing out that the relationship between a certain space and all of space is that of part to whole, not particular to universal, that ***the principles of geometry*** *cannot be derived from universal concepts, and that while space is intuited as infinite no concept can embrace infinity."*[56]

Like many of his contemporaries (including Nishida) at the end of the 19th century, scientist Henri Poincaré discussed the idea that our interest in three-dimensional Euclidian geometry is a characteristic we are born with and which we need for survival, without seeing geometry as property of nature in a literal sense. "Poincaré analyzed how organisms construct the principle of a relativity of space thus: I can only defend myself against a menacing object, A, if I know where it is relative to my body."[57] Poincaré saw that "... this complex system of associations [is] so to speak ... our whole geometry."[58]

Konrad Lorenz explained in his 'Deszendenzlehre' that we are born with an understanding of space, because otherwise our ancestors, the apes, while jumping around, would have fallen out of the trees.[59] More recently, physicist and philosopher Carl Friedrich von Weizsäcker justifiably questions whether our inborn notion of space is

---

[55] Hermann von Helmholtz, "Origin and Significance of Geometrical Axions", 1870. See David Cahan, "Science and Culture - Popular and Philosophical Essays - Hermann von Helmholtz" (Chicago: The University of Chicago Press, 1995), p.245. Emphasis mine.

[56] See Kitaro Nishida, "Intuition and Reflection"(New York: State University of New York Press, 1987 - orig. "Jikaku ni okeru chokkan to han sei", 1941), p.18. Emphasis mine.

[57] See Arthur I.Miller, "Imagery in Scientific Thought - Creating 20th Century Physics" (Cambridge, Mass., London: The MIT Press, sec. print 1987 - orig. Birkhäuser Boston inc. 1984), p.24. A highly recommendable book. These ideas have been furthered by Miller. See Arthur I. Miller, "Insights of Genius - Imagery and Creativity in Science and Art" (Cambridge, Mass., London: The MIT Press, 2000 - orig. Springer Verlag New York, 1996).

[58] See Arthur I. Miller, "Imagery in Scientific Thought - Creating 20th Century Physics" p.25.

[59] Konrad Lorenz published his "Deszendenzlehre" in "Gestaltwahrnehmung als Quelle wissenschaftlicher

necessarely geometrical - not to mention Euclidian. In my opinion, three-dimensional geometry is indeed a part of our sense of space, but also other facts play comparable and simultaneous roles; for instance, the perception of colour accents, the perception of depth caused mainly by colour and form contrasts and by distortion of perspective, the perception of movement, the memory of previous experiences and especially our whole motoric activities.[60]

5.6 THE RECEPTIVE FIELD - THE PROJECIVE FIELD

Because in neurobiology 'the receptive field' only concerns the combination of sources of input for an individual neuron in the brain, I would like to extend this notion in a way to better understand our total perception. Therefore, I propose that the whole field supplying us with all input, our immediate environment, can be called 'the receptive field'.[61]

This receptive field, however, is only part of the process of perception, because our continuous scanning of the environment involves a seemingly opposed process, namely a process proceeding from our brains and from the rest of our bodies out into all directions of the environment around our bodies. This outgoing process is illustrated by our body-temperature, the magnetic radiation of our bodies or our breathing process. It is also illustrated by our way of interpreting and associating. A process certainly not only evolving inside our heads, as our senses cannot be disconnected from interacting with the environment. We might say that we project our thoughts into our immediate environment. Hence we can speak of 'a projective field'.

Neuroscientist Terrence Sejnowski proposed the notion of the projective field and described it as a polarisation of the receptive field (as mentioned above, the field of incoming impulses concerning one particular neuron).[62] He understands the projective field as that towards which a certain neuron projects its output, towards other neurons with which his axon makes synaptic contacts. Although Sejnowski limits his notion of the projective field to the interaction between individual neurons in the brain, I propose to extend this notion into the immediate environment *outside* our body. With this concept, I imply that the receptive field and the projective field overlap and, in fact, concern both our immediate environment and ourselves. I make this proposal especially because the input to our thinking (and, thus, to our neurons) as a process is definitely not

see picture 66

Erkenntnis" ("Perception of Gestalts as source for scientific acknowledgement") published 1959 in "Über tierisches und menschliches Verhalten" See Carl Friedrich von Weizsäcker, "Zeit und Wissen" (Munich, Vienna: Carl Hanser Verlag, 1992), p.164.

60 What I mean by 'motoric activities' is the activity of moving the body, the continuous swinging of the head, the scanning of space by our hands, feet and other body-parts, but especially the manual handling - the manipulating - of objects.

61 See Thomas Vargish and Delo E. Mook, "Inside Modernism - Relativity Theory, Cubism, Narrative" (New Haven and London: Yale University Press, 1999), p.105: "A field is a spatial and/or temporal model or representation in which all constituents participate and interrelate without privilege."

62 See Francis Crick, "The Astonishing Hypothesis - The scientific search for the soul", p.146-147. Sejnowski works at the Salk Institute.

restricted to the confinement of our skulls.

The notion of the projective field does not only cover this important part of our thinking process, but certainly it also covers our brain output (into our environment), obviously exceeding the output of a single neuron. At an international symposium, several computer-scientists acknowledged the importance of the space outside the body as the space where creativity takes place.[63] For instance, William Goldwin spoke of the transitional space posited by psycho-analyst Donald Winnicott, which lies between the creative subject and the objective world.[64] James Ambach and Alexander Repenning discussed 'participatory theater', regarding the end-user of the computer as puppeteer or director.[65] Here it is also important to recall the description of our brain-processes earlier in this chapter, which do not allow a clear-cut separation between in-coming and out-going impulses in our thinking process. This makes the notion of the projective field even more justified.

The American experimental psychologist James J. Gibson suggested a distinction between the visual world and the visual field.[66] The visual world is reality as we perceive it everyday. The visual field is what we see after reflection on the impressions of the visual world when we try to understand the actual nature of the acquired visual information.[67] Gibson concluded (maybe with the problems of painting on his mind): "The visual field has boundaries, whereas the visual world has none."[68]

In art and art theory, one can find more examples of an understanding that thinking and perception are not one way or rectilinear processes, but are extended into our environment. For instance, perception involves the space between the body and the

---

63 The conference "Creativity and Cognition 2" was organized in 1996 at Loughborough University, UK, initiated by Ernest A. Edmonds and Linda Candy. ("Creativity and Cognition 1", April 13-15, 1993, Loughbourough University, UK). See also Linda Candy and Ernest Edmonds, "Explorations in Art and Technology" (London: Springer Verlag, 2002).

64 See William Goldwin and co-researchers, "Objects in Transition: a Spatial Paradigm for Creative Design", in Ernest A. Edmonds and Linda Candy, "Proceedings Creativity and Cognition 2" (Loughborough, UK: Loughborough University, 1996), p.37-44.

65 See James Ambach and Alexander Repenning, "Puppeteers and Directors: Supporting Artistic Design by Combining Direct-Manipulation and Delegation", ibid., p.67-76.

66 James J. Gibson (1904-1980), "The Perception of the Visual World" (Boston: Houghton Mifflin, 1950). See Paul Overy, "Kandinsky - The language of the eye" (London: Elek Books Ltd, 1969), p. 35-36.

67 See Paul Overy, "Kandinsky - The language of the eye", p.36: "It is hard to explain scientifically how exactly we see the visual world; it is much easier to explain how we see the visual field. And yet almost all the time we see the visual world and only rarely, and by an effort of concentration, do we see the visual field. In fact the visual field is really a rather sophisticated way of seeing that depends on the ability to introspect our sensations - to watch ourselves seeing. Most people are aware of the visual field at certain times but painters in general seem to be particularly sensitive to this."

68 See Paul Overy, "Kandinsky - The language of the eye", p. 118. Comparably, Frank Stella refers to the difference between the perceived images and the pictorial images. See Frank Stella, "Grimm's Ecstasy", p.68: "The first difference, and perhaps the most important, is that pictorial images have boundaries and perceptual images do not (or at least not the same obvious kind, since they are always after the fact). The physical and temporal boundaries of a perceived image are difficult to secure. In the case of pictorial images the opposite is true. They are confined and static. They are perpetually apprehensible, the opposite of all of our visual

observed artwork.[69] The classic example is Kandinsky's description how he was blown away by a visit to farmhouses decorated with highly coloured non-mimetic ornaments. He had the intense sensation that, "They taught me to move into the picture, to live in the picture..."[70] Early in his life he formulated his ideal thus: to create paintings into which the observer was drawn, paintings that seemed to extend in both directions, offering a depth in front of the observer, but also reaching out to engulf the observer.[71] In my opinion, Kandinsky had his moment of 'enlightenment' when he stepped into that farmhouse, sensing (more than understanding) the importance of the projective field for finding the truth about the essence of reality. Much later, Kandinsky exemplified the interactive functioning of the projective field, writing: "As soon as we open the door and step out of the seclusion and plunge into the outside reality, we become an active part of this reality and experience its pulsation with all our senses."[72]

Art theorists like Konrad Fiedler and, more recently, Michael Bockemühl or Gottfried Böhm have stated that the observer is absorbed into the painting. Böhm writes on the German painter Gotthard Graubner: see picture 29

"In the end Graubner's painting must (as all art) be measured against the plausibility and evidences that it conjures up in the viewer. Of course, this relationship possesses very special features because the symbiotic incorporation of pictorial volume and colour process offers the viewer a narrowly defined symbiosis of his own. Standing in front of these paintings, the viewer senses an allusion to his own corporeality, he reacts to the resonances. These correspondences are not merely cognitive, they demand reenactment through the body-sense, its visual, tactile and synaesthetic capacities. This distinction of the physical aspects of both work and viewer is highly remarkable. It creates an experience of interdependence, the character of which can be gauged from the human body belonging as it does both to the world and to itself." [73]

The perception of this interdependence takes place in the projective field, as I have proposed. One can experience this interdependence in many great works of art, but in some especially. In addition to the great works by Graubner and the amazing wall works

perceptions, which are always fleeting, inexplorably slipping away from memory and touch. What the best art does is give us the best of both worlds - the perceptual and the pictorial."

69 Compare physicist David Bohm's observation of his own response to a Georges Rouault painting as will be mentioned later. Or, compare Nishitani's concept of the middle. See §5.2.

70 See Paul Overy, "Kandinsky - The language of the eye", p.119, 120. Kandinsky, at that time still studying law, visited in 1889 on behalf of the Society for Natural Science, Ethnography and Anthropology of Moscow the northern province of Vologda to report on the peasant laws and the survival of paganism among the Syryenian tribes.

71 Obviously compare Matjushin's concept of "SorVed", earlier in this chapter.

72 From "Point and Line to Plane", see Paul Overy, "Kandinsky - The language of the eye", p.121.

73 See Gottfried Böhm, "Gotthard Graubner - painting" (Cologne: Galerie Karsten Greve, 1995), p.29. On Bockemühl, see for instance, Michael Bockemühl, Uta Mitschke, Ulrich von Gizycki, "Das Kunstwerk und die Wissenschaften - über die unterschiedliche Art, sich ein Bild zu machen"(Edition Tertium, 1994).

by Stella, I have had similar profound experiences standing in front of and sometimes very close to one of Monet's amazing 'Nymphéas' paintings.[74] I have also had that intense experience letting myself be absorbed by the powerful and very cosmic paintings of Natvar Bhavsar and the 'Gauge Field' paintings of Richard Purdy.

One can find similar experiences of art expressed in the writings by Frank Stella. Stella studied and lectured about Caravaggio. In these lectures he describes how he understands the spatial structure of his own wall-constructions of the late 1970's and 1980's as a kind of spherical space that provides a spatial experience of painting that does "... not seem to end at the framing edges or seem to be boxed in by the picture plane ...". Stella further calls this spherical space a 'working space'.[75]

As you may expect, in my opinion the working space of a work of art is the equivalent to the field where the receptive and the projective field both occur. Working space here obviously does not mean the artist's studio in a literal sense, but the immediate environment of an artwork embracing both the artwork and the perceptive field of the observer. The difference between Stella's working-space and my proposed projective field is more or less trivial. Stella (and Böhm on Graubner) discusses the field extending outwards from the artwork engulfing the observer. In my concept, the observer himself is the starting point of the field of perception reaching outwards, meeting and assimilating the field of energies radiating outwards from the artwork. My concept is more or less comparable to Nishitani's concept of 'the middle'. The process of becoming absorbed by, or engulfed by, a work of art can be understood as a process of intense concentration of vision, in which attention is focussed to a degree that we do not perceive a difference between our selves and what we perceive. This process is comparable to what is called in eastern philosophies a self-nullifying process of finding the 'true self'. It is an experience of the sublime.

Here it seems a good idea to refer to the scientific concept of a field. Professor of English Thomas Vargish and professor of physics and astronomy Delo E. Mook write:

"Physicists sometimes use the mathematician's field, but in physics the term commonly assumes a more empirical meaning, as illustrated by this discussion taken from a mathematical physics text: 'Many physical quantities have different values at different points in space. For example, the temperature in a room is different at different points: high near a register, low near an open window, and so on ... Similarly, the gravitational force acting on a satellite depends on its distance from the earth ... In all these examples there is a particular region of space which is of interest for the problem at hand; at every point in this region some physical quantity has a value. The term "field" is used to mean both the region and the value of the physical quantity in the region (for example, electric field, gravitational field)."[76]

[74] Especially the painting that is in the collection of the Foundation Beyeler.

[75] See William Rubin, "Frank Stella 1970-1987" (New York: The Museum of Modern Art, 1988 - orig.1987), p.88. See Frank Stella, "Working Space, The Charles Eliot Norton Lectures" (Cambridge, Massachusetts and London: Harvard University Press, 1986).

One can translate the region and value aspects easily into artistic terms: region as the location in a composition and value as the emphasis a pictorial element gets by its colour or shape. The whole composition of a work of art is itself part of the field that engulfs the observer. This, in my own interpretation, does not only seem to connect to Stella's ideas, but also brings to mind Cézanne's 'modulations', Signac's Pointillism, Monet's expressive brushstrokes spread rhythmicaly over his large 'Nymphéas' canvasses, and Mondrian's typical Neo-Plastic compositions. A work of art can be defined to be a field itself, but (like all fields) is part of a larger field, including the observer.

see pictures 15, 16, 19

Providing additional proof that the above-mentioned function of the field is correct in the context of a work of art, it seems important to mention the notion of 'Raumwert' (the meaning of an object in the particular space where it is located) proposed by sculptor Adolf von Hildebrand in late 19th century.[77] To understand the meaning of objects, Hildebrand considered it important to consider the particular appearance of these objects in space, their interactions and relationships (basically, the disposition of these objects). Local colour, light illuminating these objects and the position in space of the observer all influence the appearance of these objects. Art theoritician Hans Heinz Holz summarizes that Hildebrand's 'Raumwert' is the expression of the ontological quality of the field of an object. An example of the importance of the right handling of the 'Raumwert' is the famous group of statues "The Burghers of Calais"(1884-95), by Auguste Rodin. The perfect handling by Rodin of the 'Raumwert' of the six individuals makes this group into the amazing coherent and dynamic whole that interacts so well

---

[76] See also earlier in this essay. For this quote, see Thomas Vargish and Delo E. Mook, "Inside Modernism - Relativity Theory, Cubism, Narrative", p.105, where they quote Mary D. Bon, "Mathematical Methods in the Physical Sciences".

[77] Proposed in 1893. See §2.6, footnote 102. Hildebrand is quoted by Hans Heinz Holz while discussing the influences of Hildebrand on Wölfflin, see Hans Heinz Holz, "Strukturen der Darstellung - Philosophische Theorie der bildenden Kunst II" (Bielefeld: Aisthesis Verlag, 1997), p.45,46 (my own translation): "We wish to understand every product of apparent oppositions, which decides on a spatial image, to define the expression of spatial values, being different from those impulses, that exist in the images of the process... As the appearance of space itself is the product of several elements co-operating in nature, as for instance the object as being, its local colour, the source of illumination as direction of light and quality, the view angle taken by the observer in relation to the object, so the spatial values mean more or less rich crossing points or knots of these natural phenomena. In them a co-operation evolves of natural moments that are in principle separated, in them a unity is presented, which only includes vision and which makes it a simultaneous statement of separated relations, causing a spatial orientation of images to exist, an understanding of the spatial situation. In this lies the opportunity to bring individual objects, which based upon realistic reasons do not exist in and by themselves in necessary relationships and poses no necessary spatial position towards each other, in a necessary, conditioned coherance. Now it becomes easily understandable, that in the discovery of the spatial values of the appearance lies the specific artistic power and talent of the painter, and that in the picture the spatial values include the actual creative and unifying capacity." ("Das jeweilige Produkt von Erscheinungsgegensätzen, welches eine räumliche Vorstellung ausmacht, wollen wir zum Unterschiede von den Anregungen, welche in den Vorgangsvorstellungen bestehen, mit dem Ausdruck Raumwerte der Erscheinung bezeichnen ... Da nun die Raumerscheinung selbst das Produkt verschiedener in der Natur zusammenwirkender Elemente ist, wie zum Beispiel der Gegenstand als Daseinsform, seine Lokalfarbe, die Beleuchtungsquelle als Lichtrichtung und Qualität, der Standpunkt, den der Beschauer zum Gegenstand einnimmt, so bedeuten die Raumwerte mehr

with any observer from any angle. Rodin did not only accomplish this with the dynamic expressions of the individual figures, but especially by their precise positioning in context to each other, by the shapes and sizes of the empty spaces between the figures, framed by the expressive gestures.[78]

It is my interpretation that because of the 'Raumwert' of objects, imaginable as field, the objects in our environment interact with the projective field of the observer and thus the object becomes perceptable and gets its particular meaning. The interactive process between our bodies (including our brains) and our environment is also responsible for the phenomenon that different people perceive the same sunset, work of art or tea-pot seemingly in the same way, but nevertheless interpret them quite differently. Interpretation is based on memory and affects what we perceive. A sunset can be a romantic highlight for one, causing him or her to keep staring until the sun has disappeared. But for the other it can recall such bad memories that he or she turns his or her head away in frustration.

5.7 FOCUS OF ATTENTION AS A PROCESS OF TALKING TO ONESELF

The continuous confrontation of ourselves with the things in our environment, or, in other words, our continuous interaction with things in the space in which we live, demands attention to our environment. We will now discuss our need to project things outside our bodies into space while thinking (hence, our projective field).

Literally talking to oneself, but also humming or singing to enhance our concentration or our thinking, a kind of self-argumentation, are well known examples. Another example is the tendency during meetings, conferences or telephone-conversations to make schematic notes or scribbles, which are quite often illegible and have no other meaning but to enhance or focus our attention, and therefore, our thinking. Other examples of thought made spatial include the design of sketches, diagramms and graphics, which allow us to understand highly complex problems at one glance.

---

oder minder reiche Kreuzungs- oder Knotenpunkte dieser Naturwirkungen. In ihnen kommt ein Zusammenwirken zustande an sich auseinander liegender Naturmomente, in ihnen offenbart sich eine Einheit, die nur der Gesichtssinn erfaßt und die ihm von getrennten Verhältnissen eine gleichzeitige Aussage macht, wodurch ein räumliche Orientierung der Vorstellungen entsteht, ein Erfassen der räumliche Sachlage. In ihnen liegt die Möglichkeit, Einzelgegenstände, die an und für sich aus realen Gründen in keinem notwendigen Zusammenhange stehen und keine notwendige räumliche Stellung zueinander einnehmen, in einen notwendigen, sich bedingenden Zusammenhang zu bringen. Es ist nun leicht begreiflich, daß in der Entdeckung der Raumwerte der Erscheinung die spezielle künstlerische Kraft und Begabung des Malers liegt, und daß im Bilde den Raumwerten die eigentliche gestaltende und einigende Fähigkeit innewohnt.")

78 This becomes very clear when one compares an original cast of the whole group, for instance, in the Metropolitan Museum in New York, with the presentation of this sculpture-group at the main building of the campus of Stanford University, CA, where the distances between the figures seem to be cut and extended, causing the group to come apart into individual bronzes interacting in a strange loose combination (probably done to allow one to walk in between the figures). Unfortunately Rodin's precise 'Raumwert' is completely disturbed. The German poet and writer Rainer Maria Rilke, who worked with Rodin as his secretary, describes the importance in Rodin's sculpture of 'empty air'. See Rainer Maria Rilke, "Auguste Rodin" (Frankfurt, Leipzig: Insel Verlag, 1984 - orig.1913).

The importance of talking to one's self - not only aloud, but also without sound - visually or in our minds - has recently been acknowledged scientifically as an important part of our learning process. Philosophy acknowledged its importance much longer ago. For every conscious being the confrontation of the self with the environment for the purpose of understanding the self is important, but equally important is the capacity to learn by reflection on experiences. This capacity is crucial for survival. Learning is a process of self-dialogue. That is why learning is a necessary feature in our quest starting at birth, to finally 'see the self'.

As with so many of our ideas, the origin of a concept of a dialogue with the self can also be traced to Greek philosophy. Plato, for instance, believed language itself functioned best in its social activity of speaking, especially in talking to oneself.[79]

In Renaissance occultism the original Hebrew language was seen as a natural language. Van Helmont, the alchemist and philosopher who was of great influence on Leibniz, thought original Hebrew was an alphabet based on pictorial representations of the physical movement made by the tongue.[80] The moment a thought is expressed in a spoken word, it is projected into the material world as sound and as physical movement of the tongue. In this sense, language can be considered a bridge between mind and matter. In a similar way, Leibniz and his contemporaries (following Plato) believed that creation was a process of emanation from an intelligible world of ideas. A basic harmony between nature and the human mind exists a priori, knowledge consists in remembering archetypal ideas, and intuition is the highest form of knowledge.[81] The a priori presence in one's brain of the basic harmony of one's self with nature, or, the existence of an inborn Ur-memory of immersion in nature, is a very interesting way of thinking, especially in context to notions of creativity or the search for the self, as discussed here in the various philosophies. Creativity, and the search for 'the true self' consist of processes

79 Philosopher Carl Friedrich von Weizsäcker writes on Plato, see Carl Friedrich von Weizsäcker, "Zeit und Wissen" p.67: "He defines the daiona as a dialogue of the soul with itself. Thus Plato, not unlike modern linguistic philosophers, defines language not as the expression of thinking, but acts of thinking through the social process of talking in the specific form of the talking to oneself". ("Er definiert die dianoia als einen Dialog der Seele mit sich selbst. So definiert also Platon, nicht unähnlich modernen linguistischen Philosophen, nicht die Sprache als Ausdruck des Denkens, sondern Denkakte durch den sozialen Vorgang des Sprechens, in der speziellen Form des Selbstgesprächs.")

80 See Allison P. Coudert, "Leibniz and The Kabbalah", International Archives of the History of Ideas 142 (Dordrecht: Kluwer Academic Publishers, 1995), p.149. See Allison P. Coudert, "Leibniz and The Kabbalah", p.145: "The anonymous author of the Sefer Yezirah considered the letters of the Hebrew alphabet building blocks with which God had constructed the universe." (would this explain the Biblical notion "in the beginning was the Word" ?). The Sefer Yezirah is the Book of Creation, written in Palestine between 3rd and 6th AD. Mercurius van Helmont published "Alphabeti veri naturalis Hebraici brevissima delineatio", 1667, proposing a method to learn deaf and dumb people to speak. This Van Helmont based on a similar assumption as the Sefer Yezirah, that Hebrew is the 'lingua sancta' or natural Ur-language of man, which would refer to the true essence of all things and to the same God that gave Adam the perfect language. He understood the shapes of Hebrew symbols to miror the shape of the tongue while speaking Hebrew. For examples of Van Helmont's pictures illustrating this theory, see Umberto Eco, "Die Suche nach der Vollkommenen Sprache", p.94.

81 See Allison P. Coudert, "Leibniz and The Kabbalah", International Archives of the History of Ideas, p.152.

of becoming conscious of a fundamental knowledge that already exists in our memory at birth.

An interesting feature of language is that although talking to someone else can help one make up one's own mind to do something, it seems that hearing oneself talk aloud - or writing one's own thoughts - actually enhances one's own thinking or reflection. Hegel emphasized the importance of reflection: "Being is not real: it is the first immediacy; its reflection, therefore, is a becoming and transgressing into something else ... The real, therefore, is manifestation."[82] The process of talking to oneself is a fundamental way of becoming conscious, of learning and understanding. For obvious reasons this does not imply there are only empirical or rational things to be learnt by talking to oneself.[83] Trusting one's intuition and pure experience is quite essential.[84]

Nishida, in discussing the idea of psychologist William James that the present as conscious act should possess some kind of continuity in time, writes: "This means that the present always is in the focal point of consciousness. Thus the field of pure experience always coincides with the field of attention."[85] Nishida further explains: "Originally for experience there exists no inside nor an outside. What makes it *pure* lies in this unity, not in its character."[86] An example of this unity lies in coming to understand one's immersion in one's environment, in the world, in the cosmos, in the whole of nature. This can be understood according to many individual interpretations. For one this is a religious experience, for another it is an intuited or scientific fact. Whatever the interpretation, it is always a result of a process of talking to oneself.

That the process of talking to oneself will lead to a better understanding of self in the world is also why in various Oriental philosophies a search for the true self is discussed. It is clearly not only a matter of seeing this connection with one's eyes or hearing a verbal explanation with one's ears, but a process involving all senses interacting with thought and the physical processes of our bodies. Nishida writes,

---

82 Hegel, "Logik", quoted in Hans Heinz Holz, "Der Ästhetische Gegenstand - Philosophische Theorie der bildenden Kunst I" (Bielefeld: Aisthesis Verlag, 1996), p.74: "Das Sein ist noch nicht wirklich: es ist die erste Unmittelbarkeit; seine Reflexion ist daher Werden und Übergehen in anderes .... Das Wirkliche ist darum Manifestation." Holz states that reflection on reality has naturally led in art to an oscillation between the humanization of nature and the naturalization of man. Hans Heinz Holz, "Der Ästhetische Gegenstand - Philosophische Theorie der bildenden Kunst I", p.181. This seems quite reasonable. It provides further ideas for understanding why both figurative art and abstract art will always exist simultaneously.

83 It is interesting to note here that something can only be decided to be rational, objective or empirical by talking to someone else (as opposed to only talking to one's self!).

84 I understand pure experience as immediate or direct experience, without being effected by verbal analyses. Nishida understands pure experience as immediate thinking, connecting immediate perception, immediate experience and immediate thinking. See Kitaro Nishida, "Über das Gute", translated by Peter Pörtner (Insel Verlag, 1990, first ed.1989 - orig. "Zen no kenkyu", 1911), p.48. This is definitely not to be mistaken for the impossible notion of pure thinking in the sense Descartes intended.

85 See Kitaro Nishida, "Über das Gute", p.32: "Das heißt, im Fokus des Bewußtseins liegt immer die Gegenwart. Somit fällt der Bereich der Reinen Erfahrung immer von selbst mit dem Bereich der Aufmerksamkeit zusammen."

86 Ibid., p.34: "Ursprünglich existiert für die Erfahrung weder ein Innen noch ein Außen. Was sie rein macht, liegt in eben dieser Einheit, nicht in ihrer Art."

"Real religious enlightenment is not an abstract consciousness based on thought nor is it blind feeling; it is the personal acknowledgement of the deep unity that is the basis of knowledge and will. But that implies a kind of intellectual consideration. A deep self-acquirement of life."[87]

That all processes of learning, all processes of acquiring knowledge and conscious experience are processes of talking to oneself also explains why every person can only follow his or her own path, at his or her own pace, to acquire knowledge of life itself and of him or her as self.[88]

The quantum physicist and philosopher David Bohm has extensively studied the phenomenon of dialogue. By dialogue he does not mean a discussion, which is merely a confrontation of opinions, but a value-free comparison of different opinions, in which an understanding on an unconscious or tacit level can emerge.[89] "If the individual can hold all the meanings together in his own mind, he has the attitude of the dialogue."[90] Although this is an interesting idea, it seems to me to be too utopian to be possible. Because people are no holy men, and with a few exceptions will never be, in any dialogue some kind of powerplay or competition is involved, destroying all pure dialogue. These disruptions of dialogue are often so unnecessary that one wonders how people can get along at all - not to mention can govern a democracy. I did not even refer to the unavoidable problem that we often speak of the same thing, but individually understand something entirely different.[91]

Small children tend to talk aloud to themselves. Parents think they need to reprimand them for talking to themselves, because talking aloud to oneself is considered foolishness. Important research on children, however, shows how essential talking to oneself is to a child's development. Already in the 1920's the Russian psychologist Lev S. Vygotsky published that his research proved the strong relation between social experience, speech

---

[87] Ibid., p.68: "Wahre religiöse Erleuchtung ist weder ein auf dem Denken gründendes abstraktes Bewußtsein noch ein blindes Gefühl; sie ist das Selbsterfassen der tiefen Einheit, die dem Wissen und dem Willen zugrundeliegt. Aber das meint eben eine Art intellektueller Anschauung. Ein tiefes Sich-Bemächtigen des Lebens." See also §2.

[88] An interesting example that this kind of concept is probably as old as mankind was found in the scroll "The Eigth and the Ninth Level", Codex VI found at Nag Hammadi, including the statement of Hermes and his pupil "I see my self"; and in the "Armenian Aphorisms": "He who knows himself, knows the All." See Prof. Dr. G. Quispel, "De Hermeneutische Gnosis in de loop der eeuwen - Beschouwingen over de invloed van een Egyptische religie op de cultuur van het Westen" (Baarn: Tirion, 1992), p.47-48. This concept is explained by Hermes as the result of being (spiritually) born again. Could Oriental enlightenment as mentioned by Nishida be compared to this kind of concept of being reborn? The role of 'the path' in religions and life-philosophies like Tao or Japanese Zen (like 'wabi' or path of tea) is also intriguing. Remember also Vivekananda exclaiming the Vedantic definition of finding "Thou Art That!" See §2.2.

[89] A confrontation of opinions, according to Bohm, can never lead to a mutual understanding, only to fragmentation and greater differences. This is something one can experience at many if not at all symposia, panel-discussions, conferences.

[90] See David Bohm, "On Dialogue", David Bohm Seminars (Ojai, California, 1990), p.17.

[91] For instance, structure to a philosopher is something different than to an artist and even more different to an engineer.

and learning. Vygotsky's research could well have been inspired by Karl Marx, who, in the mid-19th century, emphasized that practice is more real than passive contemplation, and a more genuine source for acquiring knowledge. Vygotsky considered it most important when speech and practical activity converge.[92]

In my opinion, Vygotsky is referring to the importance of the relation between thinking, speech and acting. Speech might be understood in a more metaphoric sense, as a medium for communication, including non-verbal attention by projection exemplified by the process of visual thinking.[93] The visualization functions as an enhancement to the thought processes. This is, in principle, what the artist Charles Biederman means when he refers to art as the evolution of visual knowledge. Speech and visual thinking might formally be different notions, but in our perception, in our thought processes, they cannot be separated. Try to read a text without seeing images. Try to look at a painting without 'talking in your head'.

An interesting analogy can be drawn here to the role of calligraphy in Zen. The making of scrolls and paintings is a process of meditation that takes many years of practice and self-control (self-attention or focussing of the self), including motor-control. Although these scrolls often present poems, the appearance of the text and the composition of the signs in delicate gestures handpainted in black ink seem more important than their readability.[94] This, of course, is not something that happened by chance, but is based in the Zen tradition of using words to indirectly evoke what is not literally said and cannot be explained in words. This coincides with how we might generally understand abstract art: we can appreciate abstract art as we sense it has meaning, although we cannot literally read or retrieve this meaning. We might agree with each other on the meaningfullness of a certain work of art, but as soon as we start discussing this meaning in words, we will find that we often hardly agree. That is why Zen follows the concept of using words to go beyond words. Zen-master Fukushima Keido writes,

"It is not simply a negation of words and letters. Rather, what is being negated is the attachment to the word. This is because words and letters both consist of something having to do with intellectual knowledge, so to transcend words implies the transcendence of

[92] See Laura E. Berk, "Why Children Talk to Themselves", Scientific American November 1994, p.60-65: "The most significant moment in the course of intellectual development", Vygotsky wrote, "... occurs when speech and practical activity, two previously completely independent lines of development, converge." As a result from the political circumstances of the Cold War, Vygotsky's work did not become known in the west until the 1960's.

[93] See the ideas of Chalmers, described earlier in this chapter. See also my own paper "The Process of Self-Argumentation in the Projective Field", in Ernest A. Edmonds and Linda Candy, "Proceedings Creativity and Cognition 2" (Loughborough, UK: Loughborough University, 1996).

[94] I found out that the texts in this specific Zen-calligraphy are even too abstract for most Japanese to read, but nevertheless highly appreciated for their esthetic value and significance. This was also the purpose, as the short explanation on Zen in the text above explains. For a very good discussion on calligraphy, see Yujiro Nakata, "The Art of Japanese Calligraphy" (Weatherhill/Heibonsha, 1983 - orig.1973). Audrey Yoshiko Seo and Stephen Addiss, "The Art of Twentieth Century Zen - painting and calligraphy by Japanese Masters" (Shambala Press, 1998).

knowledge. So to not rely on words means to not be attached to the words; it does not mean to not use them or negate them. On the contrary, it means that you can truly, freely use them." [95]

The strength of Zen-calligraphy lies in its use of a visual presentation to amplify the attention. As such, it stimulates the process of talking to oneself and focuses one's immediate perception onto the wholeness of nature. In Japan this is not only accomplished by looking at a calligraphic scroll, but also by one's interaction with the gardens, the lay-out of the temple complexes and the design of the temples' interiors.[96] The focussing of attention in a process that demands the immediate involvement of one's own actions is also the most important objective of the manual handling of tea-bowls in the tea-ceremony. For obvious reasons, such experiences are not limited to the Japanese culture. One can find in many cultures similar combinations of visual stimuli with physical activity to enhance the attention necessary for the desired experience.[97] All religious rituals are based on combinations of the visual with the physical, enhancing one's capacity for an inner dialogue, or talking to one's self. This is not merely a philosophical or theological explanation.

The importance of the capacity to focus attention seems to be proven by the applications developed by modern industries. Scientific research, for instance, is performed by controlling computers with neural signals in which vision plays an important role. This research is based on the detection of very small electrical currents in our brains. Physiologist Emil Heinrich Du Bois-Reymond discovered that the contraction of muscles (in our arms, for example) causes minute electrical charges. With modern electrodes and electronic amplifyers, these tiny muscle impulses can easily be registered. This has enabled researchers to develop computers that can be controlled by small muscle-activity and by eye-ball movements.[98] Psychiatrist Hans Berger proposed the term 'electroencephalogram' to describe the voltage fluctuations of the brain that can be recorded by using electrodes attached to the scalp.[99] The new challenge is to use these recordings to control a computer. This technology is already used to control a flight-simulator or an actual plane by the brain-waves of the pilot.[100] Although it is expected to

[95] Fukushima Keido is from the Tofuku-ji monastery. See Audrey Yoshiko Seo and Stephen Addiss, "The Art of Twentieth Century Zen - painting and calligraphy by Japanese Masters", p.14.
[96] In the ancient temples one can find that the entrances offer a kind of detour, like by a small road going up and around one or several corners, a series of stairs, etc. that allow the visitor to get rid of the burden of everyday life and start focussing his attention. This is applied today by Japanese architects like Tadao Ando or Mio Shibuya (who is also working on a theory for a 'Architecture of the Path').
[97] This also seems valid as explanation for the experience you might have in an excellent exhibition of fine art in a museum or gallery.
[98] Du Bois-Reymond did his discoveries in Germany, 1849. Small muscle activity are called EMG or electromyographic signals. Eye-ball movements concern the corneal-retinal potential, creating the electrooculographic signal or EOG.
[99] Discovered in Germany, 1929; known today as EEG.
[100] This research is done at the Alternative Laboratory of Wright-Patterson Air Force Base in Dayton, Ohio,

become much more complex, currently scientists delineate the following brain-waves: Alpha-waves (caused by unfocussing, as by closing one's eyes), Beta-waves (resulting from heigthened mental activity), Theta-waves (which accompany feelings of emotional stress), Delta-waves (occurring during deep sleep), Mu-waves (apparently connected to motor control, as they diminish with movement or the intention to move). Extraordinary for our discussion is the fact that the pilots in the mentioned example also need visual information projected on the transparent canopy of their plane to focus their attention on the task at hand. By doing so they enhance the involved brain-waves, making these signals strong enough to control the computer. Here the concept of re-entry clearly is decisive.[101] This enhancement seems to happen in other experiments as well: when one tries to control a computer by brain-waves, one is simultaneously focussing one's attention on the visual information on a monitor to decide what to do next and to see if the orders function properly. These ongoing experiments are exciting proofs of the applicability of the concepts of self-argumentation and the projective field!

5.8 VOLITION, SELF-ARGUMENTATION AND MANIPULATION

In the Renaissance philosophers like Van Helmont or Leibniz were very intrigued by a different aspect of projection, the concept of volition: thoughts could be projected into the material world by willing.[102] Schopenhauer, as discussed before, argued that we are but a tiny part of a much larger whole and thus our own will is but a reflection of the will of nature. The power that generates our individual will is virtually projected from the outside onto ourselves. This seems to diminish the importance of personal volition, which comes from the inside and is projected outwards. In Schopenhauer's opinion, we should begin by knowing the aspect of will inside ourselves, because our own body is the only phenomenon in the world that we know from both sides, from the inside and from the outside. Such a search for the will in one's self is a process directed from the inside outwards, and is founded in the acknowledgement that our own will is subjected to the will of a large whole, making individual volition less important than the will of the world. Remembering the discussion of the process of our thinking as a process of talking to oneself, one may assume Schopenhauer's process of exploration of

USA. See Eugene E. Covert, "Evolution of the Commercial Airliner", Scientific American September 1995, p.82. This technology is already applied in the newest generation of fighter jets, like the Eurofighter, whose steering has become so complex no human could master it without computer-enhancement.

101 See the discussion on 're-entry' in §5.1.

102 They considered the creation of the world by God an act of volition. See Allison P. Coudert, "Leibniz and The Kabbalah", p.145-148. Creation started with thoughts in God's mind and thus became materialized. These ideas can be found in the Kabbalah, in Renaissance Neoplatonism and Hermeticism (and in the art of Lull). Raymond Lull or Ramon Llull or Raimundus Lullus (appr. 1232-1316) was a Catalan born on Mallorca in an environment where the Islamic, Jewish and Christian cultures verged. Lull developed a sophisticated system or language using letter-symbols and words in complex combinations. His main publications was titled "Ars Magna". See Umberto Eco, "Die Suche nach der vollkommenen Sprache" (Munich: C.H. Beck - Europa Bauen, 1994 - orig. "La ricerca della lingua perfetta nella cultura europea", 1993), p.65-76.

the will inside ourselves to also be an argument with one's self. I use the notion 'argument' (or, better, 'self-argumentation') on purpose, because it can have the character of a struggle. Self-argumentation is definitely meant to support and enhance the development of our knowledge on reality (as such, self-argumentation is survival oriented) and our own body as 'seat of one's self' is definitely the starting point to look at reality. In my opinion the desire for more knowledge could very well be defined as the ultimate desire to overcome the limitations of human life by getting the whole picture of reality. When we understand reality we will understand the reason for our limited existence. The acceptance of this limitation is then of course still a different matter. While discussing reflection and intuition Nishida wrote in 1917:

> *"When I stretch out my hand, this is a matter of will if looked at from within, but from without it is a movement of the body. The will is the body of the spiritual world, and the body is the will of the material world;* ***our body, as the fusion of mind and matter, is a work of art.*** *"* [103]

I propose considering the reverse of Nishida's statement as well, viewing art as a fusion of mind and matter and confirming that the work of art in our projective field results from the process of self-argumentation.

As I mentioned before, a commonly underestimated aspect of our perception concerns the manual handling of objects - like taking up a pencil and drawing, or using a brush for painting, or picking up all kinds of materials for sculpture and manipulating these by hand.[104] It might be interesting to add to the various concepts already discussed by referring to the special value given in certain philosophies in Korea and Japan to the tea-bowl. From the point of view of handcraft itself one would imagine that the potter's aim is the highest level of formal perfection. However, this is not the point in these philosophies.[105] The tea-bowl should reflect reality in its shape, and because reality is apt to change, the tea-bowl cannot be visualized as a perfect symmetrical shape. The individual properties of such a tea-bowl become very important for focussing one's attention to its basic properties. This happens because we simply have to take it up in our hands and in waiting for the tea to cool off, we unconsciously study and admire its shape and touch. Thus in a very simple but extremely effective way our attention is led away from everyday troubles into a meditative state. The handling of such a tea-bowl may lead to an unforced focussing on the essence, on no-thingness. Again, the tea-bowl allows one to focus on what can be considered 'no thing' with help of a thing.

see picture 56

[103] See Kitaro Nishida, "Intuition and Reflection in Self-Consciousness" (New York: State University of New York Press, 1987 - orig. "Jikaku ni okeru chokkan to han sei", 1941), p.122. Emphasis mine.
[104] 'Mani' comes from manus, meaning hand and is, therefore, quite appropriate.
[105] It should be considered beside the point that in Korea and Japan one can also find enough potters who try to accomplish the perfection of the form in the same sense as accomplished by ceramic industries. This is not the approach meant here - it is a difference in basic philosophy, to a certain level comparable to the difference in painting a portrait and making a portrait by use of a camera.

It is hardly surprising that the potters who are capable of creating the right tea-bowls for this experience are not just manufacturers, but considered artists who have consciously applied this philosophy. Early 20th century master potter Kawai Kanjiro was intrigued by the question, "Who is moving this hand of mine?"[106] His conclusion was that we do not work alone. With this statement he meant that it is not only the artist's mind that determines the final work of art, but also the interaction of the artist's hands with the material and the involved manufacturing-process (like the fire in the kiln in the potter's case). The final work of art is also influenced by our intuited relationship with 'sunyata', the 'no thingness' or the eternal whole of nature in which we are immersed. Or, as Schopenhauer would say, the will of nature influences the motive and moves Kanjiro's hand.

Contemporary artist Richard DeVore's ceramic sculptures exemplify a similar though still different approach from the Japanese and Korean tea-bowls. His vase-like sculptures are much larger than these tea-bowls and by their size demand a different kind of perception. The sculptures make one desire to touch them, but even more, to gently touch the thin and sensous skin, to look inside and walk around (they are too big to just pick up). DeVore understands himself 'between Japan and Greece'. He does not understand himself as a potter nor as a ceramic artist, but as artist. This makes sense, because his sculptures are not vases but more (comparable to Oriental thought) objects that make one's mind wander, by pondering with eye and hand about the colours and distortions in the shape. Without the ritual of the Oriental tea-ceremony, DeVore's ceramic sculptures provide a similar experience of forgetting all troubled secular thoughts. Such an experience is evoked by the natural though man made appearance of the artifact. Clay happens to be the material that currently answers best to his ideas.[107]

see picture 58

Some years ago I became especially conscious of the importance of manual handling or manipulating while trying to accomplish a first artistic experiment in Virtual Reality (also referred to as VR).[108] In spite of the fact that VR-technology at the time was still visually primitive, the illusion of this virtual environment was not only quite strong because I could move through this virtual space, but especially because I could directly manipulate objects in that space with my (virtual) hand! This is an opportunity that is

[106] See Yoshiko Uchida, "We do not work alone - The thoughts of Kanjiro Kawai" (Kyoto: Kawai Kanjiro House and Nissha Printing Company Ltd, 1973 - first edition 1953).

[107] In May 2004 I had the fortune to briefly talk to Richard DeVore at his opening at the Max Protetch Gallery in New York, and learn about his ideas.

[108] During an artist-in-residence week at Loughborough University in England in 1995, where I co-operated with Professor Roy Kalawsky and his assistant Simon Berr. In context to the "Creativity & Cognition 2" symposium organized by Linda Candy and Professor E.A. Edmonds, LUTCHI-Research Center, see Ernest A. Edmonds and Linda Candy, "Proceedings Creativity and Cognition 2". See Ernest Edmonds, "Into Virtual Space and Back to Reality", in "Fré Ilgen - The Search" (Alphen a/d Maas: The Foundation for the New Arts, 2001). See my own paper "CRAVE - Creative Virtual Environment - Die Bedeutung der direkten Manipulation", on Kai-Uwe Hemken, "Texte zur virtuellen Ästhetik in Kunst und Kultur", CD-ROM (Weimar: Kunstgeschichtliches Institut der Ruhr Universität Bochum, VDG-Verlag und Datenbank für Geisteswissenschaften, 1998). V-R (Virtual Reality) is also known as 'Virtual Environment'.

still missing from the typical personal computers, where it is quite difficult for many users to use the full capacity of their computer.[109] There is some discussion in contemporary computer-science that near-future programming will concern this kind of actual and direct manual handling.[110]

It seems that computer-science or computer-technology can learn a lot from artists, who basically always think with their hands. But scientists should not merely observe artists or artworks. Mere observation is a quite crude and highly naive research method still fashionable among cognitive psychologists and ergonomists. The researchers should at least try to directly discuss the various aspects of the creative process with the artists themselves. They may find that quite a few artists can actually talk about and are also interested in learning more about creativity and cognition. A very good example is the English artist Michael Kidner. In an interview with art historian Patricia Railing Kidner says about his work, see pictures 30, 31

> *"... when I was trying to deal with logical structures, I was persuaded that feelings might confuse communication. Rather it is the other way about. After the Systems Group disbanded,[111] I began a series of drawings that concerned wavy line lattices. When the measurements involved became too critical to handle I went in search of a computer and actually did make two computer aided drawings, but at the same time I discovered some elastic cloth, which served very well as tracing paper and solves the problem I was having with the lattices. I **could watch the transformations** as they occured on the elastic **while physically manipulating it**. In short, I could feel what I was doing while I was doing it and I liked the feeling. I did not go back to the computer."*[112]

[109] See my own paper, "Virtual in Reality - Real in Virtuality", in Ernest A. Edmonds and Linda Candy, "Proceedings Creativity and Cognition 2", p.278-279.

[110] I received this information from personal talks with Prof. E.A. Edmonds, at that time executive director of LUTCHI-Research Center, Loughborough University, UK. Throughout the international symposium, "Creativity and Cognition 2", 1996, at Loughborough University, cognitive psychology's notion that thinking occurs in the hands was repeatedly mentioned, as for instance by Richard Coyne (Department of Architecture, University of Edinburgh). Coyne, referring to the analytic philosopher Gilbert Ryle, writes that he and like-minded philosophers "... have eloquently argued for a broader conception of thinking that extends the mental to include the body." See Richard Coyne, "Creativity as Commonplace", in Ernest A. Edmonds and Linda Candy, "Proceedings Creativity and Cognition 2", p.7. Still, it was disappointing to see at this symposium on computer-science that most if not all computer-scientists understood manipulation as improving the handling of the graphics (the icons or menu's) on the screen, while still moving the computer-mouse around - which because of its restrictions is something entirely different than actually using one's hands!

[111] The "Systems Group" was a group of English artists in the late 1960's and early 1970's that aimed for an objective way of working by trying to discard any method of artistic creation that allows a personal 'touch'. To accomplish this they used systems that were considered objective and allow at random decision making, like designing a grid with numbers along the horizontal and vertical axis. Numbers were decided by throwing dice. Combination of numbers (which could also result from other processes) were connected with lines, squares or planes and decided the composition. This ambition failed, because in the end none of the artists could avoid idiosyncrasy.

[112] See Patricia Railing, "Michael Kidner - Interview", in PRO-NR.9 (Dordrecht: Pro Foundation, 1993), p.27. Emphasis mine.

By emphasizing the feeling of direct manipulation in the thinking process, Kidner puts his finger exactly on the most important aspect of understanding our creative process! The result in these examples is not only evaluated (meaning: critically reviewed) when the process of self-argumentation, either in a spoken or visualized way, is finished. No, there is a continuous evaluation process - a jumping back and forth of one's attention between that perceived (outside one's body) and one's brain with the senses as intermediaries. Although sound - including music - certainly plays an important role in our perception, here I am concentrating on visual perception - visual consciousness.[113]

Visual consciousness obviously plays a very important role in understanding fine art. We encounter or see a work of art which causes a process in the immediate connection of our eyes and brain. For a large part this process happens unconsciously at a very high speed inside our brain, but at some point the processed signals become strong enough to virtually emerge as an image in our consciousness - hence our visual consciousness. This is the moment we become (visually) aware of the work of art. Because this process is so crucial in understanding our perception of art, maybe even our appreciation and need for art, it is hardly surprising that many artists and philosophers have formulated ideas on this subject, but also that scientists have started to explore our visual consciousness. We perceive ourselves, the environment and the world from the position of our bodies, and to be able to perceive we explore our environment, we undertake certain actions (we open our eyes, 'start' our senses, move around, touch, etc.).[114]

---

[113] It should be mentioned that an interest in sound has been studied in direct relation to aspects of visual perception, like perception of space and interpretations of colour. The Dutch architect Jan Hoogstad understands hearing to be important for judging a space. He also has a profound interest in music and has experimented to translate music into architecture. He emphasizes the importance of perception by moving through a space for defining architecture: "If it is so that experiencing space is made up of a group of space-determining images, then it can be concluded that: space can only be experienced by moving through it. In other words: Space = (Time + Memory) x Movement, S= (T + Me) x Mo." See Jan Hoogstad, "Ruimtetijdbeweging - Prolegomena voor de architektuur" (Den Haag: SDU, 1990). English translation published in PRO-NR.9, p.30-32. Movement through a space without a sound or a perception of sound under normal conditions is impossible and thus involves automatically the quality of sound. The level of importance of hearing to our orientation in space is shown in scientific research like that by Masakazu Konishi on owls. See Masakazu Konishi, "Listening with Two Ears", Scientific American, April 1993, p.34: "In a process called binaural fusion, the brain compares information received from each ear and then translates the differences into a unified perception of a single sound issuing from a specific region of space." And: "We find that the owl combines aural signals relating to location not all at once but through an amazing series of steps. Information about timing and intensity is processed separately in parallel pathways that converge only late in those pathways." Although owls and human beings are different it still is a good example showing that the process of orientation in a space is not a matter of a singular stimulus or input and a resulting singular response or output, but a continuous jumping back and forth of new information between perceived and perceiver, screening/analysing of new information, adjustment of conclusion (of one's opinion), renewed scanning, etc. In my opinion this reflects a form of self-argumentation, for which the '8' or lemniscate is therefore a good metaphor indeed. The topic sound and space can also be related to the topic sound and colour as we perceive space visually by the existence of colour. Sound and colour have been studied by many philosophers and artists since ancient Greece. Recent scientific research on light captured in airbubbles has shown that this brings forth sound. These subjects are discussed elsewhere. It would be interesting to have a closer look at the relation sound - colour - space and what consequences it might have for architectural spaces.

[114] Henri Bergson understands the body as the center of activity and perception as the translation into action

To find some profound backing for the discussion of the importance of visual consciousness we will look again at more contemporary facts and ideas proposed by modern neurophysiological research, in which visual consciousness is the central issue. The following discussion may seem a bit technical, but in my opinion is essential for finding more substantial information to appreciate what art has to offer. Francis Crick and Christof Koch, for instance, propose using visual awareness to understand consciousness. They write,

> *"We choose visual consciousness rather than other forms, because humans are very visual animals and our visual percepts are especially vivid and rich in information. In addition, the visual input is often highly structured yet easy to control."*[115]

Neurobiologist Semir Zeki emphasizes that the complexity of this research does not imply the merely finding of empirical facts, because a lot of interpretation is needed to be able to understand the processes of perception.[116] In my opinion, this seems to support profound reasons for more substantial interdisciplinary dialogue on the subjects of perception and visual consciousness.

Zeki criticizes the opinion that the different tasks of the brain (like speech and vision) are localized in a certain part of the brain or in a certain hemisphere of the brain. For instance, he criticizes the idea that colour, form, movement, and other possible attributes of the visual world are processed separately. This means that the brain functions in

by which we influence our environment. The body as such cannot produce a representation. It needs an action to achieve a better understanding of reality, which it achieves through the interaction of thought, action, and everything around us. The understanding does not merely follow some process inside the head or body, but the understanding interacts with the environment. See Henri Bergson, "Matter and Memory", p.21: "Here are the images which compose the universe in general, then those which are near to my body, and finally my body itself. In this last image the habitual office of the centripetal nerves is to transmit movements to the brain and to the cord; the centrifugal nerves send back this movement to the periphery." American philosopher John Dewey describes in a related way the necessity to understand the creation of art as a process of interaction between the various aspects of one's self (sense, need, impulse, action, plus consciousness) and the world. See John Dewey, "Art As Experience" (New York: Perigee Books, 1980 - orig. 1934), p.25: "Art is the living and concrete proof that man is capable of restoring consciously, and thus on the plane of meaning, the union of sense, need, impulse and action characteristic of the live creature. The intervention of consciousness adds regulation, power of selection, and redisposition. Thus it varies the arts in ways without end. But its intervention also leads in time to the idea of art as conscious idea - the greatest intellectual achievement in the history of humanity." Nishida, who also read Bergson and Dewey, writes, see Kitaro Nishida, "Intuition and Reflection in Self-Consciousness", p.115: "Immediate experience, as developmental, is a movement from universal to particular, the process of self-determination of a universal, simultaneous existence. The universal concept of color is a reality of immediate experience. Physically color may be defined as the vibration of ether, but experientially it is a concrete universal operating on itself; it is one inner continuum."

115 See Francis Crick, "The Astonishing Hypothesis", p.203.

116 See Semir Zeki,"Inner Vision - An exploration of Art and the Brain", p.69: "The study of the visual system is a profoundly philosophical enterprise; it entails an inquiry into how the brain acquires knowledge of the external world, which is no simple matter. The visual stimuli available to the brain do not offer a stable code of information. The wave-lengths of light reflected from surfaces change along with alterations in the illumination, yet the brain is able to assign a constant color to them."

a much more complex way than was proposed by the old concept of a linear stimulus-response process in relation to a supposedly precisely located speech-centre, a supposedly precisely located visual center, etc.[117] This theory assumed that we only see something when we can associate it with an earlier experience. It therefore assumed there was a difference between perception and understanding, each with its own localization in the brain. Zeki compares this classical duality with Kant's duality of perception and understanding, which he opposes with proof from his experiments.

Charles Biederman uses a very clear example of how conditioning through learning is quite important for our understanding of perception. He writes,

> *"Consciousness and visualization - this is the crux of any kind of seeing. For example, if one is a doctor, he may be able to observe at once that a particular person is ill with a particular disease; or, if one is an auto-mechanic, that a motor is at fault at a particular place or places. But the observer who is unfamiliar with the particular visual structures involved in each case, will probably only see a sick person or a defective machine, although all the visual data available to the doctor and the mechanic are present to the untrained observer ... Visual activity makes special demands in art as in other fields, in that it requires special training in the cortical area. It is not simply a matter of 'feeling', as so many artists and others unfortunately assume."*[118]

It is important to keep in mind, in connection to this quote from Biederman, that most if not all neuroscientists only study consciousness in very general terms. This means that, complex as their theories and discoveries may seem, they exclude all individual characteristics that are slightly different for each person. Individual characteristics that clearly play such an important role in art.

Most of the research on the brain, however exciting, seems to focus on a search for a pure mechanic or behavioristic functioning of our conscious being. I agree with the notion that in the end everyone generally consists of the same mechanical, biological or chemical structure, but nonetheless we are all different. I can imagine that the same basic structure has grown towards individual diversity as a result of differences in information in our genes, differences of personal experience[119] and even differences of environment[120] and of space/time.[121] Although research certainly has shown differences

[117] The here described concept of a simple causal understanding of perception is also known as 'S-R Theory' (Stimulus-Response) and considered to be the basic mechanism of Behaviorism in psychology.

[118] See Charles Biederman, "Art as the Evolution of Visual Knowledge" (Red Wing, MN: Charles Biederman, 1948), p.32.

[119] Since learning is a process of focussing, I can imagine it has some influence on the development of the brain.

[120] The social and cultural environment, but also the actual immediate environment, in terms of climate, sufficient space and the right facilities to develop oneself, enough nutrition, or lack of these basic conditions, etc.

[121] The different times and locations - differences in space/time - where we are born and grow up together with many social circumstances have a clear and direct influence on the emergence of one's personality and as a result, our brains are all different.

between the functioning of female and male brains, these differences do not concern the main activities of certain isolated brain-parts for particular tasks (like logical reasoning or creativity). In summary, it is not that simple to split the brain into a left and a right part, designating one hemisphere as the locus of certain functions the other hemisphere does not have, as if one hemisphere could include all female characteristics and the other only male characteristics, or that creativity is processed in only one hemisphere and rational thinking in the other.

New brainscanning devices using state of the art technologies show this cliché to be utter non-sense. To accomplish any task (for instance, the processing of the looking at a work of art) it seems that almost always different parts in both hemispheres of our brains are involved. This, however, should not be misunderstood as a suggestion that there are no differences between the two parts of the brain. There are differences, but there are no black/white or clean-cut differences in functionalities between both parts.[122] Like so many things in nature, it is much more complex. For instance, more research has shown that not only conscious perceptions, but also unconscious perceptions play a role in our visual consciousness.[123]

This process obviously implies that we can respond to things we see without knowing or understanding our own response consciously. This kind of unconscious response can emerge at various levels between absolute unconsciousness and absolute consciousness. These differing levels of consciousness help explain why we can appreciate an abstract artwork without consciously understanding it or, without experiencing our appreciation consciously and immediately (meaning: without having acquired more knowledge by longer reflection first). This should offer many readers an adequate explanation to the often heard response to art: "Well, I do not know anything about art, but I kind of like it." The hypothesis of the existence of both conscious and unconscious useful perceptions in neuroscience provides evidence that we should learn to trust our unconscious responses more often.

---

122 Research has shown that when a part of the brain is damaged, the tasks earlier processed by this part may be taken over by several other parts in the brain. Other research shows for instance that both sides of the brain can perceive illusory contours, but only the right hemisphere seems able to grasp certain perceptual groupings. Cognitive neuroscientist Michael Gazzaniga emphasizes the mistake researchers often make in following Darwin to compare animals' brains with the functioning of the human brain. Evidence has been found that there are too many differences. See Michael Gazzaniga, "The Split Brain Revisited", Scientific American, issue July 1998, p.39: "Our uniquely human skills may well be produced by minute and circumscribed neuronal networks. And yet our highly modularized brain generates the feeling in all of us that we are integrated and unified. How so, given that we are a collection of specialized modules? The answer may be that the left hemisphere seeks explanations for why events occur." Gazzaniga and his research group conclude that the left hemisphere has a higher or more advanced consciousness than the right hemisphere.

123 Research that gives reason to assume that in primates there are two systems concerning the functioning of the brain: the on-line system that is unconscious and the seeing system that is conscious. Research by Milner and Goodale, 1995. See Crick/Koch, "Consciousness and Neuroscience", in Special Issue "Mind and Brain", Scientific American, September 1992, p.152-159: "In short, the neuroanatomy does not suggest that the sole pathway goes up to the highest levels of the visual system, and from there to the highest levels of the prefrontal system and then down to the motor output. There are numerous pathways from most intermediate levels of the visual system to intermediate frontal regions."

5.9 EXTENSIONALISM

As our train of thought and its essentially connected process of argumentation with ourselves is not restricted to our own bodies, but extends from our bodies outwards into our environment, I introduced the notion of 'extensionalism' in 1992 in an attempt to define a basic theory of all creativity.[124] Extensionalism is the result of my desire to update the ideas in art - design - architecture - urban design in direct relation to science and philosophy, which first became known through constructivism.[125] We now know that it is no longer relevant to suppose that the key-factor of our perception of reality concerns constructing an image in our mind on the basis of received impulses.[126] The new and more realistic paradigm concerns the continuous interaction between ourselves and our immediate environment outside our body.[127]

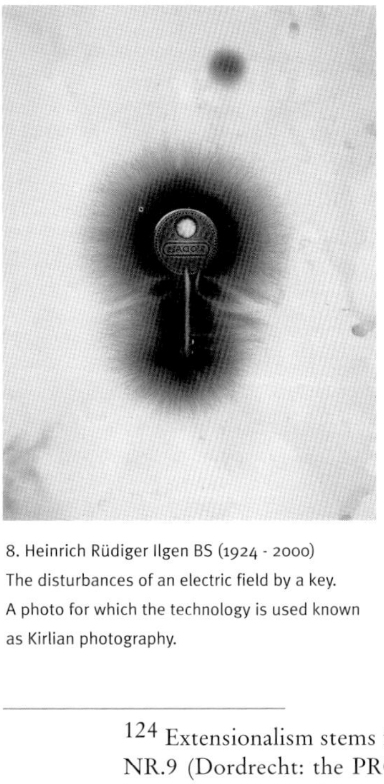

8. Heinrich Rüdiger Ilgen BS (1924 - 2000) The disturbances of an electric field by a key. A photo for which the technology is used known as Kirlian photography.

We know now that any kind of re-construction of reality based on logical reasoning and empirical evidence will ignore many aspects of reality that are just beyond words, including the impact processes in nature have on one's whole being. Such influences we hardly can escape because of our immersion in the complex processes of nature.[128] Mind and, therefore, aesthetic experience, are not events isolated within our bodies.[129] Therefore, extension is a much more adequate notion than construction, and makes the notion extensionalism much more relevant than constructivism. It is true that the images that enter our brain through the eyes are first fragmented in our eyes, after which they are processed in several parts of the brain, before being assembled or re-constructed again in still inexplicable

124 Extensionalism stems from extension. See my paper "From Constructivism to extensionalism", in PRO-NR.9 (Dordrecht: the PRO Foundation, 1993), p.4-23. Extension as in extend: reach or stretch out, make longer, in space or time.

125 See §3 on constructivism.

126 Although the so-called 'binding-problem' in neuroscience seems still to suggest this as a possibility, but - as was discussed in this chapter - more with the character of simulation which is open to misinterpretations of physical reality.

127 I mean not only in our brain, or head, but involving our whole body.

128 For instance, Faraday, who studied light and magnetism in the first half of the 19th century, concluded that the magnetic force had to be present in all things, in all forms of matter. See Gerrit L. Verschuur, "Hidden Attraction - The Mystery and History of Magnetism" (Oxford: Oxford University Press, 1993) p.97. When everything radiates magnetic forces, their fields will undoubtedly interact with each other and interact with much larger magnetic fields, for instance, from earth itself or cosmic magnetic 'winds' as the solar wind. In the 19th century an extensive interest emerged in occult knowledge, including many theorists who became interested in the extension of the body in all directions caused by vibrations. See Maurice Tuchman, "Hidden Meanings in Abstract Art", in Maurice Tuchman, "The Spiritual in Art: Abstract Painting 1890-1985" (New York: Abbeville Publishers, 1986), p. 20. For instance, Baudelaire was very interested in this. See also §14.

see picture 9

129 Dewey emphasizes that ignorance of the continuous interaction between the mind, the body and the environment makes art worthless to man. See John Dewey, "Art As Experience" p.264.: "Mind that bears only an

ways. However, as has been discussed in this chapter before, this is only one aspect of the perception of reality.[130]

Extensionalism finds itself in a long tradition of thinking about the extension of the human body in all directions.[131] For instance, cultural philosopher Vilém Flusser wrote:

> *"We no longer believe in the reality of a self, a mind, a spirit. What we now begin to feel is that there are numerous virtualities around us and within us, that there is no difference between around and within, and that those virtualities are opportunities for us to become concrete according to specific projects. By thus realizing ourselves we also realize those next to us and the environment within which those realizations occur."*[132]

Flusser describes the interaction of the self inside our body with the environment, including other selves, outside our own body. This interaction is more important than the body as such or the world as such. This interaction is a result of the virtual extension of our perception and of our thinking into the environment, reminding us of the projective field. Extensionalism, therefore, is a justified term for the approach that studies this interaction, tries to understand it and, finally, hopes to suggest ways for the application to improve society.

A modern development that will make further understanding of self-perception and of the world even more complex is promised by the research about the human genome.[133] We may conclude that nothing, not the brain, the body, or the genome are in total control of our brain processes, our consciousness, our behavior, our whole being. This means we cannot try to understand our functioning, perception of reality, and visual consciousness, by attempting to reduce our functioning to the working of an

accidental relation to the environment occupies a similar relation to the body. In making mind purely immaterial (isolated from the organ of doing and undergoing), the body ceases to be living and becomes a dead lump. This conception of mind as an isolated being underlies the conception that esthetic experience is merely something 'in mind', and strengthens the conception which isolates the esthetic from those modes of experience in which the body is actively engaged with the things of nature and life. It takes art out of the province of the live creature."

130 This is the 'binding problem' in neuroscience.

131 This tradition includes Aristotle, Cusanus, Leibniz, Descartes, Schopenhauer, Goethe, Bergson, Dewey, Whitehead, Nishida, Von Weizsäcker ("The thinking substance is really also extended." - "Die denkende Substanz ist wesentlich auch ausgedehnt", see Carl Friedrich von Weizsäcker, "Zeit und Wissen", p.350), to scientific theories from Bohm, Penrose, Prigogene, the Santa Fé Institute, and can be connected to the interests in the continuum, in duration, direction, the process, structure, coherence, order-fluctuations and concepts of space/time; to analogies between art, philosophy and science; to analogies in knowledge and cultural expressions between human cultures.

132 See Vilém Flusser, "Man as Subject or Project", in catalogue 3rd PRO Conference'89 Rotterdam-Dordrecht-Vlissingen (Dordrecht: The PRO Foundation, 1989).

133 So far scientists have already found that quite a few motivations for our actions are not based on our own decisions but on decisions made for us by our genes, for instance by a specific hormone. Science journalist Matt Ridley describes the sheer depth of complexity of this new development, by refering to the fact that genes are not isolated entities, but "... part of an enormous confederation called the body..." "The brain, the body and the genome are locked, all three, in a dance. The genome is as much under the control of the other two as they are controlled by it. That is partly why genetic determinism is such a myth. The switching on and

individual neuron in the brain or to the properties of certain genes, studied in isolation.
In my opinion this confirms what philosophers like Schopenhauer, Nishida and Dewey already sensed and many artists sensed through their work: we need to accept the complexity of being a self as part of and emerged in a large whole. Our own bodies are the starting point for this understanding. Projection of objects - like works of art - into the environment around us are the means for our understanding of reality. This is an understanding that is located in the 'field' between our minds and the whole of nature, the location where the receptive field and the projective field overlap. This location is also the arena of the humanities, such as psychology and sociology.

The process of perceiving reality involves space and time. That I am not alone in considering this subject very important will become clear in the next chapter.

off of human genes can be influenced by conscious or unconscious external action." See Matt Ridley, "Genome - The autobiography of a species in 23 chapters" (London: Fourth Estate Ltd, 1999), p.148. Ridley illustrates this by discussing the level of cholesterol and other steroids in our bodies. These levels are partly controlled by a chromosome, but clearly influenced by our decisions about eating, which partly are influenced by our culture, social position and general environment.

§6 SPACE/TIME

We live in space. Life evolves through time. Even the slightest motion we make happens in time and in space. Any understanding of reality, therefore, has to consider the implications of space and time. Science and philosophy have taught us that space and time are two notions that in their experience (and measurement) cannot be separated. Hence, we may still speak of space and time as individual entities but also can discuss these notions combined in one notion, as the duality of 'space/time.'[1]

All scientific theories of space/time that will be described in this chapter are based on studying the properties of light, non-local connections and the shape of paths through space/time. Because a work of art exists in front of us in reality and the making and perceiving of art takes place in a lapse of space/time, this subject does matter in understanding the meaning of art. When confronted with a blank new canvas for a new painting or the vacant space for a new sculpture, the artist has to deal with the same properties of space/time as science: the properties of light and the shape of the paths through space/time. Painting involves applying many properties of light through colour. Sculpture involves all properties of light in a three-dimensional space. This obviously does not imply that sculpture is a better medium for portraying reality, because in our perception, painting, with its capacity to simulate space (as was discussed in the previous chapter on 'pictorial illusionism'), becomes the equivalent to phenomena in real space. For any artist, the application of intervals is important in the creation of a composition. Intervals are the interrelationships between parts that are not actually connected, but are nevertheless connected in our perception, connected at 'a deeper level'(in scientific space/time theories one speaks not about intervals but about non-local connection). This obviously is relevant to both figurative and abstract art. The visual appearance of the work of art is based on contrasts of colour, contrasts of shape and/or contrasts of size. Though in general one considers these to be properties of static artworks, I suggest that they also simulate the pictorial elements' paths through space/time. This comparison should become clear in this chapter. Besides, there are quite a few artists who have consciously and seriously studied change in their art. Change is an important feature of the process of space/time.[2]

Both scientists and artists try to understand reality. This chapter will attempt to show

[1] See Brian Greene, "The Elegant Universe - Superstrings, Hidden Dimensions, and the Quest for the Ultimate Theory" (New York: Vintage Books, 2000), p.298: "Physicists use the term duality to describe theoretical models that appear to be different but nevertheless can be shown to describe exactly the same physics." For more general information on the various concepts and ways of dealing with time, including the measuring of time, see Kirsten Lippencott, "The Story of Time", including essays by Umberto Eco and E.H. Gombrich (London: Merrill Holberton Publishers in association with the National Maritime Museum, 1999). See Marie-Louise Franz, "Zeit-Strömen und Stille" (Kempten: Kösel, 1992 - orig. "Time-Rhythm and Repose", series "Art and Imagination", Thames and Hudson Ltd, editor Jill Purce, 1978).

[2] Change as an important paradigm is discussed in §8. Good examples are to be found in the the kinetic sculptures by Jesus Rafael Soto, Jean Tinguely, George Rickey, and in the mobiles by Calder, Tim Prentice and my

how the subject of space/time is also a very important example of a subject on which scientists, philosophers and artists can be of substantial support to each other's understanding. To that end, not only complex and highly abstract scientific theories will be mentioned, but also simultaneous interpretations in philosophy and art. The interest and understanding of many artists in space/time is varried, but goes deeper than is often assumed.

Any interaction with reality takes time. The processing of perceived signals in our brain takes time, as we saw in the previous chapter. In the process of our being, doing and becoming, our perception takes place at a certain moment and at a certain location in our physical reality.[3] Therefore, it is a fact that the process of perception is part of the continuity of space/time. In addition, the whole body contains many cyclic processes, often referred to as bio-rhythms, such as heart-rate, hormone- and nervous systems, etc. These cyclic processes make us part of nature's complex space/time cycles such as day/night, seasons, etc. Our desire to better understand this deep connection between ourselves and nature is itself quite natural.[4]

An understanding of space/time, however, is more complex than looking at your watch and finding your location on a map. As we will see, neither time nor space are as fixed as a watch or a map might suggest. Several examples will be discussed to illustrate how science, philosophy and art may help us understand the multi-layered complexity of space/time, especially because our understanding of space/time is interrelated with our perception of reality and of ourselves.[5] This subject also deserves so much attention because it is one of the major subjects in modern theoretical physics search to understand reality. Besides, the fine arts have expressed interest in space/time since the early abstract painters and sculptors.[6] For a long time, space/time seems to have been understood as the main property of the essence of reality and the whole of nature - and maybe

---

own mobiles and sculptures. But, in principle, change can be found already much earlier in certain paintings, like in Monet's haystack- or Rouen-cathedral series.

[3] Nishitani discusses the 'home-ground of Dasein', meaning our actual location in the particular spot in reality where we perceive our selves, from where we perceive the world around us and act accordingly, always being driven onwards by an inner drive. It is the everyday level of the self without taking any invisible higher or underlying structure into consideration. See Keiji Nishitani, "Religion and Nothingness", translated by Jan van Bragt, foreword by Winston L. King (Berkeley, Los Angeles, London: University of California Press, 1983), p. 242: "Being obligated to the infinite drive from the home-ground of the self itself to be constantly engaged in doing something and consequently being obligated also to keep entering into relation with others and co-determining the self with others endlessly, but yet remaining forever incapable of taking leave of the self that presses onerously down upon us - this, it seems to me, is by and large the state of affairs that has arisen to awareness through the concept of karma. It might be termed a self-awareness of the essence of existence in time, conceived as a dynamic nexus of being, doing and becoming." He describes karma as "The term 'karma' expresses an awareness of existence that sees being and time as infinite burdens for us and, at the same time, an awareness of the essence of time itself." See Keiji Nishitani, "Religion and Nothingness", p.221.

[4] The actual impact of rhythmic processes in nature on the rhythmic processes in our own bodies and brains will be discussed more fully in §13 and §14.

[5] Therefore, the subject of this chapter cannot be understood as separate from the previous chapter, nor from the next chapters!

[6] In principle, the more dynamic use of paint - showing the marks of the brush or pen, as in expressionistic

it is. It is a very complex subject making this chapter one of the most difficult parts of this book for readers who are less familiar with scientific theories, but also for readers less familiar with the works and theories of artists.

6.1 INTRODUCTION

It is sometimes suggested that we live in an N - dimensional world, from which we can merely experience three dimensions because of the restrictions of our senses. However, we may be able to understand a fourth dimension thanks to our capacity to reason.[7]

In this chapter, you will find out yourself how highly abstract ideas in physics have become. I will discuss notions of space/time that can also support our understanding of compositions in art. These notions have popped up through history as a result of common observations of processes in nature. They have also proved useful as metaphors. For instance, the concept of 'push and pull forces' observable in magnets or tidal motions and the concept of 'the field' can be understood as metaphors for how two or more objects interrelate. In this sense space/time could be a metaphor for the complex and continuous changing streams of energies that constitute nature as a whole - the total swirling energies in which we are a temporary cluster of energies.

The early abstract artists were not only involved in exploring space/time - inspired by philosophical and scientific ideas - but the kind of translations of space/time they developed in painting, sculpture and architecture have set the standard for most abstract art ever since. Unfortunately, very often artists' interests in science are ignored, not taken seriously or even wrongly interpreted, although evidence can easily be found in their works and in published texts to support what the artists themselves have stated on the subject. Too often researchers on the analogies between art and science project their personal conclusions on history without looking first at easily available sources in history.[8]

painting - already presents strong simulations of motion, therefore of space/time. In that sense, the calligraphy of China, Korea, Japan, the Islamic culture or Celtic enlightened manuscripts, the Venetian painters or the great painters from the Baroque, the American Expressionists or individual artists as Frank Stella, Gotthard Graubner and Gerhard Richter, can all be mentioned. Basically, one may argue that any evidence of an act, such as carving or any other kind of mark or trace a person leaves in a material, is an expression in space/time. Colour and compositional expertise have allowed powerful and complex interpretations and imaginations of space/time in real life and life imagined to exist in the heavens (angels, deities, etc.).

[7] 'N' = an undefined amount. Time is often considered to be the fourth dimension (while the first three dimensions are one-dimensional point, two-dimensional line and plane, three-dimensional shapes with a length, depth and height). Theories about other worlds or more dimensions are the result of a process of highly abstract reasoning in both theoretical science and in philosophy. The assumption that more dimensions would exist is evoked by the discovery in particle physics of some disturbing discrepancies in the accepted properties of light as consisting of a particle/wave duality that travels at a constant speed and that this speed would be the highest speed defining space/time. New discoveries demand a different understanding of space/time, as will become clear in this chapter.

[8] See Leonard Shlain, "Art & Physics - Parallel Visions in Space, Time and Light" (New York: Quill William Morrow, 1993). An interesting book by Leonard Shlain, a surgeon by profession and clearly a person profoundly interested in art. Unfortunately he allows the East-West cultural interaction only to start in 1853 when US Navy Commodore Pierce forced Japan to open trade. This did start a new eruption of trade with

The classical opinion says that we live in a three-dimensional world. These dimensions concern length, width and height that together create an image of depth. For many centuries, in many cultures, time was thought to be different for humans than for the gods or God. For humans, time was thought to have a limited character of which change (like becoming older) was an inescapable feature. In the heavens time would be eternal and unchanging. Early modern scientists, like Newton, made a connection between the heavens and the earth by proving that certain laws ruled both. The observation of change in nature emerged. Newton believed absolute time flowed equally in nature without relation to anything external, and thought it was equivalent to duration. He understood relative time as a sensible and external measure of duration by the means of motion.[9] A contemporary of Newton, the philosopher Leibniz, considered duration in relation to the ancient concept of eternal return, which presupposes that the universe experiences endless cycles, resulting in all events being repetitions of earlier events. This concept is related to the prevalent idea in his time that all planets moved in perfect circles or ellipses around the sun. Leibniz concluded: "There is no such thing as a perfect

Japan, but is not the start of the interaction between Occidental and Oriental cultures. As a result of Alexander the Great's conquests all the way through the Middle East well into India, already trade-routes between Europe and the Orient were established - for instance the Silk Route (approximately between BC 100 - AD 1600). See Heinz Spielmann, "Kunst an der Seidenstrasse - Faszination Buddha" (Ostfildern-Ruit: Hatje Cantz Verlag, Bucerius Kunst Forum Hamburg, 2003). Or the trade-chasing maritime enterprises by the Spanish, Portuguese and Dutch from the 15th centuries onwards. Early examples of the interaction in culture was the influence of the Indian mandala on the design of the rose-windows in Christian cathedrals and Leibniz's interest in the ancient Chinese "I Tjing" in the 17th century. For information on concepts of time in ancient India, see Swami Sivapriyananda, "Astrology and Religion in Indian Art" (New Delhi: Abhinav Publications, 1990). Shlain also discusses the major role of the colours red and blue in modern astronomy (like in redshift) and, interestingly, compares these preferences for certain colours to depict the sky in art. Shlain suggests Renaissance artists all painted the sky first gold as they imagined the sky to be heaven, till Giotto showed them the sky to be blue. For a part this is correct, because in the Middle Ages the application of precious materials was originally intended to illustrate how the realm of God would be much more valuable and perfect. An interpretation that gave a higher value to craftmanship and choice of materials than to artistic creativity. See Umberto Eco, "Art and Beauty in the Middle Ages", translated by Hugh Bredin (New Haven and London: Yale University Press, 1986 - orig. "Sviluppo dell'estetica medievale" in "Momenti e problemi di storia dell'estetica" vol. 1, 1959). Shlain furthermore comments, that still many artists "...continued to feel more comfortable with red than blue." See Leonard Shlain, "Art & Physics - Parallel Visions in Space, Time and Light" p.183. However, this preference for gold, blue and red in those days was not always a choice of the artists, but mainly a culturaly predecided formula (see above), besides, a choice of the rich person (or church) who commissioned the painting. Blue was made out of the purest lapis lazuli (the half gem-stone) and considered as expensive as or more expensive than gold. Red was made from purple (named Tyrean or Imperial Purple, made from the secretion of the large sea snail Purpura Lapillus) and also quite expensive, but lapis lazuli was much more expensive. Therefore in a painting the highest quality of blue was only allowed for the highest deity or saint in that particular painting or for a king (but only when there would not be a saint in the same image). Therefore, every rich person tried to impress by commissioning a painting with as much blue, gold and red as he could afford (contracts still exist prescribing exactly the quantities of blue, gold and red that the artist should use). This means, that in fact, artists in the late Middle Ages and the Renaissance were hardly as free as today. Comparably, today artists are restrained in their creativity for commissions for public or private buildings. The economic factor always has influenced the possibilities for art (as well as for science!).

[9] See Thomas Vargish and Delo E. Mook, "Inside Modernism - Relativity Theory, Cubism, Narrative" (New Haven and London: Yale University Press, 1999).

return such as in circles or ellipses, and it will not happen that one time or place in the universe will perfectly resemble another, although they appear similar to the senses."[10] Leibniz's genius thus sensed the importance of eternal change as a major feature of space/time.

In the 17th and 18th centuries, the period that gave birth to modern science, there was not always such an extreme difference in the activities and subjects of philosophers and scientists, as we can expect nowadays. Not much later, the philosopher Immanuel Kant proposed a theory for the origin of our solar system, which he considered to have emerged in a purely mechanical way out of a primal mist, caused by pushing and pulling forces, resulting from the rules of gravity.[11] Kant thought time and space were subjective forms of intuition, in contrast to earlier opinions that space and time were objective and absolute. According to Kant, space and time are not properties of things but are ways of observing:

> *"Time is the form of 'inner sense', that is, of all states of mind, whether or not they are referred to an objective reality. There could not be a mental state that is not experienced in time, and time is made real to us through this organization of our experience. Space is the form of 'outer sense' - that is, of those 'intuitions' which we refer to an independent world and which we therefore regard as 'appearances' of objective things ... Space, like time, forms part of the organisation of my sensibility."*[12]

Kant's contemporary, the philosopher, scientist, dramatist, novelist and poet Johann Wolfgang von Goethe, had a clear idea about the fundamental character of the push- and pull forces of nature and the connectedness of all things when he wrote:

> *"Loyal observers of nature, how different they might be otherwise, will agree with each other, that everything that is meant to appear, that will meet us as phenomenon, must refer to and present itself to us as: either an original division including the capacity to unite, or as original unity that can become divided. To divide what has become one and to unite what is divided is the life of nature, this is the eternal systole and diastole (the contraction and extension), the eternal syncrisis and diacrisis, the breathing in and out of the world in which we live, weave and are."* [13]

---

[10] See Allison P. Coudert, "Leibniz and The Kabbalah", International Archives of the History of Ideas 142 (Dordrecht: Kluwer Academic Publishers, 1995), p.113. This discussion on the ancient concept known as the platonic year, was written by Leibniz as early as 1701.

[11] Kant 1724-1804. This theory was later re-invented by Laplace, who did not know Kant's theory and which has become known in our time as the Kant-Laplace theory.

[12] See Martin Hammer & Christina Lodder, "Constructing Modernity - The Art & Career of Naum Gabo" (New Haven and London: Yale University Press, 1999), p.66.

[13] Goethe 1749-1832. See Johann Wolfgang Goethe, "Verhältnis zur allgemeinen Physik", in "Entwurf einer Farbenlehre" (1810), in Rudolf Steiner, "J.W. Goethe - Naturwissenschaftliche Schriften", Dritter Band (Dornach: Rudolf Steiner Verlag, 1982, orig. 1890), p.281-282: "Treue Beobachter der Natur, wenn sie auch sonst noch so verschieden denken, werden darin mit einander übereinkommen, daß alles, was erschienen, was

A little later, in the early 19th century, Schopenhauer argued that space, time and causality are necessarily linked to allow for the existence of real objects. He discussed real objects as objects that 'perdure'. Perdurance demands both time and space. To perdure, these objects must retain their identity coexistently with change around them.[14] To be more than an empty existence in space and time, they must be virtually filled with something. This something is what Schopenhauer calls 'matter'. Furthermore, he understood matter as identical to causality. An object can only exist in space and time when it is acted upon by other objects and acts upon other objects itself. Thus objects are not only perceivable by our senses, but must also be understood in a larger interconnected whole, a totality of experience, or what Schopenhauer calls 'empirical reality'. This is reality in which all objects are temporally, spatially, and causally interrelated: the world as we perceive it everyday.

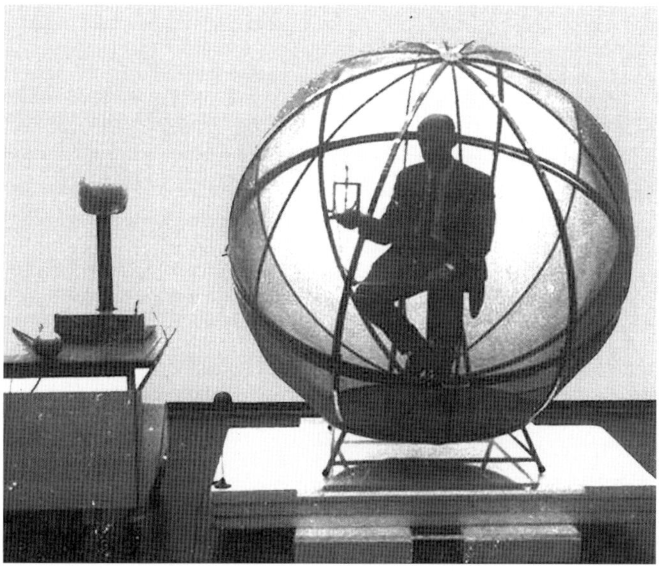

9. Heinrich Rüdiger Ilgen BS (1924 - 2000) **Faraday Cage** demonstration model, ca. 1972
My father designed this cage for the Technical University Eindhoven. A complete cage of metallic meshwork effectively screens ambient electromagnetic waves from the enclosed region. This was discovered by Michael Faraday (1791-1867) in 1836 using a much smaller version merely containing a measuring instrument, not a person.

In light of these philosophies, it is hardly surprising that a scientist like Michael Faraday, while discussing magnetic forces, used the notion of the field, setting the tone for all future discussions on the magnitude and direction of a force on some entity at a specific location in space/time.[15] The field can be visualized most simply as a fishing net. The knots in the net represent objects in reality. We can try to pick up one knot to study it, but we will always have to include the other knots that are connected - the knots we pick up at the

uns als Phänomen begegnen solle, müsse entweder eine ursprüngliche Entzweiung, die einer Vereinigung fähig ist, oder eine ursprüngliche Einheit, die zur Entzweiung gelangen könne, andeuten und sich auf eine solche Weise darstellen. Das Geeinte zu entzweien, das Entzweite zu einigen, ist das Leben der Natur, dies ist die ewige Systole und Diastole (das Zusammenziehen und Ausdehnen), die ewige Synkrisis und Diakrisis, das Ein- und Ausatmen der Welt, in den wir leben, weben und sein."

14 See F.C. White, "The Fourfold Root", in Christopher Janaway, "The Cambridge Companion to Schopenhauer" (Cambridge: Cambridge University Press, 1999), p.66.

15 Made public by Michael Faraday in 1845. See Thomas Vargish and Delo E. Mook, "Inside Modernism - Relativity Theory, Cubism, Narrative", p.105-106. See §7.

same time so to speak. That is also how we can visualize objects and their interconnections in space/time. The field is also an apt concept for describing the functioning of a work of art.[16] Many artists were and are conscious of the important feature of interconnection and push and pull forces in their works, while studying and analyzing the relationships between forms and between colours, etc. I will include just one example here. Kandinsky, clearly referring to an idea that recalls Goethe, wrote: "The recession and advance of the form elements draw the basic plane forward (towards the observer) and backwards in depth (away from the observer) in such a manner that the basic plane, like an accordion, is pulled apart in both directions."[17] Let us not forget that Kandinsky made two-dimensional (flat) paintings. Therefore, he is talking about the strong simulation of push and pull that happens in perception.[18] This does not only relate to the earlier discussion in this book on the importance of visual illusion, but it is also interesting to remark that most push and pull forces in nature itself are not clearly visible to us. Gravitational forces in the universe are for instance only comprehensible by measuring and using simulations. When we look up at a clear moonless starry sky we cannot even perceive depth.

Later in his paintings, Kandinsky developed complex compositions with many shapes that seek to destroy the picture-plane as a static flat plane and virtually seem to float. Paul Overy writes of Kandinsky: "One of the results of the 'destruction' of the picture-plane, according to Kandinsky, is a 'change in the feeling for time'."[19] Kandinsky comments on the impact of this strong illusion as an aspect of our perception, writing, "The transformation of the material picture-plane into indefinable space offers the opportunity of increasing the span of time."[20]

Just before Kandinsky's generation, an important popular promotor of scientific ideas in the 19th century was Hermann von Helmholtz,[21] who started his career by studying Goethe's scientific theories and philosophy. Von Helmholtz was a pioneer in physiology and physics with a keen interest in the possible implications of new ideas from both these fields for philosophy and art (painting as well as music). Therefore, it is hardly surprising that many artists knew his writings on vision, colour, optics and painting, physiology and music, the interaction of natural forces, conservation of force, geometry and perception in general. In his paper, "On the Origin and Significance of Geometrical Axioms", 1870, Von Helmholtz describes geometry's progress in the 19th

16 See §5.

17 See Wassily Kandinsky, "Point and Line to Plane", in Paul Overy, "Kandinsky - The language of the eye" (London: Elek Books Ltd, 1969), p.122.

18 Another influential example was the originally German painter Hans Hoffmann, who first taught in Munich before coming to New York. He always spoke to his students about the importance of "push and pull" in painting. Hoffmann was of large influence to the first generations of major 20th century artists in the USA, like the American Expressionists.

19 See Paul Overy, "Kandinsky - The language of the eye", p.124.

20 Ibid, p.124. Compare Frank Stella's descriptions in §5.3.

21 See David Cahan, "Science and Culture - Popular and Philosophical Essays - Hermann von Helmholtz" (Chicago: The University of Chicago Press, 1995).

century in getting near to a first understanding of a fourth dimension.[22] He describes geodetic lines as the straightest lines between points (to be distinguished from the shortest line), the curvature of surfaces, the invention of projective geometry, the concepts of geometry by Riemann,[23] new concepts of spherical space and the necessary distortion of shapes - and organisms - in a curved space. Clearly these ideas helped lead to Einstein's famous concept of a distorted curved space/time. Quite an interesting analogy can be found in Cézanne's ideas about the emergence of projective geometry, concepts of spherical space, and premonitions of an Einsteinian concept of space/time. Charles Biederman discusses Cézanne's interest in concentric vision, referring to Leonardo da Vinci, who already stated that the air "... is filled with circles ..." and many virtual lines.[24] Cézanne writes that every object has a culminating point in our perception - we could also say that when we focus on an object we get the illusion this object has a certain point that attracts our vision foremost:

---

[22] Ibid, p.226-245.

[23] The curvature of surfaces by Gauss (1828), the invention of projective geometry by N.J. Lobachevsky, published in "Prinzipien der Geometrie" (Kasan, 1829-30), the concepts of geometry by Riemann, published in "Über die Hypothesen welche die Geometrie zu Grunde liegen"(1854). See Hermann von Helmholtz, "On the Origin and Significance of Geometrical Axioms", in David Cahan, "Science and Culture - Popular and Philosophical Essays - Hermann von Helmholtz, p.234: "The numbers of measurement necessary to give the position of a point, is equal to the number of dimensions of the space in question. In a line the distance from one fixed point is sufficient, that is to say, one quantity; in a surface the distances from two fixed points must be given; in space, the distances from three; or, we require, as on earth, longitude, latitude, and height above the sea, or, as is ususal in analytical geometry, the distances from three co-ordinate planes. Riemann calls a system of differences in which one thing can be determined by n-measurements an 'n-folded aggregate' or an 'aggregate of n-dimensions'. Thus the space in which we live is a threefold, a surface a twofold, and a line a simple extended aggregate of points. Time also is as an aggregate of one dimension."

[24] See Charles Biederman, "The New Cézanne - From Monet to Mondriaan" (Red Wing: Charles Biederman, 1958), §4 and p. 71: "The air is filled with an infinite number of lines, straight and radiating, intercrossing and weaving together without ever coinciding; and they represent for every object the true Form of their reason (of their explanation) - la vera forma della lore cagione." In my interpretation, Leonardo already sensed the lines of force - of energy - the concept discovered in the late 19th century by Maxwell. The concept that everything follows circles seems related to similar ideas in ancient philosophies, like in the Veda's. In this context one can mention the attempts for a concentric vision by Kandinsky's virtual destruction of the flat picture plane to open to infinite space and El Lissitzky's concept of 'PAN-Geometry', briefly discussed later in this chapter, but also the traditional construction methods of perspective in painting can be mentioned, which - in the Renaissance - were based on a linear construction using one central point at the horizon to which all other perspective lines lead - so also a concentric vision, not with a culminating point per object, but for the whole of nature. Erwin Panofsky described how the choice of perspective through all ages has everything to do with a sense of self in the immediate relationship to nature as a whole. See Erwin Panofsky, "Perspective as Symbolic Form", translated by Christopher S. Wood (New York: Zone Books, 1997 - orig. "Die Perspektive als 'symbolische Form'", in Vorträge der Bibliothek Warburg, 1924-1925), p.67: "Perspective subjects the artistic phenomenon to stable and even mathematically exact rules, but on the other hand, makes that phenomenon contingent upon human beings, indeed upon the individual: for these rules refer to the psychological and physical conditions of the visual impression, and the way they take effect is determined by the freely chosen position of a subjective 'point of view'. Thus the history of perspective may be understood with equal justice as triumph of the distancing and objectifying sense of the real, and as a triumph of the distance-denying human struggle for control; it is as much a consolidation and systematization of the external world, as an extension of the domain of the self."

"To realize progress there is only nature, and the eye is educated by contact with her. It becomes concentric by dint of looking and working. I mean that in an orange, a ball, a head, there is a culminating point and this point is always in spite of the powerful effect - light, shadow, coloring sensations - it is always the nearest to our eyes. The edges of objects flee towards a center placed on our horizon."[25]

In Cézanne's words, there is one point that is closest to our eyes. The rest of the object's shape and its environment are located on lines that radiate from this point in every direction, resulting in concentric vision.[26] This theory of vision led Cézanne to search nature - in his case the landscape - for various culminating points showing a combination of virtual streams of lines of force. This results in Cézanne's famous so-called unfinished paintings after about 1900.[27] One of his greatest works that illustrates his deep understanding of the pulsating forces of nature found in our immediate perception

25 See Emile Bernard, "Souvenirs Sur Paul Cézanne", in R.G. Michel, "Une Conversation Avec Cézanne", 1926, in Charles Biederman, "The New Cézanne - From Monet to Mondriaan", p. 29. And quoted in Françoise Cachin and Joseph J. Rishel, "Cézanne" (London: Tate Publishing, 1996), p.288. A slightly different translation of the same letter by Cézanne to Émile Bernard, see Michael Doran, "Conversations with Cézanne", translated by Julie Lawrence Cochran, introduction by Richard Shiff, Documents of Twentieth-century art (Berkeley, Los Angeles, London: University of California Press, 2001), p.45-46.

26 This concept of radiating lines is definitely part of the tradition of considering vision in terms of following lines, as was already formulated by Euclid. See §12.3. Biederman says about Cézanne's concept, referring to Cézanne's interest in forms of roundness, like the apples and oranges in his still lifes, although he does paint in planes (his brushstrokes - structure or 'modulations') and not in roundness, see Charles Biederman, "The New Cézanne - From Monet to Mondriaan", p.29: "Therefore, the references are to some relations that exist between nature and a sphere and painting and planes. Let us do, then, to the sphere what Cézanne does to nature; namely, consider the sphere as transformed into continuous series of planes. Accordingly, when the artist refers to a 'culminating point' on the sphere which, in spite of all effects of light and color, is always the closest to our eyes, and since he is no more a painter of points than of roundness, he would seem to be referring to that plane on a sphere which would be the 'nearest to our eyes'." Biederman explains - and illustrates it wonderfully showing a ball covered with small squares of cardboard (Ibid., figures 4-5-6) - that the plane nearest to our eyes is basically parallel to the picture-plane while all the others are in a kind of angle towards the horizon. Biederman correctly concludes that the plane parallel to the picture-plane gives the impression of being static, while the other planes (under an angle) simulate different kinds of dynamics - something Biederman clearly adopted in his own reliefs in the 1940's and onwards.

27 Of course this development did not just happen. In the paintings, watercolours and drawings prior to 1900 one can see a gradual understanding of the dynamics of nature emerge slowly. The first signs are his discovery of molding painting in his modulations, a free hand variation of Pointillism. A second large step one may notice in how Cézanne paints trees - especially from about 1882 (for example "Farm in Normandy, Summer (Hattenville)", see Françoise Cachin and Joseph J. Rishel, "Cézanne", p.248). Their liveliness seems to have been inspired by trying to depict the confusing motions of the leaves under a rush of wind - comparable to how the Futurists later depicted motion of machines, animals and people using rhythmic painted brush-strokes in groups ordered along curved rows. Cézanne's struggle is visible in these trees: sometimes it shows a more spontaneous ordering of colourpatches in all directions, sometimes a more dogmatic - rationalized - ordering along strict lines, as in "The Great Pine", 1889 or "Large Pine and Red Earth", 1890-'95 (see Françoise Cachin and Joseph J. Rishel, "Cézanne", p.373). This process can also be wonderfully found in the catalogue for the great exhibition at the Kunsthaus Zürich from 2000. See Felix Baumann, Evelyn Benesch, Walter Feilchenfeldt, Klaus Albrecht Schröder, "Cézanne - Finished - Unfinished" (Ostfildern-Ruit, Germany: Hatje Cantz Publishers, 2000).

is the fabulous painting "Forest".[28] Cézanne went through a gradual process of first exploring painting as technique,[29] then exploring various themes,[30] desperately searching nature for its true property, and finally reaching the genius level of combining experience, knowledge, and a better use of colour than he ever did before. This resulted in only a few paintings, like the amazing "The Garden at Les Lauves",[31] which shows an incredible simulation of push and pull forces and concentric vision using bright freehand geometric colour patches and a few line-segments in a calculated but dynamically structured composition. The principle difference between the Impressionists and Cézanne is that, while the first try to catch the immediacy of 'l'impression'(a slice of time), Cézanne tries to depict the *duration* of space/time.[32] Needless to say, this involves tackling the problem of depicting *change*. Like many of his contemporaries, Cézanne was quite interested in the philosophy of Schopenhauer.[33]

see picture 15

In the context of this chapter on space/time, it is interesting to recall Schopenhauer's earlier mentioned ideas on objects in empirical reality in space and time. Schopenhauer believed that nature as a whole (empirical reality) has a will that overrules everything. A fragment or echo of this worldwill is an essential part of every object or being's individual will. Every action that is 'willed' is preceeded by a motive to do so. This motive acts as the impetus to do anything; to act, to move, to change. To act means to be part of a causal world, to be influenced by and to have influence on. To act means to be. Describing how one can understand one's own motives and actions, Schopenhauer writes, "I must recognize the inscrutable forces that manifest themselves in all the bodies of nature as identical in kind with what in me is the will, and as differing from it only in degree."[34] When we see a plant, we recognize the inner force that makes it grow and extend. We may also recognize this force as comparable to the inner force, or will, inside

28 "Forest", (orig."Sous-Bois") 1894. See Françoise Cachin and Joseph J. Rishel, "Cézanne", p. 378. Collection of the Los Angeles County Museum of Art.

29 The development of regular brushstrokes into his more and more geometrized colour patches.

30 His motive, changing from overall landscapes to individual trees, and back again, with the newly acquired knowledge, to the landscape. In my humble opinion, his more idealistic 'bathers', portraits and still lifes are a kind of more popular side-track. These were probably his attempts to become an acknowledged artist, but also to clear his mind for his 'real stuff' (my own conclusion being an artist myself - sometimes you just have to do something really different to clear one's head).

31 "The Garden at Les Lauves", c.1906. See Felix Baumann, Evelyn Benesch, Walter Feilchenfeldt, Klaus Albrecht Schröder, "Cézanne - Finished - Unfinished" p. 381. This painting is in Washington DC, The Philips Collection.

32 See §2.4.

33 See §7. Schopenhauer has refered to reading the 'Bhagavad Gita'. See Christopher Janaway, "The Cambridge Companion to Schopenhauer". Vivekanda, describes that this Vedantic book speaks of the world as we know it to consist of a turmoil of intense activity, but in the midst of it eternal (psychological?) calmness is possible caused by the balance of mind - the balance we should try to acquire. See Swami Vivekananda, "Jnana Yoga" (Almora: Advaita Ashrama Mayavati, 4th edition, 1930), p.293. One might say that a painting depicting an intense motion, is frozen motion (as the painting is not actually moving) and exemplifies 'eternal calmness'?

34 Arthur Schopenhauer, "The World as Will and Representation", quoted by Christopher Janaway, "Will and Nature", in Christopher Janaway, "The Cambridge Companion to Schopenhauer" (New York: Cambridge

ourselves that is exemplified or expressed in our own actions. This connection with Schopenhauer makes Cézanne's often quoted search in the landscape for 'his motive' so much more interesting.[35] It makes sense that, inspired by Schopenhauer, he knew he had to go into the landscape and look hard at nature's appearances to try to find the 'motives' of nature's actions and, thus, to find the motive of our own actions, of our own being. Because the translation from a mere philosophical concept into a visually perceptable concept (a painting) is not so simple, it also explains why he had to follow a road riddled with so many frustrating disappointments to come to find his culminating points in all objects, searching for a translation of the dynamism of harmony in nature into painting. Cézanne wished "... to lose myself in nature, grow again with nature, like nature, ..."[36] Compare this to the earlier quote by Schopenhauer![37]

It is no wonder an intelligent and serious artist like Charles Biederman, understanding what Cézanne accomplished, developed his own reliefs.[38]

I hope it is clear why I have brought up Cézanne. His particular interest in concentric vision and his understanding of this concept relates not only to the 19th century discussion on projective geometry and to Schopenhauer, but also exemplifies how artists searching to create artworks reflective of our perception of nature's changing dynamics cannot avoid creating a strong simulation of space/time (the process of continuous change in nature in fact causes space/time never to freeze, but to follow its path, creating

University Press, 1999), p.145. See Arthur Schopenhauer, "The World as Will and Representation", quoted by Christopher Janaway, "Will and Nature", in Christopher Janaway, "The Cambridge Companion to Schopenhauer", p.146: "What appears ... as plant, as mere vegetation, as blindly driving force (blind treibende Kraft), will be taken by us, according to its inner nature, to be will, and it will be recognized by us as the very thing which constitutes the basis of our own appearance, as it expresses itself in our actions."

35 In Joachim Gasquet's book on Cézanne we find many references to ideas described by Schopenhauer, including a reference to Schopenhauer himself by Cézanne (p.169), to statements like "everything is connected" (p.165), to Buddhist and Hindu ideas (p.160, p.169), etc. See Joachim Gasquet, "Cézanne - A memoir with Conversations", translated by Christopher Pemberton, preface by John Rewald, introduction by Richard Shiff (London: Thames and Hudson Ltd, 1991- orig. 1921). There is of course a slight but important difference between 'motive' and 'motif' (motive says more about the drive for an action while motif is more a subject of decorating) - as I am sure Cézanne meant it in a Schopenhauerian way, I stick to 'motive'. See chapter 8.2, footnote 33, for more on the difference between 'motif' and 'motive'.

36 See Joachim Gasquet, "Cézanne - A memoir with Conversations", p.168.

37 One may be tempted to also relate Cézanne's 'modulations' - his rhythmic repetitive use of certain sized colour patches, to Schopenhauer, because Schopenhauer described space and time as fragmented parts that by their systematic interrelations make being possible. To me this seems a bit too far fetched, because on one hand it is not clear how deeply Cézanne understood Schopenhauer and on the other hand, it is more natural he knew about Pointillism in painting, as was developed by the painter Seurat based on Chevreul's colour theories for the gobelin industries.

38 Biederman concluded that Cézanne's greatest accomplishment was the emphasis on the plane - meaning Cézanne's plane-like brushsstrokes. I do not completely agree, because in my opinion the discovery of how to depict the pulsating forces in the whole of nature in an amazing ordering and structuring of colour by Cézanne is a greater discovery. Without that aspect, painters like Kandinsky, Kupka, Delaunay, Malevitch, Matjushin, etc. would have had a hard time before finding this out. In Biederman's own art one can also find simulated motions that clearly show a similar complex composition of centrifugal and centrepetal motions like Cézanne already explored.

the steady 'stream' of space/time).[39] Our capacity to perceive change in nature every single moment and every day shows that space/time problematics are fundamental aspects of perception itself and not merely a problem for theoretical physics or a result of a pseudo-scientific interest of artists.

The major difference between art and reality is that art is a simulation - which is no fault, given the importance of illusion for our understanding of reality.[40] It might be interesting to briefly mention here that all artistic approaches to space/time concern a kind of frozen segment of space/time, involving the described simulation of change.[41] The interest seems to be that by focussing our attention on such a frozen simulation of change we unconsciously or more or less consciously sense the eternal processes of change in nature in which we are emerged. This deeply attentive sense leads to a brief forgetting of the self, a momentary forgetting of the time-schedules we live in, a virtual dissolution of the self in the whole of nature, a temporary intense union of the self with the world, dissolving the usual sense of duality. To really understand Cézanne's culminating points, Kandinsky's painting in front of the plane, Biederman's structure of nature, or so many examples from art we perceive as 'good', one must sense this experience onself. It is not so strange to draw a parallel between the experience of art and deep meditation. It is the intense experience of the sublime.

6.2 THE CONTINUUM

After a lot of interest during the 19th century in the continuum[42] as equivalent to duration and infinity, especially in the field of mathematics, at the start of the 20th century the continuum was considered important for the new ideas of space/time. As a subject, the continuum itself is an old topic. Already Aristotle showed an interest in the continuum, which he understood as a something that can be divided infinitely into even parts and the general structure of unlimited partiality and extension as space.[43] This

39 This is better reflected in Cézanne's own words: "There are some days when it seems to me that the universe is nothing but a continuous stream, a river of aerial reflections around the ideas of man." See Joachim Gasquet, "Paul Cézanne", Bernheim-Jeune, Paris, 1921, quoted in Charles Biederman, "The New Cézanne - From Monet to Mondriaan", p. 13. Cézanne here is obviously referring to the age old interest in the flow of nature as process and, therefore, of time (as Heraclitus said, or in Tao-philosophy has been stated). Cézanne was also interested in Buddhism, which might partly explain his desire to become one with nature, to become whole: "The great buddhist trick: nirvana, the consolation without passions, without stories: colors! The thing would be to absorb it, to let oneself flower here." See Joachim Gasquet, "Paul Cézanne", Bernheim-Jeune, Paris, 1921, quoted in Charles Biederman, "The New Cézanne - From Monet to Mondriaan", p.12.

40 See §5 for the discussion on 'pictorial illusionism'.

41 In my point of view, this can even be applied to kinetic art - art that involves real motion - because kinetic sculptures show a closed circle of motions and nature does not. This is something Leibniz already concluded (see earlier this chapter). See Frank Popper, "Licht-Kunst-Licht", exhibition catalogue (Eindhoven: Stedelijk Van Abbemuseum, 1966). See Frank Popper, "Origins and Development of Kinetic Art" (New York: New York Graphic Society, 1968 - orig. Studio Vista).

42 The continuum in general means a continuous and cohesive series involving only gradual changes, or a continuous unlimited cohesion in structure, motion and development in matter and thought. In philosophy the notion of a continuum led to a discussion about the confrontation between continuity and discontinuity of processes in nature. In science this confrontation is studied as processes of motion, change, stagnation, etc.

concept is also related to Euclid's definitions of the point, line and plane. Discussions on these subjects can be followed through history and can be connected to the discussion on Non-Euclidian geometry in the early 19th century. Non-Euclidian geometry in fact has been developed simultaneously by János Bolyai, Carl Friedrich Gauss and Nikolai Ivanovich Lobachevsky, and seeks a solution to the classical geometrical problem known as the parallel postulate.[44] This concerns the problem that in two-dimensional Euclidian geometry no definition and no clear proof can be formulated for the existence of two parallel lines: as they point towards infinity, they can never be found and thus can never be checked. You cannot find or show infinity, you can only point in its direction or simulate its concept. In Non-Euclidian geometry, the third dimension (depth) is included by projection onto a plane. This is obviously not literally true, because the projection still is studied on a two-dimensional plane - so it is the simulation of a third dimension that is used (visualized along a diagonal axis). Thus we speak of a projective geometry. Since Einstein's theories, we know that lines in space are in principle curved lines. Therefore, we currently speak of a hyperbolic geometry. Interest in the continuum in combination with Non-Euclidian geometry has stimulated interest in a better understanding of time.

Several philosophers have repeatedly warned about overestimating the notions, rules and definitions of mathematics and geometry. Mathematics and geometry are very useful tools, but neither can be found 'lying around' in nature itself. The danger is that in our thinking about subjects of reality we are tempted to allow mathematics and geometry to replace an actual perception of reality. Schopenhauer considered geometry a direct non-empirical perception of the parts of space, including its relationships. He viewed geometry as an intuitive sensing of space, distance and depth. He criticized playing around with precise definitions of geometry and the attempt to create and solve geometrical problems that are not actually problems.

Philosopher Henri Bergson, who influenced many early abstract artists, discussed the vortices and lines of force (and the field) as metaphors in physics, which are analyzed by philosophy because of their convenience as symbols for experiencing space and time.[45] He asks whether these symbols in our experience are so real and effective because they can be understood to be real in their own right:

Both in philosophy and in science the discussion about the continuum is linked to the discussion about evolution and progress. The continuum can be seen as the realm of multi-dimensional space/time that constitutes infinity and continuous change.

43 See Carl Friedrich von Weizsäcker, "Zeit und Wissen" (Munich and Vienna: Carl Hanser Verlag, 1992), p.151.

44 See Marvin Jay Greenberg, "Euclidian and Non-Euclidian Geometries - Development and History", (New York: W.H. Freeman and Co., third edition, 1994).

45 Henri Bergson influenced for instance the Futurists, and Frantisek Kupka, Wassily Kandinsky and Naum Gabo. Kandinsky even met Bergson. See Will Grohmann, "Über das Geistige in der Kunst - Erkenntnisse und Erfahrungen", in the exhibition catalogue Kunsthalle Tübingen, "Kandinsky - die Welt klingt - Hauptwerke aus dem Centre Georges Pompidou Paris" (Cologne: Du Mont Verlag, 1999), p.33. On the impact of Bergson on Kupka's ideas, including Kupka's familiarity with Bergson, see Pierre Brullé and Marketa Theinhardt,

"Could we, working with them, get back to experience, if the notions to which they correspond did not at least point out the direction in which we may seek for a representation of the real? Now the direction which they indicate is obvious; they show us, pervading concrete extensity, modifications, perturbations, changes of tension or of energy and nothing else. It is by this, above all, that they tend to unite with the purely psychological analysis of motion which we considered to begin with, an analysis which presented it to us not as a mere change of relation between objects to which it was, as it were, an accidental addition, but as true and, in some way, independent, reality."[46]

One can see how Bergson's questioning if vortices and lines of force could be seen as real notions in our thinking about real space and time must have inspired artists to explore these abstract notions in painting. It becomes even more obvious why artists became interested in exploring motion in space and time in the following extraordinary quotation from Bergson that almost reads like a directive on how to proceed for modern artists:

"In short, try first to connect together the discontinuous objects of daily experience;[47] *then resolve the motionless continuity of their qualities into vibrations on the spot;*[48] *finally, fix your attention on these movements, by abstracting from the divisible space which underlies them and considering only their mobility (that undivided act which our consciousness becomes aware of in our own movements):*[49] *you will thus obtain a vision of matter, fatiguing perhaps for your imagination, but pure, and freed from all that the exigencies of life compel you to add to it in external perception. Now bring back consciousness, and with it the exigencies of life: at long, very long, intervals, and by as many leaps over enormous periods of the inner history of things, quasi-instantaneous views will be taken, views which this time are bound to be pictorial, and of which more vivid colors will condense an infinity of elementary repetitions and changes.*[50] *In just the same way the multitudinous successive positions of a runner are contracted into a single symbolic attitude, which our eyes perceive, which art reproduces, and which becomes for us all the image of a man running."*[51]

"Trotz allem Malerei - Frantisek Kupka über die Schöpfung in der bildenden Kunst", in Dorothy Kosinski and Jaroslav Andel, "Frantisek Kupka - Die abstrakten Farben des Universums" (Ostfildern-Ruit: Verlag Gerd Hatje, 1997), p.155-156.

[46] See Henri Bergson, "Matter and Memory", translated by N.M. Paul and W.S. Palmer (New York: Zone Books, 5th edition, 1996 - orig. "Matière et mémoire", 1908 - written in 1896), p.201.

[47] Compare Pointillism, Impressionism, Cézanne or Cubism.

[48] Compare Monet, Van Gogh, Pointillism, Rayonism, Orphism.

[49] Compare Kupka, Kandinsky, Futurism, Suprematism, Van Doesburg's Elementarism.

[50] Compare Constructivism, Mondrian's Neo-Plasticism, Biederman's Structuralism, Lohse's interpretation of konkrete Kunst.

[51] See Henri Bergson, "Matter and Memory", p.208-209.

As an example that early pioneers of abstract art, comparable to Bergson, understood pictorial elements as singularities of force, interconnecting the various pictorial elements in a composition, Kandinsky wrote: "A composition is nothing other than an exact law-abiding organization of the vital forces which, in the form of tensions, are shut up within the elements."[52]

Studying the continuum, a discrepancy soon was discovered. Understanding the continuum merely as a constant arrow of time through eternal space became doubtful. The perception of a continuum with a constant direction and speed viewed by one observer from one particular point in space is a correct perception. But as soon as more than one observer is involved, the continuum is viewed very differently by observers who are standing at different locations in space. By the difference of their location, time will be differently interpreted by these observers. Here is a very simple example: someone who is born in a certain village, spends all his life there and hardly moves around, has a profoundly different notion of space/time than someone who continuously flies around the world experiencing many differences in time, culture and climate. Already this simple example illustrates how our notion of time is connected to the location of the observer in eternal space, obviously also influencing any opinion about the continuum. Needless to say, the observation of space/time might be an individual property, but in general space/time stays the same. As with many phenomena, there is a difference between what a phenomenon is in general and how the same phenomenon is perceived in particular.[53] Our position or localization in space is not absolute in relation to time, but is relative in relation to time![54] Hermann Minkowski was Albert Einstein's mathematics professor at the ETH Zürich, Switzerland. In 1908 Minkowski proposed understanding the separate notions of time and space as one and the same notion: space/time. We perceive reality especially because of the existence of light. This is why the sun as the source of all light, colour, warmth and energy, as the virtual source of life itself, has always been admired, honoured and pictured through all centuries and cultures.[55] Because light is so important to our perception, it is only logical that light has been a major topic of discussion in physics ever since Newton, and in philosophy since Euclid.[56] Because our vision

52 See Wassily Kandinsky, "Point and Line to Plane", translated by Howard Dearstyne and Hilla Rebay (New York: Dover Publications Inc, 1979 - orig."Punkt und Linie zu Fläche", 1926). Compare also further in this chapter remarks on Moholy-Nagy and Kemeny.

53 In principle, classical science studies the general while art studies the particular. A contemporary problem is that one had to conclude that we should combine both approaches to be able to understand reality better. This also is the result of the acknowledgement of various fields of science that one cannot study anything in perfect isolation anymore (the classical attitude to study something while assuming the rest stays more or less the same cannot be applied anymore).

54 In the 1990's film "Microcosm" about insect-life in a meadow, it is stated that the period we perceive as only one day is to insects a month, a month in our perception a season to the insects' perception, a season a life-time.

55 See Madanjeet Singh, "Die Sonne - Das Gestirn in der Kulturgeschichte", translated by Théresa-M. Bullinger (Tübingen, Berlin: Ernst Wasmuth Verlag and UNESCO, 1994 - orig. 1993).

56 Euclid wrote about light-rays projecting from one's eyes in his optical theory, the collision of these rays with an object would make this object perceptable to our eyes. Examples of light-emanating images of gods

depends entirely on light, unaided eyes cannot perceive anything quicker than the speed of light, and because this speed seemed to be the same for anyone anywhere, the speed of light became the constant in the discussion on space/time.

This discussion shows that the debate that followed focussed mainly on two aspects of space/time: the basic properties of light itself and the path through space/time. Einstein, for instance, proved in his Theory of General Relativity that the straight path of light becomes curved as the particles of light are influenced by the presence of matter and energy. They are attracted or repulsed by other particles (and on a larger scale in the universe by gravitational forces). Therefore, stars are not located where they appear to be, as the path of their light is distorted so many times before it reaches the eye's retina.[57]

It must be noted that Minkowski's and Einstein's theories concerned concepts of space/time at a certain moment in the continuum, meaning their concepts were metaphorically a kind of flat model of space/time. Though space/time is much more complex, let me propose, for the sake of clarity, we consider space/time continuously evolving in three-dimensional reality, allowing us to imagine the continuum as a three-dimensional tube. The scientific theories of Minkowski and Einstein focus merely on a thin two-dimensional slice of this tube. That is, they studied space/time when time was not changing or passing and three-dimensional space did not exist (a change of time brings forth space).[58] This clearly was a theoretical assumption and not based on perceiving space/time in everyday reality, but nevertheless, it was important for the attempt to understand the processes of space/time.

---

and holy persons one can find for instance in the Catholic, Hindu, Buddhist cultures. See Umberto Eco, "Art and Beauty in the Middle Ages", p.47: "The image of God as light had an ancient pedigree, from the Baal of Semantic paganism, from the Egyptian Ra, from the Persian Mazda - all personifications of the sun or of the sun's beneficent action - to the Platonic 'Sun' of the Ideal, the Good. This image passed on to neo-Platonism, Proclus in particular, and entered the Christian tradition through Augustine, and then through the Pseudo-Dionysius who constantly praised God as 'lumen', fire, or the fount of light. Yet another influence on later Scholastics was that of Arab pantheism - Avenpace, Hay ben Jodkam, Ibn Tofail - which passed on its visions of glittering essences of light, its ecstacies of brightness and beauty." Today we know of course that we see indeed because our eyes catch the light-rays colliding with objects, but the source of the light-rays are not our eyes, but the sun or a lamp.

57 See Nathan Cohen, "Gravity's Lens - Views of the new Cosmology" (Wisley Science Editions, 1989), on the phenomenon called 'gravitational lenses'. When we see a star at some place in the sky, this star in fact has moved already further some time ago. This means that we always look into the past when we look up at the sky. The mind boggling complexity becomes clear when one thinks a bit longer about the relationship of the distance of a star to one's eyes with the actual whereabouts of this star in space/time. It implies that when we look upwards into a starry sky, we look into many levels of history, because the deeper we look and the longer the distance between the star and our eyes, the longer ago that star was actually at the spot where we see it.

58 Because time obviously does change or pass, more complex space/time theories became necessary.

6.3 SPACE/TIME IN ART

The various aspects of space and time have always been present in art, because every human action involves space and time, especially when such action leaves some mark in a material or changes material into a certain shape, as in painting or sculpture. Conscious simulation of motion through space and time have been explored in art as long as mankind has existed; from rotation symbols, the bronzes and wall paintings of walking persons, fighting soldiers or equestrians in Antiquity, to the angles and mythical figures soaring through the skies in great Baroque ceiling paintings, the depictions of the great forces of sweeping seas and whipping clouds in nature in 19th century Romanticism, the strong simulations of changes of light in Impressionism, and the power of the sculptures of Auguste Rodin.[59] Both Cézanne and Rodin artistically (meaning, neither theoretically nor scientifically) explored the notion of duration of space/time in art and made the birth of abstract art seem a natural next step. Because here it is useless to attempt a complete historical review of the development of space/time in art, I will mainly focus on the relatively short period from 1910-1960, in which an extraordinarily intense discussion existed amongst artists exploring the artistic implications of Einstein's theories about space/time.

see pictures 1, 13, 14

In principle, Einstein's Theory of Relativity already proved that more than one path through space/time exists. Because of the distortions or curvatures of that path, it became conceivable that in simultaneous processes more speeds of the continuum are

[59] Auguste Rodin knew how to depict motion in a figure. He understood well how to make a static statue move in one's perception. The secret is to understand the difference with a photo. A photo expresses a frozen moment of a moving figure. This is unnatural, because in our perception we perceive an ongoing motion. Artists like Rodin have always known how to express an ongoing motion by not chosing to depict a frozen movement, but a combination of a sequence of motions. One can accomplish this by showing a striding figure instead of a figure with one foot actually lifted of the ground, the right tensions in the muscles of legs, arms, the slight turn of the body, the slightly turned head in one direction, the shoulders not level, the hips in opposite direction. Movement is shown not as a frozen single moment in space/time, but in fact as strong simulation of the transition from one attitude to another. See Paul Gsell, "Rodin on Art and Artists", translated by Mrs. Romily Fedden (New York: Dover Publications Inc., 1983), Chapter IV "Movement in Art". See the same book, p.92, Rodin describing the principles of movement in Greek sculpture (of Phidias) using a model he made himself: "My statuette offers, from head to feet, four planes which are alternatively opposed. The plane of the shoulders and chest leads towards the left shoulder - the plane of the lower half of the body leads towards the right side - the plane of the knees leads again towards the left knee, for the knee of the right leg, which is bent, comes ahead of the other - and finally, the foot of this same right leg is back of the left foot. So, I repeat, you can note four directions in my figure which produces a very gentle undulation through the whole body." Rodin in fact searched in sculpture for what Cézanne searched for in painting, namely, no 'l'impression' (see §2), but duration, which clearly is a property of space/time. One can experience a comparable artistic accomplishment in portrait-painting. Great portrait-painters have always understood that faces also slightly and often delicately change and move continuously. Therefore, it is no use to depict a single moment of someone's face (the reason why one can experience that a photo of someone is not like one knows that person), but to find a more or less timeless depiction - a picture showing how a particular person looked at a certain age, not at a fraction of a certain moment. Besides, it will be interesting to notice, that the above mentioned quotation of Rodin shows that principles of abstract art exploring space/time have always been present in figurative art (just consider how Rodin describes the change of directions and angles of the planes and compare this to paintings of Cubism and Suprematism).

possible and, as such, multiple histories could exist, each with a different time-schedule. Logic teaches that light following a straight path through time moves faster than light following a curved path, as the curve presents a detour. Research in modern quantumphysics has proven that this is an illusion.[60] It is interesting to note that Kandinsky, who had quite a serious interest in scientific ideas, considered curved lines originally to be straight lines that were put under horizontal pressure and had a different dynamic than straight lines.[61] Lesser known are the theories of a fourth dimension by the American mathematician C.H. Hinton published in 1904. Inspired by this book, another book on the fourth dimension was published by P.D. Ouspensky in Russia in 1909.[62] These ideas were studied by artists like the Russian painter and musician Matjushin. Also translated into Russian before 1910 were the ideas by Maurice Bucke, who discusses his analysis of time by using significant numbers.[63] Bucke also developed a theory on the perception of colours, in which he concluded that the real basic colours are red and black, which clearly influenced early abstraction in Russia.[64] In his magnus opus, "Tertium Organum - The Third Canon of Thought, A Key to the Enigmas of the

---

60 This astonishing research-result will be discussed later in this chapter.

61 See Wassily Kandinsky, "Point and Line to Plane", translated by Howard Dearstyne and Hilla Rebay (New York: Dover Publications Inc, 1979 - orig. "Punkt und Linie zu Fläche", 1926), p.79: "(The simple curved line) It is really a straight line which has been brought out of its course by constant sideward pressure - the greater was the pressure, the farther went the diversion from the straight line and, in the course of this, the greater became the outward tension and, finally, the tendency to close itself." And, Kandinsky writes, p.98: "The element of time, in general, is discernable in the line to a much greater extent than it was in the case of the point: length is a concept of time. On the other hand, the time required to follow a straight line is different from that required for a curved one, even when the lengths are the same; the more animated the curve becomes, the longer is the span of time it represents. Thus, the possibilities of using line as a time element are manifold. The application of time has a different inner colouration in horizontal and vertical lines, even if of equal lengths, and perhaps it is in reality a matter of different lengths which, at any rate, would be psychologically explainable. The time element in a purely linear composition must not, therefore, be overlooked and in the theory of composition it must be subjected to an exact examination". It may certainly have been that Kandinsky became aware of this concept by reading Vivekananda (see §2.2), whose lectures were translated into Russian and read by Kandinsky. Vivekananda said in a lecture delivered in the USA, probably in 1896, see Swami Vivekananda, "Jnana-Yoga" (Almara: Advaita Ashrama, Mayavati, 4th edition 1930), p.218: "There is no motion in a straight line. Everything moves in a circle; a straight line, infinitely produced, becomes a circle." This is based on Vedantic philosophy that in the end everything moves in circles.

62 C.H. Hinton, "The New Era of Thought"(1888), "The Fourth Dimension" (1904). These were translated into Russian in 1915. P.D. Ouspensky had used Hinton's ideas in his own publication "The Fourth Dimension"(1909) and in "Tertium Organum - The Third Canon of Thought, A Key to the Enigmas of the World"(1912). See Patricia Railing, "On Suprematism - 34 Drawings" (Forest Row, UK: Artists Bookworks, 1990), p.8, 9. Rodchenko had a copy of the Russian edition of 1917 of Hinton's publications in his library. See Alexander Lavrentiev, in "Alexander Rodchenko - Spatial Constructions" (Cologne: Galerie Gmurzynska, with Hatje-Cantz Verlag, 2002), p.27.

63 Number can be defined as a unit belonging to a numerical system and subject to its laws. Significant numbers are numbers that have a specific meaning. In case of a rounded number one reduces the numbers to those that provide sufficient information, these numbers are considered 'significant'. It will be of no surprise that theories exist about certain 'significant numbers' being symbols with a mystical or secret meaning. See, for instance, Daniel Tyradellis, Michal S. Friedlander, "10 + 5 = Gott - Die Macht der Zeichen" (Cologne: DuMont Literatur und Kunst Verlag, Jüdisches Museum Berlin, 2004).

64 See Maurice Bucke, "Cosmic Consciousness", originally published in 1905, in Patricia Railing, "From

World", 1912, Ouspensky discusses scientific, religious, philosophical and artistic subjects, such as theories about space and time in 19th century science.[65] He also discusses the books by Hinton, four dimensional space, the ether, perception, language (of humans and animals), the new physics by Minkowski and Einstein, infinity, a great variety of occult concepts, theosophy and the cosmic consciousness by Bucke. Ouspensky believed the cosmic consciousness was the highest level (the fourth level in his theory) of development, from which we also perceive four dimensional space, higher emotions and, finally, self-consciousness. He was quite popular amongst early abstract artists, especially in Russia and Poland, but also amongst later generations of artists. Mathematician and poet Velimir Khlebnikov[66] and the painters Kasimir Malevitch and Michael Matjushin,[67] also studied and published about the continuum, Non-Euclidian geometry and the fourth dimension at the beginning of the 20th century. Malevitch, inspired to appreciate the importance of space and time by the theories of the Futurists and especially informed by Ouspensky, considered the planes or masses on his canvas as pure 'force forms'. He understood colour as pure energy, and therefore, as an important element in itself to explore space and time. Malevitch compares the analoguous property of colour as pigment to the wave/particle duality of light: colour in painting also consists both of matter - we can pick up the pigment with a brush - and lightwaves - we perceive colour in painting by receiving the reflected lightwaves. Malevitch wrote: "The form of suprematism consists of constructing various forces as colours and it is painted by material; it therefore contains a multitude of moving states."[68]

There seems to be a general consensus that the Cubists Pablo Picasso and Georges Braque were the first artists to translate ideas about space and time into painting. But it

Science to Systems of Art - On Russian Abstract Art and Language 1910 - 1920 and other essays" (Forest Row, UK: Artists Bookworks, 1989), p.29. Bucke considered the evolution of language to be a reflection of the evolution of consciousness, an idea also to be applied to our perception of colours. He constructed a colour theory based on the wave-length theory of colour, implying that red and black are the real primary colours. The influence of this theory one can see oneself in the clear preference of so many early abstract painters, especially in Russia, for the colours red and black. Later these became also the major colours of graphic design (as we would see red and black first, meaning, in already very poor light, the contrast between these colours function best for signs; a knowledge applied today for road-signs). The Nazis clearly took their strong red-black signs directly from this development.

[65] See P.D. Ouspensky, "Tertium Organum - The Third Canon of Thought, A Key to the Enigmas of the World". Ouspensky was a student of Gurdjieff, and published in 1913 "Iskaniia novoi zhizni: Chto takoe Ioga" ("Search for the new life: What Yoga is"), discussing the various Yoga schools. See Charlotte Douglas, "Beyond Reason: Malevitch, Matjushin, and their circles", in Maurice Tuchman, "The Spiritual in Art: Abstract Painting 1890-1985" (New York: Abbeville Publishers, 1986), p.187.

[66] Khlebnikov studied at the same university where Lobachevsky, one of the discoverers of projective geometry, taught a century earlier. In a letter Khlebnikov mentioned to prefer the Lobachevsky Jubilee collection of essays published by The Mathematical Society of Kazan. See Railing, "On Suprematism - 34 Drawings" (Forest Row, UK: Artists Bookworks, 1990), p.13. Khlebnikov, inspired by analyzing Malevitch's first suprematist compositions, wrote "The Head of the Universe, Time in Space" in 1919.

[67] Matjushin introduced the fourth dimension into Russian artistic thinking. See Alla Powelichina, "Michael Matjushin - Die Welt als organisches Ganzes", in Heinrich Klotz, "Matjuschin und die Leningrader Avantgarde" (Stuttgart-Munich: Oktogon Verlag, 1991), p.30.

[68] See Railing, "On Suprematism - 34 Drawings", p.28.

seems instead that there was a more general interest by many people - including other artists - between 1905-1910 in the possible implications of the revolutionary ideas about space and time. Although Picasso and Braque definitely were inspired by discussions about space and time, there is not much evidence for how deeply their understanding reached. There is a lot of evidence available that they were involved in discussions about space and time and the fourth dimension, which resulted in their focus on painting objects fragmented and seen from different angles at once.[69] Much clearer evidence for how artists tried to explore this highly abstract subject can be first found with Italian, Russian, Hungarian and Polish artists, followed by abstract working artists all through Europe. All of these artists were very well informed about what was going on in France. One should not forget that a kind of artistic isolation or separation only existed during the Cold War, which was much later.

Quite an extraordinary example was the Russian artist Naum Gabo, who studied a diverse variety of subjects from 1910-1914 in Munich, including physics with Wilhelm Röntgen, the discoverer of X-rays (1895), and later with Gustav Herz. Gabo attended physics lectures on Einstein's theory in 1911 or 1912 and wrote: "Einstein's principle was discussed among the dons, among the professors, and among the students."[70] Matjushin, as early as 1911, worked on the fourth dimension and developed his Theory of Extended Vision (SORWED), based on the continuum.[71] Matjushin understood SORWED to contain and connect both Occidental logic and rationality with Oriental a-logical wisdom. His concept of perception as 360° vision can be translated as an attempt to make possible the comprehension of no-thingness or 'sunyata'.[72]

see pictures
5, 22

The combination of logical reasoning with a non-verbal understanding of reality

---

[69] For an eloquant discussion on this subject concerning Picasso, Braque and their scene, see Arthur I. Miller, "Einstein, Picasso - Space, Time, and the Beauty That Causes Havoc" (New York: Basic Books, 2001). See especially §5. The mathematician Maurice Princet was a participant in the Montmartre art scene in 1907 and following years. Miller discusses Princet's crucial role in explaining in café's new theories to many artists, like the fourth dimension. Miller mentions as sources for Princet: Poincaré's "La Science et l'Hypothèse"(1902) and Esprit Jouffret's "Traité élémentaire de géometrie à quattre dimensions"(1903). Besides, Miller describes that around 1905 there were popularized publications in newspapers and journals on these new scientific and on new technological discoveries (like X-rays and new atom-theories) available to a larger public.

[70] See Martin Hammer and Christina Lodder, "Constructing Modernity - The Art & Career of Naum Gabo"(New Haven and London: Yale University Press, 2000), p.471, note 113. Gabo probably has attended a colloquium organized by physics professor Arnold Sommerfeld, who was one of the first supporters of Einstein's theory and who lectured on the subject 1908-1909 and in a seminar in 1911. See also §3.

[71] In his "Studies of Experience of the Fourth Dimension", Matjushin based his ideas on Lobachevsky, Riemann, Minkowski, Gauss and Hinton; and he published with Jelena Guro as early as 1913 their "The Sense for the Fourth Dimension". See §5.2 on Matjushin's "SORWED".

[72] Matjushin did actually study Yoga-concepts. See Charlotte Douglas, "Beyond Reason: Malevitch, Matjushin, and their circles", in Maurice Tuchman, "The Spiritual in Art: Abstract Painting 1890-1985" p.186-187. Vivekananda distinguishes in the lecture "The Cosmos - The Microcosm" the eyes from "the real organ of vision". He understands the eyes to be merely "the instruments of vision" and the brain the real organ. On top of this he adds the presence of the mind to be decisive for actual perception. This lecture was delivered in New York, 26 January 1896. See Swami Vivekananda "Jnana-Yoga" p.196, p.197: "The mind, too, is only the carrier; it has to carry the sensation still forward, and present it to the intellect. The intellect is the determining

seems to have grown in popularity in both art and science, especially in the past decades, leading to a revival of interest in Oriental thought, including Tibetan Buddhism, Taoism or Zen. One can find more early abstract artists with an interest in space/time and the essence of movement in Analytical Cubism and in some paintings in Synthetic Cubism, Orphism, Rayonism and Futurism - later also in the De Stijl. Some say Cubism started in 1907 when Picasso painted "Les Demoiselles d'Avignon". Recently, it is more widely believed that a group of other artists between 1900-1910 moved from traditional painting towards Cubism.[73] One also knows now that the terms Analytical and Synthetic Cubism were invented afterwards to explain the development of Picasso and Braque, ignoring the variety of Cubist developments visible in the works of the other artists.[74]

In 1912 the theoretical manifesto on Cubism was published by the artists Albert Gleizes and Jean Metzinger. This manifesto was translated into Russian and published by Matjushin in Russia in 1913. Gleizes and Metzinger write: "A painting carries within itself its raison d'être .... It does not harmonize with this or that ensemble, it harmonizes with the totality of things, with the universe: it is an organism."[75] Illustrating their interest in non-Euclidian geometry, they continue: "If we wished to tie the painter's space to a particular geometry, we should have to study, at some length, certain of Riemann's theorems."[76] Finally, demonstrating some knowledge of space/time notions: "In short, the science of design consists in instituting relations between straight lines and curves. A picture which contained only straight lines or curves would not express existence."[77]

faculty and decides upon what is brought to it. Still this is not sufficient. The intellect must carry it forward, and present the whole thing before the ruler in the body, the human soul, the king on the throne." Vivekananda adds that in Hindu philosophy the (physical) instruments are part of the external body, while the mind and intellect are part of the 'finer body' (comparable to 'spiritual body' in Christianity). Besides, the soul is considered to be eternal, therefore part of 'sunyata', while the body is not (hence, reincarnation). Chinese philosopher Wu Ching-Hsiung writes on (Chinese) Zen, see John C.H. Wu (= Wu Ching-Hsuing), "The Golden Age of Zen, introduction by Thomas Merton (New York, London, Toronto, Sydney, Auckland: Image Books Doubleday, 1996 - orig. 1967), p.30: "Realizing that what is expressible in words, colors, and sounds must always fall short of reality, the Chinese spirit finds its home in what is beyond words, colors, and sounds. It uses words to evoke the indefinable, sounds to evoke silence, and colors to evoke the formless Void." Compare the discussion of 'sunyata' in §2.2.

73 Robert Delaunay, Albert Gleizes, Henri Le Fauconnier, Jean Metzinger.

74 See Fritz Metzinger, "Introduction", in "Albert Gleizes/Jean Metzinger - Du'Cubisme'/On'Cubism'/Über den'Kubismus' ", translated by Fritz Metzinger (Frankfurt: R.G. Fischer Verlag, 1993 - orig. 1912). Analytical Cubism is considered the first stage of development of Cubism, initiated around 1908 by Braque and Picasso with paintings in which all forms in a still-life or portrait are translated into cubic shapes (after Cézanne), after which these cubes are dissolved into planes of tonal colour (allowing these forms or portraits to became one with space). Important and clearly recognizable properties of Analytical Cubism were linear structuring, play with illusion by inserting very realistic fragments into quite abstract compositions (like parts of newspapers) and the use of browns and greys, disregarding the importance of colour. The next stage of Cubism was Synthetic Cubism, starting around 1912, in which no existing subject or object was the theme, instead all available plastic means were composed in a kind of collage-style. This movement included Juan Gris.

75 See Fritz Metzinger, "Albert Gleizes/Jean Metzinger - Du'Cubisme'/On'Cubism'/Über den'Kubismus' ", p.81.

76 Ibid. p.84.

77 Ibid., p.86.

Albert Gleizes developed a method of transforming and rotating planes, allowing him to create highly complex compositions simulating simultaneous movements. He accomplished this in 1922, as a result of his renewed interest in modern science. This coincides with the popularizing of Einsteins' theories in France, for instance, by French mathematician Charles Henry, whom Gleizes knew. Henry was especially interested in extending Einstein's description of the role of the observer to include aesthetics.[78]

One of the greatest pioneers of early abstract art, Frantisek Kupka, is also quite probably one of the very first artists who was most serious about the relationship between art and science.[79] Kupka published his main theories in "Tvoreni v umeni vyvarném" ("The creation in fine art") in 1923.[80] He advised every artist to study science, especially physiology and biology and execute some research through the microscope. Kupka understood

---

78 See Peter Brooke, "Albert Gleizes - For and Against the Twentieth Century" (New Haven and London: Yale University Press, 2001), p.95: "In december 1922, the French mathematician Charles Henry, ..., published an account of the theory of relativity in which he suggested that Einstein had not taken sufficient account of the point of view of the observer. He was, Henry argued, treating the phenomena he describes as if they could be known independently of the operation of the senses. Earlier in the same year, Henry published a series of articles under the general title 'La Lumière, la couleur et la forme' in Ozenfant and Jeanneret's journal, 'L'Esprit nouveau'. Henry's interest in aesthetic questions derived from his conviction that since the world could only be known through 'representations' in the mind, any attempt to express reality mathematically must take account of the human sensibility. Physics must become 'psycho-physics' and must be prepared to consider the aesthetic sense - whether phenomena are pleasing or displeasing. Henry used the terms 'rhythmic' and 'non-rhythmic', in relation to pleasing and displeasing, giving them a very precise meaning that is of great interest to the long-term development of Gleizes's thought. Gleizes had known Henry since 1920 or 1921,..." They had numerous discussions on collaborating until Charles Henry died in 1926. Gleizes published an article in hommage to Henry in the journal 'Les Cahiers de l'étoile', 1930. Charles Henry lived 1859-1926. In the late 19th century Henry had influenced 'Pointillism'. See §7, footnote 50. On Gleizes, see also Rudolf Indlekofer, "Albert Gleizes et le Cubisme/und der Kubismus/and Cubism", with introduction by Jean Chevalier (Basel, Stuttgart: Basilius Presse, 1962).

79 Kupka (1871-1957) grew up in East Bohemia. He became a spiritual medium for some time, earned a living by making illustrations, lived some time in Vienna but got fed up with all the exaggerated and highly trendy interests in the spiritual, the occult and the negative. In 1898 he moved to Paris, where again many were interested in the occult. In 1905 he started to be seriously interested in science and technology. At the Sorbonne University he took courses in physics, biology and physiology, and he worked as assistant in a biological laboratory at the university. His favorite quote is "Man is nature, conscious of its self" ("L'homme est la nature prenant consience d'elle-même") from Elisée Reclus, 1905 - Kupka was commissioned to make the illustrations of Reclus' "L'Homme et la terre". See Ludmilla Vachtová, "Frantisek Kupka", (Prague: Odeon, 1968). See Thomas M. Messer, "Frantisek Kupka 1871-1957 A Retrospective" (New York: The Solomon R. Guggenheim Museum, 1975). See Dorothy Kosinkski and Jaroslav Andel, "Frantisek Kupka - Die abstrakten Farben des Universums" (Ostfildern-Ruit, Germany: Verlag Gerd Hatje, 1997 - also available in English). See Konrad Oberhuber, Christoph Vitali, "Two Pioneers of Modern Art I - Frantisek Kupka, from the Jan and Meda Mladek Collection" (Vienna-Prague-Munich: Graphische Sammlung Albertina Wien, Haus der Kunst München, Ceske Muzeum Vytvarnych Umeni, 1996). See Arnauld Pierre, "Frank Kupka - In White and Black", facsimile reprints of 'Abstractions' 1933/48 and "Four Stories of White and Black" 1926, introduction by Arnauld Pierre (Liverpool: Liverpool University Press and Artists Bookworks, 1998). See Bruno Racine, Alfred Pacquement, "Frantisek Kupka - 1871-1957, Eine Retrospektive", Centre Pompidou, Kunstmuseum Liechtenstein, (Ostfildern-Ruit: Hatje Cantz Verlag, 2003).

80 Published by SVU Mánes, in Prague. For a complete German translation, see Noemi Smolik, "Frantisek Kupka - Die Schöpfung in der bildenden Kunst" (Ostfildern-Ruit: Hatje Cantz Verlag 2001). In this publication he refers to several scientific publications, like William Nicatti, "La psychologie naturelle", Louis

nature as a continuously changing process of becoming, both at macro and micro-levels. As an example, he used the perception of space that, in his opinion, is a process of reconstructing a whole image out of fragments of space and time. Though everything is continuously changing, we can perceive nature as a large whole, because of the organic character of everything, including ourselves. Kupka wrote:

> *"When we consider for instance microscopic observations, we find, that every living matter moves; in a hand that for a moment does not seem to move, blood is circulated from one cell to another, the molecules orbit around each other, the vibrating air cannot leave the surface unmoved, everything is different as it appears to our uneducated eyes."*[81]

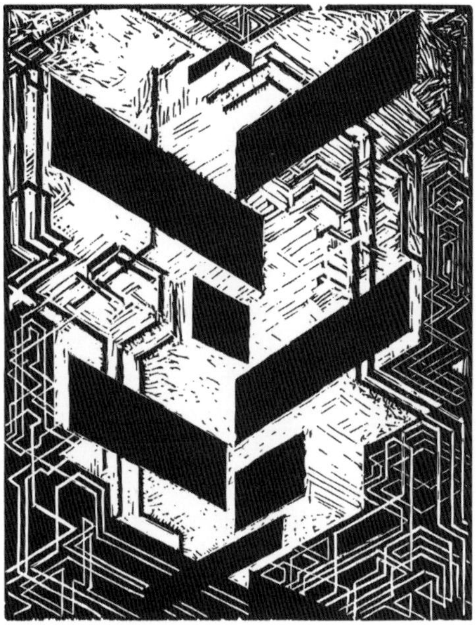

10. Frantisek Kupka (1871-1957)
From **Four Stories of White & Black** 1926
Woodcut, ca 28 x 28 cm (11 x 11 inches)
©) c/o Beeldrecht Amsterdam 2004

Considering visualization of the notion of time impossible in art, Kupka concluded that space would be the domain of fine art and time would be the domain of music.[82] This is interesting, because in his own paintings space is simulated and his compositions look wonderfully dynamic. So why accept the illusion of space but not of time?

Some of Kupka's major paintings have been connected to the Orphism of Delaunay - they have even been understood as copies after Delaunay, although Kupka made them earlier and based them on classic Orphism.[83] Orphism, in the more popular version in

see picture 21

Foucault, "Étude optique de surface", the number theory of Henri Poincaré, and refers to the theories of his day about space/time and the fourth dimension.

81 Published in his major book, quoted by Pierre Brullé and Marketa Theinhardt, "Trotz allem Malerei - Frantisek Kupka über die Schöpfung in der bildenden Kunst", in Dorothy Kosinkski and Jaroslav Andel, "Frantisek Kupka - Die abstrakten Farben des Universums", p.159: "Wenn wir z.B. von mikroskopischen Beobachtungen ausgehen, stellen wir fest, daß jegliche lebende Materie sich bewegt; in einer Hand, die für einen Moment unbewegt erscheint, zirkuliert das Blut von einer Zelle zur anderen, die Moleküle umkreisen sich, die vibrierende Luft kann die Oberfläche nicht unbewegt lassen, alles ist anders als es unserem ungeschulten Auge erscheint."

82 See Pierre Brullé and Marketa Theinhardt, "Trotz allem Malerei - Frantisek Kupka über die Schöpfung in der bildenden Kunst", in Dorothy Kosinkski and Jaroslav Andel, "Frantisek Kupka - Die abstrakten Farben des Universums", p.159: "The fine arts are a narative of forms in space, time here is impossible ... To define a rule, we may say, that the domain of music is time and the one for fine arts is space." ("Die bildenden Künste sind eine Narration der Formen im Raum, die Zeit is hier ausgeschlossen ... Um eine Regel aufzustellen, können wir sagen, daß die Domäne der Musik in der Zeit ist, die der bildenden Künste im Raum.").

83 Especially Kupka's "Amorpha"-series from 1912, the couple of "The Newtonian Discs" paintings from 1911/12, and the glorious "Form of Yellow, Notre Dame" from 1911. Dorothy Kosinkski and Jaroslav Andel, "Frantisek Kupka - Die abstrakten Farben des Universums", p 182. This is one of those sad stories in art

modern art, began around 1912. Robert Delaunay explored the principle of simultaneous contrast by Chevreul, in almost entirely abstract pictures that he expected to cause experiences of rhythm and vibrations in the perception of the beholder. His friend, the poet Guillaume Apollinaire, named this style 'Orphism', inspired by his own new publication of poems about the Greek mythological figure Orpheus. Apollinaire thought Orphism combined colour and light, while Kupka was more concerned with the creative forces of nature.

Chevreul was the Director of Dyes, of the famous and royal gobelin-tapestry factory in France. He researched the improvement of the quality and sustainability of the brightness of the colour dyes for the textiles his industry used.[84] One can imagine he must have searched for a method that would allow the smallest amount of different basic colours to still manufacture tapestries with complex coloured images. This is comparable to how one makes full colour reproductions in the printing industries using only yellow, magenta, cyan and black. Such a method would undoubtedly make the production of the gobelin much cheaper, because the fewest differently dyed textiles would be needed. This would help explain how Chevreul's research for the gobelin-tapestry industry also inspired the Impressionists, Seurat and Signac, to develop their technique of Pointillism, which later became paintings swirling with colourmotions.[85]

Focussing entirely on the phenomenon of light-rays, Rayonism was a movement inspired by the discovery of X-rays in 1895 by Röntgen, by the theories of the mathe-

---

history in which one artist came to be better known than the other, though the artistic accomplishment of the lesser known artist just seems better. Apollinaire described Delaunay's Orphism as pure expression of colour and light. Kupka's concept of Orphism reached deeper. He was very intrigued by the interpretation of Orphism by Lucien Dhuys, who applied the strong influence of archaic spiritual traditions to Aeschylus' trilogy, including the myth of Prometheus (the sculptor who fell in love with the statue of the girl he created himself, which was brough alive by divine decision). Kupka's fascination was clearly in the artist's transformation of dead into live matter, by adding or projecting some of his own energies into the work of art (comparable to a musician bringing sound to live playing a 'dead' instrument). Kupka thus interprets Schopenhauer's important concept of the motive (see earlier this chapter, see chapter 8 footnote 33). One of the essays in Kupka's book from 1923 is about "The Motive". See Noemi Smolik, "Frantisek Kupka - Die Schöpfung in der bildenden Kunst", "Das Motiv", p. 29-45. The other two themes of classic Orphism are: wholeness of nature and Eros. See also §7. Kupka consciously understood the powers of colour to develop a visual language analogous to music. For more on the origin and differences between Kupka and Delaunay about Orphism, see Arnauld Pierre, "Orphism to Construction", in his "Frantisek Kupka - In White and Black", Facsimile Reprints of "Abstractions" 1933/48, "Four Stories of White and Black" 1926 (Liverpool: Liverpool University Press and Artists Bookworks, 1998).

[84] Chevreul, 1786-1889, was a trained chemist, who published hundreds of books and articles. See Faber Birren, "The Principle of Harmony and Contrast of Colors and their Application to the Arts - M.E. Chevreul", newly revised edition with essay by Faber Birren (London: Schiffer Publishing, Ltd, 1987 - orig. 1854).

[85] Pointillism means painting fields of little dots of a small selection of different pure colours that optically are mixed in our vision, comparable to the pixels in the graphic industries or tv - technology. It was meant to repeat all colours everywhere on the canvas to enhance a sense of harmony. See Robert L. Herbert, "Seurat - Drawings and Paintings" (New Haven and London: Yale University Press, 2001). See Marina Ferretti-Bocquillon, Anne Distel, John Leighton, and Susan Alyson Stein, "Signac 1863-1935", catalogue by the Metropolitan Museum of Art (New Haven and London: Yale University Press, 2001), p.10, Signac wrote: "All

maticians Arthur Cayley and Felix Klein, the theories of physicist/philosopher Ernst Mach and later by Einstein's Theory of Relativity.[86] Rayonism started around 1911 and stated that we perceive everything around us by the linear paths of light that travel from our eyes outwards to scan objects and are crossed by the linear paths of reflecting light by all other objects around us. The idea of light rays projecting from our eyes outwards seems to mirror Euclids' theory of optics. The concept of painted straight lines from and to objects also seems to substantiate Cézanne's theory of concentric vision and clearly relates to Italian Futurism. Futurism, at first only a literary concept in 1908, proclaimed the destruction of all historical evidence of culture (like libraries, museums, academies, etc.) and focused on the beauties of revolution, and the speed and dynamism of modern technology. Futurists believed these ideals had the 'cleansing' effect and dynamism, of which the modern war-machine would be the greatest manifestation.[87]

De Stijl was founded in 1917 by Theo van Doesburg, who studied possibilities of translating the notion of a fourth dimension into a new architectural concept. The Dutch artist Joost Baljeu wrote about Van Doesburg:

that is involved consists of four or five precepts enunciated by Chevreul which elementary school pupils should know." The fragmentation in colour quantities similar in size as invented by Seurat, was further explored and extended by Signac. Signac also made this approach a popular trend in many countries in Europe (Belgium, Holland, Germany, Switzerland, England). It led to painting with similar colour-patches (a bit like Cézanne already had done) in a more free painterly style than Seurat. Examples of such a further development after Pointillism are, for instance, the works of the formative years of the Fauvists, Cubists, Futurists, German Expressionists, but also of Kandinsky, Kupka and Mondrian. In principle, Mondrian stayed loyal to the basic concept of Signac of uniting very fragmented parts of colour into one harmonious whole. For an outstanding study, see Erich Franz, "Farben des Lichts - Paul Signac und der Beginn der Moderne von Matisse bis Mondrian" (Edition Tertium, 1996). The unprecedented brightness of colour, accomplished in Pointillism by the careful combination of small fragments of highly contrasting colours was furthered by the Fauves - like Derrain, young Matisse, Braque, and Kandinsky. Signac emphasized that Pointillism is not a mere fragmentation of colours into small units, but a fragmentation in a certain specific way, based on colour contrasts. Therefore, Signac prefered the name 'Chromoluminarism'. See Walter Hess, "Das Problem der Farbe - in den Selbstzeugnissen der Maler von Cézanne bis Mondrian" (Munich: Mäander Verlag GmbH, 1993 - orig. 1953), p.18.

86 The Russian painters Larionov and Gontcharowa were the key-figures of Rayonism. The discovery of "X"rays showed that matter did not actually exist. This obviously made new concepts of perception of space - and thus of time - necessary. One could expect that some artists understood this would imply also a new concept of painting reality. Thus it is hardly surprising that the popularization of "X"rays has inspired the use of overlapping shapes that seems transparent in Rayonism, Cubism, Futurism. See Marlene Lauter, Beate Reese, "FormSchichten - FarbStrahlen, Aspekte russischer und osteuropäischer Kunst - Eine Ausstellung aus Anlaß des Jubiläums '100 Jahre Röntgenstrahlen' ". See Dorothy Kosinkski and Jaroslav Andel, "Frantisek Kupka - Die abstrakten Farben des Universums", p.74. Going deeper, including the news on the atomic model (Rutherford) and its implications for seeing reality on top of what "X"rays had shown, Kandinsky "... wrote in "Reminiscences" how the division of the atom had seemed to destroy the whole basis on which science was founded. Later he was to see that what happened was that science had abandoned positivism for a theoretical position which it was quite possible to reconcile with his own spiritual values." See Paul Overy, "Kandinsky - The language of the eye" (London: Elek Books Ltd, 1969), p.50.

87 Futurism was inspired by the philosophies of Bergson and Nietzsche. Futurism's proponents in painting were Marinetti, Boccioni, Carrà, Russolo, Severini, Balla. Boccioni published his writings of 1913 in 1914 as "Plastic Dynamism", emphasizing the importance of motion as derived from 19th century theories of electricity like in the notion of lines of force. For more on Futurism, see §8.1.

"Van Doesburg was attempting to restore the element of the fourth dimension stemming from Analytical Cubism with its overlapping of various points of view in space which then interpenetrate one another by using interacting lines, thus suggesting the interpenetration of open plane areas, or 'open' planes." [88]

Van Doesburg understood the fourth dimension could best be studied and applied in architecture.[89] The bases for his architectural concepts were formed by three-dimensional crosses called tesseracts.[90] These are conceived as plastic forms that indicate a combination of centripetal and centrifugal movements. Van Doesburg wrote,

"The new architecture calculates not only with space but also with time as an architectural value. The unity of space and time will give architectural form a new and completely plastic aspect, that is, a four-dimensional, plastic space-time aspect."[91]

A year later, El Lissitzky, who was friends with Van Doesburg, wrote,

"Time now becomes a factor of prime consideration as a new constituent of plastic F. In the studios of modern artists it is believed that space and time can be formed into a direct unity, and therefore that they can replace each other. Space and time are different in kind. Space in our physical science is three-dimensional. In time, however, one cannot wander into depth, height, breadth; time is one-dimensional. We differentiate between three-dimensional, physical space and the multi-dimensional mathematical spaces. There is but one time, both in physics and in mathematics. We know no space outside of objects and no objects outside of space. To form space means to form objects. Objects can be resolved into elements. Time is constant, it cannot be decomposed into elements. Space factors are ***divergent****, time factors are* ***sequential****. This we must grasp clearly."*[92]

The artists mentioned so far in this chapter experimented with presenting the fourth dimension by simulating change of localization in their composition, inspired by ideas from philosophy and science. One can simulate change of localization in a two or three-dimensional visualization by using a set of similar elements or units (Van Doesburg referred to these units as 'cells'). When the units are put on a line and are similar in size, shape and colour, already some motion is suggested. This is enhanced when they vary greatly in position, size, shape and colour. Another possibility is to draw a line after an

---

88 See Joost Baljeu, "Theo van Doesburg" (Studio Vista, 1974), p.31-32. See Ad Petersen, "De Stijl", parts 1+2, the complete reprint (Amsterdam: Athenaeum, Bert Bakker, Polak & Van Gennep, 1968.

89 Compare to the ideas of for instance Strzeminksi and Kobro, later in this chapter.

90 See Joost Baljeu, "Theo van Doesburg", p.75 + 145.

91 Theo van Doesburg, "Towards Plastic Architecture" (1924), in Joost Baljeu, "Theo van Doesburg", p.144.

92 El Lissitzky, "A. and Pangeometry" 1925, in Sophie Lissitzky-Küppers, Herbert Read, "El Lissitzky - Life-Letters-Texts" (London: Thames and Hudson, 1992 - orig. Dresden: Verlag der Kunst, 1967), p. 355. With "F." El Lissitzky meant Form.

object. This is based on a simple optical effect: when you draw a point, this will not simulate motion, but as soon as you draw a line starting from this point the line will provide you with the simulation that the point is moving (or, that the picture shows a frozen moment of motion). This phenomenon is familiar from comics. You can also study this phenomenon while looking at the stills of a film. When an object moves through space it changes position, when it retreats from us it seems to change in size.[93] Obviously, working in three dimensions offers more dynamic possibilities, although in a two-dimensional picture the absence of gravitational forces can be simulated, while in three dimensions it cannot. One can see in many artworks how artists have applied these methods to simulate space/time.

Coinciding with the general interest in his day in the organic, Van Doesburg translated his interest in cells and the fourth dimension into an interest in artistic principles of growth.[94] Van Doesburg's own concept was best accomplished in the study-model 'Maison d'Artiste', Paris 1923, a co-operation with the young architect Cornelis van Eesteren. This exciting model is probably one of the first architectural models using separate modules for every single room and combining these by stacking them in a rotational motion around a vertical staircase.[95] The boxes of the room-modules of the Maison d'Artiste are visually dissolved by extending balcony-roofs and painting rectangles on their sides in contrasting colours, allowing a dynamic play of vertical and horizontal lines, suggesting a continuous motion in space/time. This stands in contrast to the opinion of Piet Mondrian, who (like Kupka) thought it was impossible to process time as an aspect into art.[96]

The fabulous and famous Rietveld-Schröder House shows similar properties, clearly

---

[93] Sometimes it seems to change in shape or colour. Something near seems brighter in colour and its shapes more detailed and sharp.

[94] Comparable to these artistic interpretations of growth, philosopher John Dewey wrote, see John Dewey, "Art as Experience" (New York: Perigee Books, 1980 - orig. 1934), p.23: "Time as organization in change is growth, and growth signifies that a varied series of change enters upon intervals of pause and rest; of completions that become the initial points of new processes of development." See also §3. On some more interpretations of growth in constructive art, see also §4 on Biederman, and see §11.

[95] Dutch artist Joost Baljeu furthered in the 1950-1980's Van Doesburg's ideas, while also referring to cells and growth as properties of the fourth dimension. In the 1960's architects were inspired by new democratic and social incentives and focussed on architectural concepts based on modules that could be produced in serial production (the architectural equivalent to Minimal Art?). This so-called 'pre-fab' architecture was created by architects like Moshe Safdie, R. Dietrich, Arato Isozaki, Wolfgang Döring, Yona Friedman, Kisho Kurokawa. See Heinrich Klotz, Volker Fischer, "Vision der Moderne, Das Prinzip Konstruktion" (Frankfurt: DAM, Prestel Verlag, 1986). In the late 1980's Frank O'Gehry became famous with his architectural concepts based on providing every main function in a house with its own separate volume and shape. Their final assemblage gives the impression to consist of a group of connected, but still individual entities. Gehry and architects like Rem Koolhaas, Zaha Hadid, Daniel Liebeskind, Peter Eisenman and Coop Himmelblau were baptized by Philip Johnson to be "Deconstructivists". Just another example of the irony of history: this deconstructivist architecture is actually very similar to utopian designs by constructivist architects some 70 years earlier, like Chernikov in his fabulous "101 Architectural Phantasies", 1933. See Margit Rowell, Deborah Wye, "The Russian Avant-Garde Book 1910-1934" (New York: MOMA, Harry N. Abrams Inc., 2002), p.227.

[96] Mondrian considered the fourth dimension to be just a mental affair and, therefore, no property of plastic

reflecting how Gerrit Rietveld's architectural talents were influenced by Van Doesburg's ideas about space/time and the growth of cells applied to architecture.[97] It is interesting to note here that several artists between 1919-1921 changed their art dramatically into compositions that rotate or curve back into themselves, suggesting a more conscious exploration of Einstein's theory of space/time. El Lisstzky, for instance, wrote:

> *".. we see the transition of curvature from the two-dimensional into the three-dimensional, but the transition of the three-dimensional curvature into the four-dimensional is a factor which neither our sense of sight nor our sense of touch can grasp. Time is apprehended indirectly by our senses; it is indicated by the variation of an object's position in space. When the speed of these variations had reached that of modern rhythms, artists saw that they were obliged to record this."*[98]

Artists like Russian painter and sculptor Gustav Klucis understood that, according to the Theory of Relativity, three-dimensional space is a *cut* in the space-time continuum.[99] As a result, these artists explored ways to illustrate movable phenomena in three-dimensional systems of coordinates by situating themselves in the centre of the four coordinates. This kind of representation was understood as a fourth dimension.[100] Klucis read a lot and studied metaphysics. He explored new models of space/time, such

---

expression. He disagreed with the idea of suggesting depth and dynamics in painting by visual illusion, illusion that is created by the overlapping of shapes or the use of the oblique in a composition. This led to his famous disagreement with Van Doesburg on using the oblique in painting. Van Doesburg introduced the oblique as it suggests a higher dynamic and simulates the fourth dimension better than in a pure orthogonal composition. See Harry Holtzman, Martin S. James, "The New Art - The New Life - The Collected Writings of Piet Mondrian" (New York: Da Capo Press, 1993), p.206. An interesting note here is to refer to Alexander Calder's meeting with Mondrian in Paris in 1930. The story is only known by Calder, who said that while he was inspired by a visit to Mondrian's studio, and seeing some paintings and some pure coloured rectangles on the walls, he desired to make them actually oscillate in different directions. On the other hand Calder has said in 1966 that he told Mondrian his impression. Mondrian's answer was: "No, it is not necessary, my painting is already very fast." See Martha Prather, "Alexander Calder 1898-1976", catalogue exhibition National Gallery of Art Washington (New Haven and London: Yale University Press, 1998), p.57. Of course, it cannot be sure if Mondrian was merely joking or if this refers to any interest of Mondrian in space/time. In any case, Mondrian's later - New York - paintings actually do simulate strong motions (like the "Boogie Woogie" paintings).

97 This house was built in 1925-26 in Utrecht, Netherlands, thanks to the inspiring co-operation of Gerrit Rietveld with Truus Schröder-Schräder. It is now an architectural monument and can be visited as part of the Centraal Museum Utrecht, an experience that comes highly recommended! See Paul Overy, Lenneke Büller, Frank den Oudsten, Bertus Mulder, "Het Rietveld Schröder Huis" (De Haan Uitgeverij). See Paul Overy, "De Stijl - Art.Architecture.Design" (London: Thames and Hudson, 2000 - orig. 1991).

98 El Lissitzky, "A. and Pangeometry" 1925, in Sophie Lissitzky-Küppers, Herbert Read, "El Lissitzky - Life-Letters-Texts", p.356. Other artists consciously considering space/time were Klucis, Rodchenko, and Moholy Nagy.

99 See Larissa Oginskaja, "Das Phantastische und die Realität in den Konstruktionen von Gustav Klucis", in Hubertus Gaßner and Roland Nachtigäller, "Gustav Klucis - Retrospektive" (Stuttgart: Gerd Hatje Verlag, 1991), p.105-106. Klucis' concept is similar to the Japanese concept of 'kire-tsuzuki', to be be discussed later.

100 Compare the earlier mentioned tesseracts in relation to Van Doesburg.

as the hypercube and the hypersphere,[101] in his paintings, photo-montages and sculptures.

Russian artist Naum Gabo and his brother Natan Pevzner wrote in their influential 'Realistic Manifesto': "Space and time are born for us today. Space and time are the sole forms in which life builds itself and in which, therefore, art should be built."[102] They proclaimed that all static art was just wrong. Gabo was intrigued by the scientific view of space and time as the basic elements of life. As was mentioned in this chapter, Gabo knew about Einstein's theory early on, but he also knew of Rutherford's model of the atom (published 1909-1911), and the popularized notions of the fourth dimension showing geometric diagrams disintegrating solids into linear webs.[103] Additionally, Gabo was inspired by Henri Bergson's theories of constant transition[104] and he was familiar with scientific proof that solid and static matter do not exist. Gabo writes,

> *"Space invades and links all matter, as does time, as change or inner rhythm."*[105]

> *"Constructive sculpture is not only three-dimensional, it is four-dimensional insofar as we are striving to bring the element of time into it. By time, I mean movement, rhythm: the actual movement as well as the illusory one which is perceived through the indication of the flow of lines and shapes in the sculpture or in the painting."*[106]

---

[101] Compare this to the earlier mentioned hyperbolic geometry. See Hubertus Gaßner, "Aspekte der Fotomontage", in Hubertus Gaßner and Roland Nachtigäller, "Gustav Klucis - Retrospektive" p.184-186.

[102] The Realistic Manifesto was published on 5/10/1920. See Ryszard Stanislawski and Christoph Brockhaus, "Europa, Europa - Das Jahrhundert der Avantgarde in Mittel- und Osteuropa", Band 3 (Bonn: Kunst- und Ausstellungshalle der Bundesrepublik Deutschland, 1994), p.190: "Raum und Zeit sind für uns heute geboren. Raum und Zeit sind die einzigen Formen, in denen sich das Leben aufbaut und in denen sich deshalb die Kunst aufbauen muß." See Stephen Bann, "The Tradition of Constructivism" (New York: Da Capo Press, 1990 - orig.1974), where a slightly different translation is published on p.9: "The realization of our perceptions in the forms of space and time is the only aim of our pictorial and plastic art." Nathan Pevzner is the same as Antoine Pevsner (agian: differences in Russian artists' names is the result of differences in translating from cyrillic writing). See Alfred Pacquement, "Antoine Pevsner dans les collections du Centre Georges Pompidou/Musée national d'art moderne", catalogue (Paris: Éditions du Centre Pompidou, 2001.

[103] For instance, W.I. Stringham, "Regular Figures in n-Dimensional Space", 1880. See Steven Nash and Jörn A. Merkert, "Naum Gabo - Sixty Years of Constructivism" (Munich: Prestel Verlag, 1987), p.14. See Daniel Tyradellis, Michal S. Friedlander, "10 + 5 = Gott - Die Macht der Zeichen" (Berlin: Jüdisches Museum Berlin, DuMont Literatur und Kunst Verlag, 2004).

[104] Bergson's philosophy was around 1910 well-known, also in Russia. On Bergson, see §8.1. Bergson, for instance, emphasized the essence of understanding continuous change in nature caused by the continuous interactions at the micro- and macro levels of nature. See Henri Bergson, "Matter and Memory", p.200: "Moreover, if there is a truth that science has placed beyond dispute, it is that of the reciprocal action of all parts of matter upon each other. Between the supposed molecules of bodies the forces of attraction and repulsion are at work. The influence of gravitation extends throughout interplanetary space."

[105] See Steven Nash, "Naum Gabo: Sculptures of Purity and Possibility", in Steven Nash and Jörn A. Merkert, "Naum Gabo - Sixty Years of Constructivism", p.13. See also Zeki, "Inner Vision - An exploration of Art and the Brain" (Oxford: Oxford University Press, 1999), p.152.

[106] Quoted in George Rickey, "Constructivism - Origins and Evolution" (New York: George Brazilier, 1967). See Naum Gabo, "The Problems of Space and Time and their Falsification", 1925, in Martin Hammer and Christina Lodder, "Gabo on Gabo - texts and interviews" (Forest Row, UK: Artists Bookworks, 2000), p. 40-45.

Gabo fiercely criticized Van Doesburg and El Lissitzky's theories about translating space and time into architecture. Gabo thought their theories were unnatural projections of theoretical reasoning onto architectural space. Because architectural space always has been a 'space-shaping' activity, Gabo argued it did not need the new interpretations Van Doesburg and El Lissitzky championed.[107] In Gabo's opinion, Van Doesburg and El Lissitzky's new interpretations only promoted their 'interior decorating', clearly referring to the efforts by De Stijl artists to visually and virtually break open enclosed architectural spaces from within by painting geometrical shapes on walls, floors and ceilings. Gabo stated that the real notion of space/time must be found in the relationship to exterior space or eternal space (of the cosmos), translated in sculpture in which rhythm, rather than volume or mass, are important features. Gabo believed time was a purely philosophical concept for movement, without reference to cause and effect.

Considering the debates by artists on the possible consequences of new scientific theories on space and time for art, it makes sense one of them started to wonder about the consequences for perspective in art. Central perspective was the method used since the Renaissance of defining a point on the horizon to which all perspective lines would lead. El Lissitzky discredited traditional central perspective and stated, quite correctly, that such a point cannot be true in reality, because in reality everything is moving all the time. Central perspective is a method designed for painting that forces us into looking at a painting from a frozen position - the perspective only works when seen from one particular spot. In principle, El Lissitzky concludes, there are two pyramids of perception: one which has its apex in our eyes, the other which has its apex at the designed spot for central perspective on the horizon. The base of both pyramids begins at the surface of the painting. However, because in reality space is not limited as such, El Lissitzky described the surface of the two-dimensional plane as the zero-level, the direction into simulated depth behind the surface as towards 'minus infinity' and the direction into actual space in front of the surface towards 'positive infinity', going straight through the observer. Thus, for El Lissitzky, the influence of actual space on created space is important. This concept is clearly related to Matjushin's concept of extended vision and Kandinsky's concept of painting in front of the canvas.[108] It explains the interest of

---

107 El Lissitzky described his ideas about a new concept of space in his essay "K. und Pangeometrie" ("A. and Pangeometry", A. = art) from 1925, quoted earlier in this chapter. See Yve-Alain Bois, "From -8 to 0 to +8 - Axonometry, Lissitzky's mathematical paradigm", in Jan Debbaut, "El Lissitzky, architect, painter, photograph, typograph", catalogue Van Abbe Museum (Eindhoven: Stedelijk Van Abbe Museum, 1990. See Kai-Uwe Hemken, "El Lissitzky - Revolution und Avant-Garde" (Cologne: DuMont Taschenbücher, 1990), p.18, referring to El Lissitzky's interest in Einstein and Minkowski.

108 Evidence that these artistic translations of scientific and philosophical concepts of space/time and the consequences for understanding our perception of space found a wider audience is provided by Alexander Dorner (1893-1957), who was the director of the Department of Painting in Hannover (today the Sprengel Museum), Germany. In 1937 he became director of the Museum in Providence, Rhode Island, USA. In Hannover Dorner supported these early attempts by artists, bought works, organized exhibitions and commissioned El Lissitzky's famous 'abstract cabinet'. See Manfred Fath and Christoph Brockhaus, "Malewitsch - Mondrian, Konstruktion als Konzept - Alexander Dorner gewidmet" (Ludwigshafen: Wilhelm Hack

artists like El Lissitzky, Van Doesburg or Moholy Nagy in axiometric drawing as a better means of simulating motion and more dynamic and complex space/time than central perspective could ever be.[109] Hungarian avant-garde multi-media pioneer László Moholy-Nagy wrote in 1922, together with Alfred Kemény:

"Vital constructivity is the representation of life and the principle of all human and cosmic unfoldings. Translated into art this means today the activation of space by dynamic-constructive systems of force, meaning the interlocking construction of the forces that are actually opposed in physical space and their construction into the space that also works as force (tension) itself." [110]

In the 1920's Polish pioneers of abstract art, Wladyslaw Strzeminksi and his wife Katarzyna Kobro, developed a special interest in the unification of man with space. They understood art - painting, sculpture, architecture - to be helpful media for realizing this unification.[111] They called their concept 'Unizm':

"The union of man and space is the action of man in that space. We come to know space through our actions. The vectors traced by the actions of man in space are: the vertical station of man and every object, the horizontal of the environment that he encounters on both sides, and the depth, before him, of forward movement." [112]

Museum, 1978), see especially the reprint of Dorner's lecture of 1931, on p.3, discussing the change of the concept of space from Romanticism to Cubism to Constructivism. In (late) Constructivism, space was explored by dissolving it into lines and pure planes. Without mass and transparant, they virtually fly through each other, exemplifying the streams of motion and energy streams of space/time.

[109] There were more artists who changed their compositions under influence of Einstein's theories on curved space/time. For instance, Swiss artist/architect Hans Hinterreiter, who introduced curved movements and lines in his paintings. See Hans Hinterreiter, "Die Kunst der reinen Form - Eine Formenlehre für moderne Künstler, Band I - Ordnung und Taufe der Elementarformen." (Ibiza, Amsterdam: Ediciones Ebusus, 1978 - orig. 1941). Hinterreiter was inspired by a combination of cristallography, islamic tiling and the colour- and form theories of Ostwald. One may compare also the curved architecture by Friedrich Kiesler in his studies for'the Endless House'. See Dr. Dieter Bogner, "Friedrich Kiesler Architekt Maler Bildhauer 1890-1965" (Vienna: Löcker Verlag 1988). See Frederick J. Kiesler, "Towards the Endless Sculpture" (1956), in Siegfried Gohr, Gunda Luyken, "Frederick J. Kiesler - Selected Writings", (Ostfildern: Verlag Gerd Hatje, 1996), p.53.

see picture 25

[110] In the manifesto "Dynamical - Constructive - System of Forces", published in 1923 in the German magazine "Der Sturm", see Veit Loers, "László Moholy Nagy" (Ostfildern-Ruit: Verlag Gerd Hatje, 1991), p.10: "Die vitale Konstruktivität ist die Erscheinungsform des Lebens und das Prinzip aller menschlichen und kosmischen Entfaltungen. In die Kunst umgesetzt bedeutet sie heute die Aktivmachung des Raumes mittels dynamisch-konstruktiver Kraftsysteme, d.h. die Ineinander - Konstruierung der in dem physischer Raume sich real gegeneinander spannenden Kräfte und ihre Hineinkonstruierung in den gleichfalls als Kraft (Spannung) wirkenden Raum." On Moholy Nagy, see also the reprint of his Bauhaus book. See Hans M. Wingler, "Vom Material zu Architektur", Neue Bauhausbücher, introduction by Otto Stelzer (Mainz, Berlin: Florian Kupferberg, 1968, orig. 1929).

[111] See Franciska Clausen, "Tre Pionérer for Polsk Avant-Garde" (Helsinki: Fynsk Kunstmuseum, 1985). See Yves Alain-Bois, "Painting as a Model" (Boston: MIT Press, 1995 - orig. 1993). See Dieter Ronte and Jaromir Jedlinski, "Wladyslaw Strzeminski" (Bonn: Kunstmuseum Bonn, 1994). See also §5.3.

[112] See Wladyslaw Strzeminski and Katarzyna Kobro, "Composition in Space, Calculations of Spatio-Temporal Rhythm", 1931, in Yves Alain-Bois, "Painting as a Model", p.146. See Yve Alain Bois, "Strzeminski

Strzeminski and Kobro believed sculpture, in Unist Theory, was an art that mobilizes time: "The spatiotemporality of the work of art is related to its variability. We call spatiotemporal the spatial changes produced in time."[113] They thought these changes occured when the observer changed his point of view, as by moving around the sculpture. It is thus natural that they became interested in applying their ideas to architectural spaces. As you will have noticed from the different examples, this was also the obvious thing to do in those days. Strzeminski and Kobro thought the purpose of architecture was "... an organization of the rhythm of consecutive motions and stops, and thereby the forming of the whole of life."[114] They exemplified the translation of the scientific understanding of space/time into an artistic theory to be applied to the design of the environment of everyday life.

A contemporary of these artists, philosopher John Dewey, wrote:

"Time as empty does not exist; time as an entity does not exist. What exists are things acting and changing, and a constant quality of their behavior is temporal ... Place, position, determined by distribution of intervals through spacing, is a great factor in effecting the individualization of parts already spoken of ... The feeling of energy and especially not just of energy in general but of this or that power in the concrete is closely connected with rightness in placing. For there is an energy of position as well as of motion."[115]

Dewey's comment on the energy of position matches well with how the artists of his time were exploring simulations of the necessary dynamics in painting and sculpture to enhance the image of a fourth dimension. The positioning of pictorial elements is decisive for this purpose. In painting and sculpture this includes the importance of the distribution of intervals - the spaces between the pictorial elements - as Dewey correctly understood.[116]

---

and Kobro: In Search of Motivation", in Yves Alain-Bois, "Painting as a Model", p.146: "Unist sculpture does not produce sculptures. Unist sculpture sculpts space, condensing it within the limits of its sculptural zone. The unist sculpture, based upon the organic unity of sculpture and space, does not want the form to be a goal in itself, but only the expression of spatial relationships."

113 Ibid.

114 Ibid.

115 See John Dewey, "Art as Experience" (New York: Perigee Books, 1980 - orig. 1934). This concept of space and time seems inspired by 19th century thinking, for instance by Schopenhauer.

116 This idea is furthered in 1950 by experimental psychologist James J. Gibson, quoted in Paul Overy, "Kandinsky - The language of the eye", p.105: "When we are attending to the visual world ... we do not attend to the spaces between the objects - the gaps or background - and we are almost unaware of their existence. But a little attention to the visual field shows that these interspaces are just truly parts of it as the areas respresenting objects. In the field as a projection, the background is not different from the objects in the compelling way it is when you observe the world. The interspaces, like the objects, are areas of colour, and the field therefore approximates the appearance of an irregular patchwork." This concept reminds one of Biederman's explanation of Cézanne's concentric vision applying little planes towards culminating points - also a kind of patchwork.

You can test the importance of positioning and the interval yourself. Draw two squares on a sheet of paper. These each become a virtual centre of force. This phenomenon emerges from the fact that your eyes are attracted to them. When you draw one square much larger then the other, you will experience a difference in 'force' between both squares, as your eyes are involuntarily drawn to one of the squares first. When you draw these two squares on several sheets of paper, while you change the interval - the distance between them - on every sheet, you will also notice this effects your experience. Now, try the same experiment with three squares. These are by definition the basic features of com-*positioning* in art![117]

In art these ideas about space/time have been furthered in the 1950's and well into the 1960's.[118] As a model of that generation and one of the artists interested in searching for a furthered theory of art and space/time, one should mention the Dutch artist Joost Baljeu. He was interested in the aspect of space/time that we today would define as the path of space/time. Baljeu believed a form - say a rectangle - existed in space/time, but as space/time continuously moves onwards (even when this rectangle lies still on a table, it still moves because the table moves together with all motions of the earth), one can imagine this particular form changing its location in space/time as a sequence of different positions in space/time - because Einsteinian space/time follows a curved path, one can understand seeing here a repetition of rectangles ordered along a curved path. Baljeu thought the attempt to connect these different positions was the 'vision of formation', which, when applied in a work of art, would make the fourth dimension comprehensible, while it is not actually moving and thus emphasizes the continuous experience of 'now'.[119] Baljeu thus created three-dimensional reliefs exemplifying a dynamic but not actually moving composition, consisting of retangular shapes diagonally ordered along curved lines.

His ideas clearly connect to earlier artists' theories, like those by Gleizes, El Lissitzky

117 Remember the ideas by Malevitch, Kandinsky, Moholy-Nagy and Kemeny or Kupka as mentioned in this chapter. Kandinsky wrote, quoted in Paul Overy, "Kandinsky - The language of the eye", p. 101: "The dynamic moment begins with the juxtaposition of at least two emotions: elements, colours, lines, sounds, movements, etc. (contrast). 'Two inner sounds'. Here is to be found the root of composition ..." Please, remember the discussion about my hypothesis that our preference for contrast and complexity in art can be based on the need for higher and more complex neural activity to allow conscious experience. See §5.1.

118 By artists like Jean Gorin, Kenneth and Mary Martin, Victor Pasmore, Richard Paul Lohse, Max Bill, Eli Bornstein, Anthony Hill and Joost Baljeu. Joost Baljeu quite literally followed and furthered Van Doesburg's ideas in his wall-constructions, sculptures and architectural models. Concerning his architectural studies he worked together with the architect Dick van Woerkom.

119 See Joost Baljeu, "Attempt at a Theory of Synthesist Plastic Expression" (London: Alec Tiranti, 1963), p.10: "The vision of formation is not interested in form, counterform or inside form, not in initial or result-form as static form, but takes these as space entities interrelated by their movements in time, between the beginning and the final phase, thus revealing certain formative principles in space-time. Thus the vision of formation ranges from macro- to microcosmos and vice versa. In doing so, it does not loose itself in a past or a future aspect, but presents the dynamic functioning of reality in the present which, however, is then seen as a dynamic 'now'. The vision of formation taking reality as a dynamic equilibrium of tangible and environmental space under the influence of force and counterforce, thus arrives at the building method of natural reality."

or Van Doesburg, but also to the philosophic ideas of Bergson and Dewey. Baljeu thought nature was permanently changing, straightness[120] was the basic principle of matter in motion, obliquity was a temporal process and the formative principle of the inequality of the forces of matter in motion, and force expressed time. These were ideas he, like Van Doesburg, or Strzeminski and Kobro, believed were best realized in architecture.

The interest by so many artists in space/time led to kinetic art. Although Gabo is seen as the actual inventor, kinetic art secured its position as a phenomenon in the art world by the exhibitions of the magnificent mobiles of Alexander Calder starting in 1932. Kinetic art concerns art that is set into motion by a natural source (wind) or by a mechanic device. Therefore, kinetic art uses real motion, and as motion evolves in space and time, it is definitely related to a further thinking about space/time. However, it also connects strongly to our perception of natural motion and to how motion is processed in our brain.[121]

Kinetic art really took off in the 1950's and 1960's.[122] Sculptor Nicolas Schöffer describes the purpose of kinetic sculpture:

> *"The essential goal of spatiodynamics is the constructive and dynamic involvement of space in the plastic work of art. A minimum of space contains unexpected energies ... The spatiodynamic sculpture exists first as a scaffold. Its mission is to describe and envelop a part of space and, then, to define the rhythm of the work of art. To this scaffold another rhythm is added with help of flat elements or thin and transparent bodies, that serve as*

120 In this emphasis on straightness, Baljeu disagreed with Gleizes, who stated, as we saw earlier, that in one work both straight as well as curved shapes should be used to reflect reality. Nevertheless, in Baljeu's reliefs and sculptures the curves slipped in - not in a real sense but as optical phenomenon - caused by his use of the oblique and his interest in a growing cell-like structure. This application of curved motions is similar to Van Doesburg or Biederman's works, in which there are no actual curved shapes to be seen, but the way the elements are mounted in the composition strongly evoke a curved motion in your eyes.

121 Semir Zeki, whose fascinating ideas in the previous chapter were mentioned, explains our perception of the dynamics of a Calder-mobile by describing how certain brain-cells operate. Because of its movement, a mobile is continuously changing position in relation to our eyes. Therefore, perception cannot be limited to one group of brain-cells. There is a particular group of cells in the brain-area called V5 that respond differently from the majority of cells to a stimulation changing from one eye to the other. See Semir Zeki, "Inner Vision - An exploration of Art and the Brain", p.156: "Collectively, these cells are able to signal motion towards or away from the organism. [.......] when a point or line is displaced towards the viewer, its image is displaced in the opposite direction in the two eyes and, in the same way, when it is displaced away from the viewer its image is also displaced in the opposite direction in the two eyes. This, then, is a mechanism for signalling motion towards or away and would, one presumes, be the neural way of indicating the displacement of the elements of the Calder mobile in the centrifugal and centripetal directions." It is one of Zeki's remarkable intuitions that he suspects many artists more or less unconsciously explore aspects of perception that our brain 'demands' and, therefore, make art that is of high interest to neurobiology.

122 The early abstract artists like Naum Gabo and Moholy-Nagy had already experimented with kinetic sculpture much earlier. See §3. George Rickey, himself a pioneer of modern kinetic sculpture, quotes what Gabo told him, see George Rickey, "Constructivism - Origins and Evolution", p.191: "There are statics and dynamics, then there is kinetics." See also Frank Popper, "Origins and development of Kinetic Art" (New York: New York Graphic Society, 1968 - orig. Studio Vista).

> *counterweights and disclose all energetic and dynamic possibilities of the captured space. Thus the sculpture becomes an airy, transparent work of art open to all sides making the pure rhythms of the proportions and the logical clarity of a rational well-considered structure tangible ... The essential goal of spatiodynamics is the overcoming of matter, as does modern physics."* [123]

Even in the 1960's, in the Cold War isolation of the USSR, there existed a group of artists making kinetic art, huge kinetic installations in public spaces and organizing kinetic performances and films. This group was called 'Dvezhenye'.[124]

Another approach to kinetic art has been offered by neurobiologist Semir Zeki. Discussing how brain cells respond to stimuli provided by objects in general - also by the properties present in artworks - he shows that the brain scans reality for constants and essentials. He also shows that brain cells process information at a diversity of speeds, implying that there are limitations to perception based on the speed of objects that we can perceive.[125] Simplified, this means, when something moves too quickly, the information it carries is lost on us.

A good illustration is provided by a comparison between two proponents of 'time-based art', which is considered a new variation of kinetic art. The Korean Fluxus artist, Nam June Paik, makes installations with piles of tv-screens all flashing random sequences of images recorded from tv-programs, movies, performances, etc. The observer is continuously bewildered by the visual bombardment of flashing colour, while the brain catches barely recognizable parts of the multitude of images. The complete opposite is offered by the digital works of artists like Ernest Edmonds and Manfred Mohr: very still geometric compositions using beautiful colours that change in very slow and long sequences. The artist duo localStyle (Marlena Novak and Jay Alan Yim) in their digital work, "Dancing Cranes", accomplish a different kind of sequence

see pictures
36, 38, 39

123 Quoted from "Die drei Entwicklungsstufen der dynamischen Skulptur", 1963, in Ryszard Stanislawski and Christoph Brockhaus, "Europa, Europa - Das Jahrhundert der Avantgarde in Mittel- und Osteuropa", Band 3, p.112+113: "Das wesentliche Ziel der Spatiodynamik ist die konstruktive und dynamische Einbeziehung des Raumes in das plastische Kunstwerk. Ein Minimum an Raum enthällt ungeahnte Energien .... Die spatiodynamische Plastik besteht zunächst aus einem Gerüst. Dessen Aufgabe ist es, einen Raumausschnitt zu umschreiben und einzufangen und dann den Rhythmus des Kunstwerks zu bestimmen. Diesem Gerüst wird ein weiterer Rhythmus aufgesetzt, und zwar mit Hilfe von flachen Elementen oder dünnen und durchscheinenden Körpern, die als Gegengewichte dienen und dem eingefangenen Raum alle seine energetischen und dynamischen Möglichkeiten erschließen. Damit wird die Plastik ein lüftiges, durchsichtiges und nach allen Seiten offenes Kunstwerk, das den reinen Rhythmus der Proportionen mit der logischen Klarheit einer rationell durchdachten Struktur greifbar werden läßt .... Das Wesentliche Ziel der Spatiodynamik ist die Überwindung der Materie, und das gleiche will die moderne Physik."

124 See §3. The average age of the artists of the group 'Dvezhenye' (='movement'; also written as 'Dvijenie') was around 20. This group was initiated by Lew Nussberg and existed 1962-1977. Artists outside the USSR working with kinetic sculpture were Jean Tinguely, Pol Bury, Gianni Colombo, Len Lye, Walter Linck, Günther Haese, Takis, Julio le Parc, Hans Haacke, Norbert Cricke, Harry Kramer, Yaacov Agam, Angel Duarte, Alexander Calder and George Rickey.

125 This was described in §5.

of images and sound based on perceptible rhythmic and geometric patterns. The comfort of change slow enough for our brain to catch can be compared to observing how a traditional painting changes in colour during the slow process of natural change in daylight. In my opinion, Zeki's neurobiological research provides a convincing reason why we might be attracted by the sheer power of the speed of Paik's image-explosions, but then loose interest at the same speed, and why Edmond's, Mohr's and localStyle's digital works seem to capture our attention for a much longer time.[126]

As was said at the start of §6.3 I focussed on the period 1910-1960. This was indeed the period in which one finds the most intense discussions of artists about space/time, especially in their translation of space/time into the fourth dimension. Though space/time keeps attracting artists' attention, this is not so much based on the fascination for a fourth dimension anymore. Time as fourth dimension became so exhaustively explored that the artistic implications of suggesting a fourth dimension just became part of the artistic vocabulary. Notions such as rhythm, structure, process, nets, grids, change, repetition, intervals, and the acceptance of notions of 'action' and 'process' in painting and sculpture, all have become part of the artistic vocabulary since the 1950's and 1960's. Besides, in recent decades one could see the introduction of the notion 'time-based art', concerning film-, video-, and computer generated art. Artists keep following the newer developments of scientific theories on space/time, which go far beyond understanding space/time as only a fourth dimension, and some artist try to figure out the possible implications for art.

6.4 SPACE/TIME IN SCIENCE: THE BASIC ELEMENTS

Let us now return to the development of scientific concepts of space/time, while keeping in mind what has been said about the interests of artists. This seems necessary to better understand what these artists were exploring parallel to science, but also to appreciate the growing abstraction of scientific theory on the complex subject of space/time.We will see why it has become plausible to assume that science and art are closing the gap between their very different approaches to this major topic of perception of reality. This gap seems to become especially smaller and smaller because of the growing level of abstract thinking which always has been essential in art, and in the past decades has become essential in theoretical physics as well.

Though we briefly have to discuss the development of the main ideas in the 20th century, it is not essential here to describe all developments in detail. To provide some additional details, in the footnotes one can find some references and suggestions for further reading.[127]

---

126 Zeki's point also proves why traditional painting and sculpture will never loose their importance, regardless of the wild claims of the advocates of the 'new media'.

127 See David F. Peat, "Superstrings and the Theory of Everything" (Abacus Books, 1992 - orig. 1988). See Brian Greene, "The Elegant Universe - Superstrings, Hidden Dimensions, and the Quest for the Ultimate Theory" (New York: Vintage Books, 1999). See Lee Smolin, "Three Roads to Quantum Gravity", (New York: Basic Books, 2001).

The foundation of all scientific theories on space/time perception is the idea that, for our perception, we are dependent on the existence of light. Originally light was assumed to have a constant speed - which is therefore the maximum perceptible speed. In recent decades this concept of light has changed dramatically.

In the days modern science was born, around the 17th century with Isaac Newton, light was thought to be composed of small entities or particles, though soon other scientists started to wonder if light consisted of waves. New experiments in the 19th century seemed to prove that the wave-theory was correct.[128] Also in that century, the first theories were developed on electromagnetic force, gravity, and conservation of energies. All of these theories forced a reconsideration of what was known about the properties of energy, and particularly of light. The discovery of more rays than only visible light (as radio-waves and X-rays) meant more complex features became part of the discussion about understanding the duality of space and time and how it can be possible to combine both space and time into one new notion.

New theories emerged, concerning connections in space/time that are not perceptable to our eyes and are related to a deeper structure of nature, like Quantum Theory.[129] This theory suggests that all energies are neither built by small particles nor by waves, but by small indivisible quantities of energies.

Thomas Vargish and Delo Mook discuss the remarkable analogy between the concept of quanta and the discovery of applicable quanta in the form of units, strokes or patches of paint in Cubism.[130] I see this analogy holding for almost all, if not all, art, because all art forms do basically nothing else than create rhythmic patterns of certain quantities of material.[131]

The theories of Albert Einstein were new steps that triggered an avalanche of theories and understanding of space and time. Light became understood not as mere wave (or as particle), but as consisting of 'photons', both wave and particle, that consist of small

---

128 The duality or complementarity of light as wave/particle emerged from studying the experiment by Thomas Young that has become legendary as the 'Two-Slit Experiment'. Young studied light in 1803 in an experiment in which he let (sun)light fall through a curtain with two slits onto a flat surface. Although one would expect to see only two stripes of light on this flat surface, this did not happen. Instead more stripes could be observed with less light stripes next to each other. This pattern of stripes is called the interference pattern. Interference names the way two waves add up to each other. In constructive interference the waves enhance each other's wave pattern, in destructive interference they annihilate each other's wave pattern. Without going into technical details, this experiment showed that light does not travel in straight lines, otherwise there would only be the two expected stripes. The only feasible explanation was that light travels in waves.

129 The quantum was proposed by Max Planck in December 1900. Max Planck discovered that energy comes not in particles or in waves but in indivisible units, which are called quanta. Planck also showed that energy, for instance from heated material, is not transmitted at a constant speed, but in a rhythmic pattern of jumps of small quantities.

130 See Thomas Vargish and Delo E. Mook, "Inside Modernism - Relativity Theory, Cubism, Narrative", p.113. Thomas Vargish is professor in English at the University of Maryland and at the University of Gothenburg, Sweden. Delo Mook is professor in physics and astronomy at Dartmouth College.

131 Exceptions are monochrome painting, when done with a roller, spray-gun or other device.

packages of electromagnetic energies.[132] A further important implication of Einstein's theories was the aspect of relativity. Without going into this notion in detail, it is sufficient for our discussion to briefly recall a famous example.

When we stand somewhere and see a train moving past, we have a certain perception of space and time. However, when we travel in a train parallel to another train moving in the same direction, with almost the same speed, in our perception the other train will hardly seem to move, while to someone standing at the station both trains will move at high speed. This example is useful for helping to explain why all motion that we perceive around us or, for instance, in the universe, cannot be judged by one's perception alone, but is always relative to where we are, relative to our position in space/time. In my opinion, one can find analogies to this phenomenon in the abstract art of Einstein's day. Kandinsky's "Improvisations" and Malevitch's Suprematist paintings do not provide a single focal point. Their compositions can only be viewed by a jumping of the eye between the pictorial elements that are juxtaposed in such a way that they express their meaning 'relative' to each others' location in the composition. Einstein also showed how the properties of light create the plausibility that light, as electromagnetic energy itself, will bend under the influence of other electromagnetic forces, like gravity. This led to the concept of space/time being curved and distorted in the universe. This idea, as explained in this publication, had quite an impact on artists like El Lissitzky and Moholy-Nagy, who incorporated a distortion in their artistic compositions under the influence of a 'curved' pictorial space.

Further scientific theories reinforced the discussion about the dilemma that the properties of the processes of the macro-universe did not match the properties of the micro-universe, and led to the complex wish to unify the world of particles with the universe.[133] In the decades that followed, further scientific theories developed in quick succession. Most theories came about as results of logical 'Gedanken-Experiments' (thought experiments) and mathematical calculations, other theories as results of empirical experiments.[134] All of these developments were based on studies of the prop-

---

132 In 1905, Albert Einstein, seeking to explain why certain solids generate electric currents when struck by light (the photoelectric effect), published in the German "Annalen der Physik" that light sometimes acts as a stream of particles. This implied that light could be particle and wave, an extension of the standard opinion of the 19th century that light comes in waves. Einstein showed that at a certain moment we can observe light consisting of particles and at another moment consisting of waves.

133 In 1913, Niels Bohr published how atoms are composed of heavy nuclei with a positive charge around which light electrons with a negative charge orbit as if they were small galaxies. See Erwin Schrödinger, "What is Matter?", Scientific American Special Issue September 1991, p.16-21. Bohr thus provided reason to believe that all processes in macro-nature are mirrored at a micro-level.

134 In 1923 Louis de Broglie turned Einstein's concept of the photon around and stated that electrons themselves also can act as waves. In 1925 Quantum Theory was officially formulated, confirming the acceptance of the wave/particle duality of atomic objects. In the same year Einstein published his new ideas on Quantum Statistics, inspired by a letter from Satyendra Nath Bose, which has become known as the Bose-Einstein Condensate. It was the result of Einstein's research of electromagnetic radiation, especially the radiation trapped in a heated container that at a certain temperature attains the same temperature as its walls. This phenomenon seems also to be a result of synchronization of rhythmic patterns (heat also follows a wavy or rhythmic

erties of light and their implications for understanding how we perceive space/time.

One problem is that our ways of calculating space/time do not seem to work everywhere in the universe. This has led to new theories, growing even more in complexity and abstraction. These theories seem plausible from our relative position on earth, but cannot necessarely be proven yet, like for instance the concept of black holes.[135] It is very important to the discussion in this publication, especially to all that has been said about the functioning of the processes in our brain, to understand that in this scientific development it became gradually more clear that every process in nature is fundamentally a rhythmic or oscillating process consisting of waves. This is so important, because in this conclusion lies the reason why I emphasize the importance of synchronization as the basis for assuming the various influences on our thinking, behaviour and, therefore, on our appreciation for art.

In art one can find examples of painters who have studied compositions that seem to reflect the 'black hole' phenomenon. One example is Kliun's "Spherical Painting" from 1923. The contraction of energy in a kind of singularity seems also exemplified in Rodchenko's fascinating black paintings from 1918 and 1919. However, there is reason to assume these artists were more inspired by concepts from Buddhist and Hindu philosophies, like the void and sunyata.[136] As I mentioned before, evidence was found that the speed of light was not constant. Understanding light became more complex once again. It was, at first, mainly a mathematical debate,[137] then led to experiments that

pattern) and is called the black-body radiation. The photons left over from the Big Bang, the supposed original blast that created the universe, (therefore, including life itself) with the entire universe as a container, are understood as examples of black-body radiation. See Jeremy Bernstein, "The Reluctant Father of Black Holes", Scientific American June 1996, p.66-72. In 1927, at an international congress for science in Brussels, the final conclusion was presented under the presidency of Niels Bohr: the electron is either wave or particle, depending on the experimental apparatus you use, but not both. (As Bohr came from Copenhagen this declaration is known as the Copenhagen Interpretation) It became accepted that anything is both particle and field of waves. Werner Heisenberg formulated in 1928 the Uncertainty Principle: you cannot know the position of an electron without disturbing the electron's speed or direction of motion. See Erwin Schrödinger, "What is Matter?", Scientific American Special Issue September 1991, p.16-21: "The wave phenomenon forms the 'body' proper to the atom. It takes the place of the individual pointlike electrons which in Bohr's model are supposed to swarm around the nucleus." In studying the Two-Slit Experiment again, it was decided, that if it were possible to shoot one photon at a time through the slits one could not foresee where the photon would hit the back wall, meaning it is impossible to know how the photon will travel. In other words: according to Quantum Mechanics, interference occurs whenever there is more than one possible way for a given outcome to happen while the ways are not distinguishable by any means.

135 In 1916 the German astronomer Karl Schwarzschild showed how complex it is to try to understand space/time with our instruments of knowledge. He discovered that at a certain distance from the center of a star mathematics does not function anymore. At this distance time seems to vanish and space becomes infinite. This phenomenon is known as the Schwarzschild radius. The interpretation of this phenomenon in mathematics led to the theory that all energies at some point converge in a single point in space, called a singularity, leading to the development of black holes. A new concept initiated by J. Robert Oppenheimer and his students in 1939.

136 See §2 and §3. Not without reason one can find some natural resemblance between the mentioned painting of Kliun and works by contemporary painter Natvar Bhavsar, whose works are partly based upon his Indian background.

137 In 1949 Richard Feynman published his famous diagrams for the first time. These very abstract visualizations

proposed to see the photons or light-particles as certain quantities of electrons with a certain charge, a charge that could change, and electrons that consisted of certain percentages of the properties of 'waviness', in combination with properties of 'particulateness'. The combination of waviness and particulateness in the same electron was a much more complex and new concept of the electron than the earlier concept that an electron was either wave or particle, not both. The confusion about either photons or electrons as basic elements of light still continues. But this is still not the last of more complex discoveries. In the previous decade experiments showed that light particles may even follow unseen and undetectable paths. These are called 'tunnelling photons'.[138] Illustrating the vast complexity of the attempts to understand particle 'behaviour', experiments have even shown that particles might unpredictably change their charges.[139] The probability that light and other streams of energy may follow more paths through space/time than in the three-dimensional universe perceptible to our eyes

---

became methaphors for a new theory called Quantum Electrodynamics (or QED). See Richard P. Feynman, "QED - The Strange Theory of Light and Matter" (New York: Penguin Books, 1990 - orig. Princeton University Press, 1985). Based on a more advanced knowledge of light, for example, that light travels at different speeds through warmer or colder air or through water, Feynman described with a high degree of accuracy how electrons as particles with a certain electrical charge interact with photons, the particles of light. QED made the debate over the wave/particle duality irrelevant. Only mathematics mattered. See Hans Christiaan von Baeyer, "The Quantumeraser", Scientific American January/February 1997, p.12-14: "Electrons and photons were replaced by symbols that physicists can manipulate to generate quantitative, verifiable predictions." Mental or other images would not matter excepting diagrams. New names were proposed for the wave/particle duality: 'wavicle' and later 'quanton.' These experiments showed that particles, like the electrons, act as waves, making Einstein's theory even more complex. Ibid., p.12-14: "Thus arises the exceedingly curious behaviour of the denizens of the quantum world: until it is detected, the electron is a wave; the act of detection converts it into a particle."

138 In 1993, the Two-Slit Experiment in an adapted version (with mirrors instead of slits) was realized and proved that photon's behaviour is unpredictable, somehow passing through a mirror-barrier that is not supposed to let photons through. See Raymond Y. Chiao, Paul G. Kwiat and Aephraim B. Steinberg, "Faster than Light? Experiments in quantum optics that show that two distant events can influence each other faster than any signal could have traveled between them", Scientific American August 1993, p.38-46. This experiment led to the idea that quantum jumps do exist, and implied that there might be more paths through space/time than we can perceive or observe. Photons seem to disappear and pop up unexpectedly somewhere else. In this experiment evidence was found for the so-called tunnelling photons, which reached a recorded speed of 1.7 times that of light. The problem became more complex and confusing when new methods were introduced, using streams of electrons instead of a beam of light in the Two-Slit Experiment.

139 Experiments done by several institutions in the past decade have already shown that the interference pattern disappears without evidence that the uncertainty principle (of Von Heisenberg) effects the process. Theoretical implications were published in 1996 by German physicist Berthold-Georg Englert, associated with the Max Planck Institute for Quantum Optics. The major conclusion was that light does not consist of a mere duality of wave/particle, but of a combination of a certain percentage of waviness and a certain percentage of particulateness. Similar research has been done in Quantum Optics. See Paul Kwiat, Harald Weinfurter and Anton Zeilinger, "Quantum Seeing in the Dark", Scientific American November 1996. This research has shown how objects can be detected without being hit by light. New research should focus on this complex new property of quanta instead of still headbanging over the wave/particle duality. Comparably, it would be narrow-minded while studying sound to only focus on extreme loudness and softness, as every sound is a mixture of these, or, while studying colour, it would be silly to only focus on black/white contrasts. In my understanding this new evidence and new theory can much better explain the differences in brightness of light and of colour, maybe even helping to explain our impression that certain colours seem to be heavier (to have more

has also been confirmed by theories in astrophysics.[140]

It becomes plausible that all motions through the vast cosmos only follow curved paths and, in very, very long intervals, return approximately to the same spot in space/time. As a result, the cosmos could indeed exist in a large sphere instead of a linear kind of infinity. For instance, there are theories that state that the vast quantities of energy trapped in black holes travel through 'wormholes' that somehow connect them to so-called 'white holes', where the energy erupts again into the cosmos that is visible to us (comparable to vast streams of tunnelling photons). White holes are very large clusters, or bursts, of great quantities of young white stars. This circulation of energy seems to be additional proof of the principle that conservation of energy is indeed a critical property of all processes constituting nature.

New discoveries of the band of waves of energy that make nature into what it is, and resulting new imaging technologies, have shown that there is much more to nature than visible light allows us to perceive, making these 'tunnelling' activities of streams of energy an understandable concept.[141]

We see by the existence of daylight and perceive objects, such as works of art and colours, by reflections of daylight. We also sense that artworks have a meaning, which cannot only be explained by mechanical descriptions of the reflections of light. Therefore, these scientific theories do matter for our quest to understand art. For one thing, art is about colour. Therefore, it certainly makes sense not only to try to

particulateness?). They also open the door to even more complex theories about space/time. In any case, since QED and the here described recent experiments, including the proof of tunnelling photons it cannot be stated anymore that light travels at a constant speed nor that it is an absolute entity. Tunneling-photons are photons that travel faster than light, therefore, seem to disappear and pop up somewhere else when they slow their speed back to 'light speed', thus giving the impression to dive through an unseen tunnel. As has been stated before, our perception of space/time is unavoidably connected to the perception of light. Therefore, it is quite possible that other speeds and other paths of space/time exist that we cannot perceive consciously, which make unexpected sightings and phenomena possible. These might even include sightings and phenomena which were formerly discarded as mystical events and religious experiences.

140 The possibility of different paths through space/time has also been confirmed by the famous scientist Stephen Hawking in his detailed theories about space/time and black holes as singularities. To the contrary of public knowledge, black holes were defined by Oppenheimer and co-workers in 1939 and not in the 1960's by Hawking, although Hawking defined them more properly. A singularity is a point from which energy leaves and towards which it loops back; it is the switch point of energy's lines of force. Obviously these theories have had major consequences for how we look at the universe. As the developments in astrophysics and astronomy would take too great a detour to describe, I hope the reader forgives me for not elaborating these. The only thing that should be of interest here is that black holes are considered to be extremely dense objects that by powerful gravitational forces attract all matter, including light and form distortions of space/time. Hawking stated that the universe can very well be imagined as a large spherical shape in which all phenomena move along curved paths creating a sense of infinity (of the continuum) that is not linear. An interesting analogy of this concept is the "Egg of Brahma" in Hinduism, from which the universe is supposed to be born. In Buddhism the sphere is the metaphor for the All.

141 New technological developments in the 1980's have allowed the translation of ultra-violet and gamma-rays of the cosmos into pictures. Earlier this was accomplished by the discovery of the photography of natural X rays in the universe and since the 1950's by the discovery of natural bursts of radio-rays. These pictures show a much more complex universe than is shown in pictures made by normal optical instruments and prove that there are indeed more differences in space/time than perceptable by our daylight-vision! Not to mention

understand how our brains process our vision of colour, but also to understand what colour, as a phenomenon of light and energy, is. If science shows that streams of energy can disappear and pop up somewhere else, why should this natural phenomenon not have an impact on our creation of and appreciation of art?

We will continue our discussion on developments in science to illustrate how scientific explorations into the core of reality have become highly abstract in a way that seems to make the leap to abstract (visual) thinking in art smaller.

6.5 SPACE/TIME IN SCIENCE: SHAPE AND PATH

So far I have discussed the developing knowledge of light's basic properties and some odd aspects scientists have come across, like the unpredictable and temporary disappearance of lightparticles. If we want to understand the complexity of space/time, we also need to know more about the paths through space/time and their possible impact on our perception of reality.

A basic fact is that when we perceive an object as stationary in our environment it is not stationary at all. It looks stationary as we travel together with the object, our environment, and the whole earth at a very high speed (some 100,000 km per second) through the continuum of the universe.

The movement through the universe is of course a motion through space/time. Every position an object takes in space through its lifetime can be connected in our imagination as an ordered collection of pictures. This relates to the repetition of forms I described earlier when I discussed the translation of space/time by early abstract artists.[142] This order forms the object's path through space/time and is called the object's 'world line'.[143] If the earth rotated only and perfectly around its north - south pole axis, all world lines for two-dimensional objects would be perfectly circular, and the world lines for three-dimensional objects would be curved tube-like shapes. But as the axis of the earth is not only wobbling, but also gradually changing its position, and because earth orbits together with the moon in an elliptical path around the sun, the world lines of all objects on earth (including ourselves) are not straight lines or circles but very complex curved shapes with properties of both an elipse and a spiral, following a kind of oscillating motion.[144]

Coming back to the evidence and theories discussed before, it seems justified to

---

that there might even be more kinds of waves that we currently are incapable of detecting.

142 See §4 on Bohm and Biederman. See also the discussion on Van Doesburg and Joost Baljeu, earlier in this chapter.

143 This is not to be mistaken for a geodetic line. A geodetic line is the straightest connection between two points (not the shortest connection) in three-dimensional curved space, like the lines of longitude and lattitude.

144 In art this makes not only geometry, but also certain kinds of free-hand calligraphic and organically flowing shapes almost a natural result of these non-linear cosmic motions. I suggest this might be what Matjushin sensed in the expression of sheer swirling power captured in the growth structure of roots of trees. Trees that grow upwards in a spiralling fashion under the influence of gravity and earth's complex rotations. This makes tree-roots - or their branches - into historical displays of nature's motions.

expect that there are also world lines or paths through space/time that are not always visible to our perception, but which more or less explain invisible phenomena.[145] Further ideas about the connections between phenomena that seem to exist, although according to our perception they clearly are not connected, have led to theories about the connections of all phenomena at a deeper level. Experiments showed sufficient evidence for acceptance of the existence of some underlying structure at a level of reality. This underlying level is so deep into the micro-world that existing technology can neither measure nor prove the existence of the tiny particles, which one assumes must exist as building stones of this structure. This dilemma has sent theoretical physics on an insecure journey at the highest level of abstract thinking in science's history. Examples of such theories were the initial attempts for Superstring Theory[146] and

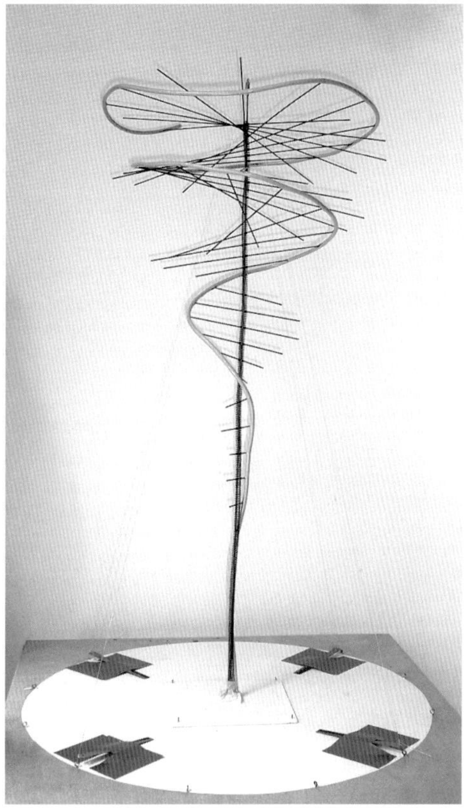

11. Michael Kidner (1917-) **Fleeting Time**, 2004
Extension spring, wire armature, fibreglass rods, polythene tubing, nylon stays, plywood base 94 x 66 x 66 cm (37 x 26 x 26 inches)

"The diminishing spiral was prompted by my sense of time (at the age of 80) getting shorter. What had not occurred to me was as the diameter of the coile diminishes the vertical distance between then increases. Perhaps the vertical distance represents movement, in my case slowness. What used to be a short way now seems a long way or time seems shorter."
Michael Kidner August 2004

145 See David Deutsch and Michael Lockwood, "The Quantum Physics of Time Travel (common sense may rule out such excursions - but the laws of physics do not)", Scientific American March 1994, p.50-56. This kind of theorizing has led to the many-universes interpretation, first proposed by Hugh Everett III in 1957, long before even the most recent Two-Slit experiments proved the existence of 'tunnelling photons'.

146 In 1970 the Japanese/American physicist Yoichiro Nambu proposed that elementary particles can be described as extended, one-dimensional objects. Just as all objects have their world lines, all particles have their complex paths through space/time (their traces through time) that can be imagined as strings. Visually one can compare this to a sequence of dots on paper building a line. As we move through space/time at an identical speed to the speed of these particles, we perceive only the tips of these particles (that is, those that move at the same speed through space/time as we do). One might imagine a pointillist painting as the level of our eye-perception, and under all the tiny dots, strings swirl through space/time. All objects we see in our environment are composed of large quantities of these strings. These particles appear to us as basically one-dimensional. As we learned earlier in this chapter, particles do not stand still, but oscillate or vibrate at high frequencies. These particles make phenomena perceptable to our vision by synchronizing their frequencies with the frequencies of (day)light. Yoichiro Nambu thus stated that particles are strings that whip around at the speed of light and called them lightstrings. Superstrings are strings that posses supersymmetry. Symmetry in particle-physics is a property of a physical system that does not change when the system is transformed in any way.

Twistor Theory.[147] New developments in Superstring Theory have become of special interest again in the last decade and seems to be the prevalent theory for the near future. For one thing, this theory has reconfirmed as fundamental the notion of rhythm or vibration, even at the smallest levels of particles. These theories differentiate between force-particles and matter-particles, exemplifying the connection between the microworld of particles with the macro-world of the universe, with the purpose of understanding the fabric of space/time.[148]

The general scientific objective is clear: the desire to find an explanation for reality, containing the perceptible world we live in, the universe, and also the invisible world of possible other dimensions that explains the underlying structure through which everything seems to be interrelated. In other words, the general scientific objective is the search for a Theory of Everything.[149]

Einstein predicted that all objects that move near the speed of light are shortened or become flatter until they reach the speed of light and become completely flat or one-dimensional. We can only perceive space and three-dimensional objects in space through the lapse of some time. This implies that if we were able to see, frame by frame, pictures taken at the speed of light, we would see every individual frame as absolutely flat. Compare this to a film in which the film maker walks around an object. The picture-frames will show you slices of existence in space/time of that object in relation to the motion of the camera. All our ways of perceiving space visually, be it by the movements of our eyes, the constant motions of our heads, the swinging motions of our whole bodies

---

147 Einstein's Theory of General Relativity is based on ideas about the geometry of curved space, which physicist Roger Penrose extended by trying to include the processes of Quantum Theory. Penrose proposed, that in order to unite Quantum Theory and space/time, a more complex space was necessary. In such a complex space, the fundamental objects are not points but twisting lines. He named his concept 'Twistor Theory', which is related to String Theory. According to Roger Penrose, a point in reality becomes a twisting line in space/time, a line in reality becoming a distorted plane in space/time, etc. Penrose imagined this curved space of space/time as one composed of a patchwork of small, flat spaces, in contrast to the linear representations of space/time advanced by String Theory. When the overall space is curved, their individual segments will not join smoothly at their edges. The individual segments are considered flat, as they mark a certain two-dimensional slice of space/time.

148 In these recent developments the string is understood as a tiny loop of vibrating or oscillating energy. These strings do not only have a different charge from the classical particles (as electrons), but can have different tensions as well as differences in their vibrational behaviour. The differences in their vibrational patterns give rise to different masses and force charges. See Brian Greene, "The Elegant Universe - Superstrings, Hidden Dimensions, and the Quest for the Ultimate Theory" (New York: Vintage Books, 1999).

149 More theories emerge. Some scientists have proposed to replace String Theory for an even more complex theory with the name M-Theory. 'M' comes from membrane. A membrane being a two-dimensional slice of space/time. See Duff, "The Theory Formerly Known as Strings", Scientific American February 1998, p.54-59. See Brain Greene, "The Elegant Universe - Superstrings, Hidden Dimensions, and the Quest for the Ultimate Theory". Like String Theory, M-Theory relies on the idea of supersymmetry. It refers to the theory from the early 1920's by Polish physicist Theodore Kaluza and his Swedish colleague Oskar Klein, who suggested that space/time may have a fifth dimension that is not infinite as the other four are, but closes into itself, forming a circle. It is striking that most artists who have explored space/time in their abstract art in the end create compositions that simulate a motion looping back into itself. Following M-Theory, this feature of such a closed but dynamic composition could be quite well understood as the fifth dimension in art. Furthermore, I

or our tactile actions, are time-based! Therefore, one can imagine that all events that occur at the same moment in space/time are flat segments of space/time or thin slices of the world lines of all objects in our environment. When enough of these flat segments overlap like transparencies in our perception, we perceive space as if there has been a lapse of time.

Physicist Roger Penrose proposed picturing space/time as trying to cover a large ball with a set of flat cards. A picture that illustrates this quite literally has not been published by Penrose, but by the artist Charles Biederman in 1958.[150] Biederman obviously could not have intended to explain Penrose's theory - that theory was not yet born - but aimed to explain the structuring of Cézanne's paintings. Chance or not, this example shows another analogy between art and science that seems worthwhile to explore. For instance, the mathematics involved in fitting regions of space together to cover some larger space is called 'cohomology', and plays an important role in Penrose's ideas.[151] In fine art one can find many more examples of artists doing exactly that (fitting regions of space to cover a larger space) and what I have earlier proposed calling 'visual cohomology'.[152]

Another interesting analogy between scientific ideas and fine art is another idea by Penrose related to the above-discussed problem of space/time. At a certain moment Penrose developed an illustration of null-lines (the paths taken by light and massless objects, comparable to the twisting world lines) of the Robinson-Congruence, a mathematical understanding of the electromagnetic field, which inspired Penrose for his ideas about complex space/time.[153] When one looks at this drawing of complex lines of force, it shows that these null-lines move in three dimensions in a combination of centrifugal and centripetal forces in an almost spiral-like, or oscillating fashion. It becomes quite

suggest that the interpretation of a fifth dimension in science as well as in art reflect the conservation of energy, which seems to be the major process of nature. In 1978 this was furthered by Cremmer, Julia and Scherk of the École Supérieure de Paris into a concept containing 10 spatial dimensions and 1 temporal dimension. After some harsh criticism this idea of 11-dimensions was forgotton. Only in the late 1990's did it surface again as M-Theory, bringing the long sought unification of the geometry of space/time with Quantum mechanics closer. Another recent development is called Quantum Gravity. See Lee Smolin, "Three Roads to Quantum Gravity".

150 See Charles Biederman, "The New Cézanne". See §4.

151 This clearly also happens in Cézanne's paintings and can be found in the famous Penrose tilings.

152 See my article, "Extensionalism and Twistor Space: Similarities and Relations between Art and Twistor Theory", in Leonardo magazine, Vol.2 8 Nr .3 (Boston: MIT Press, 1995). Examples of 'visual cohomology' one can find in the artworks by Cézanne, Augusto Giacometti, Exter, (certain paintings by) Mondrian, Freundlich, Hinterreiter, Biederman and Escher. More recently one can find examples in the drawings and sculptures by Michael Kidner, the kinetic curtains of Tim Prentice, the paintings of Jean-Pierre Maury, the disc-installations of Paul Dacey, the paintings and installations by Richard Purdy. You will also find 'visual cohomology' as an important feature of my own artworks, especially in the large wall-sculptures and paintings of "The Dragon Series". Pointillism, the development in painting initiated by Seurat and Signac through inspiration by Chevreul, also provides a foundation for this idea, even more by the developments in painting following the lead of Signac: fragmenting colours in similar colour-patches or brushstrokes all over the canvas and fitting them into one harmonious whole again. Mondrian with his Neo-Plastic and Boogie-Woogie paintings perhaps illustrates the ultimate solution, but also Pollock in a similar, but different way.

153 It is a good example of how a visualized theory can be easier and quicker understandable than a complex mathematical formula.

revealing to compare Penrose's illustration of the Robinson Congruence to the simulations of highly complex movements in artworks by so many artists described in this publication.[154] Richard Purdy, in his artistic vocabulary, used some shapes that seem to be oscillating in a similar way to Penrose's visualization of the electromagnetic field. Resemblances like this are not wishful thinking by artists, or projections afterwards. Penrose himself not only emphasized the importance of thinking visually, but also was inspired by his interest in projective geometry and cristallography. This combination has also fascinated and inspired quite a few abstract artists, like Hans Hinterreiter or M.C.Escher some 50 years before Penrose.[155]

Thanks to Einstein, one knows that gravitational forces will influence - will bend - the path through space/time of light. Any attempt to try to understand the properties of space/time will have to become much more complex, as evidence from cosmic research shows. For instance, the fluctuating magnetic storm from the sun (the solar wind), which also influences the rotation of our earth and therefore of our perception of time, seems to show a certain cyclic behaviour. However, in the meantime research has shown that many other stars also project their own cosmic winds through the cosmos, undoubtedly also colliding and interacting with the solar wind and magnetic field of the earth![156] These forces have to be taken into account when one wishes to further understand the paths through space/time.

One can imagine the path of a slice through time forming a distorted volume, of which the outlines are based on the outlines of this slice. This is called its 'world volume'.[157] Some years ago I suggested the possibility of including in this discussion the aspect of colour for an even more complete theory of space/time.[158] Because null-lines consist of the movement of light and light makes colour possible, perhaps actual three-dimensional coloured forms can be virtually or metaphorically understood as references to the movement of two-dimensional colour planes through space/time, just as points in Penrose's twistor space are a complex structure of null-lines in space/time and lines in twistor space are distorted planes in space/time. An abstract, coloured, three-dimensional shape could thus be understood as the 'world volume' of the shape in real space/time.[159] Because colour is so important in our space/time, and as I am an artist using colour also in sculpture, this seems very plausible to me.[160] This seems especially plausible, because

---

154 See also the discussion by Semir Zeki on the processing of our brains while seeing a Calder-mobile, earlier this chapter.

155 Penrose was in touch with Escher. See Hans Hinterreiter, "Die Kunst der reinen Form - Eine Formenlehre für moderne Künstler, Band I - Ordnung und Taufe der Elementarformen. " See Doris Schattschneider, "M.C. Escher - Visions of Symmetry" (W.H. Freeman and Co., 1990).

156 See §14 on the cosmic influences on the rhythms on earths, which have a great probability of affecting our space/time perceptions.

157 Compare the concept of the world-line earlier in this chapter.

158 See my article, "Extensionalism and Twistor Space: Similarities and Relations between Art and Twistor Theory".

159 The "Colour-Form" sculptures from 1929/30 by Matjushin seem very good metaphors for this idea. See Alla V. Povelikhina, "Organica" (Cologne: Galerie Gmurzynska, 1999).

all space/time ideas include properties of light, and light and colour are basically equivalent.

6.6 SUMMARY AND CONCLUSIONS

Although one certainly finds many works of art through all centuries that seem to incorporate a certain concept of space/time, from early abstract art onwards artists, parallel to scientists, have gradually explored and still study space/time quite seriously.[161] Since the 1970's it seems that space/time and the notion of a fourth dimension in art are not researched as solitary subjects anymore, but more or less accepted as important properties of making art. In many modern works of art one will find a form- and composition language clearly simulating aspects of space/time, although the artist may not even be aware of this.[162] Though not all artists consciously study the various aspects of space/time, all artists are, as are all other human beings, part of the processes of space/time. Therefore, to incorporate aspects of space/time into their artworks is just natural (besides being unavoidable). Another reason for this to happen is because the modern language of form and composition is related to what the first pioneers of abstract art developed. However, it is primarily a logical result of how human knowledge advances. It seems that the moment some knowledge is accepted, it becomes adopted and, as such, from then on is applied without one being consciously aware of what it is and how it was developed. In any case, space/time has become a natural feature of art's depiction of reality.

The big difference between art and science is and continues to be that artists depend on trusting their visual argumentation, including their own process of visual argumentation. This is the process of focussed seeing and continuous reflection that we could call intuition. Additionally, it is intuition that is mostly non-verbal.[163] The trouble for scientists is that they cannot trust their intuition for sensing a solution, but must in

160 Colour changes continuously in three-dimensional space under the influence of changes in light through time. This property of colour seems a powerful tool to further explore complex space/time.

161 It should be remarked here, that depictions concerning a certain (unconscious?) understanding of space/time are as old as mankind, for instance in the rotation-symbols, all kinds of celestial charts and models of the skies, much later in Michelangelo's 'serpentine' figure-stands, in Rubens', Tiepolo's and other Baroque paintings, or in Turner's swirling masses of paint. Of course one could argue that space/time has always been a subject in art while looking at the explorations of light and depth in paintings, for instance Rembrandt or the Impressionists, but they did not include a more conscious exploration of space/time concepts analogous to scientific interpretations to the degree the abstract artists did and do. One often encounters artists who do not explore actual motion, but such a strong simulation of motion it seems their paintings and sculptures are continuously moving at high speed: examples are Roberto Matta, Charles Biederman, César Domela, Joost Baljeu, the artworks by Manfred Mohr, who explores the hyper-cube in growing complexity or the sculptures by Hartmut Böhm, who explores infinity, quite a few sculptures by Anthony Caro and Chillida, the fabulous works of the last two decades by Frank Stella, Jean-Pierre Maury, Michael Bette, Al Held, Natvar Bhavsar, Gotthard Graubner, Richard Purdy, and my own works.

162 A big exception is the growing interest of artists in so-called 'time-based art', meaning art animations generated with the help of a computer, video- or 8mm film camera. One may ask oneself if the majority of these artists are actually aware of aspects of space/time beyond a sequence of events.

163 We do have many experiences and thoughts without actually hearing them in words in our minds, like the

principle depend on knowledge that can be communicated by using a specific linear language like mathematics. Although many innovative scientists have also learned to trust their visual communication capacities, or non-verbal means of spontaneous intuition (a kind of enlightenment?), they are still obliged to prove or justify their conclusions with traditional methods.[164] It is revealing that the scientific search for understanding the fabric of space/time has forced a change in the scientific process itself. The traditional process has always been that experimental physics leads the way, while theoretical physics lagged behind in figuring out what was found in the experiments.[165] Since research has entered the realms of micro-nature that cannot be explored by available experimental technologies, theoretical physcis has taken the lead. It is very interesting to the whole argument in this book that this has led physicists to trust their aesthetic intuition to pursue their quest, instead of building only on the traditional empirical experiments.[166]

The big irony of course is that although artists are accepted when they follow their intuition, in our modern civilization it is still thought that only science brings forth knowledge. Art might seem in theory to take a short cut to truth, but in the end it takes an even more difficult road and much longer time to make its point. Artists need science and philosophy to enhance their own understanding of what they are doing and what they are searching for. They do not need science to merely produce illustrations of scientific theories or to copy a scientific kind of research. Artists, scientists and philosophers do not live in perfect isolation, but under the influence of the existing knowledge they find on their paths. Under the influence of the 'Zeitgeist' they search for the same thing: to better understand reality, to better understand our being, to better understand our individual self, 'to see one's self', using a combination of visual and non-visual means.

In this chapter we have seen how even a highly abstract notion like space/time, in the

---

immediate experiences of beauty and the sublime, or sensing that something is good or wrong. This will be explored in §7 and §8. See §5.4 on 'blindsight' and 'sublimal perception.'

164 See Arthur I. Miller, "Imagery in Scientific Thought - Creating 20th Century Physics" (Boston: Mit Press, 1987 - orig. 1984). Miller discusses how scientists like Einstein initially virtually saw the solution to complex problems, like the duality of light, but needed many years to work on the mathematical proof.

165 In contradiction to what one would understand, 'experimental' physics implies a branche of physics that is specialized in creating and executing empirical experiments.

166 See Brain Greene, "The Elegant Universe - Superstrings, Hidden Dimensions, and the Quest for the Ultimate Theory", p.166-167: "While a theory is being constructed, its incomplete state of development often prevents its detailed experimental consequences from being assessed. Nevertheless, physicists must make choices and exercise judgements about the research direction in which to take their partially completed theory. Some of these decisions are dictated by internal and logical consistency; we certainly require that any sensible theory avoid logical absurdities. Other decisions are guided by a sense of the qualitative experimental implications of one theoretical construct relative to another; we are generally not interested in a theory if it has no capacity to resemble anything we encounter in the world around us. But it is certainly the case that some decisions made by theoretical physicists are founded upon an aesthetic sense - a sense of which theories have an elegance and beauty of structure on par with the world we experience." And: "...as we enter an era in which our theories describe realms of the universe that are increasingly difficult to probe experimentally, physicists do rely on such an aesthetic to help them steer clear of blind alleys and dead-end roads that they might otherwise pursue. So far, this approach has provided a powerful and insightful guide."

end, has to be understood in terms of our perception, meaning before our eyes. Therefore, it is no wonder that in science computer simulation has become such a convincing tool. Computer simulation, for obvious reasons, brings science closer to the realm of fine art, because in these simulations large parts of the substantial information are communicated visually between scientists, without necessarely showing ultimate empirical proof. This development makes artists' endeavours to explore space/time additionally important, although perhaps not as important as the various highly abstract scientific or philosophical interpretations and theories. Because of the various aspects of artistic experience in visualizing intuited knowledge about nature's processes, the artist can offer the scientist alternative (additional) means for his scientific research. Finding analogies between art and science must therefore be understood as a justified and useful approach. To perceive analogies in another discipline certainly supports one's own efforts. It should, therefore, finally become natural that scientists, philosophers and artists keep an open mind for each others' professions.

§7 OBJECT AND SELF

Today a physicist no longer can distinguish significantly between matter and something else.
Erwin Schrödinger, 1953 [1]

When we wish to understand reality we soon discover that we need to understand the confrontation of our selves with this reality. If there was something like completely empty space, there would hardly be a confrontation - maybe only within our own minds - and hardly a reality as we know it. If there was not such a confrontation between what is within ourselves and what is outside our bodies, one might wonder if anything like a self or consciousness could be possible. Objects in space, such as trees, cars, houses, mountains and works of art allow this confrontation, make us conscious, make individuality a possibility and establish how we experience reality. Because of the clear importance of objects to our everyday perception, this chapter focusses on the object and the self. As such, this and the next chapter are immediate extensions of §2, but of course also in direct relation to all other chapters. The duality this chapter addresses is necessary for understanding art as object and therefore needs specific attention. What else does art concern but the 'object and self', or, as we will see, the self through the interaction of object and self?

The interaction between oneself and an object in principle concerns two processes: first, the process of this interaction itself, and secondly, the necessity or meaning of this interaction and our understanding of the object as such. Neither can be separated from the other. Because it is my conviction that through a deeper understanding of this interaction we can find clues for understanding ourselves and our appreciation and need for art, this chapter will try to cope with the highly philosophical and abstract level of this subject. Unfortunately, it seems unavoidable to include a wide variety of difficult subjects, artistic concepts, philosophies and scientific theories that seem to have nothing in common at first. However, each are of critical importance for understanding the interaction with reality, the world and objects, in which artworks as objects themselves seem to play such important roles. It is precisely in the confrontation with the object that the dilemma can be found between the image we have of ourselves as objective observer and as participant.

In principle objects are three-dimensional appearances emerging in our perceptive field and possessing a certain materiality.[2] Matter is characterized by extension, weight, mass and movement and is defined by space/time. These properties already show that

---

[1] See Erwin Schrödinger, "What is Matter?", Scientific American Special Issue 1991 (orign. Scientific American September 1953), p.16.

[2] Let it be clear from the start: all artworks, including drawings, computer prints, even video or computer animations are 'objects' in the strict sense: they all need material (including devices to project or show on a monitor) to present them in reality to our eyes.

the discussion about matter entails a discussion about energy and automatically concerns subjects like the elementary particle, fields of force, movement, continuum, space/time, extension and interaction, and thus a diversity of topics in science, philosophy and art. The reader is kindly requested to recall §2, because all through human history matter has been understood as equal to substance or essence.

7.1 KINESIS AND EXTENSION

In philosophy one distinguishes between *materia prima* (primary matter) and *materia secunda* (formed matter). The first evolves from Aristotelian thought,[3] the 'hylemorphism' (hyle as duality matter-form), through which Aristotle tried to find an explanation for the changeability of things by stating that the primary matter relates to its form as potentiality and act. In other words: change in all objects around us happens because these objects contain a certain primary matter that causes its individual form as it appears to us while it also causes the form to change at some point.

The primary matter is universal, the form is specific. In case of change only the form changes, not the primary matter. The formed matter is the matter that we perceive with our physical being.[4] The existence of primary matter we can only try to acknowledge without actually perceiving it with our senses.

Early Ionian thinkers and, later, Aristotle understood that the physical existent, the being, must necessarily be extended.[5] An existent is a body existing at a certain moment, including living and non-living appearances like objects. *Existo* is the Greek notion for emergence, to raise oneself, to appear, to be perceivable, to be manifest. Aristotle understood the infinite as an attribute of substantial being, and body as substantial being, as existent with an extension in every direction. Bodies interact as a result of the principle of extension.[6] When we briefly imagine the extension of all objects or bodies as waves being catapulted in every direction starting in a body, we can imagine the waves of a particular object colliding with the waves of another object.[7] This process is interaction. Extension in every direction automatically introduces the notions of movement, time and force into the discussion.

Aristotle wrote: "... physis (nature) in the primary and strict sense is the ousia (beingness, essence) of things which have in themselves, as such, an arche (principle, source) of kinesis (change, movement).[8] The Greek notion kinesis refers to a process of change and development and is therefore inseparably connected to being. Ivor Leclerc writes: "The *ousia* of things is to be identified with *eidos*, form, rather than with *hyle*, matter,

[3] See also §2.
[4] See Dr. J. Waldram, "Encyclopedie van de Filosofie" (Baarn: Tirion, 1993), p.154.
[5] This view was also held by Anaximander of the Milenian School, around 450 BC.
[6] See §5 on the notion of the projective field.
[7] This is well illustrated in paintings by the Futurists and Rayonists; or by the various circular ripples on the surface of a pond caused by rain drops.
[8] See Ivor Leclerc, "The Nature of Physical Existence" (Lanham, MD: University Press of America, 1986), p.107.

and it is accordingly in *eidos* and not in hyle that is to be found the source, the spring, the impetus, of *kinesis*."[9] The real essence of reality must not be sought in the material components of an object, but in the composition of its form. Here we can find reasons for the eternal change that we perceive around us everyday. For example, when we do not look at the elementary properties of wood, but look at the appearance of a tree, we can see that the twisted way the roots, trunk and branches have grown through time show (or, in a sense, they simulate) the power of continuous change of nature. In rotation symbols and repetitive, rhythmic designs and patterns in ancient and folk art, and later, especially since the Baroque in fine art, many artists understood the importance of kinesis as reflecting the essence or eidos and deliberately simulated motion in their artwork.[10] The notions of infinity, extension and movement were already quite early keys in our thinking about reality. The kinesis of the physical universe is infinite in the sense that physical being is a continuing process, decided by a coming into being, while the force of kinesis guarantees that the being never comes to a stand still, but always develops further.[11]

Since the Greeks, these considerations have been extended and adjusted into theories that try to explain the resemblances between aspects of the totality with every entity in that totality. Cusanus, who influenced many of the important thinkers of the 16th century,[12] understood the universe as a contraction of God (the universe incorporating God's powers in a denser form than the eternal vastness of God himself), and the world as an explicatio Dei, an expression of God. Ivor Leclerc writes about Cusanus:

> *"The universe, as the very word indicates, is a one or unity, but it is a contracted unity, a contraction of the infinite absolute unity to a particular form. This contracted unity, the universe, is then further contracted to the many actual individual existents, which are thus each a contracted unity."*[13]

Today we would speak of researching the analogies between the macrocosms and the microcosms.

Object and subject are two poles that can only be understood in their relationship. In the Middle Ages, clearly still under influence of Aristotelian philosophy, subject was considered equivalent to substance, because it was seen as the bearer of properties and

---

[9] Ibid., p.120. Ivor Leclerc is Fuller E. Callaway Professor of Metaphysics and Moral Philosophy Emeritus, Emory University.

[10] This relates to the treatment of kinetic art in §3 on constructivism and §6 on space/time. Also compare the discussion on the continuum.

[11] Compare this to Whitehead's notion 'becoming a being'. See Alfred N. Whitehead, "Process and Reality", corrected edition, edited by David Ray Griffin and Donald W. Sherburne (New York: The Free Press, 1978 - orig. 1929), p.22. This relates quite well to most contemporary theories in science concerning the continuous changing circumstances, like by Prigogene or the Theory of Complexity, discussed later in this chapter.

[12] Cusanus influenced Paracelsus and later Leibniz.

[13] See Ivor Leclerc, "The Nature of Physical Existence", p.79. Compare Bohm's Implicate Order and wholeness, and Bohm/Hiley's "Undivided Universe", discussed later in this chapter.

actions. Subjects existed independently of man and of his knowledge, though man himself was perceived as a subject (and as a carrier of knowledge). René Descartes understood a body as res extensa (extended substance) and the human soul as res cogitans (thinking substance), introducing the duality of body and soul, of object and subject. Because Descartes believed matter to be mathematical, it was his conviction that a body is the real essence of the physical, and thus, the extension of matter is caused by everything being a thing with extension in length, width and depth, and must be continuous and homogeneous. Therefore, a physical existent must be one sole continuing 'res extensa'.[14] Isaac Newton followed Descartes' considerations.[15]
Leibniz wrote:

> *"I do not think that substance is constituted by extension alone, since the concept of extension is incomplete. Nor do I think that extension can be conceived in itself, but I consider it an analysable and relative concept, for it can be resolved into plurality, continuity, and coexistence or the existence of parts at one and the same time."*[16]

The way Leibniz understood extension is that it could only exist in a plurality of appearances, co-existing simultaneously. By their extension, these appearances shape continuity or the continuum. He did not see extension as a property of matter itself, but as an aspect of how matter exists, viewing extension as a relationship between substances. Extension itself is incomplete, because it is not a physical substance, but a relation between substances.[17] Furthermore, it is a relation that can change through time.

[14] Descartes lived from 1596-1650. See Ivor Leclerc, "The Nature of Physical Existence", p.187. René Descartes, in "Space and Matter" (orig.1644), in Richard Coyne, "Technoromanticism - digital narrative, holism, and the romance of the real" (Cambridge, MA: MIT Press, 1999). p.91: "The nature of matter, or of a body considered in general, does not consist in its being a thing that has hardness or weight, or color, or any other sensible property, but simply in its being a thing that has extension in length, breadth, and depth." Coyne continues: "So a property such as hardness can be described in terms of resistance to movement through space. Furthermore, all properties such as hardness, color, heaviness, coldness, and heat can change. The one constant is that the object occupies space." This concept is analogous to Giordano Bruno's (1548-1600) concept of objects immersed in space, space as extended universal matter. See Ivor Leclerc, "The Nature of Physical Existence", p.162: "The general meaning of *spatium* at the beginning of the modern era was still that of 'extent, stretch, interval', and when this is borne in mind together with Bruno's conception of the extent vacant of body as filled with the universal matter, his new use of *spatium* becomes clear: 'Space therefore is a certain continuous physical quantity consisting in a triple dimension, in which the magnitude of bodies is captured, by nature before all bodies, and subsisting without all bodies, indifferently receiving all things, without conditions of action and passion, intermixed, impenetrable, not formable, not locatable, exteriorily embracing all bodies, and incomprehensibly within, containing all bodies.' " Bruno understands space as three-dimensional extent that is the universal matter itself, in which all objects and beings (all 'bodies') are immersed, while these can only be as they are by their immersion. Here, one may draw an interesting analogy to Oriental philosophies, especially Taoism and 'no thingness' (see §2).
[15] See §6 on space/time where I mention how Newton understood absolute time as an independent entity equivalent to duration - which is another word for continuity, or for Descartes' res extensa.
[16] See Ivor Leclerc, "The Nature of Physical Existence", p.243.
[17] Ibid., p.244. Leibniz wrote: "Extension is itself, for me, an attribute resulting from many substances existing continuously at the same time."

Leibniz proposed a direct connection between movement and body, movement and plurality, and gave potential force fundamental importance. He called this a science of dynamics.[18] His ideas belong to the very first theories that proposed thinking about reality as composed of something else than appearances determined by the separation between objects and subjects.

In the early 20th century, Leibniz's ideas were furthered by philosophers such as Alfred North Whitehead. Whitehead, discussing Leibniz, emphasized the impossibility of isolating any element ('privacy'= isolation). He wrote,

> *"The order of nature, prevalent in the cosmic epoch in question, exhibits itself as a morphological scheme involving eternal objects of the objective species. The most fundamental elements in this scheme are those eternal objects in terms of which the general principles of coordinate division itself are expressed. These eternal objects express the theory of extension in its most general aspect. In this theory the notion of the atomicity of actual entities, each with its concrescent privacy, has been entirely eliminated. We are left with the theory of extensive connection, of whole and part, of points, lines, and surfaces, and of straightness and flatness."*[19]

From studying the statements by the early abstract artists, contemporaries of Whitehead, we can find evidence that this kind of thinking also had its analogy in art. It can only be repeated that this is no strange thing or mere chance, as many of these early abstract artists read, studied and discussed ideas from science and philosophy - as also is the case today. For example, Matjushin followed the method or system of a perception of the world as an organic whole. In his opinion, in the organic world a tree, stone and man do not exist separately but can only evolve in a system of a whole and exist in a general mutual connectedness and movement, even involving the connection of the globe with infinite space.[20] In the first two decades of the 20th century, one can find in painting quite a few variations of such an emphasis on the connectedness of an object or being with the whole. Some of these artistic concepts were inspired by the scientific concepts of lines of force originally proposed in 19th century electromagnetic theory and furthered by new theories about space/time.[21] Because a line - any line - on a paint-

---

18 This is comparable to the Greek notion 'dynamis'. Ibid., p.259.

19 See Whitehead's notion of 'extensive connection'. See Alfred N. Whitehead, "Process and Reality", corrected edition, edited by David Ray Griffin and Donald W. Sherburne (New York: The Free Press, 1978 - orig. 1929), p.294-301. For the quotation, ibid., p.292. Compare this last sentence to Kandinsky's "Point and Line to the Plane", which will be discussed later in this book. You will find that the idea of points, lines and planes (Whitehead's 'surfaces') is not related only to problems in art or mathematics, but a crucial topic in discussing the order of space and time since the early Greek. See §12.3.

20 This clearly is related to Oriental thought, which should come as no surprise because artists like Matjushin were well informed about this. See §3 on constructivism, §2.1 and §2.2.

21 There are quite a few paintings one can find with titles referring to 'lines of force', by Rodchenko, Popova, Gontcharova or Larionov. One can also find paintings with references to 'vortices' and matrix-like compositions by Balla, Boccioni and the other Futurists or Cubists.

ing or drawing attracts and leads the eye, it also gives the impression of being a line of force. The visual tension it evokes in the viewer's perception has everything to do with force. Of course, this can be enhanced by using very expressive lines or rough brushstrokes. This is the genius of strong calligraphy. Twentieth century Japanese artist Yu-Ichi's paintings offer a magnificent example, but clearly also artworks by Kandinsky, Jackson Pollock or Frank Stella.

In my own work I am fascinated by the strong power of two- and three-dimensional coloured lines of force. I am also quite involved in studying the play of virtual lines of force, meaning the visual connections between separated entities (or objects), through which a fragmented whole is still understood as one whole in our perception. In such cases, the colours, shapes and contrasts of the various entities cause the viewer's eyes to 'jump', virtually drawing lines of force between these separated entities. Thus they make them perceptable as a group with a combined meaning as one whole - a composition. This obviously also happens in figurative or representational art. Other artistic interpretations that shape such optical 'lines of force' are realized by repetitions or sequences of certain units, like the sequences of colour and squares used by Richard Paul Lohse and Richard Purdy, the highly complex meshworks by Leonardo Mosso, Michael Kidner or Jean-Pierre Maury, the patterns of Philip Taaffe, the paintings of fragments of a matrix by Philippe Jahanguir, or the complex compositions by Paul Dacey using painted discs that are only visually connected in a system. Because of my own artistic research, I am convinced that 'lines of force' automatically result in extension as an important paradigm for studying reality.

see pictures 31, 40, 41, 43, 47, 49

7.2 PARTICLES OR WAVES

Discussing our confrontation with objects, with anything outside our own bodies, raises a question about on what level this confrontation takes place. The level of visual perception is but one level. The interaction on a particle level is another.[22] The particle level is especially important, because to one's eyes it might seem that one's own body and a building or table are very clearly separated, but at a particle level this becomes less obvious. Although I discussed this subject in §6 in relation to our understandings of space/time, let's look into some more ideas that have everything to do with the previous discussions of extension and our subject here, and also help us understand how we think about object and self today.

Leibniz defined his ideas in his theory of monads.[23] Monads are an infinite number of mutually independent points of force that are characterized by different levels of con-

22 For an extensive historical discussion, see Bernard Pullman, "The Atom in the History of Human Thought", translated by Axel Reisinger (Oxford: Oxford University Press, 2001 - orig. 1998). Bernard Pullman (1919-1996) was a Professor of Quantum Chemistry at the Sorbonne University, France. For a discussion on ideas of basic particles in ancient Indian thinking, see Swami Sivapriyananda, "Astrology and Religion in Indian Art" (New Delhi: Abhinav Publications, 1990).

23 See Gottfried Wilhelm Leibniz, "Monadologie", reprinted in original german/french text (Stuttgart: Philipp Reclam, 1998 - orig. 1714). For an english discussion of origin and contents, see Allison P. Coudert,

sciousness, up to the highest kind of soul-life. The monads each reflect the universe in a different way. It might be interesting to briefly note here that for a very long time, because of the ruling dogma of religion, philosophers and the early scientists always had to think twice before offering a theory that opposed the church. Thus, in the early 18th century in Europe, one was still not completely allowed to think about anything other than God as the start and end of any theory about reality. Under the influence of ancient knowledge from other cultures, like the Kabbalah, sparked by a general interest of the intelligentsia in occult knowledge,[24] and coupled with emerging doubts about determinism and fate, the problem of individuality and freedom in a larger framework slowly and carefully became a central philosophical issue. In this context we must understand that Leibniz tried to propose a theory in which not God, but a particle-like entity, the monad, was the starting point, without criticizing the absolute position of God. He simply placed God far above, and allowed everything else to contain a tiny reflection of God.[25] Thus, after first emphasizing his loyalty to the church's doctrine, he then could focus on a new concept of the world, consisting of entities that interact in one large whole. In Leibniz's own words at the very beginning of his "Monadology" he writes: "1. The monad, which we will discuss here, is nothing else than a simple substance, that enters in compositions; it is simply without any parts."[26] Leibniz emphasized the logic of all parts that cannot be understood as separate entities, but as immersed in a whole.[27] Leibniz' brilliant approach avoided clashes with the church and simultaneously developed a new way of thinking, allowing him to slip in ideas about the existence of individuality and how all individuals are immersed in the whole of reality.

"Leibniz and the Kabbalah" (Dordrecht: Kluwer Academic Publishers, 1995). Some influences on Leibniz were theories by occultist philosophers Francis Mercury van Helmont, Henry More and Jan Amos Komensky (better known as Comenius). Giordano Bruno is the philosopher most often cited as the source of Leibniz's monadology, also of importance was the symbolic language of Plotinus and Nicholas of Cusa (Cusanus). See Allison P. Coudert, "Leibniz and the Kabbalah", p.26: "... Nicholas of Cusa, whose concept of a universal centre as the point of coincidence of individual centres Leibniz translated from theology into anthropology and biology;....".

24 This was an interest shared by nobility all through Europe, partly motivated by the curiosity of their intellect, but surely for a larger part caused by rumours about the possible benefits of occult knowledge. For instance, caused by a fascination for early experiments with chemicals (the combining of different chemical substances to study surprising, magical reactions), including the suggestion that it would be possible to find ways to make gold. The promise of cheap gold inspired many to become sponsors and protectors of alchemists. See Allison P. Coudert, "Leibniz and the Kabbalah". See §2.3.

25 See Allison P. Coudert, "Leibniz and the Kabbalah", p.136: "Thus God alone is the primitive unity or the first simple substance; all created or derivative monads are products, and are generated, so to speak, by continual fulgurations of the divinity from moment to moment, limited by the receptivity of the creature, to which it is essential to be limited."

26 See Gottfried Wilhelm Leibniz, "Monadologie", reprinted in original german/french text (Stuttgart: Philipp Reclam, 1998 - orig. 1714), p.10-11: "1. Die Monade, von der wir hier sprechen werden, ist nichts anderes als eine einfache Substanz, die in Zusammensetzungen eingeht; einfach heißt: ohne Teile" ("1. Le Monade, dont nous parlerons icy, n'est autre chose qv'une substance simple, qvi entre dans les composés; Simple, c'est à dire sans parties.")

27 Leibniz writes, in Allison P. Coudert, "Leibniz and the Kabbalah", p.83: "... all bodies have parts. Consequently they are nothing but a swarm or multiplicity, like a herd of sheep or a pond full of drops of

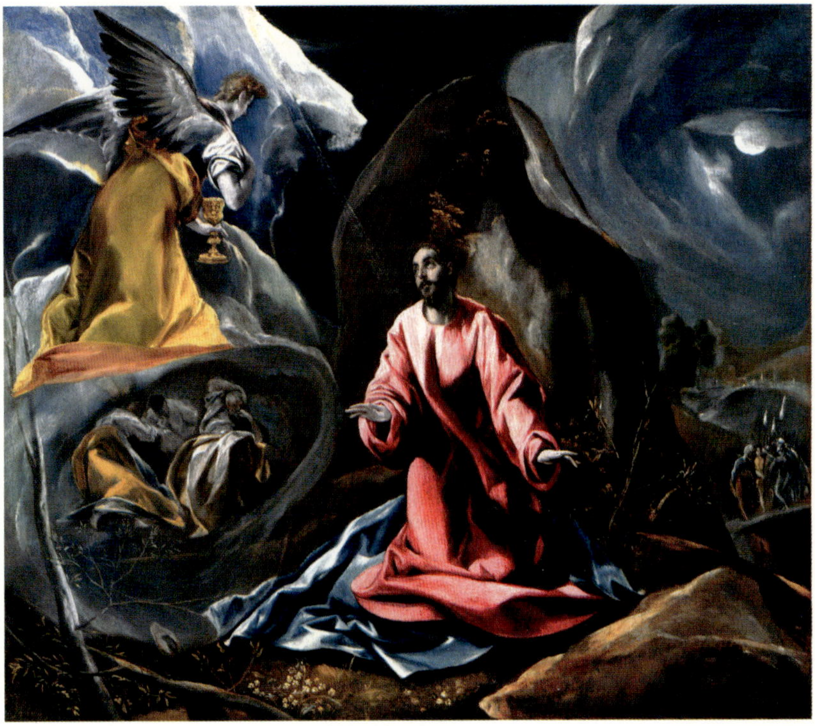

12. El Greco (Spanish, born Crete, 1541-1614)
The Agony in the Garden, about 1590 - 95
Oil on canvas
102,2 x 113,7 cm (44 1/4 x 44 3/4 inches)
Toledo Museum of Art
Purchased with funds from the
Libbey Endowment
Gift of Edward Drummond Libbey, 1946.5
Photo: © Image Source

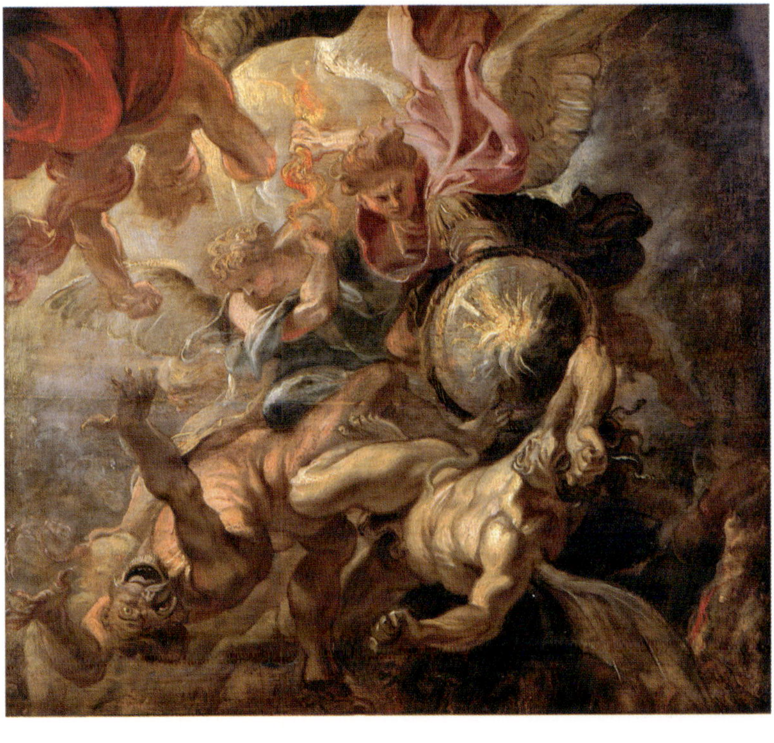

13. Peter Paul Rubens (1577-1640)
De aartsengel Michäel verslaat de opstandige engelen, ca. 1620
Oil on wood, 42 x 52 cm
(16 1/2 x 20 1/2 inches)
Koninklijke Musea voor Schone Kunsten
van België, Bruxelles
Photo: Speltdoorn

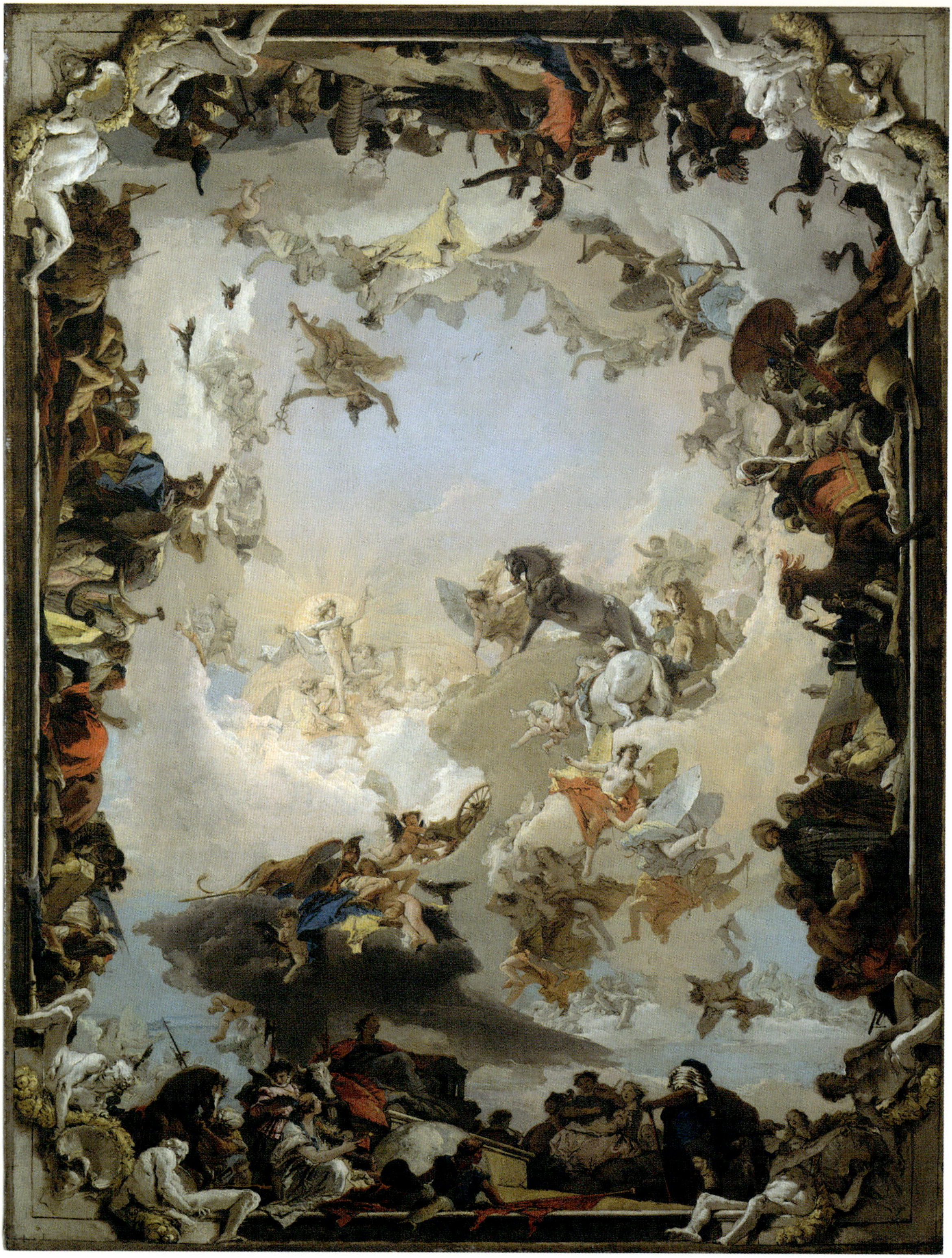

14. Giovanni Battista Tiepolo (1696-1770)
Allegory of the Planets and the Continents. Sketch for the fresco above the staircase of the Residenz, Würzburg, 1752,
Oil on canvas, H185,4 x W139,4 cm (H73 x W54 7/8 inches),
The Metropolitan Museum of Art, Gift of Mr. and Mrs. Charles Wrightsman, 1977 (1977.1.3)

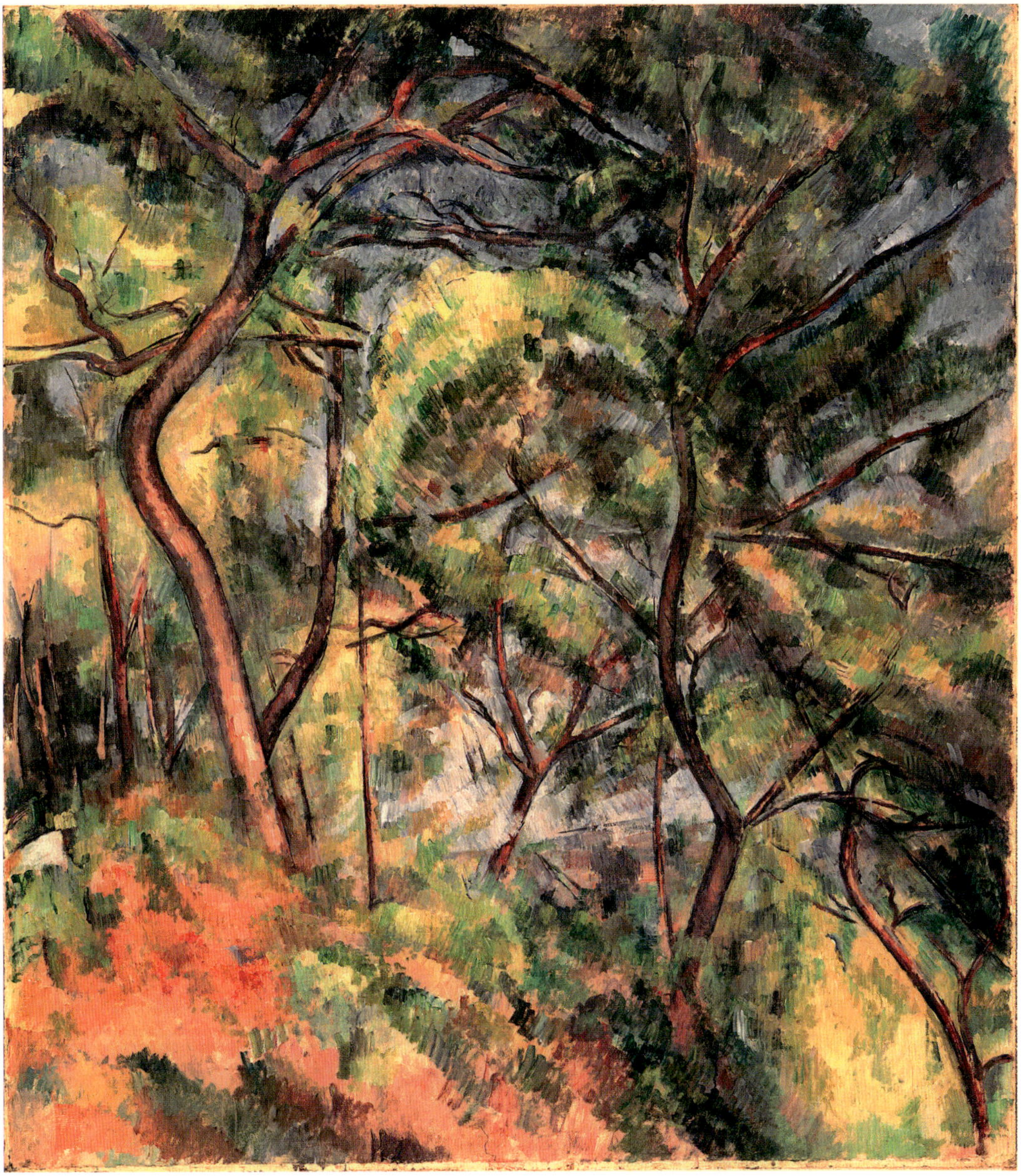

15. Paul Cézanne (1839-1906)
Sous-Bois (Forest), ca 1894
Oil on canvas, 116,2 x 81,3 cm (45 13/16 x 32 inches)
Los Angeles County Museum of Art, Wallis Foundation Fund in memory of Hal B. Wallis

16. Claude - Oscar Monet (1840-1926)
Water-Lilies (Nymphéas), after 1916, Oil on canvas, 200,7 x 426,7 cm (79 x 168 inches)
Photo © The National Gallery, London

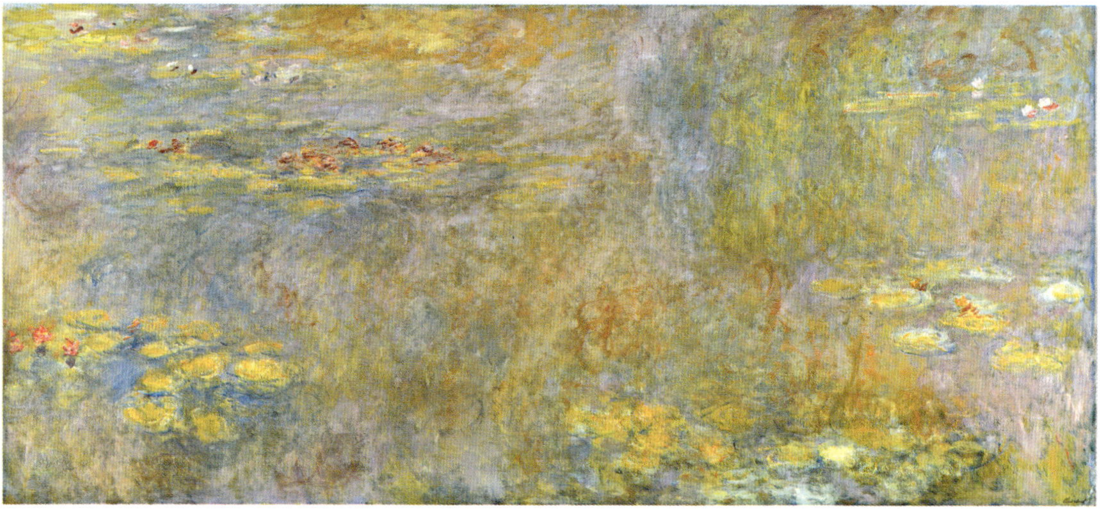

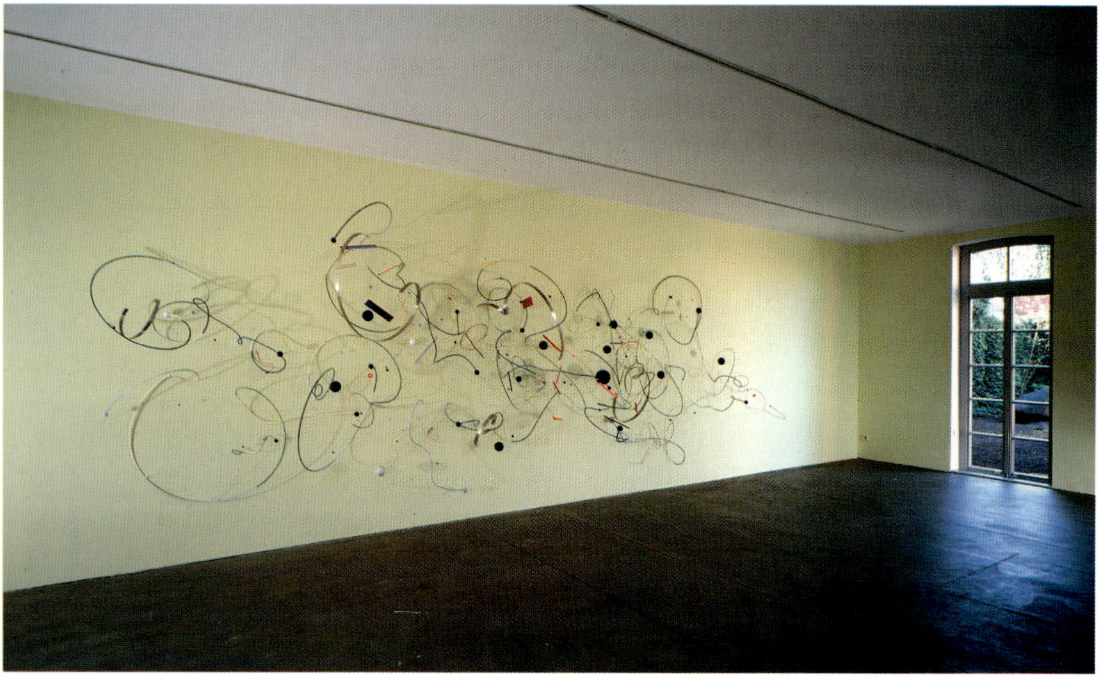

17. Fré Ilgen (1956-)
Ssssh!, The Dragon Series, 2002
Acrylic paint, stainless steel, steel wire, wood, 647 x 229 x 77 cm (250 x 90 x 30 1/4 inches)
Photo: Holger Niehaus
www.ilgen.com/fre.htm

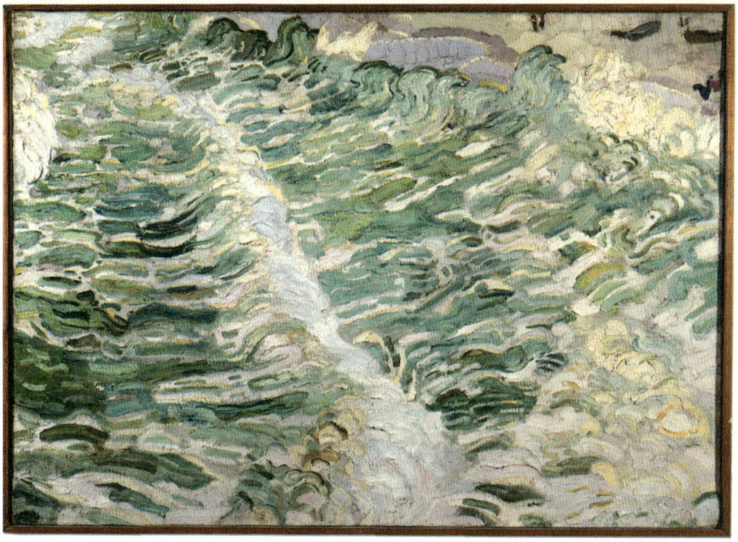

18. Max Beckmann (1884-1950)
Sonniges grünes Meer 1905 Jütland
Oil on canvas, 81 x 110 cm (31 7/8 x 43 5/16 inches)
private collection

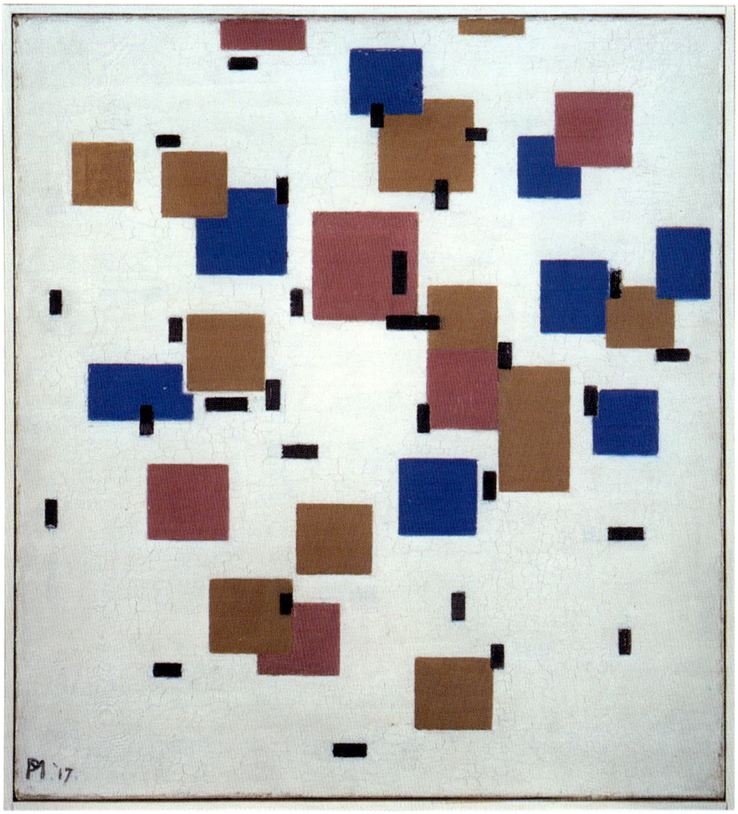

19. Piet Mondrian (1872-1944)
Composition in color A, 1917
Oil on canvas, 50,3 x 45,3 cm (19 3/4 x 17 14/16 inches)
Collection Kröller-Müller Museum, Otterlo

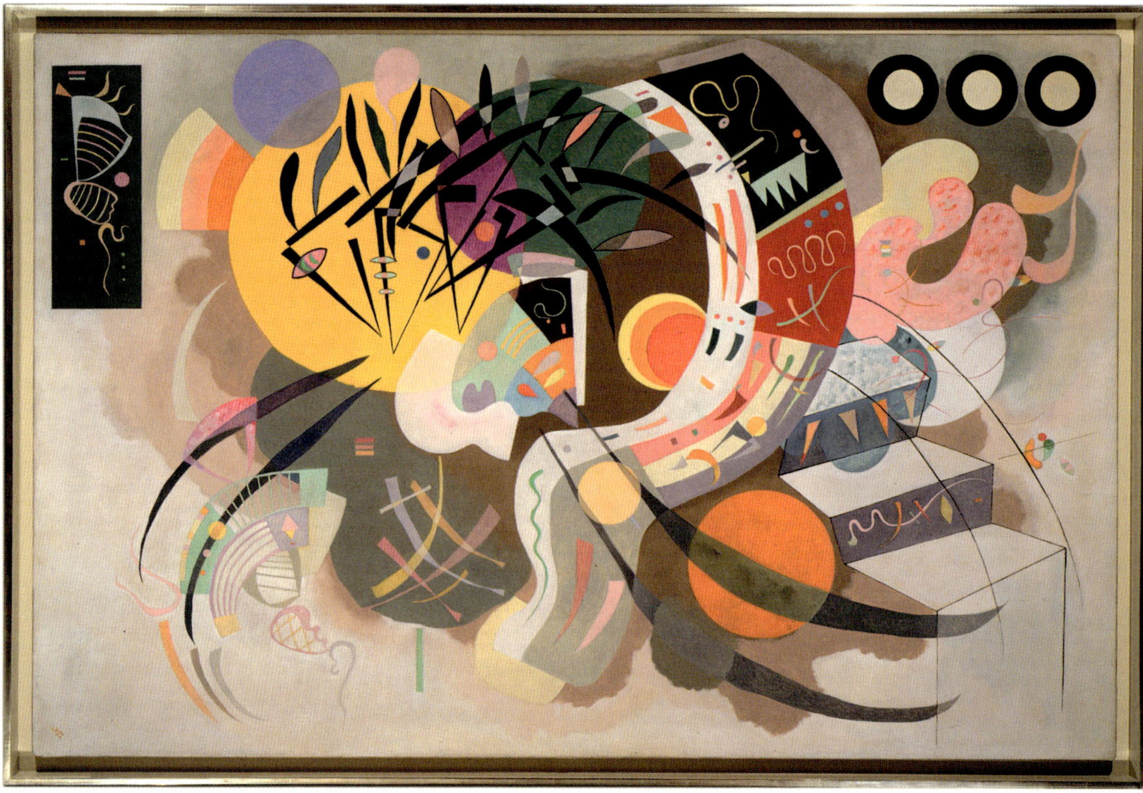

20. Vasily Kandinsky (1866-1944)
Courbe Dominante (Dominant Curve), April 1936
Oil on canvas, 129,4 x 194,2 cm (50 7/8 x 76 1/2 inches)
Solomon R.Guggenheim Museum, New York, 45.989

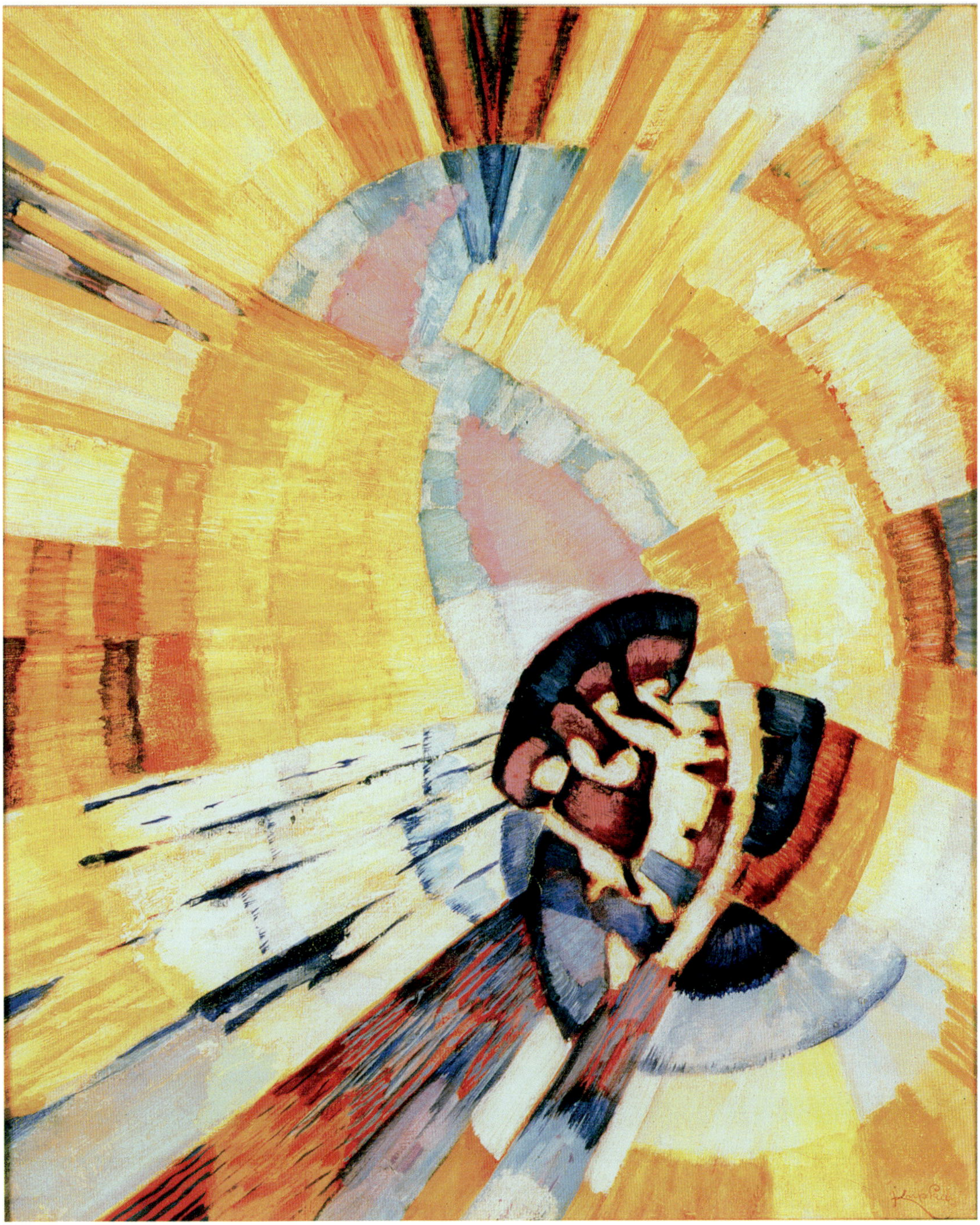

21. Frantisek Kupka (1871 - 1957)
Form de Jaune (Notre Dame), 1911,
Oil on canvas   73 x 59,5 cm (28 3/4 x 23 7/16 inches),
The Merzbacher Collection

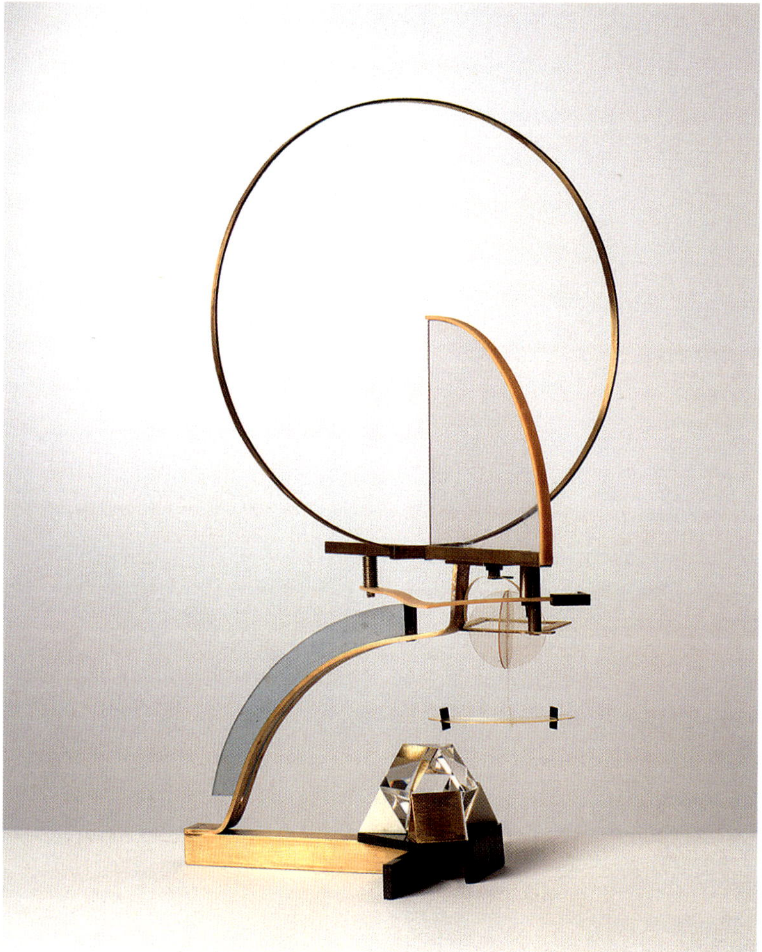

22. Naum Gabo (1890-1977)

Monument for an Institute of Physics and Mathematics,ca.1924, reassembled 1990

Glass, Bronze, Plastics, H44 cm (H17 5/16 inches)

Berlinische Galerie, Landesmuseum für Moderne Kunst, Fotografie und Architektur

Photo: Ilona Ripke, Berlin

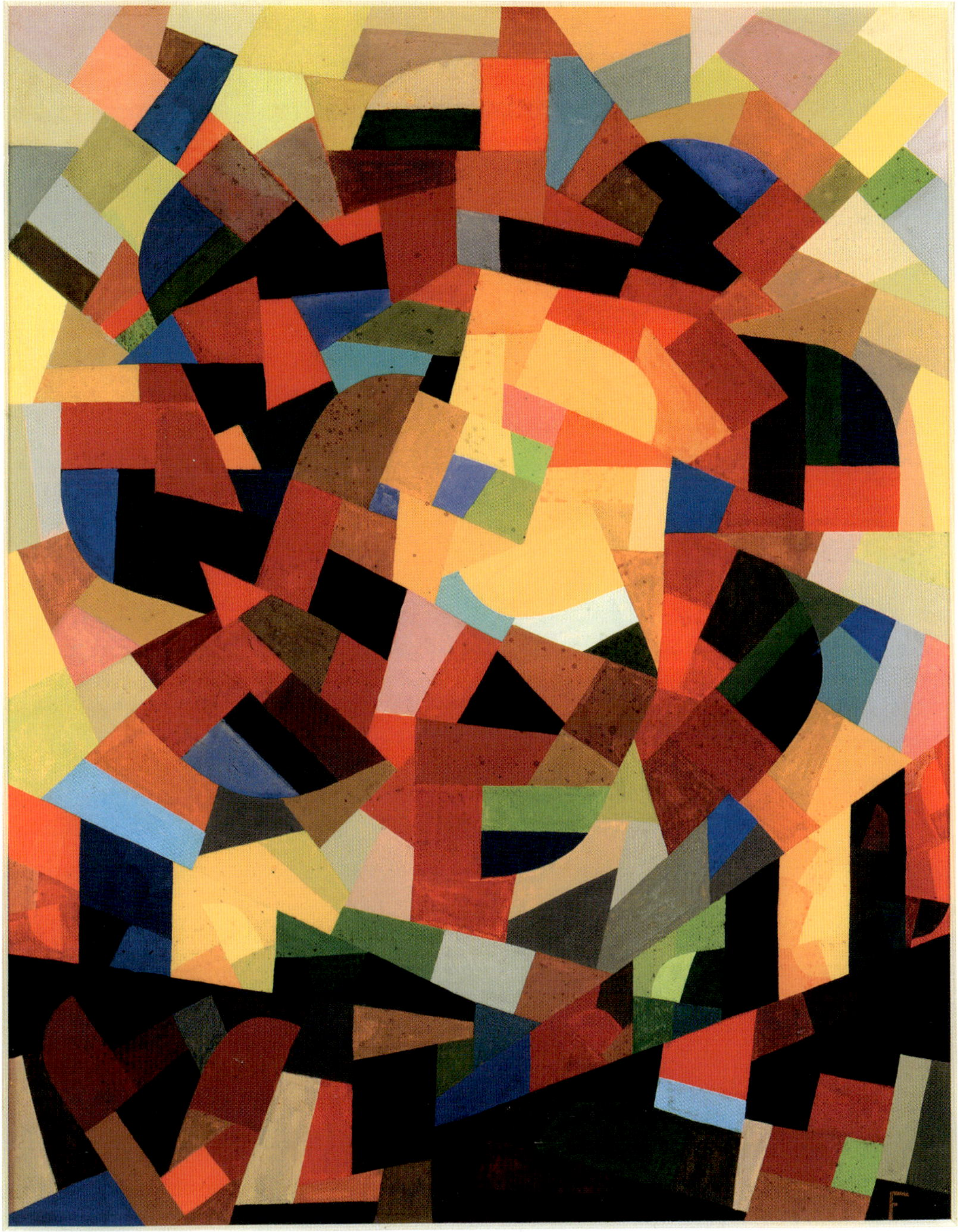

23. Otto Freundlich (1878-1943)

La Rosace II, 1941

Gouache sur carton, 65 x 50 cm (25 9/16 x 19 11/16 inches)

Donation Freundlich © Musée de Pontoise, France

www.ville-pontoise.fr

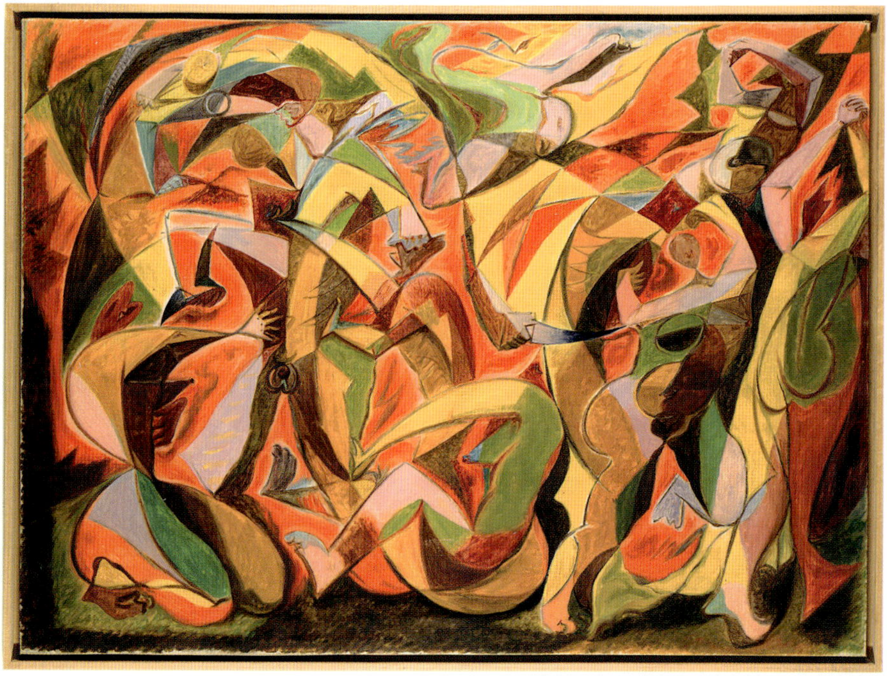

24. André Masson (1896 - 1987)
Massacre, 1931,
Oil on canvas, 120 x 160 cm (47 1/4 x 63 inches)
Sammlung Ulla und Heiner Pietzsch, Photo: Jochen Littkemann, Berlin,

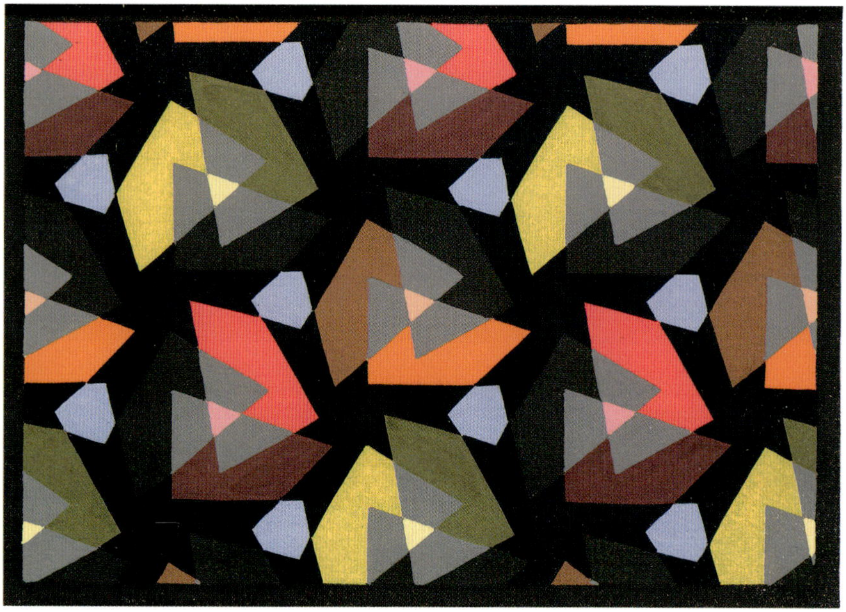

25. Hans Hinterreiter (1902 - 1989)
Study 367, 19.8.1949,
Tempera on paper, 11,3 x 16 cm (4 1/2 x 6 6/16 inches)
Private collection, Zürich

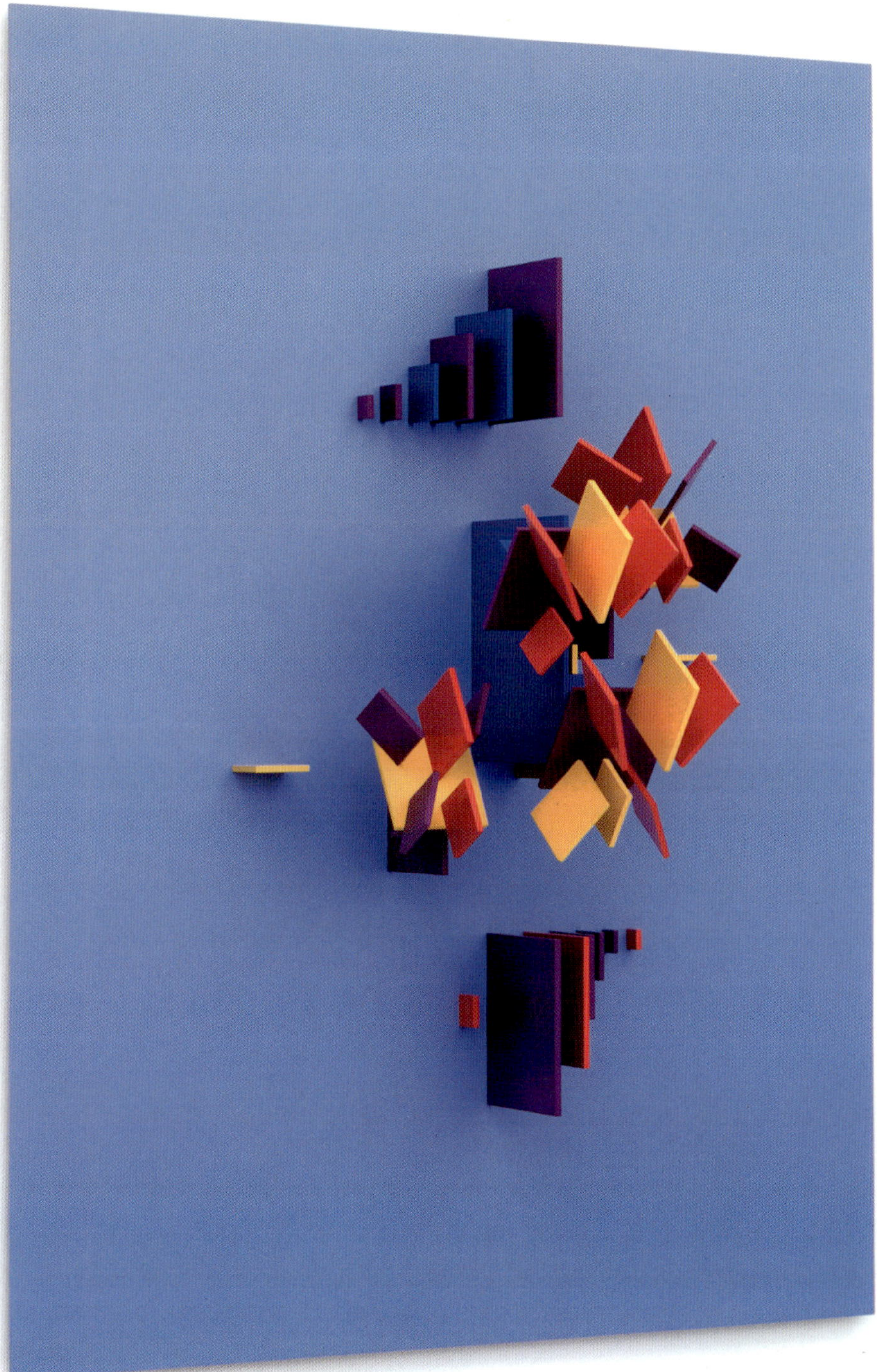

26. Charles Biederman (1906 -)
#1, 1981-1983
Aluminum relief and oil paint, 105 x 75 x 26,7 cm (41 5/16 x 29 1/2 x 10 1/2 inches)
Collection Foundation for the New Arts - FNA
www.charlesbiederman.net

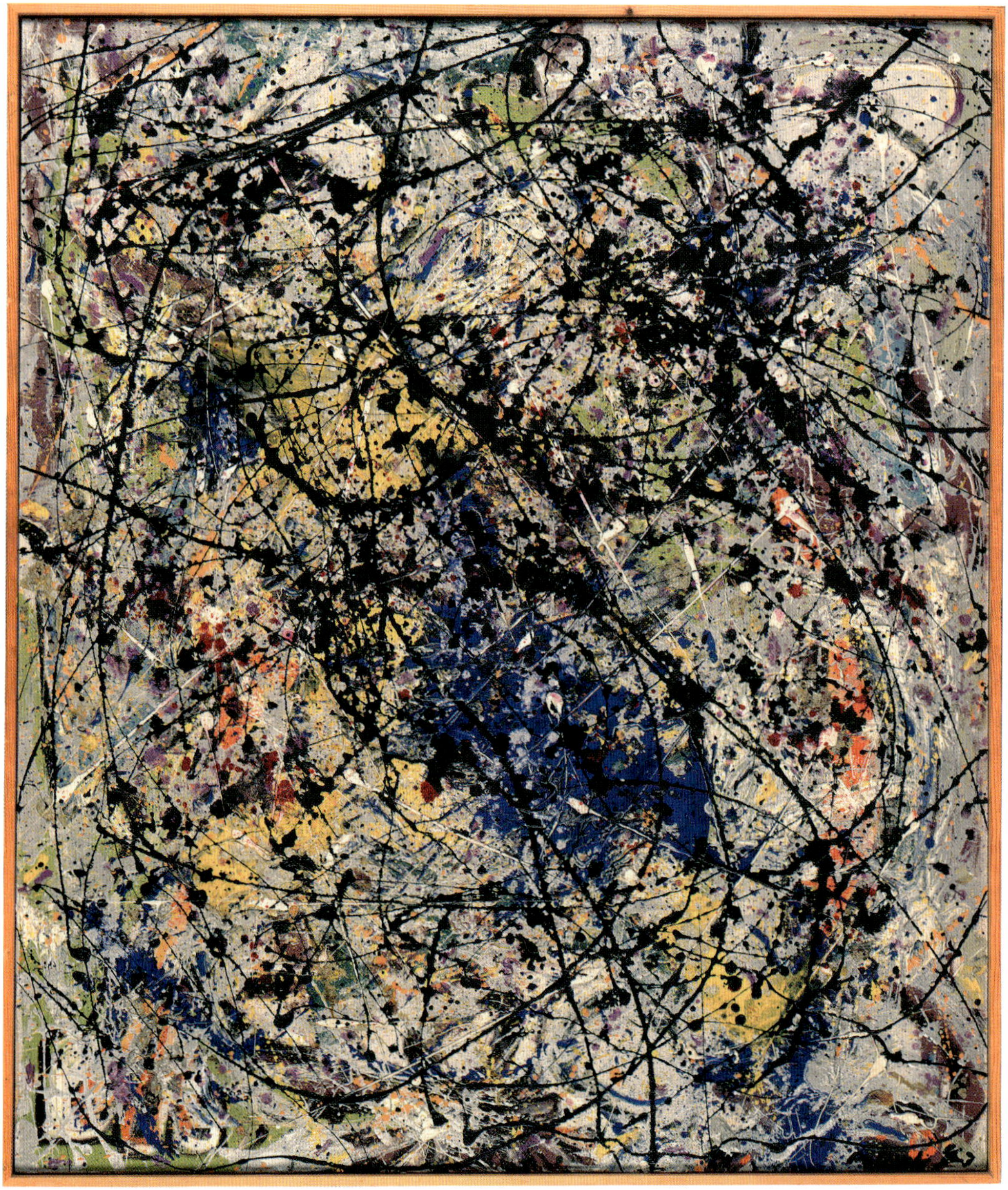

27. Jackson Pollock (1912-1956)
Reflection of the Big Dipper, 1947
Oil on canvas, 111 x 92 cm (43 3/4 x 36 1/16 inches)
Stedelijk Museum Amsterdam

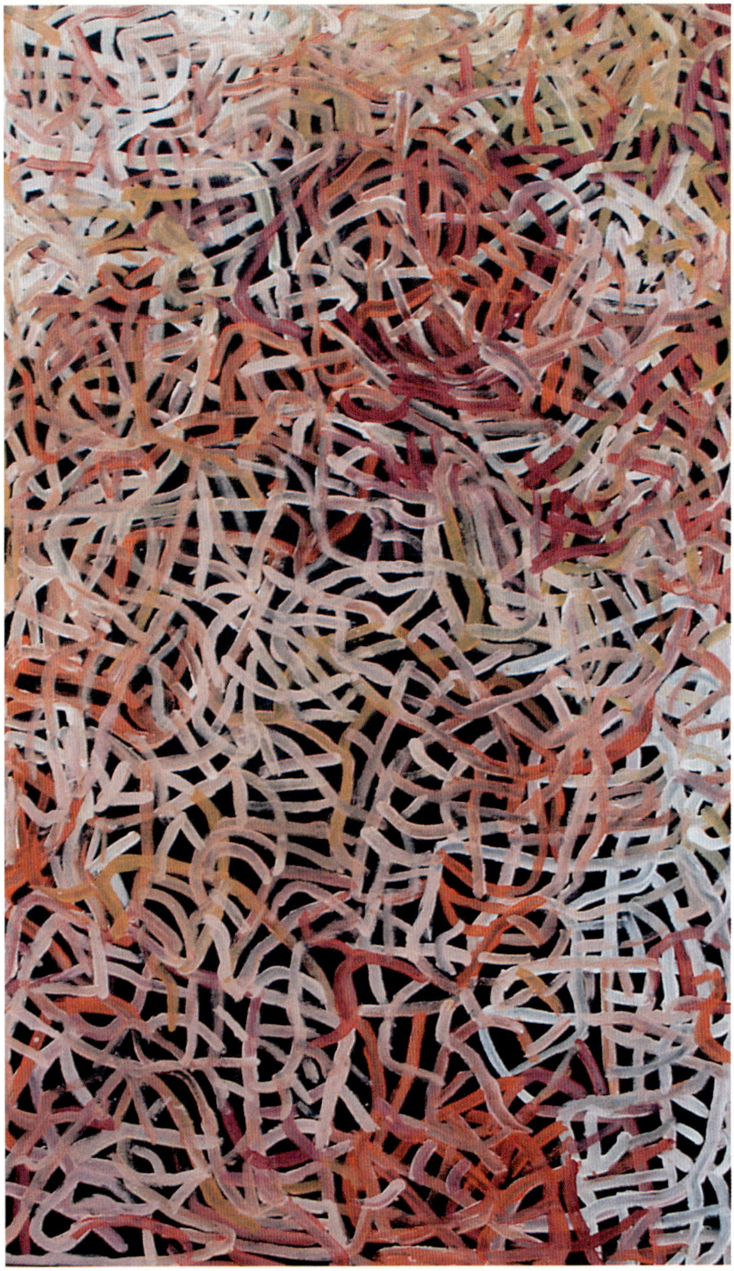

28. Emily Kame Kngwarreye (ca.1910-1996)

Anooralya Awelye, 1996

Acrylic on canvas, 213 x 121 cm (83 7/8 x 47 5/8 inches)

Private collection, on loan at Aboriginal Art Museum, Utrecht, NL

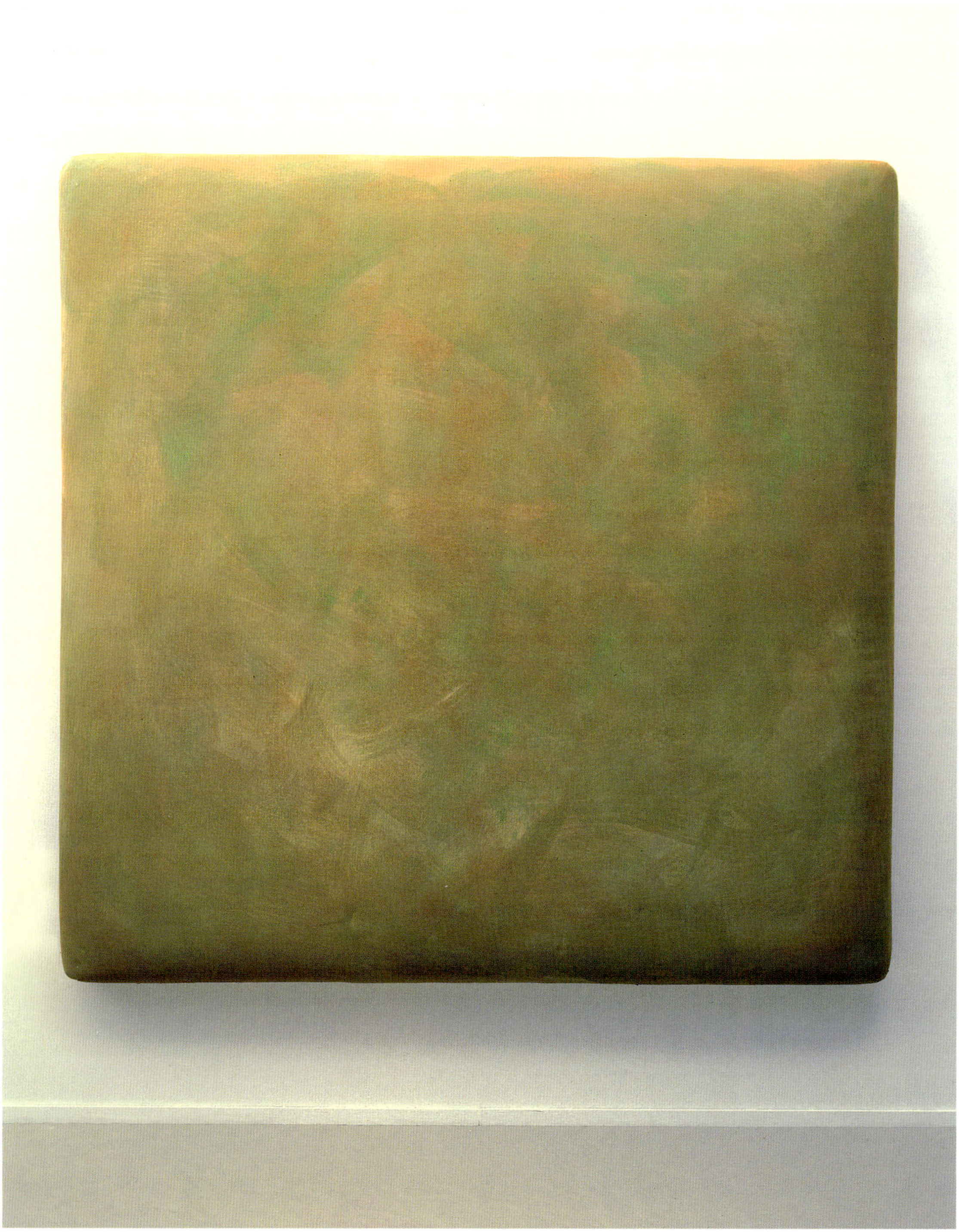

29. Gotthard Graubner (1930 -)

Hortensie, Farbraumkörper (colour space body), 1998

Acrylic on canvas on synthetic cotton on canvas, 203 x 203 x 14 cm (80 x 80 x 5 1/2 inches)

Photograph Achim Kukulies, Düsseldorf

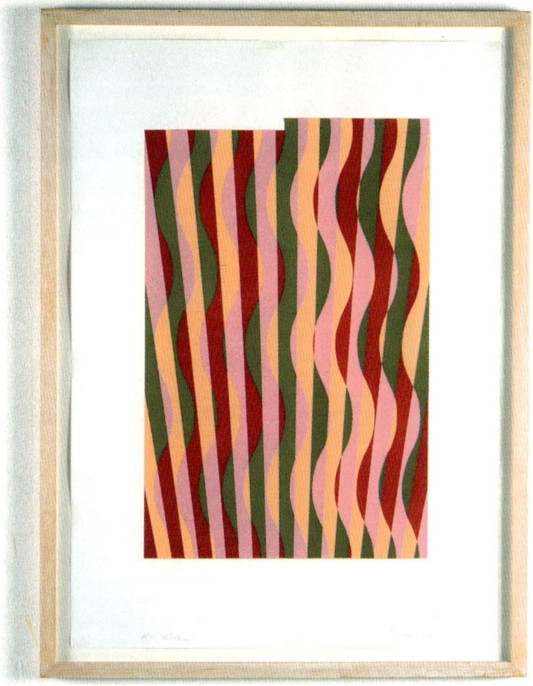

30. Michael Kidner (1917-)
Red China, 1966
Lithograph on paper. 84 x 58,4 cm (33 x 23 inches)
Photo: Ton Aartsen, Leeuwarden

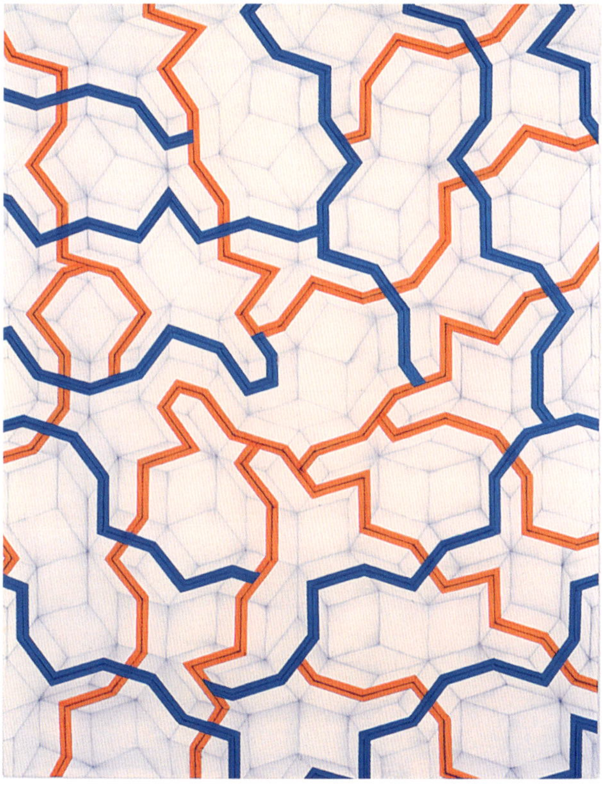

31. Michael Kidner (1917 -)
Crossroads, 2001
Acrylic on board, 135 x 102 cm (53 1/8 x 40 1/8 inches)

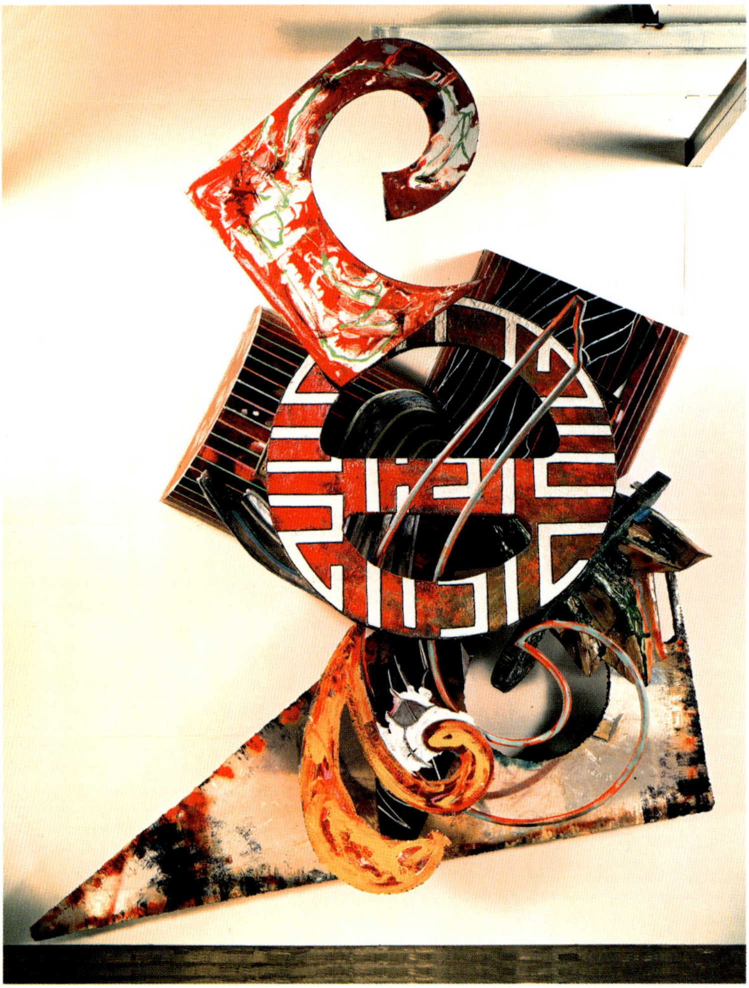

32. Frank Stella (1936 -)

Knights and Squires (s-4, 3x 2nd version), 1989

Mixed media on cast aluminum, 455,93 x 391,16 x 170,18 cm (179 1/2 x 154 x 67 inches)

New York, The Archive of Frank Stella © Photo SCALA, Florence

Photo: Steven Sloman, 1989

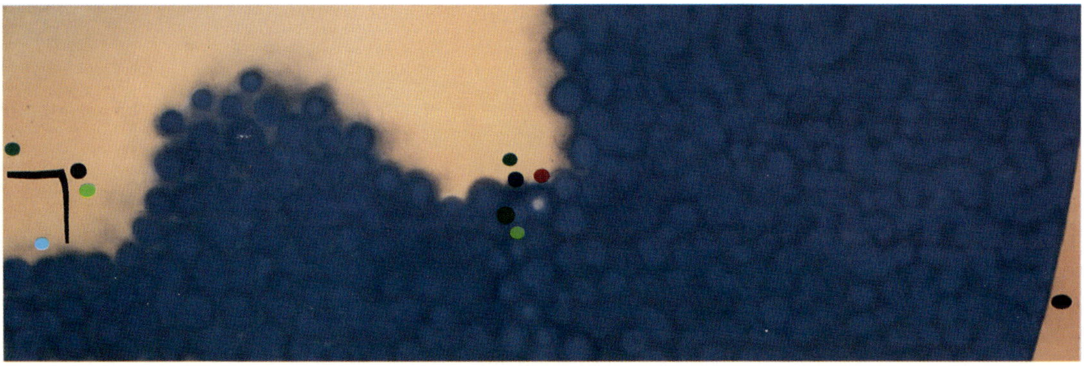

33. Victor Pasmore (1908 - 1998)

Senza Titolo 10, 1989

Etching and aquatint, Plate 67 1/2 x 200 cm (26 1/2 x 78 3/4 inches); paper 92 x 258 cm (36 1/4 x 101 1/2 inches)

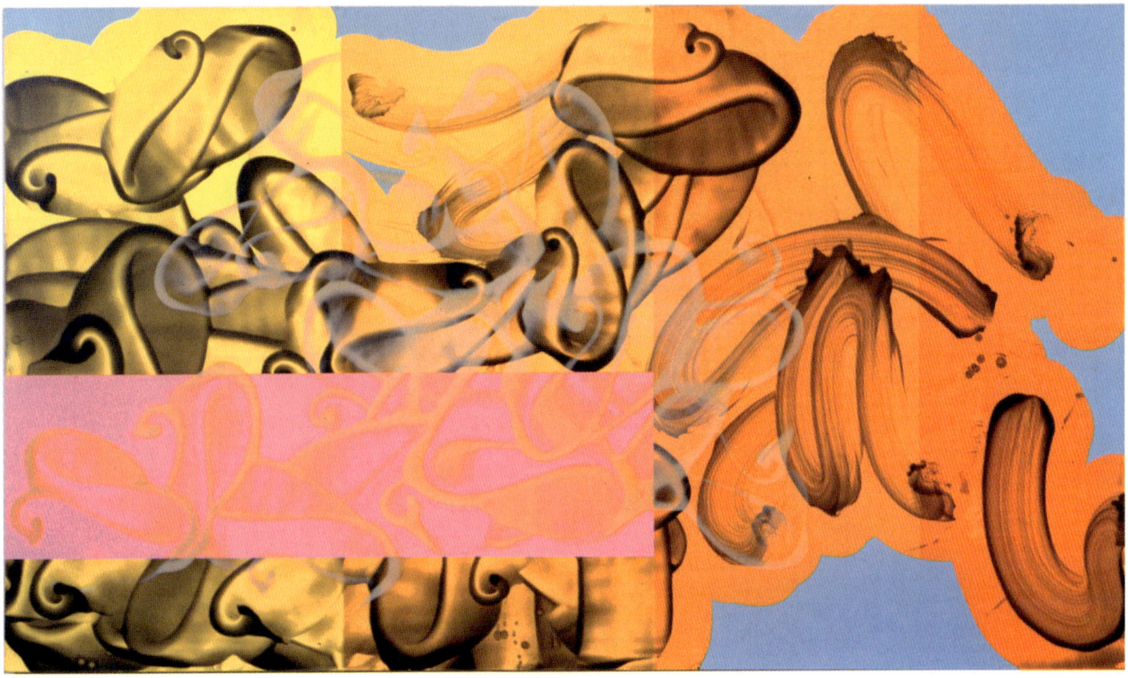

34. David Reed (1946-)
#445, 1995-1999
Oil and alkyd on linen, 155 x 259 cm (61 x 102 inches)
Courtesy of Max Protetch Gallery, New York
www.maxprotetch.com

35. Natvar Bhavsar (1934 -)
SOORA II, 1999
Oil on canvas on board, 100 x 34 1/2 cm (39 3/8 x 13 9/16 inches)
Photo: Ton Aartsen, Leeuwarden
www.sundaramtagore.com

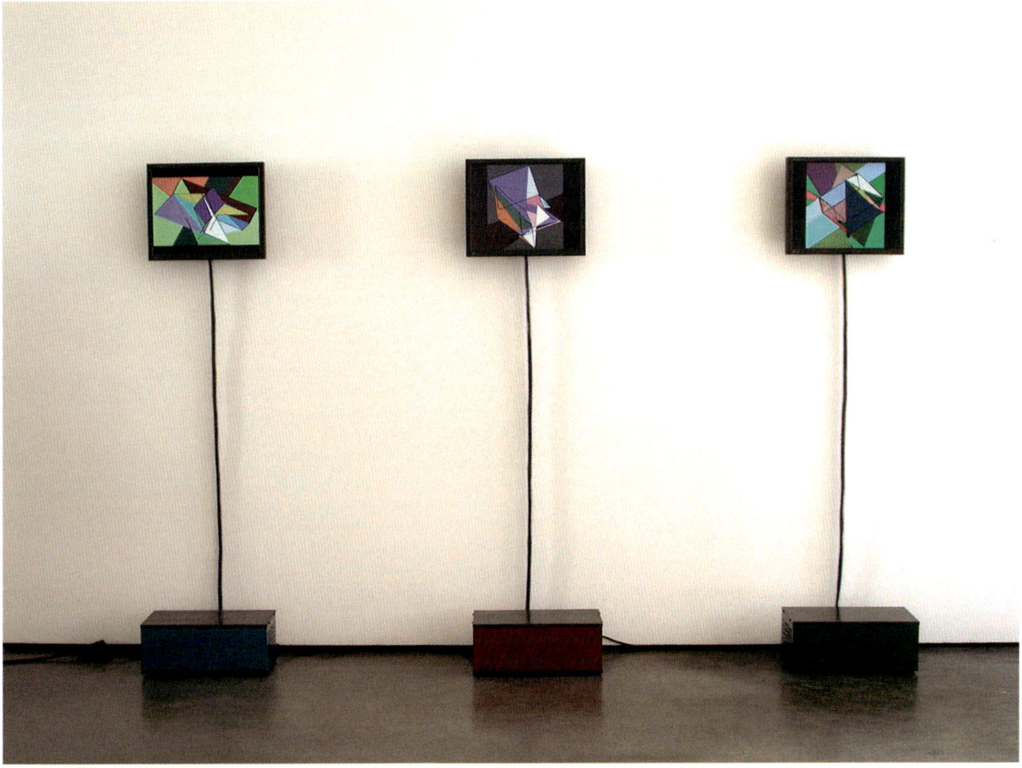

36. Manfred Mohr (1938-)
Installation **space.color** at Galerie Müller-Roth, 2004
Computer-monitors and customized computers
www.emohr.com

37. Megan Craig (1975-)
Blizzard, 2004
Oil on panel, 20,4 x 25,5 cm (8 x 10 inches)
Photo: Ton Aartsen, Leeuwarden
www.megancraig.com

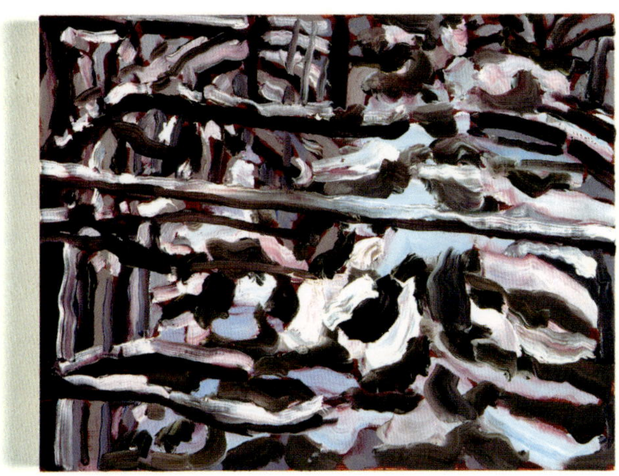

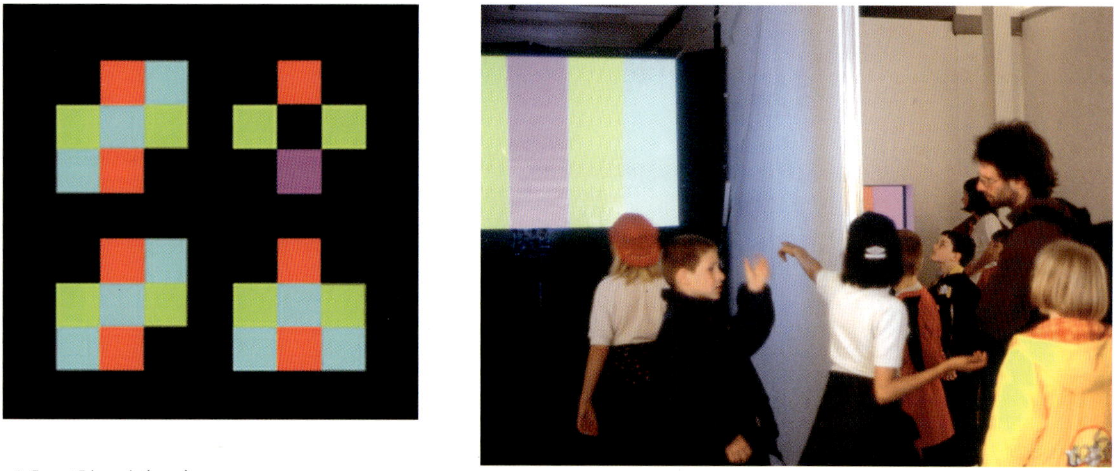

38. Ernest Edmonds (1942-)
Video Construct **Carbière 2000** (data projection onto suspended screen):
Children reacting to the changing image in the exhibition "Constructs and Re-Constructions",
Loughborough University Art Gallery, UK, 2000
Partly in view, the Video Construct "Nagoya 1998" (42 inch plasma display)
www.ernestedmonds.com

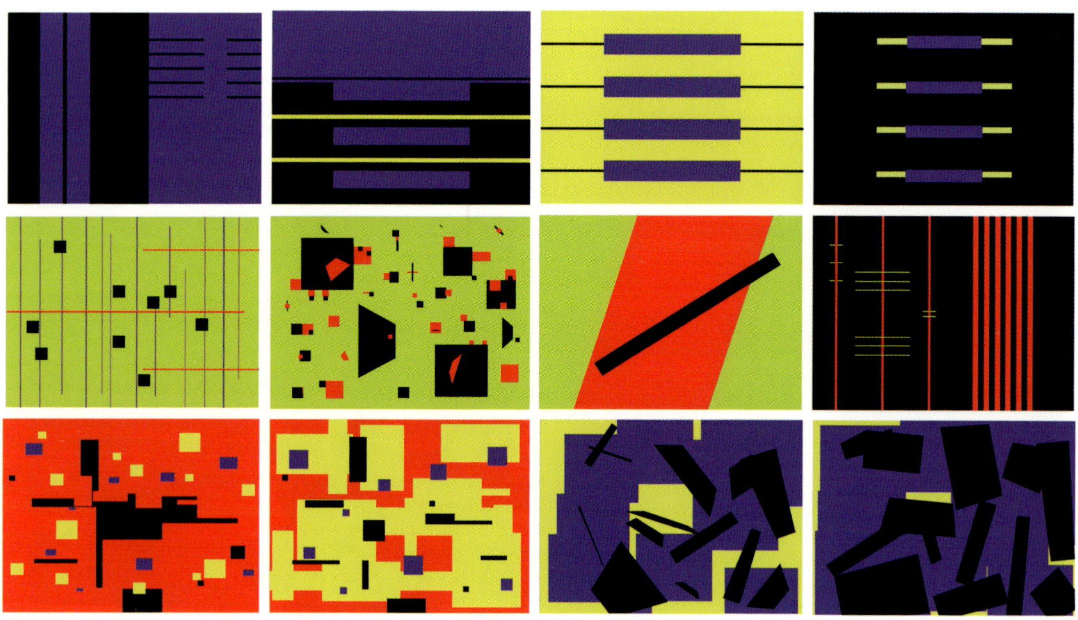

39. localStyle: Marlena Novak_visuals, Jay Alan Yim_audio
Dancing Cranes, 2002/2003; duration 6 minutes
Digital Animatography with Sound (12 stills from 10,000)
www.art.northwestern.edu/faculty/novak.html

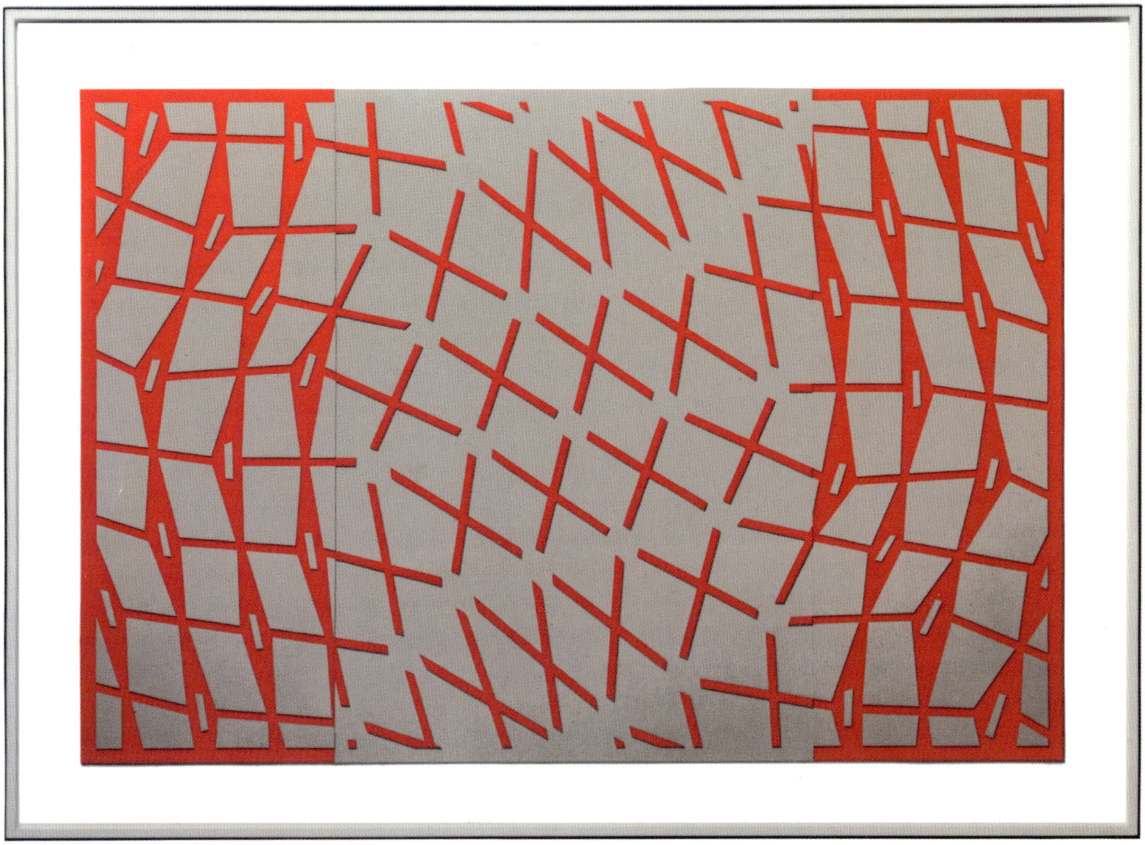

40. Jean-Pierre Maury (1948-)
De l'Été 91, le 6 juillet, rouge, 1991
Acrylic on board, 85 x 115 cm (33 1/2 x 45 1/4 inches)
www.monsite.wanadoo.fr/mauryjp

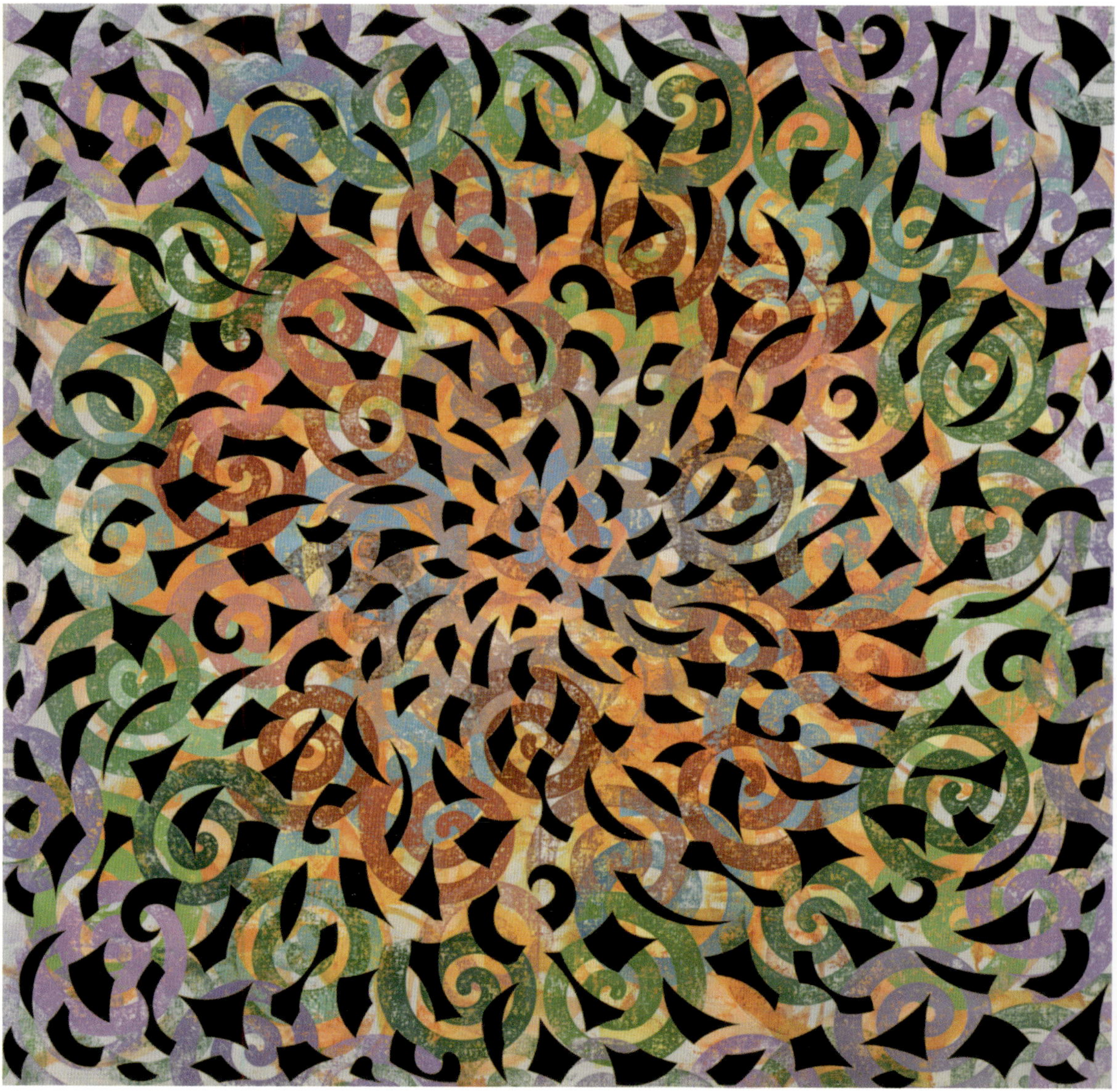

41. Philip Taaffe (1955-)

Mandala 2001-2002

Mixed media on linen, 293 x 295 cm (115 1/4 x 116 inches)

Courtesy of Jablonka Galerie, Cologne

Photo: Steven Sloman, New York

www.jablonkagalerie.com

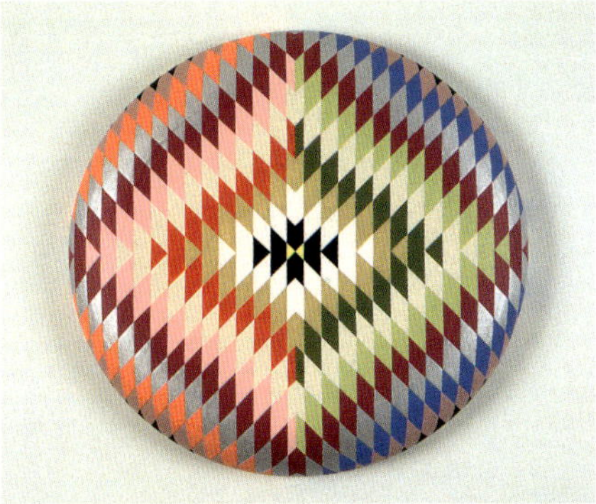

42. Paul Dacey (1960-)
Untitled - Navayo, 1996
acrylic on plastic disc,
diameter 27,5 cm (10 13/16 inches)
www.pauldacey.com

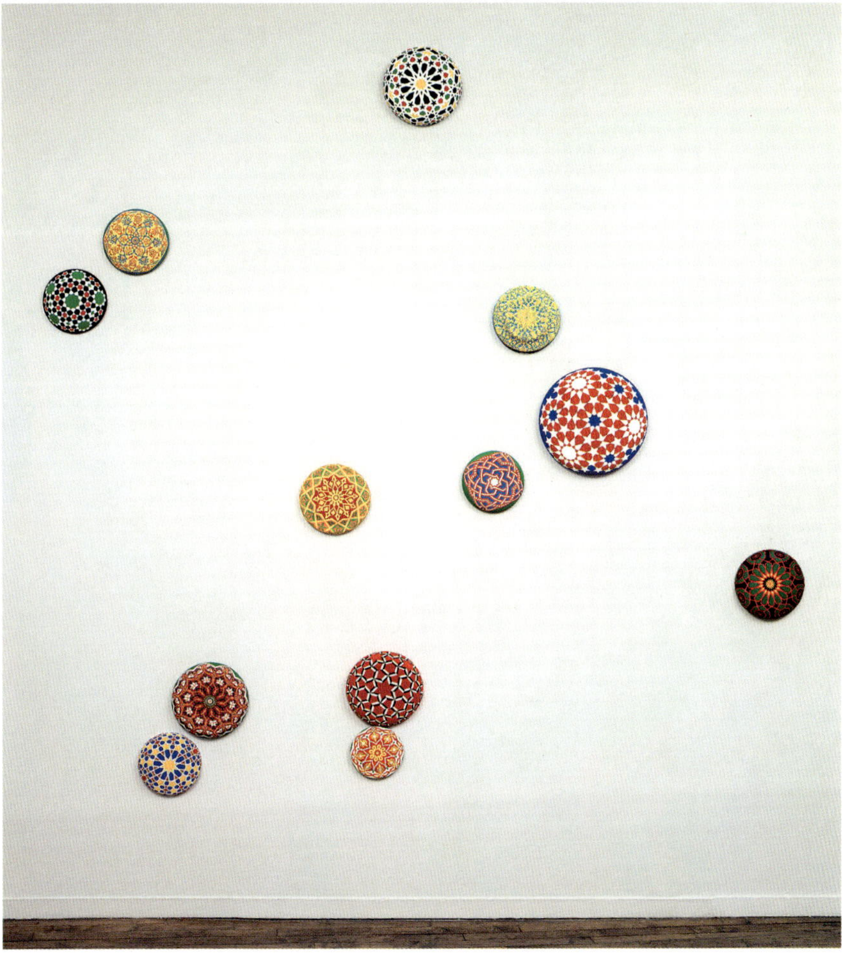

43. Paul Dacey (1960-)
Lyra/Vega II, 2004
acrylic on 12 plastic discs,
254 x 254 cm (100 x 100 inches)
Toledo Museum of Art
www.pauldacey.com

This work is based on an actual constellation, LYRA, which in western mythology represents Orpheus's Lyre, Arab astronomers saw the same pattern of stars as a swooping eagle. Utilizing Islamic design, this piece embodies the tension of Western and Arabic world views projected onto these stars that can be viewed as irreconcilable 'difference' or cultural 'synthesis'.

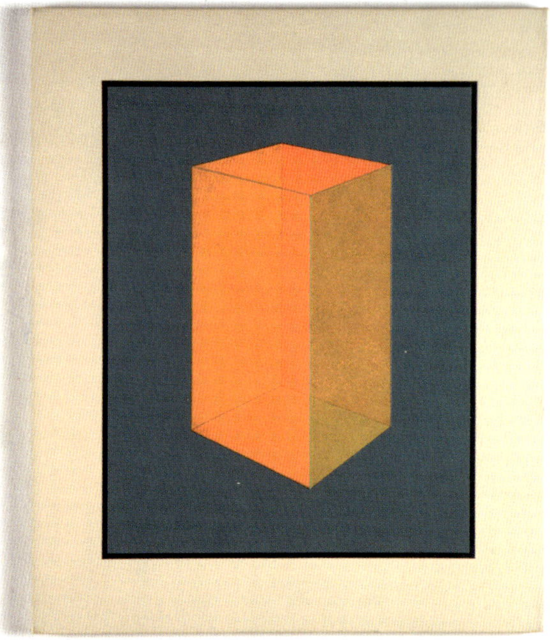

44. James Juszczyk (1943-)
Simplicity, 1996-97
Acrylic on canvas,
68,5 x 55,8 cm (27 x 22 inches)
Photo: Ton Aartsen, Leeuwarden
www.james4j.com

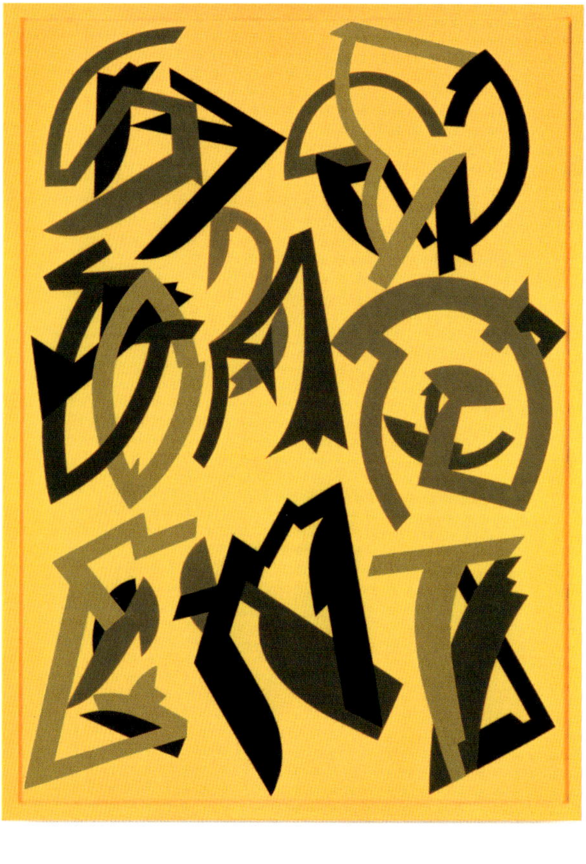

45. Michael Bette (1942-)
Nov 2001, 2001
Acrylic on canvas, 104 x 74 cm (41 x 29 1/8 inches)
Photo: Ton Aartsen, Leeuwarden

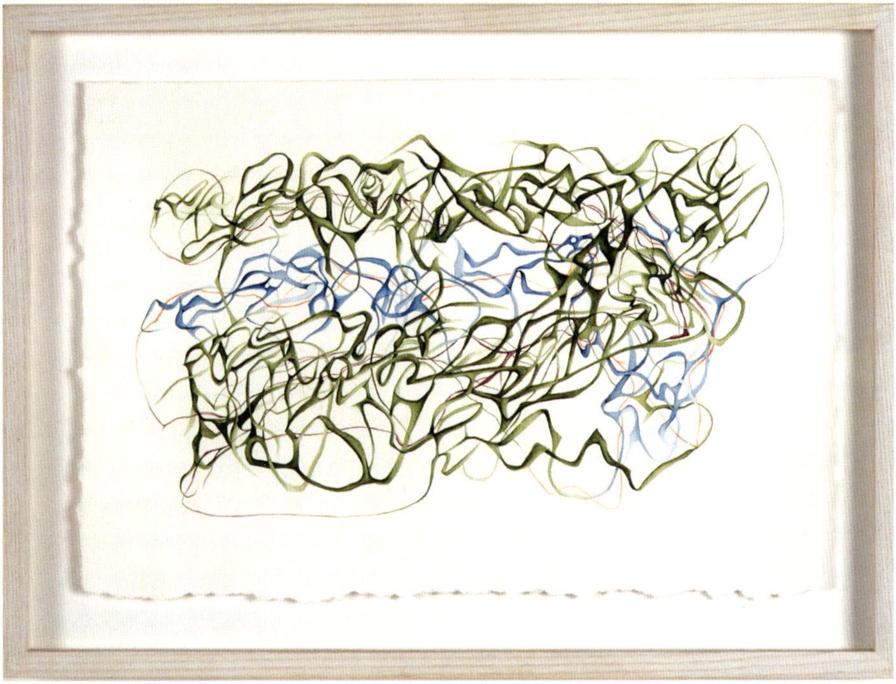

46. Megan Olson (1971 -)
Ebb, 2001
Watercolor on paper, 26,7 x 36,8 cm (10 1/2 x 14 1/2 inches)
Photo: Ton Aartsen, Leeuwarden
www.meganolson.com

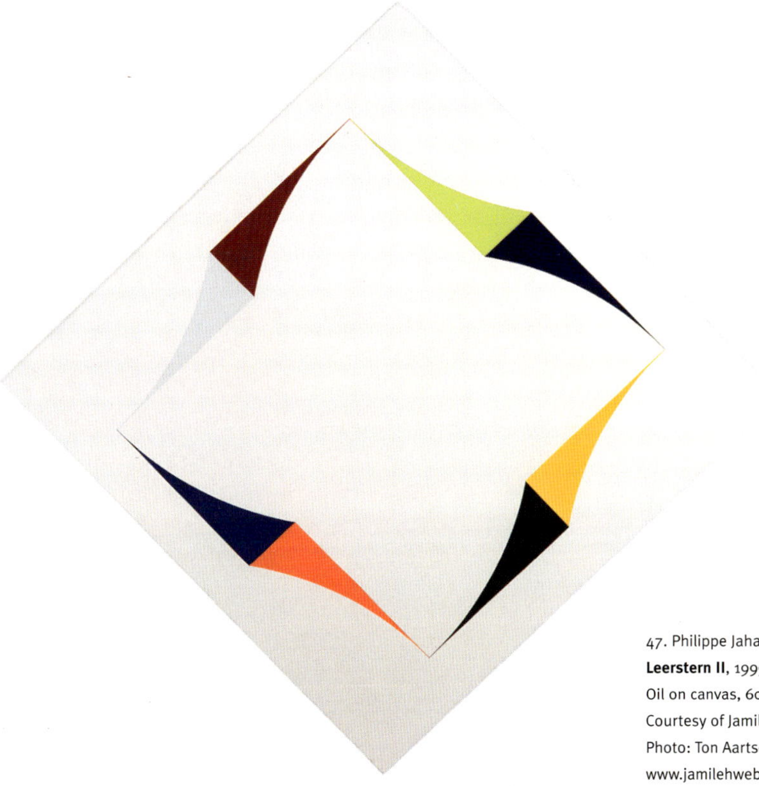

47. Philippe Jahanguir (1963-)
Leerstern II, 1999
Oil on canvas, 60 x 60 cm (23 5/8 x 23 5/8 inches)
Courtesy of Jamileh Weber Galerie
Photo: Ton Aartsen, Leeuwarden
www.jamilehweber.com

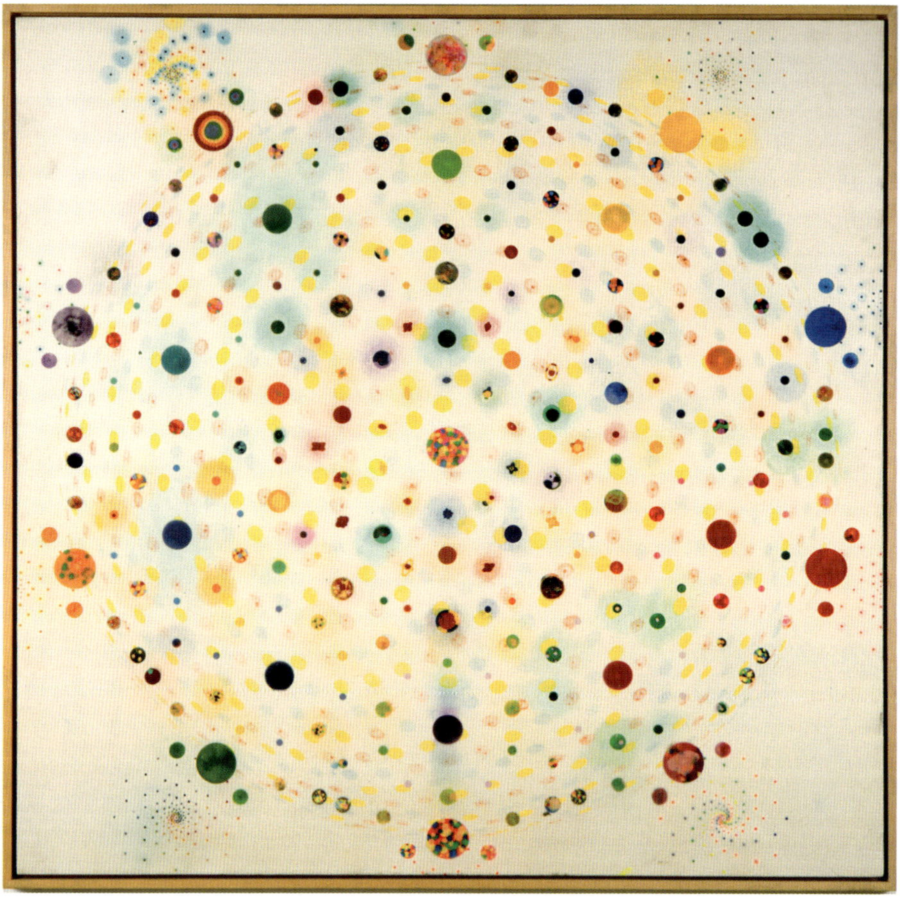

48. Richard Purdy (1956-)
Inflation, 1994
Encaustic on plywood, 122 x 122 cm (48 x 48 inches)
Photo: Ton Aartsen, Leeuwarden
www.gaugefield.net

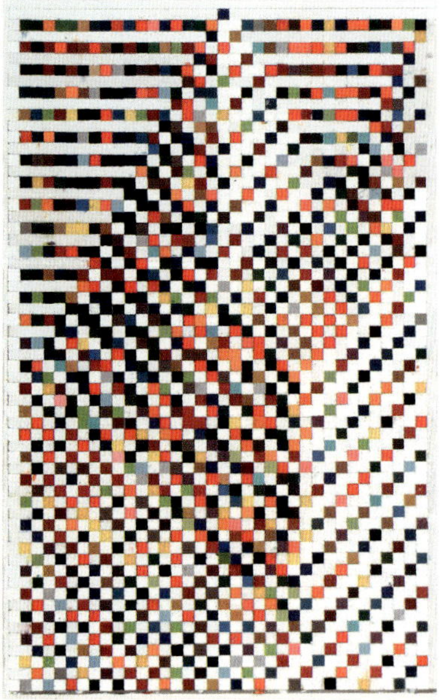

49. Richard Purdy (1956-)
156, 2004
Encaustic on plywood
72,7 x 45 x 5 cm (28 5/8 x 17 3/4 x 2 inches)
www.gaugefield.net

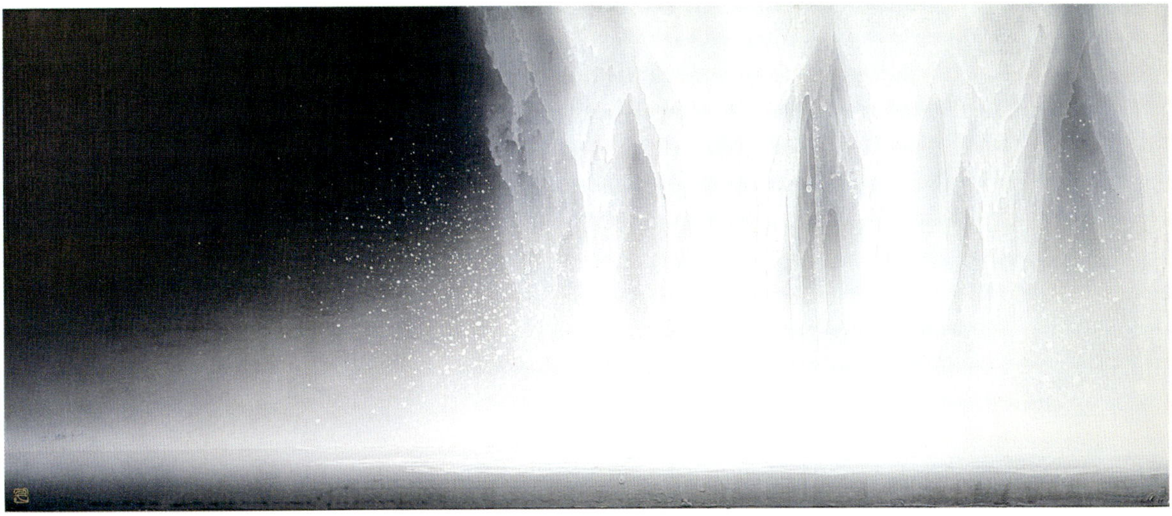

50. Senju Hiroshi (1958-)
Waterfall, 2003
Pigment on rice paper
33,4 x 72,9 cm (13 1/8 x 28 11/16 inches)
www.hiroshisenju.com

51. Megan Craig (1975-)
Manhattan Night, 2003
Oil on panel
22,8 x 22,8 cm (9 x 9 inches)
Photo: Ton Aartsen, Leeuwarden
www.megancraig.com

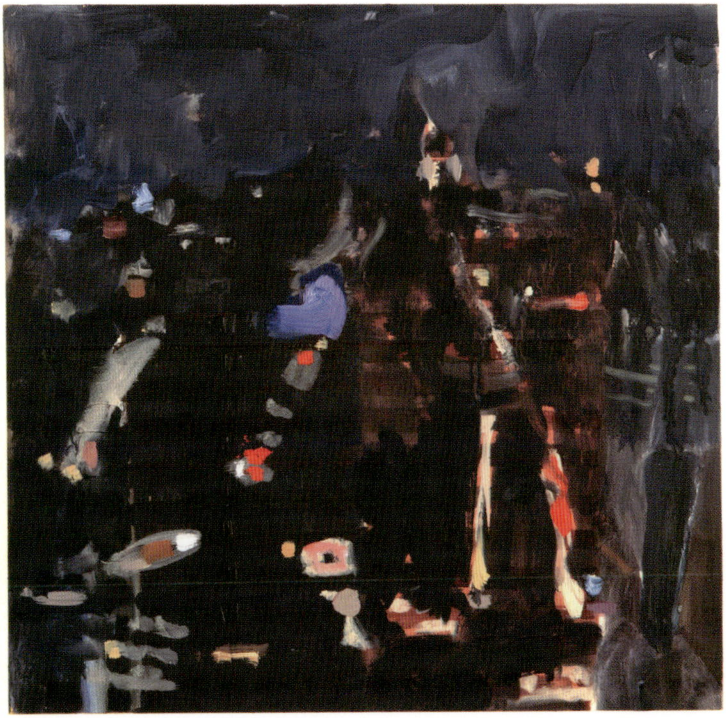

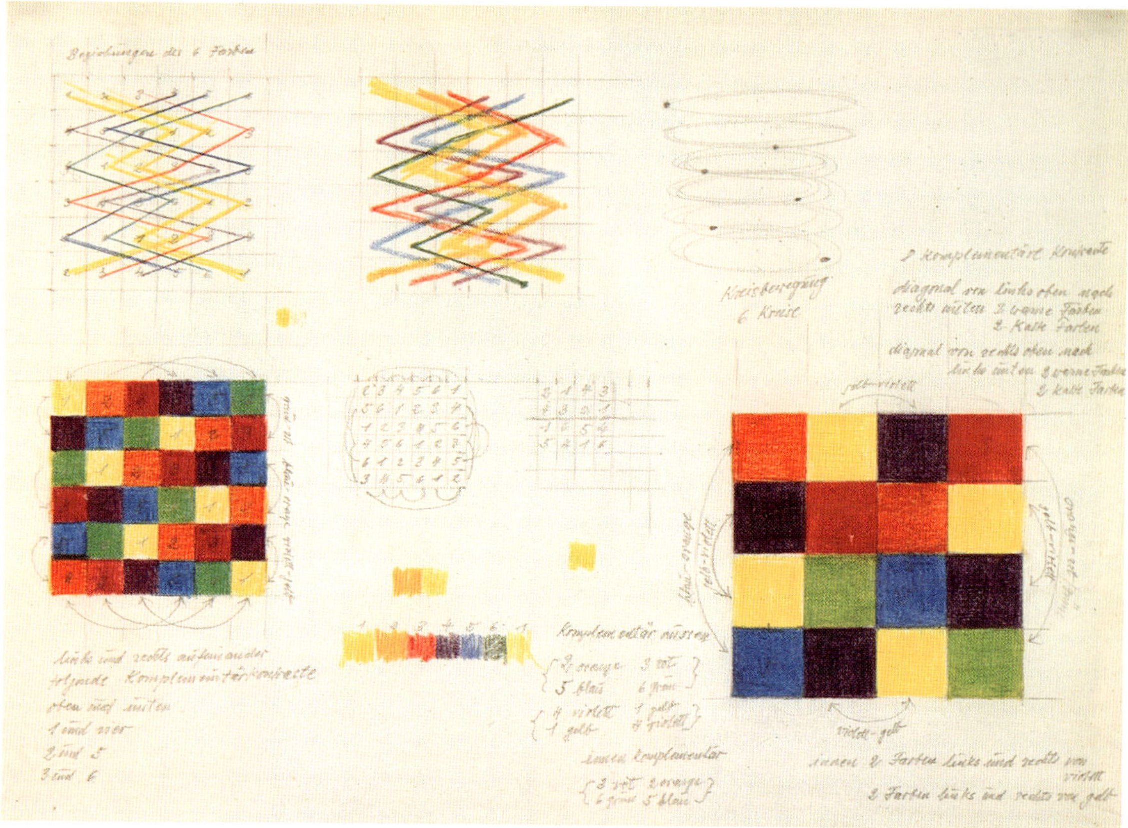

52. Richard Paul Lohse (1902-1988)
Serielle Gruppen (Groups of Series), 1950
Lead pencil and coloured pencil on paper
23,5 x 32 cm (9 1/4 x 12 5/8 inches)

www.lohse.ch

Notice in this sketch Lohse's concept of connecting the colored squares into an eternal series 'behind' or 'in front of' the picture plane. This illusion occurs in the perception of the viewer, bringing the work to life and making these non-hierarchical, highly structured and colorful paintings good metaphors for eternal change.

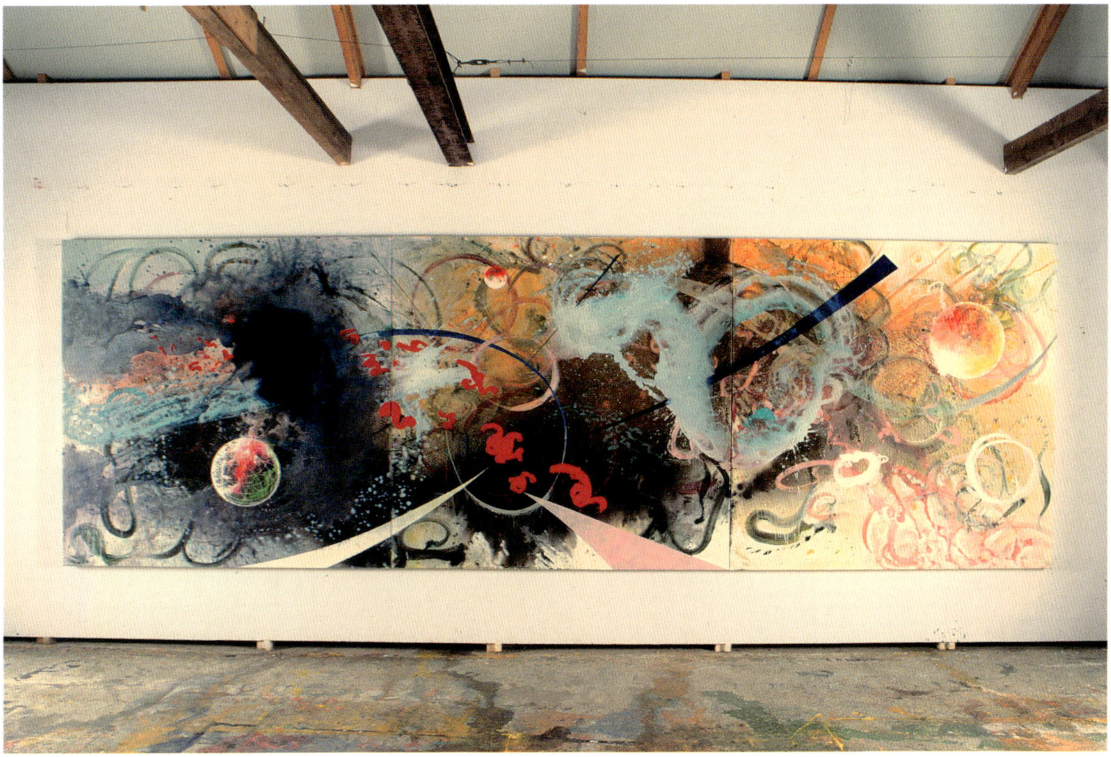

53. Fré Ilgen (1956-)
A Bird That Whistled, 2004
Acrylic on canvas, 180 x 540 cm (70 7/8 x 212 5/8 inches)
Photo: Ton Aartsen, Leeuwarden
www.ilgen.com/fre.htm

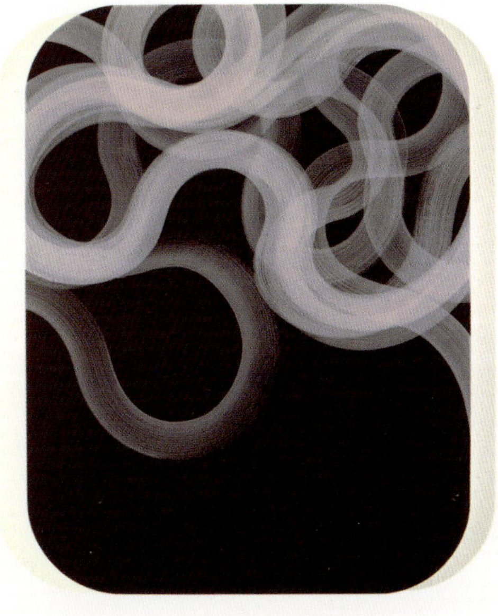

54. Christoph Wedding (1967-)
Nr.5, 2000
Oil on MDF, 87 x 65 cm (34 1/4 x 25 9/16 inches)
Courtesy of Galerie Aurel Scheibler, Cologne
www.aurelscheibler.com

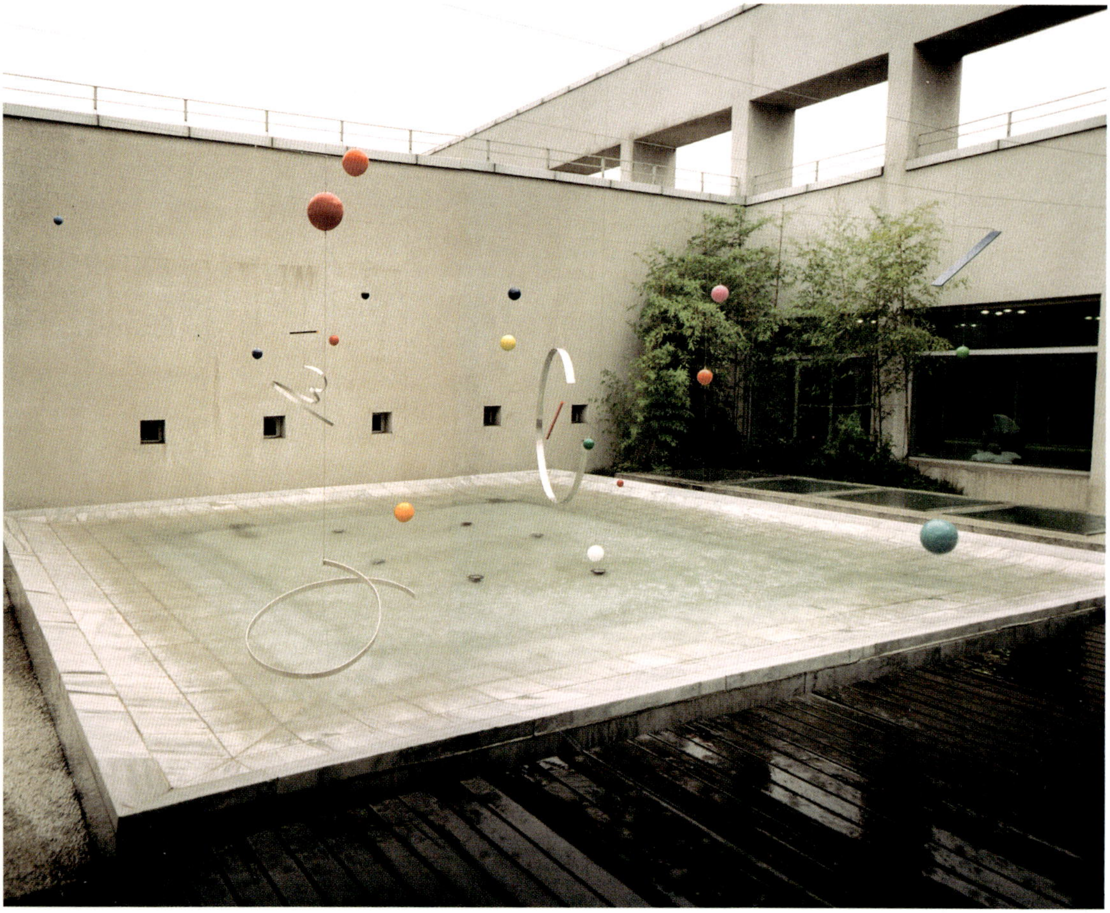

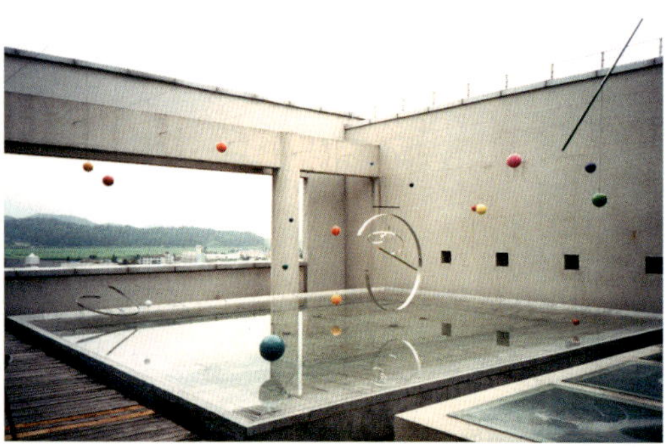

55. Fré Ilgen (1956-)
Seven Steps to Heaven, 2001
Stainless steel, aluminum, industrial paint
Corporate collection SindoRicoh Asan, South-Korea
Courtesy of Park Ryu Sook Gallery, Seoul
www.ilgen.com/fre.htm

57. Claus Goedicke (1966-)
C 1996-143, 2/3, 1996
Photograph on board
110 x 36 cm (43 5/16 x 14 3/16 inches)
Courtesy of Galerie Ulrich Fiedler
www.ulrichfiedler.com

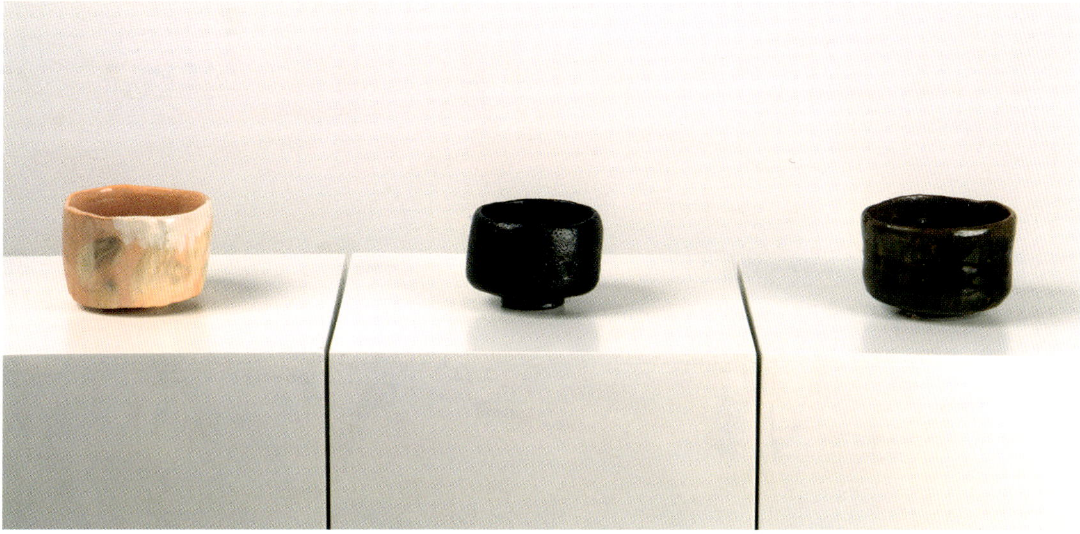

56. Attributed to Sasaki Shoraku
Pink Glaze Chawan

Sasaki Shoraku (1944 -)
Black Raku Chawan
Photo: Ton Aartsen, Leeuwarden

Hunchung Lee (1967-)
Green Glaze Kiln, 2002
Courtesy of Park Ryu Sook Gallery, Seoul
www.parkryusookgallery.co.kr.

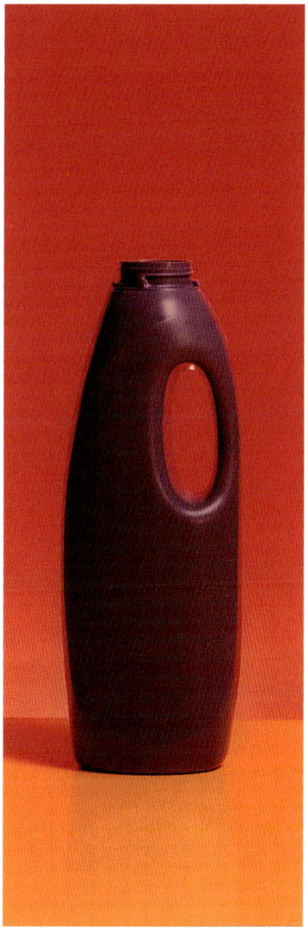

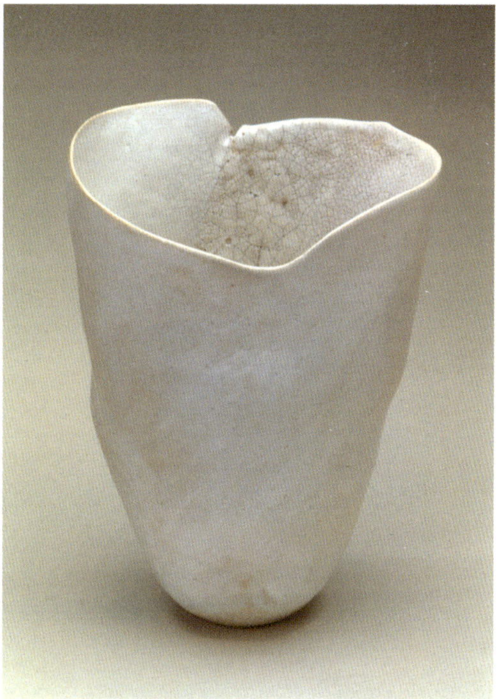

58. Richard DeVore (1933-)
#940, 2000
Stoneware, 38 x 27,3 x 20,2 cm (15 x 10 3/4 x 8 inches)
Courtesy of Max Protetch Gallery, New York
www.maxprotetch.com

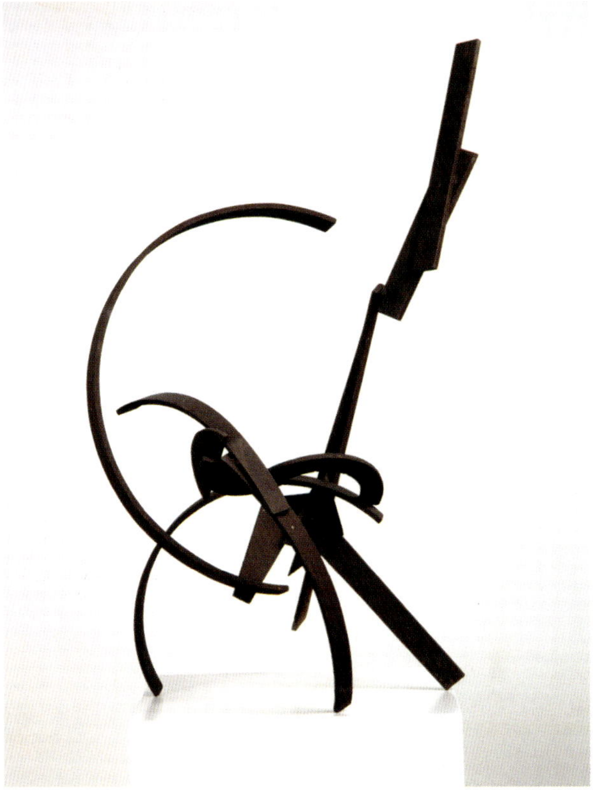

59. Paul Suter (1926-)
Vancouver, 1989
Steel, 70 x 45 x 35 cm
(27 1/2 x 17 3/4 x 13 3/4 inches)
Photo: Ton Aartsen, Leeuwarden

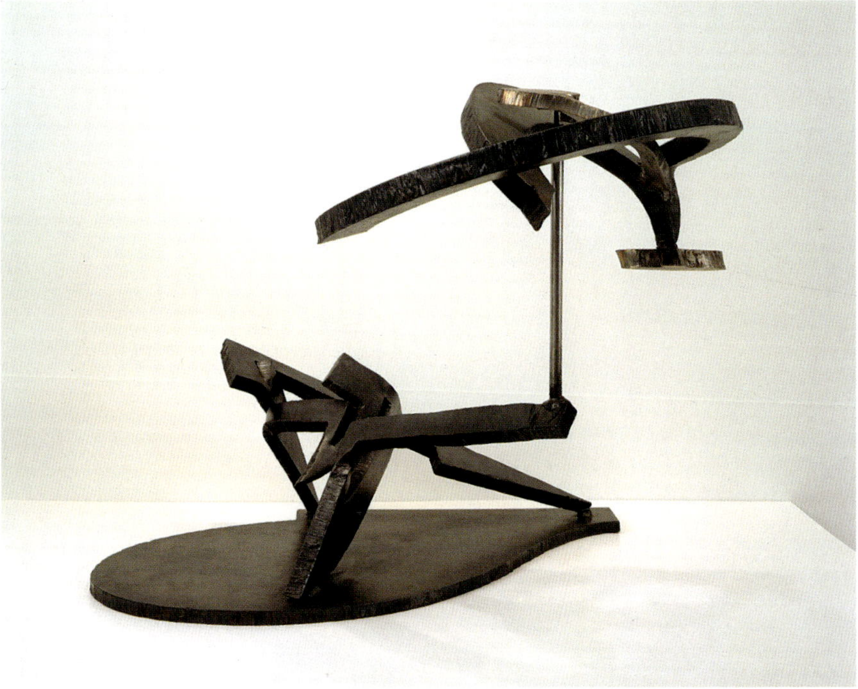

60. Mark di Suvero (1933-)
Untitled, 1994
Steel and stainless steel, 71 x 102 x 93 cm (28 x 40 x 36 1/2 inches)

This contradicted somewhat the official hierarchy as advocated by the church, but was so cleverly built around an abstract theory that its revolutionary content was not so obvious.

The monad, therefore, can be understood as a metaphor for the relationships between microcosm and macrocosm. The monad is not necessarely an actual atomic particle, though in its logic it is related to our current ways of thinking about particles and quanta. Remember Cusanus's ideas earlier in this chapter. Substance, by the way, was in Leibniz's days understood in terms of activity, perception and unity. Simultaneously it was believed that no substance disappears, but merely changes into something else.[28] This comes remarkably close to our modern thinking about the conservation of energy.

It is quite clear that a further discussion about object and self has brought us to a brief consideration of the composition, or matter, of both. To avoid too much confusing repetition, you are kindly asked to recall what was written in §6, especially in §6.4. The complexity is caused by the fact that in understanding our encounter with a work of art, not only do all kinds of aspects of object and self play important roles, but these aspects all take place in space/time. Thus, to some extent, a certain amount of repetition of knowledge from the previous chapter is necessary.

Isaac Newton, the grand early physicist on who's theories and laws so much of modern physics is based, was a contemporary of Leibniz. Einstein wrote about Newton,

> *"In Newtonian physics the elementary theoretical concept on which the theoretical description of material bodies is based is the material point, or particle. Thus, matter is considered a priori to be discontinuous. This assumption makes it necessary to consider the action of the material points on one another as "action at a distance". Because the later concept seems quite contrary to everyday experience, it is only natural that the contemporaries of Newton - and indeed Newton himself - found it difficult to accept."*[29]

Einstein continues to explain that, because of the success of Newton's physics, it took a long time before new concepts emerged. This only happened in the 19th century by

water and fish or a clock full of wheels and attachments. But just as all numbers are derived from one plus one, so must all multiplicity be derived from unity. For this reason unity is the proper root and seat of all existence, of all force, and of all sensation; and these constitute the soul. From this one has irrefutable proof that souls exist, that everything must be full of souls, what the nature of a soul is, and, finally, why each soul is indestructable. For unity has no parts, othwerwise it would be multiplicity."

[28] Leibniz writes in his "Discourse", in Allison P. Coudert, "Leibniz and the Kabbalah", p.78: "... no substance perishes, although it can become completely different. They also express the whole universe, although more imperfectly than minds do. But the principal difference is that they do not know what they are nor what they do, and consequently, since they do not reflect on themselves, they cannot discover necessary and universal truths."

[29] See Albert Einstein, "On the Generalized Theory of Gravitation - An account of the newly published extension of the general theory of relativity against its historical and philosophical background", Scientific American Special Issue "Science in the 20th Century", 1991, p.40-45 (orig. Scientific American April 1950).

Young's Two-Slit Experiment, the discovery that light consists of waves and, above all, by the discovery of electromagnetism. This discovery led James Clerk Maxwell to find the existence of waves of energy, whose properties corresponded to those of light as far as they were known at the time.[30] Waves united into fields of energy. Einstein wrote,

"A consistent field theory requires continuity of all elements of the theory, not only in time but also in space and in all points of space. Hence, the material particle has no place as a fundamental concept in a field theory. Thus, even apart from the fact that gravitation is not included, Maxwell's electrodynamics cannot be considered a complete theory."[31]

Einstein, who searched for an explanation for the phenomenon called the photo-electric effect,[32] accepted, for the time being, the duality of matter as wave and particle. He explains that the particle exists, but because it is a local concentration of energies, the field, not the particle, is the fundamental phenomenon:

"According to general relativity, the concept of space detached from any physical content does not exist. The physical reality of space is represented by a field whose components are continuous functions of four independent variables - the coordinates of space and time. It is just this particular kind of dependence that expresses the spatial character of physical reality. Since the theory of relativity implies the representation of physical reality by a continuous field, the concept of particles or material points cannot play a fundamental part, and neither can the concept of motion. The particle can only appear as a limited region in space in which the field strength or the energy density is particularly high."[33]

This discussion about matter, when translated into notions of the material point and the continuous field, is equivalent to the visual and theoretical research by artists, who like mathematicians and philosophers are trying to understand the point, the line, and the plane as basic 'tools' for building a picture of reality. Again, composition in art is

---

[30] See Gerrit L. Verschuur, "Hidden Attraction - The Mystery and History of Magnetism" (Oxford: Oxford University Press, 1993), p.120: "The stunning conclusion was that electrical and magnetic forces, under the umbrella of a new description, *electromagnetism*, traveled at the speed of light. The corollary was also true, and this too was a wonderful insight. Light had to be an electromagnetic phenomenon! "We can scarcely avoid the interference," Maxwell said, "that light consists in the transverse undulations of the same medium which is the cause of electric and magnetic phenomena." " Gerrit L. Verschuur is a professional radio astronomer studying interstellar matter and magnetic fields.

[31] See Albert Einstein, "On the Generalized Theory of Gravitation", Scientific American Special Issue "Science in the 20th Century", 1991, p.40-45.

[32] The photo-electric effect is waves of light being able to cause electric currents in an object.

[33] See Albert Einstein, "On the Generalized Theory of Gravitation", Scientific American Special Issue "Science in the 20th Century", 1991, p.40-45.

equivalent to the composing of a virtual picture of reality in scientific or philosophical reasoning.

Quantum Theory concluded that matter consists of small, continuously vibrating quantities. Starting at the end of the 1920's, Einstein and Dirac extended this theory into the idea that all matter is built from (quantum) fields. Quantum physicist Erwin Schrödinger wrote: "Today a physicist no longer can distinguish significantly between matter and something else. We no longer contrast matter with forces or fields of force as different entities; we know now that these concepts must be merged."[34]

At the center of these considerations one finds the idea that the electromagnetic lines of force and fields of force are the basic elements, and the duality of the wave/particle is the central problem. David Bohm has proposed it is likely that the wave itself is not merely a mathematical property, but the actual physical form.[35] All matter is continuously in motion and not solid, but consists of a certain composition of vibrating quantities of energy. It is highly intriguing that a man like Chu Hsi wrote already in the 12th century: "To the man who is intimately aware of Creative Mind, there is not an iota of matter throughout the whole earth."[36] Though clearly meant in a methaphoric sense, Chu Hsi's quotation is a good example of how intuition, observation and clear thinking can lead to an understanding that is only much later confirmed by scientific proof!

Certain three-dimensional appearances do not have a materiality in a strict sense, like the sky above us, the space in an open landscape or the public spaces in a city. As a rule they become perceptable to us by the objects in that space or surrounding that space. These objects define restrictions, sightlines, or perspectives. In our interaction with these objects, quite often we neglect the importance of the changes of light, as it is in our perception of depth. The changes of light on trees, on bushes, on grass, on stones, on buildings, on earth and on clouds make landscapes, cities and skies appear the way they do in our perception. In fine art one can find impressive examples of how artists understood this.[37] In sculpture this seems to come naturally without applying certain simulated light-effects used in two-dimensional painting, but becomes especially effective when using colour. For instance, Greek, early Christian and medieval sculpture (like the statues on the facades of cathedrals, statues of saints) were all brightly coloured. And, because sculpture is three-dimensional it is 'vulnerable' to actual changes of light, just as all appearances in reality are (from chair, tree, truck, building to cloud). The sheer

[34] See Erwin Schrödinger, "What is Matter?", Scientific American Special Issue 1991 (orign. Scientific American September 1953), p.16.

[35] See David Z. Albert, "Bohm's Alternative to Quantum Mechanics", Scientific American May 1994, p.32-39.

[36] Chu Hsi, 1130-1200, a Zen or *Ch'an* master from the House of Fa-yen in China. See John C.H. Wu, "The Golden Age of Zen", (New York: Image Books - Double Day, 1996), p.182. This thought can be understood in the tradition of 'sunyata' and nothingness, see §2.

[37] For instance the great painters of light, like Vermeer, Rembrandt, Titiaan, Courbet, Turner, Constable, Monet, Cézanne, Hodler, Kupka, (early) Kandinsky, and more recently one can experience this in the paintings of Lohse, Rothko, Graubner, Bhavsar.

mention of an 'interaction' already shows that there is no such thing as a fully autonomous entity, as the word object in the classical sense might suggest. The word 'object' in our language is related to objective, implying the properties that are characteristic of the object, which are considered to be true and not open to any different interpretations. No influences or interactions are considered because the objective truth is supposed to be final and not open to change. This is a complete impossibility.[38]

There is only truth in the unity or wholeness, which in art is called a composition: the interaction between the pictorial elements is more important than the individual pictorial elements separately.[39] In the same way, the objects in an environment cannot really be understood without the interactions between each other and with the environment. Also the whole of the composition in art is more than the sum of the pictorial elements. Arriving at the sum of a series of elements involves isolating the characteristics of every individual element and adding these characteristics on top of each other. This may lead to a process in which those specific characteristics that concern the interrelationships between all these elements and the environment are left out. It also may engender an ignorance of the specifics of the location in space/time of these elements. In painting or sculpture, for instance, this would lead to an ignorance of the impact of light on the artwork or of the size of the space in which the artwork is displayed. In nature itself a certain tree can only be that specific tree by the interaction with the soil, the humidity, the temperature, the quality of air, the competition with other trees for light and water, the influences of wind, rain, lightning, fire, natural disasters and influences from animal and man, and so on, in combination with the growth- or life cycle of such a tree. A tree, therefore, can never be understood as an autonomous object disconnected from these influences. We can, however, create an image concerning some general characteristics of a tree, but we should always be aware of the fact that these will never suffice to explain one particular tree completely. This fact underscores the problem of the fusion of universality and individuality, a problem that is evident in the confrontation between subject and object.

---

[38] The concept of 'the objective', of being able to name the objective properties of an object, seems related to the interpretation in several cultures, like in ancient China, that names and words for objects are important tools for grasping the meaning of these objects and subsequently acquiring power over them. To emphasize that the real meaning of reality is beyond any superfluous power over any object, Taoism promoted to 'name the nameless', meaning search and find the meaning over which one has neither power nor control by merely knowing how to name it. That is also indicated by the desire to reach beyond what words offer as their literal meaning.

[39] Kandinsky wrote in "Reminiscences" (1913), in Magdalena Dabrowski, "Kandinsky - Compositions" (New York: The Museum of Modern Art, 1995), p.11: "Painting is like a thundering collision of different worlds that are destined in and through conflict to create that new world called the work. Technically, every work of art comes into being in the same way as the cosmos - by means of catastrophes, which ultimately create out of the cacaphony of the various instruments that symphony we call the music of spheres. The creation of the work of art is the creation of the world." Kandinsky continues, "The very word composition called forth in me an inner vibration. Subsequently, I made it my aim in life to paint a 'composition'."

[40] Kant (1724-1804), "Kritik der reinen Vernunft" ("The Critique of Pure Reason") 1781.

7.3 PHILOSOPHICAL, ARTISTIC AND SCIENTIFIC CONCEPTS

Kant, impressed by Newton's discoveries and inspired by British empiricists (like Hume), published a critical review of the capacities of human knowledge, its certainties and its limitations.[40] He stated that we have to understand that knowledge is not a result of things but that things are a result of knowledge (this reversal is called his 'Copernican Revolution'). Impressed by the validity in his time of mathematics and natural laws in physics, Kant stated that there is knowledge that is 'a priori' (everything that does not depend on experience; in Kant 'a priori' means necessary and universal) and knowledge that is 'a posteriori' (knowledge from experience). This led him to search for the rules of a priori knowledge. For Kant, there is no 'objective reality' apart from our rational capacity and the spatial/temporal form of intuition.[41] This development must have been enhanced by the emerging discussion at the end of the 18th century about the existence of a possible free will, suggesting all objects exist on their own. Kant expected object to contain possible properties that are outside our experience, which are 'das Ding an sich' ('the thing in-itself'), properties that are only valid for that particular object, that are its objective properties. In his opinion, the discussion about object and subject cannot be separated from the discussion about matter, which seems quite justified in the context of our contemporary knowledge of particles, fields of quanta, and so on. Kant also discussed the purpose of nature and of art.[42] In nature, the logic of causal explanation can be found (any action of an object will cause some response, will have an effect on something). Even so, reasons can be found to assume the existence of the theological explanation, which, however, will not be able to replace the causal explanation. The work of art contains an inner purpose based on our experience of the beautiful and the sublime. I will discuss this in §8.4.

Nietzsche was very much involved in new considerations that matter did not actually exist, which leads us to a different interpretation of the duality of object and self.[43] In context to the growing interest in the notion time, Nietzsche argued we cherish the illusion that things remain constant and unchanging because it allows us a sense of control. This illusion is a result of the observation that we consider ourselves, as the basis of all our observations, to be constant. Nietzsche sees this as an illusion because everything changes continuously. It is an illusion driven by our desire to escape suffering, to seek safety and understanding (change brings angst, and fear of the unknown), but which only causes deception and more suffering. Similarly, Nietzsche pointed out that the

41 This follows directly from Newtonian empiricism. To be able to find the 'objective' properties of a phenomenon, an object, one considered it should be studied under circumstances that can be 'controlled', where any influence of anything else can be avoided - the study in 'splendid isolation' in the laboratory.

42 Kant discusses the connection between nature and art explicitly in "Kritik der Urteilskraft" ("The Critique of Judgement").

43 Nietzsche in "The Will to Power" (1883-5), in Richard Schacht, "Nietzsche" (London: Routledge, 1996 - or. 1983) p.150: "If we give up the concept 'subject' and 'object', then also the concept 'substance' - and as a consequence also the various modifications of it, e.g., 'matter', 'spirit', and other hypothetical entities, 'the eternity and immutability of matter', etc. we have got rid of materiality."

belief in causality is the result of the inability to accept any event without intent. Instead, he emphasized the importance of understanding reality as a continuous flux of events, not as a causal and isolated one-after-the-other process, but more clearly a manifold one-after-another or interplay of forces constituting a continuum.[44] It is not surprising that Nietzsche develops these interests while living in the age of the first scientific theories of the conservation of energies.[45] Nietzsche proposed the notion of 'the will to power' to explain the inner driving force of all objects, beings and events to interact, compete and influence each other, causing change - sheer transformations of forces and energies. He even discusses the concept of 'quanta', illustrating the growing interest at the end of 19th century thinking in understanding reality, our world, all objects and ourselves, as composed of small interacting quantities of energies, leading to Quantum Theory in the early 20th century.[46] Nietzsche considered reality to exist only in the interactions between these individual quanta, and between them individually and the whole. Although there are systems formed, this is more or less accidental. There is no such thing as a hidden order. To Nietzsche, there are only the eternal battles between all quanta driven by their 'will to power'.[47] It is no wonder that his ideas lead him to conclude that there are no constant entities that life consists of, but that life is a continuous process of construction and destruction, growth and decay. Stability, equilibrium (or harmony) happen, but only temporarily.

In the 19th century there was a lot of serious interest in researching happiness and sadness, in the physiological processes and expressions of these emotions and how these should be translated into art. This was connected, for instance, to Schopenhauer's conviction that life was misery which can only be escaped by elevating one's mind through enlightenment or the experience of art. The desire for salvation led to a desire for harmony, which led to a search for understanding and controlling harmony. In the spirit of the 19th century, people sought a formula for beauty by describing and using laws for harmony - becoming fascinated by the Golden Section, Fibonacci, other number series, and developing a sincere interest in the powers of the line and obviously in laws for colour-harmonies. In general, the search for scientific rules for aesthetics and directives

---

44 These ideas can be linked to the concept of 'lines of force', but also have been confirmed in modern scientific theories like those by Prigogene, described later in this chapter.

45 Nietzsche in "The Will to Power", in Richard Schacht, "Nietzsche", p.243: "Not merely conservation of energy, but maximal energy in use, so the only reality is the will to grow stronger of every center of force - not self-preservation."

46 Nietzsche in "The Will to Power", in Richard Schacht, "Nietzsche", p.193: "If we eliminate these additions, no things remain but only dynamic quanta, in a relation of tension to all other dynamic quanta: their essence lies in their relation to all other quanta, in their 'effect' upon the same."

47 Nietzsche in "The Will to Power", in Richard Schacht, "Nietzsche", p.209: "My idea is that every specific body strives to become master over all space and to extend its force (- its will to power) and to thrust back all that resists its extension. But it continually encounters similar efforts on the part of other bodies and ends by coming to an arrangement ('union') with those of them that are sufficiently related to it: thus they conspire together for power. And the process goes on." One is reminded here of the process of synchronization, which Nietzsche seems to imply, when he mentions his concept of 'coming to an arrangement'.

for painting were the result. These were directly connected and motivated by an extensive interest in the duality of object and subject.[48] It seems logical that in this context discussions arose about the principle of complementarity, which concerned the dependancy of the observed on the observer.[49] This concept did not focus on the confrontation, but on the interrelation between the subject and the object, and was especially discussed by the 19th century psychophysicists, who also introduced psychological meaning to the use of and direction of lines in works of art.[50] The importance of the relationship between object and subject was taken over as a notion by art critics who clear-

[48] See also Richard Shiff, "Cézanne and the End of Impressionism - A Study of the Theory, Technique, and Critical Evaluation of Modern Art" (Chicago: The University of Chicago Press, 1984).

[49] This was similar to statements made by scientists, following Heisenberg's Principle of Uncertainty - stating that the observer influences what he observes. In 19th century thinking this was the result of Schopenhauer's famous statement of "the world as will and as representation", often interpreted to mean that the world as we perceive it is the result of who is perceiving.

[50] Because the particular psychological interest of these psychophysicists in the meaning of the apperarance of a line seems very important for the preferences of early abstract artists for certain lines (for instance in Cubism, and by Kandinsky, Kupka or Mondrian), this footnote is necessarely long. The psychophysicists were scientists in the 19th century interested in studying perception using combinations of scientific methods (like mathematics and geometry) with psychological - in this case emotional - associations. Humbert de Superville published in 1827 "Essai sur les signes inconditionnels dans l'art", including his famous linear depictions of three faces - the happy face, the neutral face, the sad face - concluding upwards movements to indicate vacillitation, agitation, dispersion, explosion, or brilliance. Horizontal movements would indicate equilibrium, calm, order, brightness, light. Downwards movements would indicate concentration, withdrawal, solemnity, depth, shadows. Duchenne de Boulogne in his "Mécanisme de la physiognomie humaine" published pictures of happy and sad faces. Following these theories, Charles Henry, who published his theories in "Introduction à une esthétique scientifique", 1884, was the most important psychophysicist who, with his theories on the importance of the direction of lines (based upon perception of lines, like lines are not static, but 'forces' with a certain direction, a circle being a movement in two directions, therefore one should better speak of a 'cycle'), compositions in art (which would be a 'composition of forces' and a 'decomposition of spectrum') and movement of colour, was very influential on artists like Seurat, Signac and the Symbolist painters and writers. For an outstanding study on the influence of colour- and other scientific theories, and the discoveries of new artist's materials (like new industrially fabricated pigments, ready made canvasses, new brushes, etc.) on the birth of Impressionism, see David Bomford, Jo Kirby, John Leighton and Ashok Roy, "Art in the Making - Impressionism" (London: The National Gallery London, Yale University Press, 1991). Henry aimed to combine scientific with artistic capacities to improve industrial art and design. The enormous impact of the Japanese prints with their flat colours and importance of lines, was also important at that time leading to a trend in painting called 'Le Japonisme', as one knows well from Van Gogh, but also Seurat and Signac. Of course at the end of the 19th century Jugendstil, Art Nouveau and the Arts and Crafts movements are quite related to these interests. The architect/artist Henry van de Velde even stated that it was the central issue to find harmony with the rhythms of nature. Charles Henry published in 1890, "Éducation du sens des formes", with illustrations by Signac. At some point Henry wanted together with Signac to analyze the linear rhythms in Japanese prints to find some rules in the angles and directions of the lines and patterns. It must be emphasized, though, that there is enough evidence that painters like Signac were very interested indeed in the various scientific theories (of for instance Henry), but also repeatedly stated that these directives for painting were of limited value. See Robert L. Herbert and Ferretti-Bocquillon, "Seurat - Drawings and Paintings" (New Haven: Yale University Press, 2001). It should be clear that the development of early abstract art in the first decades of the 20th century and the emergence of the idealism for pseudo-scientific approaches in art for the benefit of improving society (like in constructivism, see §4) are quite logical steps after these 19th century efforts. The interest in the line as described above also puts the importance of the line in early abstract art in a larger perspective!

ly influenced the ideas of artists of that century (like Cézanne).[51] Richard Shiff mentions that, as a result of the influence of Schopenhauer, the artist Maurice Denis stated in 1895 that the final goal of art was the synthesis of object and subject, which can be understood as sort of dissolving of the duality between object and self.[52] After this conclusion, painting could never be the same again. It was no longer merely nice pictures of certain scenes, but images reflecting the new understanding of reality. I think I can safely say that these ideas about a synthesis of the object and subject, the dissolving of the duality between object and self, or even more clearly, Schopenhauer's union of the individual and the universal, make the interest of early abstract artists in the existence and relevancy of universal principles a natural and really timely topic.[53] This is emphasized

---

51 A result at least partly of the popularity of Schopenhauer in France - see also in §6 on Schopenhauer. See Richard Shiff, "Cézanne and the End of Impressionism - A Study of the Theory, Technique, and Critical Evaluation of Modern Art", p.27, (emphasis mine): "According to Charles Lévêque's explication (1874), Schopenhauer's famous statement, 'the world is my representation', indicated that the objective world could never be free of the subject perceiving it: the world perceived was a phenomenon of the mind. Lévêque further explained that Schopenhauer sought a way out of this epistomological impasse. To eliminate the illusions created by the mind and to discover a more fundamental reality, he sought the 'most immediate perception', the point of experience at which subject and object cease to be distinguished and union of the individual and the universal is achieved. This philosophical speculation came to bear upon the subject of art not only for Schopenhauer, but - more significantly for present purposes - also for Jules Laforgue, an admirer of Schopenhauer and his disciple Eduard von Hartmann and a friend of Charles Henry and a number of symbolist critics." On Charles Henry, see the previous footnote.

52 Besides the evidence one finds in history about Schopenhauer's influences on developments in 19th and early 20th century art - art that became of pivotal importance to modern art - to connect Schopenhauer with art not only in a philosophical but also in a practical sense, is not so strange, because Schopenhauer himself was quite interested in understanding colour. Schopenhauer published in 1816 his "Das Sehen und die Farben" ("Vision and Colours"). Kandinsky had a copy of this book in his library. See Magdalena Dabrowski, "Kandinsky - Compositions" (New York: The Museum of Modern Art, 1995), p.18. This is no big surprice, because Kandinsky was very influenced by French symbolists (who in their turn were influenced by Schopenhauer). Kandinsky discussed his interest in Schopenhauer with Franz Marc. See Magdalena Dabrowski, "Kandinsky - Compositions", page 18.

53 Discussing the discoveries in Cubism and of the Theory of Relativity, Naum Gabo wrote (remember that Gabo and contemporaries knew also about X-rays, proving objects, our bodies and matter in general not to consist of solid material) in "The Constructive Idea in Art", 1937, in Martin Hammer and Christina Lodder, "Gabo on Gabo - Texts and Interviews" (Forest Row: Artists Bookworks, 2000), p.100: "The borderline which separated the external world from the artist and distinguished it in forms of objects disappeared; the objects themselves disintegrated into their component parts and a picture ceased to be an image of the visible forms of an object as a unit, a world in itself, but appeared as a mere pictural analysis of the inner mechanism of its cells." Gabo then explains that this resulted in the Cubist artist "... [transferring] the entire inner world of his perceptions with all its component parts (logic, emotion and will) into the interior of the object penetrating through its whole structure,...". Kandinsky wrote in 1937, in Max Bill, "Essays über Kunst und Künstler" (Bern: Benteli Verlag, 1963 - orig. 1955), p.213: "Abstract painting leaves the 'skin' of nature, but not its laws. Allow me the 'grand notion', the cosmic laws. Art can only be great, when it is in immediate connection to the cosmic laws and is submitted to it. One senses these laws unconsciously, when one does not approach nature from the outside, but - internally - one must not only be able to see nature, but also to experience it." ("Die abstrakte Malerei verläßt die 'Haut' der Natur, aber nicht ihre Gesetze. Erlauben Sie mir das 'große Wort', die kosmische Gesetze. Die Kunst kann nur dann groß sein, wenn sie in direkter Verbindung mit kosmischen Gesetzen steht und sich ihnen unterordnet. Diese Gesetze fühlt man unbewußt, wenn man sich nicht äußerlich der Natur nähert, sondern - innerlich - man muß die Natur nicht nur sehen, sondern erleben können.")

here as an example of the importance of always trying to understand any artist's statement in the larger context of history.

Because the interaction between object and self is dependent on the behaviour of matter as material of which everything, including ourselves, is composed, and on how everything in reality seems to be connected, I will discuss several basic aspects of the properties of matter and of these (hidden) interconnections. One will see that theories from science are mixed with philosophical concepts to explain the many interactions between objects, beings and phenomena and to throw a different light on the discussion about object and self. The manifold interactions and interconnections in reality also cause change that continuously affects object and self. Understanding change involves both scientific and more philosophical issues. It will be pointed out that both have an impact on understanding works of art.

The modern notion of matter as consisting of small quantities (quanta) of energy, and not as solids, makes the interaction, extension and interaction between an object and its environment unavoidable. Solids are objects that rely completely on themselves - their existence is limited within the outlines of their shape. Quantities of fluctuating energies in principle go beyond their visually assumed outlines and thus interact continuously with the energies of their immediate environment.

In addition, the properties of a certain object are only considered to be 'objective' when different persons who study a particular object at different times define exactly the same properties. I propose that we might speak of the 'objectedness' of an appearance. This is only a theoretical assumption, because objective properties cannot possibly be definite. They are open to change by the continuous interactions in reality, although at eye-level we still will have the impression of perceiving objects standing 'objectively' by themselves, without any perceptable interactions (or even without any perceptible change). All circumstances change and make any absolute objectedness or objectivity - in the meaning of an absolute autonomy - definitely impossible and merely of theoretical interest. Therefore, it is natural that an interest in the notion of changing circumstances is not merely a modern development! Since man has been able to think and communicate, all kinds of oracles, religions, philosophies and theories have been developed in an attempt to find an explanation for the changing circumstances and to look into the future, with the sole purpose of having a better chance of surviving.[54]

[54] One of the oldest examples of such oracles that has become quite popular again in our times is the I-Ching or "Book of Changes". The pictorial strength of the I-Ching clearly has not escaped artists. In modern times examples can be found in the very large installations from the early 1980's by American artist Walter de Maria showing 64 I-Ching combinations using stainless steel rods. See Wim Beeren, "Walter de Maria" (Rotterdam: Museum Boymans-van Beuningen, 1984). More recent examples of interest in the I-Ching can be found in the works by German sculptor Birgitta Weimer, American painter Marlena Novak, or in the 'chance operations' of American composer John Cage. The ambition of the I-Ching was to develop a system or language of signs that could accurately explain the future. To fullfill this ambition, the inventors of the system had to understand the functioning of the human mind, based on the knowledge that the mind reflects on the world in pictures, signs, words, notions. The rules that define the interrelations between these aspects form something like a language. Therefore, for every regular aspect of human existence a pictorial symbol should be developed

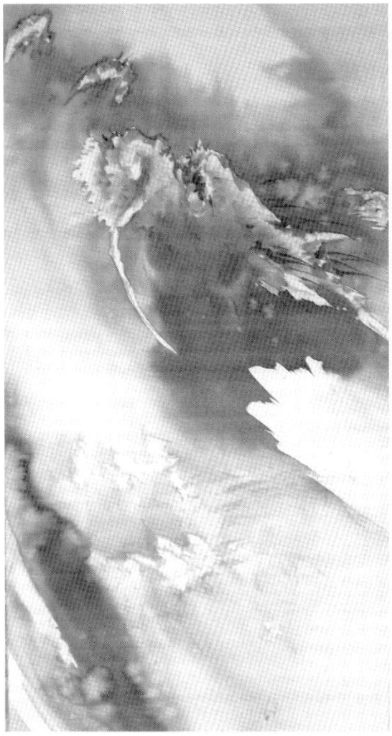

61. Kida Kado (1812-1877)
detail **Dragon**, metaphor for eternal change.
The dragon emerges from nothingness and
disappears into nothingness

For instance, a better understanding of the weather and seasons will improve methods for agriculture and thus avoid periods of famine.

In modern science in the 20th century one can discover an emerging tendency to finally and definitively get rid of Newtonian determinism, meaning accepting that in reality everything does not proceed according to strict and determined laws of nature, but is open to results from changing circumstances. This indicates that an objective observation is impossible. Nevertheless, some phenomena seem to follow laws of nature. Therefore, one of the important themes of the 20th century has been, and still is, to find out to what degree phenomena are determined by laws and to what degree they possess the potentiality to change unexpectedly. This involves really everything from particle-physics, cosmology to economics and indeed should include art. If the impact of changing circumstances was not so important, then the outcome of all processes in nature would be predetermined. In other words, outcomes could be predicted exactly, implying that oracles like the I-Ching are indeed true. The unpredictablity of the weather or the unpredictability of how a particular tree will grow are perhaps simple examples that reality is more complex than that. The development of Quantum Theory with all its complex uncertainties has stimulated this tendency to rethink determinism.

Information Theory provides an additional angle for contemplating object and self. This theory furthers the discussion on the impact of the various properties - hidden or not - and the interactions and interconnections between everything in reality. This seems of specific interest in context to our perception of a work of art being based on the assumption that a focus of one's attention on the work of art is an attempt to retrieve certain information. Information Theory has also developed and has become of

---

that could also be defined in context to the whole systems. It took the ancient Chinese several centuries to develop the I-Ching system. Although it seems difficult to date its origin, it is known to have existed in the era of the western Zhou - dynasty, 1045 - 770 BC. See Frank Fiedeler, "Yin und Yang - Das kosmische Grundmuster in den Kulturformen Chinas" (Cologne: DuMont Verlag, 1993). As I mentioned in §2.3, Leibniz got in touch with Father Joachim Bouvet who informed him about the 64 hexagrams of the I-Ching. Leibniz published the results of their discussions and his analysis of this binary system in his "Explication de l'arithmétique binaire" from 1703. See Umberto Eco, "Die Suche nach der vollkomenen Sprache" (Munich: C.H. Beck-Europa Bauen, 1994 - orig. "La ricerca della lingua perfetta nella cultura europea", 1993), p. 290-293. In 1968 the psychologist Marie-Louise von Franz discovered that the basic structure of the 64 hexagrams of the I-Ching coincides in a structural and a numerical sense perfectly with the 64 nucleodtriplets of DNA; DNA which is the basis of the genetic code of life. This alone gives a lot of reasons to speculate on the level of knowledge in ancient China. See Frank Fiedeler, "Yin und Yang - Das kosmische Grundmuster in den Kulturformen Chinas", p.82.

renewed interest. Information Theory gives the notion of 'information' formal meaning, basing the number of choices one has on a collection of data.[55] In summary one might say that information is something with a certain meaning contained in a medium, and it acquires its meaning when it is obtained out of this medium by a recipient. 'Obtaining' is meant in a metaphorical sense, since it will mean retrieving ('unpacking') information by a process of thinking sparked by visual perception, by visual or verbal reading. It is not far-fetched to consider Information Theory as an additional angle for understanding the interaction between object and self, since perception is pure information gathering if nothing else. As we learn from Henri Bergson; perception is a result of the confrontation of the object and self.

Analogues to Information Theory, David Bohm has proposed that information is something 'in a form', which seems very related to both Plato's understanding of 'to inform' and to the Aristotelian idea of 'ousia'. Carl Friedrich von Weizsäcker writes "Information is the measure of the quantity of form."[56] In other words: the higher the quantity of a form, the more complex a form is, the more information it contains. He uses for form also the notion Gestalt:

> *"In the ontology of classical physics one would understand form as a logical notion, that can imply a fundamental reality: the form of a body or of a force, form in space, maybe also in time. In the origin of the concrete Quantum Theory, however, (localized) space is introduced as a mathematical property of the 'primordial', also as a continuum of possibilities for the Yes-No decisions and particles and fields, described in a classical sense as bodies and forces as representations of the symmetry-group of this continuum. **Information** then is the basic notion from which the traditional understanding of matter (res extensa) has been retrieved."*[57]

According to Information Theory, the quantity of information is in most cases meas-

[55] Originally from Claude E. Shannon, 1948. See Richard Coyne, "Technoromanticism - digital narrative, holism, and the romance of the real" (Cambridge, MA: MIT Press, 1999), p.96: "Information is what is there underlying the sentence, with the sentence as a carrier of information. In some respects this use of 'information' accords with the etymology of the word to 'inform', commonly taken as 'to impart some essential characteristic to'. The word is derived from the Latin 'informare', which is 'to give form to'. To inform is to imprint a lump of wax with a form, in the sense in which Plato spoke of the forms of the Intelligible realm being imprinted on the material of the sensible form."

[56] See Carl Friedrich von Weizsäcker, "Zeit und Wissen" (Munich, Vienna: Carl Hanser Verlag, 1992) p.292: "Information ist das Maß einer Menge von Form."

[57] See Carl Friedrich von Weizsäcker, "Zeit und Wissen", p.292: "In der Ontologie der klassischen Physik würde man 'Form' als ein logisches Prädikat auffassen, das einer fundamentalen Realität zukommen kann: Form eines Körpers oder einer Kraft, Form im Raum, vielleicht auch in der Zeit. In der Herleitung der konkreten Quantentheorie wird jedoch der (Orts-) Raum als mathematischer Zustandsraum des 'Urs', also ein Kontinuum von Möglichkeiten für die Ja - Nein - Entscheidungen eingeführt, und Teilchen und Felder, also klassisch gesagt, Körper und Kräfte als Darstellungen der Symmetrie Gruppe dieses Kontinuums. Information ist dann der Grundbegriff, aus dem der traditionelle Begriff der Materie (res extensa) erst hergeleitet wird." (Emphasis mine)

ured in bits, which are units with only two values.[58] Claude E. Shannon introduced in his theory also the notion of entropy from thermodynamics.[59] Like a painting composed in such a way that in every part it looks the same (such as a repetitive overall pattern or a monochrome painting), a system in a state with a uniform equilibrium does not show any hierarchal order. Entropy can be understood as the degree to which a system exists in chaos. In his concept of Information Theory Shannon understood entropy as the degree of choice during the process of defining a message, the process of the attempt of the recipient to obtain the offered information. Until the moment the recipient has been able to formulate the information, the message, in his head, the offered information may seem so complex that it seems mere chaos or entropy. The most simple messages are those messages that have a crystal clear organization, and easy readable structure. When a symbol in a message allows much freedom of choice, this must be the result of a low degree of organization - a high degree of entropy - of the message. In such a case the choice will present a lot more information. Such an understanding of entropy is, in an artistic composition, exactly the same. In art, a composition that resembles a state of absolute uniform equilibrium is highly ordered, or structured in a simply readable symmetrical way. Compositions involving complexity and clear contrasts, although they may give the impression of being chaotic, merely present a complexity of information exceeding information that can be grasped in one glance or put into words and that can only be retraced by trusting one's intuition or after some effort and time.

Continuing the cross-cultural historical progression of concepts of the interconnectedness of everything in the world at an imperceptible level, in the 1960's physicist David Bohm developed the Implicate Order Theory (or enfolded order), which he kept developing until the early 1990's.[60] This theory offers a scientific explanation of what was intuitively intended by Taoism, Schopenhauer, or Nietzsche much earlier. The basic and simplest illustration of this theory, which aims to explain a lot about the perception of phenomena in our world that sometimes seem to pop up around us, is an experiment

see picture
7

58 These sets of two values are called 'binary codes'. For instance, plus or minus, black or white, zero or one. Obviously this has been used for and still is the basis of all computer technology as long as it continues to work with binary logic of sets of 1's and 0's.

59 Entropy, originally a mathematical notion, meant the chaos of a system. It was a notion that evolved out of studying heat and was understood as the amount of heat that could not be translated into labour. The Second Law of Thermodynamics states that the entropy in a closed system will always grow, causing all closed systems to end in a thermal equilibrium or dead end. Entropy also means the state in which a structure dissolves into fragments that then become parts of various other structures - the virtual flowing back from an object or being into the whole of nature after its dissolution or death. Entropy was perceived as unstructured, uncontrolled or even chaotic at such a moment, because of the classical assumption that during a study of the structure of an object or being all other things and phenomena around it do not change (a concept called 'ceteris paribus'). Ignoring this basic fact made it impossible to view the dissolution of a structure into entropy as a step that can be understood. The conscious neglect of the influence of the interactions with other phenomena around the studied process prevented one from 'seeing' the logic of these interactions. One could only perceive unexplainable chaos, instead of understanding it as a next phase in a complex continuous process of not one isolated, but of many interacting structures.

60 Most of his work, David Bohm accomplished in close co-operation with physicist Basil Hiley.

with two concentric glass cylinders. The inner one is fixed and the outer one can be rotated slowly. Bohm and David Peat wrote,

> *"The space between the cylinders is filled with a viscous liquid such as glycerin. When the outer cylinder is turned, fluid close to it is dragged along at nearly the same speed, but fluid close to the inner, stationary, cylinder is held nearly at rest. Hence fluid in different regions of space moves at different rates, and in this way, any small element of the glycerin is eventually drawn out into a long thin thread. If a drop of indissoluble ink is placed in the liquid, then it becomes possible to follow the movement of the small element by watching how the drop is drawn out into a thread until eventually it becomes so fine as to be invisible. At first sight one may be tempted to say that the ink drop has been totally mixed into the glycerin so that its initial order has been lost and is now random or chaotic. But suppose that the outer cylinder is now rotated in the reverse direction. If the fluid is very viscous, like glycerin, and the cylinder is rotated too quickly, then the fluid element will in fact retrace its steps exactly. Eventually the element will return to its original form and the droplet of ink will appear as if from nothing."*[61]

This implies that a phenomenon can disappear from our visible reality into a hidden order of sorts, only to re-appear at another moment. David Bohm, introducing new notions, proposed that the visible order might be understood as the 'explicate' order that enfolds into a hidden or 'implicate' order. Or, vice versa, out of the hidden or implicate order the visible or explicate order unfolds. Shortly before his death Bohm put down his last ideas about connectedness in collaboration with Basil Hiley:

> *"... the key new feature here is that of* ***the undivided wholeness*** *of the measuring instrument and the observed object, which is a special case of wholeness to which we have alluded in connection with quantum processes in general."*[62]

Bohm and Hiley emphasize the unavoidable interaction between ourselves and the perceived. When we study something we focus our attention on this something. Because we never can observe with an empty head, but with former experiences, with prejudices, associations, and expectations, we influence beforehand the outcome of what we observe. Our focussed attention is not a one-way process of one signal from ourselves towards an object, but a continuous jumping back and forth of attention between the object of attention and ourselves. Through this process, the observed becomes such a part of our projective field that we only can agree with Bohm and Hiley's concept of an

61 See David Bohm and F. David Peat, "Science, Order & Creativity" (London: Routledge, 1989 - orig. Bantam Books 1987), p.172-173.

62 See David Bohm and Basil Hiley, "The Undivided Universe - An ontological Interpretation of Quantum Theory" (London: Routledge, 1995 - orig. 1993), p.6.

undivided wholeness. This sense of undivided wholeness is a phenomenon that can be experienced quite well while observing art, while feeling absorbed by a good work of art. Bohm/Hiley's theory is clearly related to the problem of quantum jumps and tunnelling photons that resulted from the famous Two-Slit Experiment.[63] If there is such a thing as Bohm's 'implicate order' - an enfolded order with potentialities to partly unfold into the 'explicate order' of reality as we see it - then all phenomena indeed are connected at a deeper level. As we have seen in the discussion on space/time perception, and on matter, there is enough evidence to take this theory seriously.

7.4 CHAOS

Chaos in context to Information Theory has been mentioned. In the 1970's 'chaos' became the hot topic when Chaos Theory became fashionable through Benoit Mandelbrot and science-journalist James Gleick. Chaos as a concept was already discussed by the ancient Greeks, who considered chaos to be the extensive empty space that existed before all else. The Pre-Socratic thinkers considered chaos to be the structuring form that was the original beginning of the universe. The thinkers of the Stoa understood chaos as disorder underlying all things.[64] Nietzsche understood chaos as the moving force. At the beginning of the 20th century the philosopher Alfred North Whitehead understood chaos as the particular point of disorder from which order and the cosmos evolve.[65] Ideas about chaos are universal. They illustrate the relationships between Oriental and Occidental thought, and how different they are in their interpretive details.

Eiko Kawamura describes how the relationships between chaos and cosmos are understood in Zen-Buddhism:

> *"Zen sees in the actual world, which normally is understood as chaos (Hun-tun), a functioning of creativity and freedom for a world of true reality. This chaos is expressed as creativity in very different ways - meaning differently in every period and differently by every individual human being. If we explain the word chaos with different words, in a certain way it becomes ordered. In this sense creativity and cosmos are not diametrically opposed to each other, as expression of chaos, but each describe reality. The relationship of chaos and cosmos in Zen can therefore be understood as analogous to the understanding of Heidegger's 'being self' and 'Being of being'. Or in the best possible precision of words: in the end it can be understood as absolutely contradictory and also as absolutely self-identical."*[66]

---

[63] See §6.

[64] The Stoa was a school of philosophy founded by the philosopher Zeno in Athens, Greece, about 4th - 2nd centuries BC. The name came from the "Stoa poikilè", a colourful, with wall paintings decorated gallery with columns. This philosophy school was further developed until about 2nd century AD.

[65] Whitehead inspired Ilya Prigogene, who will be discussed later in this chapter.

[66] See Eiko Kawamura, "Das Problem von Chaos und Kosmos im Zen-Buddhismus", in "Strukturen des Chaos" (Munich: Wilhelm Fink Verlag, 1994), p.90: "Zen sieht in der faktischen Welt, die normalerweise als

In my interpretation, this relationship of creativity and cosmos as an expression of chaos is analogous to the ideas of scientist Ilya Prigogene. Besides, it seems to reflect the whole idea of art as a search for the essence of reality! When one combines this short reference to Zen ideas about chaos with the broad interest in Eastern philosophies in the late 1960's and early 1970's in western countries, it helps to explain the popularity of Chaos Theory.

In modern science this theory concentrates on the before-mentioned Second Law of Thermodynamics, trying to understand unpredictable behaviour like turbulences in smoke or liquids. Mandelbrot and his fellow chaos researchers concentrated on mathematical models, which led them to develop the well-known 'fractals', computerized pictures based on algorithms. Beautiful as these fractals may be,[67] they say nothing whatsoever about real life - except in a metaphorical sense. It was Albert Libchaber who offered a first look into real chaotic behaviour in an experiment in 1979, when he discovered in a tiny cell of liquid helium how a fluid's flow becomes disordered.[68] Stimulations to study chaotic behaviour in nature came from the desire to tackle processes that seem to be impossible to predict, like the weather. To do this, Chaos Theory ambitiously crossed the boundaries of many different disciplines in science and technology. This was a natural reaction to the exaggerated specialization in science. Chaos tries to understand and incorporate in a theory the so-called 'butterfly effect'. This notion refers to the phenomenon of unexpected chain reactions in the weather: the tiny strokes of the wings of a butterfly that disturbs the air in Peking today can provoke a storm in New York next month.[69]

Another phenomenon studied and discussed widely in Chaos Theory is the existence of strange attractors that create a kind of cyclic behaviour in the processes of reality. Everything is in a state of flux, everything is vulnerable to change. A change of circumstances may cause the disturbance of the order of a group of moving parts in a cyclical process. Attractors are centers of attraction that pull these parts back into some order (not necessarely exactly the same, but a similar order as the one which was initially disturbed).[70] The most famous diagram of an attractor is the '8' shaped computer-simula-

Chaos (Hun-tun) betrachtet wird, ein Wirken von Kreativität und Freiheit für eine Welt der wahren Realität. Dieses Chaos wird als Kreativität auf verschiedenste Weise zum Ausdruck gebracht - nämlich in jedem Zeitalter un von jedem Menschen anders. Wenn wir das Wort 'Chaos' mit anderen Worten erklären, dann wird es in gewisser Hinsicht geordnet. In diesem Sinne stehen Kreativität und Kosmos als ein Ausdruck des Chaos einander nicht dualistisch gegenüber, sondern bezeichnen jeweils die Realität. Das Verhältnis von Chaos und Kosmos im Zen kann daher parallel zum Verhältnis von Heideggers 'Sein Selbst' und 'Sein des Seienden' verstanden werden. Oder in den nach Möglichkeit präzisesten Worten: Es kann letztendlich als absolut kontradiktorisch und als ebenso absolut selbstidentisch verstanden werden."

67 Especially the coloured ones developed by Otto Peitgen.

68 See Madhusree Mukerjee, "Profile: Albert Libchaber - Seeing the World in a Snowflake", Scientific American March 1996, p.23-25.

69 Today this phenomenon is studied through computer simulations of artificial life as the phenomenon of emergence.

70 See Prigogene's notion of adaptive organization further in this chapter.

tion by Edward Lorenz from 1963,[71] which shows a remarkable resemblance to the '8' motions simulated in so many artworks. Chaos Theory primarily made unsolved multidisciplinary themes subjects of discussion that had been avoided in the classical (Newtonian) science of specializations. When one reads about the interests in very different fields of science, for instance particle physics, theoretical physics, neurophysiology, cognitive science, biology, medicine or computerscience, as a lay person one can only wonder why the representatives from the various fields do not talk more to each other. Benoit Mandelbrot was so succesful because he knew enough about various fields to be taken seriously by the academics in these various fields. Thus, he showed that real multidisciplinary approaches can be very fruitful for all involved. Although in philosophy and religion the notion of chaos is as old as the world, in the 1970's Mandelbrot's chaos was the right Zeitgeist-related notion that appealed to a very broad public, especially because of its mystical touch.[72] The aesthetic power of the fractal-pictures has inspired quite a few amateur and professional artists. For instance, the Swiss painter, designer and colour-specialist Karl Gerstner or German Op-Art artist Ludwig Wilding.

Many more artists got interested in studying chaotic behaviour, but not in copying fractal-images, for example French computer-artist Vera Molnar, or artists like German painter Horst Rave and American painter Richard Purdy, all of who really try to understand the principles of Chaos Theory. Instead of merely copying fractals, they search for their own pictorial elements and compositions exemplifying chaotic behavior. Still, as unfortunately always seems to happen when there is a certain trend in popularized science, large groups of not-so-serious artists merely pasted the lable 'chaos' onto their work. However, besides focussing general attention on topics like the complexity and diversity of nature - this theory did not come up with any real solutions to explain everyday reality.[73] The fractals as illustrations are ultimately mathematical presentations that only have in common with reality that they show how processes in nature tend to develop from the simple to the complex.

[71] See James Gleick, "Chaos - de derde wetenschappelijke revolutie", translated by Patty Adelaar (Amsterdam: Uitgeverij Contact, 1991 - orig. "Chaos: making a new science", 1987).

[72] Mandelbrot's theory was undoubtedly also the right timed answer to the frustrated emotions after the chaos of the Vietnam-war, that seemed so illogical.

[73] This is true with the exception of certain applications in computing and engineering, like in 'fuzzy logic'. Fuzzy logic is a notion from computer technology. It tries to escape the linearity of binary Yes/No computer logic and aims to offer a greater variety of choices more comparable to the degree of choice our own brains offer. Fuzzy logic is a branch of machine intelligence that can model and control nuances overlooked by normal computers. This technology is used in consumer electronics like coffee-machines or washing-machines; their programms can be more custom-made based almost on individual preferences. Machines programmed with fuzzy logic can be more energy efficient. See Bart Kosko and Satoru Isaka, "Fuzzy Logic - The binary logic of modern computers often fall short when describing the vagueness of the real world. Fuzzy logic offers more graceful alternatives", Scientific American July 1993, p.62-67.

7.5 ORDER FLUCTUATION - ADAPTIVE ORGANIZATION - CHANGE

In the 1970's new theories emerged, continuing the century-old search for the coherence of events through a structure or order in nature to find a Theory of Everything, a theory that could explain the whole of nature. These theories sought an explanation for something like nature's will, which reminds one of Schopenhauer's 'world will' and thus presents us with another loop back into history. Physicist Ilya Prigogene played a key-role in this development. His theories, clearly furthering the philosophies of Nietzsche and Whitehead, belong to the scientific ideas that sparked my own train of thought concerning a larger meaning of art beyond being merely a cultural product of some possible artistic or market value. This expanded meaning is not only provided by psychological associations of the human mind, but also is, at least partly, a result of our living as biochemical beings in the world, too. Besides, Prigogene's interdisciplinary ideas have everything to do with the subject of this chapter: the confrontation between object and self in a larger context.

Since the 1960's Prigogene developed revolutionary research with his theories of self-organization, chemical clockworks in organisms, order - fluctuations and breaking points. A living organism is highly complex, especially when seen from a thermodynamical viewpoint. Certain behaviours approach a situation of pure equilibrium, others do not. Prigogene and his fellow researcher, biologist Isabelle Stengers, compare the streams of energy that flow through an organism to the erratic behaviour of a river, which can mainly be calm, but still can sometimes rush down in a waterfall, releasing some of its energy. Prigogene and Stengers discuss for instance the remarkable periodic behaviour of the amoeba *Dictyostelium discoideum.* When a group of these amoeba is distributed at random on a flat surface they show a clear process of self-organization towards the centre of the group in the form of concentric or pulsating waves.[74] Prigogene and Stengers also discuss how nutrition can play an important role in the process of self-organization.[75] When not enough nutrition is available (anymore), the organization of the organisms changes. New centres of attraction seem to emerge, whose existence and location the amoeba seem to communicate to each other. The chemical clocks inside the amoeba seem to provide this communication and result in the behaviour described as 'order-fluctuation'. There is evidence for order-fluctuations to be

---

[74] The chemotactual factor causing this is called cyclic AMP (cAMP), a substance that is involved in several biochemical processes, like in the regulation of hormones.

[75] It might be a coincidence, it might not be so, but Prigogene and Stengers' experiments seem to confirm Schopenhauer's ideas about 'will as inner nature' present in all beings and things. Schopenhauer thought that at any given moment an organism will tend to some localized 'telos', an aim, goal or purpose. See Christopher Janaway, "The Cambridge Companion to Schopenhauer" (Cambridge: Cambridge University Press, 1999). Janaway writes on this subject, p.143: "Whatever localized telos it tends towards, its functioning is governed by enduring ends that must be secured repeatedly - nutrition, for example - and the single overarching telos which explains them all (to which they all are instrumental) is that of being alive and perpetuating life. This pattern of tending towards ends which provide the explanation for behaviour is common throughout the natural world. And human willing is one among a multitude of ways in which organisms tend towards a telos."

found, just as a gravity field (for instance from our earth) can influence the order of a certain field, even at a macroscopic level. Detailed calculations show that these influences can be extremely dramatic when they are close to a breaking point. Even very small gravity fields can result in a choice of pattern. This means that the order of even the smallest of organisms, the bacteria, will be disturbed (will fluctuate) under the influence of electrical and magnetic fields, and thus can be considered to be in a state-far-from-equilibrium (what today is called a situation on the edge of chaos). The sensitivity and adaptation to outside influences is called adaptive organization.[76] That this adaptive behaviour can and undoubtedly will influence our interaction with reality - therefore, also with an object - should be clear. Just remember the influence a low pressure area in the weather or a full moon may have on your feelings. However, once more it seems to be even more complex. I discussed in §5 the influence processes in the body have on the brain, like the fluctuating flow of hormones, therefore in principle affecting our perception of an object.

Let us now turn to another interesting phenomenon, that definitely also has to be considered. Quite an interesting property of organic cells that is being researched more extensively is the death of cells, which seems to happen according to a fluctuating order and exemplifies Prigogene's chemical clocks. Obviously this research is stimulated by the search for better treatment of the infections that threaten modern civilization, like HIV and cancer. In cells, division and death are interrelated in a never ending Yin-Yang battle. It is surprising, though human, that biologists in the first 150 years of cell theory have only focussed on the positive side of cellular life. An initial step towards cell-death research was taken as late as the early 1970's, when pathologists discovered that normal cell-deaths look different from the cell-deaths caused by acute injuries. Normal cell-death was called 'apoptosis'[77] and thought to be an act of suicide activated by the cell through an internal program for self-destruction.[78] An example of the usefulness of such programmed cell-death is that a cell that is infected by a virus will kill itself to pre-

---

[76] This seems to have a lot in common with the phenomenon of synchronization. See §5.1. Biochemical scientist and molecular biologist Friedrich Cramer discusses this phenomenon extensively. See Friedrich Cramer, "Symphonie des Lebendigen - Versuch einer allgemeinen Resonanztheorie" (Frankfurt a/M, Leipzig: Insel Taschenbuch, 1998). At the core of his argument is that in the whole of nature, at every level in macro and micro-nature, there are rhythmic and cyclic processes that influence each other's rhythmic behaviour and/or are influenced by other rhythmic processes. The difference in our bodies between day- and night processes is only one obvious example, the complex variety of hormone-processes another one. Cramer discusses how, according to current knowledge, about 3000 metabolic cycles are active in our bodies, each swinging at their own frequencies. As long as they act in harmony (in synchronisation) we are healthy and we do not notice a thing. Also the communication between individual cells happens by a rhythmic transmission of energy (in the case of cells, the transmission of certain chemical substances). For an outstanding discussion on synchronization as the growing field in science, see Steven Strogatz, "SYNC - How Order Emerges from Chaos in the Universe, Nature, and Daily Life" (New York: Theia Books, 2003).

[77] Apoptosis is Greek for falling.

[78] See Martin C. Raff, "Death Wish - All cells come primed for self-destruction. The challenge for medicine is to make them die on cue.", The Sciences, July/August 1996, p.36: "It is estimated, for instance, that in the developing brain about half the nerve cells die soon after they are formed, and many other developing organs

vent the virus from spreading. Research has shown that cells communicate information to their neighbouring cells and that this process is essential in the process of apoptosis (as it is essential for cell-division, too). Could the natural death of cells be compared to the Greek 'kinesis', and function as inborn drive for change and renewal, allowing the possibility of living tissue to adapt and survive?[79]

That this phenomenon is open to rhythmic or fluctuating influences from outside the body should be considered a logical conclusion of Prigogene's ideas about adaptive organization and self-organization. Try for instance to imagine the immense influence on the cells of the organism, that we call our body, by gravity, the quality of air that we breathe, the quality of light that warms and illuminates our bodies, the kind of food we eat, the amount of stress we put ourselves in! These are all aspects capable of affecting the interaction object and self. Again, it is beside the point here that these factors will not completely decide our response to an object or why we prefer the one work of art above the other. The logical implications of our bodies being biochemical organisms open to outside influences play a role nevertheless and - if nothing else - prove how simplistic it is to merely lean on pictorial analysis for finding the sole reasons for our appreciation of art!

There is a general belief that man (and animal) always prefer repetitive procedures, which enhance a feeling of understanding because they can be recognized by memory and thereby judged as harmless or threatening. This preference for repetition results in a continuous search for finding some repetitive structure in what we perceive, which is projected into art and explains repetitive patterning and structuring in all kinds of cultural expressions throughout human history.[80] But, it should also be remarked here, that when one briefly considers how important the notion of change is to understanding life on the cellular level in our brain and the rest of our body, it seems not so far fetched to propose the hypothesis that we desire to understand change in life - as an aspect of life - by looking at simulations of change in works of art. This desire to understand change is at least as important as finding structure. One may also understand change as process, because all change happens as a process.[81] Works of art are created by people subject to

are thought to undergo similar rates of cell death. Those suicides help shape the body as well as the mind."

[79] Richard Purdy made a beautiful small painting on this theme: "Death by Design", 1999. It has been stated that all cells in our bodies are replaced during periods of only 7 years.

[80] This point is very well made and extensively documented by Gombrich. See E.H. Gombrich, "Sense for Order - A study in the psychology of decorative art" (London: Phaidon, second edition, 1984 - orig. 1979). This fact also clearly inspired many early constructivist artists. See §4.

[81] Process as phenomenon has always been an important aspect of art - as for instance when the brush-stroke of a certain master is discussed. Ever since philosophers like Nietzsche, see Richard Schacht, "Nietzsche", p.229-243, and Whitehead - his major book "Process and Reality" - in science, philosophy and art, process has been an important paradigm. In art process became a topic especially since the DaDaist experiments with chance (Hans Arp's at random dropping of pieces of paper to decide on a composition), Surrealist experiments - Wolfgang Paalen's "Fumages" (paintings realized using smoke prints from candles), Max Ernst's paint experiments, the so-called 'automatist techniques' aiming to avoid conscious artistic decisions, also explored by Masson, Baziotes, Klee, Matta, etc. or the experimental workshops in New York in the 1930's led by Mexican muralist Siqueiros, Mark Tobey's and Miro's experiments with free calligraphy, but especially

all discussed aspects of change, just like any observer. Because works of art are, by definition, specifically human interpretations of change, these interpretations are probably more accessible than expressions of change that one may find in nature itself. Of course, we can find changes in nature everywhere; in the clouds, the patterns of grass in a field, the winding growth pattern of a tree, the everchanging colour and intensity of day light, but it seems that in our everyday life we do not notice these as consciously as when expressed in a work of art. Besides, there are numerous changes in nature we cannot perceive with the speed and limited capacities of our vision, as for instance cell-growth and motions of the planets.

see picture 45

Being subject to the complexities of change in nature also makes a desire for harmony - for temporal stability or security - very natural. Artworks seem to function so well, because most works of art simulate change without actually changing. Therefore, they offer the notion of change as well as harmony.[82] This phenomenon is very well expressed in the poetic 'freehand' geometrical structures of Jean-Pierre Maury, but also in the precisely painted and sensitively coloured paintings of Michael Bette.

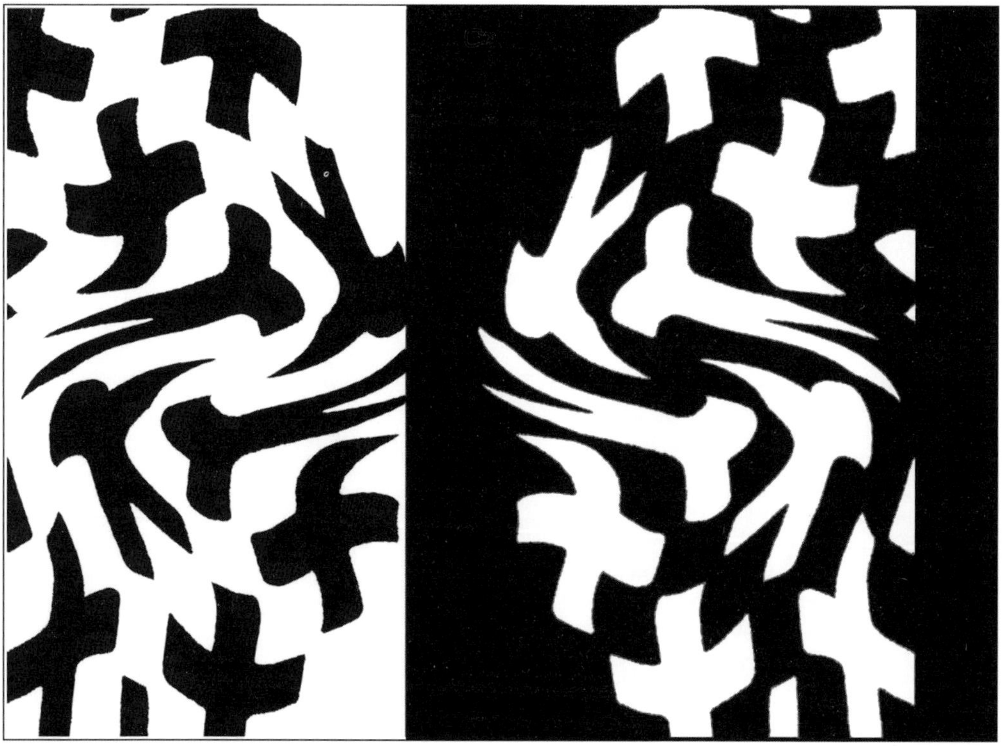

62. Jean-Pierre Maury (1948-)
MDF 2003050, envol stationnaire, noir et blanc 2003, Acrylic paint on MDF 150 x 201 cm (59 x 79 1/8 inches)
www.monsite.wanadoo.fr/mauryjp

This tension between change and harmony in a work of art seems to mirror Prigogene's moment of a breaking point, which one can imagine as a kind of cross-road. This concept explains how in reality, with all our knowledge, we can only predict a limited part of a process, after which changing circumstances cause a moment when the stability is broken, and a moment of instability follows. Or, as we do not know how the process will proceed, this moment of instability involves a moment of insecurity (metaphorically understood as a breaking point). This is a moment when we cannot predict how things will go. After this moment is passed, a virtual choice for further proceeding is somehow made or caused, and we will be able to predict the process in another limited stretch of time, following the laws of classical science. Prigogene calls the moment of the metaphorical breaking point an 'order-fluctuation'. This is the notion of breaking symmetry. In principle symmetry involves two forces or quantities, which, as each others' polarities, are in perfect harmony or equilibrium and destroy each others' forces (in the same way that every particle has its anti-particle). Reality shows that moments of equilibrium do occur, but that because of the 'kinesis'[83] of changing circumstances these moments never exist very long nor can they be permanent. The symmetry is soon broken. Biology provides the right metaphor: a moment of absolute symmetry or equilibrium is equivalent to death (when for instance both chambers of the heart are in absolute equilibrium, meaning the pressure in both is the same, the heart stops pounding, an unfortunate stagnation we call a cardial arrest). The Theory of Everything should be able to explain all these phenomena. Such a theory must not be confused with David Bohm's concept of wholeness, which implies not an everything but a coherence of the whole, as he considered it feasible to understand the whole but denied that we will ever be able to understand every individual thing.

In the 1980's the Santa Fé Institute[84] was founded in the United States as multi-disciplinary research center in the field that has become known as the 'Theory of Complexity'. This field represents a first attempt to research the complexity of order-fluctuations as a result of changing circumstances involving the fields of particle physics, economy and artificial life. Artificial life, which is a part of the research on artificial

since Jackson Pollock, the later 'action painters' and expressionist 'tachist' painters. In the developments of certain installation, performance or conceptual art, but also in more system-related art in the 1960's and 1970's, a certain process became more important than the final visual result. For some artists, the most essential seems that the very process of creation is of higher value than the final result and the process provides the artwork's whole meaning. This emphasis on process being more important than the visual result seems to have been used too often as an excuse for poor visual results. Besides, I absolutely disagree that the process of making a work of art should be the sole content and meaning of art. Therefore, I choose not to use the word process too much, and prefer 'change' as paradigm.

82 All works of art do in fact change when seen in a different space or when the light changes, but these of course involve changes of context and of interaction with the environment and are not actual changes of the work itself.

83 'Kinesis' is the Greek term for the inner drive to keep moving, as was discussed earlier in this chapter.

84 See M. Mitchell Waldrop, "Complexity - The Emerging Science at the Edge of Order and Chaos" (New York, London: Viking/Penguin Group, 1992).

intelligence (AI), is the study of life by studying computer-simulated entities and societies of these entities, defined by properties analogous to properties of actual living organisms. Key-words in these studies are 'emergence',[85] 'on the edge of chaos'[86] and 'autocatalysis'. The Santa Fé Institute, however, has not been able to come up with real solutions yet. It has to be repeatedly discovered how difficult and slow the road to understanding the complexity of reality is, because for a large part it is dependent on the capacity of the supporting technology. It seems for instance that we can only develop the perfect computer to study life, even define its parameters, after we first are able to describe life itself, including individual-, group- and social behaviour with all its intricacies, external influences and conflicts. And that is exactly what we wished to use the computer for in the first place! The central issue in this understanding continues to be the acceptance of the overwhelming influence of the changing circumstances, the search for a possible theory and the acceptance of possible uncertainties that are 'beyond words'. When everything changes or continuously changes this affects all phenomena to different degrees and causes all information to change. C.F. von Weizsäcker wrote: "We move in an unfinished and possibly unfinishable field of never completely clear notions."[87]

This seems also to be proven by recent research in Quantum Physics. The classical notion is that electrons rotate around the nucleus like tiny planets around their sun. Quantum Theory has shown that this process is much more complex, still not providing an agreed concept. For instance, Werner Heisenberg felt that classical orbits had no place in Quantum Theory, while Erwin Schrödinger was of a different mind. Today, scientists believe that elements do orbit around the nucleus, but that these orbits do not lie in one phase (meaning: they cannot be imagined to follow linear paths, like perfect circles or ellipses). Instead, the electron moves in many orbits. Physicists speak therefore of wave-packets, which define the trajectory of these complex orbits and show the probable location of an electron. Visualized with computer technology, the classical orbit would indeed show a circle on a flat plane. The wave-packet shows the same flat plane with a kind of circular form, but with some parts lifted upwards like small mountains rising from a plain. Wave-packets show the orbiting electron's tendency to complex changes in localization and emergent factors.[88]

With justification it may be concluded that the current state of scientific knowledge

---

[85] One is reminded that the Greek notion 'existo' meant emergence, hence emphasizing emergence as a phenomenon of existence.

[86] The notion of instability would be more useful than chaos, as the latter seems to be too mystical for its purpose, something the English artist Michael Kidner pointed out to me when we discussed this matter

[87] See Carl Friedrich von Weizsäcker, "Zeit und Wissen", p.344: "Wir bewegen uns in einem unvollendeten und vermutlich unvollendbaren Feld von niemals völlig scharfen Begriffen."

[88] These mountains in wave-packets are often compared to shell-shapes. See Michael Nauenberg, Carlos Stroud and John Yeazell, "The Classical Limit of an Atom - By creating ultra large atoms, physicists hope to study how the old physics of the quantum world becomes the classical mechanics of everyday experience.", Scientific American June 1994, p.24-29.

confirms once again that the last thing has not yet been said about the basic properties of the particles that constitute the object, the subject, the self, the world. However, what seems to be certain is that cohesion and interaction at a particle level of reality are facts, which puts our eye-level perception of separation between object and self at least in a more complex light. Clearly, our vision does not tell the whole tale about reality and we need additional knowledge from philosophy and scientific research, including thought experiments. Art offers very good possibilities for combinations of visual perception and 'thought perception'. Thought perception might be proposed as a useful concept for the complex combination of actual scientific knowledge, mere logical reasoning and intuition that seem to come together in visualizations - or visualized theories.

Since modern science had to leave the solid ground of absolute empirical facts, and was forced to also accept uncertainties and approximations, for the first time since Leonardo da Vinci scientific theory has become equivalent again to the mixture of certainties and uncertainties comparable to art and philosophy.[89] All that has been said in this chapter shows that a desire to understand the interaction of 'object and self' leads to an attempt to understand the desire for simulations of change, movement or fluctuation in works of art. It should have become clear that these simulations in art have nothing to do with a mere temporal or cultural reflection of the speed and anxiety of current modern technological society, but relate to a much deeper, older and often unconscious memory of the very structure of our own physical being.

It seems apt to finish this chapter with a quote from Nietzsche, emphasizing that to communicate with each other, but also with ourselves we need to 'fix' our impressions in a visual language (signs):

> *"In brief, the development of language and the development of consciousness (***not** *of reason but merely of the way reason enters consciousness) go hand in hand - The emergence of our sense impressions into our own consciousness, the ability to fix them and, as it were, exhibit them externally, increased proportionally with the need to communicate them to* **others** *by means of signs. The human being inventing signs is at the same time the human being who becomes ever more keenly conscious of himself."* [90]

[89] It is quite interesting to study the developments in the fine arts during the same periods as the briefly mentioned scientific theories. One will find quite a lot of interrelations, like the studying of chance in the arts of the 1950's and 1960's, the search for understanding how we actually perceive structure (see §3), the involvement of chaotic or unstable aspects in rational concepts (in the 1970's, like by Rickey, Stella or Kidner) and the acceptance of a combination of structure, breaking of symmetry, order-fluctuations and edge of chaos (in the 1980's and 1990's by artists like Maury, Bette, Purdy, myself and many others).

[90] Nietzsche in "The Gay Science" ("Die Fröhliche Wissenschaft"), 1882-87, in Richard Schacht, "Nietzsche", p.286.

§8 DISSOLVING DUALITY

Every real artistic representation is itself and the universe, the universe in this individual form, this individual form in the universe. Benedetto Croce, "Brevarioli Estetica"[1]

Continuing the discussion of the last chapter, we will now further explore some consequences of the confrontation between ourselves and our environment. If we wish to more fully understand what happens when our attention is attracted by a work of art or even when we find ourselves absorbed by a work of art, we need to explore our psychological interaction with the work as object. This interaction can be described as virtually dissolving duality. This does not only include the duality between self and object, but also, in a larger sense, the duality between self and world (or nature).

As we discussed in the previous chapter, we cannot isolate anything in reality. For instance, when we try to isolate the characteristics of an object that are unique to this object alone, we ignore another set of characteristics important to the same object; namely, the properties of the enormous number of complex interactions by which this object is a part of our reality. Comparably, one cannot understand a particular form or colour in a part of a painting without studying it in the context of the whole composition. One may call those properties that seem unique for a specific object (or part of a painting) its individual poperties, and those properties of the object that are not only unique for this object alone, but also for all objects, its universal properties. Taking a closer look we will always find that we cannot clearly separate the individual properties from the universal properties. Individual properties are at least in part defined or caused by universal properties. Thus, they are so entirely mixed that one should speak of properties that only differ in degree of universality or individuality.[2] Although in general we are quite capable of appreciating its shape and colours, we can hardly really understand a certain vase with flowers by merely trying to understand it as something with a certain size, content, shape, with certain characteristics of colour, material, or what particles or quanta it is composed of. We have to include in our process of understanding the impact of gravity or the influence of light on this vase and flowers, of what use it is to us, and what association it recalls - making it into what it is that appears to us.[3] Besides,

---

[1] See Umberto Eco, "Die ästhetische Botschaft", in Dieter Henrich und Wolfgang Iser, "Theorien der Kunst" (Frankfurt a/M: Suhrkamp Taschenbuch-Wissenschaft #1012, 1992 - orig. 1984; Eco's essay orig. "La struttura assente - introduzione alla riceraca semiologica", 1968), p.404. Benedetto Croce lived 1866-1952.

[2] See Swami Vivekananda, "Jnana-Yoga" (Mayavati, Almora: Advaita Ashrama, 4th edition, 1930), p.51: "To stop death, we shall have to stop life also." Vivekananda meant in context to the duality of life-death that we must understand life and death to be the same and only to differ in degree and intensity. This is, as we saw in the previous chapter, backed up by modern biology (remember the phenomenon of death-cells, death-commando's incorporated in living cells).

[3] Remembering the person who gave you the flowers or the occasion when you were given the flowers or the vase.

our perception of any entity can never be objective in the strict sense, because we ourselves are continuously open and vulnerable to changing circumstances and we all are very different individuals indeed. It may be a banal example, but because our hands all differ in size and strength we will all perceive the discussed vase differently when we pick it up, although we still might agree on non-specific general values like 'it is heavy'. Also, we will perceive the same vase with flowers differently in a room with a comfortable temperature and in comfortable light than in a room with a freezing temperature and in such a strong light that we hardly can see anything!

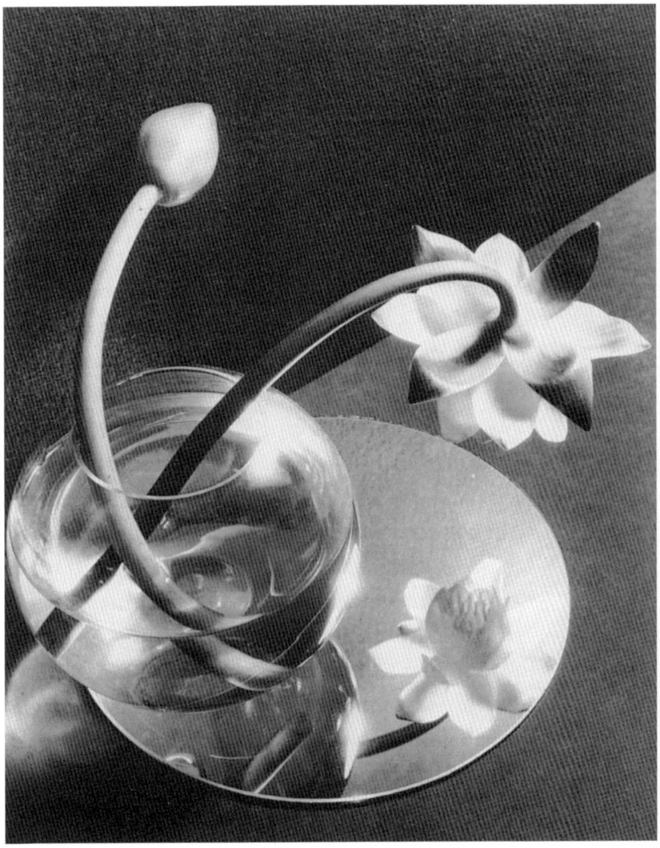

63. Edward Quigley (1898-1977) **Flowers in Vase** 1935
Photograph, 35,5 x 28 cm (14 x 11 inches)
Photo: courtesy of Barry Friedman Ltd, New York

Perception and understanding always are a combination of knowledge, interpretation and sense-information of the context, of the perceived circumstances. What we can do is attempt to research the generalities of the perceived object and its interrelations with all processes in our world, while accepting and certainly not forgetting the described non-objectivity. In such a process, testing each others' opinion, through publication or every other kind of dialogue, is obviously an essential part of our personal learning process. We do learn by virtually throwing our ideas and feelings in a particular form - words, music, fine art - into the perceptible world before us and by repeatedly studying it, while also studying the responses of other persons. We learn by studying whatever other persons also throw into our world. We may learn that appearances which we perceive as entities with a certain materiality can be unconnected free-standing objects to the senses, although they can be interrelated or connected at a deeper level to everything around them at the same time. Learning is a combination of sense-brain-perception, storage in memory, and a more abstract process of logic or reasoning that evokes an understanding of intricate interrelationships. This capacity obviously also works the other way around, allowing us to virtually see or hear things evoked by reading. Again, sense-perception and abstract thinking can only formally, theoretically be separated, because in everyday life they concern the same complex process of consciousness, merely differing in degree and intensity.

The notion of connectedness at a deeper level has been mentioned repeatedly, but is much older than often is known. Because of its crucial and basic importance for understanding the actual essence of the process of dissolving duality, we will now look into connectedness at a deeper level from yet another angle, focussing more on the desire to understand coherence by finding a comprehensible structure. This coherence can certainly be understood as a synthesis of the individual with the universal and as such also continues the discussion on 'no thingness'.[4]

8.1. SELF-NATURE, INTUITION AND MEMORY

Such a synthesis or union is analogous to the notion of the self-nature in Zen and continues to be a major topic in modern philosophy and science in the ongoing quest to understand the complexity of reality. In line with both Occidental and Oriental philosophies, Nishida puts the specific properties of the self at the core of understanding the object and the objective world.[5] The notion of self-nature in Zen-Buddhism

---

[4] See §2.2. Kandinsky in "Abstract Painting" (published originally in "Kroniek van Hedendaagse Kunst en Kultuur", Amsterdam, 1935) writes, see Kenneth C. Lindsay, Peter Vergo, "Kandinsky - Complete Writings of Art", (New York: DaCapo Press, 1994 -orig. Editions Denoel, Paris, 1970), p.789: "... the abstract painter derives his 'stimulus' not from some part of nature, but from nature as a whole, from its multiplicity of manifestations, which accumulate within him and lead to the work of art. This synthetic basis seeks its most appropriate form of expression, which is called 'non-objective'. Abstract form is broader, freer, and richer in content than the 'objective' [form]." See also "Abstrakte Malerei", in Max Bill, "Kandinsky - Essays über Kunst und Künstler" (Bern: Benteli Verlag, 1963 - orig.1955), p.190: "... der abstrakte Maler bekommt seine 'Anregung' nicht von einem X-beliebigen Stück Natur, sondern von der Natur im ganzen, von ihren mannigfaltigsten Manifestationen, die sich in ihr summieren und zum Werk führen. Diese synthetische Basis sucht sich eine für sie am besten geeigneten Ausdrucksform, das heißt die 'gegenstandslose'. Die abstrakte Form ist breiter, freier und inhaltreicher als die 'gegenständliche'.")

[5] In 1915, see Kitaro Nishida, "Intuition and Reflection in Self-Consciousness", translated by Valdo H.Viglielmo with Takeuchi Toshinori and Joseph O'Leary (Albany, NY: State University of New York Press, 1987 - orig. "Jikaku ni okeru chokkan to han sei", 1941), p.70: "If knower and known are represented as separate realities, the universal and the individual are independent of one another. But the individual thus objectified cannot be the real subject, for as the constructive unifying activity of consciousness, this cannot be made an object of reflection. It is rather the maintainer and the center of the objective world. Thus the etymological primacy of the 'subject' as the foundation of 'object' is restored." And on the same page: "In the real world of immediate experience, thus, the subject is a genuine dynamic development, the knower includes the known within itself, and subject fuses with object in a dynamic unity where in the subject is immediately object and object is immediately subject." In agreement with Schopenhauer, Nishida wrote in 1917 on the object of knowledge and free will, in Kitaro Nishida, "Intuition and Reflection in Self-Consciousness", p.142: "We commonly think of the object of knowledge as standing over against us, but what gives objectivity to cognition is the concrete background to the act of knowledge, the subject in the sense of <u>subjectum</u>. Objective knowledge is a return to the foundation of the self and a looking back behind the self. Thus <u>the ultimate object of cognition is absolute free will</u>." and: "... there is no standpoint from which we can reflect on will itself. When we think we are reflecting on will, on personal unity, we are dealing only with a relative affirmation, which belongs not to the true self but to the external world. <u>The world of absolute will is essentially one of mystery, inaccessible to cognition, but approached in art and religion</u>." See also §5.8 on Nishida's statement "... our body, as the fusion of mind and matter, is a work of art."

means the finding of the true self by understanding its relationship to the wholeness of nature, the huge process of the cosmos, which is beyond our comprehension and thus is implicit ('the implicate order'), while accepting and understanding the events of everyday's reality, which are explicit ('the explicate order'). Such an understanding in Zen is considered to be beyond words and considered to be the experience of enlightenment.[6] In Zen this obviously does not mean a kind of attempt to avoid or escape reality by concentrating on the beyond. Zen is an understanding of reality as it comes to our perception in combination with the abstract understanding of a coherence at depth.[7] Put very simply: keep living in your own rhythm of everyday while also attempting to acknowledge in general the huge and eternal processes of the whole universe. Understanding this is a profound attempt to understand the essence of reality itself.

However different Occidental and Oriental culture might seem to be in detail, the general drives and aims for knowledge on the essence concern very much the same things. This essence cannot be explained in words, because words are capable of discussing only phenomena that we can translate into words. A verbal text will never suffice for explaining the coherence in nature at depth, which we cannot see and cannot understand by merely reading.[8] I am aware of the irony while I try to make what is 'beyond words' accessible to you by merely using words. Any deeper understanding of life is based on a sensing of truth beyond what is said, though it can be triggered by what is said or written. A blind quoting or sheer repetition of ideas from religion, philosophy, politics or science is not actual understanding. The 'self-nature' is a concept meaning a clear and deep understanding by a self in its position in the world, being a tiny entity immersed in an extremely large whole. This is an understanding that can only emerge in oneself when one is capable of virtually looking beyond one's ego - the moment we can overcome the egocentric focussing of our personal attention on our own mind, body, needs and desires, we can glimpse the larger reality of which we are but a part.[9] This can

[6] See John C.H. Wu, "The Golden Age of Zen" (New York: Image Books, Double Day, 1996), p.58: "All external things are but a reflection of our 'original face', and all external teachings are but an echo of the true music of our self-nature. Let no one identify himself with his mere reflection or echo; it is only by seeing one's self-nature that he becomes actually what he is in essence." The notion 'beyond words' comes from the original Chinese Zen notion 'pu li wen tze' - meaning 'no dependence on words and letters'.

[7] It should be mentioned here that this thoughtful concept is not the privilege of Zen and can be found in other religious and natural philosophies as well, for instance in Vedantic thinking and Taoism.

[8] The many symposia, conferences and panel discussions I was fortunate to attend either as speaker or as part of the audience, have repeatedly shown to me how little words seem to be capable of communicating actual contents - too often, too simple, public discussions slide off into little word war games focussing on the formulations of a speaker's presentation instead of on her or his actual point, obviously also influenced by all kinds of social processes.

[9] In the history of Japanese philosophy one can find two very important early thinkers who each were very concerned with dissolving duality to understand actual reality: Shinran and Dogen. Shinran (1173-1262) was the important Japanese innovator of the Pure Land School, in Japan called 'Jodo Shinshu', today the large Shin-Buddhist sect. For an excellent discussion see James C. Dobbins, "Jodo Shinshu - Shin Buddhism in Medieval Japan" (Bloomington and Indianapolis: Indiana University Press, 1989). The concept of The Pure Land originates in China and can be understood as a metaphor for the virtual level of absolute no-thingness that is eternally changing, eternally developing, giving me reasons to assume an analogy to Schopenhauer's

and should be accomplished by pure thought (including art as visual thought) and not by any artificial means, for example, drugs or escaping life as we know it. This is an experience words can hardly, if ever, grasp.[10] Confirming the need to acknowledge the importance of visual thought as a result of this dilemma, Charles Biederman wrote:

> *"With thought we abstract perceptions which evolve into the speakable of knowledge, with sensory awareness abstractions become unspeakable, what Goethe called 'visual thought', the experience of visual perception evolving."*[11]

'World Will'. Shinran spoke of the aim to be reborn, which he metaphorically understood as a 'return to the city of Dharma-nature', which is the world of effortless naturalness (how one is by nature - nature as the complex proccesses of the universe outside and inside ourselves - not how one can try to become by calculation, pure logical reasoning or following religious dogma, etc.), while he emphasized that one can never expect extrication from 'conditioned naturalness' (everyday life). See Masao Abe, "A Study of Dogen - His Philosophy and Religion", edited by Steven Heine (Albany, NY: State University of New York Press, 1992), p.164 and following, and p.191. Shinran's basic concept was as simple as it was brilliant: he said one only needs to keep reciting the name of 'Amidha' (Buddha's name) - a practice called the 'nembutsu' - which will focus the mind to abandon the level of ego-focussing towards the level of 'other-power' (allowing oneself to completely be absorbed by nature at large) and thus allow one to virtually be born in (enter) the Pure Land. This was brilliant, because it made religion very accessible to every person, not only to a religious elite (no complex liturgical ceremonies were required anymore). Besides, a rhythmic repetition of basically any word has the capacity to meditatively focus one's mind into deeper unconscious thought. This obviously is temporary - we are always 'betrayed' by the various aspects of everyday human life, therefore the need for a re-newed desire for enlightenment is necessary, a last and final one happening at the end of one's life. Shinran emphasized that the experience of being re-born can be attained in everyday life (immediate attainment of rebirth or 'sokutokuojo'), because the Pure Land is not some after-life or heaven, but a state of acknowledgement of nature that can be found deep in one's subjective self. Dogen (1200-1253) was the founder of the Japanese Soto Zen sect, his main work was the "Shobogenzo" ("A Treasure of the Right Dharma Eye"). See Eido Shimano Roshi and Charles Vacher, "Dogen - Shobogenzo - yui butsu yo butsu shoji", a reprint and translation in English and French (Fougères, La Versanne: Encre Marine, 1999). Dogen emphasizes that the Dharma is present in every person, but one can only become conscious of this by practice, one can only attain it by many years of practicing sitting in meditation ('zazen', which Dogen calls 'the casting off of body-mind' or 'shinjin-datsuraku'). For Dogen, practice and attainment are one. He speaks of practice as 'becoming a buddha' and of its goal, the attainment of the awakening of 'Buddha-nature'. To emphasize there is no 'Buddha' as a person functioning as role-model whose appearance or behavior one merely should try to copy, Dogen speaks of the '<u>no</u>-Buddha nature' - a notion typical for Zen philosophy meant merely to emphasize not desiring to find a personified Buddha-nature, not to stare at the word but to attempt to grasp the meaning beyond the word. Dogen emphasizes that attainment still is more important than practice, though practice is the means. This seems quite comparable to art in that learning one's craft does matter, but certainly is not the goal itself. It is interesting that Dogen repeatedly mentions one should practice 'zazen' for at least some 20-30 years, which is also in general the average amount of years one needs in art to mature. Traditional Buddhism stated in the Nirvana Sutra 'Tathagata' (Buddha) as something that 'abides forever without change', but Dogen understands it to be 'permanent, nonbeing, being, and change'. Thus he does not see life and death as a process of living that will end (a process of generation and extinction) but a continuing process of appearance-disappearance ('kimetsu') or being-nonbeing ('umu'), leading him to advocate that we should desire to acknowledge 'whole-being' ('shitsuu'): not to understand our own being as temporary phenomenon with our focus on purely egocentric interests of everyday life with death at the end of the road, but to overcome our egocentrism, even our sentient being-centrism, to be able to deeply understand our being a part of the ongoing process of eternal changing forms. The actual profound and deep experience of this understanding of 'whole-being' happens on the level of conciousness known as 'nirvana' ('nirvana' is no other place, no heaven above, but a state of consciousness). Like Shinran, Dogen also emphasizes that true understanding leads to true com-

Furthering 19th century ideas, Henri Bergson stated that the real source of philosophical insight is the immediate contact with the real, which is not objectively observed, because it cannot be perceived autonomously.[12] Bergson thought that to be able to get at the deeper meaning of reality, to understand one's individual self within the larger perspective of the world, no objective observation or pure logical rationalization restricted by the symbols of language would suffice. Something else was needed. This something he called intuition, lacking a better concept.[13] Being an artist myself I relate to Bergson's interpretation of intuition, because it could also function as a definition of artistic intuition. His metaphysical experience of intuition seems related to the previously discussed 'self-nature' in Zen. Also coinciding with Oriental philosophies, Bergson understood reality not to contain separate isolated things, but as an endless stream of becoming.[14] For Bergson, duration is the paradigm, not a static status quo, while memory is the very medium and result of duration. The only actual reality understandable to any person is the perception of one's self and one's own duration through time, what Bergson called 'real time'. This perception of being has to be continuously adjusted, because of the many interactions with our environment and the involved emotions, associations, expectations, etc. Therefore, our own being is also a continuous becoming. Needless to say, only because of memory and consciousness can we perceive duration, while consciousness simultaneously consists of change, and therefore of duration itself.

Bergson acknowledged the value of artistic intuition, because artists and poets have the talent to present their intuited experiences of reality in perceptible forms, in con-

---

passion and that can only happen when one transcends nirvana and returns to work in the midst of the sufferings of everyday world.

10 See John C.H. Wu, "The Golden Age of Zen", p.64: "In itself, the self-nature is identical with the non-dual real, which is beyond space and time and above all attributes that human language can offer. Human language is at home dealing with the things of the phenomenal world, the field of relativity where all things seem to go in endless pairs of opposition."

11 See Charles Biederman, "Art, Science, Reality" (Red Wing, MN: Charles Biederman, 1988), p.26. On the same page he refers also to a remark by Whitehead, who comparably to Goethe wrote: "Thought about nature is different from the sense perception of nature ... sense perception has an ingredient or factor which is not thought. I call this ingredient sense awareness." This notion as proposed by Whitehead clearly connects to the before mentioned ideas of what is beyond words, compare also 'the unspeakable' by Kuspit in §9.

12 Henri Bergson (1859-1941): the searcher for knowledge is absorbed by what he studies while his own individual being is the starting point of all observations - the duality individual truth versus universal truth. This understanding is also reflected in the early 20th century scientific notion that the viewer influences what he observes.

13 Henri Bergson described this in "L'évolution créatrice" (1907), in Bertrand Russell, "The History of Western Philosophy" (London: Routledge, 1991 - orig.1946), p.758: "By intuition ... I mean instinct that has become disinterested, self-conscious, capable of reflecting upon its object and of enlarging it indefinitely."

14 On duration and memory, see Bertrand Russell, "The History of Western Philosophy", p. 760: "Duration is the very stuff of reality, which is perpetual becoming, never something made. It is above all in memory that duration exhibits itself, for in memory the past survives in the present." See also Bertrand Russell, "The History of Western Philosophy", p.758. This is taken up by Whitehead with his organic philosophy understanding reality as a continuous process in which everything is becoming a being. See §4 on Biederman-Bohm.

trast to the average person.[15] Following his idea about the importance of memory and intuition, allowing us to combine experiences of the past with experiences of the present, we may understand the artwork as a materialized intuited memory, especially because art is the combination of intuition, pure perception and - by its sheer material form - also of duration.[16] Bergson wrote, "In pure perception ... we are actually placed outside ourselves, we touch the reality of the object in an immediate intuition."[17] This also seems an adequate description of how, through an intuitive process like making art, art being the medium for pure perception and involving a projection outside ourselves, we can touch the essence of the studied object - of reality. As an example, I like to refer to the painter Frantisek Kupka, who actually was influenced by Bergson, as well as by Schopenhauer. He wrote:

> *"The viewer should have the feeling in front of a work of art, that something happened here and that further things will happen as long as the work exists .... The form- and colour compositions offered to the viewer by him (the artist) are not only for his retina, but for his inner world. Here, he touches, impresses and fascinates him ... Artist and viewer communicate in the agreement about what is, eye to eye with the cosmic will."*[18]

---

15 Bergson in "Das Lachen", Jena 1914, quoted by Francesca Talpo, in Norbert Nobis, "Der Lärm der Strasse - Italienischer Futurismus 1909-1918", (Hannover: Sprengel Museum, 2001), p.71: "Between nature and ourselves, ah, what do I say: between ourselves and our own consciousness lies a veil, a veil that is opaque to normal people, but is easy and almost transparent to artists and poets." ("Zwischen die Natur und uns, ach, was sage ich: zwischen uns und unser eigenes Bewusstsein legt sich ein Schleier, ein Schleier, für den gewöhnlichen Menschen dicht, leicht aber und fast durchsichtig für den Künstler und Dichter.")

16 See Henri Bergson, "Matter and Memory" (New York: Zone Books, 1988, from the 5th edition - orig. "Matière et mémoire", 1908 - first edition was published in 1896), p. 73: "Memory, inseparable in practice from perception, imports the past into the present, contracts into a single intuition many moments of duration, and thus by a twofold operation compel us, de facto, to perceive matter in ourselves, whereas we, de jure, perceive matter within matter." Referring to the mere fact that the substance of our brains of course also consists of matter, he also wrote, p.139: "If matter, so far as extended in space, is to be defined (as we believe it must) as a present which is always beginning again, inversely, our present is the very materiality of our existence, that is to say, a system of sensations and movements and nothing else." This would obviously explain the deep feeling we can experience in a work of art - a work of art definable as a 'system of sensations and movements' in some material form, thus expressing our existence itself.

17 See Bertrand Russell, "The History of Western Philosophy", p.760. Bergson worked his ideas out into more detail, emphasizing the mere fact that we need objects to establish our perception, 'object and self' (see §7) indeed, in his famous book "Matière et mémoire". See Henri Bergson, "Matter and Memory" p.179: "The body, by the place which at each moment it occupies in the universe, indicates the parts and the aspects of matter on which we can lay hold: our perception, which exactly measures our virtual action on things, thus limits itself to the objects which actually influence our organs and prepare our movements." Because pure perception causes us to decide a next action, as novel experience pure perception causes changes in our knowledge (on reality) that is based on memory and inspires our intuition.

18 Quotation from the manuscript of the book "La création dans les arts plastiques" (the original French text published in 1989 by Cercle d'Art, Paris), in Pierre Brullé and Marketa Theinhardt, essay "Trotz allem Malerei - Frantisek Kupka über die Schöpfung in der bildenden Kunst", in Dorothy Kosinski and Jaroslav Andel, "Frantisek Kupka - Die abstrakten Farben des Universums" (Ostfildern-Ruit: Verlag Gerd Hatje, 1997), p.164: "Der Betrachter soll vor einem Kunstwerk das Gefühl haben, daß hier etwas geschehen ist und daß auch weiterhin etwas geschehen wird, solange das Werk existiert ... Die Form- und Farbkompositionen, die er (der

Other examples of important developments in art inspired by Bergson's understanding of duration include the dissolving of space and time (and the dissolving of other dualities), the emphasis on the intuited moment as the source of artistic creativity, the concept of painting 'states of the soul', and the simultaneity or the general dynamics we can find in Italian Futurism.[19] The Italian Futurists were the group of artists who also understood that the discoveries and new theories about space/time, the virtual non-existence of matter and the concept of quantum mechanics meant that everything is indeed continuously in motion and that the appearance of every object is not the only or real truth. The Futurists stated that the artists should become an actual part of the stream of life, because "...everything moves, everything runs, everything changes at high velocity".[20] The artist should therefore no longer focus on illustrating a particular scene at a particular moment seen through a lens or frame, but on the process of becoming, on the changing interaction of the object with the viewer in a wider perspective.[21] Art should no longer be merely about colour and form. The painterly gesture on the canvas must not be understood as a frozen moment of universal dynamism, but as the most dynamic

Künstler) dem Betrachter bietet, sind nicht ausschließlich für seine Netzhaut bestimmt, sondern für seine innere Welt. Hier berührt, beeindruckt und fasziniert er ihn ... Künstler und Betrachter kommunizieren im Einverständnis von dem, was ist, Auge in Auge mit dem kosmischen Wollen." The reference to the inner world of the artist is obviously connected to Bergson's intuition, but also to late 19th century and early 20th century interests in theosophy, early modern psychology and taken up by quite so many artists in early 20th century, like by Kandinsky or - later - by the Surrealists who prefered this inner world or inner voice to prevail over any other perception or experience.

19 For an excellent essay on Bergson's influence on Italian Futurism, see Francesca Talpo, "Der Futurismus und Henri Bergsons Philosophie der Intuition", in Norbert Nobis, "Der Lärm der Strasse - Italienischer Futurismus 1909-1918", p.71, quoting from a letter by futurist essayist Enrico Prampolini to Bino Seminatelli from 3 February 1917: "Motion is spiritual, intellectual and material life. Also the concept of immediate life is a very open notion, like Bergson sensed in his 'Philosophy of Intuition', from which the Futurists acquired a large part of the concepts for their poetry and art."("Bewegung ist spirituelles, geistiges und materielles Leben. Auch der Gedanke des augenblicklichen Lebens ist ein ungemein weitläufiger Begriff, wie dies Bergson in seiner 'Philosophie der Intuition' erahnt hat, aus der dann die Futuristen einen großen Teil der Konzepte für ihre Poesie und Kunst übernommen haben.")

20 Ibid., p.65: "... alles bewegt sich, alles rennt, alles verwandelt sich in rasender Eile." This is a quotation from the statement "The futurist painting. Technical manifesto. 11 April 1910" ("Die futuristische Malerei. Technisches Manifest. 11. April 1910") signed by U. Boccioni, C. Carrà, L.Russolo, G. Balla, G. Severini. For a complete translation of this manifesto (original title "La Pittura Futurista - Manifesto Tecnico") in German, see Norbert Nobis, "Der Lärm der Strasse - Italienischer Futurismus 1909-1918", p.375, 376. See Uwe M. Schneede, "Umberto Boccioni" (Stuttgart: Verlag Gerd Hatje, 1994). See David Elliott, "Balla - The Futurist" (Milan: Nuove edizioni Gabriele Mazzotta, 1987).

21 In the catalogue of the Futurist exhibition organized in Berlin in 1912 by the magazine 'Der Sturm', Boccioni writes about his painting "The Street invades the House" ("Die Straße dringt ins Haus"). See Francesca Talpo, "Der Futurismus und Henri Bergsons Philosophie der Intuition", in Norbert Nobis, "Der Lärm der Strasse - Italienischer Futurismus 1909-1918", p.66: "The painter does not restrict himself like a photographer to only reproduce what he sees through the small square frame of his window. He brings everything into his picture that one may view in all directions from an open balcony." ("Der Maler beschränkt sich nicht darauf, wie ein Fotograf, das wiederzugeben, was er von dem kleinen viereckigen Ausschnitt seines Fensters aus sieht. Er bringt alles auf das Bild, was man einem offenen Balkon von allen Seiten übersehen kann."). This concept of multi-vision reminds one of Matjushin's 360° 'extended vision', see §6.3.

experience itself.[22] No artist, however, can 'touch' a viewer with a work of art if it does not relate to aspects of that viewer's own memory.

Memory is partly constituted by personal - individual experiences of one's life, but most certainly also partly built up by more universal experiences present in the genes and matter of our physical being.[23] It is at this level of universal memory where artist and viewer temporarily meet, temporarily because of the ever changing circumstances, the eternal flux. Although the notion 'universal memory' is correct, it cannot be understood as a memory that is exactly the same for everyone. It must be seen as a very general reference to the universal properties of existence that are similar but still translated differently in each of our individual perceptions and minds. For instance, when I say 'red', everybody knows the colour I mean, but only by approximation. If you actually had to choose from colour samples the one I meant, you would most likely pick a different hue of the colour red than the one I was thinking of.[24]

8.2 ON COHESION, ORDER, STRUCTURE, HARMONY

All religions that have ever existed or still exist create a certain set of rules about how everything works. They create more or less a kind of system, structure or order with a god or hierarchy of gods and tell us how to behave. The ultimate aim is to see and accept a certain structure and to understand how to come into harmony with that structure, or how to synchronize with the structure of the gods.

Religion comes from the Latin 'religere', meaning to perceive a certain order with a specific hierarchy. Religion is a way of connecting creator and created - and reconnecting the individual with the universal. It is easy to understand why this kind of structure has

---

22 It makes sense that the Futurists were so intrigued by the movements of new technological machines, like cars, trains, planes, but also by the sheer abstract notion of 'lines of force' as discussed by science, see §6. They could be seen as metaphors of the notion of continuous change and movement which science had taught them. Very often one finds articles on Futurism only discussing briefly their fascination for the machine, ignoring the fact that their understanding of the modern physics of their time was the real origin and drive of this interest. The Futurist manifestoes were very emotional and aggressive statements, like so many artists' manifestoes they meant to get attention by shocking. The Futurists went so far as to glorify the 'cleansing' effect of war, and there exists evidence that some of the Futurists actually took part in the Italian pre-fascist movement (during and immediately after WW I) as result of their desire for the unification of Italy as one great nation. This explains for an important part why their importance is differently valued than other early modernist art developments (though the fascination for the machine as such was really a Zeitgeist phenomenon, like works from several Russian constructivists - Tatlin, Gabo - or French artists - Delaunay, Léger - show). It is very interesting that the Futurists started using the pictorial means of Impressionism - the painting of rhythmic repetitions of little quantities of colour, even exploring pointilistic techniques - but developed quickly a very different sense of paint handling (not based on the Impressionist 'vibration of light', but more the contrasts of colours by itself, often adding black) including the importance of the curved line, which was partly inspired by scientific theories (compare Kandinsky).

23 As you will find repeatedly in this publication, it is this kind of an understanding that led 19th century artists and philosophers to look for the unification of self and world, but the early abstract artists tried to develop a visual language to make this understanding more accessible. These efforts can be related to the theory of archetypes in Jungian Psychology.

24 This is an example earlier used by the philosopher Wittgenstein.

provided - and still provides - mankind with a lot of comfort, but the structure of nature does not possess any hierarchy in this sense. Therefore, it is hardly surprising that through all centuries, as a shared property of all human cultures, we can find a more general search, analogous to, but different from, religion, for a better understanding of a coherence of the self with the whole that we call reality, meaning the rest of nature.[25] One can find examples of structure as a major subject in art ever since the very first abstractions.[26] In anthropology, examples of an interest in structure can be found in all cultures and periods. One is reminded that many abstract artists have always been intrigued by abstract images from all kinds of cultures. It is crucial for such a notion of structure that the totality of interrelations remains more important than the single parts of the structure.[27]

While studying different cultures, we will soon find evidence that the search for structure in all cultures emerges as a combination of verbal and visual concepts. This is proved by the fact that religions and philosophies do not only contain written or spoken text, but communicate their contents, meaning or messages (information) in combinations of text with ornaments on peoples' bodies, on buildings, in the landscape, in visual rituals or as object (artifact).[28] The desire for structure or cohesion is a desire driven by the expectation of having better opportunities for survival (by a precise understanding of one's position in relation to others one can better judge possible danger), but also motivated by the frustration caused by doubting the structure offered by religion and its attempt to tell the whole tale.[29]

[25] It is beyond the scope of this book to dig very deep into the many ways of expressing our need for structure or system. I recommend the curious reader: E.H. Gombrich, "The Sense of Order - A study in the psychology of decorative art" (London: Phaidon, second edition, 1984 - orig. 1979). Gyorgy Kepes, "Struktur in Kunst und Wissenschaft" (Bruxelles: Éditions de la Connaissance, s.a., 1967 - orig. "Structure in Art and Science", George Brazilier, Inc., NY). Peter Checkland, "Systems Thinking - Systems Practice" (Chilester, New York, Brisbane, Toronto: John Wiley & Sons, 1991 - orig. 1981). Oleg Grabar, "The Mediation of Ornament" (Washington DC: Princeton University Press, 1992). See also §3.

[26] See §4 on Constructivism. One of the probably oldest examples of abstractions in fine art from 1900 is by Augusto Giacometti, the uncle of the famous sculptor Alberto Giacometti, beautiful examples (gouaches) one can find in the Museum of Chur, or in the Kunstmuseum Zürich, both in Switzerland.

[27] This is studied by theoretical science since the 1920's and early 1930's the idea of fields, nets or wholeness - like by David Bohm - emerged. In art such structures have been explored all through the 20th century. Well known examples in early abstract art can be found with Larionov, Klee, Mondrian, Rodchenko, Popova, Balla, Kandinsky, Freundlich, and later in the art of Lohse, Kelly, Morellet, Nemours, Mosso, Kidner, Maury, and numerous other artists. In principle, even in the complex dripped and splashed meshworks of Jackson Pollock or intricate meshworks by Mark Tobey! More recently it has emerged in the paintings of Paul Dacey, Richard Purdy, my own artworks or in the works of young artists like Christoph Wedding or Megan Olson.

[28] Examples can be found through all cultures and episodes. To name just a few: Ancient-China, Japan, India, Mesopotamia, Middle East, Africa (like the Kuba in the Congo or the Ndebele in South Africa), Greek, Romans, Celts, Vikings, the Hebrew, Christian, Muslim, Hindu and Buddhist cultures, but for instance also the Native Americans from North-, Central and South America (like the Aztecs, Yanomamö or Kaiapo), or the Maori and Aboriginal (see list of literature).

[29] Nevertheless, religion is and will always be a great and effective way to comfort many people and help them understand the limitations to the importance and duration of their existence.

It can hardly be denied religion always has played an immense role in the development of our knowledge about reality. The development of knowledge has always been and will always be a process of rational and logical facts mixed with a lot of irrationalities, superstition, uncertainties and beliefs. Religion functions quite well between these polarities. Belief, by definition, implies no complete rationalization. Leibniz saw himself as a philosopher of the 'harmonia praestabilita', understanding that there is a harmony between everything that is independent from man and is decided by God.[30] As a result of the new discoveries in astronomy, the Church could not continue to suppress logical conclusions made by man after observing nature, even when these conclusions contradicted the dogma of the Church. Obviously the Reformation stimulated this trajectory towards more free thought. At the end of the 18th century the philosophers of the Enlightenment understood reason to be the primary constituent of thinking. Voltaire wrote: "God has given us a principle of universal reason....".[31] The Enlightenment thus also gave the definitive impetus for scientific, objective, logical truth to be the only real truth - something that unfortunately still is too often seen as absolute fact. Hegel viewed the apparant self-subsistence of finite things as an illusion and stated that nothing is real but the whole (the real is rational, and the rational is real).[32] To avoid too much repetition, you are kindly asked to recall what I have written in previous chapters on the development of 19th century thought and art, for example on Schopenhauer and Cézanne.

Joachim Gasquet reported a meeting with Cézanne in Aix, when Cézanne explained to him that he was getting a grip on his 'motive':

> *"Well then ..." (He repeated his gesture, holding his hands apart, fingers spread wide, bringing them slowly, very slowly together again, the squeezing and contracting them until they were interlocked). "That's what must be achieved ... If I pass too high or too low, the whole thing is botched. There shouldn't be a single weak link, a single hole through which emotion, light, or truth can escape. I advance my entire canvas at once,* ***as a whole****, if you get my meaning. I bring together, in one impulse, with one conviction, everything that's*

[30] Leibniz lived 1646-1716. See the summary on Leibniz's monadology in §7.2.

[31] See Richard Coyne, "Creativity as Commonplace", in Ernest Edmonds and Linda Candy, "Creativity and Cognition 1996 - Proceedings" (Loughborough: LUTCHI Research Centre, Loughbourough University, 1996), p.3. For an extensive study of the development of creativity and the computer in contex to romanticism from the Enlightenment onwards, see Richard Coyne, "Technoromanticism - digital narrative, holism, and the romance of the real" (Boston, Ma: MIT Press, 1999).

[32] Reality is according to philosopher Georg Wilhelm Friedrich Hegel (1770-1831) a coherent system in which everything that was, is and will be, has its own specific location, while cohering with the whole. The final truth is the whole of reality coinciding with the coherent whole. The truth does not pre-exist at the start of the path to truth, but evolves at the end, because this path to truth belongs to truth itself. Perceived from the level of the coherent whole the start and end are the same. Hegel considered it important to acknowledge reality to be this coherent whole, and the subject as part of the coherent whole. The subject is identical to the system by which the whole is coherent. Thus, the system itself is subject. He considered logic to be the most useful approach to understand this concept.

scattered ... Everything we look at disperses and disappears, doesn't it? Nature is always the same, but nothing remains of it, of what appears to us. Our art should set out to convey the thrill of its permanence along with the elements, the appearance of all its changes. It should give us a taste of nature's eternity. ***What's underneath it?*** *Perhaps nothing. Perhaps everything."*[33]

Cézanne was clearly trying very hard to find the cohesion in nature that must be found underneath the apparantly separated objects and beings visible in nature. Going out into the landscape must have been one of the major factors in Cézanne's understanding of going beyond a depiction of the immediacy of the 'impression' and exploring instead the duration of change in the confrontation of the eternal flux of phenomena in the calmness of a fixed composition. Thus he was using artistic means to catch the kinesis in nature in combination with the permanence of nature (similar to Bergson's later concept of duration). Cézanne quite well formulated the major tasks for the next generations of art that we have come to know as the Modernist Tradition: more or less abstract art that is not really in motion, but explores all the visual means to simulate continuous change. Recall Cézanne's exploration of culminating points in our perception.[34]

see picture 15

If one wishes to understand the early abstract artists' profound interest in the line as a medium for expressing the dynamics and spatial properties of reality (three-dimensional reality is where the duality between self and world happens), one needs to acknowledge the interests in the line that emerged in the 18th century in immediate combination with the general ideas in science, psychology and philosophy at the start of the 20th century, when space and time were understood as a cohesion of lines of force or vortices.[35] As example one can name Futurism, which applied the use of rhythmic repetitions of lines to explore the new understandings of space/time and the non-existence of solid matter

33 Quotation in The Tate Gallery, "Cézanne" (London: Tate Publishing, 1996), p.52 (emphasis mine). I witnessed the Dalai Lama using exactly the same gesture with both his hands as Cézanne to explain connectedness. This was in his opening speech at the international symposium "Art and Science meeting Spirituality in a Changing Economy", organised by Louwrien Wijers, Amsterdam, 1990. On Schopenhauer's 'motive', see §6.1. Joachim Gasquet (1873-1921), was a writer and friend of Cézanne (Cézanne painted his and his father's portraits). The original French word is 'le motif', which in English should be 'motive' (= that which causes an act) and should not be confused with the English 'motif' (= main idea or design in a work of art) - probably an unintentional human error in the translation of Gasquet's text into English, but very important nevertheless. Importantly, in the academic essays on Schopenhauer one should use the correct word, 'motive'. The English meaning of 'motif' is too shallow to encompass Cézanne's understanding of Schopenhauer. It seems interesting to note that in German only the word 'das Motiv' (comparable to the English 'motive') exists. Therefore in German this confusion does not exist.

34 See §6.1.

35 See §6.2. See §7.3, footnote 50, on the psychophysicists, Japonisme and Jugendstil. Several paintings and studies by Italian Futurist Giacomo Balla carry titles like "Vortice". He mentioned in "Pittura, Scultura Futuriste" (1914) "vortice travolgente della modernità". Also Boccioni mentioned the word 'vortice'. Inspired by the Futurists (Marinetti presented a lecture in 1910 in London), in England around 1913 an artist group was formed with the name "Vorticism", vortex understood as energy to be consumed 'futuristically' "through the incessant struggle in the complex city", as stated by sculptor Gaudier-Brzeska. They published two issues of their magazine "Blast" (1914-1915). See Phil Mertens, "Vorticism - ICSAC Cahier 8/9", edited by Andrew Wilson (Bruxelles: Internationaal Centrum voor Struktuur Analayse en Constructivisme, 1988). In general a

in painting.[36]

Another example is Rayonism, which was an early abstract approach to painting that was inspired by the discovery of X-rays, ultraviolet and radioactive rays, later also inspired by Einsteins Theory of Relativity and by new photographic technologies (like photograms) in the first two decades of the 20th century. Michail Larionov was quite conscious of the fact that how an object exists or how it is presented in a picture is not the way it is perceived by our eyes, because we perceive light rays bouncing off the object in rhythmic motions.[37] The whole notion of 'rhythm' was very much in vogue at the end of the 19th and start of the 20th century, and was not only an interpretation of scientific discoveries like Maxwell's lines of force, or a result of developments in painting like Pointillism, or advocated by Theosophy.[38]

---

vortex is a system, pursuit, viewed as something that absorbs things.

36 Futurist Boccioni describes that the spaces between objects are not really empty, but filled with rhythmic vibrations of energies, caused by the continuous changes in the intensity of the energies that are contained in matter. This is the reason, Boccioni writes, why in the Futurist paintings one cannot find empty space but lines emanating from objects that depict the interactions between everything caused in various grades of intensity. See Francesca Talpo, "Der Futurismus und Henri Bergsons Philosophie der Intuition", in Norbert Nobis, "Der Lärm der Strasse - Italienischer Futurismus 1909-1918", p.68 This concept of lines virtually connecting all objects in space/time, is clearly inspired by the scientific notion of a 'vector'. See Gerrit L. Verschuur, "Hidden Attraction. The Mystery and History of Magnetism" (New York, Oxford: Oxford University Press, 1993), p.113: "The notion of a vector as displaying the direction in which the potential acts also comes from Maxwell's works. The vector potential of the magnetic field was described by a direction and a strength of the field at any point in space. These field vectors, as Faraday had found, had a circular shape around the current carrying wires." When one looks again at a Futurist painting (or a painting by Kupka), the relationship between these artistic creations and the scientific theories are crystal clear.

37 In Russian 'Lucizm', published in April 1913, in French called 'Rayonism', in Italian 'Radiantismo', in German around 1920 also known as 'Strahlenkunst'. X-rays were discovered in 1895 by Röntgen. See Graham Farmelo, "The Discovery of X-Rays", Scientific American November 1995, p.68-73. The artist Michael Larionov, considered to be the most important exponent of Rayonism together with the artist (and his wife) Gontcharowa developed his early ideas around 1909-1910. Larionov wrote, in Felix Ingold, "Strahlenkunst", in Dr.István Schlégl, "Michael Larionow Rayonistischer Werke 1912-1914 und illustrierte Bücher russischer Futuristen" (Zürich: Gallery & Edition Dr.István Schlégl, 1987), p.7: "We perceive merely the whole of the rays from a lightsource, which are reflected by the object and thus gets into our field of vision. This implies that if we wish to paint exactly what we see, we need to paint the whole of the rays that are reflected by the object..." ("Wir nehmen lediglich die Gesamtheit der von einer Lichtquelle ausgehenden Strahlen wahr, die vom Objekt reflektiert werden und so in unser Gesichtsfeld gelangen. Folglich müssen wir, wenn wir genau das malen wollen, was wir sehen, die Gesamtheit der von einem Objekt reflektierten Strahlen malen...") For an extensive monography on Larionov, see Anthony Parton, "Mikhail Larionov and the Russian Avant-Garde" (Princeton, NJ: Princeton University Press, 1993). Parton prefers to speak of 'rayist painting' instead of 'rayonism'. In his book on Larionov, Parton says Einstein's Theory of Relativity became known to artists around 1919, when this theory was popularized as result of the observation that the sun eclipse of May 1919 proved the bending of light-rays. See Anthony Parton, "Mikhail Larionov and the Russian Avant-Garde" p.131. In 1914 Larionov wrote, in Anthony Parton, "Mikhail Larionov and the Russian Avant-Garde" p.133: "In rayist painting the intrinsic life and continuum of the colored masses form a synthesis image in the mind of the spectator, which slips outside of time and space. One glimpses the famous fourth dimension - since its length, its breadth, and the density of the superposition of its colors are the only signs of the visible world - and all other sensations born from an image are of another order."

38 Theosophy studied and analyzed existing and accessible occult ideas, concepts and theories, aiming for a spiritual way of life based on the assumption that all knowledge has the same fundamental roots. Theosophy

Moritz Geiger, while studying principles of aesthetic value that everyone notices, discussed the importance of the formal principle of a rhythmic pattern, which he called eurhythmy:

> *"The facts of symmetry and harmony, or rhythm and balance, of proportion and of unity in variety - there is no realm of art or natural beauty which is not given unity and form by this principle. The beauty of the proportions of the human body, or the harmony of colors and tones, follows this principle as well as the structure of music and the form of verse; without an inner distribution of emphasis, an artistic prose is as little possible as a painting; eurhythmy is the backbone of architecture and the nerve of the dance. It is the foundation of everything which we call artistic form."*[39]

Furthermore, Geiger considered the fundamental function of eurhythmy to be an ordering and articulating. It should come as no surprise that similar interests can be found in art in the same period. For instance, in Orphism or Futurism ideas about rhythms in colour, light, music and poetry were understood as connected.[40]

see picture 19

The Dutch group 'De Stijl' considered pure harmony expressed in art to be something

became known by the publications in 1875 by the Russian Helena Petrovna Blavatsky. She emphasized the rhythms inherent in nature, like the seasons and the aging of a person, and concluded that there are cycles of reincarnation as paths to spiritual perfection - inspired mainly by Hinduism. Theosophy was very popular among early abstract artists (earlier among the Symbolists painters in the 1880-1890's) and had quite an influence all through modern art history. See Magdalena Dabrowski, "Contrasts of Form - Geometric Abstract Art 1910-1980", p.17. See Maurice Tuchman, "The Spiritual in Art: Abstract Painting 1890-1985" (New York: Abbeville Publishers, 1986).

39 See Moritz Geiger (1880-1937), in Klaus Berger, "The Significance of Art- A Phenomenological Approach to Aesthetics" (Washington DC: Center for Advanced Research in Phenomenology and University Press of America, 1986 - orig. "Die Bedeutung der Kunst", 1944), p.113. It seems that Moritz Geiger is furthering the interest in rhythm and harmony of the 19th century French psychophysicists (see §7.3) but also the main interest of Jugendstil with the rhythmic whiplash line as its central motif.

40 French painters Sonia and Robert Delaunay are considered to be the founders of 'Orphism'. Also considered to belong to Orphism were certain works by Duchamp, Picabia, Léger, Picasso, Villon, Herbin, Marcoussis, Le Fauconnier. Robert Delaunay wrote in "On Light", see Hajo Düchting, "Robert and Sonia Delaunay - Triumph der Farbe" (Cologne: Benedikt Taschen Verlag, 1993), p.39 (emphasis mine): "Light in nature creates the motion of colours. The motion is caused by the relation of different sizes, of colour contrasts between themselves. Thus she creates reality. This reality has depth (we can see up to the stars) and then becomes rhythmic simultaneously. The simultaneity in light means harmony and the rhythm of colours, which enables human vision. Human vision possesses the largest sense of reality, because it emerges from the observation of the universe." Later the Delaunays concentrated more on 'pure colour'. After the observations of natural and artificial light phenomena, Robert Delaunay focussed on curved shapes. The name 'Orphism' was originally coined by Delaunay's friend, the poet Apollinaire around 1911-12, referring to his collection of poems on Orpheus. This is not to be confused for the Orphism as followed by Kupka. See §6, footnote 83. A further confusion arises in trying to distinguish French Orphism from Italian Futurism. This confusion is understandable when one knows it existed also in those days in such a way that the Italian Futurists accused Apollinaire of copying and transforming their Futurist statements into a neatly modified 'pseudo-new' or stolen statement. See Enrico Crispolti, in Norbert Nobis, "Der Lärm der Strasse - Italienischer Futurismus 1909-1918", p. 55, discussing Boccioni's accusation of this appropriation in an article of 1 April 1913, published in the magazine 'Lacerba'.

different from harmony in nature. Harmony in art is a temporarily succesful expression, because the limited capacities of the artist have to be continuously revised. Harmony in nature depends on an equivalence of opposites, an equivalence of duality.[41] By emphasizing in art contrasts or oppositions of basic or universal forms and colours in pure universal equilibrium, "De Stijl" sought to exemplify universal beauty; beauty expressed not by words or by the chosen forms, but by the compositional rhythms of the artworks.

8.3. ON AUTONOMY AND WHOLENESS

German art historian Dietrich Mahlow correctly pointed out to me that current knowledge about reality proves that there is no such thing as autonomy, but only interactivity.[42] He advised me that I better stop using the notion of object for my artworks. These essays are not only partially a result of my own 'quest for knowledge' caused by his remark, but will also show that there are still relevant reasons to continue using the notion of object. These reasons become clear only when one accepts that the objectivity of an appearance exists at the eye-level of perception, while simultaneously there is an unavoidable interaction of this appearance with other appearances at a deeper level. This must be understood as the non-objective property of appearance! This duality of the notion of the object is quite comparable to the long debated duality of light as wave/ particle in physics. The objectivity of an object as it appears at eye-level compares to the 'particle' with a certain substance. The non-objectivity of an object as it is at a deeper level compares to the 'wave', connecting to all other waves into the complex network of reality!

Islamic buildings are decorated with geometrical motifs, tilings and patterns to emphasize that which is between the self and the other - like the holy.[43] The Amazone Kaiapo-indians paint their skins with geometrical patterns not merely to communicate

---

[41] Piet Mondrian in "Natural Reality and Abstract Reality: A Trialogue (While Strolling from the Country to the City)", published like a dialogue between two persons walking, in the magazine De Stijl 1919-1920, in Harry Holtzman and Martin S. James, "The New Art - The New Life - The Collected Writings of Piet Mondrian" (New York: Da Capo Press, 1993), p.96: "As I said before, 'harmony doesn't have the same meaning for everyone.' It depends on our conception of it. In the naturalistic there is natural harmony, to be sure, but the equilibrated relationship of the abstract is another conception of harmony. That the conception of harmony is relative and perfects itself in time - this is shown not only by the successive expressions of art, but also to a greater or lesser extent by the life of every artist. The beauty of the artist's effort is precisely his constant striving for a purer expression of harmony. In the expression of each new vision of beauty, he discovers more and more that the harmony manifested in reality is so strong that mere visual reproduction is inadequate to represent it. He constantly transforms the visual toward greater plastic harmony. You know this yourself. After ecstasy, dissatisfaction follows - and thus a new plastic expression. Reflection and comparison make the artist dissatisfied with the harmony he has established. Although the New Plastic expression of harmony is after all the most satisfying, it too always falls short of our most inward but, alas, still too unconscious idea of harmony. If the harmony of reality is so strong, this is due to the living beauty of nature that acts on all our senses simultaneously: it is not the visual aspect of natural appearance alone that moves us."

[42] During the Kulturtage Dreieich 1995, Dreieich, Germany.

[43] See Oleg Grabar, "The Mediation of Ornament" (Washington DC: Princeton University Press, 1992).

the hierarchy in the tribe, but also to emphasize the skin as the medium between the self and the other - the outer world.[44] Does art also function as a metaphor or intermediary between our selves and the other, between the self and the essence of reality? Art as the medium to intensely connect the individual with the universal was not only sought by several 19th century artists like Cézanne or by early abstract artists, but also in philosophy by Benedetto Croce, for example, who emphasized the relationships of art to the cosmos. Additionally, Umberto Eco wrote:

"According to this teaching in the artistic representation one breathes the total life of the cosmos, the individual would be pulsating with the life of the whole, and the whole revelates itself in the life of the individual: 'Every real artistic representation is itself and the universe, the universe in this individual form, this individual form as the universe.' "[45]

To approach the problems concerned with autonomy and wholeness in the world, one needs verbal and visual concepts as explicit directives towards approaching the essence. In part, the drive to understand reality by combining visual and verbal information can be reduced to a desire to survive: more knowledge about the position of the self or of the group in that reality, as acquired for example by a better understanding of how reality is structured, provides an advantage over other beings and can provide us with a better sense for danger, extending the chances for survival. Quite probably this original motivation was soon mixed with a more general, and probably more conscious, drive for more knowledge that in principle is based upon pure frustration. Frustration or dissatisfaction about the fact that we do not know why we exist or what we basically are. Curiosity is also an important drive, but not as powerful as frustration. Frustration is a

---

[44] See Gustaaf Verswijver, "Kaiapo - Amazonië, de kunst van de lichaamsornamentiek" (Tervuren: Koninklijk Museum voor Midden-Afrika, 1992). However obvious, it is good to remind ourselves that our own bodies are always the starting point of perception. This is something that does bring to mind what was discussed earlier in this chapter in context to Zen and what David Hume (1711-1776) called 'the withness of the body' - meaning the presence and involvement of the body. David Bohm considered it possible to find all knowledge of the physical world within our own body, because the body as part of nature should naturally contain this knowledge. This seems based on Hegel's and on Vedantic philosophy - to which David Bohm had plenty of access through his friendship with Krishnamurti.

[45] See Umberto Eco, "Die ästhetische Botschaft", in Dieter Henrich und Wolfgang Iser, "Theorien der Kunst", p.404: "Nach dieser Lehre atme man in der künstliche Darstellung das ganze Leben des Kosmos, das Einzelne sei durchbebt vom Leben des Ganzen, und das Ganze offenbare sich im Leben des Einzelnen: 'Jede echte künstlerische Darstellung ist sie selber und das Universum, das Universum in dieser individuellen Form, diese individuelle Form als das Universum.'" To the Italian philosopher Croce reality is the historically developed spirit: everything that exists is a concrete expression of spiritual life; living nature is the first expression of spirit; the abstract systems designed by man are therefore substracted and minor variations of the original. Aesthetics is to be understood as reflecting self consciousness that has as subject the intuitive and sensing self-consciousness. A natural drive urges intuition towards expression, feeling develops into form, art thus is formed expression of the intuitive experiencing spirit, every artwork must be built like a language: it is the language of the soul. See Dr. J. Waldram, "Encyclopedie van de Filosofie" (Baarn: Tirion, 1993).

strong drive, naturally connected to the desire to abolish this frustration and, as such, leading towards the search for an ideal.

Schopenhauer saw life mainly as a suffering. Ethics and art were the only means of salvation, which he considered man capable of because of his intellect. According to Schopenhauer, man can detach from the individual by concentrating himself without any ambitions on the universal, on ideas.[46] The ascetic way of life will bring the highest salvation. It will not surprise anyone that Schopenhauer saw relationships between his ideas and Buddhism.[47]

8.4. THE BEAUTIFUL, THE SUBLIME, PERFECTION

Art offers revelation and relief from perceiving everyday suffering by experiences we have named 'the beautiful' and 'the sublime'. While the experience of the beautiful may offer a delightful distraction and makes everyday life enjoyable, the experience of the sublime is so intense that it can completely dissolve the duality between self and the world. The desire for perfection is implicit in the desire we feel to repeat experiences of the beautiful and the sublime. What are the differences in these experiences? Is sheer perfection the final frontier? These are questions I will attempt to answer.

We all perceive certain things, events, and occurances as beautiful. They can be phenomena as different as a burst of terrific sunlight through dark clouds, a flower in spring, a smile or gesture by a beloved person, a song, a philosophical thought, a scientific theory, a poem, or a work of art. Experiencing beauty can be, but is not necessarily, related to a deep appreciation of relationships of form, size or colour. Most of the time the experience of beauty is an instantaneous, immediate sensation. But is a sense for beauty, the sublime, or perfection, really only a fleeting and very personal experience? The analogies between our experiences give reasons to assume there is some deeper cohesion between these different experiences. It would be beyond the purpose of this book to try to describe all the ideas about beauty, the sublime or perfection, but it will be interesting to mention a few. As always, theories might help enhance our own thinking.[48]

In early Greek philosophy beauty and the sublime coexisted in the same worldview. They were seen as each other's complement. The sublime was categorized as the high-

---

46 This is clearly a Platonian concept, see §2. Hegel furthered this Platonian concept and stated that through art we express ideas that will bring us to higher levels of self-awareness. See Hegel, "Aesthetics", quoted in Richard Kuhns, "Psychoanalytische Theorie als Kunstphilosophie", in Dieter Henrich and Wolfgang Iser, "Theorien der Kunst", p.184.

47 Like Leibniz already a few centuries before. See Moira Nicholls' splendid essay "The Influences of Eastern Thought on Schopenhauer's Doctrine of the Thing-in-Itself", in Christopher Janaway, "The Cambridge Companion to Schopenhauer" (Cambridge: Cambridge University Press, 1999), p.171-212, including a list of Oriental literature found in Schopenhauer's personal library.

48 This discussion unavoidably overlaps and partially repeats §2.4 and preceeds §9. It is not very easy to find good and interesting literature on beauty. It is one of those subjects about which a lot of nonsense has been written. In contrast, it is worthwhile to explore Kant, Schopenhauer, Nietzsche, Santayana, Dewey, Whitehead, Nishida, Gadamar, Adorno, and more recently Fons Elders and Donald Kuspit in general. And,

est order and the most intense experience.[49] Beauty was often seen by the Greeks as equivalent to the notion of 'symmetria', meaning proportion. Plotinus rejected this and thought beauty was something contained in bodies. Beauty in a body causes 'symmetria' to emerge, but it is not 'symmetria' itself. Good proportions are the result of beauty radiating from the inside out. The recognition of beauty through the appearance of 'symmetria' is the immediate perception of one's soul and the mutual origin in the Realm of the Good.[50] The perception of beauty is experienced as positive, because it is an immediate experience of feeling re-united with the larger whole from which we come and in which we are immersed.[51] Plato thought every individual object and being contained an inner drive aiming towards a re-unification with the larger whole of nature. This inner drive cannot be perceived by merely considering the objective properties of an object or being. The inner drive becomes perceptable when the object or being awakens an experience of beauty in the perception of the viewer. Because the object or being excites a pleasurable experience within the viewer, Plato believed the experience of beauty was an activating property of an object or being. An experience of beauty arouses desires and pleasures, dissolving all kinds of suffering. Plato's interpretation of beauty can be understood as a kind of active (emergent) idea for which he uses the word 'ekphainestaton'. Plato understood this as a process of becoming into being.[52] Aristotle extended Plato's concept of the experience of beauty as an active experience with his

---

on specific artists, Robert C. Morgan, Carter Ratcliff, and Irving Sandler.

[49] In an excellent essay inspired by the dramatic terrorist disaster in Washington DC, Pennsylvania, and New York on 11 September 2001, Dutch philosopher Fons Elders, describes the actual need to re-establish the link between the sublime and the beautiful, a link that started to dissolve in 19th century thinking and has become completely lost in the current world as is exemplified by the intense experience of the television coverage of the Twin Tower disaster that illustrated the dangerous connection between the sublime and deep horror. Elders describes, that Plato distinguished four forms or stages of beauty: the beauty of the body, moral beauty, intellectual beauty, absolute beauty. See Fons Elders, "The Sublime and the Beautiful - On Ontology and Creative Imagination" (Brussels: VUB Brussels University Press, 2001), p.30: "Or in a different presentation: beyond the order of the particular forms, the world of phenomena, one might become conscious of the general ideas behind the particular ones, in order to reach the Idea of Beauty and the Idea of Truth that coincide in the Idea of Goodness. The sublime coincides in Plato's world view with the highest stage."

[50] See James Kirwan, "Beauty" (Manchester and New York: Manchester University Press, 1999), on Plotinus, p.57: "Beauty, for him, is not proportion itself but rather that which 'illuminates' proportion; a thing is beautiful by virtue of its communion in 'Ideal-Form'. Beauty, in this system, is the aspiration of primal matter towards its perfect form, a form we recognise because its Idea is inherent in ourselves. Thus the soul is awakened from its stupor and drawn toward the Absolute, the source of this illumination, and towards, therefore, a beautific knowledge on what really is." This clearly refers to the ideas on the 'eidos,' as discussed in §2.

[51] Ibid., p.28: "This beauty is perceived at first glance by the soul, which, as a fragment of the divine fallen into matter, names as from an ancient knowledge that which reveals any trace of kinship with itself. The delight of beauty lies in the soul taking its own to itself, in its being stirred anew to the sense of its own nature." Quoting Plotinus, Kirwan continues: "The Good is also the Primal Beauty, and in our act of recognising beauty we express the desire to be reunited with this absolute which is 'the Apart, the Unmingled, the Pure, that from Which all things depend, for Which all look and live and act and know, the Source of Life and of Intellection and of Being'. Beauty is, then, for Plotinus, at once token and presentiment of the Authentic-Existence, it flows from the real which is 'There'."

[52] See Hans-Georg Gadamer, "Bildkunst und Wortkunst", in Gottfried Boehm, "Was ist ein Bild?" (Wilhelm Fink Verlag, 1994), p.100: "... from beauty as the emergent" ("...vom Schönen als dem Hervorscheinenden...")

introduction of the notion of 'energeia', which hangs between actuality, reality and activity. He believed there was a difference between becoming into being, which is linked to the notion of kinesis or internally generated movement that is never complete, and energeia, which is both static (actuality) and dynamic (activity). This seems very suitable for describing an emerging but never stable, and often fleeting experience of beauty. Aristotle interpreted seeing and have-seen or thinking about something and having thought, including experiences of beauty, as simultaneous processes (which has been proven by the modern understanding of the functioning of the brain). Philosopher Hans-Georg Gadamer compares this to our observation of art:

> *"The experience of art is also not like one thing after the other, but evolves as a waiting sojourn, during which the work of art emerges. What thus emerges 'appeals to us', like we say, and thus the appealing as such is with what emerges as in a dialogue."* [53]

Beauty and harmony seem to be linked, if not each other's equivalent. This also seems to be reflected in the original meaning of the word 'cosmos'. Cosmos was the Greek notion of interaction resulting from the understanding of the duality of the unlimited and the limiting as a harmony.[54] The Greek word 'kosmos' is an aesthetic term for a fitting order, a right arrangement, and includes meanings like becomingly, decently, honorably. The Stoics used cosmos for the 'anima mundi' or soul of the world, also implying an aesthetic meaning. Comparably, thinkers like Plotinus considered something to be ugly when it lacked a pattern or structure. The Romans translated the kosmos into the Latin word 'universum', transforming its original meaning as general order into one revolving around only a specific order (which is expressed in the Latin 'unus-verto').[55]

Gadamer (1900-2002) was a pupil of Heidegger and Jaspers. One is advised to read Hans-Georg Gadamer, "Die Aktualität des Schönen - Kunst als Spiel, Symbol und Fest" (Stuttgart: Philipp Reclam, 1995 - first edition 1977).

53 Ibid, p.103: "Die Erfahrung von Kunst ist auch kein Nacheinander, sondern vollzieht sich wie ein wartendes Verweilen, in dem das Werk der Kunst herauskommt. Was so herauskommt, 'spricht uns an', wie wir sagen, und so ist der Angesprochene mit dem, was da herauskommt, wie in einem Gespräch."

54 Gadamer wrote on Plato and harmony, ibid., p.97: "He had to make up his mind what the unlimited (apeiron) and the limiting (peras) in fact are, about which the thinking spoke. The one obviously cannot exist without the other. For this insight we are obliged to Plato, when he showed that in the limited there is always both. Only in the vicinity of the unlimited the exactness of the limiting is possible. In this sense one can actually say, that it concerns here basic categories which today we would call the 'order of being'. The Greeks called it cosmos and, above all, 'harmonia', a word that at first was acquired from music." ("Er mußte sich nur darüber klar werden, was das Unbegrenzte (apeiron) und das Begrenzende (peras) eigentlich sind, von dem das Denken sprach. Das eine kommt offenbar ohne das andere nicht aus. Diese Einsicht verdanken wir Plato, als er zeigte, daß im Begrenzten immer beides ist. Nur im Umkreis des Unbegrenzten ist ja die Genauigkeit der Begrenztheit überhaupt möglich. In diesem Sinne kann man also wirklich sagen, es handle sich hier um Grundkategorien dessen, was wir inzwischen 'Seinsordnung' nennen würden. Die Griechen nannten sie Kosmos und, vor allem, Harmonia - ein Wort, das zunächst aus der Musik gewonnen war.") Compare this to Leibniz's notion of a 'harmonia praestibilita': there is a harmony between everything that is independent from man and is decided by God.

55 See for an excellent discussion James Hillman, "The Practice of Beauty", in Bill Beckley and David Shapiro,

As can be expected, with the emerging power of the doctrine of the Christian church, concepts of beauty and the sublime as the highest order of experience became translated as direct references to God.[56] The universe and everything in it are seen as God's handiwork, therefore in principle as good and beautiful (a huge contrast to the actual circumstances in the 'Dark Ages'). Umberto Eco mentions, for instance, how Dionysius the Areopagite in the "De Divinis Nomibus", "...describes the universe as an exhaustible irradiation of beauty, a grandiose expression of the ubiquity of the First Beauty, a dazzling cascade of splendours."[57] Because of this concept, beauty is to be found in the substance of which a thing is made, in handcraft, proportions and choice of materials, not necessarely in the artistic quality. This concept led to precise definitions of the properties of beautiful artifacts, which led to the formulation of ideal objects and the preference for ideal systems, as number series, geometrical constructions and perspective constructing methods. Eco writes: "... art was the science (ars sine scientia nihil est) of constructing objects according to their own laws. Art was not expression, but construction, an operation aiming at a certain result."[58] Additionally, a separation was understood between the sensuous beauty of an object that pleases the eye and interior beauty that pleases the soul. Aesthetic experience was not seen as

"Uncontrollable Beauty - Towards a New Aesthetics" (New York: Allworth Press, 1998), p269: "Cosmos does not present itself as an all-embracing whole, but as the appearance of fittingness of each thing as and where it is; how well, how decorously, how appropriately it displays. And its beauty is that very display; cosmos in each, as each, grain of sand." Hillman, debating the described original meaning of the cosmos in a contemporary context, quite correctly describes the search or desire for beauty as the equivalent to the desire to feel one with the cosmos, on p.268 of the same essay he writes: "If the cosmos itself implies beauty, if we live in an aesthetic world, then the primary mode of adjustment to the cosmos would be through the sense of beauty, the aesthetic response. For this reason alone, the repression of beauty has cosmic proportions. No wonder civilization is in disarray, and no wonder the terrible burden on the individual artist to find his or her own way back to the innate demand that the cosmos places on an individual talent. We are each out of order and in need of therapy because we have forgotten that life is essentially aesthetic, cosmologically so. In Whitehead's words: 'The teleology of the universe is directed to the production of Beauty.'"

[56] In the 15th century Ficino wrote "De Amore" ('amore' understood as 'the desire for beauty') in response to Plato's Symposium on Love and inspired by Plotinus, Dionysius and scholastic tradition. See James Kirwan, "Beauty", p.31: "Beauty is the attraction of the soul back to its origin in God, it is God as attraction."

[57] See Umberto Eco, "Art and Beauty in the Middle Ages", translated by Hugh Bredin (New Haven and London: Yale University Press, 1986 - orig. "Sviluppo dell'estetica medievale" in "Momenti e problemi di storia dell'estetica, vol.1, 1959), p.18. Eco quotes Dionysius the Areopagite on that same page: "But the Superessential Beauty is called 'Beauty' because of the quality which It imparts to all things severally according to their nature, and because It is the Cause of the harmony and splendour in all things, flashing forth upon them all, like light, the beautifying communications of Its originating ray; and because It summons all things to fare unto Itself (from whence It hath the name of 'Fairness'), and because It draws all things together in a state of mutual interpenetration."

[58] Ibid, p.93. How remarkably similar to Constructivism in modern times! See §3. Leon Battista Alberti defined in "On Painting" (1436) precisely how an artist should make a good painting, describing how to combine standing persons with seated persons, some naked, some half-clothed, some with hands upwards, others with arms by their sides, some turned to the viewer, some turned away, etc. It is known that his essay was read and used by many artists, for instance, by El Greco. See David Davies and John H. Elliott, "El Greco" (New Haven and London: Yale University Press, 2003), p.46.

instantaneous intuition, but as a 'dialogue' with the object.[59] The effort necessary to perceive beauty in an object is rewarded by experiencing joy and satisfaction of desire. A deep and profound experience of beauty provoked by the appearance of an artifact may dissolve one's self, elevating one closer to God.[60]

Mystic writers in 15th century Spain promoted the concept of 'mental prayer', an 'ascent of the mind to God', furthering the concept of beauty in the Middle Ages. This 'ascent' could be accomplished by an immersion first in meditation and then in contemplation. David Davies writes:

> *"Meditation involved the application of the senses in order to imagine, for example, the size of the garden of Gethsemane, or the physical suffering experienced by Christ on the cross. In contemplation, the higher form of mental prayer, the spiritual reformers would seek to transcend the physical world, and hope to attain through Grace a union of the soul with Christ. Initially they would attempt to purge their minds of physical images since these would prevent them from attaining that state of quiet which was spiritual, and in which they hoped to receive infusion and illumination from supernatural sources. Subsequently their understanding might be illuminated with supernatural light. Beforehand they would be in a state of blindness and darkness - the despair of the 'dark night of the soul' (Saint John of the Cross). Then, possibly God would make his presence felt to them and their souls would experience mystic union with God. Mystic writers could find no words to express this union adequately, yet common to their reminiscences were images of the flame and a brilliance of light and colour, as in the poem 'The Living Flame of Love' of Saint John of the Cross."*[61]

see picture 12

The concept of 'mental prayer' helps to explain why El Greco developed his famous style using elongated persons in dramatic compositions.[62] It is a brilliant way of painting to provoke in the viewer the necessary connection between everyday reality through a kind of 'visual mental prayer' (including the brilliances of light and colour) to offer a

[59] It is interesting to briefly refer to aesthetic theories in the 10th century in India when Kasmiri pandit Abhinavagupta emphasized that pleasure or delight are the principal objectives of aesthetic experience, which he understands as an inner or mental perception. See Pratapaditya Pal, "Himalayas - An Aesthetic Adventure" (Chicago: The Art Institute of Chicago in association with the University of California Press and Mapin Publishing, 2003), p.19: "...(*manaspratyksa*), i.e. it is perceived through the mind or inner sense. Such a perception is self-knowing ... The fact of tasting (*asvadana*; aesthetic perception being conceived as a particular form of tasting) is of a mental order: it differs from the fact of eating, which is a purely material act ... The mind of him who tastes must be *ekagra* (concentrated) absorbed in the tasting to the exclusion of all else." In my understanding one may interpret this exclusion as dissolving of self.

[60] See also Archbishop Damianos, "The Icon as a Ladder of Divine Ascent in Form and Color", in Helen C. Evans, "Byzantium - Faith and Power (1261-1557)", The Metropolitan Museum of Art, NY, and Yale University Press (New Haven and London), 2004, p.335.

[61] See David Davies and John H. Elliott, "El Greco", p.61.

[62] It should be added that elongated figures were common in Byzantine icons, and El Greco started his career as icon painter on Crete (which was part of Byzantium). Still El Greco's elongated figures are much more dramatic and expressive than the ones one finds in icons.

'mystic union with God' equivalent to an experience of the sublime. El Greco's paintings are great works of art because they allow one today to still experience the sublime (while not necessarily causing a union with God but a more general dissolving of the duality between self-world, or body-soul in Christian thought). The capacity to offer the experience of the sublime in art became fully generated in the great Baroque art like by Tiepolo.

see picture 14

In all theories it is commonly accepted that the experience of beauty is of a temporary character, necessitating the desire to continuously restore the experience. One of the difficulties obviously is that pleasure is experienced as inseparable from the experience of beauty. The notion of 'pleasure' opens the door to an even more difficult mine-field of definitions and ideas, involving also 'desire' and the complexities of physical and psychological desires.[63] The yearning for beauty is in principal not object-related, but leads the mind to the absolute beyond the appearance of reality around us. Therefore, beauty will not actually alleviate suffering, but it takes the mind off suffering nevertheless. There are of course very different levels of experiencing beauty, which differ in intensity. When the intensity of the experience of beauty reaches the level one may call the sublime - however short this may be - this experience instantaneously dissolves the duality of self and world, making the causes of suffering disappear for a moment. The experience of beauty is not self-centered or object-related, though it can be caused by an object. It is a sensation of pure being. It is logical that in religion this experience is seen as brief moment of intense unification with the divine. It also makes sense that beauty is experienced as equivalent to 'truth' and 'good' or to experiencing the essence of life and of self.[64] The artist is thought to be the one who is disclosing wisdom in beauty.[65]

A distinction between the sublime and the beautiful emerged, though at first still

63 This is not even to mention that pleasure or desire were often seen as sins by institutionalized religions, and therefore, definitely not understood as positive objectives. Goodness or truth were much more acceptable notions.

64 It is also quite logical that in the 1950's, when 'structure' was the leading paradigm, the desire for beauty was understood to be the desire for order. See James Kirwan, "Beauty", p.55, on Eric Newton's (not to be mistaken for the 17th century physicist Isaac Newton!) "The Meaning of Beauty" (1959): "Beauty, he writes, is a 'law-abiding behaviour' that can be expressed in mathematical terms, and our response to beauty is an instinctive recognition of that law. The desire that beauty satisfies, according to Newton, is the desire to understand and correlate, it is the pleasure we feel at intuiting the mathematical behaviour of the universe, a behaviour so complex that it can only be grasped intuitively; 'The remarkable feature of this process is the power of the mind to arrive at a verdict without being conscious that the evidence on which it is based comes from so many different sources.' "

65 Ibid., p.140 (discussing Maritain's "Art and Scholasticism" of 1920): "However, for Maritain, the ontological splendour, or 'brilliance of form', that beauty manifests is not conceptual clarity; rather the more substantial and profound the secret significance of a thing the more concealed from us it is; the artist is on the track of wisdom, pursuing its perfume, but never possessing it." Fons Elders mentions that for classicist authors like Boileau and Bossuet, Beauty was the splendour of Truth and Goodness. See Fons Elders, "The Sublime and the Beautiful - On Ontology and Creative Imagination", p.31: "In his 'Réflexions critiques sur quelques passages du rhéteur Longin', 1694, Boileau stresses the undefinable and unspeakable aspect of the sublime in the experience of art. In his words , 'je en scay quoy de sublime', it is not something that can be demonstrated with proofs, but what makes itself felt. It is an aesthetic response, a value-judgement based

within the Platonic notion of beauty - truth - goodness. Already in some Baroque paintings beauty, the sublime and horror were combined, for instance in some of Rubens' paintings.[66]

At the end of the 18th century, clearly in the Zeitgeist-related interest in a logical understanding of a free self, Diderot proposed understanding the experience of beauty as an experience of relationships and the adherent sensation of pleasure as a property of feeling rather than reason.[67] There came a shift in thinking at least in part caused by the emergence of a general liberation from the suffocating doctrines of the past centuries. The resulting resistance to any theories about beauty and the sublime made a shift away from understanding beauty as an experience and the sublime as the highest experience. This shift happened through the exploration of the object as it is by itself, and an emphasis on sensing the essence in every object through the contemplation of its aesthetic appearance. Edmund Burke proposed that the sublime was a manifestation of power and intensity; intensity that cannot be reached without a certain amount of suffering and terror. This meant that an experience of the sublime as an intense negative experience was separated from an experience of beauty as an experience of good.[68] Burke thought art's mission was to arouse and effect the passions. Because of the difference in intensity, in art a search for the sublime became more important than a search for beauty.[69] This attempt to create a break between beauty and the sublime may have been a natural result of the 18th century conviction that the universe is governed by divine rules (and therefore beauty and the sublime are controlled) and an 18th century interest in 'discovering' free will, exemplified by the Enlightenment. The idea of free will made men aware of being on their own more than ever and without divine protection against the brutal forces and play of nature. The process of becoming conscious of one's immediate submission to nature's forces without any divine intervention was emphasized by the new scientific discoveries presented as 'laws of nature' and the vulnerability to diseases, famine, etc. This shift led to a kind of fascination for experiences of deep horror and misery in life.

Kant disagreed with Burke that the experience of the sublime is based on fear of the unknown. Instead, he described the experience of the sublime as a positive, deep and

upon good taste and sensibility."

see picture 24

66 Rubens painting "Massacre of the Innocents", ca 1611-1612, at The National Gallery, London. A great painting showing a group of persons in one swirling dynamic motion. The viewer is initially enthralled by the dynamics and the beauty expressed by the colours, composition and craft, until one sees the corpses of children and the ongoing slaughter. A similar though much milder experience is offered by André Masson's great painting "Massacre" from 1931.

67 Diderot in "The Beautiful" from 1752. See James Kirwan, "Beauty", p.140.

68 Edmund Burke in "A Philosophical Enquiry into the Origin of our Ideas of the Sublime and the Beautiful", 1757. See Fons Elders, "The Sublime and the Beautiful - On Ontology and Creative Imagination", p.33-34.

69 Ibid., p.33-34. Elders correctly implies that this new tendency to focus on intensity of experience, seems reflected in a lot of 20th century and current main-stream art to attract attention by sheer negatively shocking pictures or actions (in my own opinion also a close relation to developments in the entertainment industries and news media). This seems well based on the assumption that the intensity of such an experience definitely does not need to be a positive experience - as Burke already had implied.

grand experience of something that is too big to grasp. This was an experience he understood as a profoundly deep aesthetic experience. Kant distinguished between the experience of the beautiful and the experience of the sublime: the beautiful needs a perceivable object as a vehicle (incorporating not necessarily deep aesthetic properties, while aesthetics still decides its appearance), the sublime does not have a material quality.[70] By emphasizing the object as a thing in itself, Kant emphasized the role of the viewer, not of the participant in or creator of art. In my interpretation this means understanding experiences of beauty as experiences aroused by an object that gives us pleasure without any intense involvement. The experience of the sublime demands a deeper involvement. Schopenhauer's ideas have been discussed at length in other parts of this publication. It should suffice here to recall that in contrast to Kant he emphasized the necessity of acknowledging that we are tiny parts of a large whole and are tiny reflections of the all-encompassing world will. He concluded that the experience art provokes is one of the few means of escaping the suffering of reality. The experience of art allows the experience of dissolving the duality between self and world.[71] Schopenhauer and Hegel considered the contemplation of the Idea or essence of reality crucial, as it is given to perception by the aesthetic form that generates beauty. As I have said before, through the experience of beauty we feel unified with the essence of the world. In 19th century art, one can trace the shift away from an understanding of the sublime as a mere connection to the divine, as a new understanding of the sublime emerged in the experience of the phenomena of nature itself. For instance, one can see this shift in Joseph Mallard William Turner's, in Caspar David Friedrich's or in Claude Monet's paintings.[72] Late 19th century Symbolism shows that looking for experiences of the sublime was based on intensity and not necessarily on the beautiful with subjects like death, suffering and sorrow. This is clearly related to the understandings of important philosophers like Schopenhauer and Nietzsche that life is suffering and can only be temporarily escaped by the intense experience art offers us.

Much more than Schopenhauer, Nietzsche tried to understand the eternal essence of reality while including individual emotions. Nietzsche thought art presented an illusion,

[70] Ibid., p.33, discussing Kant: "The sublime is first of all an experience, not a material quality. The infinity of the sublime remains a barrier for our sense-bound intuition. The sublime obliges us to conceive of nature in her totality without being able to realise this reproduction objectively." Elders himself, ibid, p.15: "The sublime likes to hide itself; it negates any definitive form, while the beautiful needs matter, colour, sound, rhythm to manifest itself."

[71] Schopenhauer proposed the allegory as an effective vehicle in art, because it presents to us some contents which are evoked by what we see in the painting, but is not literally what we see. An allegory leads our perception to what is beyond what we actually see - it shows a figurative story, but we know the story and its proper morale or meaning hidden 'beyond' the narrative of the story. In an odd way this seems comparable to calligraphy in Zen: the symbols seen provide just enough associations to recognize what poem is written while the meaning is hidden 'beyond' the narrative of the poem.

[72] On Turner, see for instance his fabulous sketchbooks, like "J.M.W. Turner - The 'Ideas of Folkstone' Sketchbook 1845" (London: The Tate Gallery, 1987). On German Romanticism, see Werner Hofmann, "Caspar David Friedrich - Naturwirklichkeit und Kunstwahrheit" (Munich:Verlag C.H. Beck 2000 - orig. Editions Hazan Paris, 2000).

but a necessary one to overcome the suffering of life.[73] He also believed art was not a self-contained or isolated object or experience detached from life, but quite involved and immersed in life, which explains the value of art in life and for understanding life. He based his complex theory of art on the duality of the Dionysiac and Apolline. Dionysiac represented the creative intoxication, and Apolline the controlled and stabile reason in the creative process. Nietzsche considered art's purpose to be the overcoming of the self and connection to the one-ness of nature, to be "...for a brief moment primordial being itself ".[74]

Experiences of beauty are so essential to life, because they are temporary experiences, fueling the desire to live on to experience the next moments of beauty. The artist is the creator of tragedies who can make life bearable by transforming the suffering and terror of the world into the sublime and magnificent.

A new development that really changed the discussion about beauty and the sublime through the 19th century is the strong advance of science and technology. New discoveries in physics, biology, astronomy, and the resulting inventions like the engine, train, radio, and electric light, changed the vision we have of the world completely. This naturally caused a further shift in the relationship between beauty and the sublime. The sublime increasingly became merely an intense experience, frequently more negative and shocking than positive. Beauty in art increasingly became merely entertainment: simple straight forward pleasure. Quite probably it is not coincidental that during the 19th century a larger art market erupted, including the so-called 'salon-artistes'. Fame, fortune and public exposure gained importance.[75] Needless to say, despite this trend, many artists kept exploring the original goal of finding beauty in our understanding of the world, and seeking the actual core of nature without assuming it should be merely entertaining or shocking. Their mission was to re-establish the original and positive experience of the sublime. As times change, the approach of these artists has also changed.

It is fascinating that as result of the shift of interest from a concept of the universe

---

73 Nietzsche often spoke about the artwork as a dream. It will be clear that and how his theories influenced certain tendencies in art to search for 'truth' in dream-like subjects, like in Symbolism, later in Surrealism and even in spiritual paintings such as those by Mark Rothko (who said he was inspired by Nietzsche).

74 Quote from Nietzsche "The Birth of Tragedy", in Richard Schacht, "Nietzsche" (London: Routldge, 1996 - orig.1983), p.493. See Nietzsche, "The Birth of Tragedy" (New York: Penguin Group, 1993 - orig. 1872), p.25: "The more aware I become of those omnipotent art impulses in nature, and find in them an ardent longing for illusion and for redemption by illusion, the more I feel compelled to make the metaphysical assumption that the truly existent, the primal Oneness, eternally suffering and contradictory, also needs the delightful vision, the pleasurable illusion for its constant redemption: an illusion that we, utterly caught up in it and consisting of it - as a continuous becoming in time, space and causality, in other words - are required to see as empirical reality." The concept of the "Übermensch" is often misunderstood and misused, he originally did not mean some super-human being, better than other persons, but merely a person that rises to the mental level of understanding reality beyond individuality, the level he considers presented by art. The "Übermensch" thus can be well compared to the 'enlightened' person in Oriental philosophies.

75 For a very interesting and illuminating psychological analysis, see Donald Kuspit, "Psychostrategies of Avant-Garde" (Cambridge: Cambridge University Press, 2000), including a feature about Manet. Kuspit clearly shows how this development has created the perimeters for avant-garde art until today.

decided and ruled by divinity to one that is constituted by 'laws', in the 19th century not only scientists and philosophers, but also artists started to emphasize the hidden order of nature, a positive evolutionary process beyond the mere mimetic appearances around us, or the cohesion of everything in the complex interrelationships of reality.[76] As the interest in more abstract notions of perceiving the world and nature evolved, it was only natural and logical that the need also evolved for finding the real essence of reality without being distracted by any story-telling picture. The times were ready for abstract art.

George Santayana exemplifies the change of understanding beauty, the sublime and perfection. He understood that there is a natural drive in all phenomena of nature towards perfection. This was a thought clearly related to the belief of his age in evolutionary processes and universal progress. He believed beauty was pleasure, regarded as the quality of an object. He discussed our perception of beauty in nature at length.[77] This capacity for perceiving beauty leads us to the meaning of things. Santayana understood the artist as the person who can fix our general understanding of beauty in a materialized form and thus make it accessible. Art provides us with a medium for contemplating all aspects of life, including death. He considered the ornament an important feature. Because of its complexity the ornament enhances the aesthetic essence of the form and also attracts our attention better than a form without ornament. The complexity of the use of ornaments should be combined with our desire to find structure and our search for the equilibrium.[78] Following Kant, Santayana distinguishes

[76] In 1898 scientist Felix Klein had a plaster copy made of the Greek sculpture "Apollo of Belvedere". On the face of this copy Klein drew the border lines basic to the Greek laws of proportion. Klein wished with this method to mathematically analyse the Greek formula of beauty. The experiment failed. See Daniel Tyradellis, Michal S. Friedlander, "10 + 5 = Gott - Die Macht der Zeichen", (Cologne: DuMont Literatur und Kunst Verlag, Jüdisches Museum Berlin, 2004), p.174.

[77] See Georg Santayana, "The Sense of Beauty - Being the outline of Aesthetic Theory" (New York: Dover Publications, Inc., 1955 - orig.1896), p.32: "Further, this pleasure must not be in the consequence of the utility of the object or event, but in its immediate perception; in other words, beauty is an ultimate good, something that gives satisfaction to a natural function, to some fundamental need or capacity of our minds. Beauty is therefore a positive value that is intrinsic; it is a pleasure. These two circumstances sufficiently separate the sphere of aesthetics from that of ethics. Moral values are generally negative, and always remote. Morality has to do with the avoidance of evil and the pursuit of good: aesthetics only with enjoyment." Santayana continues to explain the differences between pleasures of the senses with the perception of beauty. The perception of beauty is a deeper experience than mere simple sensation and maybe a more conscious experience than an experience, that can be qualified as a pleasure for the senses.

[78] Ibid, p.102: "We may thus oscillate between decorative and structural motives, and only in one point, for each style, can we find the ideal equilibrium, in which the greatest strength and lucidity is combined with the greatest splendour." One may recognize in this description the works by Kupka, Kandinsky, Pollock, Stella, Maury, Taaffe or Purdy - I certainly identify myself with my art with this approach! This concept is in my opinion not merely Zeitgeist-related (the age of both Jugendstil or 'Wiener Sezession' with its ornamentations, the interest in the ornament in Germany by various art theorists as Lipps and Worringer, and the emerging interest in structure in physics), but can also be understood as follows: an art that provides us with highly complex images, as through ornaments, in combination with a still accessible structure, reflects our brain's need to be stimulated to be more active, to think longer (and thus deeper) about reality (see §5) much better than an art that merely shows a few very simple relationships in a very purified, reduced composition. Complex pictures demand more focussed attention from the brain.

between the experience of beauty and the experience of the sublime. Beauty allows us to identify with the world, the sublime raises us above it.[79] He considered the impossibility of action as an important condition of the experience of the sublime.

If we could count the stars, our perception of a starry sky would be one of reason and beauty, but not of the sublime. In my own interpretation this acknowledges the importance of searching for complexity in art. The more complex a work of art is, the closer it comes to evoking an experience of the sublime, because we sense structure and cohesion but cannot grasp it and can only stand in awe before such a work of art. Santayana concludes, while describing first that our heart and reason often remain unsatisfied about what is offered to us as truth or good, but that our eye more quickly finds satisfaction, that beauty seems the clearest manifestation of perfection: "Beauty is the pledge of the possible conformity between the soul and nature, and consequently a ground of faith in the supremacy of the good."[80] This definition clearly stands in the long line of concepts of inner beauty as have been described earlier (especially in Hinduism and the concepts of beauty in the Middle Ages), which also was mirrored by Kandinsky, who proposed through the notion of 'inner vision' we could obtain direct access to the union of self and nature in an object.[81] Something is beautiful because it contains an 'inner beauty'. The beautiful comes from the inside out, so to speak.[82] This clearly is not Kandinsky's discovery either, but seems to reflect Plotinus' ideas described earlier, a common interpretation in art that the essence, truth or beauty is already present inside the material and the artist merely has to 'get it out into the open'. Rodin understood a

[79] Ibid, p.144: "But there are always two methods of securing harmony: one is to unify all the given elements, and another is to reject and expunge all the elements that refuse to be unified. Unity by inclusion gives us the beautiful; unity by exclusion, opposition, and isolation gives us the sublime. Both are pleasures: but the pleasure of the one is warm, passive and pervasive; that of the other cold, imperious, and keen. The one identifies us with the world, the other raises us above it."

[80] Ibid,p.164.

[81] See Wassily Kandinsky, "to retninger", in the Danish journal "Konkretion" ("Two Directions", 1935), see Kenneth C. Lindsay, Peter Vergo, "Kandinsky - Complete Writings of Art", (New York: DaCapo Press, 1994 - orig. Editions Denoel, Paris, 1970), p.779: "This experience of the 'hidden soul' in all the things, seen either by the unaided eye or through microscopes or binoculars, is what I call the 'internal eye'. This eye penetrates the hard shell, the external 'form', goes deep into the object and lets us feel with all our senses its internal 'pulse'." See also "Zwei Richtungen" in Max Bill, "Essays über Kunst und Künstler" (Bern: Benteli Verlag, 1963 - orig. 1955) p.193: "Dieses Erleben der 'geheimen Seele' der sämtlichen Dinge, die wir mit unbewaffnetem Auge, im Mikroskop oder durch das Fernrohr sehen, nenne ich den 'inneren Blick'. Dieser Blick geht durch die harte Hülle, durch die äußre 'Form'zum Inneren der Dinge hindurch und läßt uns das innere 'Pulsieren' der Dinge mit unseren sämtlichen Sinnen aufnehmen." Compare Kandinsky's 'inner vision' to the Indian concept of 'inner perception', see footnote 59, this chapter.

[82] See Wassily Kandinksy, "Concerning The Spiritual in Art", translated by Sadler (New York: Dover Publications Inc., 1977 - orig. "Über das Geistige in der Kunst", first title in English "The Art of Spiritual Harmony", 1914), p.55: "If the artist be the priest of beauty, nevertheless this beauty is to be sought only according to the principle of the inner need, and can be measured only according to the size and intensity of that need. That is beautiful which is produced by the inner need, which springs from the soul." In the original German version this reads slightly different - especially the last sentence, "was innerlich schön ist" is entirely missing. This means "what has an inner beauty" (this is corrected in Kenneth C. Lindsay, Peter Vergo, "Kandinsky - Complete Writings of Art", p.214.; this translation speaks of 'inner value' instead of Sadler's

work of art as 'true', either ugly or beautiful when it had character, which he based on the translation of 'the inner truth' into 'the outer truth'. Said otherwise: the appearance of a work of art can only evoke a sense of beauty when the artist is capable of letting the power of beauty burst forth from the inside out. Rodin understood the artist as capable of virtually 'reading' the inner truth of nature, therefore its sheer beauty.[83] Being an artist myself, I understand this can be accomplished when one puts enough visual tension in a work, applying the right contrasts and relationships of colours, forms, sizes, directions, etc. or as in Rodin's case: emphasizing gestures, grimaces, muscles and simulating motion.[84]

In direct relation to the growing interest in connectedness in the 19th and early 20th centuries, stands the positive attitude of the philosopher and mathematician Alfred North Whitehead. Whitehead considered beauty to be an important and natural binding factor in the complex interrelationships in reality.[85] Beauty, in my interpretation, is the experience of happiness in the temporary harmony (equilibrium, moment of symmetry) with the whole. The moment of experiencing the sublime is the moment of a deep acknowledgement of the essence of reality.[86] Could, then, the search for beauty and the sublime in art be analogous to experiencing a beautiful solution or truth in science?

'inner need'. Lindsay and Vergo also translate the mentioned quote from Kandinsky as: "Whatever arises from internal, spiritual necessity is beautiful. The beautiful is that which is inwardly beautiful."). "Soul"- in German "Seele" - is mentioned in the fore last sentence of the original text as "was einer innerseelischen Notwendigkeit entspringt" is correctly translated as Sadler's last sentence. See Nina Kandinsky, "Kandinsky und Ich - Mein Leben mit einem großen Künstler" (Munich: Knaur Verlag,1999 - orig. 1976), p.74: "Wenn der Künstler Priester des 'Schönen' ist, so ist auch dieses Schöne durch dasselbe Prinzip des inneren Wertes zu suchen, welchen wir überall gefunden haben. Diese 'Schöne' ist nur durch den Maßstab der inneren Größe und Notwendigkeit zu messen, welche uns bis jetzt überall und durchweg richtige Dienste geleistet hat. Das ist schön, was einer inneren seelischen Notwendigkeit entspringt. Das ist schön, was innerlich schön ist."

83 See Rodin, in Paul Gsell, "Auguste Rodin - Rodin on Art and Artists" (New York: Dover Publications Inc., 1983), p.20: "In fact, in art, only that which has character is beautiful. Character is the essential truth of any natural object, whether ugly or beautiful; it is even what one might call a double truth , for it is the inner truth translated by the outer truth; it is the soul, the feelings, the ideas, expressed by the features of a face, by the gestures and actions of a human being, by the tones of a sky, by the lines of a horizon. Now, to the great artist, everything in nature has character; for the unswerving directness of his observation searches out the hidden meaning of all things." And, on the same page: "To any artist, worthy of the name, all in nature is beautiful, because his eyes, fearlessly accepting all exterior truth, read there, as in an open book, all the inner truth." For Rodin, the most horrible and most ugly are also beautiful, as long as they have character.

84 One is reminded of the studies of some psychophycisists of facial expressions in Rodin's time. See §7.3, footnote 50, on Humbert de Superville and Duchenne de Boulogne.

85 See Alfred North Whitehead, "Adventures of Ideas" (New York, London: Free Press, 1967 - orig.1933), p.265: "Beauty is the internal conformation of the various items of experience with each other, for the production of maximum effectiveness. Beauty thus concerns the inter-relations of the various components of Reality, and also the inter-relations of the various components of Appearance, and also the relations of Appearance and Reality. Thus any part of experience can be beautiful. The teleology of the Universe is directed to the production of Beauty. Thus any system of things which in a wider sense is beautiful is to that extent justified in its existence."

86 Such a profound experience in my opinion can be seen as equivalent to what is often described as a moment of 'enlightenment' in various Eastern philosophies/religions, for instance, in Vedantic thinking, or as 'entering The Pure Land (Shinran)' or 'attaining Buddha nature' (Dogen). See §2 and this chapter footnote 9.

Especially, because beauty plays such an important role in the confrontation of the self with an object, with the actual world?

The temporality of harmony is currently being discussed again in relation to new scientific ideas about the importance of changing circumstances and order-fluctuations. Whitehead already wrote, "Progress is founded upon the experience of discordant feelings."[87] Discordant feelings are feelings of unease or frustration that will stimulate a desire to improve the situation and, therefore, will provoke progression in our perpetual search for the essence of existence. This perpetual search is obviously a process of continuous change. It is always a major problem that too few artists have written down their own theories and thoughts, making it difficult to find who was and who was not conscious of the sublime. In my own opinion, great art of the Baroque (especially the magnificent ceiling paintings of Tiepolo and Domenichino, the swirling compositions of Rubens, or the late paintings by El Greco) definitely evoke experiences of the sublime, as do the late Monet "Nymphéas" paintings and Kandinsky's "Compositions". Furthermore, the best paintings by Jackson Pollock and Mark Rothko also make reference to the sublime. Artists like Barnett Newman and Robert Motherwell actually published on the sublime, although neither understood the experience of the sublime as a dissolving of duality between self and the world caused by an experience of beauty resulting in an acknowledgement of the one-ness of self and the world, an experience of feeling at peace with reality as it actually is.[88] Motherwell and Newman understood the experience of the sublime as an escape out of a world of suffering, caused by the overwhelming power of large sized paintings, which are not necessarily based on beauty. They continued the tradition of viewing the sublime as a negative experience, following the lead of Edmund Burke.[89] Motherwell wrote, ".... painting becomes Sublime when the artist transcends his personal anguish, when he projects in the midst of a shrieking world an expression of living and its end that is silent and ordered."[90] Motherwell translates the experience of the sublime into experiencing the greatness of the artist, which may provoke a complete absorption in the work of art (hence, a temporary escape from

see pictures 16, 27

[87] See Alfred North Whitehead, "Adventures of Ideas", p.257. See on Prigogene in §7.6.

[88] In the magazine 'The Tiger's Eye', which published in 1948 a syposium titled "Six Opinions on What is Sublime in Art?". See Arthur C. Danto, "The Abuse of Beauty - Aesthetics and the Concept of Art" (Chicago and La Salle, ILL: Open Court 2004 - orig. 2003), p.143.

[89] See footnote 67 earlier this chapter.

[90] See Robert Motherwell, "A Tour of the Sublime", (original title "Against the Sublime", 1948), in Stephanie Terenzio, "The Collected Writings of Robert Motherwell" (Berkeley, Los Angeles, London: Univeristy of California Press, 1999), p.51-54. In the same article Motherwell also wrote: "The Sublime I take to be the emphasis of a possible felt quality in aesthetic experience, the exalted, the noble, the lofty, 'the echo of a great mind', as the treatise formerly described to Longinus phrases it." In this article Motherwell emphasizes the sublime artwork to be an opposition to the sublime 'in the social sense', with which he meant a definition of the sublime as described by any institutional authority (a museum, politics), and sees the change in art in the 19th century as a revolt to previous 'dead' art, a change he describes as a "decisive attack on the Sublime". He finishes this article, writing: "In the metaphysical sense, it cannot be a question of intent, one experiences the Sublime or not, according to one's fate and character."

suffering), standing in awe of the artist's accomplishment, instead of experiencing the dissolving of the duality between self and world, feeling unified with reality (offering a long-lasting acknowledgement of reality as it is). In Motherwell's interpretation, this means the work of art itself is the final destination of the focus of our attention, in the original meaning of the sublime the work of art is the intermediary that triggers our focus on a deep experience of self and reality. This is a small but essential difference.

A negative experience of the sublime can also be provoked by, for instance, the sheer horror and threats in war or by the devastating power of the atom-bomb. The separation between the experience of beauty and the experience of the sublime has led to a very negative interpretation of the sublime, spiralling downwards. This seems reflected by the common attitude of the news media to introduce the most shocking and negative into our homes, and certain tendencies in modern art to shock under the banner of 'political-correctness'. Having said this, I am most conscious that no clear definition for the sublime can exist, because every precise definition in art would merely lead again to academism. Art critic Irving Sandler mentions that Newman, again comparable to Edmund Burke, understood the 'pure idea' as equivalent to the sublime, while being incompatible with 'beauty'. Based on an academic concept of beauty he saw around him, Newman stated that notions of beauty had to be renounced if one wished to suggest the sublime. He claimed to find the sublime within himself and instantaneously - an experience he called a pure idea or the 'Now'.[91] Irving Sandler describes how the color-field painters were also inspired by Burke's idea that the 'effect of infinity' and 'greatness of dimension' were important attributes of the sublime. The preference for large sized paintings was made famous by the art critic Clement Greenberg, who emphasized the concept of 'all-over', implying painting without any hierarchical composition on such a large scale that it cannot be taken in with one glance as easel-painting does. Greenberg believed these large pictures created the sensation of real space stretching beyond one's immediate vision (not to be mistaken for the illusion of space in easel-painting which is considered to be merely a virtual 'opening of a window').[92] From my own artistic experience I also have learned that size does matter. When a work of art is relatively small,

[91] See Irving Sandler, "The Triumph of American Painting, A History of Abstract Expressionism" (New York: Praeger Publishers, Inc, 1970), p.148-157. Sandler discusses the Amercian expressionists, the color-field painters and the sublime. Newman called the concept of beauty he criticized 'the Greek ideal', exemplified in his opinion in the perfection of Mondrian's paintings. Newman's 'pure idea' can be related to the aspect of immediacy - the 'now' in Zen philosophy. He and other artists in New York understood Zen through the publications and lectures by D. Suzuki. Many incorrectly understood the notion of 'nothingness' being just a vacant space (instead of something 'full of meaning'), discussed in §9. On Newman and his statement "The Sublime is Now" (1948), see Carter Ratcliff, "The Sublime Was Then: The Art of Barnett Newman", in Bill Beckley, "Sticky Sublime" (New York: Allworth Press, 2001), p.226. See Arthur C. Danto, "The Abuse of Beauty - Aesthetics and the Concept of Art", p.143-160.

[92] This concept of Greenberg was a result of his great insight that art is not about the precious thing in a neat limited frame on the wall but should enhance the acknowledgement of life in the world (clearly inspired by his interest in Marxist ideology), hence his understanding that large sized paintings offer a better chance to relate the viewer to space itself beyond a limited 'window'. Greenberg also promoted the concept of art for

one has the sensation of looking into it as outsider. When a work is of large size, one gets the immediate sensation of being part of the artwork. The actual sizes of Baroque paintings, of Monet's "Nymphéas", the works by the American Expressionists and works by artists like Frank Stella, Natvar Bhavsar, Gotthard Graubner, or the large coloured wire-works and paintings of my own "The Dragon Series" seem to imply that large sizes improve and intensify an experience of the sublime. The sheer overwhelming properties of a large size seem to result in a faster dissolution of the duality between self and world caused by the artwork. Does size do it all? No, not at all, as also many large sized works merely dwarf the viewer or are experienced as a boring mass of matter - like quite a few huge Minimalist sculptures, some 'installation art' or large screen projections of boring video- or computer-generated art.

see picture 17

Not mere size, but aesthetic innovation is required to overcome the frustration caused by the change of time, which demands a 'tool' for repeatedly finding a re-connection to reality. Donald Kuspit writes:

> *"The idea that one must perpetually renew desire to exist in the fullness of one's being, work with fresh desire, desire that has been liberated from its sedimentation in semiosis, and that can be a source of new semioticization of existence - is the motivation for art, or rather aestheticity, which at its best is experienced as desire rejuvenated and re-energizing life. Every aesthetic innovation is an attempt at the restoration."*[93]

The desire, as in art, for a moment of non-frustration can also be translated into a search for a moment of harmony with the essence of nature, which is equivalent to the search for a moment of symmetry.[94] This can also be understood as moment of dissolving duality and can be related to Santayana's previously discussed desire for perfection: the search for perfection being an intrinsic part of the process of nature. The status of perfection

---

art's sake. Art would be 'pure' when it only concerned itself - neither a depiction of a narrative nor a representation of anything that exists. See Clement Greenberg, "Art and Culture - Critical Essays" (Boston: Beacon Press, 1965 - orig. 1961), p.139. This concept of purity cannot only be related to his political convictions but also emerged in the natural flow of art history. For instance, in the 19th century in Impressionism painting already became about painting itself and not primarily about a depiction, while Kandinsky in 1910 had mentioned that every material has its own properties that the artist should discover and apply. It makes sense that someone like Greenberg understood the next step would concern 'pure art'. Unfortunately this triggered in modern art history a complete fixation on the materials used for artworks and a forgetting of the need for content and perceptual substance.

93 See Donald Kuspit, "Art as the Morale Imperative", in New Art Examiner, January 1991, p.23-25. Kuspit's description, "one must perpetually renew desire to exist in the fullness of one's being", recalls once again the Oriental philosophies of Shinran and Dogen, but also of Vivekananda, etc. They all state more or less the same process: desiring to proceed towards an intense experience leading to the dissolving of the duality of self and world, returning at some point into the 'real world', starting up this process anew, etc.

94 Harmony implies a situation of at least two different forces that are not opposed to or working against each other, but are more or less complementary, forming together a whole. As such, contrast can mean a situation of harmony (like complementary or simultaneous contrasts in colour or form 'work' opposed to each other, but simultaneously enhance each other and thus keep each other in balance). Contrast is not the same as

should be understood as the moment desire is fullfilled, which can be seen, in a metaphorical sence, as a moment of absolute symmetry, a moment in absolute balance, and therefore completely static. A moment one may call a status quo. The ending of this status quo is actually the breaking of this absolute symmetry (or the breaking point) after which desire is rejuvenated, implying that the artist is driven or motivated to reach for the next moment of symmetry by creating a new work.[95] The making of art thus can be compared to a process on the edge of chaos or - even better - on the edge of stability.[96] In direct relation to this stands Donald Kuspit's idea that a search for harmony can also lead naturally to a focus on perfection for it's own sake, ignoring its real meaning. As a result it becomes decadent.[97] This can emerge, for example, from a perfecting of the use of material or of perfecting a certain shape or form and will lead only to a levelling of quality and a kind of mannerism.[98] In my opinion, the serious artist is conscious of this danger and will always balance on the edge of 'an imperfect perfection', which is on the edge between imperfection and perfection, but as close as possible to perfection, an equivalent to working on the edge of chaos.[99] It also refers to the difference between searching for the merely beautiful or searching for the intensity of the sublime. To find the sublime one has to push the limits of the beautiful and cannot stay on secure, safe ground.

Perfection itself - even if it could be accomplished - is no actual option, because real perfection does not allow any change and we can see all through this publication that even though all statements in science, philosophy or art may differ, they all agree that change is the primary, ultimate and basic paradigm for understanding reality! Imperfect perfection is nothing less than doing one's best - delivering the best that is possible given one's capacities. The 'best' is equivalent to a temporary perfection, but as it is temporary it is an imperfect perfection nevertheless. The danger of becoming decadent is real, as the desire to reach the ideal is indeed a search for a kind of perfection.

Leibniz wrote: "To act less perfect than in principle one is capable of, is called acting

opposition. If they were actually opposed, they would annihilate or level each other - if they are not of equal power or force, there is no harmony but an 'unequal contrast' (the balance would tip over, one force would outrule the other). Harmony as such can be understood as a situation of perfect symmetry synonymous to a perfect balance between two equally contrasting forces. There must still always be a contrast, as without contrast there is no change, no difference in force, no life. A moment of symmetry is a moment in which two contrasting forces keep each other in absolute balance, meaning both are of equal strength and the virtual separation between the two tends to become temporarily nil or disappear. Thus in a moment of absolute symmetry the potentiality exists for the unification of the two parts in one whole, the dissolving of duality. Because this is only temporary one may better speak of an asymmetrical-symmetrical process instead of continuous symmetry.

[95] See Prigogene's ideas in §7.6.

[96] Remember the notion of dynamic stability in biology as is found in the centrosome in cells. Compare also the Japanese concept of 'kire-tsuzuki' in §9.

[97] Like certain tendencies in art, for instance some 'concrete art' and some Minimal Art.

[98] See Donald Kuspit, "Dialectic of Decadence" (New York: Stux Press, 1993).

[99] Or, as discussed before, on the edge of stability - stating that pure stability is equivalent to decadence. See also §9.

imperfectly.'[100] In my opinion, Leibniz underscores the necessity of searching for the ideal and thus always offering the best possible. The best possible is still imperfect. Again, not perfection itself, but one's best must be offered. This leads Leibniz's remark back to Kuspit. The continuous desire to offer one's best leads to the result that 'best' can be seen as a 'frozen' moment of the best one could offer. After further development, one will see one may do better, meaning the previous result needs improvement. This coincides with Kuspit's description of the continuous process of rejuvenating desire.

At least since the 19th century, when various persons considered philosophical and artistic implications of the suffering in the world, a conviction emerged that if artists wish to show reality they should not present beautifications of the world, but show the actual world with all its brutality, making everybody conscious of the problems in the world. Philosopher and art critic Arthur Danto describes this process quite well, describing how especially after WWII generations of artists took up their responsibility to answer to social and political tasks.[101] Danto thus describes the need to exemplify disgust in art, meant to make the viewer feel disgusted about the subject expressed by the artwork. This kind of moral task of art is clearly important when art is the sole source of information one has, comparable to how painting functioned in the days before the invention of book-printing, or when the Baroque paintings were informing the illiterate about the suffering of the martyrs. But, since the late 1960's everyone is bombarded every single day by all the bad news in the world through tv news-programs, talk shows, 'reality tv', expressing the suffering in such an overload that it is only natural that a kind of general weariness evolved about art trying to beat the newsmedia by 'examining' ugliness in the world. Life in the world is indeed no 'sublime experience', no joy even, the world will never become a Utopia. No individual in the world can escape the traumas of life, which are for one person more real and more horrible than for another. But if we wish to live at all, while not ignoring nor even attempting to escape the ugliness in the world, we desperately need experiences that provide positive mental incentives.[102] If art ever had any moral obligation, that is where the task lies. One cannot fight ugliness with ugliness. Those who think so are ignoring important features of being human.

---

[100] As early as 1686. See Gottfried Wilhelm Leibniz, "Metaphysische Abhandlung" (Hamburg: Felix Meiner Verlag, 1991 - orig. "Discours de Métaphysique", 1686), p.7: "Et c'est agir imparfaitement, que d'agir avec moins de perfections qu'on n'auroit pu." - "Weniger vollkommen zu handeln, als man eigentlich gekonnt hätte, heißt unvollkommen handeln."

[101] See Arthur C. Danto, "The Abuse of Beauty - Aesthetics and the Concept of Art".

[102] See Donald Kuspit, "The End of Art", (New York + Cambridge UK: Cambridge University Press, 2004), p.190: "Only when art is truly beautiful can it defy the ugliness in life - resist if not defeat it (although modern art sometimes seems like a Pyrrhic victory over life). This creates a small space of momentary happiness within the larger depressing and everlasting ugliness, even if that space is only a stay of execution and illusion. Thus, the aesthetic transformation of ugliness creates the sense of being in subliminal control of the feelings aroused by our consciousness of our own destruction and death - which confirms that we are part of the ugliness of the world. The tragic aura ugliness acquires in art makes us less susceptible to it even as it confirms that it is the permanent flaw in existence."

Our brain, our whole biological system and resulting psyche demand positive incentives for survival. The general need for beauty is also exemplified, in my opinion, by the success of recent exhibitions that show beautiful and well crafted works of art. For instance the Beyeler Foundation in Switzerland is more succesful than many a museum of contemporary art. The Beyeler Foundation doesn't show 'mainstream' art, but good and great art.[103]

It is time that artists become conscious of the danger of the interpretation of the experience of the sublime as an intense negative experience based on horror, or on experiences provoked by works of art that merely offer a temporary escape from suffering. This emphasis on the negative, which was caused by the separation of experiences of beauty and experiences of the sublime in the past two centuries, will never allow one to understand life in reality as being worthwhile. Again without wishing to imply that one should blissfully ignore all suffering in the world, nor to suggest that problems should not be addressed, one cannot avoid acknowledging that it is crucial for one's being to find an explanation for being itself, which fundamentally should be sufficiently positive to allow one to cope with the negative experiences of the world, but also with limited life and death itself. This implies that the renewed combination of beauty and the sublime is essential for a profound positive experience, if we wish to understand and explore our being in the world.[104]

It will be interesting to see if in the future the astonishing development of scientific knowledge relating to the functioning of our brains - or the further explorations of the impact of our genes on our thinking - will throw even more or rather, other, lights on our understanding of the notions beauty and the sublime. An interesting example could be if certain chemical reactions in our brain involved in experiences of beauty and the sublime have some meaning for our physical well-being and health. The information provided in §5 on the close relationships between the functioning of the brain, body, and the perceived (the object, phenomenon or work of art) seems to offer reasons why such a neurophysical explanation is not an entirely strange hypothesis.[105] This would also

[103] For instance the fabulous exhibition on colour and light. See Ernst Beyeler, Markus Brüderlin, Reinhold Hohl, "Farbe-Licht" (Riehen, CH: Fondation Beyeler, Hatje Cantz Verlag, 2000).

[104] See Fons Elders, "The Sublime and the Beautiful - On Ontology and Creative Imagination", p.40: "The principle of the Sublime has found refuge in the desire of humans toward the Sublime, the world of Orgasm, the contempt of Death. But if the principle of the Sublime is linked to the Death-principle, it needs the principle of Beauty for a companion. It needs a guide who takes care that the desire for the sublime does not end in total destruction, either of one self, or other humans. Art that chooses a priori to be present within the walls of a museum, is not the art to guide us within the domain of the sublime." See also Donald Kuspit, "The End of Art", p.160: "Art becomes empty and hollow when it no longer makes life feel timely and vivid - when it no longer seduces us to life, as Nietzsche said - and when it no longer makes us the gift of immortality by suggesting it through its own aesthetic substance."

[105] After having finished this manuscript, I found further reasons for this hypothesis in a scientific discussion on the implications of melatonin for understanding our daily rhythm of being awake and sleeping. See Steven H. Strogatz, "SYNC - How Order Emerges from Chaos in the Universe, Nature, and Daily Life" (New York: Theia Books, Hyperion, 2003), p. 99. Melatonin is a brain hormone produced by the pineal gland

imply that there are physical reasons for having experiences comparable for every human being from whatever culture and time, though not exactly similar (cultures are obviously still different). It would provide new meaning to 'universal experience' and would show that metaphysics in art is not just a preference of the individual artist, not a cultural or temporal phenomenon, but a necessary and natural result of our human condition. The way our bodies and our brains work demands concepts of a metaphysical character.

8.5 SOME THOUGHTS FROM INDUSTRIAL DESIGN

In industrial design a concern exists related to this discussion about perfection, making this discussion as realistic and applicable to everyday life as discussing economics, trade or politics. Regarding the decision-making process in the designing of industrial products, there are designers or design-managers who really and critically are concerned about the perception-value of the product.[106] It certainly is meaningful that to guarantee a market-success it does not seem to be enough for a product to merely offer new or technologically improved user-possibilities, to be shaped and produced perfectly, or just to be cheaper. This is exemplified for example by Dr. Stefano Marzano, who as senior-director of Philips Corporate Design is reponsible for the design qualities of all products from this large multinational: "Somewhere along the way, the relationship between the consumer and the product has gone wrong. There is a considerable disaffection with products that are overdesigned and over-complicated."[107] This mirrors quite well the same thing that happened in art: 'overdesign' as equivalent to perfection for its own sake. Marzano has lead Philips towards a new vision for the industrial product. His ideas are related to Alberto Alessi's opinions.

The Italian design philosopher, design- and industry manager is not without reason so succesful with his specially designed utensils. He has thought a lot about the importance of objects in our environment, and he understands the importance of feeling and desire in design. This becomes clear in a publication on a workshop in which the products are not photographed as usual, in splendid isolation, as if they were artifacts in a museum, but in their natural environment in our homes, among many other products and furniture. Alessi advocates that designers should be concerned with what he calls 'the language of objects', which he considers to be a universal language.[108] It is, therefore,

---

and is highly responsive to light (the secretion of melatonin plummets when the eyes receive day light). When one just briefly recalls that colour and light are the same phenomenon and that contrasts of colours and forms can enhance or dim the brightness of any phenomenon (or artwork) in our eye-sight, it may indeed not be a mere hypothesis to expect that one day scientists will find 'the sublime' - brain hormone.

106 Most persons that are interested in fine art or philosophy might find this a surprise. It should not be so, because of course industrial (consumer) products are objects in our environment, therefore, all that has been said in §7 and §8 should also concern industrial or architectural design.

107 See Stefano Marzano, "Flying over Las Vegas" (Eindhoven: EDC News Special September 1993), p.14 (emphasis mine).

108 See Alberto Alessi, "F.F.F. Family Follows Fiction - Workshop 1991-1993" (Centro Studi Alessi, 1993) writes in relation to this workshop with the theme "SMI" (Sensoriality - Memory - Imagination), emphasis

hardly surprising that Alessi advocates design with properties similar to a mixture of poetry and novels, appealing to all the senses and to deeper sentiments (perhaps to the essence?), and is quite wary of mannerism or dead perfection, which does not communicate anything. The Japanese industrial designer, philosopher and Shin Buddhist priest Kenji Ekuan writes:

> *"The idea to become a designer comes from the wish, phantasy, and a desire to escape the original insecurity* ***caused by a lack of understanding life by expressing a world image.*** *Salvation of the world through tools - the benefit of tools is to put people at rest and make them feel secure through the medium of a world image."*

And:

> *"The birth of a new tool gives rise to desire for the next one in the human world of Utopia. A questioning of the act of creation. With response as a shield, the will to go on to the next creative act is born. This constitutes the eternal movement of creativity. The catalyst of creation is desire. The catalyst of desire is phantasy, and the catalyst of phantasy is wish."*[109]

In a metaphoric sense, a tool is a very useful notion for exemplifying the property of man-made objects, including consumer products and works of art, to support our efforts to do something, like trying to get a hold on reality. As such, Ekuan emphasizes the need to create objects for acquiring an idea of the world or of the essence. He clearly agrees with Kuspit's emphasis on desire and the rejuvenation of desire as the drive for creativity and - exemplified here also by Alessi - the need for the object.

---

mine: "Its [the industrial product] purpose is to gauge the sensorial pleasure and the grip on the public's imagination which, though in very different ways, are inherent in all the things we make. I would say that its objective is to find out better when and why people 'like' a particular product; in short, to substitute for 'Beauty' a number of cognitive data, likewise certainly arguable and approximative, but at least more complex and I believe more stimulating. Implied here would be the postulate that people are sensitive and permeable to the language of objects, in a much deeper and subtler way than is usually supposed; and that this language is much more universal, direct and (perhaps) democratic than we, particularly we who operate in 'cultivated' design, have believed so far."

109 See Kenji Ekuan, "Theory of Desire - Concerning the Source of Creation", in "A Prayer Design", SD Space Design Special Extra Issue No.19, "A Design Declaration - GK's 30 Year History", January 1988 (emphasis mine). Kenji Ekuan has been a major influence on Japanese design since the 1940's and he is an advisor of multinational industries and the Japanese Ministery of Culture and the Ministery of Economics. In my interpretation, Ekuan's use of the notion 'tool' can also be understood as product or artifact, because any artifact can help you as an intermediary like a virtual tool (like understanding space) or accomplishing something (like eating). Ekuan has accomplished a translation of Shinran's philosophy into the pragmatics of industrial design. For an introduction into the ideas of Shin Buddhism or Shinshu, see Takashi Hirose, "Lectures on Shin Buddhism" (Kyoto: Higashi Honganji Publication Department, revised edition 1988 - orig.1980). See footnote 9, earlier in this chapter. On Ekuan's ideas, see Kenji Ekuan, "The Aesthetics of the Japanese Lunchbox", edited by David Stewart (Cambridge, MA: MIT Press, 2000 - orig. Tokyo: Goma Shobo, 1980). A brilliant and very readable set of essays explaining the capacity of the compactness and beauty of the Japanese lunchbox to focus one's attention on the joy of life, every single day again (Ekuan argues that the Japanese lunchbox is both metaphor and prototype for the best design in Japan, offering also non-Japanese simple, straigtforward enjoyment and excitement in everyday life based on sophisticated principles of structure and beauty).

8.6 SOME THOUGHTS FROM BIOLOGY

Quite an interesting similar/different view on our desire for repeatedly finding a renewed equilibrium is presented by modern biology, showing that this process is not merely a psychological or philosophical interpretation of the human mind. Biologist William J.M. Hrushesky writes,

"Why do all living organisms do virtually everything cyclically? Daily cycles of life, as well as seasonal and monthly ones, arose, quite simply, because life evolved on this planet. The waxing and waning of light, heat and electromagnetic and gravitational forces caused rhythmic changes both in the availability of energy and in the physical medium in which evolution was unfolding. But even more basic than the happenstance of geophysical location to evolution, the rhythmic organization of temporal processes maximizes the stability of living things and ensures that they not waste precious energy. ***Life's absolute need for stability requires continuous readjustment to external and internal dynamic requirements.*** *The adjustment can be pictured as cyclical: a phase of activation or production; then an assessment of stability; a 'midcourse correction', based on feedback from the outcome of the activity in the first phase of the cycle; and a return to the beginning of the cycle. A second cycle of activity then begins at the optimum time if it would promote stability. If stability is already optimum, the first phase of the new cycle begins with minimal or non-existent productive activity. The breakdown of such cyclical temporal ordering has lethal consequences for the organism. One of the most important and practical applications of the emerging understanding of the role of cycle in biology is the treatment of disease."*[110]

The search for renewal of an equilibrium adjusted to the changing circumstances is of importance for survival.[111] We may see Hrusheshky's description also as a successful definition of the creative process. Would it be very far-fetched to consider the drive of a biological system to fight a disease as equivalent to the psychological drive in our minds to fight frustration - to find happiness - especially because happiness clearly is also a 'health-issue'?[112]
Once more it is of interest to quote Ekuan:

---

[110] See William J.M. Hrushesky, "Timing is Everything", The Sciences, July/August 1994 (emphasis mine), p.32. See also about Friedrich Cramer, §7, footnote 76.

[111] So, our frustration over a given situation could well be a built-in mechanism to survive by searching for this renewal!

[112] See Donald Kuspit, "Happiness, Health, and Related Anomalies of Avant Garde Art", in Lynn Gamwell and Donald Kuspit, "Health and Happiness" (Ithaca, NY: Cornell University Press, 1996), p.25: "It [happiness] is a peculiarly dynamic kind of equilibrium, with a strong sense of purpose and identity, autonomy and energy. Above all, in my opinion, it is self-analytic, and as such a form of self-regulation - a resolution of conflict without the resulting stasis and dead end associated with the usual concepts of happiness (mentioned above). In other words, happiness involves resolving the tension between the death and life instincts, their mutual acknowledgement and acceptance." Again, this seems quite well related to principle thinking in Eastern philosophies and religions, like the finding of the 'True Self' in the combination of the dynamics of

"Temporary culture - a system of emptiness. Metabolism and succession - the structure of health. The structure of preservation of freshness. A structure that leaves nothing behind. Fascination with change brings about the joy of creation. The urge towards reproduction brings about happiness. ***Reproduction and change*** *are the two aspects of creativity."*[113]

He clearly emphasizes that *change* is not a bad thing and that change will turn frustration into joy. And as we have seen previously, joy has everything to do with experiencing beauty.

The moment we are able to describe the clear but changing coherence between ourselves - our group - and the whole (of nature), we will have found the essence and have understood being. One may also say: at that moment we understand the concept of nature and of life itself, we will loose our sense of frustration. Of course, we experience moments of some understanding, moments in which we experience beauty and joy - as Ekuan mentions. However great, these are not lasting. If we already possessed a complete understanding then we would no longer have a need for collecting knowledge. The dissatisfaction with the level of knowledge we do have - based also on the conviction that there is more knowledge to be obtained - motivates our search for more and better knowledge. Besides, it is a given fact that in the very structure and composition of our biological being there is an eternal drive for action. The flow of blood and other fluids, our whole bio-system, our actual breathing process, all demand motion. Desiring to avoid all physical or mental action would be suicide. One might also say that it would indeed be against our existence as natural beings to continuously have a happy smile on our faces - and an intrinsic impossibility (how can one have a profound and deep experience of happiness when one has never experienced unhappiness?). The fluctuations between happiness - sadness - happiness are a natural result of our very being. Therefore, frustration and desire have to be accepted as natural processes that are not to be avoided. Artworks seem to work so well in their capacity to help us come to terms with this strange contradictory process.

8.7 THE OBJECT AS MEDIUM IN THE HOLO-MOVEMENT

The projection of our conclusions, our reactions, our interpretations, outside our body as object - for instance as artifacts or artworks - forms an important part of the development of knowledge.[114] Just as in every other process of argumentation in which

continuous change in nature at everyday level with the sheer infinite calmness of the eternal continuation of this process at the largest macro level (when we look around us, all and everything continuously changes, when we look up at a clear night sky, we apparently think we are seeing total calmness).

113 See Kenji Ekuan, "Concerning Appearance of Change", SD Space Design Special Extra Issue No.19, "A Design Declaration - GK's 30 Year History", January 1988 (emphasis mine). Reproduction brings to mind the need to relate artifacts to memory, in the sense of Bergson.

114 See §5 and §7.

this projection is evaluated continuously during the process of perception, objects play a fundamental role in our individual search for coherence. The notion of object is meant here as both two-dimensional and three-dimensional object. A good example of our need for creating objects to focus our mind is the Kalachakra-Mandala ritual by Tibetan monks, building a mandala on a cloth lying on the floor. This ritual concerns an elaborate and predetermined process using coloured sand. The spiritual concentration plays an important role during this ritual and is enhanced by the act of precise working. In addition, the ritual of sandcolouring is preceded by an inauguration with dance and music, with the goal of focussing attention.[115] The North American Navajo Indians also use sandpaintings as part of a performance that continues for a period varying from one to nine days.[116] Additionally, in the Tibetan and in the Navajo sandpainting rituals one can find a clear use of geometry, bright colours, colour contrasts and a breaking of symmetry. These are religious rituals that are quite interesting, because their essence is so close to our everyday functioning: a combination of thinking and acting, for which the action of doing enhances and focuses thinking (heightening attention). Bertrand Russell writes on Karl Marx:

"In Marx's view, all sensation or perception is an interaction between subject and object; the bare object, apart from the activity of the percipient, is a mere raw material, which is transformed in the process of becoming known. Knowledge in the old sense of passive contemplation is an unreal abstraction; the process that really takes place is one of handling things."[117]

Marx's emphasis also confirms the importance of manipulation in the process of self-argumentation. Making, creating art obviously concerns basically a handling of materials but also as Donald Kuspit says: "Instead of conceiving art as total transformation, it is best conceived, more subtly, as a mode of transition or mediation between the self and the work."[118] The art critic Clement Greenberg insisted that a work of art should have an identity. This identity allows the object to virtually speak to the viewer by becoming related to the identity of the viewer. When the object has no clear identity in the perception of the viewer it will never be more than a mere object. In such a case the object provokes no unique experience for the viewer and one can only consider its material and

---

115 See Martin Brauen, "Das Mandala - Der Heilige Kreis im tantrischen Buddhismus" (Cologne: DuMont Verlag, 1992). See also §5, especially §5.7, §5.8.

116 These performances are referred to as a 'chant' or a 'sing'. See Franc J. Newcomb and Gladys A. Reichard, "Sandpaintings of the Navajo Shooting Chant" (New York: Dover Publications, Inc., 1975 - orig. published by J.J. Augustin, NY, 1937). Quite often these sandpaintings also are built in a circular composition including rotation symbols, magnificent examples are the "Whirling Snakes" and "Whirling Mount".

117 See Bertrand Russell, "The History of Western Philosophy", p.749.

118 See Donald Kuspit, "Signs of Psyche in Modern and Post-Modern Art" (London, New York: Cambridge University Press, 1995 - first edition 1993), p. 298. Compare also the fascinating parallel between the meaning of geometry by the Islam and by the Kaiapo-indians as described earlier in this chapter.

handcraft properties.[119] These properties are obviously very important, though not enough to allow just any well made artifact to provoke the experience of art. Simultaneously, because a work of art is realized in our projective field, an artist cannot avoid using media that answer to the characteristics of our perceptable reality, meaning the use of material, energy, light, colour, sound, form and space. Furthermore, obviously every viewer is an individually different self. In a simplified way this means that the self consists in part of universal properties and in part of more unique properties, which we consider to be individual. Universality concerns those characteristics that are similar to all people, that define us as part of a group, of mankind, of the fauna, of nature. Individuality is a result of the fact that all of us are born at different locations and times in the complexity of space/time and grow up under continuously changing circumstances that vary from each other.[120] Through time, along the roads of evolution, these differences have become more complex and extended; for example through the evolution of genetical codes.

Therefore, individuality in fact is a sort of subdivision of universality, explaining why we all feel ourselves to be individuals, but have still so many things in common with other human beings and the rest of nature. Many ideas and theories discussed so far in this publication show how essentially everything, every phenomenon, including ourselves, consists of quantities of energy - kinds of knots in the complex and N-dimensional fields of energy that continuously flow through space/time - electromagnetic energy. Nishida wrote:

> *"If we were able to explain all physical phenomena in terms of electromagnetic energy, matter would be identical with electricity and objects would no longer be defined primarily in tactile terms, but in terms of the phenomena of light perception."*[121]

Early on Nishida seems to have hit the nail on its head. The self, on this reading, would also be a certain amount of energy (paths of waves) connected to all other things, though still unique because of the circumstances of its birth and localization in space/time.

Philosopher Vilém Flusser described the self - the important property of individuality - as a unique entity, but simultaneously as a junction in a complex net of streams of information.[122] Is the emergence of individuality in the world analogous to the phe-

---

[119] See Clement Greenberg, "Art and Culture - Critical Essays", p.67: "Modernist pictorial art, with its more explicit decorativeness, calls more attention to the immediate physical qualities of painting. But like any other kind of picture, the modernist one still assumes that its identity as a picture shuts out awareness of its identity as an object. Otherwise it becomes, at best, sculpture, at worst, a *mere* object."

[120] Circumstances that may differ fundamentally in social, cultural, economical or political conditions. Conditions that have an impact on the availablity of, the access to and the choices of nutrition, education, and other basics of general development - which all have a profound impact on individuality.

[121] See Kitaro Nishida, "Intuition and Reflection in Self-Consciousness", p.118.

[122] See Vilém Flusser, "Ins Universum der technischen Bilder" (Göttingen: European Photography, 1992),

nomenon of a single thought emerging in our brian? Individuality is a result of continuously changing circumstances and can be immediately understood as proof of the impossibility of autonomy and as a result of the complexity of interactions in the holomovement of the macro- and microcosmos in which we partake.[123] Autonomy would be possible only if there could be a being unaffected by changing circumstances, which is not possible. The idea of a possible autonomy feeds the still popular belief in the duality of mind and body. This duality is nonsense and only a theoretical assumption. It implies that mind, soul, spirit and body can be imagined as separate entities, apparently without any interaction with the environment. Clearly this is unlikely. Mind, soul, spirit and body as separate notions were invented by man to proclaim and emphasize religious dogmas. By advertising the doctrine that mind, soul, spirit and body are separate entities, one can condemn the weakness of the body and, simultaneously, one can offer salvation through the possibility of an escape for the soul. This may lead to a system by which one can offer hope to the suffering. History has taught us that this allows for a totalitarian power over believers.

All man-made notions (including specially designed languages like mathematics) seem always to lead to academic definitions that introduce endless discussions about their meaning and implications, endless adjustments of the definitions. However interesting these discussions can be, they tend to miss the point of the essence of reality completely. Many, if not all, of these notions are human inventions as means to some end, but often become ends in themselves. The danger is evident: the original reason for the creation for these notions (to support a better understanding) gets lost in the debates. Notions we adopt often become doctrines, aspects of our culture, which influence our perception of reality and of ourselves.

Nevertheless, we will always need such notions (or a scientific language like mathematics) to be able to discuss with ourselves and with others our ideas for extending our knowledge, but we should never forget that these notions do not offer the final or precise knowledge about reality all by themselves. They are the tools for finding knowledge.

---

p.100: "The so-called 'I' is a junction in a net of dialogically flowing information and a storage for information that passed through (meaning it is inherited as well as also, to a much greater extent, collected information), and at this junction there emerge unexpected, illogical computations, new information. This new information is experienced as purposeful, freely decided, because every 'I' is an unique junction and distinguishes itself from all other junctions in the net by its position and by the information it has stored. Such a picturing of 'purpose' is not only implied by neurophysiology, but also reflects many other visions that we receive from other disciplines."("Das sogenannte 'Ich' ist ein Knotenpunkt in einem Netz von dialogisch strömende Informationen und ein Lager für durchgegangene Informationen (und zwar sowohl von ererbten als auch, zum weitaus größeren Teil, von erworbenen Informationen), und an diesem Knotenpunkt entstehen unvorhergesehene, unwahrscheinliche Komputationen, neue Informationen. Diese neue Informationen werden als beabsichtigt, frei entschieden empfunden, weil jedes 'Ich' ein einzigartiger Knotenpunkt ist und sich von allen übrigen Knotenpunkten im Netz durch seine Stellung und die in ihm gelagerten Informationen unterscheidet. Eine derartige Schilderung der 'Absicht' drängt sich nicht nur von der Neurophysiologie her auf, sondern sie entspricht auch vielen anderen Einsichten, die wir aus anderen Disziplinen gewinnen.")

123 Holomovement is a notion proposed by David Bohm and Basil Hiley. See David Bohm and Basil Hiley,

Therefore, we should always be open to arguments that show that the notions we are familiar with are just wrong. The existence of a word or a notion does not prove by itself that it exists as a real phenomenon! This illustrates one of man's difficulties: we need to communicate, but at the same time we have to accept the limited precision of all our communication!

Experiencing truth, goodness, beauty or the sublime all happen in the duality of the object and self. Our being able to be perceptive of all actual objects around us, while also having the capacity to virtually look beyond this, allows us to find truth in understanding our limited individual existence within the eternal and infinite process of nature. The experience of beauty is our inborn sensibility for finding our individual access to beauty. The beauty of objects focuses our attention to the level that the duality of ourselves and the world - nature - dissolves in an intense experience of the sublime. Only when we can realize that an experience of the sublime is introduced or accompanied by beauty will we be able to find consolation in our being and in our self. Simultaneously, it is evidently important to understand, acknowledge and accept that such experiences are not long lasting and continuously have to be renewed.

"The Undivided Universe - An Ontological Interpretation of Quantum Theory" (London: Routledge, 1995 - orig. 1993), p.357: "We may suppose that the universe, which includes the whole of existence, contains not only all the fields that are now known, but also an indefinitely large set of further ideas that are unknown and indeed may be never known in their totality. Recalling that the essential qualities of fields exist only in their movement we propose to call this ground the holomovement. It follows that ultimately everything in the explicate order of common experience arises from the holomovement. Whatever persists with a constant form is constantly renewed by enfoldment and dissolved by unfoldment. When the renewal ceases the form vanishes."

§9 GREATNESS UNDER THE THREAT OF DECADENCE

Don't think of what you have to do, don't consider how to carry it out! Kenzo Awa[1]

Decadence in a work of art exists when the appearance of the work offers so little or so much information that we cannot find any information in it. For our perception to be sufficiently stimulated and our attention to be sufficiently focussed we need neither too little nor too much visual impulse provided by a work of art. The scale between both extremes is defined by a natural sense of visual attraction, which is an attraction of the (biological) eye-brain perception, not by a process in which the brain first rationalizes whether what one is seeing is interesting. When a work of art does not arouse our perception in a natural way, when a work of art does not function in a way that helps us to focus our minds, then we may call that work of art decadent.

The threat of decadence looms above all serious creativity, but nevertheless must not be exaggerated. There are more serious problems in life. It is beside the point whether decadence as a phenomenon has a reason to exist, because it can be quite entertaining, amusing, simply fun or answer to basic drives like lust for power or lust itself. Thus, interests in decadence may also distract from everyday problems and, like any form of entertainment, offer some short escape, though it can never offer any deep experience. Needless to say, if one wishes to find consolation in more profound experiences, one has to be aware of the threat of decadence to be able to avoid it. When we take art as experience serious it becomes important to understand the why and how to push to the very limits and achieve greatness in art. Greatness is the opposite of decadence, but still lies very close to it. Push a little too far and a great work becomes a decadent one. The limits towards which artists have to push cannot be precisely defined, but still one can sense them to be more or less defined by the threat of decadence.

In this context it will be easy to understand that human creativity is driven by the search for an ideal.[2] We desire to find truth about ourselves by searching to expose the truth of nature's reality. Our immersion in nature defines our perception and acknow-

---

1 Sword master Kenzo Awa. See Eugen Herrigel, "Zen in the Art of Archery" (New York: Pantheon Books Inc., 7th printing, 1963 - orig. "Zen in der Kunst des Bogenschiessens", Munich: Otto Wilhelm Barth Verlag, 1953). Awa clearly implies to trust one's intuition based on a 'giving ourselves' over to the immersion in nature as a whole that can only be accomplished by being able to go beyond the self-inflicted restrictions of the ego-centric attitude - to let our acts of creativity (the combination of 'head and hands') virtually flow with the flow of continuous changing nature. When we reason too much from the ego-centric level we desire too much to follow the kind of logic that we prescribe in words to ourselves and thus will lead to decadence, because whatever art will be the result, it will fail the vividness of life.

2 It will be obvious that I am concerned about serious art based on profound and sincere motivations of the involved artists to mature towards 'greatness' - a difficult notion that I will attempt to define later in this chapter; though the large quantity of exhibitions in galleries and museums show there are also reasons for the existence assumed for art with very different objectives - like purely political activist or commercially motivated or plainly entertaining or with no apparent objectives at all - I am <u>not</u> concerned with these kinds of art.

ledgement of what is real. There is no such thing as an objective opinion outside the realm of the processes of nature. Again: nature not merely as landscape, but as the all-engulfing process including everything from macro- to micro-nature. The search for the ideal - in science, philosophy or art - always has been a search for mutual conclusions of individual approaches in which intuition plays an important role. Intuition is the combination of conscious and unconscious decisions in an open but still structured process of focussing attention, involving memory, logic and feelings. As discussed before, beauty (sensing beauty, looking for beauty, experiencing beauty) is the leading motive of our intuition in this search for the ideal. The experience of the sublime is the highest experience of being close to intuitively acknowledging the total immersion in the whole of nature. Searching for the experience of the sublime is difficult to orchestrate. One cannot exactly define what one is looking for. Simultaneously there is only a thin line between an experience of the sublime and mere dramatic spectacle. The search for the ideal always must involve high risks of reaching - stretching oneself - towards the limits of what one is capable of. Reaching for greatness makes the threat of decadence immanent.

We experience beauty when we experience some truth in or unification with nature. We experience the sublime when we experience a moment of the eternal process of harmony and dissonance (a breaking of harmony) within the dynamics of nature. Experiencing beauty is sensing the existence of truth, but still from the outside. Experiencing the sublime is so overwhelming that it can be described as feeling truth while being immersed in it, feeling from the inside unified with what is outside ourselves. One can recall this feeling by imagining experiences one can often have in nature (here understood as 'landscape'): walking for hours through a drizzling rain, standing in a meadow and letting gusts of strong wind virtually flow through oneself, diving in the crashing waves of the surf.[3] Obviously one may also experience this while listening to music or focussing on a work of fine art.

[3] Swiss painter Ferdinand Hodler (1853-1918) standing on the edge of a tranquil lake referred to the experience as if one stood on the edge of the universe, an experience of unision with the universe one can find especially in his later paintings of lakes, blurry mountains and clouds like his "Landschafticher Formenrhythmus (Genfersee)" (1909) "Grüner Abendhimmel am Genfersee" (1915), "Sonnenuntergang am Genfersee von Craux aus" (1917). These are experiences he also must have felt standing high on mountain tops, exemplified in his magnificent "Eiger, Mönch und Jungfrau im Mondschein" (1908). See Beat Wismer, "Ferdinand Hodler, Piet Mondrian: Eine Begegnung" (Baden, CH: Verlag Lars Müller, 1998), p.37, quoting Johannes Widmer who reported on a walk with Hodler along the Genfersee (Lake Geneva): "Do you see how on the other side everything dissolves in lines and space? Is it not to you as if you stand on the edge of earth and can freely roam the universe? That is what I will paint now!" ("Sehen Sie, wie da drüben alles in Linien und Raum aufgeht? Ist Ihnen nicht, als ob Sie am Rand der Erde stünden und frei mit dem All verkehrten? Solches werde ich fortan malen!") - besides the point here, but this final conclusion of Hodler is also almost where Mondrian started his important quest, like in his famous "Pier and Ocean" drawings and paintings - this point is made by Beat Wismer in this very interesting catalogue of a magnificent show, while emphasizing both artists did not actually meet. See also Stephen F. Eisenman and Oskar Bätschmann, "Ferdinand Hodler - Landscapes" (Zürich: Swiss Institute for Art Research, 1987 - a catalogue of a show touring the USA).

Beauty should not be mistaken for the many degrees of aesthetic experiences we have. Although I am well aware of the danger of trying to define in words what, as experience, actually cannot be put into words so precisely - regardless of the long history of complex and often highly academic aesthetic or semiotic theories - I will still try to approach the difference between beauty and mere aesthetic experiences. Aesthetic experiences, provoked for instance by very well done handcraft, perfect industrial production, fashion or by pure symmetrical compositions in art or monochrome painting, are not to be undervalued, because they provide different levels of pleasure. Nevertheless, they are not very deep experiences.[4] Although in truth all experiences of beauty and aesthetics do not seem to last, truly deep experiences of beauty can lead to experiences of the sublime that can be so intense that they stand out from simple aesthetic pleasure. Probably this is so, because simple aesthetic pleasure provides us only with a sense of pure perfect harmony on an easily accessible level, which is too poor a picture of the dynamic harmony in nature as we know or as we sense it. A state of perfect harmony can be translated into a situation of perfect symmetry. The dynamics in nature make us always aware that harmony can exist, but always temporarily, and perfect harmony is an unnatural ideal. This means that in nature, in reality, in life, a situation of symmetry will always be broken. One may sense harmony, one may long for harmony, but only while one acknowledges that this harmony will be a temporary state. One therefore cannot speak of harmony as a moment of perfect symmetry but as a moment that is on the verge of breaking symmetry.[5] The sensation of a harmony on the verge of being broken is triggered in our perception by works of art that contain various contrasts. That is also why often artifacts that are meant to evoke easy aesthetic pleasure avoid glaring contrasts, while in artifacts that evoke beauty large contrasts are essential. Not only in artifacts, but in general (like in the play of sunlight, the wind, and the clouds), contrasts might exist within the subject or object that produces the experience of beauty or between it and its environment. Such contrasts grasp our attention and open us to the deep experience.

Beauty is a situation experienced on the verge of change, like a beautiful smile or a stroke of sunlight. If everyone was continuously happy, smiling, joyful and dancing, we could not experience happiness. Happiness and suffering are naturally linked and are properties of the same experience of changes in life, differing merely in degree and intensity. We need dualities in everyday life. If there was no duality, life would be 'monochrome', and we would not be capable of experiencing anything, definitely not the sublime. Of course, already our biological bodies provide evidence that without dualities we

[4] This is one of the reasons for the existence and need for rapid change of trends - besides the obvious sales - pushing and promoting. It must be emphasized that this definition cannot be seen as dogmatic rule or law, because for instance the tradition of Zen-inspired ceramics in Japan and Korea are also based on handcraft, but clearly do incorporate everything that also makes fine art stand out from any serial products! Although it sounds rather cliché, vague or too abstract, basically the criterium is with what intention the artifact is created, indeed what for instance Kenzo Awa meant!

[5] See on Prigogene in §7.6.

could not even exist.[6] Duality can be understood as 'contrast in a certain relationship', thus also proving the essential application of contrast in art, including contrasts of colour, form, size and space.[7] The sublime is the experience beyond the moment of dissolving duality and is absolute quietness - even if it is only for a moment. While a deep experience of beauty still involves looking at an object, an experience of the sublime is feeling part of it.[8] It should not be necessary to point out that it is still rather naive to only distinguish between simple aesthetics - beauty - the sublime.

There are too numerous in-between variations - again differing in degree and intensity, something everyone may experience while walking through a museum. In the end what matters are the varying degrees of experienced intensity provoked by a work of art. The intensity will be caused by contrasting relationships of colours, forms, sizes, and shapes. When no or too few of these contrasting relationships exist in a composition, any degree of intensity will be nullified in our perception. Too many contrasts will only annihilate the desired effect of contrasts, resulting in the absence of contrast (this is often the case in decorations). While we still will 'see' the work, there are no impulses that focus our attention. The artifact is unable to touch us deeply, it is merely boring, and can be considered 'decadent'. Such works of art may provoke one to turn inwards, to retreat into oneself, comparable with looking at a blank wall. If, however, one wishes not only to momentarely escape reality but desires to acknowledge one's temporary existence in reality and one's part in the eternal flow of space and time, one needs an experience that allows an incorporation of one's self inside and outside one's mind and body. This can only happen in a deep experience of the sublime, opened by an artifact that incorporates the right amount of contrasts. One may imagine the experience of the desired degrees of contrasts and intensities as a wavy pattern, consisting of highs and lows allowing combinations of virtual cuts and continuums in our experience (while a boring or decadent work of art merely mirrors a straight linear pattern - a non-changing continuous line).

To illuminate this concept from another angle it seems relevant to discuss a few notions from Japanese culture. This will also emphasize that this description of experiences in cuts and continuums does not only exist in western thinking. The first notion is the

[6] The necessary differences of force between left and right chambers of your heart, the actual presence of both life and death in the 'commando-chain' in our very cells, the necessary differences in force between hormones or cells can be understood as dualities.

[7] With justification one can argue that contrast always means one thing in opposition to another thing. For example, a colour can only be called 'in contrast' when it is juxtaposed against another colour. I define duality as 'contrast in a certain relationship' for the sake of emphasizing the necessity of understanding the importance of all things in relation to other things. As an illustration, Piet Mondrian emphasized the necessity of acknowledging relationships, which clearly forms the foundation of his Neo-Plastic paintings.

[8] Will Grohmann, the art historian who personally knew Kandinsky, wrote, see Will Grohmann, "Wassily Kandinsky - Life and Work" (New York: Harry N. Abrams Inc., 1958), p.31: "Kandinsky had the impression of moving about inside his pictures, of living inside pictures - an experience of which he later became conscious when he invited the beholder to 'take a walk' in his pictures, and tried 'to compel him to forget him-self, to dissolve himself in the picture'."

Japanese notion 'katachi', which cannot be translated precisely. It refers to specific relations and to connectedness. It concerns notions like form, shape, pattern or Gestalt.[9] In contemporary Japanese thinking it can also be understood as a combination of symmetry and a state of dissymmetry, which in my opinion seems similar to a breaking of symmetry or the edge of stability. I do not mean symmetry here strictly in a geometrical sense, but as being in equilibrium.[10] Ryosuke Ohashi describes how in Japanese culture the notion kire-tsuzuki, literally cut-continuum, plays an important role through Zen-Buddhism:

> *"Kire-tsuzuki is a structure in which opposed events each infiltrate into the interior of the other and disassociate both from each other simultaneously. The art that expresses such a structure is the art of* ***kire****."*[11]

In contemporary art in Japan one can find examples in the sculptures by Jiro Sugawara. Sugawara breaks a stone open to re-assemble all parts again in a different way, confronting the viewer with the characteristics or powers of the stone present on the inside as well as on the outside. 'Kire-tsuzuki' does not only seem analogous to Prigogene's notion of breaking points (a break being similar to a cut), but also seems equivalent to a temporal equilibrium, because of its paradox of being a cut and a continuum.[12] Cut can be understood as a moment of stagnation in an ongoing process or as a moment of symmetry (a moment opposing forces hold each other at bay, cutting off any further process). This moment of stagnation is temporary. At some point in time (in the continuum) a change in the circumstances may have an effect on this stagnation causing the process to continue again. This is the moment symmetry is broken.[13] Everyone experiences the continual change in their own environment, including the process of aging, and seeming to pass through time unconscious of one's own changes. Kitaro Nishida, wrote:

> *"When we say that experience is discontinuous, we already presuppose the continuity of the self; without consciousness of continuity we could not conceive discontinuity."*[14]

---

[9] See T. Ogawa, K. Miura, T. Masunari, D. Nagy, "Katachi u Symmetry" (Tokyo: Springer Verlag, 1996). Compare also §2.

[10] Ibid., p.27-46.

[11] See Ryosuke Ohashi, "Kire - Das 'Schöne' in Japan - Philosophisch-ästhetische Reflexionen zu Geschichte und Moderne" (Cologne: DuMont Verlag, 1994), p.66: "Kire-tsuzuki ist eine Struktur, in der einander Entgegengesetztes sich jeweils bis ins Innere des Andern durchdringt und sich beide zur gleichen Zeit vollkommen von einander abheben. Die Kunstfertigkeit, die eine solche Struktur gestalterisch zum Ausdruck bringt, ist die Kunst des kire."

[12] See §7.6.

[13] Arnold Mandell, stated in 1977 that in biology an absolute equilibrium, quite comparable to perfect symmetry, means death - and death is certainly a cut in life. See James Gleick, "Chaos - de derde wetenschappelijke revolutie" (Amsterdam: Uitgeverij Contact, 1991 - orig. "Chaos: making a new science", 1987), p.268.

[14] In 1915. See Kitaro Nishida, "Intuition and Reflection in Self-Consciousness" (Albany, NY: State

This is a clear example of how duality functions in Japanese thinking. Discontinuity can be understood as the equivalent of a cut ('kire'). The tradition of free style and expressive calligraphy or 'sho' is a good example. The strong dynamic brushstrokes put down in an immediate gesture show power and motion, while their sheer frozen immobility cuts this motion off (after the brush-stroke sinks in, it obviously will never move again). Koichi Nasu made geometric paintings in which lines and very sensuous colour planes are combined on shaped canvases. The lines are clear references to continuity, but not infinity, as they are cut or seem to bounce back from the sides of the canvas. The use of a traditional Japanese method of glueing a special kind of paper onto a canvas-like carrier and then painting planes between in layers of very soft tones of whites and yellows in contrast to a highly tempered ultramarine blue and in contrast to the black lines, enhance the visual simulation of a space that opens up and closes into itself.

Based on the same technique, Hiroshi Senju's incredible screen-paintings for Jukoin-Betsuin of the Daitokuji temple in Kyoto show the endless continuation of waterfalls in a frozen stillness.[15] The stillness in these and related waterfall paintings serves as a virtual cut between being and sheer nothingness. The sheer grandeur of the image leads one's mind and vision towards the experience of the sublime. Senju is an exceptional artist who exemplifies in his art that greatness is not necessarely related to large sizes only.

see picture 50

The notion of nothingness has been discussed before.[16] In art it has often been misunderstood. It is one of those typical problems of language, that when concepts are translated into words, the automatic process of associations takes off. This becomes even more confusing when such a concept is translated from other cultures. In the previous chapter it was already mentioned that some of the American Expressionists had an affinity with Zen, exemplified in Barnett Newman's concept of the 'pure idea'. The information he and others obtained about Zen was mainly through the publications and teaching of Daisetz T. Suzuki.[17] Information on Japanese culture and art in general was

University of New York Press, 1987 - orig. "Jikaku ni okeru chokkan to han sei", 1941), p.65.

[15] See Robert G. Edelman, "Hirsohi Senju - The Waterfall Paintings", exhibition catalogue 1995. Hitonari Tsuji, Kazuya Yamaguchi, "Hiroshi Senju - Screen Paintings for Jukoin-Betsuiin, Daitokuji", 2002. "Hiroshi Senju", Japan, 2002.

[16] See §2.

[17] Although Suzuki's texts are good as general introductions to Zen, they will not be sufficient enough to understand Zen. One obviously cannot understand Zen by merely reading about Zen - or by merely drinking tea or sitting in Zen (by merely copying Zen rituals). One can find more understanding by studying the books by Nishida, Nishitani, or Abe. Suzuki's essays were published from 1921 onwards, like in The Eastern Buddhist. See Helen Westgeest, "Zen in the fifties - interaction between east and west" (Zwolle: Waanders Uitgeverij, 1996), p.29. See: D.T. Suzuki, "Manual of Zen Buddhism" (New York: Grove Press Inc., 10th print 1960- orign. published 1935). See D.T. Suzuki, "Zen und die Kultur Japans" (O.W. Barth Verlag, 1994 - orig. "Zen and the Culture of Japan", New York: Bollingen Foundation Inc., 1959). Earlier, in 1906 "The Book of Tea" by Kazuko Okakura was already published and popular in the USA. This book was published some 20 years later in France. See Helen Westgeest, "Zen in the fifties - interaction between east and west", p.38. Westgeest mentions, p.39, that the first publication in the west on Zen is considered to be "The Religion of the Samurai" by Nukariya Kaiten, published in 1913. I wonder if one day some researcher will find earlier

available already much earlier.[18] Zen philosophy, however, only became popular in art in the 1950's in the USA, France and Germany.[19] For a large part one may attribute this popularity to frustrations after WWII, including the gloom and doom atmosphere in relation to the atom-bomb and connected loss of the ideal of art being able to support any improvement of society.[20] A desire to retreat into oneself seems a natural result.

I will now select and describe certain aspects of Zen philosophy, because from all Eastern philosophies certain basic principles of Zen have had the most profound impact on modern art and keep being important for our understanding of the meaning of art, the creative process, and our quest to understand ourselves in reality.

Several western artists were interested in the aspect of the 'now' in Zen and developed western variations in painting and drawing analogous to Japanese expressive and highly abstract Zen - calligraphy. Eugen Herrigel attempted to explain this notion of 'now'. He describes from his own experience in Japan the process of a student interested in Zen who followed the process of submitting himself to a master, starting to practice, and after endless practice, slowly and gradually proceeding to understand the long and

---

dated material or other evidence, because in the 19th century there were frequently Japanese students of philosophy studying in Europe, for instance Nishida, who after all became the father of the School of Kyoto of modern Zen. Besides, as an immediate result of Zen-master Shaku Soen, abbott of the Rinzai monastery in Kamakura, touring the USA after his speech at the International Religious Conference, Chicago 1893, in the USA Zen study centers were initiated from about 1900 onwards. See Heinrich Dumoulin, "Zen Enlightenment - origins and meaning", translated by John C. Maraldo (NY, Tokyo: Weatherhill, 7th print 1995 - orig. "Der Erleuchtung des Zen im Buddhismus", Fischer Taschenbuch Verlag, 1976), p.4. More books were "Zen Buddhism and Its Relation to Art" by Arthur Waley (1922) and "Die ostasiatische Tuschemalerei" by Ernst Grosse. In 1929 Suzuki's first book was published in London, from 1949 onwards his books became also published in the USA. In 1948 the before mentioned book by Eugen Herrigel, "Zen in der Kunst des Bogenschießens" ("Zen in the Art of Archery") was published, translated in 1953 into English and into French. It seems Robert Motherwell for instance refers to this last book ("... that book 'Zen and Archery' - that's much closer to what I'm concerned with in certain ways.") in an interview with Richard Wagner, 14 June 1974. See Stephanie Terenzio, "The Collected Writings of Robert Motherwell" (Berkeley: The University of California Press, 1999), p.220. Art critic Irving Sandler recalls the presentations in 1954 of Zen stories by Sabro Hasegawa, a Japanese painter (and by John Cage) at the Club in New York, an association of artists in the 1950's. See Irving Sandler, "The Sweeper-Up After Artists - a memoir" (New York: Thames and Hudson, 2003), p.41.

[18] See §10 and §11, footnote 52.

[19] See Helen Westgeest, "Zen in the fifties - interaction between east and west". Some well known artists had an interest in one way or another in Zen, but only a few - like Mark Tobey - actually visited Japan. Artists with various interests in Zen, in the USA: Mark Tobey, Barnett Newman, John Cage, Ad Reinhardt, Rollin Crampton, Philip Guston, Abram Lassaw, Theodorus Stamos, Robert Motherwell, Alcopley, Philip Pavia, John Ferren, Franz Kline, Sam Francis. In France the art known as 'Art Informel', with artists like Georges Mathieu, Henri Michaux, André Masson, Pierre Soulages, Pierre Alechinsky, Jean Degottex, Yves Klein, the German Hans Hartung and the Spaniard Joan Miró. In Germany the art known as 'das Informel': Emil Schumacher, Karl Otto Götz, Julius Bissier, Willi Baumeister, and the group 'Zen 49': Rolf Cavael, Gerhard Fietz, Rupprecht Geiger, Willy Hempel, Fritz Winter, Theodor Werner, Brigitte Meier-Dennighoff, Hann Trier, Bernard Schulze, K.R.H. Sonderborg, Gérard Schneider, and a bit later Günther Uecker. One might also mention Gerhard Altenbourg. See Jutta Penndorf, "Silence, Silence, Silence - Gerhard Altenbourg - Die Sammlung Wilfried und Astrid Rugo" (Lindenau: Museum Altenburg, Saarland Museum Saarbrücken, 2002).

[20] For an outstanding eye-witness report on the volcanic art world in New York after WWII, see Irving Sandler, "The Sweeper-Up After Artists - a memoir" (New York: Thames and Hudson, 2003).

painful exercises as a process with the sole purpose of discarding all logical reasoning, trusting one's intuition to go beyond one's individual or ego-centric desire for control, not only mind but also body, to just let go, to trust and let happen what and when it happens. The goal is to get to the level of being fully attuned to nature itself, the level where one does not know if one acted oneself or some 'higher power' actually made one act. Herrigel explains this in learning the art of archery, in which the way of Zen is to get to the level beyond ego-centric control, where one lets the arrow fly in a way and at a moment one does not consciously choose, without controling where it goes, still finding out it is not just going anywhere, and occasionally hitting the bull's eye of the target. This exemplifies a level of 'self-detaching immersion', which one only can get to through lengthy and painful exercises, involving a union of mind, breathing process, muscle-control and the whole body.[21] This is not an easy objective. Though hopefully obvious, it still must be emphasized that the discipline of archery itself is not the objective, it is 'merely' the ceremony for the purpose of acquiring the described level of a deep feeling of immersion in nature. Acquiring a deep sensing of immersion in nature by letting oneself act fully according to one's non-rationalized, uncontrollable, intuition is thought to exemplify the 'Great Doctrine'. In terms of archery, an important part of the 'Great Doctrine' is that not every shot will hit right on target - this would reflect an overly controlled desire and is considered 'devilry'.[22] As always in Zen, it is not about what one sees or does, but about what the act (including the act of perception) evokes in oneself!

It will be clear, especially I hope to artists, that the process described here mirrors the creative process of the sincere artist: a lengthy process of learning one's craft, learning to step this up by gradually trusting one's intuition, slowly and painstakingly trusting - risking - more fully one's intuition to go beyond logical reasoning to acquire the level that one feels the creative process, the act of creation, the painting, the sculpting, happens in a way one cannot always define. One cannot even say how it came about. This is neither an unconscious process nor a trance-like process. It is 'merely' a process of actions in which conscious acts are made 'open' for unconscious influences. In this process the physical actions do not just play a role, but can be considered crucial in the process of focussing attention.[23] I have noticed that in my own process of working as

21 See Eugen Herrigel, "Zen in the Art of Archery" (New York: Pantheon Books Inc., 7th printing, 1963 - orig. "Zen in der Kunst des Bogenschiessens", Munich: Otto Wilhelm Barth Verlag, 1953). p.72.

22 Ibid, p.81. Herrigel quotes Zen Master of archery Kenzo Awa, who responded when Herrigel asked him whether there should be a relationship between the target, the tip of the arrow and thus an approved method of sighting to allow succesful hitting: "Of course there is", answered the Master, and you can easily find the required aim yourself. But if you hit the target with nearly every shot you are nothing more than a trick archer who likes to show off. For the professional who counts his hits, the target is only a miserable piece of paper which he shoots to bits. The 'Great Doctrine' holds this to be sheer devilry. It knows nothing of a target which is set up at a definite distance from the archer. It only knows of the goal, which cannot be aimed at technically, and it names this goal, if it names it at all, the Buddha."

23 See §5.7 on speaking to one self and self-argumentation.

an artist a disciplined controlling of my breathing process plays an important role in concentrating my attention.

One must trust the brush to go where it 'wants' to go - while simultaneously applying all one's artistic experience, including enough craftmanship, to keep a conscious but also unconscious 'eye' on all the relationships in the composition and the impact on the whole composition of what one does in that particular moment. This combination of conscious (rational) and unconscious (purely intuitive) decisions must be understood as being quite different from the intentions of the Surrealists, who wanted to make decisions solely with their unconscious psyche. The above-described level of conscious and unconscious decision making in a process of abstract, non-verbal reasoning takes quite a lot of practice to obtain. This approach in art seems very similar to the art of archery in that one just needs to pratice one's various crafts from the level at which that craft is still an obstacle to the level at which one is not consciously applying the knowledge while working. Therefore, it seems that the 'Great Doctrine' is quite a useful analogy for the road to creating greatness in art in a process of 'kire-tsuzuki' (the study of the road or path is called in Zen 'satori'[24]). This analogy seems especially useful because no great art can come about without taking risks, without accepting that not every single piece can be a master piece.

One can indeed understand the 'Great Doctrine' as analogous to the approach to greatness in art, while the mentioned 'devilry' can be seen as equivalent to decadence in art. The moment the artist is too concerned with the final result, meaning that the final result should be 'on target', should be 'great', this self-inflicted control will ruin the possibilities for great art and give way to the 'threat of decadence'. Artists should not underestimate this dilemma, because while searching for greatness they also have to live, meaning to sell, and it has often been that the acceptance of artists' new steps in their works are only acknowledged much later in the market. Frank Stella is one great example of an artist who keeps pushing himself regardless of the success of previous kinds of work.

Quite a few of the western artists exploring a calligraphic style did not actually understand the sense of deeper meaning in the more creative Japanese calligraphy (like by

---

[24] Dogen wrote in "Shobogenzo", see Eiko Kawamura, "Das Problem von Chaos und Kosmos im Zen-Buddhismus", in "Strukturen des Chaos" (Munich: Wilhelm Fink Verlag, 1994), p.122: "To study the road (satori) means to study the self. To study the self means to forget the self. To forget the self means to be enlightened by all things. To be enlightened by all things means to remove the barricades between the self and others. In this moment no trace of enlightenment can be found, although the enlightenment goes further into infinity (into everyday life)." ("Den Weg (satori) zu studieren, bedeutet, das Selbst zu vergessen. Das Selbst zu vergessen, bedeutet, von allen Dingen erleuchtet zu sein. Von allen Dingen erleuchtet zu sein, bedeutet, die Hindernisse zwischen dem Selbst und anderen zu entfernen. In diesem Moment ist keine Spur von Erleuchtung zu finden, obwohl die Erleuchtung unendlich weitergeht (bis ins alltägliche Leben)."). Compare the quote from Kandinsky in this chapter footnote 8! Kandinsky knew a lot, including about Oriental philosophies, but he cannot have know anything about Dogen's ideas - Dogen was only re-discovered by the School of Kyoto, founded around 1921, and presumably not available in Europe right then. On Dogen see also §8.

[25] Working myself incorporating splashed, dripped and poured paint in my own art, I am very aware of the

Shiruya Morita or Yu-Ichi, or early masters like Nantembo) and made manneristic (too rationaly calculated) splashes of paint.[25] Artists who understood nothingness as negative emptiness, completely empty void or pure negation in painting, missed the deeper issues of the original Oriental concept of 'nothingness full of meaning'.[26] Offering empty nothingness works to a certain degree, because it throws one's perception back onto one's self, like a 'soul-mirror'. As has been mentioned before, this can also be accomplished by focussing all our attention on a spot on a blank wall (a method used for meditation in monasteries) which certainly can have a meditative result and bring one's inner self to rest. But as the ultimate goal should be to accomplish this for the self within the immediate context of the complex world as we perceive it every day, one can doubt if such a retreat into oneself could lead to access to the sublime. One has to offer an artifact that incorporates the complexity our everyday experiences tell us we need (a complexity our brain needs to make experiences conscious). Only thus can one have access to 'no-thingness' as it actually exists in nature: full of life, colours and forms in compositions expressing the complex streams of energies.[27] Merely copying works or ideas because they are thought to contain the right content, without finding the proper content oneself, will only make way for decadence.[28]

Sincerity, commitment, self-criticism, lots of hard study, trial and error are ways of avoiding decadence. Still any sincere artist should not feel restrained by a threat of deca-

continuous danger of making it too beautiful or too calculatingly expressive, loosing the necessary controlled spontaneity (when one studies artists like Kandinsky one can also find they had often similar worries if the artwork would still be 'great' or over the top and be merely 'decorative'). One must also remember that a lot of 'informal' art in the 1940's and 1950's was simultaneously inspired by the Surrealist notion of 'automatic writing' - as advocated by Masson, Paalen, Matta, Ernst - making it rather too complex to limit any critical review to Zen as its sole source.

26 Irving Sandler discusses the supposed empty nothingness in the white paintings by Robert Rauschenberg of 1951 and the musical composition "4'33" later by John Cage, which in the audience's interaction in exhibitions and performances were not empty after all, because shadows, different lights and sounds by the audience always add to the supposed nothingness in these works of art. See Irving Sandler, "A Sweeper-Up After Artists - a memoir", p. 254, 255. Cage intended to make an audience aware of everyday sounds. In my opinion, Sandler correctly noticed that there is a discrepancy between a supposed nothingness within an artifact that (re)presents nothing and what one actually perceives, because the same work of art still begets a meaning in one's experience, which is an interaction with the artifact. The experience of nothingness in the art by Rauschenberg and music by Cage (or Minimal Art later) is different from an experience of 'no thingness' intended in Eastern thinking. Rauschenberg's and Cage's interpretation are focussed on making manifest the everyday (hence limitations in time and space, no sublime needed), while in eastern thinking the intention is deep experience of the now in combination with the flow of eternity (hence, the need to dissolve the duality of self and world in an experience of the sublime) of which for instance Hiroshi Senju's waterfall paintings are grand examples.

27 In contrast Mark Tobey said about empty space: "It's all loaded with life." See Helen Westgeest, "Zen in the fifties - interaction between east and west", p.74. That is also why, in my understanding, Jackson Pollock's complex paintings reflect nothingness much better than the empty colour fields by Barnet Newman or for instance Elsworth Kelly, while Clifford Still seems to offer an interesting solution for nothingness in his large colour field paintings that still are not monochrome by virtue of the way they are painted (much more alive than Newman's!).

28 Unfortunately repeatedly it happens that because of the mystic appeal of Zen, artists are attracted to copy Zen principles whithout having a deeper understanding of these principles. One may doubt the assumed

dence, while being aware of its danger. Taking necessary risks means pushing one's creativity to the often thin borderline between the sublime and the decadent, allowing for the potentiality of producing great art - or failing.[29] The drive is the continuous process of dissatisfaction - finding temporary satisfaction - dissatisfaction, etc. - at least in part pushed onwards by the dynamics of nature and as such by the continuously changing biological processes in our own bodies.

Dissatisfaction with a given situation generally motivates us to search for improvement. The only other option is resignation. Resignation is equivalent to an acceptance of the dissatisfaction as an unchangeable fact. By learning to live with dissatisfaction it can be minimalized or even annihilated. The search for improvement is by definition the search for an ideal. The final ideal is the sublime that can only be reached temporarily in an instantaneous and intense experience. We may experience the sublime - even once in a while - but we cannot stay in the sublime. We always at some point will be pulled back (by our consciousness?) to the realm of the everyday duality between self and world. How else can we survive but in the realm of dualities?

You may wonder what the purpose is of lifting yourself out of the everyday world of dualities, with its problems and suffering, by a dissolving of self and world in an experience of the sublime, when one will be 'pulled back' anyway. Though tough to answer, for an important part it is the possibility of repeating the intense experience of the sublime that makes life bearable by really feeling united with the ongoing processes of nature. It gives life a grander purpose than that acquired by mere introspection, because it makes it clear that one is an actual part of both everyday life as well as of eternity. Art plays such an important part in this, not only as a medium to spark this experience, but also because this process of acquiring the experience of the sublime and subsequently loosing it again, is very similar to the creative process. A creative process also is a search that brings a sense of psychic elevation when a satisfactory result is accomplished, but only for a while, after which the process is started again.[30] Searching for an ideal has always

---

relationship between Zen and Yves Klein's early 1960's performances using beautiful naked female models as an alternative 'brush' to make spontaneous impressions of immediacy on paper. These are considered to be inspired by his praxis of judo and seeing the impression of the bodies made on the judo-mat. Ibid., p.126. Or performances by Georges Mathieu, who dressed up in a kimono to make huge paintings before an audience. Ibid., p.130. Zen-entertainment?

29 Longing for greatness in art always poses the same problem: by desiring to reach 'beyond everyday' to find the eternal essence of reality one still has to use artistic means that can only be found in everyday reality, and are needed to explore properties of the everyday. We desire to understand the 'beyond' while obviously still being in this world.

30 As already mentioned in the previous chapter, it seems possible that science will discover a hormone that plays a crucial role in providing us in our consciousness with such a feeling of psychic elevation - maybe even explaining our experience of the sublime and thus our need for such experiences in a very different way. This may be comparable to, though different from, the rush of endorfine caused by sports activities? Processes that basically will be influenced (defined even?) by synchronization with rhythmic processes in nature at large - as explained in §5? If so, it would also throw quite a different light on the ideas of artists like Kandinsky, who stated they were exploring art expressing the inner vibrations of the artist's soul (that match the vibrations of nature) and thus will evoke a vibration in the 'soul' of the beholder. Kandinsky wrote in "On Stage

been an important property of every search for more knowledge and better communication.[31] But, it is not an open process towards the ideal. A formulation of and focus on an ideal may put one on the right path, but obviously does not garantee one actually will get there. An ideal also leads to the temptation to fabricate or simulate the ideal itself or the path by trusting a clear definition of form without content, misleading oneself and finally leading to pure decadence.

Decadence in art or design is the application of certain forms and shapes without the power of their meaning, aiming for superficial and easy entertainment. The notion of decadence can be related to academism in art.[32] In art decadence has only an aesthetic value without any connection to the essence of reality - Kandinsky's 'inner vividness' -

Composition", 1912, see Robert Motherwell, "Documentary Edition by The Documents of 20th Century Art: The Blaue Reiter Almanac, edited by Wassily Kandinsky and Franz Marc", edited by Klaus Lankheit (New York: The Viking Press, 1974), p.191: "When the artist finds the appropriate means, it is a material form of his soul's vibration, which he is forced to express. If the method is appropriate, it causes an almost identical vibration in the soul of the audience." German original text: "Über Bühnenkomposition", 1912. See Max Bill, "Kandinsky, Essays über Kunst und Künstler" (Bern: Benteli Verlag, 1963 - orig. 1955), p.50.

31 This is something discussed at length by Charles Biederman in his book "Art As The Evolution of Visual Knowledge". Umberto Eco decribes how man through all centuries has been fascinated by the idea of developing a universal language as the ideal language that would connect people and improve the world. Typical for the 19th century, Arthur Rimbaud wrote for example, see Eco, "Die Suche nach der vollkommenen Sprache" (Munich: C.H. Beck - Europa Bauen, 1994 - orig. "La ricerca della lingua perfetta nella cultura europea", 1993), p.14: "For the rest, as every word is an idea, the time will come for a universal language (...). This language will be one that speaks from soul to soul and will contain everything, smells, tones, colours ..." ("Im übrigen wird, da jedes Wort ja Idee ist, die Zeit einer universalen Sprache kommen (...) Diese Sprache wird eine sein, die von der Seele zur Seele spricht und alles zusammenfaßt, Gerüche, Töne, Farben (...)"). Around the change from the 19th to the 20th century hope emerged for actually finding this universal language. Linguists Couturat and Léau thought this to be possible in 1903 because of the extensive progress in communication and transportation, the telephone and wireless telegraphy. These new communication media enhanced international trade around the world, stimulated by the strong relationships of the great powers with their colonies. Politics became globalized, making co-operation between nations a necessity. Couturat and Léau saw too many problems to choose an existing language as the universal language and stated that a simple artificial language should be developed, which is similar to the natural languages, but that can be perceived as neutral by anybody (all existing languages being somehow politically stained). They expected that a universal language would provide everybody with the means to communicate freely and openly with everybody else. A utopian enthusiasm, that seems to repeat itself at the end of the 20th century in the form of the hype in the electronic highway of the Internet and World Wide Web with similar claims!

32 See Richard Shiff, "Cézanne and the End of Impressionism - A Study of the Theory, Technique, and Critical Evaluation of Modern Art" (Chicago: The University of Chicago Press, 1984), p.XV. While discussing the artistic climate in 19th century France, Shiff wrote that familiar academic styles often appear as dead metaphors: "Now, if technical practice transforms its object - that is, its 'subject' matter - the 'original' is in some sense lost. But perhaps technique merely transfers the original, carrying its essence, so to speak, from one location to another, as if it could pass unchanged from nature to culture. Even so, originality is diminished; it is weakened in that the original is repeated. Existing in two places, or in two formal slates, it becomes not only reiterative, but static." The notion of being 'static' can indeed be understood as academic or decadent, because static implies no motion, no change, and implies, therefore, no desire or creativity. Remember that in biology a static situation is considered to be the equivalent of death. Shiff mentions that Cézanne and other impressionists lived in a culture where the creation of the original was emphasized. He emphasizes that originality seems to emerge in art which has no definite model. One can only agree, because any fixed model always will result in dogmatism or decadence in which any real creativity is suffocated.

and especially motivates a contra-movement towards an art which does have this connection.[33] Clearly in line with this and the various other aspects of the discussion in this chapter, Donald Kuspit supports the thought that art should be able to communicate the aspect of desire for the non-verbal, das 'Unaussprechliche', the unspeakable, of reality.[34] One might even state that if one could verbalize everything art can present, then art would not be needed. If art was still produced, then it could only illustrate what was already known verbally and thus it would be only decadent. The artist Charles Biederman seemed to agree with this idea when he wrote:

"Unlike the wordsmen of art the genuine artist does not speak 'about' art, but rather, speaks from 'within' the interior of the creative act which he alone achieves and experiences beyond the realm of words."[35]

Biederman advocates the idea that the viewer should trust and develop his own experience that is beyond words, instead of relying only on verbal explanations. Although definitely not meant by Biederman, this is comparable to Zen, and can only be accomplished by an artist through a patient and highly individual learning process.[36]

Looking for the essence will never result in a definitive and final reaching or finding, but will lead to experiences of the sublime. This search involves the attitude of the artist to offer his best - in every work anew. Similar to Kuspit and in agreement with my own understanding of this subject, the cultural-philosopher Vilém Flusser wrote in relation to Information Theory:

"The theory says that a gesture is less 'kitsch' when it contains more information, and,

---

[33] Here are some simple examples of the sublime versus the decadent: the magnificance of the Baroque paintings of Tiepolo, Titian and Rubens versus the empty decadence of the Rococo paintings of Watteau and Boucher, the power of the early Pop Art of Rauschenberg and Lichtenstein versus the kitsch of Jef Koons. But also the ever continuing development of Frank Stella versus the non-progressive absoluteness of Donald Judd.

[34] Compare §8.1., footnote 6 on the notion of 'pu li wen tze' - no dependence on words and letters in Zen. Donald Kuspit pointed at the actuality of the phenomenon of decadence in art. See Donald Kuspit, "Signs of Psyche in Modern and Post-Modern Art" (Cambridge, US: Cambridge University Press, 1995 - orig. 1993), p.348: "To experience an art scene as decadent is to give up expectation of significant satisfaction from art, which may be taken seriously as an objective cultural symptom, but is not expected to support and enhance anyone's subjective sense of self."

[35] See Charles Biederman, "Art, Science, Reality" (Red Wing, MN: Charles Biederman, 1988), p.2.

[36] In the private interviews I was fortunate to have with Charles Biederman in the late 1980's and early 1990's, I learned that he did not like his ideas to be compared to Oriental thought - just like he did not like to learn about all the theories and ideas of the Russian early abstract artists. Charles always emphasized the need for an artist to focus entirely on creating a single kind of art, comparable to how artists in former ages specialized in painting landscapes or portraits, but hardly on both. Biederman focussed himself on the relief. I do not believe myself it is so important to focus on any single medium of art, but it is important to focus on an approach towards reality which in a natural way through time becomes recognizable as one's idiosyncrasy. In my own case, working on sculptures enhances my ideas for painting and vice versa - something I know from other artists themselves is common these days - for instance Michael Kidner or Gottfried Honegger (besides earlier examples like Naum Gabo).

besides, that the quantity of information as transmitted through a gesture is connected to the code of the gesture. This statement has an important implication. The more information a gesture contains, clearly the more difficult it is for a receiver to read it. The more information, the less communication. It follows that the less a gesture informs (the better it communicates), the more empty it is and the more nice and 'pretty' it is, because it demands less effort to be read."[37]

Flusser emphasized the importance of a creative person finding a balance between too little and too much information, between pleasing quickly (easy aestheticism) and offering more experience at depth. This seems to be very much like the previously mentioned state of imperfect perfection or edge of chaos (or edge of stability).[38] The search for this equilibrium is a search for the ideal. Flusser's definition of something with (too) little information being more comfortable ('angenehmer') and prettier ('hübscher') connects quite well to the emerging criticism by Kuspit and others of the easy and empty aesthetics in modern art of the last decades, which led a lot of art to merely show quick and very simple kind of jokes, so-called political statements, the celebration of appropriation, glorifications of emptiness and lots of neo-neo art.[39] Simple, easily accessible, easily consumed, easily forgotton, entertainment. This phenomenon is, in my opinion, too easily accepted as a feature of the new information age: the need for lots of quick and easily digestable information. This kind of art is often produced for the market by artists who are desparate for income and some succes (not even necessarely 'fame and fortune'). While there is obviously nothing wrong with the art market as important arena for presenting one's art for dialogue and acquirement of an income (how else to

[37] See Vilém Flusser, "Gesten - Versuch einer Phänomenologie" (Düsseldorf, Bensheim: Bollmann Verlag, 1991), p.19-20: "Die Theorie besagt, daß eine Geste desto weniger Kitsch ist, je mehr Information sie enthällt, und außerdem, daß die durch eine Geste übermittelte Informationsmenge an den Code der Geste geknüpft ist. Diese Behauptung hat eine wichtige Implikation. Je mehr Information eine Geste enthält, desto schwieriger ist es offenbar für einen Empfänger, sie zu lesen. Je mehr Information, desto weniger Kommunikation. Folglich: je weniger eine Geste informiert (je besser sie kommuniziert), desto leerer ist sie und desto angenehmer und 'hübscher', denn sie erfordert wenig Anstrengung, um gelesen zu werden."

[38] See §7 and §8.

[39] The following publications might be of interest in this context. Arthur Danto's "After the End of Art - Contemporary Art and the Pale of History", (Princeton, NJ: Princeton University Press, 1997), concerns an approach based on the philosophy of Hegel. Danto's theory is mainly aimed at understanding an end to the classical narrative in art and attempts to provide a basis for everything that happened in art ever since Pop Art. See more on Danto in the next chapter. In a very different way, Robert C. Morgan offers an intelligent, thorough and critical analysis of the mechanisms of the art market and art world, exemplifying the powers at play which decide on what art is put forward and what art is ignored, decisions that have nothing to do with quality in art. See Robert C. Morgan, "The End of the Art World" (New York: Allworth Press, 1998). See also the various articles and interviews with Frank Stella concerning his critical opinion on museums, published in relation to his exhibition of new works at Paul Kasmin Gallery, NY, in 2003. See Donald Kuspit, "The End of Art" (Cambridge, MA: Cambridge University Press, 2004) for a brilliant analysis of the origins, causes and emergence of the loss of meaning in art. Kuspit argues that the main problem is that art has become too succesful to be part of everyday life and is now nothing more than everything else, has thus lost all meaning specific to art and cannot offer anything at all (Greenberg mentioned this as a possible problem earlier, but without the

proceed creating new art?), it seems there have never before in history been so many economical interests, and, therefore, manipulations, in art as in the last couple of decades.

Art critic Robert C. Morgan analyses this international situation well. He warns for the apparent loss of interest in the experience of the artwork.[40] The artist should keep reminding him/herself to desire real substance in art and not merely a substantial price. After all, 'market' has two meanings: a place to sell, but also a public place for dialogue. I propose that as a result 'market value' also has two meanings: an economic one and one of communication.

It makes discussion about idealism, beauty, the sublime, decadence and what art should really address all the more important.

Summarized once more: pure aesthetics is pleasing for a short moment, the experience of beauty makes a real impression that may last, the experience of the sublime engulfs one completely and has an everlasting impression that may change one's vision of (everyday) life. This, as I briefly discussed, can be experienced by greatness in art which often lies very close to decadence. It is the challenge and agony of every serious artist to explore the borderline.

---

convincing arguments Kuspit offers). Kuspit calls for a return to deeper meaning in art.

40 See Robert C. Morgan, "Cultural Globalization and the Artist" ("Sztuka w Wieku Kultury Globalnej") (Lodz, Poland: Muzeum Artystow dia Lodz Biennale, 2003), p.12: "A major issue for artists in this impending globalized arena is how we are going to adapt the virtual world to the tactile world on the basis of everyday reality - including our emotional reality which unless I missed something is still largely based on tactile experience. Human conscience will have a part in how we determine the ethical consequences of our actions."

§10 THE NARRATIVE OF BEING

This morning - rather, the whole of nature, life, the whole world surrounding the artist, as well as the life of his soul - is the only source of his art. Wassily Kandinsky, 1935[1]

That's what I paint: Whole lot. Emily Kngwarreye, 1991[2]

Before we explore a few of the main artistic approaches to the search for the sublime and the essence of reality, there is a feature of art that seems quite relevant to introduce into our more and more complex discussion about the meaning of art: the narrative.

The American contemporary philosopher and art critic Arthur C. Danto makes a distinction between three periods of the narrative in art: the Vasarian narrative, the Modernist narrative and the period 'after the end of art'.[3] The Vasarian narrative in art concerns a precise depiction of reality as we see it around us, which Danto assumes started with Vasari.[4] The modernist narrative concerns the major shift from attempts to depict reality to an art that only deals with itself. As advocated by Clement Greenberg, this exchange of examining the world to examining the self led to painting about painting. Danto assumes that the modernist narrative started in late 19th century more or less

[1] From "Today's art is more alive than ever", 1935, in Will Grohmann, "Wassily Kandinsky - Life and Work" (New York: Harry N. Abrams Inc., 1959), p.224. A quote from Kandinsky from "Approach to Art", 1937, in Will Grohmann, "Wassily Kandinsky - Life and Work", p.224: "Who can tell, perhaps our (abstract) forms are natural forms, though they are never objects of daily use." Will Grohmann, "Wassily Kandinsky - Life and Work", p.218: " 'Art, another nature, just as mysterious, but more understandable, for it springs from the understanding,' Goethe said. The laws of art and nature, Kandinsky infers, will ultimately lead to understanding the laws of the world's composition."

[2] From essay "Terry Smith, "Kgwarreye Woman Abstract Painter", in Donald Holt, "Emily Kngwarreye - Paintings" (Sydney: Craftsman House, 1997- orig. quoted in M. Boulter, "Foreword", in "The Art of Utopia: A New Direction in Contemporary Aboriginal Art", Craftsman House, 1991, p.61), p.31. Later in this chapter we will come back to Aboriginal art, attempting to show that there is a justification for considering this remark of Emily Kngwarreye not merely concerning her being busy with many subjects, but also considering this remark as a reference to her attempt to cope with wholeness in a similar way to Kandinsky (though very different in its approach of painting).

[3] Danto emerged from analytic philosophy (and neo-positivism), which after WWII and inspired by Wittgenstein's theories, emerged in two branches (one aiming at improving the structure of language, the other at improving argumentation itself) that "... were committed to the view that philosophy as it had been traditionally practiced, and most particularly that part of philosophy known as metaphysics, was intellectually suspect if not downright bogus, and that the negative task of both branches of analytical philosophy was to exhibit, to demonstrate, the emptiness and nonsense of metaphysics." Danto continues, "Metaphysics was nonsense because it was radically disconnected from experience, or from observation". See Arthur C. Danto, "After the End of Art - Contemporary Art and the Pale of History", (Princeton, NJ: Princeton University Press 1997), p.129. Danto considers Hegel most important for his own ideas. Danto's concept of 'the end of art' must not be confused with Donald Kuspit's concept of 'the end of art', nor with Robert C. Morgan's 'the end of the art world' See the last two footnotes in the previous chapter.

[4] Danto refers to the famous publication by Vasari on Renaissance artists. See Giorgio Vasari, "The Lives of the Artists", translated by Julia Conaway Bondanella and Peter Bondanella, (Oxford: Oxford University

with Manet and Cézanne. Danto considers the period 'after the end of art' to be the third important period in modern art, starting in the early 1960's (Danto repeatedly refers to Andy Warhol's "Brillo Box" as the key work of art), which forces a break with the history of the principle of narrative. After 1960 anything is possible and allowed, art may deal with anything, except with a major narrative. Danto understands this as the moment that artists started to question the difference between artworks and real things. This he calls 'the end of art' - the moment philosophy was becoming most important in answering such a question. Though I can appreciate this philosophical angle, especially in its historical context, I cannot agree with this rather bold black and white view.

In my opinion any art, any artistic expression, carries a narrative, at least the artist's particular view on what is important in life. To be more precise, I don't mean narrative in the general sense, the story telling of some daily, historical, political, social event or problem, nor fairy tales, romances, phantasies or neurotic projections and compensations, but the approach that virtually tells us the story of our personal being in the world, within the universe and incorporating the existence of the complex interconnectedness of everything. This story is not literally told to us, we cannot read it like in a novel. However, we can 'virtually' read it. Even though it cannot be completely put into words, it is made accessible in the process of interaction between ourselves and an artifact, caused by the particular appearance of this artifact. This process is a narrative process nevertheless. I propose calling this the narrative of being.[5]

Considering this, all that has been said in the previous chapters, and considering how art developed in the past two centuries, it is interesting to discuss the distinctions between abstract art and representational art more extensively.[6] This remains a prevalent and rather primitive distinction. The distinction is often based on the assumption that abstract art is a concept of a higher or more advanced culture - more related to science - or of a culture in which the artists express man's insecurity about life and the world in which he lives.[7] Although the motivation to cope with the insecurity of life

Press, 1991- orig. "Vite de' piu eccellenti architetti, pittori et scultori italiana", 1550).

[5] See §5.8 on self-argumentation! With some justification one can argue if the narrative of being should not concern the narrative of 'life' or of 'reality', but I assume this will too easily be associated with the kinds of daily narratives that are not intended. Besides, the narrative of 'being' seems more appropriate to emphasize the focus on the position of the self within the existence in reality.

see pictures 4, 50

[6] Representational art that evokes the sublime, in my own experience, are certain paintings in the Baroque, some exceptions in later representational painting like by C.D. Friedrich, Monet's almost entirely abstract "Nymphéas", only few in contemporary art like Swiss artist Franz Gertzsch's extremely large portraits and large wood-block prints of portraits and very Japanese images of water and a river ("Schwarzwasser II", 1993/94). See Josef Helfenstein, "Franz Gertsch - Die Holzschnitte" (Baden, CH: Lars Müller Verlag, Kunstmuseum Bern, 1994), p.77. But also Hiroshi Senju's grand paintings of waterfalls and deserts.

[7] This is a point made by Wilhelm Worringer (1881-1965). See Wilhelm Worringer, "Abstraction and Empathy", including an introduction by Hilton Kramer (Chicago: Elephant Paperbacks, 1997 - originally "Abstraktion und Einfühlung", 1908). Worringer's main thesis was that we prefer representational art in periods of trust and pure satisfaction in life, thus in delight in the self (example Renaissance) and we tend towards abstraction in periods of total insecurity (examples: Egyptian, Byzantine, Gothic, primitive or modern expressionist art). Worringer was the very first who looked beyond the traditional art-historical boundaries that classically separate fine art from 'primitive' art and emphasized studying their analogies instead. Though there

obviously does exist - remember the discussion in §9 - the development of art has shown that this subject is not the privilege of abstract art. However, when we recall the known functioning of the brain, §5, its preferences for information that can be more quickly processed, in combination with the philosophical and scientific notions of a connectedness at some deeper level 'under' or 'beyond' all things and phenomena around us and within us, then it seems compositions using non-representational forms and shapes are better equipped 'tools' to help us virtually 'read' and explore the essence of reality.

Abstract art in its traditional meaning, understood as using forms and shapes that have not been seen before, cannot exist in a strict sense. Any artistic expression can only communicate something, when it activates some memory stored in our brains - even if the memory concerns abstract notions like rhythm, contrast, or simulation of depth and motion.[8] Kandinsky made a useful distinction between the 'virtuoso' - the artist who creates from nature while avoiding any form of interpretation (in today's language: photo-realistic painting) - and the 'creator' or 'compositional artist' - the artist who creates works that emerge out of their own logic. This truth can easily be applied to both representational and abstract art. Basically, this insight provides the means to dissolve the 'duality' between representational art and abstract art. It certainly helps to explain why there is no actual difference between a composition by Tiepolo, Kandinsky or Frank Stella. It also explains the many forms of art that have emerged somewhere in between the assumed polarities of representational and abstract art. Again, we thus find a duality that in fact deals with the same issues and only differs in degree and intensity.

In other words: in representational as well as in abstract art, artists work with similar means, because they all use colours, manipulate materials, forms, and shapes in a specific relationship creating pictorial space, analogous to the relationships between the beholder and everything around him in reality. The representational artist generally prefers forms and shapes derived from the very appearances of daily life, while the abstract artist generally prefers forms and shapes derived from the properties of the substances and relationships of everyday life. The representational artist thus explores the

is a dispute if Worringer had any influence on early abstract artists, his ideas are at least significant for an emerging broader interest in artistic expression of other cultures. This is exemplified by Kandinsky, Marc, Macke, etc. in "The Blaue Reiter Almanac", in Kandinsky's "On The Spiritual in Art", or by Picasso's interest in African sculptures. In the mean time, about a century later, after all the various developments of abstract art, we can safely conclude that abstract art is not less 'real' than realistic art.

[8] Kandinsky wrote in "On The Question of Form", published in Robert Motherwell, "Documents of 20th Century Art: The Blaue Reiter Almanac, edited by Wassily Kandinsky and Franz Marc", edited by Klaus Lankheit (New York: The Viking Press, 1974 - orig. 1912), p.168: "Here we see that in principle it makes no difference whether the artist uses real or abstract forms. Both forms are basically equal. The choice must be left to the artist, who must know best by which means he most clearly can give material expression to the content of his art. To express it abstractly: in principle there is no question of form." The original German "Über die Formfrage" is published in Max Bill, "Kandinsky - Essays über Kunst und Künstler" (Bern: Benteli Verlag, 1963 - orig.1955), p.36. Kandinsky emphasized that it is not about the form itself one should be concerned or aware, but about the 'inner sound' or 'inner meaning', meaning what the artwork evokes in us is what is critical, not how it appears, therefore correctly criticizing all classifications, definitions of style and '-isms'.

landscape, the still life, the group of persons, the portrait, while the abstract artist explores dynamics, spatial relationships, principles of growth, light itself, expression. These features are also used by the representational artist, but as a means for making his representation visible, not as subjects by themselves. The distinction remains between the representational artist who is primarily interested in the narrative of a particular situation happening in a limited lapse of time and, secondly, in indirectly 'telling' the narrative of being, while the abstract artist is mainly interested in more straightforwardly 'telling' the narrative of being. This is the reason why abstract artists consider abstract art to be more 'real' than representational art.[9] It is also the reason why abstract art seems to be more effective in telling the whole tale, something confirmed by neurophysiology.[10]

Again, these definitions must be seen as stimuli for thinking about the subject and not as the 'truth and the whole truth', because there are so many different kinds of art exemplifying the often tiny differences in degree. The example of the allegory has already been mentioned.[11] In allegory the story visualized cannot be appreciated when one is not familiar with the actual narrative and the message hidden beyond it, while the representation should evoke the meaning. As mentioned before: in Zen calligraphy it is not about the calligraphic sign, it is not even about the poem distorted by the calligraphic sign, it is about the meaning beyond the words, evoked by the calligraphic sign, and the familiarity with the 'narrative' of the poem. The same is true for abstract art.

A great example that is analogous but still different from both the western allegory and Zen calligraphy is offered by the better contemporary Australian Aboriginal art. In particular, their paintings of recent decades bridge in a special way the assumed gap between the purely abstract and the purely narrative.[12] The 'desert' paintings appear

---

[9] Kandinsky, in a letter to Will Grohmann of 3 April 1933. See Matthias Haldemann, "Kandinsky's Abstraktion - Die Entstehung und Transformation seines Bildkonzepts" (Munich: Wilhelm Fink Verlag, 1998), p.249: "The nature of the elements present in the capacity of these elements, to free themselves completely from the material plane, to 'float' partly in front, partly behind it, provides the artist with a great power to create an immaterial world, to put the work outside 'space' and 'time'. On this rests the pure realism of 'abstract' painting, which exceeds conventional 'realism' of representational painting. Actual reality instead of delusion." ("Die in der Natur der Elemente liegende Fähigkeit dieser Elemente, sich von der materiellen Fläche ganz zu befreien, teils vor ihr, teils hinter ihr zu 'schweben', gibt dem Künstler eine gewaltige Kraft, eine unmaterielle Welt zu schaffen, das Werk ausserhalb des 'Raumes' und der 'Zeit' zu stellen. Darauf beruht die reine Realistik der 'abstrakten' Malerei, die die konventionelle 'Realistik' der gegenständlichen Malerei weit hinter sich läßt. Statt Vortäuschung reale Wirklichkeit.")

[10] See §5. Semir Zeki confirms that abstract compositions activate a less extensive part of the brain than representational art. See Semir Zeki, "Inner Vision - An Exploration of Art and the Brain" (New York: Oxford University Press, 1999), p.205-208.

[11] See §8.4.

[12] Originally the Aboriginal painted their bodies, sacred totems, carved into rocks and trees, drew in sand, on bark, and shields. The motifs are abstractions from perceived aspects of the country-side, footmarks, fires, water wells, beings, that were and often still concern repertoires of stories told from generation to generation. Since 1971 gradually more Aboriginal artists were introduced to modern paints, board and canvas, leading some to develop their artistic skills at such an extraordinary rate and to such degrees of artistic idiosyncrasies, that one clearly cannot merely label these expressions as 'tribal art' or 'ethnic art' Emily Kame Kngwarreye is

completely abstract, especially to western eyes, but to the Aboriginal they contain complex combinations of inherited tribal narratives, descriptions of the specific properties of a particular country side, and aspects of the personality of the artist. The Aboriginal call their creative process a 'dreaming'.[13] This not only explains the quote from Emily Kngwarrye at the start of this essay, but also gives further reason for assuming the analogy with the description by Kandinsky also quoted at the start of this chapter. Kandinsky and Emily Kngwarreye mean to depict the 'narrative of being', which indeed is a combination of the whole of nature and the world 'told' at the daily level of the immediate environment and the self. Both quotes illustrate that we cannot speak of a 'pure' abstraction in art devoid of any narrative, and that great abstract art always has layers of meanings.[14]

see picture 28

There is no composition in abstract art that can be appreciated when one does not see - cannot acknowledge - that the image depicted does not concern a narrative of a daily event, but incorporates the deeper meaning of the narrative of being evoked by the relationships of the applied pictorial means.[15] The simple truth is that if you are a person entirely focussed on yourself, and your horizon is centered on your immediate daily environment, then you can neither find access to nor appreciate any abstraction that provokes something deeper than straightforward aesthetic pleasure. Needless to say, this is not a matter of better or worse, right or wrong, higher or lower, it is merely an explanation of different experiences that find their sources in our various preferences

the most famous, she started creating extraordinary paintings only at high age (76), from about 1989 till she died in 1996. Other very good artists are Kathleen Petyarre, Rover Thomas, Mick Namarari Tjapaltjarri. For extensive information see Donald Holt, "Emily Kngwarreye - Paintings" (Sydney: Craftsman House, 1997). Ulrich Krempel, "ARATJARA - Art of the First Australians" (Cologne: Dumont Buchverlag Köln, 1993). Hank Ebes, "Nangara - the Australian Aboriginal Art Exhibition - from the Ebes Collection" (Brugge: Stichting Sint Jan, 1996). The Aboriginal Art Museum, Utrecht, Netherlands, www.aamu.nl. One is advised not merely to take the label Aboriginal Art for granted, because of the huge differences in levels of quality, like in any other art!

13 Terry Smith describes the several layers of meaning the desert- paintings have, typical for the part of Australia where Emily Kngwarreye lived. See Terry Smith, "Kgwarreye Woman Abstract Painter", in Donald Holt, "Emily Kngwarreye - Paintings", p.26: "Desert paintings convey their meanings on four different levels. Each of these has two aspects, and all operate simultaneously, reinforcing each other. The paintings work as a depiction through inherited forms and techniques of stories, events and figures of sacred significance: as both the broad narrative involving many related people and as specific moment or moral particular to the ancestors of the artist; as a cartography of a place owned by the dreamer - painter, including journeys across it, both by the sacred originators and by the artist as a hunter or gatherer; as a witness that the duty of representing or singing the Dreaming has been done, thus constituting a restatement of title or deed to the land indicated; and, finally, as an individual interpretation of these duties and practices, varying somewhat, and thus keeping alive, the obligations and pleasures of painting. Self-expression is important, but less so than all the other reasons for painting." See §8, footnote 73.

14 These observations seem to provide reasons to criticize Wilhelm Worringer's concept that man's impulse to abstraction results from a sense of insecurity about the world, (see footnote 4, this chapter). This seems to be contradicted by the Aboriginal's impulse to abstraction, which is based on the acknowledgement of one's life in one's environment and not on its denial. Though Worringer mentions Aboriginal Art, he must only have seen it in a museum and cannot have had access to much background information - besides Worringer published his book in 1908, while the abstract Aboriginal painting I describe only emerged in the 1970's!

15 Semiotics, as the theory of the meaning of signs, does not work, because it does not actually incorporate

and personal perceptions. One cannot see that for which one is not open.

Theory - the artist's statement, the art theoretician's or art critic's comments - is very important, because theory can provide you with just enough 'tools' to see how a particular work of art tells the narrative of being, without ever being able to clarify all the details. Theory may provide you with the 'door-handle', but you still have to 'open the door' yourself, by looking at the work of art with an open mind. If theory was able to offer you 'all there is' in a work of art, that work of art would have lost its reason to exist. In a similar sense, a theoretical text itself cannot ever communicate its meaning when the reader only stares at the individual letters of the alphabet - not even when the reader only stares at the individual words and has no knowledge or information about what work of art this text speaks. The similarities and analogies between all forms of art are incorporated in the need to be able to look 'beyond' the depiction - or 'under' the surface - to 'read' the narrative of being.

When one studies Kandinsky's "Improvisations" they look like random non - representational compositions of loose traces, handpainted lines, wild and blurry coloured spots and fields in a swirling soup of dynamic colour. A closer study reveals his many quite precise sketches as studies for the paintings. Even more conclusive is his essay on an experimental combination of stage design and theater, involving precise considerations of colours, lighting, music, voices, and moving persons.[16] It becomes clear that the way he described this experimental play is the way he painted his "Improvisations". They tell his own narrative of reality, which we as observers only can sense by first looking with an open mind, reading the mentioned essay, and then looking again.

Even when Mondrian says his Neo-Plastic paintings concern pure relationships, he is in fact composing in a similar sense, virtually orchestrating his own narrative of being, telling us that we can only comprehend the basic importance of relationships of everything around us by abstracting to only a few basic forms and colours in a reduced harmonious cohesion. This reduction allows us to appreciate that all objects, all phenomena that appear to us as individual entities, are nevertheless connected. In Mondrian's paintings a red square only can be 'itself', a particular red square, by the immediacy of its specific location within the composition, meaning in its immediate relationship and optical interaction with the black lines, the various gray squares and rectangles and possibly other primary coloured parts. A closer look at such a painting will reveal the number of layers of paint, the resulting great varieties of grays, but also the varieties of primary colours, and often partially painted-over black lines. One will easily find that for Mondrian there was no preset law for making the right composition. He struggled to

see picture 19

the aspect of change. See §2.6.

[16] Kandinsky's "The Yellow Sound: A Stage Composition", in Robert Motherwell, "Documents of 20th Century Art: The Blaue Reiter Almanac, edited by Wassily Kandinsky and Franz Marc", edited by Klaus Lankheit (New York: The Viking Press, 1974 - orig. 1912), p.207. For more information on the context of Kandinsky's stage composition, see Peg Weiss, "Kandinsky in Munich - The Formative Jugendstil Years", (Princeton, NJ: Princeton University Press, 1985), chapter IX "The Munich Artists' Theater".

'get it right', basically in a similar way that artists like Tiepolo, Monet, Kandinsky or any serious contemporary artist struggled or struggles, who also had or has to fight for the 'right' composition. When we agree that nature - reality - continuously changes, how could preset descriptions for art ever be able to provide access to the narrative of being?

A more recent example is the formidable "Moby Dick" series by Frank Stella, started in the 1980's and proceeding well into the 1990's. All these works carry titles of chapters from the famous novel by Herman Melville. Though it should be obvious that Stella did not merely produce illustrations for this story, there are links between the book and the hugely dynamic reliefs.[17] Comparable to what was discussed above concerning Kandinsky's "Improvisations", one can much better appreciate Stella's "Moby Dick-Series" when one first looks with an open mind, then reads Melville as well as Robert Wallace's analysis, then looks again. Quite clearly - again, as in the case of Kandinsky - this procedure does not explain every detail of these works, and it is clear Stella did not consciously use all details of Melville's narrative in his own narrative. But gathering all of this information allows more access than merely looking at Stella's series, and helps one understand why these works are so fabulous. It becomes quite interesting to thus perceive Stella's - as Kandinsky's or Emily Kngwarreye's - works as somewhere in between purely representational and purely

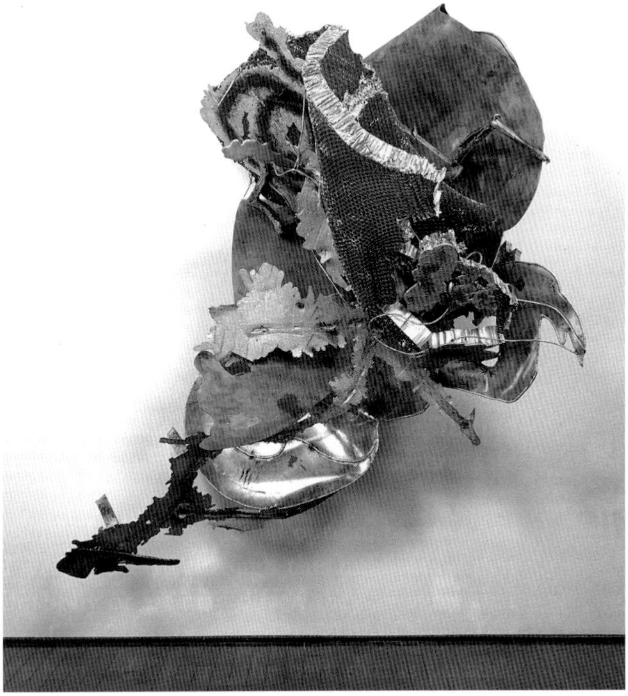

64. Frank Stella (1936-) **The Mast-Head**, 1990
Mixed media, 252,7 x 208,2 x 179 cm (99 1/2 x 82 x 70 1/2 inches)
Collection of Kawamura Memorial Museum of Art, Sakura, Japan
© c/o Beeldrecht Amsterdam 2004

see picture 32

17 See Robert K. Wallace, "Frank Stella's Moby Dick, Words & Shapes" (Ann Arbor: The University of Michigan Press, 2000). One good example is the wall construction, "The Mast-Head", which without any further information looks like a pile of junk metal succesfully composed as a huge assemblage of odd shapes into a dynamic whole, plausibly referring to the continuously changing forces of nature. After reading Wallace's analysis it becomes not crystal-clear but still clear enough, that one is looking at a ship from the top of the mast down, the swirling odd shapes of junk metal become dynamic waves, a shark appears, etc. It is no clear story that can be described in words as an illustration of this particular chapter of Melville's novel, besides there is more going on than a depiction of a mast-head in a strict sense, nevertheless the Stella piece acquires an extra dimension because of the narrative thus disclosed by Wallace!

abstract art. It makes one wonder indeed if purely abstract art is possible. I do not think so, because in my own painting - applying painted spheres that are on purpose not exactly three-dimensional spheres in a 'photo-realistic' sense, but spheres and not flat circles nevertheless - I do not sense any difference between my approach as a 'compositional artist'and Baroque painters' colour- and form dynamics in simulated coloured pictorial space.

see picture 53

Another recent interesting example here are the paintings by the young American artist Megan Craig. She paints city-scapes and landscapes in fragments or cut-outs of larger scenes, in a freehand way creating organic, amorphic and blurred geometric coloured shapes. Craig provides enough clues to see what scene it is, while the absence of details, incorporation of some high contrasts, and the right sense for colours prevent one from only recognizing a scene of everyday. One can easily sense the cohesion or connectedness of all things in her painting, with an inner power towards cohesion and potentiality to change. A potentiality that lies just beneath the surface of city-views, buildings, trees and dunes and almost erupts into our vision. Craig's narrative refers to the essence of continuous change and pure duration of reality, as we can experience in daily life, without being a simple narrative of everyday life itself.

see pictures 37, 51

In immediate connection to the discussion of §9, we can even assume that when no narrative of being can be observed in a work of art, then that work has virtually no meaning to us. The narrative might be too simplistic, comparable to the level of narratives in tv-soap series or the advertising bussiness. Such a work of art will be just plain decadent or merely decorative. This obviously is also true the other way around: when the narrative is more important by itself than what is actually presented in front of us as artifact, then such a work is not quite needed either. In such a case the artifact merely functions as display, as promotion - product, for the narrative.[18]

Art theory, art criticism, and art history are powerful means that can support our efforts to find the entrance to the narrative, but should not become ends by themselves.

To be able to study the development of the various expressions of the narrative of being, approaches to the essence of reality, their natural emergence in history (all approaches to reality do not just evolve out of nothing, but as a result of a complexity of previous or current events), their immersion in history (all approaches to reality make our history), and their various sources of inspiration, in the coming chapters I will focus on the distinction between the amorphic/organic and the geometric. Thereafter I propose the spiral oscillation as more or less the synthesis and conclusion of the first two and as the best metaphor for the narrative of being.

The amorphic concerns the shapeless or formless, the Ur-soup of life, the free clustering of 'no things' in the realm of particles, pure formless energies, the nebulae in

[18] The very reason why so much conceptual art should just not have been made and the involved artists should have instead published novels, short stories or essays.

the universe.[19] The organic concerns shapes related to shapes and principles of nature as we can observe when we stroll through a landscape, for example, botanical shapes or the principle of growth. Though one sometimes can make distinctions, basically the amorphic and the organic are so closely related that I discuss them as one.

The geometric clearly concerns shapes defined by Euclidian or Non-Euclidian geometries and is often thought to concern pure rational concepts of the mind.

To every student of nature or of fine art it will be clear that these three groups also overlap, are strongly interrelated and frequently mixed. In nature the amporhic, the organic and the geometric overlap in the appearance, structure and emerging pattern of crystals, bacteria or galaxies. In fine art they mix and overlap in a lot of painting and sculpture, from the birth of ethnic human creation and the emergence of the ornament, to the birth of modern abstract art. Although the terms are independent and unique, their applications fit together in a larger, coherent story.

19 According to the dictionary, form is seen as the equivalent to shape, the outward or visible appearance, the general arrangement or structure. Shape itself is the total effect produced by a thing's outlines, appearance or embodiment.

§11 THE SHAPE OF BEAUTY I : THE AMORPHIC/ORGANIC

Nature,
Nature anew -
Or there will be -
No art anew.
Charles Biederman[1]

The criterion of the organic is always the harmonious, the balanced, the inwardly calm, into whose movement and rhythm we can without difficulty flow with the vital sensation of our own organisms. Wilhelm Worringer[2]

Although people living in cities may still often perceive otherwise, as human beings we are part of nature. This makes it obvious that since man started to think, wholeness became an issue in religion, philosophy, science and art. Those who study reality in an effort to understand life and our selves, became interested in the amorphic/organic related to concepts of wholeness in nature at large. The great pioneers of understanding the amorphic/organic in painting, Cézanne and Monet, promised more than a mere depiction of a view of a plant or a landscape. More intuitively than consciously, they sensed what to search for. They accomplished this by painstakingly searching for clues to the structure in nature, by actually sitting in the landscape and exploring by seeing and painting - painting itself as thinking - while being inspired by ideas of thinkers like Schopenhauer.[3]

Throughout human history one can find examples of a special interest in translating the amorphic/organic into human creations in art and architecture. Often one finds examples of merely copying nature's appearances for ornamental reasons, for example in body-painting, religious decorations, architecture and generally in folk art. An early example of deeper thinking about the amorphic/organic are the ideas by the Italian architect Leon Battista Alberti, who was the first architectural theorist to formulate a doctrine of organic unity in architecture.[4] As a result of the new discoveries in astronomy, by Galilei and later Newton's great discoveries, it became clear that the dogma of the

[1] Poem by Biederman, written in the guestbook of Jacqueline and Fré Ilgen in 1988.
[2] See Wilhelm Worringer, "Abstraction and Empathy", with an introduction by Hilton Kramer (Chicago: Elephant Paperbacks 1997- orig. "Abstraktion und Einfühlung", 1908), p.114.
[3] One is reminded that during the birth of early abstract art (officially 1910, though much earlier examples of abstract studies urge one to say 1900-1911), both Cézanne and Monet were still around and very active. See §2.4, and see §6.1 on Cézanne's concept of culminating points, Cézanne painted his - in my opinion - best work around 1905. Monet made his greatest "Nymphéas" paintings 1920-1926.
[4] See Caroline van Eck, "Goethe and Alberti: Organic Unity in Nature and Architecture", in The Structurist magazine, issue 35/36, 1995-1996. Alberti lived 1404-1474. Alberti also formulated a precise definition of a good painting. See §8, footnote 58.

Church had its flaws. This opened public debates and more free opinions, theories and research. It is only natural that man has always studied nature and, therefore, organic life.[5] As long as man exists one can find examples in artworks, ornaments on buildings, clothing, furniture, utensils, and illustrations in reports from discoverers.[6] Here only a few interesting facts will be mentioned, as they seem worthy and add to our discussion of the emerging interest in the organic.

In the 17th century the first theories emerged about a certain ordering of all plants. The English naturalist Nehemiah Grew developed the idea of plant sexuality from his knowledge of animals.[7] The idea of the sexuality of plants provoked moralistic discussions at the time - a typical example how man projects his own concept of life on nature.[8] The Swedish taxonomist Carl Linnaeus became famous for proposing the system of plant classification that is still used today.[9] It was not the only system: around 1799 about 52 different systems were known, a confusion described as 'system-madness'. This drive obviously can be understood as a search for the order of nature and was a step towards the search for universal principles that really emerged in the 19th century. The Reformation added its own impact to the liberation-process from the dogma of the (Catholic) Church with the result that, at the end of the 18th century, philosophers and scientists stated that logic and rationality were the only ways towards truth. This movement became known as the Enlightenment.[10] An exception was Jean-Jacques Rousseau, who criticized objective science and the notion of progress by the Enlightenment.[11] Later he stated his famous concept of 'back to nature', meaning that in education the heart should be valued more than the mind.[12] Nonetheless, the Enlightenment further resulted in a loosening of the grip by the church on the sciences and initiated an interest in different worldviews in which possible relationships between art and science were not considered as strange. This resulted in the church losing its position as the undisputed authority on the purpose of the universe and became the beginning of the final advance of science as the new authority on reality.[13]

Johann Wolfgang Goethe was not only a writer and poet, he also contributed to geol-

[5] This is exemplified by the oldest botanic gardens all over Europe. The famous 'Hortus Botanicus', the botanic garden of the University at Leyden, Netherlands, was created as early as 1590 and meant for scientific research.

[6] For instance Albrecht Dürer.

[7] Published in 1682 "The Anatomy of Plants", see Londa Schiebinger, "The Lovers of the Plants", Scientific American, issue Feburary 1996, p.98-103.

[8] It was a great shock that female plants were fertilized by more than one male plant.

[9] In his "Praeludia Sponsaliorum Plantarum", 1729.

[10] Examples were Voltaire and Descartes. This intellectual movement must not to be confused with enlightenment in Oriental philosophies.

[11] Rousseau, the French writer, philosopher and composer (1712-1778), criticized objective science and progress in "Dialogue sur les sciences et les arts" (1750). Rousseau must not to be confused with the late 19th century primitive painter known as 'le Douanier Rousseau'.

[12] Rousseau wrote this in "Émile ou de l'Éducation" (1762).

[13] It is worthwhile to read Richard Hamblyn, "The Invention of Clouds - How an amateur meteorologist forged the language of the skies" (London: Picador, 2002 - orig. 2001). Hamblyn describes the path of

ogy, physics, biology. He wrote a very influential book on colour and art and also an important book on botany.[14] In the latter book he refers to research by contemporaries that led to the discovery of photosynthesis, the process by which plants take up carbon dioxide in a process of absorbing light and giving off oxygen.[15] Goethe searched for the laws that regulate the growth of natural organisms. In accordance with Linnaeus' ideas and those of other system-searchers, Goethe theorized that all plants stem from one single form, which he called the 'Urpflanze' (the primary plant). He applied his conclusions to his understanding of art and architecture, which was not a new thing to do. Seeing analogies between the procedures of the artist and those of organisms in nature belongs to the tradition of classical poetic and rhetorical theory.[16] Rhetoricians like Cicero and Quintilian had long ago stated that an orator should imitate nature and that natural expression in all art is more persuasive. Goethe focussed on the change of form through growth and underlying similarities, calling this research 'morphology'.[17] Disliking the Newtonian attitude of the Enlightenment, which sought to deduce or fragmentize everything that is researched, Goethe emphasized that the whole always must be researched without isolating any parts, as nature itself presents itself to us in one whole.

World views following this idea about the whole emerged a bit later, like Schopenhauer's concept of a world-will and other theories about creation, cosmic purpose, evolution and the notion of free will. In the 19th century, the quickly rising importance of biology accelerated the interest in the debate about these theories, as exemplified by Charles Darwin's ordering of nature in his evolution-theory. The philosopher and mathematician Bertrand Russell wrote about the early 19th century:

---

discovery of a system in the formation of clouds, supporting efforts to forecast the weather (accomplished by originally amateur meteorologist Luke Howard in England), but simultaneously describing the growth of popularity of scientific discoveries presented as theatrical public performances with gasses and explosions. Hamblyn describes how 'creative insight' was promoted in science in opposition to logical analysis. It is interesting to add that in Luke Howard's quest the creation of drawings and watercolors were crucial for defining his 'language of the skies'. Concerning clouds (the amorphic forms per definition!), these look amazingly abstract. Howard's observations also influenced an artist like John Constable (who, also inspired by the new emphasis on 'creative insight', said in a lecture at the Royal Institution, London, in the first half of the 19th century: "Painting is a science and should be pursued as an inquiry into the laws of nature" and: "Why, then, may not landscape painting be considered a branch of natural philosophy, of which pictures are but the experiments?" Ibid., p.222. Howard also impressed Goethe while he was working on his 'Morphology'. Ibid., p.209-210.

14 Goethe lived 1749 - 1832. See J.W. Goethe, Kleurenleer" (Zeist: Uitgeverij Vrij Geestesleven, 1991- orig. "Entwurf einer Farbenlehre", 1810). See Rudolf Steiner, " J.W. Goethe - Naturwissenschaftliche Schriften"- Band III (Dornach: Rudolf Steiner Verlag, 1982- orig. Band I 1883, Band II 1887, Band III 1890, Band IV+V 1897). Goethe published on botany the essay "Versuch die Metamorphose der Pflanzen zu erklären" ("An attempt to interpret the metamorphosis of plants") in 1790.

15 See John E. Dale, "Power Plants", The Sciences magazine, issue September/October 1994, p.28-33.

16 See Caroline van Eck, "Goethe and Alberti: Organic Unity in Nature and Architecture".

17 Published in his "Morphologie", 1830, See Rudolf Steiner, "J.W. Goethe - Naturwissenschaftliche Schriften"- Band I.

"The conception of organism came to be thought the key to both scientific and philosophical explanations of natural laws, and the atomic thinking of the eighteenth century came to be regarded as out of date." [18]

Hegel also emphasized that nothing is real except the whole, which he understood as an organism.[19] So-called Organic Theory played a major role in European Romantic philosophy in early 19th century and in Neo-Romantic art in the late 19th and early 20th centuries.[20]

Around 1850 a critical and new approach to ornament in architecture emerged. The idea was to develop ornaments one could identify as expressions of one's own time. In Germany, for instance, Gottfried Semper stated that all ornaments used in his age were not relevant, as they were either badly copied or their designs just stolen from earlier epochs and other cultural periods.[21] He became an important promotor of the idea that as a result of the development of new industrial materials - like the new steel and glass-constructions - a new kind of ornament should be developed, one that could be understood as being specific to these new materials. Not unlike the general interest in his time in the organic, certainly not unlike Goethe's or Darwin's theories, he stated that the basis for such new universal ornaments could be found in nature itself. Building on people like Grew, Linnaeus, and Rousseau, inspired by Goethe's 'Urpflanze', and comparable to Darwin, who showed how very different species can be built on the same universal principles, Semper thought the great variety of organisms can be retraced to certain 'Urformen' - 'primary shapes'. The mission would be to find, classify and translate these primary shapes for application by the technical arts. The aim was not to copy nature, but to offer technological interpretations of nature. This approach was also based on Goethe's morphology and Ernst Haeckel's natural philosophy. Haeckel formulated the so-called biogenetical constitution, according to which the development of the individual is a repetition of the history of the family to which this individual belongs.

The bridge between Darwin, Goethe and Haeckel was an interest in abstracting and reducting things to their elemental logical design, or 'inner shape'. Thus, this development was also clearly related to the emerging interest in the 19th century in the universal principles for art and design, as advocated early that century by Schopenhauer, or, in the later part of that century, studied in England by Pugin, Ruskin and Morris of the Arts & Crafts Movement, and by Jugendstil and Art Nouveau in Germany, France,

[18] See Bertrand Russell, "The History of Western Philosophy" (London: Routledge, 1991 - orig.1946), p.698.
[19] Hegel 1770-1831.
[20] F. Schelling, F. Schleiermacher, A.W. Schlegel. See Alla V. Povelikhina, "Organica - The Non-Objective World in the Russian Avant-Garde" (Cologne: Galerie Gmurzynska, 1999), p.12.
[21] Published in his "Wissenschaft, Industrie und Kunst" ("Science, Industry and Art") and in his theoretical major work "Der Stil in den technischen und tektonischen Künsten oder praktische Aesthetik" ("Style in the technical and tectonic arts or practical aesthetics") around 1852. For extensive information on scientific publications on microscopic and other biological life available to a general public in the late 19th and early 20th centuries, see Lynn Gamwell, "Exploring the Invisible - Art, Science, And The Spiritual" (Princeton and Oxford: Princeton University Press, 2002).

Belgium, and the Netherlands.[22] There was a general emphasis on universal principles that define the 'inner shape' of a work of art. Haeckel proposed a 'monism of the cosmos', meaning a principle unity of organic and non-organic nature.[23] This was quite comparable to Cézanne's notion of the wholeness of nature and to his theory that every object can be analyzed with the basic shapes of cube, sphere and cylinder.[24]

M. Meurer coordinated translating the ideas of Haeckel and Semper into pedagogic material, with the mission of educating a new generation of ornament designers.[25] He also had an unexpectedly profound impact on early abstract artists. For instance, Paul Klee and Wassily Kandinsky studied Haeckel.[26] At the time, Kandinsky still painted in his famous expressionistic or lyrical free style, his "Improvisations".[27] Though in a more blurry sense they were present in his paintings from about 1910, Kandinksy started incorporating more precisely painted amorphic/organic shapes in his paintings around 1921. In his later paintings Kandinsky aimed at developing an ideal visual language based on unique kinds of organic shapes or uni-cellular organisms, which grew into a personal calligraphic style. It might be said that, throughout his career, Kandinsky was interested in depicting life. Initially he created narratives about everyday life, then painted the sheer raw dynamics of nature's forces. In his Bauhaus period he included more rationalization, and, finally, the aforementioned amorphic/organic shapes evoking a sense of microscopic life as the basic level of all life.[28]

see picture 20

22 For excellent discussions on the importance of these movements on early pioneers of abstract art in Munich, see Peg Weiss, "Kandinsky in Munich - The Formative Jugendstil Years" (New Jersey: Princeton University Press, 1985), and Thomas M. Messer, "Kandinsky in Munich 1896-1914" (New York: The Solomon R. Guggenheim Museum, 1982).

23 Haeckel published in 1866 his "Generelle Morphologie der Organismen" ("General Morphology of Organisms"). See Ernst Haeckel, "Die Welträtsel - Gemeinverständliche Studien über monistische Philosophie" (Verlag von Emil Strauß, 1902 - orig.1899). See Ernst Haeckel, "Die Lebenswunder - Gemeinverständliche Studien über Biologische Philosophie - Ergänzungsband zu dem Buche über die Welträtsel" (Leipzig: Alfred Kröner Verlag, 1906).

24 Cézanne described these shapes independently but analogous to the theories on the education of children by Swiss education innovator Pestalozzi. Pestalozzi said that children should be taught the ABC of observation - "ABC der Anschauung" - based on the basic shapes of primary geometry.

25 To this end he published in 1889 his "Vorschlägen zur Einführung eines vergleichenden Unterrichts" ("Proposals to the introduction of an education of comparison").

26 See Gert Mattenklott, "Karl Blossfeldt - Urformen der Kunst - Wundergarten der Natur" (Munich: Schirmer/Mosel, 1994), p.17. In his book "Point and Line to Plane" from 1923, Kandinsky discusses the organic line, illustrated by a photogram of the blossom of the Clematis.

27 Kandinsky called these works "Improvisations" inspired by Arnold Böcklin (1827-1901), the Symbolist painter of allegories, who considered that a right work of art should be like a large improvisation. See Hans K. Roethel, "Kandinsky" (Oxford: Phaidon, 1979), p.21. Böcklin meant that to create a good work of art, no pre-defined properties should be used as sole basis - no basic 'rules' lead to the a good work of art, but only a process of 'open' improvisation, including the finding of harmony in a composition by the counter balancing contrasts (while still - obviously - the artist's experience, his craft and history of development play a role). One is reminded of the concept of "The Great Doctrine" in Zen, as discussed in §9, the trusting to 'let go and see what happens', while it is still based upon so much practice with the craft that the craft-part has become part of one's natural behavior - to be able to apply these without consciously knowing.

28 See Paul Overy, "The Language of The Eye" (London: Elek Books Ltd, 1969), p.106. Kandinsky owned

In 1890 Meurer's quest was rewarded by the Prussian government and the Berliner Kunstgewerbemuseum.[29] He obtained funding to educate future teachers of natural studies, and he received funding for the material and travel expenses involved in field research. This field research was accomplished with modern technologies, comparable to the methods for field research employed in earlier times, using drawing and watercolour.[30] Meurer hired the young Karl Blossfeldt, who later became famous for his outstanding photographs of all kinds of plants and flowers from Greece, Italy and North Africa.[31] These fabulous pictures explain very well how the interest in the organism paralleled the genuine interest in geometry at the end of the 19th century and start of the 20th century, and how both were closely related in the common search for the ideal (like the universal principles of shape).[32] Earlier than Blossfeldt's pictures, but in the same line of thinking, observations about animal and plant life were published by A. Koelsch in 1912 and by Raoul Heinrich Francé in 1920.[33] Francé, a biologist, was a clear advocate of his Zeitgeist when he proposed his objective philosophy that inspired artists like El Lissitzky.

The early abstract Russian and Polish artists were also inspired by the book "Tertium Organum", 1911, by Peter Demianovich Ouspensky.[34] Ouspensky combined a thorough knowledge of philosophy and the latest ideas in science to formulate his logic of infinity - the Tertium Organum: higher logic as the instrument of thought and as the key to the hidden essence of nature. Ouspensky made the late 19th and early 20th

Blossfeldt's "Urformen der Kunst". He also owned the encyclopedia "Die Kultur der Gegenwart", of which the volume "Zellen- und Gewebelehre: Morphologie und Entwicklungsgeschichte. II.Zoologischer Teil" (Berlin and Leipzig, 1913) included many illustrations of embryo's, blood cells, etc. There is sufficient evidence Kandinsky studied these often. See Vivian Endicott Barnett, "Kandinsky and Science: The Introduction of Biological Images in the Paris Period", in Thomas M. Messer, "Kandinsky in Paris 1934-1944" (New York: The Solomon R. Guggenheim Museum, 1985), p.61-87.

29 Berlin Museum for Crafts.

30 For instance, in Linaeus' time the drawings by Maria Sibylla Merian from 1699.

31 Blossfeldt's pictures were published in "Urformen der Kunst" ("Ancient shapes of art") in 1928 and in "Wundergarten der Natur" ("Miracle garden of nature") in 1932. One is really advised to study the magnificent facsimile publication on Blossfeldt's pictures. See Gert Mattenklott, "Karl Blossfeldt - Urformen der Kunst - Wundergarten der Natur" (Munich: Schirmer/Mosel, 1994).

32 It is interesting to briefly refer to the interest in photography as a new art of light emerging at the end of the second decade of the 20th century. In many examples of the early photography of artists like Rodchenko or Moholy-Nagy (and American Quigley in the 1930's) one finds the organic and the geometric both used together in one work. see picture 63

33 A. Koelsch published his observations in "Würgern im Pflanzenreich" ("Stranglers in the empire of plants"), while Raoul Heinrich Francé published his ideas in "Die Pflanze als Erfinder" ("The plant as inventor").

34 See P.D. Ouspensky, "Tertium Organum - De derde canon van het denken - een sleutel tot de raadselen der wereld", translated by Carolus Verhulst (The Hague: Servire Uitgevers bv, 1990, derde druk - eerste druk 1951 - orig. 1912, published in the USA 1922). For more detailed information on other sources concerning Organic Theory, one is advised to read the several essays in Alla V. Povelikhina, "Organica - The Non-Objective World in the Russian Avant-Garde"(Cologne: Galerie Gmurzynska, 1999). For instance, the unity of a world view was in Russia also promoted by religious philosophers. Ouspensky was a specialist in the application of X-rays to cristallography. See Nicoletta Misler, "The Crystal as Organic Matter", Alla V. Povelikhina, "Organica - The

century theories about time as the fourth dimension accessible to non-scientists. He combined these ideas with more mystical notions from occultism, Theosophy, Oriental philosophy and religions.

From early human history onwards we can find examples of mystical concepts, which explain the perceptible form of all objects and persons around us as the material and lower level of reality. A higher - or deeper - vision would allow us to see beyond material reality and find true reality to be formless. For instance, Plotinus embraced this theory describing how certain procedures and training offer one access to the formless realm.[35] This concept remained 'en vogue' and formed the mystical base for Christianity, non-Christian mysticism, and, in a comparable way, ancient Hinduism and Buddhism. It was especially important in tantric teaching, in which visualizations played a key-role. These visualizations are basically completely abstract or formless (though often geometric). In Buddhism the student is supposed to proceed through seven successive levels. The first four - considered the lower levels - are called 'rupa', meaning form or body. Thereafter follow three more - considered the higher levels - called 'arupa', meaning the formless or incorporeal.[36] This connection between Occidental and Oriental cultures was noticed and explored in the late 19th century by Theosophy and thus became one of the various inspirations for the emergence of early abstract art.[37]

Some argue that Kandinsky's serious interest in the concept of the 'formless' can be explained by the theosophic publications, and became a major impetus in his making the

Non-Objective World in the Russian Avant-Garde", p.93. Ouspensky built on the logic of infinity in the Organon by Aristotle and the Novum Organum by the philosopher Bacon. Ouspensky published his first book in 1910, "The Fourth Dimension: An essay in the study of the immeasurable". See Maurice Tuchman, "The Spiritual in Art: Abstract Painting 1890-1985" (New York: Abbeville Publishers, 1986), p.363. He published "Search for the new life: What Yoga is" in Russian, 1913. Matjushin and several Cubo-Futurists were interested in Yoga at the time. See Charlotte Douglas, in Maurice Tuchman, "The Spiritual in Art: Abstract Painting 1890-1985" p.187. The "Tertium Organum" that was translated into English and was popular in England and the USA is based on the revised version of 1915, which Ouspensky wrote after visiting India and Egypt in 1913. See in Maurice Tuchman, "The Spiritual in Art: Abstract Painting 1890-1985", p.363. Ouspensky was, for instance, read by Gordon Onslow Ford and Matta in the late 1930's. See Wieland Schmiedt, "Matta", (Munich: Kunsthalle München, Ernst Wasmuth Verlag, 1991), p.27. Matta in the early 1940's had quite some influence on young painters in New York, like Jackson Pollock.

35 Plotinus wrote this in his "Enneads", see Sixten Ringbom, "Transcending The Visible: The Generation of Abstract Pioneers", in Maurice Tuchman, "The Spiritual in Art: Abstract Painting 1890-1985", p.132-133. The described training seems to be quite analogous to the concept of meditation in religion.

36 See Sixten Ringbom, "Transcending The Visible: The Generation of Abstract Pioneers", in Maurice Tuchman, "The Spiritual in Art: Abstract Painting 1890-1985", p.133: " 'Arupa-dhyana', a state of complete freedom from forms and images, is the ultimate goal, just as imageless, intellectual vision was the objective of the Christian mystics in the Middle Ages."

37 In the period 1883-1903 eight editions were published of "Esoteric Buddhism" by Alfred Percy Sinnett, a theosophical discussion of the 'formless' in Buddhism. As mentioned before, in 1875, the Theosophical Society was founded by Helena P. Blavatksy, focussing respectively on spiritualism, the cabbala, hermeticism, Jakob Böhme's mystics, European occultism, before becoming more enthralled by Indian religions. This evolved especially when Blavatsky was succeeded by Annie Bresant, who worked closely with the English Colonel Charles W. Leadbeater. Bresant and Leadbeater published on topics like occult chemistry in "The Resolution of the Chemical Elements: Hydrogen, Oxygen, and Nitrogen" (including abstract illustrations of particles and chemical structures) and their concept of the 'ultimate atom', inspired by Edwin D. Babbitt. See

step in painting towards full amorphic abstraction.[38] While Kandinsky choose the formlessness of nearly pure chaos in a harmonious whole, Mondrian preferred to fragment a whole in a white or gray formless void into geometric parts, subsequently recombining them back into a more structured, harmonious whole.[39] Both artists understood the analogies between the concept of the 'formless' in Theosophy and the new discoveries in science that solid matter does not exist.

An interest in the capacity to reach beyond visual reality to explore 'real' reality obviously stimulated abstraction in art.[40] There are various sources to be mentioned that inspired Kandinsky's move towards complete abstraction using organic shapes in amorphic space.[41] The influential founder of modern art-science, Heinrich Wölfflin, whose lectures on the analyses of artworks Kandinsky attended, advocated treating the artwork as an independent organism.[42] Other inspirations for Kandinsky included Goethe's morphology, the philosophy of Schopenhauer and ethnography.[43] Kandinsky often mentions a concept of the 'inner sound' of persons, objects and artworks. This concept is connected to French Symbolism, which considers music to be 'outside of space', and

Sixten Ringbom, "Transcending The Visible: The Generation of Abstract Pioneers", in Maurice Tuchman, "The Spiritual in Art: Abstract Painting 1890-1985", p.149.

38 Kandinsky had a copy of Leadbeater's publication "Thought Forms", published in German in 1908. Ibid., p.135, 136. Grohmann mentions that Mrs.M. Strakosch-Giesler, who initially was theosophist before becoming an anthroposophist, when Rudolf Steiner left the theosophist movement, was one of the first pupils of Kandinsky when he started privately teaching painting in the landscape in Bavaria in about 1902, and that she introduced Kandinsky to the concepts of Theosophy and Steiner. Grohmann also mentions that Kandinsky attended several lectures by Steiner. See Will Grohmann, "Wassily Kandinsky - Life and Work" (New York: Harry N. Abrams Inc., 1959), p.41.

39 Kandinsky has said that the discovery of radio-activity (by French physicist Antoine Henri Bequerel in 1896) showed that even the atoms, the assumed basic elements of reality, can decay, which shook his confidence in science and made him think about the chaotic cohesion of everything in a formless whole. Kandinsky, quoted in Nina Kandinsky, "Kandinsky und ich - Mein Leben mit einem großen Künstler" (Munich: Knaur Nr.72226, 1999 - orig. 1976), p.32: "The decay of the atom felt similar in my soul to the decay of the whole world. The thickest walls fell instantaneously. Everything became insecure, unstabile, soft. I would not have been surprised if a stone would have melted in the air in front of me and become invisible." ("Das Zerfallen des Atoms war in meiner Seele dem Zerfall der ganzen Welt gleich. Plötzlich fielen die dicksten Mauern. Alles wurde unsicher, wackelig, weich. Ich hätte mich nicht gewundert, wenn ein Stein vor mir in der Luft geschmolzen und unsichtbar geworden wäre.") In contrast to Mondrian, it seems Kandinsky was only briefly interested in Theosophy. Mondrian was an actual member of the Theosophical Society. Mondrian's fragmentation of forms to define a kind of 'formless' can be related to the development in painting furthering the concept of Seurat's Pointillism, extended by Signac and influences by Cézanne and the Cubists. See §3.

40 This description sounds very familar to the notion that computerized "Virtual Reality" offers also a new approach to study 'real' reality! See my own article, "The Illusion and Simulation of Complex Motion", in Candy and Edmonds, "Explorations in Art and Technology" (London: Springer Verlag Ltd, 2002), p.191-196. The interest of artists to explore what is beyond everyday perception gradually emerged in various artistic approaches about reality in the 19th century, for instance in Romanticism and Symbolism.

41 See §8, §11and §12 on Kandinsky and influences of his time.

42 Wölfflin speaks of a "Ausdrucksorganismus" ("Organism of expression") of a work of art. See Heinrich Wölfflin, "Kunstgeschichtliche Grundbegriffe - Das Problem der Stilentwicklung in der neuen Kunst" (Basel, Stuttgart: Schwabe & Co Verlag, 13.Auflage, 1963 - orig. 1915), p.263.

43 See Peg Weiss, "Kandinsky and Old Russia - The Artist as Ethnographer and Shaman" (New Haven, London: Yale University Press, 1995).

understands 'sound' and 'music' not in an instrumental or notational sense, but in a wider sense of 'essentiality' or 'inner harmony'.[44]

Because of the impact on several generations of early abstract artists, I will now describe some of Wilhelm Worringer's ideas, which are relevant for understanding our sense for the organic. Kandinsky and fellow artists were interested in Wilhelm Worringer's concept of understanding abstraction as representing man's transcendental impulse - the impulse to dissolve the duality between self and world.[45] Worringer explained aesthetic enjoyment as objectified self - enjoyment. He acknowledged the contradiction incorporated in this definition. On one hand, the ego obstructs the perception of the greatness of a work of art, because one's ego is tempted to focus only on one's self. On the other hand, the ego is capable of feeling unified with the work of art; one's ego is capable of focussing one's attention outwards, opening up perception for a work of art. The work of art then begets its greatness, its very life, from the ego alone.

One might say that Worringer understood 'empathy' as the process of overcoming the individual ego that focusses only on one's self as the only center, and acknowledging one's self as part of the world. This can be understood as a process of self-affirmation, which is not an affirmation of the self as the center of the universe, but the actual self as part of the world. The absorption of our whole attention in a work of art can cause such an experience, and more or less becomes a process of self-liberation or self-alienation. This process is meant to reach beyond the ego-centric - hence the preference for representational art as medium to initially recognize the immersion in the world itself. Representational art might also allow access 'beyond' the visible world, because one can identify with recognizable forms and figures of everyday, while the composition (like a theater set) may refer to what is beyond the everyday. For instance, in the Renaissance and Baroque painting figures were set in compositions that referred to 'life in the heavens'.

---

[44] See John Bowlt, Rose-Carol Washton Long, "The Life of Vasilii Kandinsky in Russian Art, A Study of 'On The Spiritual in Art' " (Newtonville, Mass.: ORP Russian Biography Series, No.4, Oriental Research Partners, 1980), p.26. On Kandinsky's interest in 'inner sound' in relation to words, see his own volume of poems including his illustrations titled "Klänge", ("Sounds"). See the reprint by Elizabeth R. Napier, "Wassily Kandinsky 'sounds' " (New Haven, London: Yale University Press, 1981).

[45] Worringer was influenced by for instance Theodor Lipps, Schopenhauer, Wölfflin, Hildebrand, but also clearly by Vedantic philosophy - Worringer refers a couple of times to the Indian concept of 'Maya' (the eternal continuing process of reality, including good, evil, life, death and all struggles of being). Worringer refers to the Japanese, Egyptian, Greek, Arab, Byzantine, Maori and Australian Aboriginal cultures in his book "Abstraktion und Einfühlung" in 1908. This doctorate thesis (he was only 25!) evolved from a sudden recognition of the cohesion in the developments of all arts inspired by a visit in Paris to the Trocadero Museum (on ethnographic art, today called the Musée de L'Homme). Worringer emphasizes the importance of the differences in the preferences of the formal language used in the ornament through all ages, 'reading' in these repetitions or waves of interest in the more geometric (understood by him to exemplify the impulse to the pure abstract) and the more organic ornamentation (understood by him also as abstract, but still exemplifying the impulse to empathy in the world) - the arabesque he considered to be a synthesis of abstraction and naturalism with a predominance of abstraction. He glorified the Gothic (and the Gothic line) as the important development by man to transform a dead abstraction into a living movement of forces (Worringer described the Gothic more elaborately in "Formprobleme der Gothik" - "Form in Gothic", 1911). His interest in the ornament must clearly be seen in context to the Jugendstil movement in Germany.

'Abstraction' reaches further and in a more straightforward way to the beyond, because abstraction concerns the dissolving of the whole self, including acknowledging the relativity of one's own organic being, and in fact of the whole of humanity, to find the whole purpose of reality. Hence the drive for abstraction is to reach beyond the mere representation of the world (the Gothic as example).

In other words: empathy leads to the celebration of life in the everyday world, while abstraction is the acknowledgement of life as one aspect of the duration of eternity. This is a formulation very similar to Vedantic and other Oriental thought.[46] Worringer concludes that the process of recognition of one's self as connected to everything around us

"... sharpens the feeling for the inexpressible beautiful content of organic form, and paths are revealed to artistic volition, the paths of an artistic naturalism, for which the natural model merely serves as substratum to the will to form that is guided by its feeling for the organic. Now the artist learns 'to apprehend every random form as a theater within which to experience the joy of moving hither and thither in the company of nameless forces'." [47]

Worringer provides an interesting definition of the organic form discussing the structure of plants:

"All the elements of organic structure are there: regularity, arrangement round a center, balance between centrifugal and centripetal forces (i.e. circular curvature), equilibrium between carrying and burdening factors, proportionality of relationships, and all the rest of the wonders that strike us when we examine closely the organism of a plant - they it is which now make up the content and the living value of the ornamental work of art; and only a later epoch approximates this ornamental style, which has almost as little to do with natural models in principle as the geometric style, to naturalism. The process therefore consists in the subsequent naturalisation of a pure ornament, i.e. an abstract form, and not in the subsequent stylisation of a natural object. The crucial factor is contained in this antithesis. For it reveals that the primary element is not the natural model, but the law abstracted from it."[48]

[46] See Wilhelm Worringer, "Abstraction and Empathy", introduction by Hilton Kramer (Chicago: Elephant Paperbacks 1997- orig. "Abstraktion und Einfühlung", 1908), p.23-24: "These two poles are only gradations of a common need, which is revealed to us as the deepest and ultimate essence of all aesthetic experience: this is the need for self-alienation. In the urge to abstraction the intensity of the self-alienative impulse is incomparably greater and more consistent. Here it is not characterised, as in the need for empathy, by an urge to alienate oneself from individual being, but as an urge to seek deliverance from the fortuitousness of humanity as a whole, from the seeming arbitrariness of organic existence in general, in the contemplation of something necessary and irrefragable. Life as such is felt to be a disturbance of aesthetic enjoyment."

[47] Ibid., p.48. Worringer quotes Lotze from "Geschichte der Ästhetik", 1875.

[48] Ibid., p.60. This description matches the ideas by Charles Biederman, expressed in his poem at the start of this chapter.

The influence of Worringer's ideas on early semi-abstract artists will be clear. Like Worringer, Kandinsky was also interested in the ideas about the expression of the line in Jugendstil, especially in the thoughts of Hermann Obrist. He also had a profound admiration for the Belgian Symbolist dramatist Maurice Maeterlinck.[49] Kandinsky thought Maeterlinck listened to the 'inner sounds' of words. In my own interpretation, this is a way of using the meaning of a word 'beyond words' that seems quite similar to the meaning of unreadable words and poems in expressive Zen calligraphy. Such an interest emerged at the end of the 19th and start of the 20th centuries, furthered by Arts and Crafts, Jugendstil, and Art Nouveau movements, ornament in various countries and ethnography in general. A fascination with the potential expression of the line stimulated a new interest in graphology.[50]

What is less known about is a general interest in Oriental art, and the fact that artists in Munich in the early 20th century had very good access to Japanese art in Munich.[51] Though there are initially other sources for Kandinsky's concept of an 'inner sound', he also said he was taken by the 'inner tone' in Oriental art, referring to the presence of a 'universal sound' in a great variety of works that is based on an acknowledgement of nature as a whole.[52] This could explain Kandinsky's interest in the 'formless', though

[49] Obrist, one of the founders of German 'Jugendstil', prophesied the Jugenstil-ornaments one day could be applied in painting. See Rose-Carol Washton Long in "Kandinsky's Vision", in John Bowlt, Rose-Carol Washton Long, "The Life of Vasilii Kandinsky in Russian Art, A Study of 'On The Spiritual in Art' " p.46-51. Maeterlinck suggested dematerializing words to manipulate moods 'artistically', he was concerned with making contact with "the voice of the depths, 'the mystique' of beings and things", quoted in C. Giedion-Welcker, "Kandinsky the Theoritician", in Max Bill, "Max Bill: Wassily Kandinsky" (Paris: Maeght Editeur, 1951), p.166. See Peg Weiss, "Kandinsky in Munich - The Formative Jugendstil Years" (New Jersey: Princeton University Press, 1985), and Thomas M. Messer, "Kandinsky in Munich 1896-1914" (New York: The Solomon R. Guggenheim Museum, 1982).

[50] See Peg Weiss, "Kandinsky in Munich - The Formative Jugendstil Years", p.111.

[51] Franz Marc, like Kandinsky living at that time in Munich and co-editor of "der Blaue Reiter Almanak", is mainly known for his paintings with horses and deer. He created the incredible dynamic, explosive, and purely amorphic painting "Fighting Forms" in 1914.

[52] Though Japanese art and artifacts were known before - especially through Dutch and Portuguese trading facilities on the island of Decima, in the 19th century a much broader interest in Japanese culture erupted. The so-called first wave of 'Japonisme' occured in the 19th century, especially around 1860. This is exemplified in the paintings of Manet, Monet, Van Gogh, Gauguin, Seurat, Signac (see §7.3, footnote 50 on Charles Henry), who also collected Japanese prints themselves. For a good description of this exciting period involving many exhibitions on Japanese art and craft (esp. in France, but also in the UK), see Brian Kennedy, Alan R. Dodge, "Monet & Japan" (Canberra, ACT: National Gallery of Australia, 2001). For a very thorough study on the impact in the late 19th century of Japonisme on the USA, see Julia Meech, "Frank Lloyd Wright and the Art of Japan - The Architect's Other Passion" (New York: Japan Society and Harry N. Abrams Inc. Publishers, 2001). Kandinsky became part of a second wave of Japonisme. He was befriended with the artists Emil Orlik and Alfred Kubin, both knowledgable and collectors of Japanese prints (mainly the wood-block prints called 'Ukiyo-e') and knowledgable promotors of Japanese art in Germany. Kubin travelled to Japan to study wood-block printing. Kandinsky reported his impressions on a mainly Japanese exhibition in Munich in the Russian magazine 'Apollon', quoted in Helen Westgeest, "Zen in the Fifties - Interaction between east and west" (Zwolle: Waanders Uitgeverij, 1996), p.32-38: "Here one finds landscapes of tremendous variety and abstraction in the use of form and colour, subservient to the feeling of rhythm which is the pure expression of a unique, fully artistic temperament. Again and again; so much of what belongs to Western art becomes

the many other sources of inspiration for Kandinsky also point at ideas from the occult, from music,[53] from science (like cell-theory[54]) or the non-existence of solid matter. There were more artists who prefered to focus on the formless in a kind of cosmic painting. One can find magnificent examples of Hans Schmithals, Ivan Kliun, Frantisek Kupka, Robert Delaunay, Georgia O'Keefe, and Arthur Dove.[55] A close friend of Kandinsky, Paul Klee, who was also inspired by Oriental ideas, tried to make a connection between the microcosm of his art with the macrocosm of nature.[56]

see picture 21

Scientific interest in light and lines of force coincided with these artistic and more general interests in understanding the dynamics of life in the cosmos, leading to a desire for more mystical and popular translations of the concept of energy. These translations attempted to explore the relationship between energy and the assumed presence of light inside the human body with cosmic energies and cosmic light.[57] These translations explored what is beyond everyday appearance, hence not representational form but amorphic form. Visualizing forces of energies led to an interest in expressions that seem swirling or 'growing' through space/time, and could be perceived as organic. The resulting

clear when one sees the infinite variety of the works from the East, which are nonetheless subordinated to and united by the same fundamental 'tone'! It is precisely this general 'inner tone' that is lacking in the West. Indeed, it cannot be helped: we have turned away, for reasons obscure to us, from the internal to the external. And yet, perhaps we Westerners shall not, after all, have to wait too long before that same inner sound, so strangely silenced, reawakens within us and, sounding forth our innermost depths, involuntarily reveals its affinity with the East - just as in the very heart of all peoples - in the now darkest depths of the spirit , there shall resound one universal sound, albeit at present inaudible to us - the sound of the spirit of man." Though there is some speculation by various writers, one cannot be sure if Kandinsky had any information specifically on Zen, though he did have substantial knowledge on Eastern culture (at least for a part as in his family there have been roots in Asia).

53 Like Wagner's "Lohengrin", of which it is said it convinced him to become an artist, and the new music by Aleksander Skriabin and Arnold Schönberg. See Magdalena Dabrowski, "Kandinsky Compositions" (New York: The Museum of Modern Art, 1995), p.19 + 20. See Esther da Costa Meyer, Fred Wasserman, "Schoenberg, Kandinsky, and the Blue Rider" (London, New York, Paris: Scala Publishers and The Jewish Museum, NY, 2003).

54 Kandinsky always had included kinds of amorphic/organic forms in his abstract paintings, but from 1921 onwards he incorporated more precisely painted microcosmic shapes like amoebae and flagellatea, organisms that reflect the lowest form of animal life. See Hans K. Roethel, Jean K. Benjamin, "Kandinsky" (Oxford: Phaidon, 1979), p.42.

55 Hans Schmithals in "Polar Stern und Sternbild Drache" (1902), Ivan Kliun in "Red Light, Spherical Composition" (±1923), Frantisek Kupka in "Discs of Newton", Robert Delaunay in his paintings of "Orphism", Georgia O'Keefe in "Blue I" (±1917), Arthur Dove in "Abstraction No.2" (1910). For more information on artists particularly interested in the properties of light, see §13. On Kupka and his interest for instance in microscopic research like cell-theory and bacteria, etc. see §6, footnotes 79-83.

56 Klee visited Tunis and other parts of North Africa together with Macke. Kandinksy had been with Gabriële Münter in Tunisia in 1905. In Klee's great variety of poetic works one can find representational, amorphic, organic and free-hand geometric elements. Both artists incorporated in the 1920's also a more precise geometry - a period in which they influenced and inspired each other back and forth - at least for a part influenced by their involvement in teaching at the Bauhaus.

57 This specific subject will be explored in §14. Such a connection between purely scientific theories with more popularized versions also happened in the 1980's when the originally scientific Chaos Theory seems simultaneously to have inspired a stream of mystical and popular interpretations (like in a lot of New Age ideas).

art could have included geometry. The general understanding is that geometry is clearly related to science, though in occult mysticism one can find a lot of geometry used in diagrams, symbols, etc.[58] Early symbolist paintings of Piet Mondrian and the early abstract works by Wassily Kandinsky exemplify the mix of purely rational thinking inspired by science with highly mystical thoughts and symbolic language from Theosophy. When you explore their interest, ideas and theories, it becomes logical that in their art they combined amorphic, organic and geometrical shapes - sometimes preferring geometry but still in a kind of organic composition.

Mondrian, Van Doesburg, Van der Leck and Vantongerloo were inspired by the theories of Mathieu Schoenmakers to proceed in a search for understanding the whole of reality by finding and applying universal forms. Schoenmakers started as Catholic priest, but left the Church in 1903 and became interested in Theosophy and free Protestantism before developing his own theories in a kind of esoteric Catholicism.[59] He wished to develop an exact method which would allow him to construct the essence of the mystery of reality into a positive image by which he could perceive and experience the content of life and expression of life as a unity. Schoenmakers considered visual thinking - creative thinking - as the thinking of the relationship of contraries. This thinking would be the process through which the mystery of reality (the universal relationship) could be revealed as truth.

Although it would be interesting, it would take too long here to show how Schoenmakers' ideas were translated by these artists.[60] It should be clear though that Schoenmakers advocated the principle of universality in art based on a perception or experiencing of the unity of the whole of nature. He believed art could make this experience clear to us by depicting the essence of nature.

Simultaneously, Matjushin was deeply involved in wholeness, leading him to study the principles of growth of curling tree-roots, cells and crystals, seeking the original source in natural forms to find the most fundamental sign or archetype of nature.[61] Like many

---

58 See Maurice Tuchman, "The Spiritual in Art: Abstract Painting 1890-1985", for instance on Jakob Böhme.

59 Schoenmakers' (1875-1944) philosophical method he called 'christosophy' and later 'pictorial mathematics' or 'positive mysticism'.

60 In a lecture at the Academy for Fine Art, Amsterdam, 1921, quoted in M.H.J. Schoenmakers, "Het beeldende denken - leven en werk van Mathieu Schoenmakers" (Baarn: Ambo en Stichting E.C.H.O., 1992) p.133: "The artist's consciousness is universal, also because it is a consciousness that does not concern an exceptional 'feeling' or even an exceptional 'profession' but it concerns the universal construction of the world. There is no artist without a broad and deep belief that involves flowers and people and heavenly bodies. There is no artist without a broad and deep belief which connects the only one and silent Eternity with the colourful, lively and whimful world." ("Het kunstenaarsbewustzijn is universeel, ook omdat het een bewustzijn is, niet aangaande een apart 'gevoel' of zelfs een apart 'vak', maar aangaande den universeelen wereldbouw. Er is geen kunstenaar zonder een breed en diep geloof, dat bloemen en menschen en hemellichamen omvat. Er is geen kunstenaar zonder een breed en diep geloof, dat de éérne, stille Eeuwigheid verbindt met de veelkleurige, beweeglijke, grillige wereld.")

61 Matjushin (1861-1934) first followed a career as a violinist, playing in the Court Orchestra of the Russian czar till 1882, even as first violin 1881-1882. His visit in 1900 to the World Fair in Paris, especially the works by Segantini, inspired him to become a painter. See Alla V. Povelikhina, "Organica - The Non-Objective World

other artists as well as scientists in the first two decades of the 20th century, Matjushin was quite interested in pondering the distinction between the organic and the non-organic, between life and abstraction. He perceived the crystal as a fundamental object of investigation. Crystals seemed to contain organic life, as they evolve in a process that looks very much like a process of growth, but still in fact are composed of non-organic matter. As such, Matjushin and co-researchers understood the structure of the crystal to be a basis on which one should try to understand all of nature.[62] In that same time Raoul Heinrich Francé (already mentioned earlier this chapter) was quite a popular biologist and nature-philosopher.[63] Francé emerged out of a new tradition that seems to have started in the 19th century, but, like so many developments, actually had a much longer

in the Russian Avant-Garde" (Cologne: Galerie Gmurzynska, 1999), p.251-252. In Russia Matjushin had access to translated information on a great variety of Eastern philosophies and religions, especially from India, like the works of Ramakrishna (Gadadhar Chatterji, 1836-1886) and Swami Vivekananda (1863-1902), but also of the French philosopher Henri Bergson (1859-1941), the English Edward Carpenter (1844-1925; Carpenter called for a close connection of East and West), Robert Beck (who advocated a new era based on cosmic consciousness), and Charles Hinton with his ideas on fourth dimension. Matjushin was seriously interested in Yoga. Swami Vivekananda (see §2) taught a version of Advaita, a school of Vedantic philosophy, published in "Raja-Yoga", a compilation from Vivekananda's popular lectures in the USA 1895-1896 (see §6, footnote 72), translated into Russian in 1906. See Charlotte Douglas, "Beyond Reason: Malevitch, Matjushin, and their Circles", in Maurice Tuchman, "The Spiritual in Art: Abstract Painting 1890-1985", p.186. Matjushin's interests in wholeness inspired him to develop his theory of 'extended vision' or "SORWED", see §5.2 and §6.3. See Alla V. Povelikhina, "Organica - The Non-Objective World in the Russian Avant-Garde", p.13: "In order to be able to comprehend the 'connectedness' of the organic whole, you have to become co-author of nature, working in accordance with her laws, in tune with her rhythms and sounds, become the tree in the forest and not be an artist with easel on its edge." - and quoting Matjushin from a note-book in 1923: "Nature tells us - do not imitate me in depicting me. Create the way I do. Learn My Creation. Look at me differently than you have been. In observing you will see the former shape vanish."

[62] This concept inspired Matjushin to make at least two abstract paintings of a coloured crystal called "Self-Portraits Crystal" (one in ±1914-1919 the other in 1917). One should understand the crystal thus as metaphor for the spiritual purgation of the mind: just like in a crystal the colours appear caused by the breaking of light by the structure of the crystal, so do thoughts on nature's wholeness occur in the mind by impulses - impressions - experiences retrieved from any direction in reality when processed in our heads. After the Russian Revolution, Matjushin founded and directed his own institute, the Department of Organic Culture at the GINKhUK-the State Institute for Art Culture (where Malevitch was leading the Formal -Theoretical and Practical Department). There was a "Vision Laboratory", a "Hearing Laboratory", a "Touch Laboratory" and a "Color-Form Office", a "Sound-Rhythm Office" and a "Surface-Structure Office". The resulting research in visual, hearing, touch perceptions in combination with painting, music and sculptural expressions could be fused into a 'new spatial consciousness'. See Alla V. Povelikhina, "Organica - The non-Objective World in the Russian Avant-Garde", p.54. Sometime later (in the 1930's) artists Hans Hinterreiter and M.C. see picture 25 Escher were very interested in cristallography and geometric patterns in Islamic tiling, both being originally inspired by a visit to the Alhambra in the same year (not knowing each other!). Also Naum Gabo developed an interest in crystallography. He met in London in 1936-1939 with J. Desmond Bernal, a well known crystallographer who became Professor of Physics at Birckbeck College in 1938. Bernal attempted in his essay "Art and the Scientist" to find analogies between the artistic ideas and forms with those that are the basis of scientific and mathematical research. A summary is published in the magazine Circle, of which Naum Gabo was one of the editors. See J.L. Martin, Ben Nicholson, Naum Gabo, "Circle, international survey of Constructive Art", a reprint (NY, Washington: Praeger Publishers 1971), p.119-123. See §4 on a similar interest by David Bohm. see picture 44 A more recent interest in crystals is exemplified in the paintings by American artist James Juszczyk.

[63] Francé (1874-1943) was born in Vienna and grew up in Budapest. When the academic world disappointed him, he moved to Munich. He published popularized essays on subjects like ecology, evolution and culture.

history. He promoted his 'objective philosophy', considering nature to be in harmony and man's mission to acquire this harmony. In nature everything develops by functional criteria. Therefore, for man to live in total harmony, he must adapt to the laws of nature. By projecting this concept on all areas of human activity, Francé expected to find the very key to life itself.

Directly inspired by Francé, El Lissitzky and Kurt Schwitters published 'Nasci', a special edition of the magazine 'MERZ', writing on the cover: "Nature, from the Latin Nasci, i.e., to become or develop, is everything that develops, moves and forms itself out of itself through its own force."[64] El Lissitzky tried to promote a new balance between the major interest in the machine and the processes in nature, while advocating the analogies between art and modern science.[65] He was one of the first Russian artists who did not focus on either the characteristics of the material used by an artist or on the construction of parts into a machine-like whole. By focussing on 'process' instead, El Lissitzky, Nikolai Tarabukin and some others involved morphology in combination with geometry in their approach to art. This led them to the conclusion that rhythm is the key factor for expressing the 'throb of life' in an organic composition that gives the impression of a frozen process. Rhythm simulates change of shape or growth. Often curves are used that do not seem to be directly related to a perfect circle. Oscillating geometrical compositions followed, simulating this 'throb of life' - exemplifying in my opinion the search for the essence of reality.[66]

In the 1920's the German painter Otto Freundlich changed his paintings from expressionist organic compositions to very colourful geometric organic grids. He became very interested in breaking through the contours of an appearance and he understood the mission of art as making the space between appearances visible to our perception as a

He did some important experiments on the relationship between the fertility of the soil and the micro-organisms in the earth and was an early supporter of the neo-Lamarcksist concept of evolutionary teleology and the inheretability of characteristics. In 1919 he retreated to the small town of Dinkelsbühl, where he developed his 'objective philosophy'. See Peter Nisbet, in "El Lissitzky 1890-1941 Retrospektive", catalogue Sprengel Museum (Hannover: Sprengel Museum, 1988), p.21. See Kai-Uwe Hemken, "El Lissitzky - Revolution und Avantgarde" (Cologne: DuMont Taschenbücher, 1990), p.90.

64 MERZ, issue 8/9, April/June 1924. El Lissitzky illustrated Francé's booklets "Die Pflanze als Erfinder" ("The plant as inventor") and "Bios". In a letter to Sophie Küppers-Lissitzky, dated 10 March 1924, El Lissitzky mentions he would very much like to meet Francé and plans to send him a copy of Nasci (he also reminds her to buy 'Bios'). See Sophie Küppers-Lissitzky, Herbert Read, "El Lissitzky-Life-Letters-Texts" (New York: Thames and Hudson, 1992 - first edition, London: Thames and Hudson, 1968- orig. 1967, Dresden: Verlag der Kunst), p.46.

65 El Lisstizky wrote in his introduction to 'Nasci', see Sophie Lissitzky-Küppers, Herbert Read, "El Lissitzky-Life-Letters-Texts", p.351: "Modern art, following a completely intuitive and obvious course, has reached the same results as modern science. Like science, it has reduced the form to its basic elements, in order to construct it according to the universal laws of nature; in doing this, both have arrived at the same formula: every form is the frozen instantaneous picture of a process. Thus a work is a stopping-place on the road of becoming and not a fixed goal." The original German text quoted in Kai-Uwe Hemken, "El Lissitzky - Revolution und Avantgarde" (Cologne: DuMont Taschenbücher, 1990), p.90-92.

66 See §14.

fluidum with relations of force.[67] He is another one of those early abstract artists in the first decades of the 20th century who was familiar with and inspired by the new ideas in science about matter and space/time. He received a lot of information from his nephew Erwin Finlay-Freundlich, who was an astro-physicist and the director of the Einstein Institute at Potsdam - the institute founded to prove Einstein's Theory of Relativity. Freundlich was especially inspired by Maxwell's notion of a field of energy. To reach a comparable result, he proposed using curved forms in painting to break open the contours and thus visualize the dynamic cosmic forces of nature and simultaneously illustrate the concept that there is no precise border between our bodies and our environment, only flowing energies.[68] For Freundlich, coloured grids, matrixes or fields that show a visual structure in a painting, exemplified an aesthetic connection to the scientific field theory.[69]

see picture 23

One can find further examples of the general interest in the organic in the first decades of the 20th century in philosophy in the USA and England. John Dewey stated that the distinction between the mind and the body is quite dubious, instead one should speak of the organism.[70] Later in the 1920's the English philosopher/mathematician Alfred North Whitehead took this further in his philosophy of organism in which he emphasized that everything is a process, a continuous becoming into being (Whitehead's own definition: 'becoming a being'). He suggested we should look at the universe not as containing mechanistic or atomic entities, but as one organic whole.[71] While not having the space to elaborate on his theories, Rudolf Steiner's Anthroposophy should be mentioned here, if only for his ideas about a natural art and architecture based on organic shapes.[72] Steiner believed art and architecture should be based on aesthetic principles

[67] Freundlich saw them as 'Kraftbeziehungen'. On the fluidum, see §14.

[68] Otto Freundlich, quoted by Rita Wildegans, "Otto Freundlichs Werk im Kontext naturwissenschaftlicher Erkenntnisse", in Gerhard Leistner, Thorsten Rodiek, "Otto Freundlich - Ein Wegbereiter der abstrakten Kunst" (Regensburg, Osnabrück: Museum Ostdeutsche Galerie, Kulturgeschichtliches Museum Osnabrück, 1994), p.55: "To define and explain a world force, that was to which our most sincere attempt was focussed, both as artist and as human being." ("Eine Weltkraft zu deuten und zu klären, darauf war unsere innigste Anspannung als Künstler und Mensch gerichtet."). This quote is from Uli Bohnen, "Otto Freundlich Schriften" (Cologne: DuMont Verlag, 1982). Though the reason to prefer curved shapes is of course similar to Kandinsky, Freundlich was of a later generation and was involved in an artistic understanding of Quantum Theory, which Kandinsky was not - or Kandinsky might have sensed it, but there is no evidence he was informed about Quantum Mechanics as Freundlich was. Freundlich and Kandinsky knew each other and met in Paris in the late 1930's. Freundlich's paintings consist of free styled coloured grids that are a kind of synthesis of amorphic and 'free-hand' geometric shapes.

[69] See §6, §7.

[70] John Dewey (1859-1952) developed his theory around the confrontation of an organism with occurances in its environment and with the process of adaptation to these changes - a process of the mind he called 'inquiry'. See John Dewey, "Experience and Nature" (New York: Dover Publications Inc., 1958 - orig. 1929).

[71] This was inspired by Bergson's notion that reality consists of an endless stream of becoming. See Alfred N. Whitehead, "Process and Reality" (Free Press, 1979 - orig.1929). Whitehead had a profound influence on artists and scientists ever since the 1930's. See §4 on Charles Biederman and David Bohm. Scientist Ilya Prigogene also refers to Whitehead.

[72] See Walter Kugler, "Rudolf Steiner und die Anthropologie" (Cologne: DuMont Taschenbücher, 1991). Steiner (1861-1925), born in Croatia, then still a part of the Austrian empire. He worked at the Goethe-

that can be found in nature itself and will thus automatically be in harmony with nature. Architectural concepts looked like combinations of principles and proportions of crystals, the outline of mountains, while inside the building natural materials should be used. The Goetheanum at Dornach, near Basle, Switzerland, is the famous expression of these theories.

Simultaneous to the artistic and philosophical developments discussed, one can find in the 1920's and 1930's, besides Kandinsky, quite a few artists working with amorphic/organic shapes. For instance, Pablo Picasso, Hans (known also as Jean) Arp, Paul Klee, and Henri Matisse, and in the general movements of DaDa and Surrealism. Artists shared a general interest in popular and scientific publications on (micro)biology. In the early 1920's Max Ernst explored images using depictions from microbiology, and in the 1930's he made paintings inspired by scientific explorations demonstrating air flow and used a scientific diagram showing the effects of magnetism.[73]

It is interesting to follow the development of Picasso and Braque's assemblage-technique through Max Ernst's complex mystics, to a dissolution of pictorial space with amorphic blobs in the works by Hans Arp, André Masson, Joan Miró, Salvador Dali, Yves Tanguy, and with a slight geometric touch by Julio Gonzalez, Alexander Calder and Wilfredo Lam. One can see the connection in a more geometrized way in Ferdinand Léger's late 1920's paintings, which were imported and promoted in the 1930's in the USA when the Surrealists fled WWII and came to New York. Roberto Matta and Wolfgang Paalen were of great importance for the introduction of the Surrealist ideas on the amorphic.[74] This kind of amorphic/organic vocabulary became an important element

see picture 24

Schiller Archives at Weimar 1891-1897, editing Goethe's natural scientific essays. He was the leader of the German section of the Theosophic Society 1902-1913. After a disagreement with the doctrine, he initiated his own 'Anthroposophische Gesellschaft' (Athroposophic Society). Anthropos = human being; sophia = wisdom. Anthroposophy is a concept of the world that tends towards a stronger cosmic unity, while knowledge is understood as a process of harmonizing with the spirit of the essence of things, based on their mutual relationships (compare §2!). Founded on Goethe, Nietzsche, Haeckel, etc., and comparable to Francé and other Zeitgeist-thinkers, Steiner considered nature to be the example of the right harmony, to which man should adapt. Anthroposophy is a method for knowledge through which spiritual man can be led to find and connect with the spiritual in the universe. In contrast to Theosophy, Steiner considered reincarnation not a liberation from life on earth, but a way to acquire a better view and understanding of life as it is. This can be related to the interpretation of 'enlightenment' and the role of 'nirvana' by Oriental thinkers (see §8).

73 See Lynn Gamwell, "Exploring the Invisible - Art, Science, And The Spiritual" (Princeton and Oxford: Princeton University Press, 2002), p.242, and following. See Vivian Endicott Barnett, "Kandinsky and Science: The Introduction of Biological Images in the Paris Period", in Thomas M. Messer, "Kandinsky in Paris 1934-1944" (New York: The Solomon R. Guggenheim Museum, 1985), p.82.

74 Paalen, born in Austria, lived in Rome and Munich (where he followed a course by Hans Hoffmann, who later became an important teacher in New York), Berlin, Paris, traveled through Canada, British Columbia and Alaska, stayed shortly in New York and settled in Mexico in 1939. His late 1930's experimental paintings are best known. In these he 'painted' complete abstract and amorphic pictures making soot-marks with a burning candle on a canvas, and which he called 'Fumages'. See Andreas Neufert, "Wolfgang Paalen - Im Inneren des Wals" (Vienna, New York: Springer Verlag, 1999), p.117-125. Paalen was first an acknowledged member of the Surrealists, but at some point discarded by Breton. From Mexico he published the magazine "DYN". See Christian Kloyber, "Wolfgang Paalen's DYN - The Complete Reprint" (Vienna, New York: Springer Verlag, 2000). Six issues were published from 1942-1944, focussing on ethnography, poetry and fine art. Contributing

in the initial search of a new generation of young American artists to find their own contribution to art history. It was the prelude to American Expressionism.[75] Simultaneously, in the 1930's, 1940's and well into the 1950's different levels of understanding of Zen and its concept of nothingness emerged. Mark Tobey, André Masson, but also Joan Miró, probably belong to the very few artists who really and sincerely studied oriental thought and calligraphy.[76]
The Surrealist painter and sculptor Joan Miró was inspired by folk art and by shapes and forms he found in nature, like on his strolls when living on Mallorca. Miró's interest in Japanese and Chinese calligraphy (and in poetry and ceramics) is very clear in his magnificent strong and pure abstract paintings from 1960-1968.[77] He eventually visited

artists included: Roberto Matta, Alexander Calder, Henry Moore, Gordon Onslow-Ford, Robert Motherwell, Jackson Pollock. Motherwell visited Paalen in Mexico. Paalen was an intellectual, inspired by a great variety of theories and philosophies, including ethnological concepts (of the North American Indians), Schopenhauer, Kierkegaard, Tao, Chinese "I-Ching". Paalen was very interested in physicist Ernst Mach's concept of denying a distinction between matter and mind, published by Mach in "Die Analyse der Empfindungen und das Verhältnis des Physischen und Psychischen", ("The Analysis of Experiences and the Relation of the Physical and the Psychic"), 1885/1900. See Andreas Neufert, "Wolfgang Paalen - Im Inneren des Wals", p.19. Paalen stated in 1945: "Science and art both have their roots in the imagination; form and sense cannot be separated since no mental concept can become intelligible without assuring the form. But it is equally false to try to poetise science (surrealist error) as to try to make a scientific art (abstract error)." See Christian Kloyber, "Wolfgang Paalen's DYN - The Complete Reprint", p.II.

75 For an outstanding essay on this important episode in modern art, exemplifying the natural course of events resulting in European art becoming the inspiration for the birth of new independent developments in the USA, and written as experienced from the life of the involved artists (with a major role for Max Ernst), see Margret Schütte, "The Disinterested Play .... ", in Ulla and Heiner Pietzsch, "Leben mit Kunst - Sammlung Ulla und Heiner Pietzsch" (Berlin: Ulla und Heiner Pietzsch, 2000). On the formative years of the young American artists, see Irving Sandler, "The Triumph of American Painting - A History of Abstract Expressionism" (New York: Prager Publishers Inc., 1970). One can find clear references to these connections - often mixed with influences by Picasso's paintings - in the early abstract works by Pollock, Rothko, Adolph Gottlieb, David Smith, William Baziotes, Arshile Gorky, Robert Motherwell.

76 Just one magnificent example of Mark Tobey is his painting "The World Egg" from 1944 in the typical grays and whites Tobey-sensitive calligraphic style. See §9, including footnote 17. The title "The World Egg" and the ellipsoid composition clearly refer to the Hindu concept of the "Egg of Brahma", containing the "All" of world and universe. On Tobey and Masson, see Katja Blomberg, "Begegnungen des Ich mit sich selbst - Ostasiatische Kalligraphie und westliches Informel als malerische Haltung zwischen 1930 und 1960", in Hellmut Seemann, "Yu-Ichi - HIN - Werke 1954 bis 1982" (Tokyo: Tianjin Publishing Trading Corporation and Schirn Kunsthalle Frankfurt, 1995), p.45-52. As a student in 1923, Tobey was a friend of the Chinese art-student Teng K'uei and travelled to meet Teng's family in Shanghai in 1934 and to study in Japan. Though from his 17th year he was acqainted with Oriental art and philosophy, it took Masson moving to New York in 1942 to become influenced by Oriental art to introduce Oriental calligraphic elements in his works after he saw the collection of the Museum of Fine Arts in Boston. Tobey and Masson (and also for instance Hans Hoffman) used drippings and 'all-over' compositions before Pollock did. Because the latter must have seen some of it in exhibitions in New York, it is considered natural to see an indirect connection between Pollock's works and ideas with some aspects of Oriental culture.

77 For a detailed study of Miró's Oriental interests, see Pilar Cábanas, "La Fuerza de Oriente en la obra de Miró" (Spain: Electa, 2000), mentioning for instance the presence of quite a few Japanese artists in Paris with whom Miró was familiar or befriended: Tsuguhara Fujita, Ilamado Leonard Fujita, También Kanji Maeda, Yuzo Fukuzawa and Kigai Kawaguchi (who introduced Surrealism in Japan). Between 1929-1940 Taro Okamoto participated in the abstract movement in Paris before returning to Japan. It is assumed Miró was invited to 'a

Japan on two occasions.[78] Simultaneously, in the 1930's there was a trend in American art described as 'Biomorphism', based on a combination of a deep love for nature and a strong belief in the magic of man himself. This typically American trend was combined with an interest in the art of the North American Indians.[79]

Not much later, Jackson Pollock's magnificent poured and splashed paintings of sheer nothingness emerged out of his dark and brooding surrealist formative years.[80] Pollock also had a stimulating influence on European and even on modern Asian painting.[81] Pollock moved around quite a bit through the USA, starting his art education in California. As a young art student he was given a first flavour of Oriental thinking and theosophy, while being inspired by a great variety of visual influences, of which here only his early interest in ethnological art and the Mexican mural art must be men-

tea' in April 1930 at the Hotel Lutetia, Paris, the farewell party of Yoshikazu Mineguishi. This artist upon his return to Japan became the co-ordinator of the exhibition "Exposition des artistes d'avant-garde Paris-Tokyo". In his library Miró had books like "Principles of Chinese Painting" by George Rowley, "Mystique chinoise et peinture moderne" by George Duthuit, "La peinture chinoise" by Peter S. Swann, "Yi-King - Le livre des transformations" (orig. in German) by Richard Wilhelm (1968), "Poesie del Fiume Wang" by Wang Wei P'ei Ti (1956), "Le Haiku" by Georges Bonneau, and some catalogues on exhibitions of Japanese and Chinese art, like by his friends Sofu Teshigahara (known as master of ikebana, calligraphy and sculptor), Shuzo Takiguchi (1903-1979). Takiguchi was a poet, art-critic, painter, and known as promotor of surrealist 'absolute automatism' in Japan Miró collaborated on several projects with Takiguchi.

[78] Miro visited Japan in 1966 for his retrospective exhibition, and again in 1969 in context to preparations for a commissioned large outdoor sculpture for the World Expo in Osaka in 1970.

[79] See Guiltremie Maldonado, "Transferal and Synthesis - American Biomorphism of the 1930's", in Éric de Chassey, "American Art, 1908-1947 From Winslow Homer to Jackson Pollock" (New York: Harry N. Abrams Inc., 2001), p.208-215. Mentioned artists are: Charles Biederman, Ilya Bolotowsky, Byron Browne, John Ferren, Gertrude Greene, Balcomb Green, Carl Holty, Ibram Lassaw, Alice Trumbell Mason, George L.K. Morris, Ad Rheinhardt, Esphyr Slobodkina, and Albert Swinden. American Biomorphism is in this essay proposed to be distinguished from European Biomorphism as such, because they lacked the tension, violence and mystery of the Europeans (see André Masson's "Massacre", reproduced in this book). The Americans are assumed to emphasize the equilibrium in a more formal perfection. Still, they were obviously also influenced by Picasso's own 'biomorphism' and the amorphic/organic forms in combination with geometry as in Léger's paintings - Biederman's paintings of the 1930's exemplify this. A book that exemplifies the interest in the organic was "On Growth and Form" in which is discussed how many phenomena in nature are supposed to be based on certain rules of logic, rules of aesthetics that can be translated into numbers and pure geometrical shapes, like the Golden Ratio and the Fibonacci series of numbers. See D'Arcy Wentworth Thompson, "On Growth and Form - the complete revised edition" (Mineola, NY: Dover Publications, 1992 - orig.1942). For more information on these number series, see Charles Seife, "Zero - The Biography of a Dangerous Idea" (New York: Penguin Books, 2000). Thompson's book was known to artists as diverse as Naum Gabo or Jackson Pollock. Barbara Hepworth and Henry Moore also may have studied this book. "On Growth and Form" was widely popular amongst English 'systems' artists in the late 1960's and 1970's.

[80] On Pollock a lot has been published. The books I explored (see the list of literature): Alloway, Frank, Friedman, Karmel, Landau, Naifeh/Smith, Ratcliff, Sandler, Varnedoe/Karmel, Varnedoe.

[81] Pollock seems to have influenced artists like Shiraga Kazuo, who around 1955 painted on the floor using his feet smearing (oil)paint in calligraphic kind of expressions, or held performances rolling through fresh mud. Yu-Ichi Inoue was inspired by the use of black industrial enamel paint by western painters (presumably Pollock and Franz Kline) to apply in his powerful calligraphic style instead of the traditional Japanese ink. Yu-Ichi often was squatting on his paper while painting. See Hellmut Seemann, "Yu-Ichi - HIN - Werke 1954 bis 1982" (Tokyo: Tianjin Publishing Trading Corporation and Schirn Kunsthalle Frankfurt, 1995), p.106. The involvement of the body in painting in total immersion on the floor brings to memory the fashionable variant

tioned.[82] Pollock had several opportunities to hear Krishnamurti talk.[83] This is something that is not widely researched. When Pollock developed his initially dark and brooding paintings in the boiling pot of the early new York art scene in the late 1930's,[84] the interest in 'primitive art' was coupled with an interest in 'myth' by Picasso and the Surrealists - especially including the form-language of Miró - and a general interest in the occult, in Jung's concept of a collective consciousness, archetypes and their role in the creation of art. In 1942 Gottlieb, Rothko, Pollock, Motherwell and Baziotes started to experiment with automatism, primarily under the influence of Matta.[85]

Jackson Pollock's swooping motions of poured and splashed paint are achieved by

of Yves Klein using beautiful nude female models to make body marks on a huge canvas, his "Anthropométries de l'Epoque Blue" in 1960.

82 Pollock's teacher Frederick Schwankovsky introduced him to Oriental thinking, theosophy and Krishnamurti. See B.H. Friedman, "Jackson Pollock - Energy Made Visible", (New York: DaCapo Press, 1995 - orig. 1972), p.10, on Schwankovsky: "He performed experiments in extrasensory perception, especially this related to a Universal Consciousness." Friedman quotes several letters by Pollock to his brothers in which Pollock mentiones his interest in Oriental and Occult mysticism (without any clear description how deep or serious his interest was). Pollock was particularly interested in the powerful, highly expressive, representational murals by David Alfaro Siqueiros and José Clemente Orozco. Pollock owned a copy of "Yoga Explained" by F. Yeats-Brown (1937), including explanations on Hinduism. See Ellen G. Landau, "Jackson Pollock", (New York: Harry N. Abrams Inc., 2000 - orig. Abradale Press, 1989), p.66.

83 As young art student, Jackson Pollock met Krishnamurti a couple of times, staying in May 1929 at the Ojai camp, California, for about a week. See Steven Naifeh and Gregory White Smith, "Jackson Pollock - An American Saga" (New York: Clarkson N. Potter Inc., 1989), p.137-139. Though it is pure speculation if Pollock understood the notion of the 'formless' as undoubtedly Krishnamurti would have mentioned, it can be expected that it contributed in one way or another to his artistic development. Ellen G. Landau merely mentions that Indian Theosophist's Pantheism through Krishnamurti's teachings kept playing a role in Pollock's development. Persons who knew him said that "... Pollock's comprehension of the world of man and his surroundings was unusually all-inclusive.", in Ellen G. Landau, "Jackson Pollock" (New York: Harry N. Abrams Inc., 2000 - orig. Abradale Press, 1989), p.159. Art critic Carter Ratcliff discusses Pollock's sense of oneness (experienced most intensely in his creative process pouring paint) to be possibly related to Krishnamurti's ideas. See Carter Ratcliff, "The Fate of a Gesture: Jackson Pollock and Postwar American Art" (New York: Farrar, Straus and Giroux 1996), p. 70: "Pollock liked Krishnamurti's intimations of something beyond the reach of the mundane, a saving force that individuals can draw from themselves."

84 Pollock came to live in New York in the fall 1930. He studied with the painter Thomas Hart Benton. Benton's main concept was to anaylize Baroque and Renaissance paintings by reducing them to drawn arcs, bars and stick figures. He also taught his "Fundamental mechanical principles", like on rhythm. Benton: "In the 'feel' of our own bodies, in the sight of the bodies of others, in the bodies of animals, in the shapes of growing and moving things, in the forces of nature and in the engines of man the rhythmic principle of movement and counter-movement is made manifest. But in our own bodies it can be isolated, felt and understood. This mechanical principle which we share with all life can be abstracted and used in constructing and analyzing things which also in their way have life and reality". Quoted in Kirk Varnedoe, Pepe Karmel, "Jackson Pollock" (New York: Harry N. Abrams Inc., 1998), p.24. Other early influences on Pollock were the European Surrealists, Cubists (mainly Picasso), Kandinsky, and his interests in ethnography.

85 Automatism, was described in the Surrealist manifesto of 1924: "Pure psychic automatism, by which it is intended to express, verbally, in writing, or by other means, the real process of thought. Thought's dictation, in the absence of all control exercised by the reason and outside all aesthetic or moral preoccupation." quoted in Irving Sandler, "The Triumph in American Painting", p.36. Sandler mentions that though automatism in Surrealism was applied in the first years, it was temporarily abandoned in the 1930's for the 'reasoning stage', as Breton called it. Matta called for an original and abstract interpretation and started applying automatism in 1937, Paalen did so after 1939, and published in "DYN" in 1942 on this subject. Irving Sandler writes, in

great control over paint, colour, surface and size. The sense of deep space in his sensitively made meshworks have convinced me to see him as an incredible painter of space.[86] see picture 27 Pollock's painting "Reflection of the Big Dipper" is a magnificent example of his brilliance. As art critic Irving Sandler correctly observed, the paintings are done by complete immersion of the artist and also immerse the viewer in their delirium. That is why I understand Pollock's art as a great example for experiencing the sublime in a total dissolving of duality.[87] The calligraphic or more amorphic/organic and controlled use of lines interlace into complex meshworks of high power. These are sheer metaphors for the complex Quanta-fields of energies in the nothingness in nature. Sandler, referring to the introduction by Alfonso Ossorio to Pollock's show at Betty Parsons Gallery in 1951, writes:

> *"Mondrian found an absolute structure that for him symbolized the cosmic design underlying natural phenomena. Pollock, on the other hand, sought for a pattern that would embody a passionate private vision. Nevertheless, the energy that surges through his pictures suggests a universal dimension, issuing perhaps from a belief that energy is the common denominator of all phenomena."*[88]

Sandler's observation of the universal dimension in Pollock's paintings match the Chinese concept that the expression in the frozen marks of calligraphy offers a strong experience of reliving the physical action in one's mind, therefore, adding a meaningful dimension to thought.[89] We can probably relate so well to Pollock's paintings because

---

"The Triumph of American Painting", p.37: "Organic forms - as opposed to geometric ones - suggested anthropomorphic sources, inner and outer life in all of its rich, changeable, and ambiguous variety, and so pointed to a humanist content."

86 In most of Pollock's paintings, there is clearly no 'flatness' as stated so often on American Expressionism (emphasized by Clement Greenberg). Experiencing this sense of deep space in the Jackson Pollock Retrospective at the MoMA in NY in 1998, and my desire to find my own approach to what Monet accomplished in his "Nymphéas", inspired me after a period of 'digestion' to develop my large coloured wire constructions in the "The Dragon Series".

87 See Irving Sandler, "The Triumph of American Painting", p.111. I still believe that is what Pollock meant in his often quoted remark "I am nature!". He expressed this in answer to Hans Hoffmann, when this teacher/artist asked him where nature would be in his work. See Kirk Varnedoe, Pepe Karmel, "Jackson Pollock", p.42. I found confirmation for my own conclusion in Carter Ratcliff's book. See Carter Ratcliff, "The Fate of a Gesture: Jackson Pollock and Postwar American Art", p. 69: "When Pollock said, 'I am nature', he argued in short hand that empathy was unnecessary. He and the world were one, so he had no reason to look at sunsets or at anything outside himself." It makes sense that Pollock's way of totally immersed painting - which is based on pure intuition involving memory, experience, 'free reign' while still keeping a self-argumented control - is so similar to Oriental expressive calligraphy. Helen Westgeest writes on Shirya Morita, referring to an interview with Morita in Kyoto in 1991: "He describes his way of working as bringing the 'Kanji' from within himself on to the paper, by way of his arm and brush. He believes that in that way he can express his vital energy, or inner force, and so liberate himself. This is his way of trying to achieve freedom of mind and body." See Helen Westgeest, "Zen in the Fifties - Interaction between east and west" (Zwolle: Waanders Uitgeverij, 1996), p.201. Pollock and Zen, indeed a kind strong kinship while still being different.

88 See Irving Sandler, "The Triumph of American Painting", p.116.

89 The first theory of calligraphy in China was written by Chang Huai-kuan (ca. 714-760). See Wen C. Fong,

the size and action radius of the swoops of his paint are recognizably based on his physical motions - thus related to our own bodily motions.

At the time he created his major works, Pollock lived in the country side. Living myself between farm land, at some point I perceived the following. When you look at a meadow, your first idea will be of an 'empty field'. On a second look, especially when you stroll through a wild field of grass, you might notice the patterns of grass virtually streaming in the wind, intertwining in layer upon layer by growth, differences in length, colour, curve. The patterns seem to evoke a sense of precisely definable structure, though it clearly is not; it is chaotic. I understand the meadow as a great metaphor for 'no-thingness', 'full of meaning'.

Though undoubtedly pure speculation on my part, and not suggesting that Pollock would have started making his all-over patterns after seeing the grasslands, and not at all implying he merely was searching to make a depiction of grass lands, I can still imagine he had a similar experience understanding the structure of grass in a purely metaphorical sense. His paintings "Sounds in the Grass Series" seem to justify this remark.[90] It might be interesting to mention that the almost abstract and very expressive free style in Japanese calligraphy is called 'so-sho', meaning 'wild grass'.

Of the other expressionists, Clyfford Still developed a very personal style of amorphic painting. Adolph Gottlieb painted a 'sun' with amorphic shapes in a calligraphic style. Mark Rothko approached a kind of blurry geometry, resulting in immensely powerful colour realms. Hans Hoffman painted in a kind of strong 'free-style' half amorphic/organic geometry. Franz Kline developed his specific large scale calligraphic signs. Quite exceptional amorphic/organic sculptors were Seymour Lipton, David Smith (though more known for his geometric sculptures) and the great Isamu Noguchi, and later Anthony Caro, Eduardo Chillida, Bernard Heiliger, Paul Suter and Mark di Suvero. Mark di Suvero's sculpture seems to have developed gradually towards a kind of strong spatial calligraphic form language (it is quite interesting to compare in this book his sculpture with Yu-Ichi's work on paper). Often di Suvero incorporates one or more parts that can wobble or even rotate. Thus he clearly involves simulated change as well as actual change.[91]

see pictures 59, 60

Some members of the American Expressionists kept developing their work well into

"Chinese Calligraphy: Theory and History", in Robert E. Harrist Jr., Wen C. Fong, "The Embodied Image - Chinese Calligraphy from the John B. Elliott Collection" (Princeton, NJ: The Art Museum, Princeton University, 1999), p. 30: "Chang believed that through the act of writing, the artist rediscovered the vital cosmic forces that informed a character's rhythm and structure, forces that had first been revealed to the ancient sages."

[90] The "Sounds in the Grass" series, painted in 1946, was an important transition phase from almost 'free style' geometric partitioned compositions to swirling painted compositions in thick layers, like "Shimmering Substance", "Eyes in the Heat". See Kirk Varnedoe, Pepe Karmel, "Jackson Pollock", p.216-217.

[91] See Irving Sandler, "Mark di Suvero at Storm King Art Center", Storm King Art Center (New York: Harry N. Abrams, Inc., 1995). See Renato Danese, "Mark di Suvero", catalogue incl. essay by Mark Daniel Cohen, Danese Gallery NY, 2000. See Albion, "Mark di Suvero" (London: Albion, Michael Hue-Williams Fine Art Ltd., 2004).

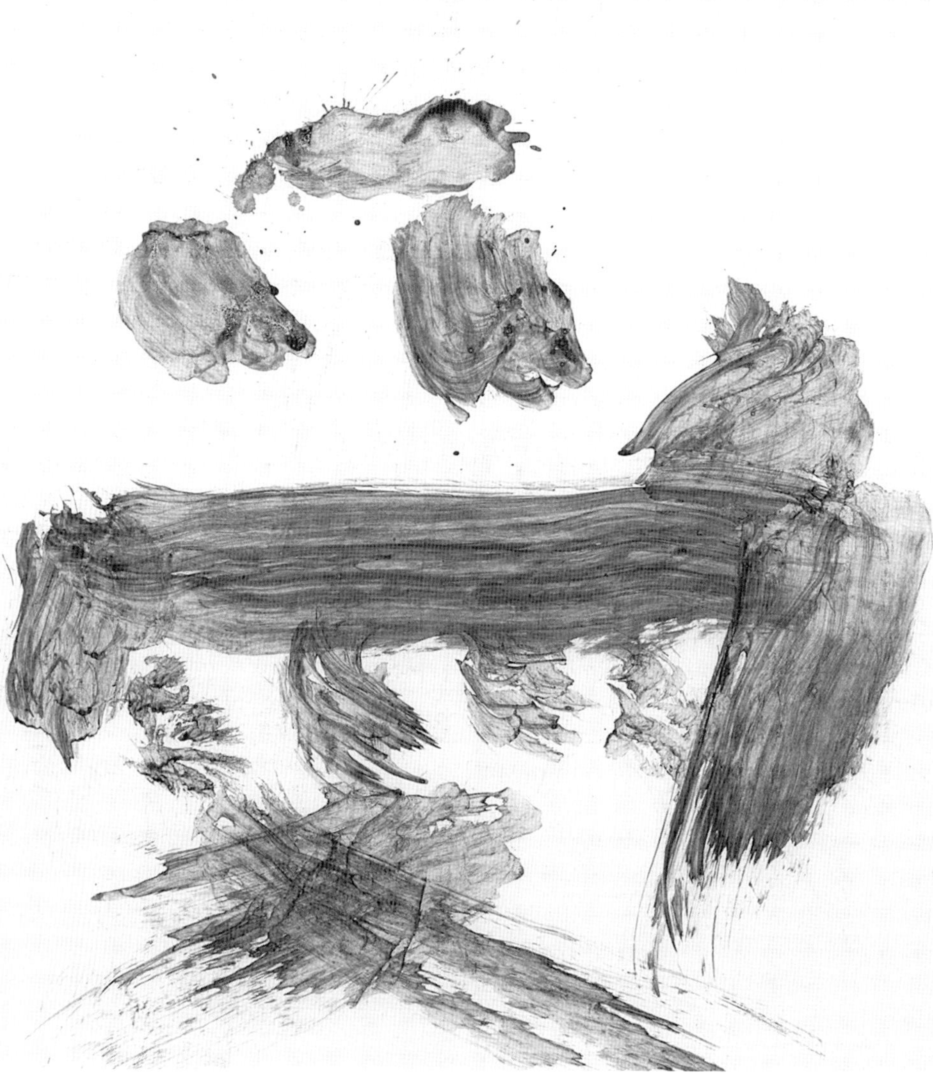

65. Yu-Ichi (1916-1985)
AI, 1972
Ink on paper, seal: Yu-Ichi; catalogue raisonné, Vol.2, #72062 91 x 126,4 cm (35 13/16 x 493/4 inches)
Private collection Frankfurt am Main, Germany
Courtesy of Galerie Friedrich Müller JAPAN ART, Frankfurt
www.japan-art.com

the 1960's, 1970's, and 1980's like Robert Motherwell, Helen Frankenthaler, and Joan Mitchell.[92]

Because I already have discussed aspects of gesture in painting, there is no reason to repeat them.[93] It just might be useful to remind one that the basic technology of painting is making and leaving a mark of paint on a flat surface. Sometimes the history of painting becomes clear in a very natural way by just studying brush-strokes from very different periods and observing them from a short distance. Brush-strokes in paintings from the Venetian School, like Titian, from Rubens and Rembrandt announce Impressionism. The brush-strokes of Van Gogh and Monet clearly announce the expressive powers of the amorphic/organic expression of the post WWII period.[94] These are in their immediate expression quite analogous to free 'sosho' style calligraphy in Japanese Zen, as in the powerful modern versions by Yu-Ichi, or the strong calligraphic and almost geometric use of paint by contemporary Korean artists Ha Chong Hyun and Lee Ufan.[95] One probably can also relate this kind of painting to the amazing last group of works by Willem de Kooning, with their flowing amorphic/organic colour shapes.[96]

When you try the close-up observation of works of art in a museum you will agree that it was only a matter of time until artists took the liberty to focus entirely on the meaning of the brush-stroke itself - or beyond the brush, merely as 'mark with paint'- considering painting as fundamentally being 'forming un-formed matter'- exploring the essence of reality in a 'world without forms and images', beyond the surface of the material world.

Based on an exceptionally thorough study and analysis of art history, in combination with a profound and deep insight into the processes of nature, the American artist Charles Biederman initially went through his own phase of 'biomorphism' before he

92 Other artists continued this line in the same period, like Sam Francis, Morris Louis, Larry Poons, Jules Olitski, etc. up to all kinds of expressionist painting in many countries and in changing waves of interest. For example German and French 'Informal' painters, and Tapies, Cy Twombly, Per Kirkeby, Raimer Jochims, Brice Marden, Gerhard Richter, Gotthard Graubner, Natvar Bhavsar, Pat Steir, Katharina Grosse, etc.

93 See §9.

94 For the brush-stroke the French word 'tache' was used already before the Impressionists. See David Bomford, Jo Kirby, John Leighton, Ashok Roy, "Art in the Making - Impressionism", (London: The National Gallery, London, Yale University Press, 1990), p.92-96.

95 See Stephen Addiss, "The Art of Zen - Paintings and Calligraphy by Japanese Monks 1600-1925" (New York: Harry N. Abrams Inc., 1989): Bankei, Sokuhi, Tetsugyu, Hakuin, Torei, Ryokan, Gocho, Sengai. See Audrey Yoshiko Seo, Stephen Addiss, "The Art of Twentieth Century Zen - Painting and Calligraphy by Japanese Masters" (Shambala Press, 1998), concerning 1850-1945: Nakahara Nantenbo, Deiryu Kutsu, Mokurai, Nishiari Bokuzan, Seki Seisetzu. Since 1945 one may mention Shiruya Morita and Yu-Ichi. More currently, for instance, Kyoko Tai, Hiroko Nakajima, Lee Ufan. See Masaomi Unagami, "Yu-Ichi, a catalogue raisonné of the works 1949-1985" Volu. I, II, III (Tokyo: UNAC, 1998, limited edition). See Dieter Ronte, "Lee Ufan - Gemälde 1973 bis 2001" (Bonn: Kunstmuseum Bonn, 2001).

96 I am referring to de Kooning's work from the 1980-ies. See Eduard Lieber, "Willem de Kooning - Reflections in the studio" (New York: Harry N. Abrams Inc., 2000). See David Whitney, "De Kooning - A Centennial Exhibition" (New York: Gagosian Gallery 2004).

developed his own view on the structure of nature and how to translate this into art.[97]

The English artist Victor Pasmore was a remarkable artist and good example of an important period of transition in modern European art. At a crucial moment in his development he was influenced by Biederman's theories and promotion of the machine-made relief as the medium for the future.[98] Pasmore went through the development from representational Post-Impressionist painting, through structural reliefs and a few architectural experiments to a very dynamic and exciting combination of (amorphic) organic and geometric/calligraphic form-language. He understood Picasso's works painted during WWII not as examples for the further development in art, but as a signal to treat painting as an independent phenomenon and thus to be able to (re)connect man with nature. Therefore, in the late 1940's, he understood the need to develop an independent morphology from a fundamental and objective alphabet of forms, changing painting from a process of visual abstraction to one of intrinsic and organic construction.[99] In the 1950's he quit painting and started making paper collages that evolved into low reliefs. Towards the end of the 1950's he developed a growing sense of space by mounting geometric bars and machine-made profiles onto transparant plexi glass planes. He accomplished the highest sense of space in his amazing geometric reliefs between about 1959-1965, like "Abstract in White, Black and Crimson".[100] It is important to know that in the 1950's artists like Pasmore understood making pure geometric reliefs as an organic way of constructing, exemplified in the often found references in statements in those years to the principle of growth, explored by constructing certain basic units or 'cells' in repetitive rhythms. Pasmore discovered that, although the relief as medium at first seemed to promise open possibilities, the surface projections in these reliefs had limitations

[97] See §3 and §4. Biederman had a deep influence on a generation of European and some American artists in the late 1950's and early 1960's, promoting the search for the structure of nature in which a (organic) principle like growth played a large role, mirrored in the magazines "Structure" by artist Joost Baljeu and "The Structurist" by artist Eli Bornstein.

[98] See Alan Bowness and Luigi Lambertini, "Victor Pasmore - with catalogue raisonné of the paintings, constructions and graphics 1926-1979" (London: Thames and Hudson, 1980). See Norbert Lynton, "Victor Pasmore - Paintings and etchings 1980-92" (London: Lund Humphries, 1992). See PRO-NR.2 (Dordrecht: the PRO Foundation, 1987). Pasmore was born in 1908. In the early 1930's he was already involved in the London avant-garde. In 1934 he became involved with the 'Objective Abstractions' movement, a group that focussed on a tachist abstract style (they choose the brush-stroke as its module). See Alan Bowness and Luigi Lambertini, "Victor Pasmore - with catalogue raisonné of the paintings, constructions and graphics 1926-1979", p.280. After several years of abstraction, he returned to traditional representational painting until 1946.

[99] Pasmore saw Picasso's works he painted in occupied France in the large exhibition in London in 1946. Pasmore, quoted in Alan Bowness and Luigi Lambertini, "Victor Pasmore - with catalogue raisonné of the paintings, constructions and graphics 1926-1979", p.94: "Henceforth the relation between artist and nature would be intrinsic and the imagery of painting a free and independent manifestation of this connection." Clearly this opinion made his mind open for Biederman's argument. Pasmore's own interest in morphology based on an alphabet of forms sounds similar to the interest of Kandinsky in the last phase of his paintings in Paris.

[100] Ibid., p.122. His interest in the relief resulted also from a renewed contact in 1948 with well-known early low relief artist Ben Nicholson. However, his decisive drive meaning to focus on the 'machine-made' relief was his reading of Biederman's 1948 book "Art As the Evolution of Visual Knowledge" in 1951. Ibid., p.14. See §4.

very similar to painting. Combined with his experience of analogous limitations in architecture, he correctly concluded that any notion of objective independence is always mixed with subjective notions.

This is something that seems logical today, but in Pasmore's time empirical rationalization and objective perception were still considered to be vital, possible and the desired objective. This makes Pasmore's conclusion that a subjective property of physical reality cannot be put in terms of dimension quite remarkable.[101] It led him back to painting and back to less geometric and more amorphic/organic shapes - in combination with strong and still very sensitively applied geometric bars/thick lines, sometimes in a quite free calligraphic style. Contrasts in rhythms, colours and organic balloon-like shapes of nothingness are important features in these works. Often they are flat paintings, like the incredible "Blue Symphony", his magnificent large prints of the 80's and 90's, or in assemblages of flat painting and low relief.[102] see picture 33

Australian Aboriginal painter Emily Kngwarreye, German painter Gotthard Graubner and Indian-American painter Natvar Bhavsar are great late 20th century artists of the amorphic/organic. Though coming from very different backgrounds, the work of these artists is related in an astonishing way and can with justification be put immediately in line with Monet's late paintings and Jackson Pollock's best work. Their coinciding interest concerns the engulfing power of colour in sheer nothingness in large scale painting, incorporating sizes of colour forms and concentrations that allow the viewer to be absorbed instead of being pushed away. Their paintings invite one to walk up to them, to virtually walk into their colour spaces, instead of walking backwards - which happens with a lot of large scale art. One can find the differences between these three painters in their various individual approaches.

Emily Kngwarreye's subjects are the dream-stories, the song-lines, which are a narrative of the Australian outback. Her magnificent and highly powered abstract paintings mostly with dots, but also with flowing brush-strokes, in principle are based on not-so-abstract stories; the painting showing a bird-eye's view of the landscape where the story happened. These paintings are very impressive examples of modern art at its best, based on the observation of nature at eye level in combination with a profoundly deeper insight.[103] see picture 28

Gotthard Graubner emerged from German 'Informel' gesture-painting and 'pure' painting. At the age of 16 he already became enthralled by Lao-Tzu's "Dao de Jing". Graubner hopes the viewer will be virtually engulfed by the flow of colour space evoked by his huge painted cushion-shaped canvasses, experiencing the sublime in continuous see picture 29

101 Ibid., p.130: "As in nature, so also in art, reality belongs to the point where subjective and objective processes meet. With the dimensional problem removed a return to painting was essential if any further development in the field of independence was to be made on my part."
102 See Norbert Lynton, Victor Pasmore, "Paintings and Etchings 1980-92" (London: Lund Humphries, 1992).
103 See Donald Holt, "Emily Kngwarreye - paintings" (Sydney: Craftsman House, G+B Arts International, 1998). Emily painted while squatting down to the side of or sometimes on the canvas, a physical immersion similar to Pollock's. See §10.

flowing coloured nothingness. Gotthard Graubner says: "The artistic initiative starts for me at the spot where the objective evolves to create a painterly organism."[104] He furthermore states that he focusses on breathing - on extension and contraction. The large cushion-shaped canvasses - which he calls "Farbkörper" ("colour bodies") bend backwards at their outline, creating the optical effect that they allow the colour-space on the canvas to become free from the flat surface and take you in. Graubner paints his works in many layers, always allowing some very small spots of a different colour to stand out, barely there but still perceptable to the true viewer. He understands these spots as important indications that pure perfection cannot equal nature and that in this way continuous change is garanteed. Graubner believes his own paintings contain 'form'. While the viewer may not perceive any actual form in Graubner's paintings, subtle differences in color evoke the sense of form in the perception of the viewer by their virtual extending and contracting motions. This clearly is related to the Oriental concept of 'form of the formless', as also exemplified in the paintings of Natvar Bhavsar.[105]

see picture 35

Natvar Bhavsar produces equal cosmic explosions of colour. He developed an extraordinary way of painting with dry pigments, without or hardly using a brush, but by screening dry colour pigments. This extraordinary technique is based partly on his Indian background, where one uses dry pigments in everyday life or rituals in various ways, and partly on Process Art, developed in the early 1970's in the USA to focus on the process of using paint as material.[106]

One may correctly wonder if the new works by Frank Stella, his wall-constructions and assemblaged paintings developed since the early 1990's, can be considered amorphic.[107] Stella's works are good examples that there is indeed not always a simple distinction to be made between the amorphic, the organic and the geometric. One may find different

104 See Uwe Schramm, "Malerei als Graphik - Graphik als Malerei", in Marlis Terlinder, "Gotthard Graubner - Radierungen - Unikate aus den Jahren 1969-1995" (Düsseldorf: Richter Verlag, 1999), p.76. ("Die künstlerische Initiative beginnt für mich dort ... wo sich das Ziel setzt, einen malerischen Organismus zu schaffen.")

105 Graubner is interested in Oriental philosophies, especially in Tao. See Gottfried Böhm, "Gotthard Graubner - painting" (Cologne: Galerie Karsten Greve, 1995). See Volker Rattemeyer, "Gotthard Graubner - Träger des Otto Ritschl Preises 2001" (Düsseldorf: Richter Verlag, Museum Wiesbaden, 2001). See Werner Schmidt, Wolfgang Holler, "Gotthard Graubner - Malerei und Zeichnung" (Düsseldorf: Richter Verlag, 2000). See Klaus Schrenk, "Gotthard Graubner - Malerei auf Papier" (Düsseldorf: Richter Verlag, Staatliche Kunsthalle Karlsruhe, 2001). See Veit Goerner, Caroline Sommer, Katharina Schmidt, "Gotthard Graubner - Farblicht" (Hannover: Kestner Gesellschaft, 2003).

106 Bhavsar's favorite Hindu-god is Krishna, exemplifying also his interest in evercontinuing change in nature. Bhavsar was born in Gujarat, India and came in 1962 to the USA to study art and finally stayed. See Irving Sandler, "Natvar Bhavsar - Painting and the Reality of Colour" (Sydney: Craftsman House G+B Arts International, 1998). Bhavsar paints while the canvas lies under him on the floor. See §2.2 on Bhavsar's concept of tuning the self to the universe. See Morgan, Robert C., "Natvar Bhavsar - The Sound of Color", Sundaram Tagore Gallery, New York, 2000. And see Carter Ratcliff, "Mutability and Metaphor" (on Natvar Bhavsar), Art in America, issue December 2003, p.80-83.

107 Here I am referring to Frank Stella's "Heinrich von Kleist" series. See Franz-Joachim Verspohl, Anna-Maria Ehrmann-Schindbeck, Ulrich Mueller, "Heinrich von Kleist by Frank Stella" (Cologne: Verlag Buchhandlung Walther Koenig, 2001. Stella's large scale non-coloured outdoor sculptures with melted splashed and dripped steel and aluminum clearly are amorphic (but also works like "The Mast-Head").

examples of these combinations in the late Kandinsky paintings and in contemporary works by Brice Marden, David Reed, David Row, Richard Purdy, Christoph Wedding, or my own. see picture 34

After discussing these developments in the amorphic/organic in art, it is interesting to briefly study some comparable developments in construction and architectural design. In the 1950's the German engineer and architect, Frei Otto, and the Russian engineer, Sergej Lebedew, began translating constructions one can find in actual organisms into new concepts for the construction of architecture. Their interests were quite comparable to those of Semper and Haeckel, and were also inspired by the ideas of the 1920's in art and architecture of combining the interest in morphology with the interest in the mechanical.[108]

The study-models of these remarkable and very experimental technical researchers sometimes come extremely close to what structural artists explored at the same time.[109] This was purely an analogous development, which is not surprising considering the interests of the artists previously discussed. Frei Otto, Sergej Lebedew, and many artists in the 1950's were interested in crystallography, and principles of the organism like growth and construction. Naum Gabo said he studied the structure of a tree to learn how to develop the engineering problem for his largest sculpture: the magnificent, vertical and 25 meter high sculpture, "Construction for the Bijenkorf Building" in Rotterdam.[110] The important pioneering work by Frei Otto has been put into practice building magnificent bridges, canopies of stadiums, large halls, and huge towers by Jörg Schlaich and Rudolf Bergermann.[111] An interesting combination of the amorphic/

108 For an interesting amount of information on the spiral in science, art, philosophy and religion, see Jill Purce, "Die Spirale - Symbol der Seelenreise" (Munich: Kösel-Verlag GmbH & Co, 1988 - orig. London: Thames and Hudson, 1974). Lebedew developed his "Biomechanism". In the late 1980's and early 1990's I had the fortune to visit both Frei Otto's institute in Stuttgart and Lebedew's institute in Moscow. Needless to say that there were quite a lot of differences between these important laboratories. While Frei Otto's "Institute für leichte Flächentragwerke" is housed in one of his fabulous tent-like constructions (making sounds like an old sailing ship when moved by the wind), Lebedew's whole institute was housed in the basement of some obscure and not exactly well maintained huge appartment building. When I met him, a highly sympathetic man, he was sitting between piles of papers, books and all kinds of research-models on all sides around him with several of his collaborators sitting next to him. Language and time did unfortunately not permit us to have a dialogue as long and deep as I had wished. I still treasure a book he gave me, which was published on his research.

109 The clearest comparison can be made with the three-dimensional structures of English artist Kenneth Martin or Russian artist Naum Gabo (1936-1946 in England), to a certain degree certainly in the 1960's in the free standing sculptures of Joost Baljeu, some 1970's and current sculptures by Michael Kidner and the 1960's architectural concepts for building with units designed to be produced in mass-prefabrication, like for instance in the architecture of Moshe Safdie.

110 The sculpture was realized in 1956-57 and stands in front of the Bijenkorf department store, Coolsingel, Rotterdam, the Netherlands. The statement by Gabo was in a letter to Herbert Read, the art historian and Gabo's friend, January 1956. Martin Hammer, Christina Lodder, "Constructing Modernity - The Art & Career of Naum Gabo" (New Haven, London: Yale University Press, 1999) p.358. There is no evidence that Gabo would have been familair with either Frei Otto or Lebedew's ideas.

111 See Annette Bögle, Peter Cachola Schmal, Ingeborg Flagge, "Leicht Weit - Light Structures, Jörg Schlaich

organic and geometric was presented by the Swiss artists' magazine "Die Spirale".[112] Typical for its time, it also gave a lot of attention to kinetic art, graphic design, poetry, and industrial design. In the 1960's many architectural concepts were based on developing cell-like units that could be mass-produced and built in organic structures.[113] For instance, the studies resulting from the co-operation of the architect Johannes Peter Hölzinger with the artist Hermann Goepfert. They developed a formative basic vocabulary, consisting of angle, wave, semi circle and spiral. Hölzinger continues his research today, exemplified in his magnificent private house in Bad Nauheim, Germany.[114]

After first making a name for himself as a kind of Minimal monochrome painter, Brice Marden changed his style completely in the late 1980's. Comparable to Pasmore, Marden at some point found it necessary to break through a phase in his art that was too dependant on an attempt to make art the expression of absolute objectivity. In contrast to most minimalists, Marden always had a high sensibility for colour in his paintings since the mid 1960's. Since 1985 he has been exploring a more intuitive painting in a kind of linear, expressive calligraphic style inspired by a personal combination of Oriental calligraphy and the radical renovations in painting by Jackson Pollock.[115] Especially in the later paintings, organic nets emerge out of the calligraphic brush-strokes of flowing colours and lines. In the early 1990's he was inspired by a growing interest in Chinese art and poetry. Marden is not merely interested in calligraphy as pictorial expression, but most certainly as understanding art as a synthesis of purpose, thought, and object. I consider one of his greatest paintings of the 1990's to be "The Muses", in tones of gray, light blue and a soft malachite green.[116]

- Rudolf Bergermann" (Munich, Berlin, London, New York: Prestel Verlag, 2003).

112 "The Spiral", published 1953-1964 in Switzerland by Eugen Gomringer, Dieter Roth and Marcel Wyss, included the artists: Kandinsky, Klee, Hans Arp, Sophie Taeuber-Arp, Max Bill, Richard Paul Lohse, Mary Vieira, Daniel Spoerri, Friedrich Vordemberge-Gildewart, Camille Graeser, Verena Wickart- Loewensberg, Kurt Blum, Laszlo Moholy-Nagy, Henry Moore, Bernhard Luginbühl, Alexander Calder, Ben Nicholson, Enio Iommi, Karl Gerstner, Josef Albers and others. See Annemarie Bucher, "Die Spirale - Eine Künstlerzeitschrift 1953-1964" (Baden: Verlag Lars Müller, 1990).

113 See Heinrich Klotz, Volker Fischer, and others, "Vision der Moderne, Das Prinzip Konstruktion" (Munich: Prestel Verlag, 1986).

114 See PRO-Nr.1 magazine (Dordrecht: PRO Foundation, 1987), p.30-35. Johannes P. Hölzinger, Gerd de Bruyn, "Der öffentliche Raum - ein Projekt des Deutschen Werkbund Hessen" (Frankfurt: Deutsche Werkbund Hessen e.V., ca. 1992). Johannes P. Hölzinger, "Synthese des Arts - The Combination of Art and Architecture in the Government Buildings on the Hardthöhe in Bonn" (London, Stuttgart: Edition Axel Menger, 1998). See Gerd de Bruyn, "Johannes Peter Hölzinger - Haus in Bad Nauheim", (Stuttgart, London: Edition Axel Menges, 2004).

115 It seems Jackson Pollock never saw Monet's "Nymphéas" in reality, as the one in the collection of the MoMA NY was purchased after Pollock's death (but in his days reproductions were available). But in context to Marden, as possible sources for inspiration, these magnificent almost abstract paintings from about 1920-1926 can certainly be mentioned. The structure of rhythmic repetitions of brush-strokes in some of these Monets come very close to modern abstract and amorphic/organic/calligraphic painting like Marden's. For instance in Monet's magnificent "Morning" from 1921-1926. See Charles F. Stuckey, "Monet - Waterlilies" (Cologne: Hugh Lauter Levin Associates Inc., Koenemann Verlagsgesellschaft mbH, 1988), p.94.

116 Marden's interest concerns the poetry and life of Han Shan, a Chinese poet from the 8th century, inspiring Marden's "Cold Mountain" series. See Charles Wylie, "Brice Marden - Work of the 1990's: Paintings,

Recent examples of the continuing interest in the amorphic/organic by a younger generation are exemplified in the paintings and works on paper by Christoph Wedding and Megan Olson. Both seem to further the tradition of Surrealist 'écriture automatique' in the frequent overlapping combination with calligraphic references. However, their work is different, much more controlled, and more plastic in a sense. Christoph Wedding's works are more stylized amorphic/organic paintings - sometimes reminding one of DNA strings swirling into nothingness. Unlike Marden, Olson does not express the brush-stroke, but the organic grown structures as image. Olson explores ideas about nature, music, and human relationships with nature. Music to her is an important inspiration for creating the rhythmic structures on the surface of her paintings, providing the painting with an energy of itself. Change, complexity and depth are everything. These are carefully, laboriously, handsomely, and sensitively painted, simulating a dynamic growth of and within space. Another painter who combines geometry with a kind of calligraphic gestural brushstrokes is Thomas Zitzwitz. Robert Yoder also combines geometry with calligraphic shapes cut out of the reflective boards of traffic signs, allowing his 'paintings' to unexpectedly lighten up terrifically. The reflection of light plays an important role in both painters' work.

see pictures 46, 54

Because morphology has become of new interest in modern physics, with new theories about complex and multi-dimensional space/time, like Inflation Theory, wrapping the flat geometrical space that symbolizes our three-dimensional space of everyday in all kinds of morphologically distorted shapes, one can expect artists to have an analogous interest in new, more complex, and amorphic/organic shaped spaces. American painter Richard Purdy, and I myself, certainly belong to this category.[117] Such concepts were earlier explored by Naum Gabo or in systematic artistic research on grids and sculptures made of fiberglass rods and stretched transparent nylon stockings by Michael Kidner.[118]

see pictures 48, 55

Modern science has shown that 'empty space' must be perceived as a complex amorphic space full of streams of fields and quantities of energies. This concept comes awfully close to mystical understandings of 'empty space', as in 'no-thingness full of meaning'. The equivalent to this current understanding of amorphic/organic space, therefore, cannot be depicted in art in sheer empty or monochrome painting or monolithic sculpture, but must deal with highly complex space, full of colours and 'formless' forms.

Drawings, and Prints" (Dallas, TX: Dallas Museum of Art, Distributed Art Publishers, 1999) p.15. Wylie notices that Marden also maintained a serious interest in further exploring Greek culture, hence the title "Muses", Ibid. p.24. Marden had been interested in ancient Greek culture ever since he went to Greece in the early 1970's. Ibid. p.29 + p.56.

117 The best examples from Purdy are his magnificent encaustic paintings "Inflation" and "Gaugefield". My own work includes the combination of amorphic/organic forms of poured pigments, calligraphic, geometric lines and forms in my 'augmented reliefs', sculptures and paintings, often involving a complex 'free-hand' style of perspective.

118 See §3 and §6.

In this chapter we have seen how, especially through modern art history, the interest in the amorphic/organic has deep roots in different but still quite similar philosophies and views about reality. Many artists who have been discussed have clearly been and clearly are exploring this subject with a profoundly deep interest in reconnecting with nature to find the essence.

I hope the reader can agree that the deeper we explore the many layers of knowledge and intriguing history of complex matrixes of creative intuition, we always come up with the same desire to reach beyond the mere limitations of the birth-death confusion of daily life, towards a sense of wholeness. This desire also leads to quite similar motivations in art, though their appearance might be very different. Though we already have seen in this chapter that often one cannot easily distinguish the amorphic/organic from the more geometric, the next chapter will explore the latter a bit deeper, because the geometric concerns some interesting additional aspects.

§12 THE SHAPE OF BEAUTY II: THE GEOMETRIC

It is, however, necessary to point out that the definitions 'figurative' and 'non-figurative' are only approximate and relative. For every form, even every line, represents a figure, no form is absolutely neutral. Clearly, everything must be relative, but, since we need words to make our concepts understandable, we must keep to these terms. Among the different forms we may consider those as being neutral which have neither the complexity nor the particularities possessed by the natural forms or abstract forms in general. We may call those neutral which do not evoke individual feelings or ideas. ***Geometrical forms****, being so profound an abstraction of form, may be regarded as neutral; and on account of their tension and the purity of their outlines they may even be preferred to other neutral forms.*
Piet Mondrian, 1936[1]

Why is a painting, in which 'geometrical' forms can be recognized, called 'geometrical', whereas a painting in which vegetable forms can be recognized is not called 'botanical'?
Wassily Kandinsky, 1931[2]

In principle, these two seniors of abstract art have said it all: we need words, but our chosen verbal concepts unfortunately do not work so well, which explains why in discussions there are so often misunderstandings and why we never should take any verbal definition or verbalized notion too literally! It is also clear from this quote that Mondrian was not a dogmatic purist to the degree that so many people think. His careful formulation shows he was conscious of the problems inherent in verbal distinctions. As he put it, the geometrical form might be preferred because of its 'tension and purity', obviously meaning its simple readability, which, as we have seen, has been confirmed by neurophysiology.

Thus it should not be a surprise that, of any form-language, geometry is so much preferred through all human cultures and centuries, often in its combination or even fusion with more amorphic/organic forms.[3] Geometry does not seem to copy nature,

[1] See Piet Mondrian in "Plastic Art and Pure Plastic Art" (1936), in Harry Holtzman and Martin S. James, "The New Art - The New Life, The Collected Writings of Piet Mondrian" (New York: Da Capo Press Inc., 1993), p.290 (emphasis mine).

[2] See Wassily Kandinsky, "Reflections on Abstract Art", Kenneth C. Lindsay, Peter Vergo, "Kandinsky - Complete Writings of Art", (New York: DaCapo Press, 1994 - orig. Editions Denoel, Paris, 1970), p. 759. See also Wassily Kandinsky, "Betrachtungen über die abstrakte Kunst", in Max Bill, "Kandinsky - Essays über Kunst und Künstler" (Bern: Benteli Verlag, 1963 - orig. 1955, this essay by Kandinsky was originally published as "Réflexions sur l'Art Abstrait" in Cahiers d'Art Nr.1/1931), p.150: "Warum wird ein Gemälde, in welchem sich 'geometrische' Formen befinden, 'geometrisch' genannt und ein Gemälde, in dem Pflanzenformen vorkommen, nicht 'botanisch'?"

[3] Of course, geometry comes in a great variety of forms, from more simple Euclidian geometry to almost organically complex fractal geometry. Fractal geometry itself already proves the folly of the cliché distinction between amorphic/organic shapes and geometry.

but seems only to be itself. Nevertheless it is willingly adopted by nature, leading to a sense of harmony with nature.[4] Because of the earlier attention on Constructivism, which deals with the main trends of the geometric in modern art, this chapter must be seen as an addition to §3.[5] We will hereafter focus on more general aspects of the interest in the geometric shape, including particular interests in aspects of visual perception and the origin and summarized history of the concept of the point, the line, and the plane.

12.1 GENERAL INTRODUCTION TO GEOMETRY

Perfect Euclidian geometry hardly exists in nature. Only on a rare occasion can one find perfect circles drawn in the sand by grassblades moved by the wind. This makes perfect geometry the idealist's tool by definition (or the more neutral, as Mondrian put it). Still, it is not only an idealist's tool, because geometry possesses the strange quality of being natural as well as not natural.[6] Imperfect geometry exists in abundance in nature. Examples are crystals, shells, plants, sand- and water patterns. In context to the limitation of the meaning of progress, it is a familiar phenomenon that anyone who studies the development of human thinking discovers how little human consciousness has progressed since the first known philosophers.[7] The more you dig into the treasure of knowledge that has been developed centuries ago, the more amazed you will become. It is plainly shocking to have to conclude how much knowledge seems to be forgotton or has merely been or become ignored.

---

[4] In 1983 on several mountain passes in Switzerland I realized the Project Switzerland using two large white and purely geometrical blocks. During the preparations in my studio in the flat Netherlands, I expected to find in the mountains an extreme contrast between these geometrical shapes and raw nature. I expected these geometrical blocks to stand out. At the same time, with the aim to heighten this contrast, I wanted to study a kind of chaotic composition. What I did find, however, shocked me. It was an almost sacred harmony between nature and pure geometry, eventually leading me to make no chaotic, but quickly finding it much more interesting to create pure symmetrical compositions. This experience inspired me to develop my monumental sculpture Eruption (realized 1984-88), consisting of two identical, serene white columns, standing near Flushing (Vlissingen, Netherlands) in the breaking waves of the tide in the sea. They have openings on the sea-side and on the top-side, allowing waves to break unseen into the columns and to become visible as they explode upwards. See Kai-Uwe Hemken, "Fré Ilgen - The Search" (Alphen a/d Maas: FNA, 2001). The sense of 'sacredness' caused by the interaction of geometry and 'wild' nature and the resulting impulse to create symmetrical compositions I now (20 years later) understand as a logical result of the optical tension of contrasts (reminding one of Mondrian's quote at the start of this chapter!), which would not have been possible to this degree of intensity when I would have stuck to my original idea to study 'chaotic' compositions. The now achieved high contrast allows an experience that 'objectifies' the self (in Worringer's sense, see §11) and thus provides an experience of the sublime (the equivalent to the sensing of 'sacred harmony'!).

[5] See §6.3. on the geometric in art in relation to the subject of space/time.

[6] 'Not natural' is not the right definition because nothing can be put outside nature - when we acknowledge nature to be more than the landscape - hence nothing can be 'not natural'. What I mean is a geometry that is not found in nature as we perceive it but is constructed by man with man-made tools.

[7] Since Thales some 2500 years ago; just recall Leucippus and Democritus, the Greek Atomists, who believed that everything consists of atoms, which are physically inseparable and undestroyable and that between them an empty space exists. These atoms would always have been and will always stay in motion. So, this theory is not for example just from the end of the 19th century, but from about 440-420 BC, meaning some 2500 years ago! See Bertrand Russell, "History of Western Philosophy" (London: Routledge, 1991 - orig. 1946), p.82-90.

When we study the history of visualization it is remarkable indeed to notice that all cultures in one way or another have used geometrical forms. To understand the full power of geometry we should not limit ourselves to studying art history, but include neurophysiology, anthropology, physics and technology.[8] Geometry comes from the Greek geos (= earth) and metron (= measure). Greek philosophy understood number and figure as subjects of mathematics, in which figure refers to geometry. In modern thinking geometry is understood as the study of space, reduced in the 19th century to a study of the continuum. Geometry is understood as an inborn aspect for orientation in space, as a logical and necessary tool for survival. Isidor of Sevilla acknowledges that long before the Greeks, the Egyptians were the inventors of geometry.[9] Plato and Pythagoras acknowledged the importance of the Egyptians, in contrast to Aristotle, who did not. It must not be forgotten that Euclid and his disciples were the first to collect and write down all the existing knowledge of geometry, adding quite a few ideas of their own. They can be acknowledged as great thinkers but not the inventors of geometry as we know it.

In the 19th century the Swiss innovator of education, Johann Pestalozzi, had quite a large influence on school education of children with his 'ABC der Anschauung'.[10] He emphasized the importance of children being able to describe a form precisely. He considered his 'ABC der Anschauung' to be based on Euclidian geometry as the appropriate

Not to mention the knowledge from Ancient China, which partially has become known in recent years, like the analogies that have been found between the I-Tjing oracle and the DNA-code. See Frank Fiedeler, "Yin und Yang - Das kosmische Grundmuster in den Kulturformen Chinas" (Cologne: DuMont Verlag, 1993). In my opinion it is interesting that Leibniz already introduced the discussion of the possible meaning of I-Tjing into western thinking (already in the second half of the 17th century!). See §2.3, footnote 49.

8 On neurophysiology, see later this chapter, and see §5. To make the power of the analogies between very different fields more accessible, I strongly prefer the notion of 'a visualization' instead of a work of art. However, because this can still lead to misunderstandings (this idea is not yet familar enough) in these essays the word art will still be used. The notion of visualization of course is disputable and could also be confusing in a sense that it also would include for instance illustrations and commercial graphics. Commercial graphics must communicate some clear and linear message (to explain to everybody what product is offered), but art certainly has more than one meaning. This is relevant for what we consider to be art, but also is relevant for other examples of man-made visualizations, like ornaments that we can find in anthropology on all kind of tools, utensils and clothing or in modern civilization applied in industrial design. Visualization to me has a similar meaning as Gestalt, but puts more emphasis on all visual qualities of the object including colour and context to its environment - certainly not limited to the 'objective' and highly formalistic connotations of modern Gestaltpsychology - and thus seems to be more appropriate. Although Gestalt should also include these properties still most people consider Gestalt to concern only shape, form or independent grouping of elements defining a sign.

9 See C. F. von Weizsäcker, "Zeit und Wissen" (Munich/Vienna: Carl Hansen Verlag, 1992), on geometry as subject of space, p.155. See §6.2. on the continuum. The idea that geometry functions as a tool to support our chances for survival was advocated by for instance Poincaré or Lorentz. Sevilla published in his 'Etymologiarum', that the Egyptians had invented geometry long before the Greeks. See Umberto Eco, "Die Suche nach der vollkommenen Sprache" (Munich: Europa Bauen, 1994 - orig. "La ricerca della lingua perfetta nella cultura europea", 1993), p.153.

10 'Anschauung' in general can be translated as observation, while in context to teaching it is often used as education by illustration. In context to scientific concepts like "lines of force", Anschauung means an

method.[11] He taught children to analyze everything based on simple geometry. This approach later became famous in a similar approach used by Cézanne, when he stated that one can analyze all shapes by using the cube, the cylinder and the sphere (which seemed to have inspired Cubism a couple of years later). The notion of Anschauung, as promoted by Pestalozzi, became of decisive importance to the scientific discoveries in the early decades of the 20th century. The development and use of geometric diagrams for instance, made it possible to make highly complex problems accessible to scientists themselves and to others. This obviously still is important today, where the computer-simulation, which is also based on geometry and mathematics, is a very powerful tool for Anschauung. In my opinion, the notion of Anschauung also exemplifies that recognition of a good solution, formula or theory in science as 'beautiful' is more deeply connected to our intuition, a combination of thinking and perception, than is normally acknowledged. Also in science, this experience of beauty is the emotion that results from a strong sense of truth, often before one is able to verbalize exactly why.[12] It has something to do with immediate perception and immediate acknowledgement. This makes Anschauung so important during the creative process of an emerging work of art for deciding what seems right and what still has to be changed. This definitely is of importance in geometric art, too. Only following rules leads to a doctrine for dead art.[13] Repeatedly in history artists and architects have experimented with translations of intuitive observations into a geometrical, formal language for the purpose of analysing what they perceive; finding structure by applying circles, squares, rectangles and triangles.

Comparable to Pestalozzi's method, famous wood-block artist, Katsushika Hokusai, in the early 19th century used geometric forms to analyse his own free-hand drawings of scenes of life to reveal the proportions and relationships in his compositions.[14] This recalls a similar method by various pioneers of modern art in the early 20th century, who

---

immediate understanding by seeing as act of acknowledgement (= seeing by the senses in combination with memory). See Arthur I. Miller, "Imagery in Scientific Thought - Creating 20th-century Physics" (Cambridge, MA: The MIT Press, second print 1987 - orig. Birkhauser Boston Inc., 1984), p.110: "In this context Anschauung refers to the intuition through pictures formed in the mind's eye from previous visualizations of physical processes in the world of perceptions; Anschauung is superior to viewing merely with senses." Miller describes also that it was very important for the maturing process of Einstein to have been at a Pestalozzi school.

[11] See Rudolf Arnheim, "Visual Thinking" (Berkely, Los Angleles, London: University of California Press, 1969). Pestalozzi published his concept in "How Gertrude Teaches Her Children", 1801. See Arthur I. Miller, "Einstein, Picasso - Space, Time, and The Beauty That Causes Havoc" (New York: Basic Books, 2001), p.47.

[12] See my discussion on beauty, §8.4.

[13] For critical remarks on the strong tendency towards a nihilistic dogmatism in geometric art, see §6, §9, §10, or my essay, "From Constructivism to Extensionalism", in PRO-NR.9 (Dordrecht: PRO Foundation, 1993).

[14] Katsushika Hokusai published this method in "Quick Lessons in Simplified Drawing (Ryakuga haya oshie)", published as two volumes (Edo: Kadomaruya Jinsuke, 1812), showing how to make 'moji-e' ('writing pictures') and methods of projecting a subject or scene using compass and ruler. See Seiji Nagata, "Hokusai - Genius of the Japanese Ukiyo-e", translated by John Bester (Tokyo, New York, London: Kodansha International, 1995), p.82. Someone like Frank Lloyd Wright was quite interested in this method. See Julia Meech, "Frank Lloyd Wright and the Art of Japan - The Architect's Other Passion", (New York: Japan Society and Harry N. Abrams Inc. Publishers, 2001), p.70-71.

abstracted from reality to depict persons, still lifes, trees or landscapes with free-hand geometrical compositions. For instance: Bart van der Leck, Piet Mondrian and Theo van Doesburg.

Swiss artist (originally architect) Hans Hinterreiter focussed his lifelong artistic research on a detailed colour and pure geometric form system.[15] He always emphasized that never the system, but the visual experience of the artist, should be decisive in the definitive choices of composition, form and colour. Acknowledging the formalistic relationships between a sequence of works of art,[16] Hinterreiter emphasized the position of nature:

see picture 25

> *"Nature remains our best teacher, even when we do not copy its outer appearances. We try with pure painterly, geometric and dynamic means to present images of the invisible laws present in the appearances, resemblances of the creative undercurrent of the visible world, its inner dimensions, that is what interests us today more than its surface."*[17]

The emphasis on nature as a teacher underlines the importance of studying nature as we can actually perceive it, and confirms the value of visual experience as a referee in the search for knowledge about the essence of reality. This emphasis obviously links Hinterreiter with other artists I have mentioned in the previous chapter. When Hinterreiter advocates his preference for a set of rules, to find the 'invisible laws present in the appearances', he clearly falls in the continuing search for the eidos. Besides, his own emphasis on placing the artistic experience above the logic of a system gives enough reason to assume that he was looking for the same kind of order as Charles Biederman, an order implicit in nature at depth like Schopenhauer or David Bohm, but visualized at our explicit eye-level of perception.[18] The difference from Biederman is that Hinterreiter always tried to be as close to a mathematical system as possible.

[15] Hans Hinterreiter (1902 - 1989) was mainly inspired by the colour and form studies by the German physicist Wilhelm Ostwald, by cristallography, Islamic art and Einsteins concept of a curved space/time. See Hans Joachim Albrecht, Rudolf Koella, "Hans Hinterreiter - Ein Schweizer Vertreter der konstruktiven Kunst" (Zürich: Edition Dr. István Schlégl, Waser Verlag, 1982). Hans Hinterreiter "Die Kunst der reinen Form - Eine Formenlehre für moderne Künstler, Band I - Ordnung und Taufe der Elementarformen" (Ibiza, Amsterdam: Ediciones Ebusus, 1978, facsimile - orig. 1941).

[16] See Hans Hinterreiter "Die Kunst der reinen Form - Eine Formenlehre für moderne Künstler, Band I - Ordnung und Taufe der Elementarformen", introduction : "As the pictures should not be connected or kept to each other by the strings of mimetic meaning, the logic of their sequence must be anchored in the formalistic."("Da die Bilder nicht durch den Faden der gegenständlichen Bedeutung aneinander gereiht und zusammengehalten werden sollen, muß die Logik ihres Aufeinanderfolgens im Formellen verankert sein.")

[17] Ibid., introduction: "Die Natur bleibt unsere beste Lehrmeisterin, auch wenn wir ihre äußere Erscheinungen nicht nachahmen. Wir versuchen mit rein malerischen, geometrischen und dynamischen Mitteln Abbilder der unsichtbar in den Dingen waltenden Gesetze zu geben, Gleichnisse von der schöpferischen Unterschicht der Erscheinungswelt, ihrer Innendimension, die uns heutige mehr interessiert als ihre Oberfläche."

[18] On Bohm's definitions of 'implicate' and 'explicate' order, see chapter 7.4.

Biederman more or less explored the process of free-hand geometry, which is more based upon visual experience and intuition of composition and sizes and less on a pre-formulated system.

Because applications of geometry can be found through all centuries and cultures, the preference to use geometrical shapes can hardly be understood as being purely rational, Occidental or male - just to name a few cliché prejudices one meets once in a while. Man has always been fascinated by understanding his position in nature with the help of geometric visualizations.[19] Throughout this publication, by 'nature', I do not mean the garden, the forest or the landscape, but the whole of macro- and microcosm in which we live.[20] Art, science and philosophy prove the necessity of understanding the wholeness and connectedness of everything, including ourselves.

12.2 ON THE BRAIN'S PERCEPTION OF GEOMETRY

We have already discussed the general functioning of the brain.[21] It is quite interesting that brain research has not been able to find physiological proof for a preference for the aesthetic of geometric compositions, but it has shown that the perception of geometrical forms costs the brain less activity. Besides, perceptual research has shown that vertical and horizontal straight lines (or outlines of planes) are the easiest to see. Simultaneously, neurophysiological research shows that curved lines offer a greater problem to the brain than diagonal lines.

Obviously it must be emphasized, that this still says nothing about aesthetic preferences, but it does say that geometry is not merely a rational tool or merely a result of pure logical reasoning, but emerged out of a natural need embedded in the brain to be able to perceive structure, depth and space at a high speed.[22] This must have been originally built in our biological system as a mechanism for survival.[23] In my opinion, this explains

---

19 Many books deal with this subject, a particular subject of geometry, or the preference for geometry in particular cultures. See Jörg Sellenriek, "Zirkel und Lineal - Kulturgeschichte des Konstruktiven Zeichnens" (Munich: Verlag Callway, 1987). Fleur Richter, "Die Aesthetische Körper in der Renaissance" (Stuttgart: Gerd Hatje Verlag, 1995). David Wells, "The Penguin Dictionary of Curious and Interesting Geometry" (London: Penguin Books, 1991). Madanjeet Singh, "Die Sonne - Das Gestirn in der Kulturgeschichte", translated by Theresa M. Bullinger (Tübingen, Berlin: Ernst Wasmuth Verlag, UNESCO, 1994 - orig. 1993).

20 It is in man's character to wish to understand what he perceives as being separate from himself and to believe he is able to watch this from a certain distance. This attitude led to the conviction that man is superior to the rest of nature and human culture opposed to nature. Quite a remarkable alternative concept is offered by evolutionist Richard Dawkins, who proposes that maybe evolution is not built with man but DNA itself as its primary player. See Richard Dawkins, "The Blind Watchmaker" (London: Penguin Books, 1988 -orig. 1986), p.126. See Richard Dawkins, "God's Utility Function", Scientific American issue Nov 1995, p.60-67. It might be illustrative for the interests of artists to mention that the English artist Michael Kidner introduced me to the ideas of Dawkins.

21 See §5, particularly §5.5. on thinking and geometry.

22 See Semir Zeki, "Inner Vision - An Exploration of Art and the Brain" (Oxford, New York: Oxford University Press, 1999), p.115-116: "... this does not address the question of how the brain distinguishes between straight and curved lines, which remains a neurophysiologically unsolved problem."

23 In August 2003, Discovery Channel presented a documentary on the functioning of the brain featuring a young Englishman who did not have any memory (as the result of a traumatic accident in his childhood) making

one of the reasons for our preference for the geometric. If we depended for basic survival on three dimensional perception every day - seeing predators or a speeding car in time and being able to judge the distance instantaneously, then one can imagine that perception in this particular context would fail if it were based on a preference for shapes that take the brain too long a time to process and analyse![24] On the other hand, because we perceive continuous change in amorphic/organic nature around us every day, it is just as natural that our perceptual preferences are influenced by the amorphic and organic and not only by the geometric. Still, it is quite interesting to note that it seems that our receptive fields - the fields of an individual visual cell in our brain during the process of our immediate visual perception - seem more often to be square or rectangular in shape than otherwise.[25] It makes one wonder if this might offer a clue to why in painting we prefer a square or rectangular shaped canvas, despite all experiments with differently shaped canvasses.

In any case, current knowledge in neurophysiology teaches us that visual perception, aesthetic experiences, Anschauung, are not experiences to be understood by the usual art-historical, art-theorical or psychological analysis or interpretations. The rhythmic processes of the brain provide their own additional input on what we see and like in the world and in art. This gives another dimension to our discussion about searching for wholeness, as it clearly is not only our own free decision to do so, but also decisions or preferences that are 'hard-wired' in our own brains. It certainly helps - at least for a part - to understand our response to art.

In context to our intense perception of a work of art, in which geometry seems to play such an important role, as also explained by brain-research, who else can I better refer to than quantum physicist and philosopher David Bohm, who during the 1960's exchanged thoughts and experiences with the artist Charles Biederman in an extensive correspondence on the relations between art and science? Through a personal experience with a Rouault painting, Bohm at some point felt immersed in the painting and was struck by a sense of flowing energies streaming back and forth between him and the work.[26] This was a very good description of a process of dissolving duality. Bohm tried

his daily functioning not easy. In this program a researcher anaylized that he did not have a memory because he could not perceive any structure in his environment - if this is a general aspect of our brain, relating memory immediately to 'perceiving structure', would this not be an interesting additional reason for our desire to perceive cohesion in everything? One can only guess at the possible implications for our desire both as artists and as art-observers for cohesion in a composition in a work of art! This is quite an interesting loop back to §5.

24 Simultaneously one can question if a kind of form-language in a work of art should be preferred that demands less brain-activities if a profound deep experience, maybe even an experience of the sublime is aimed for, because it also seems sound reasoning to expect a deep immersion into a work of art - a dissolving of the differences between self, artifact and world - if the artifact demands so much activity and attention from the brain that we can hardly be conscious of anything else!

25 See Semir Zeki, "Inner Vision - An Exploration of Art and the Brain", p.119.

26 David Bohm wrote to Biederman in a letter of 24 April 1960, in Paavo Pylkkänen, "Bohm-Biederman Correspondence, David Bohm and Charles Biederman, Volume One: Creativity and Science" (London and New York: Routledge, 1999), p.18: "I should perhaps add here that my first reactions to modern art were

to understand what Biederman aimed to research in his geometric abstract art, which this artist and theoretician called 'structurist':

> *"In this connection, it seems that a possible valid direction for the artist to explore is the problem of the unity of 'inner' and 'outer', of subject and object. In physics, this has become an important problem. Thus, because of the indivisible, quantal nature of all processes, an observation is impossible in which the observer does not merge and blend with the object observed, and participate in its very being. On the large scale, apparatus is usually too insensitive to reveal this fact. (So it does not show up.) But with very sensitive apparatus, it does show up. Nevertheless, our usual idea of separating the subject and object prevents us from understanding the indivisible character of all reality. Perhaps if our own minds became more sensitive, they could show that the subject and object are really one, so that we could see that there is a totality in which both 'I' and 'non-I' are going on, in essential relationship and interpenetration of being. Then, one might understand the similar problem in physics in a new way. Is there some way in which Structurist Art faces this problem? It seems to me that there is, in the sense that each structure seems to blend and merge with surrounding Nature, and is not just isolated inside a frame. Yet, the problem is much deeper than this. The observer should be led, in my opinion, to feel the structure to be moving outwards to the world, while the world, along with the observer, is carried into the structure. In other words, in a real masterpiece of creative art, both the creator and the viewer should have moments of understanding, in which that work becomes the very essence and principle of their being (as happens with operative truth)."* [27]

Bohm, as a physicist, thus understands the connection art offers to the essence of individual being, understanding there is no clear borderline anymore between object and subject, and indeed acknowledging the dissolution of duality in an experience of the sublime.

---

almost entirely negative. However, in some respects, I have changed my mind. For example, with regard to Rouault, I first felt that his pictures were very discouraging and depressing. Gradually, I began to see them in a new light. In particular, last year in London, I saw a picture of his, The Old Clown, part of the E.G. Robinson collection, I believe. At first, it seemed to be rather a mixed up set of patches of color. But gradually, it began to take shape. In particular two patches struck my eye, one in the face of the clown and another outside him which seemed to complement the first. My eye began to move back and forth from one patch to the other, a pulsation was established, and suddenly it ceased, to give way to a remarkable new steady vision which I can best describe as seen in a new dimension. It was not so much that the clown became visible in three dimensions, this was true but only a minor point. The major point is that there seemed to be a flow or a current in which the whole being of the clown poured to reveal itself, all his feelings, thoughts and emotions etc., and a counterflow in which the outside (including the viewer) was drawn into him, to emerge again in the outward flow. It was a very striking experience for me, one that I shall always remember." See §8.

[27] In a letter of 23 March 1962 to Biederman, ibid., p.206. Compare Bohm's doubts on the sufficient potential of the structurist relief to Victor Pasmore's doubts, which allowed him to introduce painting in his own works again, see §11. Structurist Art refers to a notion that Biederman proposed in the 1950's for the further development of art as he saw it: coloured reliefs made of machine-made materials. He abandoned the word Structurist when he found out that most artists misunderstood and misused it (they thought it would be sufficient to produce structures without any reference to deeper thoughts or contexts). Biederman

12.3 THE POINT, THE LINE, THE PLANE

The discussion of the interest in the geometric in art is strictly connected to the long history of thinking about the basics of point, line and plane. The idea that a line simulates motion is neither an invention of artists nor of comic-designers, but is linked to a much older and broader discussion in mathematics, space, continuity, infinity, direction, and even related to optics (and as such, of course a part of every discussion on art again).[28] The oldest known definition on the line was offered by the Greek, Euclid, who was a pupil of the Platonic School.[29] Euclid's famous books described every known figure from geometry. He described the line as a linear connection between two points. This idea was based only on the concept that a line is a sequence of one point after the other and was understood to be similar in concept to the idea that numbers also follow each other towards infinity.[30] Some of the most prominent of Euclid's postulates (or axioms) are: 1. a point is that which has no parts; 2. a line is something with length but no width; 3. the ends of a line are points; 5. a plane is that which has only width and length; 6. the ends of a plane are lines; 23. parallels are straight lines that lie on the same level in such a way that when one extends them into both directions they will not meet on either side.[31] These precise definitions reflect the Pythagorean universal elements, but are more abstract and without the mystical cosmology typical of the Pythagorean concept. Pythagoras was basically a mystic of an intellectual kind, who once said that all things are numbers. He was convinced that, on the basis of mathematics, thought would be superior to sense, intuition superior to observation. The objects of thought would be more real than those of sense-perception.[32] Pythagoras also believed that the world and everything in it is built up of molecules (600 BC!) composed of atoms arranged in various

since then has opted for the term 'New Art'.

[28] See §6.

[29] See §2, describing the Platonic idea that the essence lies in the idea or thought, with mathematics as its tool. Around 300 BC Euclid, with his disciples, produced a complete treatment of known (that is: earlier) and new Greek geometry and number-theory in his 'stoicheia' or "Elements", consisting of 13 volumes. See Marvin Jay Greenberg, "Euclidian and Non-Euclidian Geometries - Development and History", Third Edition (New York: W.H. Freeman and Co., 1994), p.9.

[30] The interest in these matters is founded on the ideas of the older Pythagorean School, around 600 BC, who is considered to have been the first to separate geometry from the needs of practical life with the purpose of studying geometry for its own sake as an isolated science.

[31] These numbers refer to the numbers Euclid gave his postulates. The third dimension as element of space is treated by Euclid later in his 11th book in accordance to his definition of the body.

[32] The disciples of the Pythagorean School believed that the particles of the universe consisted of the basic numbers related to the basic notions of geometry: point and number 1, line and number 2, triangular plane and number 3, pyramidial space and number 4 (the number 0 was still unknown to the Greeks). See Jörg Sellenriek, "Zirkel und Lineal - Kulturgeschichte des Konstruktiven Zeichnens" (Munich: Verlag Callway, 1987), p.49. Because the Greeks did not acknowledge or perceive the existence of 'nothing', to them no void exists, hence they had no need for the number zero. The Pythagoreans defined the supernatural link between aesthetics, ratios and the universe itself. They decided that earth is the center of the universe round which the sun, moon and planets revolved, all pinned inside a sphere. While the planets moved they were believed to make music. All shapes, all motions were defined by mathematics, thus they called the universe a 'harmony of the spheres', the heavens a mathematical orchestra, hence the concept 'all is number'. See Charles Seife, "Zero

shapes, and that he could make arithmetic the fundamental study in both physics and in aesthetics. Therefore, in Euclid's definition, the point became the uncleavable, the ultimate element, the atom. Point, line and plane became the building blocks of even figures. Mathematician and philosopher Bertrand Russell refers in the early 20th century to the fact that the whole conception of an eternal world, revealed to the intellect but not to the senses, is derived from Pythagoras's combination of mathematics and theology.[33] The debate on the point, line and plane in immediate relation to sets of numbers and in relation to the notions of continuity and infinity continues to play a returning role through the histories of philosophy, mathematics and art.[34]

Euclid described our visual perception in terms of the construction of a pyramid of vision. This must be understood as a cone of lines of light with its origin and top in the eye.[35] This pyramid of vision results from the belief that vision is evoked by linear light-rays projected from the eye outwards towards objects in our environment - objects become visible as they encounter these lightrays.[36] Euclid did not understand light as a physical phenomenon. This introduction to some historical facts concerning the point, line and plane may seem elaborate, but it is interesting to notice that even in the first ideas concerning the very basis of geometry, scientific concepts are mixed with more intuitive approaches. These are approaches we today would call artistic. Intuition, in a modern context, is considered a property of art and not primarily of science. Additionally, the concept of an eternal world is understood today more as a subject of philosophy, maybe of art, but not so much of science. Besides, the study of vision that led to the (currently scientific) field of optics was not only based on the first ideas about

- The Biography of a Dangerous Idea" (London: Penguin Books, 2000), p.31-32+34. Will Grohmann wrote that Kandinsky considered, see Will Grohmann, "Kandinsky - Life and Work" (New York: Harry N. Abrams Inc., 1958), p.92: "Technically speaking, each work of art comes into being as the cosmos did - out of catastrophe." And, quoting Kandinsky: "Out of a chaotic blaring of the instruments a symphony finally emerges, called the music of the spheres. The creation of a work of art is the creation of a world." Kandinsky clearly must be either referring to or remembering this notion from Pythagoras ('harmony of the spheres' combined with the assumed music caused by the motion of the planets). Bertrand Russell described in the early 20th century how the opposition of rational and mystical thought that we can find all through history - and in our current societies - for the first time seems to have appeared with the Greeks "... as an opposition between the Olympic gods and those other less civilized gods who had more affinity with the primitive beliefs dealt with by anthropologists." See Bertrand Russell, "History of Western Philosophy" (London: Routledge, 1991 - orig. 1946), p.51. The preference for rationality over sense-perception was repeated at the end of the 18th century by the philosophers and scientists of the Enlightenment.

[33] Our word religion is based on the Greek word 'religere' meaning seeing relations in a hierarchical system.

[34] It led for instance to the development of theories on perspective, see §14. See W. Kirk MacNulty, "Freemasonry - A Journey through Ritual and Symbol" (London: Thames and Hudson, 1991), p.15: "The 'regular progression of science from a point to a line, from a line to a superficies, from a superficies to a solid' is the way in which Freemasonry explains the process by which the Deity brings the four levels of existence into being. It is a Neo-Platonic device which can be traced through the literature of the Renaissance, via medieval Spain, to Alexandria."

[35] Euclid published these ideas in his book "Optics", building on his own definitions of the point, the line and the plane. Fleur Richter, "Die Aesthetische Körper in der Renaissance" (Stuttgart: Gerd Hatje Verlag, 1995), p.21.

[36] Compare early 20th century abstract artist Larionov and his concept of Rayonism, see §8, footnote 37.

the point, the line and the plane, but is of course also a study of the properties of light, thus of space/time and of the sun as our primary source of light, of energy and of colour - therefore: of art.[37]

When we also remember how much evidence we can find in all cultures of the natural use of simple (Euclidean) geometry in combination with colour, it is certainly revealing to relate the information from the histories of geometry, optics, colour theories, artifacts and concept of sun cultures to the histories of science, philosophy, religion and fine art! The central topics of geometry and energy are exemplified in electromagnetism and its notion of lines of force, which still today is considered one, if not the, most important fundamental concept of the processes in nature. It is, therefore, hardly surprising that the debate on the point, the line and the plane came alive once more among the early abstract artists who were inspired by science. This was especially true, because the point, the line, and the plane were also being debated in theoretical science and philosophy in the same period.[38] Nishida, who is not only an Oriental philosopher but a real intermediary between Oriental and Occidental thought, describes quite well the reasons for the inspiration of the early abstract artists. He describes the process of abstracting as an action concerning a concrete ordering of elements that are assumed to have a meaning, leading to a moment when it is experienced as a right assumption, the moment the artifact becomes something by itself.[39] In my opinion, this seems one of the better descriptions of the principle of the abstract composition in art. Influenced by the development of the interest in abstracting from nature in an amorphic/organic way,

[37] See John Gage, "Colour and Culture - Practice and Meaning from Antiquity to Abstraction" (London: Thames and Hudson, 1993), p.229, mentioning that Leonardo da Vinci, "... understood geometry as the science of continuous quantity, which was where painting began: the point becomes the line, which becomes the plane, which in turn becomes the three-dimensional solid."

[38] For instance, consider Russell's definitions of the point, line and plane, quoted in Japan by Kitaro Nishida. For Russell, points are the terms of spatial relationships and lines the relations determined by two terms. Nishida (in 1916) understood a line as a set of points at its limit and equivalent to a continuum. See Nishida Kitaro, "Intuition and Reflection in Self-Consciousness" (Albany, NY: State University of New York, 1987 - orig. "Jikaku ni okeru chokkan to han sei", 1941), p.84: "... concrete experience, or life itself, which grounds all abstract thought, can rest content with no abstract system, and always demands a more concrete position, spurring thought to advance infinitely towards the concrete." Nishida explains the urge to be more precise, which obviously is an important drive of our knowledge. A drive which has also led through history to repeatedly review the concepts on the point-line-plane while exploring the abstract.

[39] Ibid., p.84: "A set of mere points may seem very different from the concept of order, but in concrete experience its elements are no longer simple elements, but possess meaning. The concrete ordering action comprises these elements and a law of combination, and when that ordering action is complete in a perfect set it becomes, in Hegelian terms, an und für sich, in and for itself. Bergson says that no matter how many photographs of Paris we assemble we cannot know Paris itself, for no combination of discrete positions can construct movement. Yet just such a transition is made intelligible by the notion of limit, which we can relate abstract to concrete and thought to intuition." It seems interesting here to refer to Kandinsky's distinction between the virtuoso and the creational or compositional artist. See §10. Nishida wrote this after referring to the equivalence between a set of ordered points and Cantor's perfect set - the continuum. He also mentions Russell's "Foundations of Geometry" (1897), David Hilbert's "Foundation of Geometry" (1902), Julian Lowell Coolidge's "The Elements of Non-Euclidian Geometry" (1909), Luigi Cremona's "Elements of Projective Geometry" (1913).

as was described in the previous chapter, the line was the focal point of interest in the Jugendstil and Art Nouveau periods at the end of the 19th century and into the early 20th century, the 'breeding days' of abstract art.[40]

Therefore, it is not surprising that serious and well informed artists like Wassily Kandinsky became interested in the discussion of point, line and plane, and their implications for modern art.[41] He considered his book, "Point and Line to Plane", a natural extension of his earlier book, "On The Spiritual in Art", and an attempt to help define a science of art, which should be able to pass beyond painting and even beyond art altogether. He wrote, "Here I seek only to point the way, to establish certain analytical methods and, at the same time, to take synthetic values into account."[42] Besides being in line with the Bauhaus' ambition to synthesize all creative disciplines, this approach also built on pictorial analysis.[43] Kandinsky at that moment was convinced that a precise examination of the individual pictorial elements would enable one to find the essence of a work of art. Given science's preference during the early decades of the 20th century for discussing basic matters in terms of points, lines and planes, it is logical and not surprising that Kandinsky knew he had to try to apply this method in art-analysis as well. Though very useful as a foundation for teaching, for instance pointing out the analogies of considering points, lines and planes in art, architecture, music, science and nature, Kandinsky's book is also a good example of the danger of attempting to make precise definitions for artistic means: to follow the definitions in this book exactly is no garantee you will produce a good work of art.[44] Though he wanted to be very precise, Kandinsky never wanted to define a dogma and "Point and Line to Plane"

---

[40] Will Grohmann mentions that Jugendstil around 1900 created a kind of revolution in Munich. Munich became the German center of Jugendstil - Kandinksy lived in Munich at that time. Belgian architect Henry van der Velde, the main representative of the style of abstract lines and surfaces, wrote in "Lay Sermons" (1902), quoted in Will Grohmann, "Kandinsky - Life and Work" (New York: Harry N. Abrams Inc., 1958), p.35: "The line is a force, which like all elementary forces is active; forces connected by opposing lines have the same effect as several elementary forces in opposition to each other." He was quite clearly referring to the concept of 'lines of force' as discussed in the science of late 19th - early 20th century. For excellent discussions on the emphasis on the line by Jugendstil, see Peg Weiss, "Kandinsky in Munich - The Formative Jugendstil Years" (New Jersey: Princeton University Press, 1985), and Thomas M. Messer, "Kandinsky in Munich 1896-1914" (New York: The Solomon R.Guggenheim Museum, 1982).

41 See Wassily Kandinsky, "Point and Line to Plane" (New York: Dover Publications Inc., 1979 - orig. "Punkt und Linie zu Fläche", 1926, as one of the Bauhaus books edited by Walter Gropius and Moholy-Nagy - this English translation with an introduction by Hilla Rebay was published originally by the Solomon R. Guggenheim Foundation in 1947). Grohmann understands this publication deals with the elements of graphic art, mainly inspired by Kandinsky's teaching at the Bauhaus. It certainly explains the elementary, instructive or academic tone of the book and why he aimed for a pseudo-scientific approach to define the properties and pictorial possibilities of the point- line-plane. See Will Grohmann, "Kandinsky - Life and Work", p.179.

[42] Quoted from Wassily Kandinsky, "Point and Line to Plane", the foreword, p.13.

[43] See §2.6.

[44] Because Kandinsky's "Point and Line to Plane" is more or less illustrative for the approach of the Bauhaus in teaching the basic aspects of creating an artifact, the possibilities for a dogmatic and wrong interpretation of these precise definitions are some of the reasons why hardly any great artists came forth from the Bauhaus.

should not be used like dogma but as helpful, supportive tool.

As we have seen, the interest in talking in terms of the point, line and plane is the outcome of a long history and also the result of a Zeitgeist-related subject. It is especially related to the impact on society, with support of the media (newspapers), of Einstein's notion of the paths of light as lines through curved space/time. Many theories about the paths of light, the lines of force of electromagnetism and abstract ideas about space/time were discussed in the 19th century, around the turn of the 19th/20th century and even up until today in terms of points, lines and planes. As did so many of his contemporaries, Kandinsky thought that in a work of art visual tension was equivalent to perpetual motion.[45]

As an artist myself, I do recognize this equivalence quite well, as in art often a strong simulation (or illusion) of motion is apparent by the visual tension in a composition. Kandinsky's paintings also show that he did not understand the line to be only something with length and no width. His paintings depict lines under an exaggerated and sometimes distorted perspective, lines growing in width and almost becoming planes. In my opinion this is the natural result of a painter seeking to show optical motion through infinite space/time simulated on a static and two-dimensional surface (the painting). One can find this optical effect in the paintings of many of Kandinsky's contemporaries.[46]

see picture 20

Since Kandinsky numerous artists have explored and furthered the simulation of colour dynamics applying a combination of geometry and a free interpretation of the line as an independent form. One may find examples in Optical Art of the 1960's. For instance in the paintings by Michael Kidner and Bridget Riley, exploring highly coloured patterns of waves in combination with straight and circular geometry. The American artist, David Reed, is a contemporary artist who furthers the strong simulation of motion in a different way. Reed uses a very effective combination of geometric coloured shapes with very smooth calligraphic gestures. This contrast is very effective, because it allows a more dynamic result than in Optical Art. The traces of streaming energies in Reed's paintings are seductively beautiful with a magic lighting comparable to Baroque

see pictures 30, 34

[45] See Ilja Ehrenburg, "Und sie bewegt sich doch - Moskau/Berlin 1922", reprint (Baden: LIT Verlag, 1986). See Wassily Kandinsky, "Point and Line to Plane", p.81: "Whereas the straight line is a complete negation of the plane, the curved line carries with it the seed of the plane." Swami Vivekananda (see §2), said in his lecture "Immortality", delivered in America, probably 1896, published in "Jnana Yoga" (Amora, India: Advaita Ashrama, fourth edition, 1930), p.218: "There is no motion in a straight line. Everything moves in a circle; a straight line, infinitely produced, becomes a circle." Without implying Kandinsky got his idea from Vivekananda, it is remarkable at least, since it is known Kandinsky read the lectures of Vivekananda, which were published in Russian in early 20th century.

[46] For example, the Russian Cubo-Futuristic paintings by Popova. See Dmitri V. Sarabianov, Natalia L. Adaskina, "Liubov Popova", translated by Marian Schwartz (New York: Harry N. Abrams Inc., 1990 - orig. 1989). One may also mention the fabulous dynamic paintings and drawings by Rodchenko, the cosmic paintings of Frantisek Kupka and Delaunay or some Cubist paintings by Picasso, Braque, Gleizes, Metzinger, Mondrian (his fabulous tree-paintings).

[47] See Roland Waespe, Stephen Berg, "David Reed - You look good in blue", (Nürnberg: Verlag Moderne

painting.[47] Without being conscious of the ideas by Kandinsky or of his predecessors, I discovered for myself the visual power of the simulation of motion in a three dimensional composition by using bent (or curved) stainless steel strips.[48] Obviously my wall constructions and paintings from "The Dragon Series", containing curling, spiralling coloured wire, calligraphic brushstrokes, spheres like dots in all sizes and small planes, connect very well to this tradition of point, line, plane.

see picture 17

The debate in modern theoretical physics about the point, the line and the plane continues to be the leading scientific debate.[49] The major mistake in this traditional approach is that it automatically leaves colour out. As has been described before, this mistake can be traced back to the Pythagorean School of the ancient Greeks, who preferred thought above the senses and considered the products of thought to be of higher truth than perception. As has been mentioned in many places in these chapters, the current level of knowledge provides enough evidence that there are no reasons anymore to continue such an either/or attitude. Perception is just as essential as thought - basically they cannot even be understood anymore as processes that can be distinguished or separated. Therefore, it is high time that the properties of perception as studied in art (and which exist as long as philosophy and science exist) are taken seriously and become more consciously involved in our continuous search for understanding reality.

We must understand wholeness by understanding the structure of reality on a deeper level than our everyday perception allows, while discussing and exploring it with the means of and on the level of our everyday perception, therefore, including colour and contrast!

After this exploration of the geometric and especially its basic tools - the point, the line and the plane - in the next chapter we will try to find a description for the shape of beauty, based on what we have discussed so far, while adding one additional angle.

Kunst Nürnberg, Kunstverein St. Gallen Kunstmuseum, Kunstverein Hannover, 2001).

48 Before me, bent metal wire or steel strips were used by César Domela, Katarzyna Kobro, Naum Gabo, Max Bill, Enno Iommi, Georges Vantongerloo, Alexander Calder, Norbert Kricke, Walter Linck, David Smith, Bernard Heiliger, Fletcher Benton, Mark di Suvero, and Gianni Colombo.

49 In modern theoretical physics the line is understood as one-dimensional. See Brian Greene, "The Elegant Universe - Superstrings, Hidden Dimensions, and the Quest for the Ultimate Theory" (New York: Vintage Books, 1999), p.192. But in art (and in general) the line is considered to be two dimensional: one dimension for width, one dimension for length. Another example of the difficulties one encounters in multi-disciplinary studies.

§13 THE SHAPE OF BEAUTY III: THE SPIRAL-LIKE OSCILLATION

In this chapter we will explore a variety of approaches for understanding the concept of a spiral-like oscillation. Such an oscillation is a synthesis and culmination of what we discussed in terms of the amorphic/organic and the geometric, in combination with the current understanding of nature by certain fields of science. During the past century science discovered that oscillation is the most fundamental movement of nature, as expressed by the dynamics of the heart, the earth, the sun or our solar system. Everything oscillates, meaning everything shows a periodic behaviour of attraction and repulsion caused by a diversity of forces.

Oscillation, therefore, can be understood as a special kind of rhythm or cyclic behaviour. The notion of cyclic behaviour is not completely right, as this would imply a return to exactly the same location in space/time. In reality this is impossible because of the fact that through time every location in space/time is moved.[1] Therefore, a spiral-like and oscillating movement would be a more adequate description than a pure cyclic movement, because it allows for a dynamic behaviour around an approximate and everchanging center.[2] To understand, clarify and accept our position in nature and as part of nature, we seem to need images and metaphors, projecting our considerations before our own eyes to be able to reflect upon them and to be able to adjust them before making any conclusions.[3] In this process an oscillating composition seems to offer the best connections to the essence of reality.

When the first DNA-model was developed, it was convincing proof of how the actual production of a visualization - in this case the scientific model - can enhance the argumentation process and can even make a decisive difference in trying to understand a difficult and problematic phenomenon.[4] But it also became clear that in the DNA, the

[1] For instance, a fixed point on earth is being moved by the rotation of the earth, but also by the wobbling motion of the earth-axis and of course by the movement with the moon around the sun, influenced by the motion of our whole solar system around some spot in the galaxy, etc., etc.

[2] One can argue that the motions of all cycles within our bodies, like our heartbeat, glands - or hormone systems concern a process through space/time that is better described as a spiral-like oscillation. This is a complex process, especially because these complex cycles within our bodies continuously proceed (they all continue their fluctuating processes during space/time while the body ages) and simultaneously the cosmic processes that define the precise location of our bodies in endless space/time spiral onwards. In this and in §14, I will illustrate that there are reasons for assuming interactions between these various cyclic processes (rhythmic processes influencing rhythmic processes). One may wonder if this is in part the cause for the a-symmetry of our bodies and all other living things. Purely symmetrical bodies are impossible as a result of these non-symmetrical processes.

[3] I have discussed this in §5, especially §5.7.

[4] The first DNA model was developed in 1953 by Francis Crick and James D. Watson at the University of Cambridge, UK, in co-operation with Maurice Wilkins and helped by the research of Rosalind Franklin. The actual constructing of the three-dimensional model played such an important role, because the scientists had to start from scratch, from incomplete information, and bit by bit in a process of trial and error, combining

see picture 11

basic module of life, something more than oscillation is important. The final model that was developed shows not only a magnificent and aesthetically beautiful construction of a single helix structure, but of a double helix, which rotates back into itself (one movement going up, the other going down). This example also shows that the principle of direction in an oscillation must be taken into account. The phenomenon of oscillation with a direction emerges everywhere in nature through time - the direction or 'arrow' of time. For instance, our heartbeat shows a rhythmic behaviour, following not only a daily cycle of changes of rhythm, under the influence of the rhythm of day and night subject to the complex motions in our solar system, but also following the direction in time from youth to adulthood, becoming older, gradually decaying and finally dying. Analogously, our day and night cycle is subject to the rotation of the earth in its position relative to the sun, but this process, too, is subject to the influences of the cycle of seasons caused by the motion of earth through our solar system, subject again to the journey of our solar system itself through our galaxy, etc.

On whatever small or large scale, direction is the feature allowing any process to change its specific location in space/time. A change of location in space/time causes a process to unavoidably interact with other processes. These interactions cause attraction and repulsion. As such they define the spiral-like oscillation.

Direction is a concept that is an important property of Non-Euclidian geometry - also called projective geometry.[5] Direction is also strongly related to the debate about continuity, to space and (therefore) to our perception of time, and the arrow of time. Cézanne discovered the importance of a certain kind of complexity of directions involved in contracting and extending direction through painting.[6] His painting "Forest" exemplifies this observation in a most astonishing way. It presents a view into a forest and is painted in a structure of brushstrokes with a clear direction towards what seem to be several centres in a dynamic swirling motion of vibrating colours. The swirling sensation is so strong that the observer feels her or himself being virtually dragged into the concentrated and oscillating infinity of the painting.[7] Matjushin, as an example of an early pioneer of abstract art, in a way furthered Cézanne's concept of

see picture 15

the little available information on DNA consisting of numbers of calculations, chemical knowledge of the building parts of DNA and some vague two-dimensional photographs. They gradually found the beautiful conclusion by building and analysing the inner logic of the structure in a real three-dimensional model-construction. This is a perfect example that a creative process of 'self - argumentation' in science is very similar to creativity in art. See §5.7. and §5.8. Without the actual and manual building process of the model they could never have figured out the logic of the construction of DNA!

[5] See §6.2.

[6] Cézanne wrote to Emile Bernard, July 25, 1904, in The Tate Gallery, "Cézanne" (London: Tate Publishing, 1996), p.288: "To make progress there's only nature, and the eye is trained through contact with her. It becomes concentric through looking and working. I mean to say that in an orange, an apple, a ball, a head, there's a culminating point; and this point is always - despite the tremendous effect: light and shadow, color sensations - closest to our eyes; the edges of objects flee toward a center placed on our horizon."

[7] "Forest", (orig. "Sous-Bois"), 1894. See also §6.1. The main center lies just a bit above the center of the painting, it even seems marked by a cross resembling two branches. The other two centres are not so clearly

'culminating points'. By including some scientific knowledge, he developed his concept of 'extended vision'.[8] His interest in cell-theory of organic nature, in the growth of plants and the behaviour of the simplest organisms, was a real topic for biologists, philosophers and artists late in the 19th century and early 20th century. Every organic cell grows at once from its center outwards and to all directions simultaneously.[9] Accordingly, Matjushin wished to translate this concept, so fundamental to nature's growth, into a 360° vision in painting, a vision extended in all directions.

Direction is not merely a reference to the arrow of time, but especially to the vectors in space, allowing the definition of space and orientation in space. Vectors describe the imaginable lines between yourself and a building, a tree, a car, a rock, a bridge or other points of reference in space and between these points. In mathematics vectors are seen as the virtual arrows pointing in the directions through which you perceive space. Physicists call the composition of all such arrows a vector-space. By drawing these imaginary lines in your mind you can instantaneously judge distances and depth in the space where you are, information you need to be able to proceed without problems. In philosophy, direction is considered a logical result of the discussions on infinity and continuity in the 19th century and is especially relevant to understanding our fascination for geometry.[10] This discussion is obviously part of the centuries old debate about the logic of the point, line and plane, which had such a profound influence on art.[11] The spiral-like oscillation has been expressed all through history, although most of the time in a simple symbol: as a rotating cross, a spiral or whirlpool.[12] One is reminded of the double movement of the rotating helix structure of DNA mentioned before, showing

defined, but still sensed by approximation (one senses their presence mainly by the local light colour). One is a bit left from the main center, the third one in the lower right corner.

[8] See §5.2., §6.3. and §11, especially footnotes 61 + 62.

[9] See §11. See Lynn Gamwell, "Exploring the Invisible - Art, Science, And The Spiritual" (Princeton and Oxford: Princeton University Press, 2002). Gamwell describes how the public interest in the microcosm in the late 19th century was enhanced by the discovery by scientists like Louis Pasteur or Robert Koch of the microbes that cause serious diseases. Cell-theory was declared in 1838 by physiologist Theodor Schwann and botanist Matthias Scheiden - seeing so many details of intercellular bodies, they stated that all living tissue is composed of cells. We now know cell growth is controlled by an organelle called the centrosome. The centrosome was first described simultaneously in 1887 by Theodor H. Boveri and Edouard Joseph Louis-Marie van Beneden and studied by many researchers around the turn of the 19th/20th century. See later in this chapter.

[10] See Nishida Kitaro, "Intuition and Reflection in Self-Consciousness" (Albany, NY: State University of New York, 1987 - orig. "Jikaku ni okeru chokkan to han sei", 1941), p.96: ".... the idea of direction arises from the fact that one position can be determined only in relation to another position; direction is this relation."

[11] See §12.3.

[12] For an extensive explanation on the whirlpool as spiral-like oscillation and as model for the macro- and microcosm, see Dr. J.J. Lehr, "De draaikolk als model voor mikro- en makrokosmos" (De Erven Lehr, ca 1990). Ever since man exists, he created abstract rotation symbols. These symbols are basically geometric and probably refer to the sun as the major source of life itself (and, therefore, refer to the duality life-death), but they are also often considered to be a symbol for the whole, while acknowledging the drive of continous chance (symbolized in the powerful simulations of motion, like simulated rotation). Examples can be found in the cultures of the ancient Assyrians, Egyptians, Chinese, but also with the later Greeks, Romans, in the

oscillation in a kind of complex '8' motion, one movement going up and the other going down. A DNA structure seen from the top shows a remarkable resemblance to a pulsating Mandala - composition. Without intending they have the same meaning as DNA or Mandala, one can find similar kinds of compositions repeatedly in works of art and ornaments. Good examples of the spiral-like oscillation in modern art are the column-series by Michael Kidner and the sketches for the colour-ordering in the paintings by Richard Paul Lohse.[13] Purely chance? I do not think so. There is too much evidence that artists sense this basic motion of nature or consciously explore it to allow it to be merely chance.

see picture 52

Although an oscillation normally seems to result from the confrontation of two opposed forces, such as centrifugal and centrepetal forces, or contracting and extending forces, certain developments in theoretical physics seem to illustrate the importance of spiral-like oscillation in a very different context. Such an oscillation is seen as a logical result of the new developments in the Theory of Duality. This is a theory in which the notion of duality is preferred to the notion 'super', as in supersymmetry and superstrings.[14] Duality in theoretical physics concerns a certain symmetry, which allows composite entities to be viewed as equivalent to fundamental particles and vice versa. Direction and spiral-like movement are considered important features of this new theory. It is crucial to our discussion to understand the different understandings of concepts across different disciplines, which often make communication quite confusing. The notions of duality and symmetry exemplify this confusion.[15] Words are important, but unfortunately do not always clearly communicate meaning.

For many artists, the notion of duality has always been an essential condition for the

Hindu-, Shinto- (Japan), African- (like the Kuba in the Congo), Islamic-, Hebrew-, Celtic- and for instance Pre-Columbian cultures one may find similar rotating crosses. Examples include the eight legged rotation symbols of Tibet, and in other cultures four legged swastika's, three legged and two legged symbols as autonomous symbol or connected in sets or strings in ornamental frames, like in the windows of Christian cathedrals.

13 See Irving Sandler, "Art from Britain 3: Michael Kidner at-tension to the wave" (New York: Center for International Contemporary Arts, 1990). See Hans Peter Riese, Friedrich W. Heckmanns, "Richard Paul Lohse, Zeichnungen 1935-1985" (Baden: LIT Verlag, 1986).

14 See Madhusree Mukerjee, "Trends in Theoretical Physics: Explaining Everything", Scientific American January 1996, p.72-78. See Henry E. Kandrup, Stephen T. Gottesman, James R. Ipser, "Three-Dimensional Systems", Annals of the New York Academy of Sciences - Volume 75, 1995. See §6.5.

15 The understanding of duality in theoretical physics as is described here is different from how duality in art and philosophy is described previously in §6, §7 and §8. The duality of subject-object or self-world of everyday reality is a confrontation, a natural but still not so desired contrast between two entities (the desired dissolving of this duality leads to temporary relief), while in theoretical physics duality is understood as a desired situation to be able to compare two different entities in a one-to-one relationship - without any contrast or tension. See Brian Greene, "The Elegant Universe - Superstrings, Hidden Dimensions, and the Quest for the Ultimate Theory" (New York: Vintage Books, 2000), p.298: "Physicists use the term duality to describe theoretical models, that appear to be different but nevertheless can be shown to describe exactly the same physics." Hence also the difference in defining and valuing the concept of symmetry: while in theoretical science symmetry is a desired status of corresponding duality, because a lack of tension between two related or interacting entities allows them to be compared, in daily 'real life' symmetry is not desired. As has been stated

realization of dynamic compositions. Complementarity and contrast exemplify duality: complementarity of form, movement or colour is caused by simultaneous contrast.[16] There are properties of works of art that, in our vision, seem to be opposed, hence to be in contrast, in such a powerful way that they seem to be able to annihilate each other, to be each other's 'complement'. In fact, because of their capacity to annihilate each other, they cause the focus of our vision to continuously jump from one to the other, or, in other words, they evoke the experience of oscillation in our vision between forms, movements or colours. This particular optical effect has been studied both by scientists and by artists.[17] For instance, German artist Michael Bette accomplishes in his paintings a precise combination of subtle range of colours with strong geometrical calligraphic signs, causing our vision to keep wandering over the composition, never finding a center. This allows the viewer to continuously discover new relationships between colours, forms and the intervals.[18]

see picture 45

Charles Biederman not only included the complexity of contrasts of colour or of forms, but also the influence of ever changing light on form and colour-contrasts. Biederman thus incorporated actual change in looking at colour and forms. This is an often neglected or at least underestimated property of daily life and an aspect of oscillation indeed (daylight never stays the same, but changes - oscillates - all day long). Biederman himself saw this as equivalent to Monet's recording of the changes of light.[19] While Monet needed to paint the shifting light in his series of hay-stacks, poplar trees, cathedrals, etc., Biederman said the coloured relief could accomplish this in just one work by its capacity to show actual changes of light and colour under the influence of the continuous and gradual changes of daylight. The relief therefore would stand closer

see pictures 16, 26

before, in biology symmetry is considered to be equivalent to death and in art symmetry indicates a boring and dead image.

[16] According to Bernard, Cézanne has said, in Richard Shiff, "Cézanne and the End of Impressionism - A Study of the Theory, Technique, and Critical Evaluation of Modern Art" (Chicago: The University of Chicago Press, 1984), p.121: "... there is no line, there is no (chiaroscuro) modeling, there are only contrasts. These contrasts are not given by black and white, but by the sensation of color."

[17] Michael Matjushin studied the interactions of colours, inspired by Ostwald (a scientist who researched colour), and the sound and movement of colour. This led him to propose a connecting third colour as intermediary connecting two randomly chosen colours. This was a conclusion from his observations of nature. He proposed the elementary form as basic form and the contrasting form as complementary form, analogous to scientist's Chevreul's concept of a complementary colour. Matjushin believed the deformation of a form resulting from the influence of the complementary form expressed their connection and their relationship with space. The connection to its complementary form sets the form free and, at the same time, confirms the form itself by emphasizing it. Therefore Matjushin thought knowledge about the complementary forms was essential for realizing a stability or dynamics. See Faber Birren, "The Principle of Harmony and Contrast of Colors and their application to the arts - M.E. Chevreul", a newly revised edition (London: Schiffer Publishing ltd, 1987 - orig. 1854). See Faber Birren, "The Color Primer - A basic treatise on the color system of Wilhelm Ostwald" (New York: Van Nostrand Reinhold Company, 1969 - orig. "Farbenfiebel", 1916).

[18] See Gudrun Thiessen- Schneider, Perdita von Kraft, "Michael Bette", (Neuenhaus: Kunstverein Grafschaft Bentheim, Brandenburgische Kunstsammlungen Cottbus, 1998).

[19] Monet spoke of searching to depict what 'envelopes' the whole scene. His interpretation of l'impression led him to find unity in the environment created solely by light and colour. This search for the ultimate

to reality than the painting, which Biederman considered to be a mere record of a frozen impression that does not allow incorporation of actual change. This is not true, because the colours in a painting also can change dramatically under the influence of any change of light. Comparable to complementary colour and form, the changing conditions of light and colours create in our perception the sensation of an oscillation of light.This oscillation clearly focusses our mind on the work of art. This process of oscillation can be seen as the process by which the work of art attracts our attention. The work of art functions as an 'attractor'.

Attractors are locations of attraction with a stabile character. Entities that are moving around them (in this case the viewer), and are influenced by the instabile order-fluctuations of reality, will continue to show a tendency to move towards the attractor.[20] The Lorenz Attractor shows an amazing three-dimensional double spiral, which also can be found in ornamental decorations in many cultures.[21] I can imagine that these images of double spirals have a metaphorical relationship to continuous change that is perceived in nature. In nature or - maybe more clearly - in our everyday experience, we can recognize a certain structure that seems to repeat itself, like day and night rhythms or the rhythms of the seasons. After a closer look we will find that every day and season are also different. You will never find two sunsets to be exactly the same! The impossibility of accurately forecasting the weather or predicting the continuous shift of climates proves this too. In short: the structure of nature does follow a certain logic, but not one that fits into one specific set of rules. There are just too many interactions and especially unforeseen chain reactions of the many phenomena that cause the circumstances to change. This most important characteristic of nature makes the existence of strict laws of nature, if not impossible, highly irrelevant. As art is an interpretation or translation of our perception of nature, the search for strict sets of rules in art also becomes superficial.[22]

Unforeseen chain reactions can be caused by synchronization of rhythms. It is not the

---

'envelope' makes his choices very logical to depict scenes in particular weather (like the London fog) or specific moments of a day (like during a sunset or in early hazy morning light).

[20] This sounds awfully familiar to how Cézanne understood his 'culminating points', as was described earlier in this chapter!

[21] For instance, this spiral can be found among the Celts or the Maori or the Aboriginal. In my collection is a magnificent wooden carved Aboriginal shield, on one side a single spiral on the other (the side of the carrier) a double spiral. Using a computer Edward Lorenz realized a first image of this attractor in 1963. In the 1980's beautiful 'Lorentz-attractors' were realized with a computer by the German artist Georg Nees. This attractor is often used as a metaphor for Chaos Theory to illustrate the unpredictable moment of abrupt change in a process (the Lorenz Attractor shows a slow proceeding process spiralling outwards in orbit around a certain point up to an unexpected point, where the trajectory changes direction dramatically to start a new slow inwards spiral again around a new center). In my own art I already early felt a familiarity with the Lorenz Attractor before I found better analogies concerning the complex movements in a study of three-dimensional contra-rotations. See Chad Davies, J.R. Hunter, H. James, "Counterrotating Orbits and Stability in Two- and Three-Dimensional Systems", in Henry E. Kandrup, Stephen T. Gottesman, James R. Ipser, "Three-Dimensional Systems", Annals of the New York Academy of Sciences, Volume 751, 1995.

[22] Many artists who use geometry in their art still consider it important to follow a set of strict rules analogous to an old-fashioned (wrong) understanding of nature. Fortunately quite a few artists using a set of rules keep

only reason for change of circumstances, but seems to be more important than is acknowledged.[23] The phenomenon that rhythms occuring in each other's vicinity have the potential to influence each other to the level that they will start showing exactly the same rhythm, has become known as the 'synchronization of coupled oscillators'.[24] An oscillator is any system that shows a periodically shifting behavior. Synchronization happens in a process called phase-locking. A rhythm must be imagined as a certain kind of wave-pattern. Two rhythms occuring close to each other lead to the phenomenon that the waves of both rhythms become absolutely parallel, obtaining the same phases. A phase is a part of a wave showing its ascending or descending movement of peaks and valleys. These can enhance each other, but can also annihilate each other, which happens when the one wave shows a peak at the moment the other wave shows a valley.[25] It would be an interesting experiment to explore the process of observing an artwork as 'a process of phase-locking'. This does not necessarily have to be too far-fetched, as many discussions of the importance of being absorbed by an artwork seem to suggest. We might consider the experience of being absorbed as a result of the rhythms of the electrochemical processes in our brain that constitute our thinking, phase-locking with the rhythms, the frequency of the waves of light reflected from the artwork, of colours and shapes as presented to our senses by the artwork. This would imply that, when the phases enhance each other, the brain gives us the feeling that we like the artwork, and when the phases annihilate each other, the brain tells us that we dislike it (or at least that it does not capture our attention).

As an artist myself, I am deeply involved in exploring colour and form. I believe a precise use of complementary colours and forms enhances phase-locking. For obvious reasons, one may assume that there are many levels of intensity of such phase-locking. I expect that in the process of phase-locking one could find the neurophysiological explanation for an experience of the sublime, as I have mentioned before while discussing the sublime.[26] The strongest level of phase-locking evoked by a work of art will involve the majority of those parts of our brain that are involved in vision and thus will result in all our conscious thinking being absorped in processing the phenomenon that caused this phase-locking.

Obviously, with our current knowledge this is hard to prove. In the 1970's, physicist Herbert Fröhlich described the inflation-process concerning a system of vibrating and electrically charged molecules into which energy was pumped.[27] These charged molecules

the door open in their creative process for unexpected or emergent aspects, like Michael Kidner, Jean-Pierre Maury, Michael Bette, Philippe Jahanguir, localStyle, or Richard Purdy.

23 See my paper "The Synchronizing Self - A Search for Harmony as a Process of Symmetry Breaking", in T. Ogawa, T. Masunari, D. Nagy, "Katachi u Symmetry" (Tokyo: Springer Verlag, 1996).

24 See §5.1 On the complexities involved in the many cycles involving synchronization inside our own bodies, see Friedrich Cramer, "Symphonie des Lebendigen - Versuch einer allgemeinen Resonanztheorie" (Frankfurt, Leipzig: Insel Taschenbuch, 1998).

25 Compare §7.6. on Prigone and Stengers on the principle of adaptive organization.

26 See §8, footnote 105, where I discuss the possible influence of melatonin on our vision.

27 This process is described in "Long Range Coherence and Energy Storage in Biological Systems", the

are called dipoles, consisting of a positively charged end and a negatively charged end. When they vibrate, these dipoles, which are molecules in the cell-walls of organic tissue, emit electromagnetic waves. Fröhlich showed that any quantity of energy that exceeds a certain amount of energy already pumped into these dipoles will result in a united vibrating of all molecules. The addition of more energy stimulates the molecules to synchronize their rhythms and vibrate as one whole: a so-called Bose-Einstein Condensate.[28] The basic property of a Bose-Einstein Condensate is not only that the molecules synchronize their vibrations, but also that they actually become a temporary unity. Science writer Danah Zohar suggests that this physical process is a plausible explanation for the processes of our becoming conscious and our emerging individuality. The process of synchronization of neuronal (vibrating) electrochemical energies enhances thought processes to the level of becoming one (like a Bose-Einstein Condensate) and, therefore, becoming strong enough to be noticed by ourselves, culminating in the moment we become conscious. Because this is a process of gradual strengthening of the electrochemical impulse in the brain, which, as I pointed out in §5, happens by a process of re-entry or looping rhythmic process leading to a unification of rhythms by synchronization, I think it is justifiable to understand this as a process of a spiral-like oscillation.

Simultaneously, all of the separate signals in the brain lose their individual properties in the unifying process, leading to the establishment of a homogeneity that forms individuality.[29] Every individual is so unique because the circumstances for these processes in the brain of each of us are entirely different. Brains in general may look similar, but definitely are not. Following this train of thought, one could expect that the perception of a work of art, that is the reception of certain waves of energy (like the lightwaves caused by the colour and form in the artwork), evokes a process of synchronization or inflation-process in the molecules of the brain, leading to a union of a

International Journal of Quantum Chemistry, vol.2, p.641-649. Also in Hans Jenny, "Kymatik - Wellen und Schwingungen mit Ihrer Struktur und Dynamik" (Basel: Basilius Presse Basler Druck und Verlagsanstalt, 1972). Scientist Hans Jenny published his well-illustrated extensive studies at the Institut für Schwingungsforschung (Institute for Frequency - Research, at Dornach, Switzerland) on the impact of electromagnetic vibrations following changing frequencies (= electromagnetic oscillations) and on fluid and solid substances. The morphological changes in these substances clearly prove that vibrations or waves interacting with certain substances do have an impact causing these substances to change their morphological shape, to break apart, or to change into rhythmic and very geometric patterns or any other kind of regular order. The fundamental condition for such an impact is that the considered substance contains some rhythmic property itself that can relate to the 'in-coming rhythm', because this impact happens by the principle of synchronization. Jenny calls the studies of this phenomenon Kymatik (Cymatics).

28 See Danah Zohar, "Het Quantum Zelf", translated by J.P. Blokhuis (Utrecht: Aula Paperbacks, Het Spectrum, 1990 - orig. "The Quantum Self", New York: William Morrow Publ., 1990), p.87 and following. See §6.4. See Eric A. Cornell, Carl E. Wieman, "The Bose-Einstein Condensate", Scientific American, March 1998, p.26-31. The condensate is named after Albert Einstein and Satyendra Nath Bose who predicted this process in 1925.

29 The signal of an individual neuron in our brain cannot be strong enough to become a part of our consciousness. The combined forces of many neurons through synchronization can. See §5. This synchronization represents a kind of perfect democracy.

certain quantity of neural pulses as a Bose-Einstein Condensate and, finally, by the process of re-entry, to a certain conscious sensation. In biological systems, moments of synchronization do not seem to last very long, which maybe helps explain why we can have the experience that our observation of a work of art seems to rapidly change. The discussion becomes even more exciting when we briefly look at modern cell-research.

Although centrosomes were described in the late 19th century, scientists had to wait until the invention of the electron microscope to learn more about their structure.[30] At the heart of the centrosome one finds two geometric arrangements of so-called microtubules, described as centrioles. Each centriole consists of a bundle of nine rods. Though it is too far-fetched to read more into it than is actually there, when one looks at the available microscope-pictures, it is fascinating to see the strong similarity of the pinwheel structure revealed by a cross-section of a centriole to the ordering of the DNA structure seen from the top, or to the rotating kinds of Mandala-structures one can find in many cultures. From the centrosomes, microtubules, which are a kind of hollow fiber consisting of proteins, extend outwards and play their part in the actual cell-division process. They are considered dynamic structures as they continuously grow and shrink because of a phenomenon called dynamic instability. This is a phenomenon of oscillation which can be understood as the motor of life.[31] Therefore, any moment of synchronization, also understood as moment of symmetry or of harmony, is soon disturbed again.[32] Breaking of symmetry happens when the particular single symmetrical state (like in synchronization) is replaced by a variety of less symmetrical states. Translated into art, this relates to an asymmetrical - symmetrical composition. Translated into our daily reality I call this oscillating behaviour 'the continuous changing circumstances', expressing the potential for change both from the outside and simultaneously from the inside of an organism. This seems to be justified by the fact that most common circumstances at first glance do not seem to change, but after a closer observation are slightly different after all. That is why the notion of a spiral-like oscillation seems so appropriate, because it implies a kind of return to the original position in space-time, although it is not.

Briefly returning to the above mentioned hypothetical aspect of phase-locking, this could very well explain why we perceive the same artwork differently every time we see it, as we probably have to adjust our phase-locking again. In the future it might be possible to prove that this idea is not too far-fetched.[33] An oscillation's primary characteristic is rhythm, any oscillator network is in principle vulnerable to influences

---

30 The centrosome is the organelle which controls the division, motility and shape of cells. See David M. Glover, Cayetano Gonzalez, Jordan W. Raff, "The Centrosome", Scientific American issue June 1993, p.32-38. The centrosome was first described in in 1887 by Boveri and Van Beneden, who studied cell-division in the eggs of a roundworm.

31 In 1923 Tarabukin called it 'the throb of life', which is caused by rhythm and as such is used in art.

32 See §7.6. See Steven H. Strogatz, Ian Stewart, "Coupled Oscillators and Biological Synchronization", Scientific American, issue December 1993, p.68-75.

33 This seems already to be indicated by research in engineering on synchronizing chaotic behaviour with the

by rhythms of any wave-pattern hitting it from anywhere, as long as they are strong enough to cause a synchronization.

To conclude, the deeper we explore existing theories and actual knowledge in very different fields of science, and discuss the analogies in art, we repeatedly find lots of clues that our perception of the world and our appreciation of art are influenced by processes in the very cells of our bodies, in our brains, our environment and the universe. These influences are not defined by culture, but help define culture. In other words: the way we think and the location in space/time where we think, influence what we think! It all makes the desire to understand wholeness extremely logical and natural.

I have refered extensively to our being immersed in reality, in the universe. In the next chapter I will attempt to describe what kind of influences and what consequences result from that immersion.

---

aim to exploit these patterns in commercially important ways. See Elizabeth Corcoran, "Ordering Chaos - Researchers are beginning to harness nonlinear systems", Scientific American issue August 1993, p.82-83. This is naturally still far away from understanding a possible synchronization of our brain-waves with the frequencies of the light (and sound) waves of an observed object, but it is a matter of phase-locking nevertheless. The plausibility that by a process of synchronization our thinking and doing is influenced by rhythmic phenomena that occur outside our own bodies seems also to be indicated in the next quotation, in Steven H. Strogatz, Ian Stewart, "Coupled Oscillators and Biological Synchronization", p.73: "Biologists have long hypothesized the existence of networks of coupled neurons they call central pattern generators, but the hypothesis has always been controversial. Nevertheless, neurons often act as oscillators, and so, if central pattern generators exist, it is reasonable to expect their dynamics to resemble those of an oscillator network." For a completely up dated discussion on this very important topic, see Steven H. Strogatz, "SYNC - How Order Emerges from Chaos in the Universe, Nature, and Daily Life"(New York: Theia Books, Hyperion, 2003). Synchronization should obviously not be mistaken for the notion of Synchronizität by C.G. Jung. Synchronicity as by Jung concerns the temporal and perceivable parallellism of psychic and psychophysical events, which leads one to understand these events to be based on a mutual principle. See C.G. Jung, "Grundwerk-Band 2-Archetyp und Unbewusstes" (Olten, CH: Walter Verlag 1990), p.289.

§14 OUR BODIES IN THE UNIVERSE THE UNIVERSE IN OUR BODIES

After discussing the various ways to express the 'shape of beauty' and, having discussed the reasons why rhythmic processes in all varieties influence each other through synchronization, it is the right time to elaborate on our immersion in the universe. In this chapter I will attempt to describe some of the important phenomena that influence our being. In the previous chapters we saw that certain rhythmic processes, inherent in the chemistry of our brains, determine that we are not completely free to decide what we think. It seems justified to say that our concept of free will is influenced by certain natural processes. Our ideas about truth or art seem to be influenced by more processes than by our own decisions, associations or cultural preferences. Or, should we say it the other way around? Are our cultural preferences, our associations and even our personal decisions defined by the process of nature at large and the processes of nature at that particular point in space/time where we, as individuals, live?

Throughout the previous chapters I have repeatedly mentioned our unavoidable and natural participation in the complex processes of the universe. To allow us to take a closer look at what or where our position is within this complex interplay of forces, we may understand our conscious perception, our conscious thought, to occur in the realm between the macro-universe outside our bodies and the micro-universe within our bodies. Our physical being, the presence of our bodies, exists in the realm of the surface of the earth, hypothetically between the processes above us in the universe and the processes underneath us, inside the earth itself.

14.1 OUR BODIES IN THE UNIVERSE: IDEAS IN SCIENCE

Among the ancient Greeks, Aristarchus already developed a heliocentric cosmic system. This however was rejected by Hipparchos of Nikaia and by Claudius Ptolemaeus and was thus forgotten.[1] Though the geocentric cosmic system already existed in the concept of the universe by the Pythagorean School, it became more widely known through the interpretation of the Greek-Egyptian astronomer Ptolemaeus around 200 AD.[2] For Christian religious reasons this was the only accepted model in Europe for more then 1000 years. One is reminded of the conflict between the Italian astronomer, Galileo Galilei, and the Vatican, which threatened to ban him when he would not withdraw his theory that the sun, and not the earth, was the center of the universe.[3] The Church strongly opposed the change from a geocentric to a heliocentric cosmic system, because in the case of a heliocentric cosmic system, in accordance to the Church's dogma, the

1 The heliocentric universe = the sun as center of the universe.

2 The geocentric universe = the earth as center of our solar system. Remember the harmony of the spheres of the Pythagorean School, see §12, footnote 32.

3 Galileo lived 1564-1642.

presupposed highlight of God's creation - earth with man as its highest living form and ruler, and the pope as the highest intermediary between man and God - would not be the center of the universe anymore. This would thus weaken the hierarchy and power of the Church. It was believed if the sun was the actual center of the universe, then the Vatican would not rule over the most important part of the whole of creation. Besides, it was maintained that nowhere in the Bible can one find any evidence of the movement of the earth. Galilei was forced to recall his theory under pressure of the Inquisition.

After this first effort, it was the Polish astronomer Nikolaus Copernikus who put the sun again in the center, although his theory did not last in relation to the logic of that epoche. Danish astronomer Tycho Brahe proposed a compromise: earth is the center, the planets orbit around the sun, the sun orbits around the earth. German astronomer Johannes Kepler, who had been a student of Brahe and who had been in touch with Galilei by writing letters, delivered finally in 1601 the solution for science: the planets do not move in circles or in orbits consisting of parts of circles, but in elliptical orbits with the sun at their focus.[4] It is important to recall that Kepler could make this statement as he lived in a Germany where the Reformation of Luther already made an impact, allowing some freedom of thought. The Catholic Church needed much more time to acknowledge this observation as fact.[5] Kepler published his theories explaining the construction of the world based on harmonies.[6]

Later it was found that not even our sun is the center of the universe, as the sun is merely one of some 100 billion stars of the rotating galaxy of which our Milky Way is but one arm. And it has been found that there are an infinite number of similar and much larger galaxies.

It should be clear of course that the whole of nature is continuously in motion - not just as an entity, but in a complexity of many swirling forces.[7] The ancient Greek philosopher, Heraclitus, already stated that everything is flowing in a state of flux, in which he included the notion of changeablity.[8] As we saw earlier, our thinking consists

---

[4] See Kepler Gesellschaft, "Kepler-Museum in Weil der Stadt" (Weil der Stadt: Kepler Gesellschaft, 1982).

[5] It took even until the second half of the 20th century before the church formally re-established the status of Galilei!

[6] In his "Ioannis Harmonices Mundi Libri V", Linz in 1619, the "5 Bücher der Weltanschauung", in 1968 reprinted as Harmonici Mundi . See Kepler Gesellschaft, "Kepler-Museum in Weil der Stadt". Kepler furthered his ideas from his "Mysterium Cosmographicum." See Carole Stott, "Celestial Charts - Antique Maps of the Heavens" (New York: Crescent Books, 1991).

[7] Michelangelo seems to have sensed this in the translation of motion into his figurative sculpture as 'figura serpentina', which is a strong simulation of motion by a half turned posture of his model, like in his famous statue of Moses. See Donald Kuspit, "Signs of Psyche in Modern and Post-Modern Art" (New York: Cambridge University Press, 1995 - orig.1993) p.307. This simulation of movement seems to echo Plato's interpretation of genesis as a becoming into being, which is interesting to compare to Whitehead's concept of 'becoming a being' and seems to be an early representation of the notion of spiral-like oscillation (see §13). See Hans-Georg Gadamer, "Bildkunst und Wortkunst", in Gottfried Boehm, "Was ist ein Bild?", (Munich: Wilhelm Fink Verlag, 3rd edition, 2001 - orig.1994), p.97.

[8] Compare Tao or Dao in Chinese philosophy, which emphasizes continuous change and thus a continuous 'becoming' in all phenomena of nature. See Roger T. Ames, David L. Hall, "Daodejing - 'Making This Life Significant' - A Philosophical Translation" (New York: Ballantine Books, 2003). In his Theaetetus Plato

of oscillating processes of electrochemical energy.[9]

An aspect unfortunately often ignored while discussing our functioning, most certainly our thinking, is the plausibility of a phenomenon that I propose to call 'out-of-body influences'.[10] For we do not stand apart from or objectively opposite to the rest of nature. Our bodies are continuously bombarded by fields of energy that oscillate at different frequencies. As I argued in the previous chapter, it is reasonable to assume that thinking is influenced by synchronization of rhythmic processes, the level of influence depending entirely on the actual strength of the 'incoming' rhythms and on the extent to which these rhythms match - a matching that happens when the incoming wave phase-lock with the rhythmic patterns in the brain. These 'out-of-body influences' can be imagined as processes consisting of rhythmic streams of energies that come in waves towards us. To the receiver, waves are perceived as pulsating or oscillating movements - they emerge in certain rhythms that first increase in strength before decreasing and then increasing again. Compare the wave motions and tidal motions of the sea when you stand on the beach and see the waves coming towards you.

The sun continuously blasts an irregular magnetic storm known as 'solar wind' through our solar system that collides with the electromagnetic field of our earth and as such influences all streams of energy on earth. This is not only perceptable in the changes of the tides, but also in the weather and climatological changes.[11] The sun's activities show a remarkable cyclic behaviour. In recent observations and in old recordings of the sun, and of climatic changes scientists have found evidence of two cycles of magnetic activity, each of 11 years: one cycle of heating up and one of cooling down, forming a complete cycle in 22 years.[12] These cyclic changes are caused by the solar dynamo, consisting of a complex combination of oscillating magnetic fields inside and outside the sun in which sunspots play an important role. Sunspots are the locations where concentrations of energy erupt and loop through space to return through other sunspots into the sun.[13]

Evidence has been found that all stars oscillate in a similar way. Other stars also project fluctuating amounts of electromagnetic energies through the universe, comparable to

quotes Heraclitus: "You cannot step twice into the same river; for fresh waters are ever flowing in upon you." See Bertrand Russell, "History of Western Philosophy" (London: Routledge, 1991 - orig.1946), p.63.

9 See §5, see §13.

10 See §5.4. See my own paper "Gestaltung als Verbindung zwischen Denken und Handeln" ("Design as connection between thinking and acting"), 1995.

11 The solar wind can cause such a heavy electromagnetic storm that in those parts on earth where it hits, all electricity and telecommunication blacks out. This has happened in Aslaska and Canada. The best known phenomenon caused by the solar wind though is the awesome aurora borealis or Northern Lights. See Harald Falck Ytter, "Aurora - The Northern Lights in Mythology, History and Science", (Hudson, NJ: Bell Pond Books, 1983 -orig, Verlag Freies Geistesleben GmbH, Stuttgart).

12 See Kenneth R. Lang, "Sun, Earth and Sky" (Berlin-Heidelberg-New York: Springer Verlag, 1995). See Ribes Nesme, Sallie Baliunas, Dmitry Sokoloff, "The Stellar Dynamo", Scientific American, issue August 1996, p.30-36.

13 Their paths are called field-lines.

the sun, of which some will undoubtedly hit the magnetic field of our earth.[14] New measure- and visualization technologies in this century show how strong the bombardment from outer space is on the earth, consisting of gamma radiation, X-rays or Röntgen-rays, ultra-violet radiation and so-called radio-wave signals.[15] These make new observations about our universe possible, showing us that the cosmos is much more complex than is available to our vision. It has been discovered that the gamma-ray bursts originate from nearby star systems and that there are many more galaxies than was assumed.[16] Besides, researchers have found galaxies that have such low surface brightness that they emit or reflect only two percent more light than the black background of the cosmos, implying that we have only observed approximately fifty percent of all galaxies. Clearly this will have a tremendous effect on all theories about the cosmos and on figuring out what the impact of these newly discovered galaxies and their cosmic cycles of various forces have on us on earth.[17] The long terms of cyclic changes in the universe and the powerful gravitational interaction among the different planets in our solar system also seem to influence the shape, orientation and tilt of each other's orbit, including that of our earth. In the geological layers of the earth evidence can be found of these astronomical cycles.

This evidence led to a new discipline called cyclostratigraphy, which has taken up earlier attempts to research the different cycles that occur in the universe.[18] This kind of

---

14 Scientist Larry Krumenaker writes in "Rhythm Section - The pulse of planetary cycles, recorded deep in New Jersey shale", The Sciences, issue November/December 1995, p.14-17: "The cosmic influences on climate are anything but mystical. They boil down to insolation: the amount of sunlight hitting the top of the atmosphere. The more energy the atmosphere receives for each square foot, the more energy it holds. Local weather (the current, transient condition) becomes warmer, and the air flow from equator to pole gets more dynamic, causing more rainstorms, hurricanes, stronger monsoons and the like, until the energy dissipates near the poles. The principal cause for seasonal and annual variations, as every schoolchild is taught, is the tilt of the earth's axis. Other aspects of the earth's orbit, such as the earth's distance from the sun, are insignificant in the short term (in fact, the earth makes its closest approach to the sun in early January - winter in the northern hemisphere) but become much more important over hundreds or thousands of years."

15 See Nathan Cohen, "Gravity's Lens - Views of the new Cosmology" (Wiley Science Editions, 1989). See Kenneth R. Lang,"Sun, Earth and Sky". See Edward van den Heuvel and Jan van Paradijs, Niels Gehrels and co-workers, "X-ray Binaries", Scientific American, issue November 1993, p.38-45. See Corey Powell, "Trends in Astrophysics: In constant Cosmos", Scientific American, issue May 1993, p.69-76. See Raymond Jeanloz, Thorne Lay, "The Core-Mantle Boundary", Scientific American, issue May 1993, p.26-33. As I described in relation to its influence on early abstract art (§6 + §8), X-rays were discovered by Wilhelm Conrad Röntgen in 1895. See Graham Farmelo, "The Discovery of X-Rays", Scientific American, issue November 1995, p.68-73. The first radio-wave picture of the Milky Way was accomplished in the 1950's by an amateur-astronomer.

16 See Neil Gehrels, Carl E. Fichtel, Gerald J. Fishman, James D. Kurfess, Volker Schönfelder, "The Compton Gamma Ray Observatory", Scientific American, issue December 1993, p.38-45: "Gamma-ray bursts were discovered in the late 1960s by Ray W. Klebesade and co-workers at Los Alamos National Laboratory, using in order to monitor the Soviet Union's compliance with the Nuclear Test-Ban Treaty. Vela did discover short, potent bursts of gamma rays, but they originated in the heavens, not on the earth. The bursts occurred about a dozen times a year in what appeared to be random directions scattered over the whole sky. When the Vela data were declassified in 1973, the astronomical community immediately set out to determine the cause of these gamma-ray convulsions."

17 See Gregory D. Bothun, "The Ghostliest Galaxies", Scientific American, issue February 1997, p.40-45.

18 In 1754 the French mathematician Jean le Rond d'Alembert proved that mainly under the influence of the

research evidently has been sparked in the last decades by the debate about global warming. Researching the paths of the different cosmic winds is not easy, as new complexities are found all the time. For instance, it has been discovered that quite a few stars have so-called unseen companion stars, stars that follow their cosmic motions together in the same orbit while influencing each other's gravitational fields and cosmic winds.[19]

Earth itself is neither a dead solid nor a perfect sphere, but an everchanging and dented potato-shape with a relatively thin skin, fluid contents and a heavy solid core, involving a complex oscillation of huge forces, pushing and pulling at the surface.[20] The geomagnetic forces, like electromagnetic radiation, are caused by the friction between the different solid and fluid layers at the center of our earth. They erupt at the surface, distorted by so many layers of stone in the core, which differ in density. Through this distortion, one may find at certain spots higher concentrations of these geomagnetic lines of force that also influence the character of the movement of the energy fields at the surface, where we live. Migrating birds use concentrations of these geomagnetic lines of force for their orientation.[21] Even more complex factors have been discovered while studying the inner core of the earth and earth's magnetic field. It was discovered

gravitational pull of Jupiter, the earth's rotation axis wobbles counterclockwise in an elliptical motion and follows a cycle of an estimated 21.000 years. In 1845 French celestial mechanician Urbain le Verrier calculated that the eccentricity of the earth's orbit varies through a 100,000 year cycle. In the 18th century the influence of these cycles on the climate became an item of discussion, for instance in relation to the ice-ages (a subject proposed by the Scott James Scroll in 1864). In 1920 the Russian engineer Milutin Milankovitch found the 41,000 year cycle of oscillation in the tilt of the earth's orbit. This theory remained unpopular until the late 1950's, when new geological research technologies became available, such as radiocarbon dating or paleomagnetic dating. In the 1960's the American geologist Franklyn Van Houten proposed the theory that alternative patterns of colorful rock layers and results from studying the strata suggest a clear link between climates and orbital variations. In the late 1970's the Belgian astronomer André Léon Berger showed that the 21,000 year cycle is in fact composed out of two cycles: a 19,000 year cycle under influence of the planet Mars and a 23,000 year cycle under influence of Venus and Jupiter. Berger also calculated other cycles of longer duration. See Larry Krumenaker, "Rhythm Section - The pulse of planetary cycles, recorded deep in New Jersey shale", p.14-17. Berger's theory on the cycle of Mars in combination with what was said in footnote 14 seems to indicate what has been happening in the odd summer of 2003, when Europe suffered from an extraordinary heat wave, Asia had an extraordinary monsoon, there were quite severe storms in many places (in the Netherlands we even had some minor tornadoes to a size that caused damage; tornadoes normally do not occur in this country) and Mars was as close as it ever gets to earth (the reason why NASA, Europe and Japan sent satellites to Mars).

[19] See Alan P. Boss, "Companions to Young Stars", Scientific American, issue October 1995, p.38-43. Our own sun also has such a companion-star, suggested in 1984 by Richard A. Muller and called "Nemesis".

[20] An awesome natural phenomenon is that the oceans actually have 'valleys' and 'hills' of water, caused by the local differences in strength of gravity and differences in density in the layers of water in the oceans, interacting with the gravitational pull of the moon, planets and the sun!

[21] Other animals, like sharks, can locate and recognize their prey because of their capacity to sense electromagnetic currents caused by their victims. Research is concentrating on the phenomenon that organisms also can read the electromagnetic fields caused by the motions of earth. See Richard Jerome, "Animals and Magnetism", The Sciences, issue January/February 1993, p.7: "... like many rodents, reptiles, birds, fishes, insects and bacteria, newts possess a sensory mechanism that somehow keeps them oriented relative to the earth's north and south poles." and, even more interesting (emphasis mine): "... previous experiments had established *a link between the visual system and a sensitivity to magnetic fields*. For example, when migrating

that the axis of rotation of the inner core is tilted by ten degrees in relation to the earth's axis.[22] There are sufficient reasons to assume that the inner core is one solid crystal of iron almost as large as the moon, rotating in a rocky and liquid metal enclosure.[23] In addition, the earth does not merely rotate, but rotates in opposition to the earth's axis. Besides, mind-boggling evidence suggests that the magnetic field of our earth once in so many years completely flips over - the magnetic pole flipping from the north pole to the south pole! Scientists studied this phenomenon with a computer simulation to find out more about the process when this happens, every few hundred thousand years or so, including the impact caused by the known properties of the inner core.[24] The conclusion was that the inner core turned over once every 40,000 years. The inner core seems to provide the ballast for magnetic stability and functions as a kind of terrestrial dynamo (comparable to the dynamo for an electric motor). Seismologists discovered that the inner core rotates much faster than the rest of earth.[25]

Calculations have shown that the inner core is not rotating around a stationary axis, but tends to swivel eastwards at two degrees a year, the equivalent of some twelve miles. At that rate it will come full circle in about four centuries.[26] No wonder that in very different fields of science it has become accepted that life on the surface of earth is influenced by this incredibly complex play of forces.[27] It is just as foolish to think that earth and all processes on earth could be studied 'in isolation' from the universe as it is foolish to study man 'in isolation' from nature! In meteorological research evidence of the influence of these forces can be found in the influence of earth's rotation on the weather. For instance, high or low pressure areas in the northern hemisphere of the earth always rotate counter-clockwise. The same happens with the major streams of water in the big oceans. If we looked down on top of the North Pole we would clearly see that the earth rotates counter-clockwise, too.[28] One can only wonder what impact

---

birds are confined to a windowless, uniformly lighted room on an autumn day, they tend to cluster at the southern wall - following their seasonal habit of flying south even without reference to natural land marks or the position of the sun. When the room is completely darkened, however, the birds scatter chaotically, which points to *a strong connection between the perception of light and the sense of direction.*"

22 This was discovered in 1994 by Wei-jia Su and Adam M. Dziewonski of Harvard University.

23 Shown in 1995 by Lars P. Stixrude and Ronald E. Cohen.

24 This research was executed by the geophysicists Gary A. Glatzmaier and Paul H. Roberts.

25 This discovery was announced in 1996 by seismologists Xiaodong Song and Paul G. Richards. See Robert J. Coontz Jr., "Turning Point - The earth's core is found to spin faster than the crust and mantle", The Sciences, issue September/October 1996, p.10.

26 See David Schneider, "A Spinning Crystall Ball - Seismologists discover that the inner core rotates", Scientific American, issue October 1996, p.18-19.

27 See Raymond Jeanloz and Thorne Lay, "The Core-Mantle Boundary", Scientific American, issue May 1993, p.26-33: "In view of the intense dynamics taking place 2900 kilometers below the earth's surface, it should not be surprising that the forces in the core-mantle system might be making their presence felt throughout the earth as a whole. Indeed, workers have found tantalizing evidence that suggests that the core-mantle zone strongly influences two features observable at the surface. They are the wobbling in the earth's rotation, known as nutations, and the geomagnetic field."

28 In nature many examples are found of phenomena that always show a preference for a rotation in the same

the previously described complex collision of huge forces from outer space and from underneath us inside the earth actually have on our climates and quality of life!

In combination with all that has been explained about the processes of our brains and synchronization, it seems plausible to expect that these strong oscillating flows of energy - colliding with us either from deep down inside of earth or from far out in space - both unmistakenly interacting with our bodies - have the potential to influence the oscillating flows of energy in our brains. Needless to say, there are lots of serious reasons for psychology to study and analyze human behaviour, in addition to the influences on our behaviour by childhood, social and cultural circumstances, etc. There are also certain emotions, like feeling depressed or extra energized, occurring during full moon periods or caused by other natural phenomena, which are related to the influences of nature's play of forces. Analogously, the qualities that define our daily existence, for instance the qualities of nutrition, housing, health, happiness and other aspects of our biological being, also have an impact on our psychological well being.

Many 20th century artists and ancient artisans/artists have been inspired by the cosmic motions, translating them into fundamental lines and fields of energy and light.[29] This is not surprising when one takes the effort to study information that was available to the general public in the days of the birth of abstract art.[30] The analogous interest by scientists and artists to understand all this evidence of nature's forces and motions is not only exemplified in many early abstract artworks, but also in scientific theoretical models or diagrams of the early 20th century. Amazing examples are the very aesthetic models of the cosmological system by the l'Abbé Théophile Moreux from 1922, proposing an explanation for the spiral motions of attraction and repulsion in nebula's (spiral galaxies). These models are suspended and show a combination of two spirals that turn into each other.[31] If one did not know that these are meant to be purely scientific theoretical models, one would immediately take them to be early constructivist

direction, like our DNA also always shows a rotation to the left (= counter-clockwise). This is studied as the principle of chirality. It is beside the point here, but it could be interesting if we also prefer a certain direction of rotation as portrayed in art, if there was a chirality in art under influence of the motions of earth?

29 See §3, §6, §12.3.,§14.2.

30 For instance, see Alphonse Berget, "Le Ciel - Nouvelle Astronomie Pittoresque" (Paris: Libraire Larousse, 1923). This popular publication contains 710 photos and 275 diagrams; the about 310 pages present lots of information available at the time, like about Foucault's pendulum, a reconstruction of which was publicly executed in Paris in 1902 - this pendulum actually shows the wobbling motion of the earth's axis. This book also includes lots of information on gravity and the motions of the earth under influence of the rhythms of the universe, the changing position of the north pole, the solar activity. Included are photos of eclipses, of protuberances - the explosions of magnetic energies - of the sun-eclipse on 17 April 1912 with a picture of the Parisian general public looking through darkened glasses, also including very early and highly abstract photographs of the planet Mars, comets like Brooks (photographed in 1911) or Halley's comet (June 1910), very good early photographs of spiral nebula's, etc.

31 Ibid., p.175. l'Abbé Théophile Moreux (1867-1954) was an extraordinary man. Fascinated by the universe, he founded in 1899 l'Observatoire de Borges, France. He had a good relationship with Camille Flammarion, and participated in scientific expeditions (Spain, Tunisia). Moreux was particularly interested in Mars and the

artworks by Naum Gabo, Alexander Rodchenko or Katharzyna Kobro. Coincidence or not, in 1922 the artist Moholy-Nagy started to change his compositions into spiral shapes.[32]

14.2 OUR BODIES IN THE UNIVERSE: IDEAS IN ART

In the episode that has become known as the Baroque, the illusion of depth on a two-dimensional plane was altered dramatically by the development of a different kind of perspective.[33] This did not happen because something new in painting itself was required for the sake of being new. It happened as new knowledge about reality demanded a new approach in painting, but could only be accomplished at a huge scale by an amazing

see pictures 1, 14

sun. He published regularly, like "Le probleme solaire" (Éditions Scientifica, 1900), "L'avenir du soleil - Ou allons-nous?" (Paris: Bayard, 1911), "Pour Comprendre Einstein!" (Paris: Gaston Doin, 1922) and "Le Ciel and l'Univers - Origine et formation des mondes" (Paris: Gaston Doin, 1928). His publication on Einstein in 1922 seems exceptional to me. Frantisek Kupka read Moreux's observations of the sun in Flammarion's "L'Astronomie populaire" and seems to have been inspired by Moreux's drawing of the solar surface activity, and solar magnetic perturbations of 1903. See Pascal Rousseau, " 'L'oeil solaire' - Une généalogie impressioniste de l'abstraction", in Serge Lemoine, "Aux origines de l'abstraction 1800-1910" (Paris: Musée d' Orsay, Editions de la Réunion des musées nationaux, 2003), p.133.

32 El Lissitzky introduced curved and sometimes spiral forms into his compositions from 1919/20. The above described encyclopedic publication by Berget for Larousse finishes with a whole chapter on Einstein's Theory of Relativity. It can safely be assumed that many of the early abstract artists had access to a lot of this information (do not forget that many stayed at some time in Paris, so maybe some even had a look into this Larousse publication). Art historian Patricia Railing describes that El Lissitzky while using geometrical projection methods (like axonometry and isometry) added, "rhythmical arrangements of dissonance or displacement to achieve a sensation of dynamic structures stretching and bending in cosmic space." See Patricia Railing, "The Machine is more than a Brush - Morphology of Art and the Machine in Russian Avant-Garde Theory and Practice", The Structurist, No.35/36 "From the Mechanical to the Organic", 1995-1996. The result was the capability of the Suprematist architectural system to transform itself into a machine to orbit earth. Malevitch, the father of Suprematism, considered this like any organism to be the result of "the smooth harnessing of form to natural processes through some magnetic interrelations with a single form, which will comprise all the natural forces inherent in these interrelations...". See Patricia Railing, "On Suprematism - 34 Drawings - K. Malevitch" (Forest Row, UK: Artists Bookworks, 1990).

33 See Jörg Sellenriek, "Zirkel und Lineal - Kulturgeschichte des Konstruktiven Zeichnens", (Munich: Verlag Callwey, 1987). The first publication was in 1436 "De pictura" by L.B. Albert. The notion of central perspective has been put down in the "De prospectiva pingendi" (appr. 1484-1487) by Piero. An initial understanding was developed by the Florentinian architect and artist Filippo Brunelleschi (1376-1446). G. Desargues, from 1636 until 1640, tried to synthesize new knowledge from astronomy with the new ideas on perspective involving several centres in a painting. Further understandings were published in the "Traité de Stereometrie" from 1737-1739 by A.F. Frézier at the military academy of Mézieres. Officially, according to traditional art history, the Baroque existed between about 1600-1750. See H.W. Janson, "Wereldgeschiedenis van de kunst", translated by J.F. Kliphuis, Nederlandse Boekenclub (orig. Harry N. Abrams, Inc., 1976). This period indeed concerns the same epoche as the developments of new ideas about perspective. Besides, it is quite remarkable to notice how at first the impulses for the development of construction methods of perspective on a two-dimensional plane came from art and architecture, followed by new impulses from military academies and finally in the 19th century from engineering (and thus from the industrial revolution). A remarkable road of development. As, since this development of perspective has everything to do with the debate since Euclid on *the point, line and plane* and its relation to Euclid's optical theory (see §12.3), in my personal opinion, the next step in perspective-construction will be realized by computer technology, or in traditional painting and sculpture by artists with a serious but intuitive interest in new theories about space/time, in philosophy, neurophysiology, astronomy, physics and an intuitive understanding of 'no-thingness' (see §2.2).

coincidence of events in international society.[34] The Baroque emerged out of an extraordinary accelleration of the demand for great art and architecture, caused by economical, political and religious developments. The emergence of extensive trade with the accompanying explosion of colonialism resulted in new funding, new profitable professions (banking, insurance, etc. leading to a new middle- and new upperclass of non-nobility), needs for diplomatic connections, and needs to express one's new position in society. Simultaneously, the Reformation sparked further developments towards individualism. But for the arts, the Counter-Reformation in the Catholic Church made the real difference.[35]

The Vatican understood that the power of the popularity of the Reformation was appealing to the average person, because the reformers had accomplished making religious doctrine accessible. To compete with this succes, the Vatican knew it had to establish the huge change from a religion for a small elite of nobility and well educated clergy to one that could also attract and commit the crowds. A very clever concept emerged, something today we would call a professional market-strategy and promotion campaign. Churches would be built everywhere, would be large or huge and would attract by splendour. In the Baroque, painting and sculpture were understood as the right illustrative means to promote the specific interpretation of religion of the Church to an illiterate public. The sensation of the sublime was used for propaganda.[36] As has happened repeatedly in history, such important steps demanded innovations in art and architecture as symbols of the force of the new.[37]

These innovations were also sparked by new scientific theories and discoveries, like the astronomical discovery that the earth, moon and sun all move. This resulted in the gradual improvement of the dynamics in an artistic composition, by allowing for not one, but several compositional centres, replacing the central perspective with a more complex whole.[38] The ordering of people, horses and objects is structured in such a way that they seem to virtually rotate in several intertwining and overlapping movements around several centres. This can be seen quite well in some Rubens paintings.[39] When

see picture 13

34 For an excellent introduction to the Baroque, see Vernon Hyde Minor, "Baroque & Rococo - Art & Culture" (London: Laurence King Publishing, 1999).
35 This was mainly based on the Council of Trent 1546-63.
36 The Baroque in art and architecture was mainly defined in Italy by Maderno, Bernini, Borromini, and Cortona. See Vernon Hyde Minor, "Baroque & Rococo - Art & Culture", p.93. The general purpose was to "pull the worshipper right off the street, transporting him or her from the brightness and noise of city life to a region of half-light and incense." See Vernon Hyde Minor, "Baroque & Rococo - Art & Culture", p119.
37 One may compare the emergence of the Baroque with the emergence of Russian Constructivism or the emergence of American Expressionism. The first was a symbol of the new Counter-Reformation, the second a symbol for the new Russian Revolution, the third a symbol for the new American world power. Although all involved artists did well because of this link between art and politics, frequently they had their own motivations; motivations not necessarely linked to or based on any political concept.
38 This was possible primarily in paintings not commissioned for a church (with the exception of altar-pieces, which for obvious reasons still had to focus the vision of the believer on a central axis leading his view upwards or straight to the heart of the Christ figure in a painting).
39 For instance, in "The Large Last Judgment" (1615-16), "The Battle of the Amazons and Greeks" (1616-

we visually analyze his compositions by finding the major lines in the composition, the locations of the main form- and colour accents, we will find a swirling and geometrically abstract composition of circular and elliptical movements that seem to be drawn towards a mutual center.[40] This mutual center is only a center by approximation, as it cannot be exactly located.[41]

Artists have always been quite aware of the impact of the universe. Throughout art history one can find paintings depicting constellations, comets and other astronomical phenomena, based on actual knowledge and observations of the sky.[42] A magnificent example is Van Gogh's "La Nuit Etoilée" ("Starry Night") of 1889. This is a powerful painting with spiralling lights in a dramatic setting. The expressionistic style notwithstanding, it seems based on actual knowledge and careful observation by Van Gogh.[43] Around the time he created this artwork, there was intense and public interest in astronomy. People were able to see the first pictures and observations of spiralling nebulae and

1618),"The Rape of the Daughters of Leucippus" (c.1618), "The Fall of the Damned" (c.1620), "The Archangel defeats the Rebellious Angels" (c.1620, reproduced in this book) "Lion Hunt" (1621),"The Horrors of War" (1637).

40 See Harold van de Perre, "Pietro Paolo Rubens - Profeet van de moderne kunst" (Amsterdam: Elsevier, 1984). Van de Perre's pictorial analyses of Rubens' paintings are astonishing and show the described movements clearly. For instance, in Rubens painting "De marteldood van St. Lieven". These abstracted visualizations show remarkable resemblances to some early abstract paintings by Albert Gleizes, Robert Delaunay, Frantisek Kupka, Giacomo Balla, Alexander Rodchenko, Alexandra Exter, Ludmilla Popova , Kazimir Malevitch, Laszlo Moholy-Nagy, El Lissitzky or Piet Mondrian.

41 The description of this mutual and vague center brings to mind the description of the main 'culminating point' in Cézanne's "Forest", see §13. One can also mention Titian's great painting "Assumption of the Virgin (Assunta)" (1516-18). See Marion Kaminski, "Tiziano Vecellio, known as Titian 1488/1490 - 1576" (Koenemann Verlagsgesellschaft GmbH, 1998). Or the amazing ceiling paintings by Andrea Pozzo and by Tiepolo - like his "The Allegory of the Four Continents" in Würzburg, 1752-53. See William L. Barchan, "Giambattista Tiepolo"(New York: Harry N. Abrams Inc. Publishers, 1992). See Peter O. Krueckmann, "Tiepolo in Würzburg - Der Himmel auf Erden", Band I + II (Prestel Verlag, 1996).

42 For a great cross-cultural resumé from the Egyptians, the stone age carvings, depictions in East and West, see Madanjeet Singh, "Die Sonne - Das Gestirn in der Kulturgeschichte", translated by Theresa-M. Bullinger (Tübingen, Berlin: Ernst Wasmuth Verlag, UNESCO, 1993). Ever since early Christian art, one can find representations of the 'star of Bethlehem', for which Giotto di Bondone used Halley's Comet as a model. In 1609 Adam Elsheimer painted real constellations and the Milky Way, and Johannes Vermeer painted his "Astronomer" in about 1668. Tiepolo finished in 1740 the magnificent ceiling "The Course of the Chariot of the Sun". Around 1768 Joseph Wright Derby painted a group of persons looking at a table-top planetarium. In exactly the same year in the provincial town of Franeker, Netherlands, the amateur astronomer, mathematician and wool merchant Eise Eisinga finished a working planetarium in the only room of his little house, involving the bed of his wife and himself. This amazing piece of engineering and art is driven by a pendulum and works like a huge clock. It still is operational (and only has to be adjusted once every 22 years, according to Eisinga's own calculations!). Albert Boime in his analysis of Van Gogh's "Starry Night" described that many of the artists involved in astronomy lived in trading countries and/or harbour cities, for instance, Jongkind, Runge, C.D. Friedrich, Albert Pinkham Ryder, Frederic Church, and Jean-Francois Millet. See Albert Boime, "Vincent van Gogh - Die Sternennacht - Die Geschichte des Stoffes und der Stoff der Geschichte" (Fischer Taschenbuch Verlag GmbH, 1989).

43 Ibid. Albert Boime has analyzed the sources of Van Gogh's painting with incredible precision. Boime clearly shows that Van Gogh knew that he was painting a dynamic depiction of the constellations Aries and the planet Venus. Boime asked a modern planetarium to re-construct the night sky around the date (19 June 1889)

photographs of the vapour trail of comets. In May of 1889 the World Expo opened in Paris, with the Eiffel Tower as its main symbol spectacularly illuminated at night using the new technology of electrical lights. The exhibition was especially promoting the connection between geographical discoveries - including astronomical observations - and geographic conquests, a connection that was supposed to symbolize modernity.[44] In the late 19th century and early 20th century, scientific theories on space and time (and thus on the universe) gradually became more abstract. Abstract art emerged, analogously exploring the essence of reality by translating the rhythms of nature's forces into abstract and highly dynamic compositions.[45] These compositions were certainly not the result of mere artistic experimentation.

Like many of his contemporaries, the Austrian architect, artist, furniture- and theatre-designer Friedrich Kiesler was quite interested in the mechanization of stage design.[46] Kiesler, who was seriously studying perception, was inspired by the mathematics and physics of his time, such as Einstein's theories of curved space/time, leading Kiesler already in 1923 to a concept for an 'endless house'.[47] He realized this concept in the USA as an egg-shaped house and later as the famous design of the Endless House for the Museum of Modern Art New York. This Endless House consisted of a combination of several complex organic shapes melting into each other. Kiesler's plans, seen from above, show rooms in a clear combination of curvilinear motions crossing each other. The whole presents a strong simulation of the centrifugal and centrepetal forces of space/time. One can find a very similar simulation in many examples in constructive, biomorphic, organic, and surrealistic art of his time. Although artists were occasionally interested in references to astronomy before, as in the 19th century, it seems that in the 1940's and well into the 1950's a growing interest emerged in concepts that were in one

and location (Saint Rémy) where Van Gogh painted this artwork. This allowed Boime to find remarkable resemblances between the constellation depicted in the painting and the constellation in the reconstructed actual sky.

44 Boime mentions that Van Gogh wrote to his brother about exhibiting another night-sky painting of him in relation to the 1889 World Expo. Van Gogh seems also to have read Jules Verne and Camille Flammarion, founder of the Société Astronomique, publisher of several popular books on astronomy and the magazine "L'Astronomie populaire" (see footnote 31, earlier this chapter). Boime implies that Van Gogh was acqainted with this magazine. In a letter to Émile Bernard, Van Gogh described his hope for the future of science. See Albert Boime, "Vincent van Gogh - Die Sternennacht - Die Geschichte des Stoffes und der Stoff der Geschichte", p.65.

45 See §8.2.

46 Kieslers experiments, including a spiral-like stage in 1924 or exemplified by his magnificent designs for the "Endless Theater" (1923-24) show clear connections to concepts of several contemporaries, especially to El Lissitzky and Moholy-Nagy. Kiesler was involved in ergonomics, the study of the properties and motorics of the motion of the human body, necessary knowledge to improve the design of tools, furniture, machines, architecture. See Dieter Bogner, "Friedrich Kiesler Architekt Maler Bildhauer 1890-1965" (Vienna: Löcker Verlag Wien, 1988). See Antje von Graevenitz, "Endlessness and reduction, Friedrich Kieslers 'Endless House' ", Archis Magazine, issue November 1996, p.63-80. See PRO-NR.1. In the USA, in the early 1940's, Kiesler became part of the Surrealist group around Peggy Guggenheim and designed the experimental interior of her "Gallery of the Future" - a design related to the concept of the "Endless House".

47 See Siegfried Gohr, Gunda Luyken, "Frederick J. Kiesler - Selected Writings", (Ostfildern: Verlag Gerd Hatje, 1996).

way or another related to astronomy.[48] From the 1960's through the present, artists explored motions, simulations of motions, actual motion, the interaction of forces in kinds of structured complexity as intuitively understood from observing the universe, and they read about new ideas and observations in astronomy or physics.[49] The availability of new observation technologies, as provided by the Hubble Telescope or the special photography of David Malin, will keep inspiring artists, if only for the purpose of recognizing the amazing analogies between what they explore artistically and nature's actual processes.[50] The described movements have nothing to do anymore with the

[48] For instance, both Belgian artist Georges Vantongerloo and American artist Alexander Calder were quite interested in cosmology. Calder, quoted in Jean Lipman, Ruth Wolfe, "Calder's Universe" (Running Press, 1989): "The underlying sense of form in my work has been the system of the universe, a part thereof. For that is rather a large model to work from." As a young man Calder took courses in mechanical drawing, descriptive geometry, drafting, mechanical engineering and applied kinetics. Thus he became interested in the notions and relations of work and energy, which are observable in his mobiles (and, in my opinion, in his stabiles). It is not mere chance or romanticism that he gave his works titles like "A Universe" (1934), "Constellation" (1943 + 1945) or "Universe" (1974). Georges Vantongerloo was originally a member of the De Stijl-group, but only for a short period. At first he made very rigid orthogonal compositions in painting and sculpture. In 1937 he introduced curves in his painting. In 1945 he started working on sculptures consisting of curved steel and bent wire with titles such as "Espace infini", "Vecteur", in 1946 "Masses in the universe", in 1951 "Magnetic field". Paintings for which he gained inspiration from the interactions of particles and their fields of force include, "Radiation" (1949), "Deux zones de l'espace action-réaction" (1949), "Formation de matière" (1951). His last works were exciting experiments using the new material plexiglass (acrylic glass), like in "Une étoile gazeuse" (1964). All these works refer clearly to his interest in cosmology, mathematics and physics. See Koninklijke Musea voor Schone Kunsten van België; "Georges Vantongerloo 1886-1965" (Antwerpen: Koninklijke Musea voor Schone Kunsten van België, 1981). See Annely and David Juda, "Max Bill, Georges Vantongerloo - A Working Friendship" (London: Annely Juda Fine Art, 1996). See Eric Pil, "Van Tongerloo Colour theories - Reactions By Other Members of De Stijl Group", ICSAC-Cahier 10. Pil's publication includes a text by physicist Dr. H.J. Vink on Vantongerloo's elaborate colour theories. Similar interests in translating cosmological observations into art one can find in Joan Miró's crowded paintings-series "Constellations" from the early 1940's. See Walter Erben, "Joan Miro - The Man and His Work 1893-1983" (Taschen Verlag, 1998). Jean Arp made his "Four Constellations: Identical Forms Arranged on a Surface" relief in 1951. Jackson Pollock painted "Reflection of the Big Dipper" and "Comet" in 1947. One should also consider the abstract sculptures by Swiss artist Walter Linck, like his magnificent kinetic pieces "Fenêtre vers le ciel" (1958), "Points opposés/Construction mobile I" (1958), "Orbite" (1970-72). See Kunsthaus Zürich; "Walter Linck 1903-1975", 1990. More examples are the sculptures by the Argentinian artist Enio Iommi: "Continuidad" (1947) or "Curvas y lineas" (1948). Miklos von Bartha, "Arte Concreto - Invencion - Arte Madi" (Basel: Edition Galerie Von Bartha, 1991). Related are the fabulous mobiles by the English artist Kenneth Martin, "Rotary Rings" (1967) or "Screw Mobile with Tilts" (1971-72). See Annely Juda, "Kenneth and Mary Martin" (London: Annely Juda Fine Art, 1987). One may mention also the bent wire sculptures by German artist Norbert Kricke, "Grüne Kurve" (1952), "Raumplastik" (1957). See Juergen Morschel, "Norbert Kricke" (Stuttgart: Verlag Gerd Hatje, 1976).

[49] For instance, in certain works by Anthony Caro, Eduardo Chillida, Michael Kidner, Frank Stella (in his later works), Bernhard Heiliger ("Cosmos", 1970, "Orbit II" 1979, "Orion" 1980, "Kräfte der Erde" 1980). See Lothar Romain, Siegfried Salzmann, "Bernard Heiliger" (Berlin: Propylaen Verlag, 1989). Or Paul Suter, Jean-Pierre Maury, John Okulick (his work "Wraparound", 1990), Michael Bette, and Dorothea Rockburne. See Jeanne Rohatyn, Dorsey Waxter, "Dorothea Rockburne - Ten Years of Astronomy Drawings 1990-2000"(New York: Lawrence Rubin - Greenberg Van Doren Fine Art, 2000). Or David Row (his "Constellation"-series), Richard Purdy, Philippe Jahanguir, and in my own works (for instance, "The Atlas Series"). American artist Paul Dacey exemplifies in his constellation-compositions with brightly coloured discs a clear interest in astronomy. See his fabulous "Lyra/Vega II" as reproduced in this book.

see pictures 43, 47, 48

[50] See David Malin, "A View of the Universe" (Cambridge, Massachusetts: Sky Publishing Corporation and

notion of a central perspective or central rotation, but more with the notion of oscillation (a combination of centrifugal and centripetal forces). Described otherwise, these movements are the pulsating forces expressed in the concept of spiral-like oscillation.[51]

14.3. THE UNIVERSE IN OUR BODIES

Es seind ... Scintillae Animae Mundi ignea, luminis nimirum Naturae, FewrigeFuncken der Seele der Weld, ... dispergiret oder ausgesprenget in und durch das Gebew der großen Weld in alle früchte der Elementen allenthaben. Joseph Khunrath[52]

In principle, the answer to the question, 'what determines our reality?', is rather simple: energy. Fundamental and continuous change in nature has caused the discovery of the principle that no energy is lost in any process, the energies are only transformed or dissolved into other processes.[53] One example is the cycle of life. It is not so that only after our death are we taken up or dissolved into nature again, into the holomovement. From birth on we take in energy and change or translate energy continuously into bodily processes, for instance, through our metabolism, while also radiating heat, etc. While we

Cambridge University Press, 1995 - orig. 1993).

51 See §13. Through the steel sculptures of Paul Suter the process of oscillation can be understood quite well. He combines straight geometrically shaped steel strips with curved steel strips into highly dynamic compositions with a good sense of showing us the basic movements of the essence of reality. In my opinion his objects are frozen moments of the holomovement, a melting together of swirling streams of energy in space/time, that appeal so much, because Suter does not produce constructs according to any system or otherwise rational definitions, but decides on the basis of our 'real-reality' perception (not a virtual or constructed reality) by a process of seeing, touching, manual handling and self-argumentation. His works can be compared to the work of other great sculptors of the 20th century like David Smith, Eduardo Chillida, Anthony Caro and Mark di Suvero. Paul Suter distinguishes himself from them as he focusses entirely upon the oscillation. His compositions look as if they are about to dance away into the sky.

see picture 59

52 This quotation is from "Von hylealischen Chaos" (Magdeburg 1597, p.94), published in the chapter "Das Unbewußte als multiples Bewußtsein" ("Unconsciousness as Multiple Consciousness"), 1946. See Jung, "Theoretische Überlegungen zum Wesen des Psychischen" ("Theoretical Considerations on the Being of the Psychic"), in C.G. Jung, "Grundwerk - Band 2 - Archetyp und Unbewußtes" (Walter-Verlag, 1990). Although hardly possible to translate into English, this quote is roughly: "They are ... Scintillae Animae Mundi ignea, luminis nimirum Naturae, firy sparks of the soul of the world - which are dispersed or erupted in and through the canopy of the great world contained within the fruits of the elements."

53 In 1848 J.P. Joule (1818-1889) published his ideas about the conservation of heat concerning the fact that a certain quantity of heat could cause a certain amount of mechanical work. This principle of translating heat into work was soon understood as two aspects of the same entity: energy. See Arnold Koslow, "The Changeless Order - The Physics of Space, Time and Motion" (New York: Georg Brazilier, 1967), p.204-210. Although J.R. Mayer (1814-1878) had already tried to find scientific evidence for the conservation of energy it had to wait until Hermann Helmholtz proved this in 1847. Ibid., p.200: "The idea was suggested that these experiments involved various <u>forms</u> of energy: while the total energy in any one of its forms might not be conserved, the total energy in <u>all</u> its forms is conserved." The conservation of energy is quite well symbolized in the Yin Yang sign, which can function as metaphor for the conservation of energy. In the middle of the 19th century James Clerk Maxwell succesfully combined the phenomena of electricity and magnetism into the Theory of Electromagnetism. In this theory light is treated as an aspect of an oscillating electromagnetic field. Michael Faraday, before Maxwell, imagined a magnetic field as lines of force that leave the magnetic poles and return to them again, a phenomenon that is currently known in physics as 'contour integrals' (see my own

grow older and weaker we burn or translate less energy, and more energy leaves our bodies in different ways in the natural process of bodily wear and tear.[54] Our whole metabolism - our whole bio-rhythm - is a continuous interactive process with the holo-movement, in which energy continuously but irregularly enters the body, flows through the body and leaves the body. We are actually fluctuating concentrations in the complex flow of energy, which could be metaphorically described as one complex mist of energy-movements.

Before discussing the various aspects of the universe in our bodies more precisely, I will first consider some properties of the actual space in which our bodies exist. The original source for considering empty or amorphic/organic space, nothingness, could have been the emptiness observed between objects and ourselves, the perception of infinite emptiness of the sea, flat landscapes or by looking up into the skies.[55] For a long time, space was considered to be a 'vacuum', originally meaning 'empty space'. The notion of an ether originates from Aristotle, who interpreted it as the environment that contains the heavenly bodies. He classified ether as the fifth element, in addition to the four elements of Empedocles: earth, air, fire, water.[56] Much later, in the 17th century, Christiaan Huygens interpreted light as fast moving particles that move by swimming through the ether.[57] The notion of the fluidum was born in the late 18th century, explained as a fluid substance that flows through the universe and connects everything in a coherent harmony.[58] This concept found more support among those who were interested in spiritual or occult knowledge and less in science. Though it is not necessary to discuss all details, it is noteworthy that from the early 19th century on, the concept of ether continuously changed and was alternately seen as something that does not exist, that exists and is fluid, and finally led to the concept that everything, including empty

---

paper, "Extensionalism and Twistor Space: Similarities and Relations between Art and Twistor Theory", paper of symposium "Creativity&Cognition 1", Loughborough University, England, published in LEONARDO magazine, Vol. 28 Nr.3, MIT Press, 1995. Quantum Theory from 1924 was the new theory including the principles of conservation of energy and electromagnetism.

54 In the 1830's physiologist Theodor Schwann considered cells of organisms to be the possible carrier of electrical impulses. See Lyn Gamwell in "Exploring the Invisible - Art, Science, and the Spiritual" (Princeton, NJ: Princeton University Press, 2002), p.68: "Thus the body began to be seen as an electrical machine with nerves acting as wires, and by the 1860's neurology was emerging as a medical speciality." See Martin Raff , "Death Wish - All cells come primed for self-destruction - The challenge for medicine is to make them die on cue", The Sciences, issue July/August 1996, p.36-40. See §2.2 on Vivekananda and §8, footnote 9 on Dogen's interpretation of 'Tathagata' (Buddha) as 'permanent, nonbeing, being, and change'.

55 For an extensive and accessible description of this subject in science, see Henning Genz, "Nothingness - The Science of Empty Space" (Perseus Publishers, 2001- orig."Die Entdeckung des Nichts", 1998).

56 This was an assumption acknowledged since about 460 BC. The five elements, including the ether, are also described in the Hindu-cosmology in the Bhagavad Gita. See Dr. J.J. Lehr, "De draaikolk als model voor mikro- en makrokosmos", (Baarn: Tirion, De Erven Lehr), p.152.

57 Christiaan Huygens (1629-1695) in his "Traité de la lumière" (1678-1690). Sir Isaac Newton (1642-1727) also discussed the ether.

58 In the holomovement (see §8.7, footnote 123) energy is continuously moving around in smaller and greater quantities. This concerns a complexity that is difficult to imagine as it deals with a great variety of criss-crossing movements varying in direction, curvature and speed. In former times one thought there existed a nothingness between two entities, for example a fluidum or ether, that would be the carrier of energy particles like the

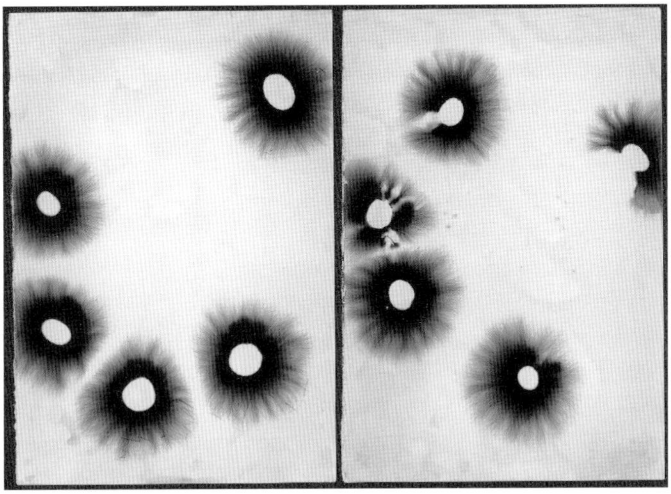

66. Heinrich Rüdiger Ilgen BS (1924 - 2000)
Two photo's, made by applying the technology known as Kirlian photography, show the disturbances of an electric field at a person's finger tips. The disturbances are caused by the electromagnetic emanation of the body. The left picture shows the finger-tips of a healthy person. The right of a person with a slight fever.

space, consists of fields of energy. Since the 1930's the field theory became more accepted, and the fields themselves were considered a new kind of entity. This theory finally replaced the ether-theory.[59] David Bohm refers to the opinion that proof for the existence of the ether has never been found, but evidence has been found for the existence of fields (of energy). Furthering Einstein's ideas about a new kind of ether, Bohm understands what before was seen as the ether to be in fact the moment of the wave of energy itself. Today we know that there is no empty nothingness, but a nothingness full with waves of energy connecting into fields of energy. With our current knowledge and imagination we can assume that the total quantity of energy comprising the macro- and microcosm does not change.

As was described in §11, the German painter Otto Freundlich is an exceptional example of an artist who seriously studied science and searched for an approach to painting that incorporates the consequences of the new physics and the understanding of ether as a field of continuous flowing energies.[60] He thus considered it essential to depict in

particles of light (photons). Franz Mesmer, Austrian doctor (1734-1815), published in "Planetarum influxu in corpus humanum" (1766) his theory that the sun, moon and stars do not merely have influence on each other as on the tides on earth, but also on all other bodies (including ourselves), and have this influence because of a subtle 'fluidum', which flows through the whole cosmos and connects everything in harmony (compare the Chinese notion of Ch'i). Mesmer believed that man can absorb this fluidum and can pass some of its energy for instance to ill people and thus cause a recovery of their disturbed equilibrium. This principle refers to the principle of magnetism. See Douwe Bosga, Martine Busch, "Natuurlijk - niet bovennatuurlijk - Parapsychologische kanttekeningen bij de ervaringen van de paragnost Warner Tholen" (Ankh-Hermes, 1984), p.181-182. It also refers to hypnosis. Kirlian photography is a scientific method studying the patterns of electromagnetic radiation through the hands by putting the hands of a test person on photographic paper, which lies on top of a thin electrified metal sheet. The image produced show the disturbances of the electrical field caused by the electromagnetic emanation from the body. It has been discovered that this pattern is different when the same test person suffers from a cold or other illness, which seems to prove Mesmer's point.

59 See David Bohm, "Causality and Chance in Modern Physics" (London: Routledge & Kegan Paul, 1984 - orig.1957), p.44.

60 Otto Freundlich's thinking was based on Kant, but also on Helmholtz. See §11. In the writings of Freundlich 1916-1924 one can find clear indications that he was interested in Relativity Theory and Quantum Theory. See Uli Bohnen, "Otto Freundlich Schriften - Ein Wegbereiter der gegenstandslosen Kunst"

see picture 23 painting the virtual breaking open of geometric contours. He believed curved and coloured shapes were the proper tools for depicting the universal forces that oscillate within the frame of a painting. Analogous to the interest in the fluidum, Freundlich understood the continuous flowing energies also to be true for human bodies - the skin cannot be the 'final frontier', because the energies stream through it in both directions, expressing the metaphysical concept of coexistence or duration.[61] He believed invisible forces from a cosmic origin caused a virtual dissolution of the skin of matter, leading to the cosmic salvation, the unification of man and universe.[62] In 1916 Freundlich thought man's ignorance of his immersion in the universe was the cause for all that was wrong in human behaviour. He was convinced that art had the potential to make man conscious again of this relationship with the universe and of mankind's cosmic dependency. Therefore, in painting, Freundlich thought one should visualize the forces that cause everything to interact and depict relationships as a better image of reality than the painting of an object. This theory was acknowledged by many of his contemporaries like Kandinsky, Mondrian, and the Constructivists. Maybe more consciously than his colleagues, Freundlich emphasized that art should offer to our visual perception a synthesis of the spaces between objects and ourselves that manifest the relationships of forces. He understood his paintings - consisting of colourful fields with patches of semi-geometric and curved shapes - as offering an aesthetic bridge between man and the scientific concept of reality as a field of energies with parts that consist of different

(Cologne: DuMont Verlag, 1982), p.27. In the essay "Der Raum" ("Space"), from 1919, Freundlich writes, ibid., p.106: "And so I say: there is no tree, there is no separate corporeality, and in this sense no nature. I consider to express the meaning of being that obliges all form to dynamically withdraw from itself and will enable our eye to perceive the interlocking space from object to object and from myself to anything else as a higher level of life,..." ("Und so sage ich: es gibt keinen Baum, es gibt keine gesonderte Körperlichkeit, und in dem Sinne gibt es keine Natur. Auszubilden gedenke ich die Seinswert, der alle Form verpflichtet, dynamisch aus sich herauszutreten, der unser Auge befähigt, die Zwischenraumdurchdringung von Gegenstand zu Gegenstand und von mir selbst zu allem andern als ein höheres Leben zu erschauen,...").

61 See Uli Bohnen "Physik und Metaphysik der Raumzeit-Erkundung in der Kunst der Moderne - Otto Freundlich im Vergleich", in "Otto Freundlich - Ein Wegbereiter der abstrakten Kunst" (Osnabrück: Kulturgeschichtliches Museum Osnabrück, 1994), p.62: "In fact, however, 'simultaneousness' represents to Freundlich the metaphysical, meaning a fluidum that cannot be matched with the theories of modern physics, a fluidum within which the separation between the world of objects and man becomes dissolvable to the benefit of a lively power-laden actualization of the emptiness which restrains all understanding." ("Tatsächlich jedoch repräsentiert 'Gleichzeitigkeit' für Freundlich das Metaphysische, d.h. ein mit den Theorien der modernen Physik nicht in Übereinstimmung zu bringendes Fluidum innerhalb dessen die Trennung zwischen den Objektwelt und den Menschen zugunsten einer lebendigen, kraftgeladenen Erfüllung der Leere, die alle Verständigung hemmt, aufhebbar wird.")

62 Freundlich was familiar with scientific experiments in the cloud-chamber (the main tool of particle physics before WWII) in which by applying X-rays the trajectories of electrons could be photographed. See Rita Wildegans, "Otto Freundlichs Werk im Kontext naturwissenschaftlicher Erkenntnisse", in "Otto Freundlich - Ein Wegbereiter der abstrakten Kunst", p.56. In this same text, same page, Freundlich is quoted: "The borders, which frame the forms, are dissolved causing the forms to be opened and to be unlocked. They are prepared by this opening and unlocking to commit to the interrelation with the free non-figurative forces." ("Die Grenzen, die die Formen umrahmen, werden aufgehoben, und dadurch werden die Formen geöffnet und aufgeschlossen. Durch diese Öffnung und Aufgeschlossenheit werden sie vorbereitet, in

intensities. Freundlich differentiated intensities of energies with slightly different shapes in different colours (assuming each colour emits a different intensity of energy). Analogous to the cyclic behaviour in nature, the composition should allow a circling play of forces - an oscillation.

Light is a result of the gigantic concentrations of energy in the universe, like in our sun. Light is essential to us as daylight-creatures and plays a major role in our perception of reality. It is, therefore, not surprising to learn that in our history we can find discussions about the (virtual) light present within ourselves. One might call this internal light the presence of the universe in our bodies. This is not actual light, but we contain streams of energies that can metaphorically be compared to light. Psychologist C.G. Jung discusses the hypothesis of a plurality of 'luminositas', to be imagined as light or energy particles inside our bodies. These were originally described by the physicists/alchemists Khunrath and Paracelsus.[63] Jung's interpretation of becoming conscious in terms of internal lights that grow in strength, coincides with our current knowledge from neurophysiology describing how our brains function.[64] Jung's theory of luminositas seems to reflect the electrochemical impulses in the neural network. The luminositas as light-sparks are quite similar to the firing of neurons. The luminositas can also be related to Euclid's ideas on optics, because Euclid also believed that light exists inside our bodies; comparable to, though different from, the luminositas of the Middle Ages.[65] Jung refers to alchemy as the origin of the image of the 'scintillae' - the sparks

Wechselbeziehung mit den freien, nichtfigürlichen Kräften zu treten.")

63 See the quote from Khunrath at the start of §14.3. The 'anima mundi' (soul of the world) understood as 'sensus naturae', a natural force which is responsible for all appearances of life and of the psyche. The Platonic scholar Guillaume de Conches (1080-1154) understood the 'anima mundi' to be equivalent to the Holy Ghost. See C.G. Jung, "Grundwerk - Band 2 - Archetyp und Unbewußtes" (Walter-Verlag, 1990). p.39. This concept is well illustrated by Titian in his painting "The Descent of the Holy Ghost" (c.1545), depicting the Apostles and holy women with little flames upon their heads, sparked by a great light emitted from a dove high above them. Paracelsus translated the mind, the psyche, as a dark sky, where thoughts light up, comparable to a sky 'full of stars and constellations'.

64 See C.G. Jung, "Grundwerk - Band 2 - Archetyp und Unbewußtes", p.35: "As we know from immediate experience the light of consciousness has many brightnesses and the 'I'- nature has many levels of emphasis. On an animalistic level a 'luminositas' merely rules, which almost does not distinguish itself from the from brightness dissociated 'I'-fragments, like at an infantile and primitive level consciousness is still no unity as it is not focussed by any structured 'I'-nature, but flares here and there, awakened by exterior or interior events, insticts and emotions." ("Das Licht des Bewußtseins hat, wie wir aus unmittelbarer Erfahrung wissen, viele Helligkeiten, und der Ichkomplex viele Abstufungen seiner Betonung. Auf animalischer und primitiver Stufe herrscht eine bloße 'luminositas', welche sich kaum noch von der Helligkeit dissoziierter Ichfragmente unterscheidet, wie auf infantiler und primitiver Stufe das Bewußtsein noch keine Einheit ist, indem es von keinem festgefügten Ichkomplex zentriert wird, sondern da und dort aufflackert, wo es äußere oder innere Ereignisse, Instinkte und Affekte gerade wachrufen."). Compare §5.

65 See §12.3.. In his "Optics" Euclid discusses optical problems in context to the idea that rays of light start within the eye, are projected outwards, and scan all objects around us. He imagined this as a cone of light of which the point is in the eye itself, also called ray-optics, (Strahlenoptik). See Jörg Sellenriek, "Zirkel und Lineal - Kulturgeschichte des Konstruktiven Zeichnens" (Munich: Verlag Callwey, 1987), p.59. This concept can also be imagined as a combination of diverging lines starting in the eye. It led to the development of central perspective in the Renaissance. Central perspective is a construction method on a two-dimensional plane of the illusion of three-dimensional reality by interpreting depth as consisting of many lines that converge in one

('Funcken'). Khunrath explains these sparks as 'radii atque scintillae', the Anima Catholica, the all-soul that is identical to the spirit of God.[66] Jung interprets one singular scintillae psychologically as the symbol for the self.[67]

Both Khunrath and Dorn built on the ideas of Paracelsus, who believed the 'lumen naturae' (the natural light) first and foremost originated from the 'astrum' or 'sydus', the firmament of stars within man himself. Paracelsus saw the firmament as the natural light that is reflected in man himself (in the 'corpus subtile').[68] Jung especially interpreted Paracelsus' idea about the reflection of the universe in man himself as a reference to the archetypes. According to Jung, 'archetypes' are the inherited, unconscious ideas and images that form the components of the collective unconscious. In my opinion, the 17th century discussion by Paracelsus, Khunrath and Dorn not only shows an early thinking about universal concepts, which are at the basis of nature and of man himself, but refers especially to two other and related aspects: the fundamental interrelation and interaction of energies outside and within man (sparks, stars or lights).

The 18th century signaled the radical shift towards understanding that there is no actual light within us, but that we see by receiving the reflected light from other sources. Goethe, for instance, also studied optics, inspiring him to write his influential book on colour. In sheer contrast to many of his contemporaries, he always emphasized trying to understand what we see as a whole and not reducing it to a combination of parts.[69] Nature presents itself as a whole to our vision. As such, Goethe understood physiological

---

point at the horizon (the horizon of our vision always being at our eye-level), whether we stand, sit, lie down, or even stand on a high building.

66 Compare Leibniz's Monadology. See §7.2. Typical for his time, Leibniz thought God had two means of causation: emanation (or radiation) and volition. Creation would happen by the emanation of (God's) light. See Allison P. Coudert, "Leibniz and The Kabbalah", International Archives of the History of Ideas 142 (Dordrecht: Kluwer Academic Publishers, 1995), p.45, p.136. Such an understanding of the emanation of light is clearly illustrated in the circular halo's of light in paintings and sculptures in Christianity, Buddhism, Hinduism.

67 Jung refers to Dorn's "Theatricum chemicum" 1602, Strassbourg, published in "De speculativa philosophia". Dorn described becoming conscious of something as a process in which the internal light slowly increases in strength. He understood the origin of this light as a spark of the light of God ('sol invisiblis respektive dei imago Dei'). Compare this with the notion of enlightenment.

68 Paracelsus wrote, quoted in C.G. Jung, "Grundwerk - Band 2 - Archetyp und Unbewußtes", p.38: "... the light of nature is rationality alone and nothing else ... the light is what provides belief ...". ("... das liecht der natur ist alein die vernunft und nichts anders ... das liecht ist das, das den glauben gibt ...");

69 Goethe has always asserted himself against the idea that light as entity can be split up according to colour theoretical implications. He beleived colour only emerges through the interaction of a body with light. He was a keen follower of the idea that nature as a whole cannot be fragmented into separate parts. See Goethe, foreword to edition from 1810, in Rudolf Steiner, "J.W. Goethe - Naturwissenschaftliche Schriften Band III" (Dornach: Rudolf Steiner Verlag, 1982 - orig. 1890) p.77: "Colours are acts of light, acts and liabilities. In this sense we may expect them to give us an explanation about light. It is true that colours and light exist in a direct mutual relationship, but we must imagine both as belonging to the whole of nature; because it is the whole of nature, that wishes to reveal itself to the vision in a specific manner through the colours." ("Die Farben sind Thaten des Lichts, Thaten und Leiden. In diesem Sinne können wir von denselben Ausschlüsse über das Licht erwarten. Farben und Licht stehen zwar unter einander in dem genausten Verhältnis, aber wir müssen uns beide als der ganzen Natur angehörig denken; denn sie ist es ganz, die sich dadurch dem Sinne des Auges besonders offenbaren will."

colours as the basis for his colour theory. In his opinion, one should not search for colours in objective processes but in the nature of the organism of our vision, our eyes, that self-sufficiently produce colourful phenomena.[70] Hence his emphasis on the (emotional) experience of colour in contradiction to the empirical analysis of colour promoted by Newton. Goethe subscribed to the idea that we can only perceive everything that we can perceive because it pre-exists as a notion in our minds. It is not so strange to understand Goethe's ideas as a further development of the concept of luminositas, because he himself refers to that 17th century concept.[71] The luminositas are, therefore, a fascinating example of concepts that were not only relevant to a certain period in history. In addition, the luminositas can be seen as a precursor to modern science and to topics that became essential as inspiration for the development of abstract art at the start of the 20th century![72]

70 See Goethe, in Rudolf Steiner, "J.W. Goethe - Naturwissenschaftliche Schriften Band III", p.88: "The eye has to thank its existence to the light. From indifferent animalistic sub-organs, light produces an organ that becomes light's equivalent, and thus the eye forms itself by means of light for the benefit of light, so that the inner light will meet the external light." ("Das Auge hat sein Dasein dem Licht zu danken. Aus gleichgültigen tierischen Hilfsorganen ruft sich das Licht ein Organ hervor, das seinesgleichen werde, und so bildet sich das Auge am Lichte fürs Licht, damit das innere Licht dem äußeren entgegentrete."). Comparable to Goethe, Kant (1724-1804) believed that some knowledge could be a priori, already existing in ourselves, and that the perception of knowledge thus includes a process of recognition. This idea builds on Plato, who already understood knowledge as a process of recognition or memory (Plato formulated this in his Theory of Recollection). This seems to be confirmed by genetic research, which shows that at birth we carry some information in our genes. Such genetically stored information allows, for instance, new born turtles to immediately find the sea.

71 Goethe quotes a verse from Jakob Böhme's "Aurora" (1612) as example of Ionian thought. See Goethe, in Rudolf Steiner, "J.W. Goethe - Naturwissenschaftliche Schriften Band III", p.88: "When the eye would not be sun-like, how could we perceive light? When not God's own power lives within us, how could the divine thrill us?" ("Wär' nicht das Auge Sonnenhaft, Wie könnten wir das Licht erblicken? Lebt' nicht in uns des Gottes eigne Kraft, Wie tönnt' uns Göttliches entzücken?"). In his comments to Goethe's writings, Rudolf Steiner remarks that Jakob Böhme suggested we can perceive the origin of things, because we carry a familiar part of this origin within ourselves. Böhme, who was a contemporary of Paracelsus and Khunrath (1575-1624), was not so much acknowledged in his own time but was extensively discussed in the 19th century and had some influence on philosophers like Hegel and Schilling. For the impact of Böhme on artists one is advised to study the essays "Hidden meanings in Abstract Art" by Maurice Tuchman and "Arp, Kandinsky, and the Legacy of Jakob Böhme" by Harriett Watts, in Maurice Tuchman, "The Spiritual in Art: Abstract Painting 1890-1985" (New York: Abbeville Publishers, 1986).

72 It seems appropriate to bring to mind the 'inner voice' Kandinksy and his contemporaries searched for in art and the involved subjects. See §8.4. Additionally, there are also clear parallels to be found with the notion of Ch'i of Ancient China. Ch'i is the principle of change and emerges out of Taoism, a philosophy of life based on rhythm and fluctuation, on the natural harmony of nature. See Michael Page, "The Power of Ch'i - An Introduction to Chinese Mysticism and Philosophy" (The Aquarian Press, Harper/Collins, 1988). Later the meaning of Ch'i became increasingly more complex and was seen as ether, breath, vapour, steam or matter/energy (comparable in a sense to Aristotle's notion of 'energeia'). A very fascinating proof that there is not nothing but still energy in 'empty' air - comes from a modern scientific experiment, making light from sound. See Seth J. Putterman, "Sonoluminescence: Sound into Light - A bubble of air can focus acoustic energy a trillion fold to produce picosecond flashes of light. The mechanism eludes complete explanation", Scientific American, issue February 1995, p.32-37: "Making light of sound is accomplished by a bubble of air trapped in a cylindrical flask of degassed water. Sound from speakers above and below the flask trap the bubble. A flash of light 50 picoseconds long emerges during the compression part of the acoustic wave. A laser measures the bubble size as it pulses in time with the sound. The light emission is rather faint." Although this research is

Frantisek Kupka, for instance, explained perception and representation as processes in which relationships are limited and energy is exchanged. Forms result from the relation between the dynamics of a particular organic whole with the whole of the rest.[73] In other words, because everything, literally every individual thing, is immersed in the whole of reality, one can understand every thing (including all organisms) as contractions of energies within the streams of energies contained in the whole we call reality. The continuous change of all things is caused by exchanges of energies, which make relationships change as well. Therefore, relationships are always limited and 'relative'. Perception is a similar process caused by the exchange of energies between perceiver and perceived.

This brings to mind colourful painting in general, but also the very special photography of Klaus Goedicke. These magnificent coloured images show simple bottles, whose forms indeed seem to emerge by a virtual 'fluidum' or stream of colours inside and outside the shape in sheer coloured nothingness.[74]

see picture 57

To conclude, on top of everything we discussed in previous chapters, we have added to the complexity of influences, the rhythmic but everchanging energies virtually bombarding us from above and beneath, from inside and outside our own bodies and minds. When one acknowledges the fundamental existence of synchronized rhythms, the crucial importance of synchronization, then one cannot avoid accepting the implications of these oscillating flows of energies. These include implications for our being, implications for the concept of human thinking, implications for our concept of art. We have seen how a part of these implications are reflected more or less intuitively by philosophy, religion and art and more precisely explored by science. The real implications can only be studied if one trusts oneself to be attuned to and incorporate the great variety of phenomena described and probably even more yet to be found. One

still at a very early stage, it seems to me to open a new field of interesting inquiry with both scientific and artistic possibilities of connecting audible tones to visual tones. It is also connected to the research in astronomy on the ejections of radio-waves emitted by stars. This discovery seems to have been imagined by Ostwald in the late 19th century, quoted in Dr. J.J. Lehr, "De draaikolk als model voor mikro- en makrokosmos", p.154: "Starting from Ostwald's pertinent conclusion, that matter is also an expression of energy, already in the 19th century one has searched for an image that would also bring matter back to a manifestation of the ether." The presence of actual energies in 'empty' air certainly provides new subjects for research and for more speculation about what energies colour in space emits and what this does to us as receivers of this energy (again, by synchronization)!

[73] See Dorothy Kosinski, Jaroslav Andel, "Frantisek Kupka - Die abstrakten Farben des Universums" (Stuttgart: Verlag Gerd Hatje, 1997), p.89.

[74] Anselm Adams and Christopher Burkett are great photographers of the exchange of energies creating form in their complex grades of tone and colour in nature. In a different way, the works of Adam Fuss, use images of the realm between the abstract and the representational. Though I could repeat the works of many artists already mentioned before, it seems appropriate to recall the great modern artists of pure colour energies Claude Monet, Charles Biederman, Willem de Kooning, Rupprecht Geiger, Gotthard Graubner, Natvar Bhavsar, but also Helmut Schober with his large paintings of explosive cosmic or alchemist energies. Dieter Ronte, "Helmut Schober - Light-Licht" (Bonn: Kunstmuseum Bonn, Electa Milan, 1998).

cannot disregard these influences on our being anymore, or label them as mere occult or spiritual concepts. Most importantly, we have to take them into account when we wish to understand art.[75]

75 After having finished the manuscript for this book, I was very excited to find a recent publication describing the growing scientific interest in synchronization, including actual evidence of brain processes being influenced by rhythmic processes from outside our bodies. One is definitely advised to read Steven H. Strogatz, "SYNC - How Order Emerges from Chaos in the Universe, Nature, and Daily Life", (New York: Theia Books, Hyperion, 2003).

§15 PROVISIONAL CONCLUSIONS
A CALL FOR A NEW BAROQUE?

The most important consideration for the future, rests on comprehending the similar-differing attitudes with which artists and scientists arrive at their determinations of nature's reality. This entails examining the means and silent assumptions each field engages in in arriving at reality evaluations. Charles Biederman[1]

The task is to actualize existence as emerging into its nature from non-ego, and to disclose the 'meaning' of such an existence, and in so doing to locate and apprehend that existence. Keiji Nishitani[2]

... nature has the power to renew life, and to make it seem worth living. The artist's devotion to and essentialization of the image of nature is a commitment to life at its most elementary. Donald Kuspit[3]

What may we have learned from the essays in this publication? The sheer multi-facetted complexities discussed in this book only offer an attempt to define provisional conclusions. There are no final conclusions, because many implications cannot yet be completely understood.

We have seen how the search to understand reality and the desire to know the essence of our own being, of life, of the world, of the whole process of the universe, of nature, is basic to our human existence. It is a search so basic that in this search all cultures in history and in the world are united, though the details of their various paths or explanations may be very different. Through the whole book we have caught a glimpse of the wealth of available information about peoples' historical translations of their concepts of the essence of reality into religion, philosophies and scientific concepts, while developing simultaneous artistic expressions. All have found the impossibility of isolating the self, the unavoidability of the interaction of the self with the world, and the immersion of the self in reality essential. All have found that being must be seen as a temporal phenomenon in continuously changing but enduring nature. Our desire, although difficult, is to accept, acknowledge and live with this knowledge without attempting to escape daily life. 'Nature' is not merely a tree, park or landscape, but the total process of macrocosm and microcosm. This means the search for the essence of reality is a search to understand your-self. The essence in art cannot be found when one seeks the essence in

---

[1] Charles Biederman, "Art-Science-Reality" (Red Wing, MN: Biederman 1988), p.1.
[2] See Keiji Nishitani, "Religion and Nothingness" (Berkeley, CA: University of California Press, 1982), p.260.
[3] See Donald Kuspit in Donald Kuspit, Lynn Gamwell, "Health and Happiness in 20th Century Avant-Garde Art" (Binghamton: Cornell University Press, Binghamton University Art Museum, 1996), p.44.

the material appearance of the artifact. Instead, one must look for the essence in the very interaction of oneself with the artifact. Because this interaction is first signaled by the artifact's appearance, one needs to take the aspects of its visual properties seriously; colour, shape, proportion, and contrast are crucial. This seems complex, but can be understood when the artwork - the artifact - is recognized as a catalyst. The work of art needs to have an identity which connects with the identity of the viewer, thus allowing a profound experience, comparable to a deep dialogue, leading to understanding. If the work of art has no such identity, we perceive it merely as an object without any deeper meaning.

In the search for the essence of reality, often knowledge and concepts from different disciplines 'cross-fertilize' other disciplines. We have seen that the artistic approach called Constructivism has been a serious attempt to synthesize the artistic concept of reality with the scientific and the philosophical concepts of reality. Related to this framework, we saw the interesting dialogue between Charles Biederman and David Bohm, between an intelligent artist and an open minded scientist, a great example of how these disciplines can have a serious exchange of ideas. We saw how we might understand the functioning of the brain, we viewed related subjects in philosophy and theories on art and by artists, and introduced some plausible and exciting implications for our perception of reality and the functioning of art, in which the projective field is a crucial notion.

Throughout, I have emphasized understanding perception as a process involving the brain, the senses, the hands and a continuous interaction with some object or artifact in our immediate environment - the virtual extension of our thinking process outside our bodies into our immediate environment, which I have called the concept of extensionalism. The need to see something 'in front of our eyes' emphasizes again the importance of visual properties. I have proposed the notion of synchronization, rhythmic processes that interact to influence each other, as an important paradigm for understanding our perception of art in scientific, biological terms. I discussed additional complexities that evidently play a role in our perception of reality, like the highly complex aspects of space/time that lead to a very different and much more abstract notion of reality than was considered before the scientific explorations and philosophical interpretations of space/time's properties. These properties cannot be seen by simply looking at nature's appearance, but only become comprehensible when these abstract concepts are put in front of our eyes - referring to what we learned about perception. Through visualization - visual theorizing - art has always had the power to explain what is 'beyond words', and has become essential for clarifying notions that are just too abstract to imagine in any other way.

The logical next complexity added to my discussion on perception was the immediate confrontation of one's self with the object, with one's environment, with the world, involving the world of particles and the fundamental concepts of change, motion, interaction, structure, harmony, and cohesion. This led to our response to this confrontation, the desire to overcome our natural restraints, the motivations for the possibilities and philosophies of the dissolution of duality, either in one's personal experience or provoked by a work of art. The aim is to feel united, to be completely absorbed by the whole of nature. This discussion necessarily led me to attempt to define the need for greatness in art and the apparent danger of crossing the line into mere decadence. Coming closer and closer to understanding our total immersion in reality, starting to understand how ridiculous it is to think we could completely retreat from or step outside reality, the hypothesis emerged that no 'objective abstraction' in fact can exist. All art concerns aspects of reality, all art contains some narrative of some part of reality, while great art concerns the narrative of actual being. To further express the exciting analogies between many artistic approaches to reality, which seem very different at first, I described the background and development of two 'shapes of beauty', the amorphic/organic and the geometric. I proposed the 'spiral-like oscillation' as a combination of these shapes, motivated by further ideas from contemporary science. The last chapter considered the processes in and impact of nature above, within and beneath us. I described synchronization as the process by which complex rhythmic processes in nature, to some degree, influence our thinking, decision making and preferences for art.[4]

All through this book I have attempted to show the analogous interests in science, philosophy and art in their quests to understand wholeness. A special attempt has been made to let a great variety of artists 'speak for themselves', to exemplify that historically there have always been many more artists with a profound interest and understanding of reality than is often assumed. More artists do not merely do, but know what they are doing!

I have tried to show the extreme complexity of understanding reality. It is of course impossible to provide you with a picture of how you as an individual with your own personal history perceive your reality. All of us, all different individuals, virtually meet in our mutual experience of reality and life, as a general phenomenon of the wholeness of nature. That is why religion, philosophy, science and art do exist and are our 'tools' to support the search for a better understanding of our individual lives. That is why wholeness is such an important theme and why I have discussed so many topics, involving so many diverse aspects involved in understanding wholeness. We have seen how important it is to understand the development of art beyond the traditional discussions of art as a temporary cultural phenomenon, beyond being merely an article for interior decorating or a commodity. To understand the developments of art, one also has to explore the actual and possible sources of inspiration, theories and considerations of the artists themselves. One must go beyond analyzing a painting or sculpture by merely describing the composition, technique or pictorial means.

---

[4] This does not imply a simple renovation of old behaviourism in psychology, which imagined all of our acting and thinking to be merely based upon 'stimulus-response' mechanisms, but it does imply that there is no such thing as a complete free will!

I have tried to indicate the richness and complexities of related knowledge, all human knowledge, religions and philosophies, through the many mentioned analogies linking Western with Eastern cultures.[5] The coherence between subjects which seem at first to be entirely different (subjects traditionally belonging to religion, science, philosophy or art) illustrates that they are in fact connected, interrelated and often flow into each other, essentially revolving around common concerns. They are examples of the highly complex meshwork of human knowledge. Knowledge gradually evolves through the centuries and generations, influenced by the historical 'Zeitgeist', by developments in politics, economy and religion - but also by nature's processes themselves.

The acknowledgement of the interrelations and analogies between art, science and philosophy, does not give us either a definitive or a total grip on the whole. It does not provide an exact understanding of how our individuality is immersed in the universality of the whole, and unfortunately does not make the world a better place. But it certainly does make this whole more accessible.

These essays are not meant to explain art in all its facets, nor to declare that only a certain kind of art should exist, but to show that our general understanding of art is much too narrow when we merely focus on distinctions in art between what is new, avant-garde or succesful in the market. Though these aspects do matter, they are not the only thing that matters or should matter in art. Obviously there will always be people who prefer to focus on their own ego, their own personal way and view of life, or to focus on their local society. There will always be people who prefer to focus on small or large political or social issues. Because artists are people too, there will undoubtedly also always be reflections of these attachments in art. Unfortunately, art also always seems tempted to put itself in the precarious position of being nothing more than a trendy tool for entertainment with little communicative power, merely eager to please.[6]

But if one wishes to understand reality as it is, then the scientist, the artist and the philosopher should try to understand the value of each others' fields for the benefit of their own development. A multi-disciplinary interest always engenders a better understanding of one's own field. This is not easy as we all are quite comfortable within the academic fortresses of our own fields.[7]

[5] An interesting side-effect of these studies has been to show how Occidental and Oriental thinking have been interrelated for much longer than normally is assumed, and that this is also reflected in art for a much longer period! Though influences between East and West can be found in artifacts since Alexander the Great, the Silk Route and Byzantine culture, in modern art (since the late 19th century) it seems to be even more clearly a kind of 'binding factor', obviously stimulated by the emergence of global trade and global communication.

[6] See §9. Though often critical people think this is a modern phenomenon, it is not. Consider, for example, Rococo art, 19th century 'salon' art, late 20th century 'appropriation art' or just 'fun art'. Besides, through all centuries one can find mediocre art that still was commissioned and sold in the days of its creation. 'Eager to please' is a different drive after all than aiming to create great art. Because through all ages artists have to eat and greatness is not always appreciated at the time it is created, one cannot just blame the artists.

[7] The many international (and multi-cultural!) meetings and publications on philosophy, art and science that emerge everywhere prove that I do not stand alone in this opinion and that a further interest in a better

We need to create a new combination of experience and thought in a new system of knowledge to become whole again.[8] While science may offer a system of thought, art may offer a system of experience. We need such a new combination to understand that we are part of the eternal fluctuating or oscillating processes of change in nature, to see ourselves as we actually are: a temporary cluster of energies in the ever flowing energy streams of nature. We are unique by our unique location in space/time, by our unique quality to be self conscious and to be able to research what we are and what life is by attempting to overcome duality, which can be accomplished temporarily through the experience of the sublime. Sublime experiences help us to understand and cope with life while still being in a world of dualities (as I have pointed out, without dualities there can be no individuality aware of itself).

Our consciousness allows us to explore the secret of life in the universe beyond the limitations of our own tiny existence as little dots in the eternity of space/time. These are explorations in which we should not only trust our rational capacities, but, founded on the acknowledgement of ourselves as whole human beings, we should trust our intuition, our sense for beauty and our capacity to experience the sublime. I think one may consider this call for a positive treatment of beauty and the sublime, in which both rational as well as intuited knowledge is taken into account, and which should be profoundly deep and accessible to all, a call for a 'New Baroque'.

The Baroque emerged out of the need of the Counter Reformation to touch the general public in immediate response to the puritan sobriety of the Reformation. In the Baroque, art was pushed to higher levels of greatness offering a large public experiences of the sublime in visually attractive works of art. Works of art that appeal to the greatness, colour and form complexities of nature's forces.

Comparably, a 'New Baroque' can be a natural response to the oversimplification of

---

understanding of the analogies between all knowledge about the essence of reality has become inevitable. The political counterpart of this idea is the concept of multilateralism - the international attempt to initiate a real dialogue by organizing meetings in which people with very different cultural backgrounds are considered to be of equal importance. This is a timely and crucially important problem to attempt to solve some global problems.

[8] See Kitaro Nishida, "Intuition and Reflection in Self-Consciousness" (Albany, NY: State University of New York Press, 1987 - orig. "Jikaku ni okeru chokkan to han sei", 1941), p.93: "When a system of thought combines with a system of experience it returns to its foundation, in accord with Cohen's principle of continuity, and this return generates a great system of knowledge, in obedience to the demand which appears as a transcendental sensation." Hermann Cohen, a student of Kant, stated in 1871 that continuity is a logical aspect of thought, an idea earlier adopted by Leibniz (see Kitaro Nishida, "Intuition and Reflection in Self-Consciousness", p.183). In my interpretation, Nishida means that a system of thought or a system of experience alone will not be able to proceed separately within the stream of knowledge that flows through all ages. This can only be accomplished in their combination, and only so will they create a new system of knowledge. Any system of experiences leads to the involvement of aspects of reality that cannot be explained with logic, creating a somewhat transcendental sensation. This I would prefer to describe as 'a sensation of the eidos', of individuality immersed in wholeness. The amount of information offered in this publication gives justification to the idea that this sensation is itself a facet of logical reasoning.

contemporary art offered the past decades. Artworks should have lasting greatness, regardless of medium, subject, form-language, concept or message. Greatness will take our breath away and will provide the viewer with a respect for life and an acknowledgement of reality.

It should have become evident in this book - supported by facts and theories from different fields of science, philosophy and art - that the meaning of art can only be comprehended in the interaction of the artifact with the processes of the brain - incorporating processes outside and inside our bodies while also being influenced by the various processes of nature outside and inside our bodies, including our own histories. Therefore, the interaction with the work of art mirrors the very interaction of one's self with the world, nature, and reality, helping one to understand the cohesion of everything, to understand wholeness.

Both to the artist and to the viewer, in the end art is about the experience evoked by a material object, but is not the object itself, it is '*no thing*'!

INDEX

A

- Abe, Masao; "A Study of Dogen - His Philosophy and Religion", edited by Steven Heine, State University of New York Press, 1992, ISBN 0 7914 0838 8.
- Abe, Ryuichi; Haskel, Peter; "Great Fool - Zen Master Ryokan, Poems, Letters and Other Writings", University of Hawai'i Press (Honolulu), 1996, ISBN 0 8248 1777 X.
- Achenbach, Nora von; Runde, Sabine; "Vier Elemente - Drei Länder - Moderne Keramik aus der Sammlung Freudenberg", Museum für Kunsthandwerk Frankfurt am Main, 1992, ISBN 3 8827 0061 0.
- Addiss, Stephen; "The Art of Zen - Paintings and Calligraphy by Japanese Monks 1600-1925", Harry N. Abrams Inc., New York, 1989, ISBN 0 8109 2774 8.
- Albert, David Z.; "Bohm's Alternative to Quantum Mechanics", Scientific American, issue May 1994, p.32-39.
- Albrecht, Hans Joachim; Koella, Rudolf; "Hans Hinterreiter - Ein Schweizer Vertreter der konstruktiven Kunst", Edition István Schlégl, Waser Verlag, 1982, ISBN 3 9080 80 02.
- Albrecht, Joachim; Fuchs, Rudi; Holz, Hans Heinz; Lemoine, Serge; Riese, HansPeter; Rotzler, Willy; Vachtová, Ludmilla; Lohse, Richard Paul; "Richard Paul Lohse - Modulaire und serielle Ordnungen 1943-84", Waser Verlag 1984, ISBN 3 9080 8011 8.
- Alloway, Lawrence; "Jackson Pollock; Paintings, drawings and watercolours from the collection of Lee Krasner Pollock", Marlborough Fine Art Ltd, London, 1961.
- Alessi, Alberto; "F.F.F. Family Follows Fiction - Workshop 1991-1993", Centro Studi Alessi, 1993.
- Ames, Roger T; Hall, David L; "Daodejing - 'Making This Life Significant' - A Philosophical Translation", Ballantine Books New York, 2003, ISBN 0 3454 4415 9.
- "Aratjara - Art of the first Australians", DuMont Buchverlag Köln, 1993, ISBN 3 9261 5417 9.
- Arberry, A.J.; "Sufism - An Account of the Mystics of Islam", Dover Publications Inc., Mineola NY, 2002 (orig, 1950), ISBN 0 4864 1958 4.
- Argelles, Jos; "The Mayan Factor - Path Beyond Technology", Bear & Company, 1987, ISBN 0 9396 8038 6.
- Arnason, H.H.; "A History of Modern Art - Painting-Sculpture Architecture", revised and enlarged edition, Thames and Hudson, 1977 (orig. 1969), ISBN 0 5002 3261 X.
- Arnheim, Rudolf; "Visual Thinking", University of California Press, 1969, ISBN 0 5200 1871 0.
- Arnheim, Rudolf; "The Power of the Center - A Study of Composition in the Visual Arts", the new version, University of California Press, 1988, ISBN 0 5200 6241 8.

B

- Baljeu, Joost; "Mondrian or Miro", De Beuk, Amsterdam, 1958.
- Baljeu, Joost; "An Attempt at a Theory of Synthesist Plastic Expression", Alec Tiranti, London, 1963.
- Baljeu, Joost; "Theo van Doesburg", Studio Vista, 1974, ISBN 0 289 70358 1.
- Baljeu, Joost; "Structure", magazine published from 1958-1964.
- Bann, Stephen; "The Tradition of Constructivism", Da Capo Press, 1990 (orig. 1974), ISBN 0 3068 0396 8.
- Barchan, William L.; "Giambattista Tiepolo", Harry N. Abrams Inc. Publishers, 1992, ISBN 0 8109 3858 8.
- Barker, Ian; "Caro", Prestel Verlag, 1991, ISBN 3 7913 1137 9.
- Barnett, Vivian Endicott; "Kandinsky and Sweden", Malmö Konsthall, Moderna Museet, Stockholm, 1989, ISBN 9 1770 4037 6.
- Barnett, Vivian Endicott; "Kandinsky - Catalogue Raisonn of the Watercolours", Volume One 1900-1921, Sotheby's Publications, Electa, 1992, ISBN 0 8566 7405 2.
- Barnett, Vivian Endicott; "Kandinsky - Catalogue Raisonn of the Watercolours", Volume Two 1922-1944, Sotheby's Publications, Electa, 1994, ISBN 0 8566 7415 X.
- Bartha, Miklos von; "Arte Concreto - Invencion - Arte Madi", Edition Galerie Von Bartha, 1991.
- Baumann, Felix; Benesch, Evelyn; Feilchenfeldt, Walter; Schroeder, Klaus Albrecht; "Cézanne - Finished Unfinished", Hatje Cantz Publishers, 2000, ISBN 3 7757 0879 0.
- Baeyer, Hans Christian von; "The Quantum Eraser", The Sciences, issue January/February 1997, p.12-14.
- Beckley, Bill; Shapiro, David; "Uncontrollable Beauty - Towards a New Aesthetics", Allworth Press, New York, 1998, ISBN 1 8805 5990 0.
- Beckley, Bill; "Sticky Sublime", Allworth Press, New York, 2001, ISBN 1 5811 5092 X.
- Becks-Malorny, Ulrike; "Wassily Kandinsky 1866-1944 - Aufbruch zur Abstraktion", Benedikt Taschen Verlag, 1993, ISBN 3 8228 9512 1.
- Beeren, Wim; Schoon, Talitha; "Walter de Maria", Museum Boymans - van Beuningen, Rotterdam, 1984.
- Berger, Klaus; "Moritz Geiger: The Significance of Art - A Phenomenological Approach to Aesthetics",

Center for Advanced Research in Phenomenology & University Press of America, Washington DC, 1986 (original title "Die Bedeutung der Kunst", 1944), ISBN 0 8191 5485 7.
•Berget, Alphonse; "Le Ciel - nouvelle astronomie pittoresque", Libraire Larousse, Paris, 1923.
•Bergson, Henri; "Matter and Memory", Zone Books, 1988 (orig. "Matière et mémoire", 1896, this version is a translation from the 5th edition of 1908), ISBN 0 9422 9905 1.
•Berk, Laura E.; "Why Children Talk to Themselves", Scientific American, issue November 1994, p.60-65.
•Bernard, Pascal; "Tadao Ando - Das Haus Koshino", Wasmuth Verlag, 1990, ISBN 3 8030 01501.
•Bernstein, Jeremy; "The Reluctant Father of Black Holes", Scientific American, issue June 1996, p.66-72.
•Beyeler, Ernst; Brüderlin, Markus; Hohl, Reinhold; "Farbe-Licht", Fondation Beyeler, Hatje Cantz Verlag, 2000, ISBN 7 7570 954 1.
•Bezzola, Tobia; Homburg, Cornelia; "Max Beckmann und Paris - Matisse, Picasso, Braque, Leger, Roualt", Taschen Verlag 1998, ISBN 3 8228 7609 7.
•Biederman, Charles; "Art as the Evolution of Visual Knowledge", Biederman, Red Wing, MN, USA, 1948.
•Biederman, Charles; "Letters on the New Art", Biederman, Red Wing, MN, USA, 1951.
•Biederman, Charles; "The New Cézanne", Biederman, Red Wing, MN, USA, 1958.
•Biederman, Charles; "Sphere and Cube", Structure - sixth series 1.1964, Joost Baljeu, the Netherlands.
•Biederman, Charles; "Search for New Arts", Biederman, Red Wing, MN, USA, 1979.
•Biederman, Charles; "Art-Science-Reality", Biederman, Red Wing, MN, USA, 1988.
•Biederman, Charles; "Art, Theology, Technology, Science", PRO-NR.6, PRO Foundation, 1990.
•Biederman, Charles; "The De-Humanization and Demoralization of Modern Art - Moreau to Picasso to Mondrian", Biederman, Red Wing, MN, USA, 1992.
•Biederman, Charles; "Nature and Art Anew", Biederman, Red Wing, MN, USA, 1993.
•Biederman, Charles; "The End of Modernism, Figurative or Abstract", Biederman, Red Wing, MN, USA, 1994.
•Biederman, Charles; "Art Mirrors Psychological Humanizing Experience of Reality", Biederman, Red Wing, MN, USA, 1996.
•Biederman, Charles; "Art as the Humanization of Science", Biederman, Red Wing, MN, USA, 1997.
•Biederman, Charles; "Visual Art Humanifies the Sciences", Red Wing, MN, USA, 1998.
•Biederman, Charles; "Re-Birth of Humanization by Leonardo da Vinci Leading to the Rebirth of what Paul Cézanne called the Beginning of a 'New Art' of 'Only Creation' ", Red Wing, MN, USA, 1999.
•Biederman, Charles; "The Visual Millenium: Leonardo to Cézanne" , Biederman, Red Wing, MN, USA, 2000.
•Bill, Max; "Max Bill: Wassily Kandinsky", Maeght Éditeur Paris, 1951.
•Bill, Max; "Kandinsky - Essays über Kunst und Künstler", Benteli Verlag Bern, 1963 (orig. 1955).
•Bill, Max; "Kandinsky -Über das Geistige in der Kunst", new edition by Jelena Hahl-Fontaine, introduction by Max Bill, Benteli Verlag Bern, 2004 (orig. Benteli Verlag 1952).
•Bill, Max; "Kandinsky - Punkt und Linie zu Fläche, Beitrag zur Analyse der malerischen Elemente", 9th edition with an introduction by Max Bill, Benteli Verlag Bern, 1964 (orig. Benteli Verlag 1955).
•Birren, Faber; "The Color Primer - A basic treatise on the color system of Wilhelm Ostwald", Van Nostrand Reinhold Company, 1969, (orig. "Farbenfiebel", W. Ostwald, 1916).
•Birren, Faber; "The Principles of Harmony and Contrast of Colors and their Application to the Arts - M.E. Chevreul", a newly revised edition, Schiffer Publishing Ltd, 1987 (orig. 1854), ISBN 0 8874 0090 6.
•Blomberg, David; Kirby, Jo; Leighton, John; Roy, Ashok; "Art in the Making - Impressionism", The National Gallery London, Yale University Press, 1991, ISBN 0 3000 5035 6.
•Boas, Franz; "Primitive Art", Dover Publications, 1955 (orig. 1927), ISBN 0 4862 0025 6.
•Bockemühl, Michael; Mitschke, Uta; Gizycki, Ulrich von; "Das Kunstwerk und die Wissenschaften - über die unterschiedliche Art, sich ein Bild zu machen", Edition Tertium, 1994, ISBN 3 9307 1702 6.
•Boegle, Annette; Schmal, Peter Cachola; Flagge, Ingeborg; "Leicht weit - light structures - Joerg Schlaich, Rudolf Bergermann", D.A.M. Frankfurt, Prestel Verlag (Munich-Berlin-London-New York), 2003, ISBN 3 7913 6011 6.
•Boehme, Gernot; Schiemann, Gregor; "Phänomenologie der Natur", Suhrkamp Taschenbuch Wissenschaft 1325, 1997, ISBN 3 5182 8925 X.
•Boehm, Gottfried; "Was ist ein Bild?", 3rd edition, Wilhelm Fink Verlag Munich, 2001 (orig.1994), ISBN 3 7705 2920 0.
•Boehm, Gottfried; "Gotthard Graubner - Painting", Galerie Karsten Greve, 1995.

B

- Bogner, Dr. Dieter. "Friedrich Kiesler Architekt Maler Bildhauer 1890 1965", Löcker Verlag Wien, 1988, ISBN 3 8540 9124 9.
- Bogner, Dieter; "Walter Kaitna - Kräftesysteme 1962-1983", Kunstraum Buchberg Wien 1994.
- Bohm, David; "Causality and Chance in Modern Physics", Routledge & Kegan Paul, 1984 (orig.1957), ISBN 0 7102 00315.
- Bohm, David; Peat, F. David; "Science, Order & Creativity", Routledge, 1989 (original Bantam Books 1987), ISBN 0 4150 3079 X.
- Bohm, David; "On Dialogue", David Bohm Seminars, Ojai California, 1990.
- Bohm, David; Hiley, Basil J.; "The Undivided Universe - An ontological Interpretation of Quantum Theory", Routledge, 1995 (orig.1993), ISBN 0 4151 2185 X.
- Bohnen, Uli; "Otto Freundlich - Ein Wegbereiter der gegenstandlosen Kunst", DuMont Buchverlag Köln, 1982, ISBN 3 7701 1263 6.
- Boime, Albert; "Vincent van Gogh - Die Sternennacht - Die Geschichte des Stoffes und der Stoff der Geschichte", Fischer Taschenbuch Verlag GmbH, 1989, ISBN 3 5962 3953 2.
- Bois, Yve-Alain; "Painting as Model", MIT Press, 1995 (orig. 1997), ISBN 0 2625 2180 6.
- Bomford, David; Kirby, Jo; Leighton, John; Roy, Ashok; "Art in the Making - Impressionism", The National Gallery (London), Yale University Press, 1990, ISBN 0 3000 5036 4.
- Bor, Jan; Petersma, Errit; Kingma, Jelle; "De Verbeelding van het denken, Geïllustreerde geschiedenis van de westerse en oosterse filosofie", Uitgeverij Contact, 1997 (orig. 1995), ISBN 9 0254 0039 6.
- Bosga, Douwe; Busch, Martine; "Natuurlijk - niet bovennatuurlijk - Parapsychologische kanttekeningen bij de ervaringen van de paragnost Warner Tholen", Ankh-Hermes, 1984, ISBN 90 2025 4421.
- Boss, Alan P.; "Companions to Young Stars", Scientific American, issue October 1995, p.38-43.
- Bossert, Helmuth Th.; "Folk Art of Europe", Wasmuth Verlag, 1990, ISBN 3 8030 5057 X.
- Bossert, Helmuth Th.; "Folk Art of Asia - Africa - Australia - The Americas", Wasmuth Verlag, 1990, ISBN 3 8030 5058 8.
- Bothun, Gregory D.; "The Ghostliest Galaxies", Scientific American, issue February 1997, p.40-45.
- Bowlt, John E.; Long, Rose-Carol Washton; "The Life of Vasilii Kandinsky in Russian Art - A Study of On The Spiritual in Art", ORP Russian Biography Series, No.4, Oriental Research Partners, 1980, ISBN 0 8925 0131 6.
- Bowness, Alan; Lambertini, Luigi; "Victor Pasmore - with a catalogue raisonné of the paintings, constructions and graphic works 1926-1979", Thames and Hudson, 1980, ISBN 0 5000 9144 7.
- Bozo, Dominique; "Matta", Les Classiques au XXe siecle, Éditions du Centre Pompidou, ADAG, 1985, ISBN 2 8585 0303 6.
- Brauen, Martin; "Das Mandala - Der Heilige Kreis im tantrischen Buddhismus", DuMont Verlag, 1992, ISBN 3 7701 2509 6.
- Brejon de Lavergne, Arnauld; "Rubens", cat. Palais des Beaux-Arts, Lille, Chr. Belser AG Verlag, 2004, ISBN 3 7630 2434.
- Brinker, Helmut; Lutz, Albert; "Chinesische Cloisonné - Die Sammlung Pierre Uldry", Museum Rietberg Zürich, 1985, ISBN 3 9070 7008 9.
- Brix, Walter; "Der goldene Faden, Bestandskatalog der Textilien aus China, Korea und Japan in Museum für Ostasiatische Kunst Köln", Wienand Verlag, 2003, ISBN 3 8790 9811 5.
- Brooke, Peter; "Albert Gleizes - For and Against the Twentieth Century", Yale University Press, 2001, ISBN 0 3000 8964 3.
- Broos, Kees; "Piet Zwart 1885-1977", Haags Gemeentemuseum, Van Gennep Amsterdam, 1982, ISBN 9 0601 2544 4.
- Bruyn, Gerd de; "Johannes Peter Hölzinger - Haus in Bad Nauheim", Edition Axel Menges (Stuttgart, London), 2004, ISBN 3 9306 9853 6.
- Bucher, Annemarie; "Die Spirale - Eine Künstlerzeitschrift 1953-1964", Verlag Lars Müller, 1990, ISBN 3 9067 0021 6.
- Butin, Hubertus; "Thomas Zitzwitz", Fahnemann Projekte, Berlin, 2002, ISBN 3 9808 0881 5.

- Cabanas, Pilar; “La Fuerza de Oriente en la obra de Joan Miro”, Electa, 2000, ISBN 8 4815 6303 X.
- Cachin, Françoise; Rishel, Joseph J.; “Cézanne”, Tate Publishing, 1996, ISBN 1 8543 7178 9.
- Cahan, David; “Science and Culture - Popular and Philosophical Essays - Hermann von Helmholtz”, The University of Chicago Press, 1995, ISBN 0 2263 2659 4.
- Candy, Linda; Edmonds, Ernest; “Explorations in Art and Technology”, Springer Verlag, 2002, ISBN 1 8523 3545 9.
- Cassou, Jean; “Wassily Kandinsky - Watercolors, Drawings, Writings”, translated by Norbert Gutermann, Thames and Hudson London, 1961 (in association with Verlag M. Dumont Schauberg, Cologne).
- Catoir, Barbara; “Miro on Mallorca”, Prestel Verlag, 1995, ISBN 3 7913 1483 1.
- Centre Georges Pompidou; “Présences Polonaises - Witkiewicz - Constructivisme - Les Contemporains”, Centre Georges Pompidou, 1983, ISBN 2 8585 0194 7.
- Centre Georges Pompidou; “Malevitch - Architectones Peintures Dessins”, Pontus Hulten, Collections du Musée National d’Art Moderne, 1980, ISBN 2 85850 0428.
- Chalmers, David J.; “The Puzzle of Conscious Experience”, Scientific American, issue December 1995, p.62-68.
- Chan-Magomedev, S.O.; “Pioniere der sowjetischen Architektur”, VEB Verlag der Kunst Dresden, 1983.
- Chassey, Eric de; “American Art, 1908-1947. From Winslow Homer to Jackson Pollock”, Harry N. Abrams Inc. Publishers, 2001, ISBN 0 8109 6363 9.
- Checkland, Peter; “Systems Thinking, Systems Practice”, John Wiley & Sons, 1991 (orig. 1981), ISBN 0 4712 7911 8.
- Chiao, Raymond Y.; Kwiat, Paul G.; Steinberg, Aephraim, M.; “Faster than light? Experiments in quantum optics show that two distant events can influence each other faster than any signal could have traveled between them”, Scientific American, issue August 1993, p.38-46.
- Choi, Min-Hong; “Comparative Philosophy - Western and Korean Philosophies Compared”, edited by the Society of Korean Philosophy, Seong Moon Sa, 1980.
- Chon, Hyebong; The National Treasures of Korea, Volume 12, Calligraphy - Old Books.
- Claisse, Genevieve; “Auguste Herbin - Vom Impressionismus zum Konstruktivismus - Ein Maler des Jahrhunderts”, Galerie Lahumiere, 1998.
- Clausen, Franciska; “Tre Pionérer for Polsk Avant-Garde”, Fynsk Kunstmuseum, 1985.
- Cohen, Nathan; “Gravity’s Lens - Views of the new Cosmology”, Wiley Science Editions, 1989, ISBN 0 4715 1054 8.
- Coontz Jr., Robert J.; “Turning Point - The earth’s core is found to spin faster than the crust and mantle”, The Sciences, issue September/October 1996, p.10.
- Corcoran, Elizabeth; “Ordering Chaos - Researchers are beginning to harness nonlinear systems”, Scientific American, issue August 1993, p.82-83.
- Corn, Wanda M.; “Mark Tobey - Works on Paper”, Stanford University Museum of Art, 1991.
- Cornell, Eric A.; Wieman, Carl E.; “The Bose-Einstein Condensate”, Scientific American issue March 1998, p.26-31.
- Coudert, Allison P.; “Leibniz and The Kabbalah”, International Archives of the History of Ideas 142, Kluwer Academic Publishers, 1995, ISBN 0 7923 3114 1.
- Covert, Eugene E.; “Evolution of the Commercial Airliner”, Scientific American, issue September 1995, p.82.
- Cowen, Painton; “Rose Windows”, Thames and Hudson, 1992 (orig.1979), ISBN 0 5008 1021 4.
- Coyne, Richard; “Technoromanticism - digital narrative, holism, and the romance of the real”, MIT Press, 1999, ISBN 0 2620 3260 0.
- Cramer, Friedrich; “Symphonie des Lebendigen, Versuch einer allgemeinen Resonanztheorie”, Insel Taschenbuch, 1998, ISBN 3 4583 3888 8.
- Crick, Francis; “The Astonishing Hypothesis - The Scientific Search for the Soul”, Simon & Schuster, 1994, ISBN 0 6717 1158 X.
- Crick, Francis; Koch, Christof: “Is Neuronal Synchronization Necessary for Fine Sensory Discrimination?”, paper on the internet: www.phil.vt.edu/ASSC/engel/crickl.html.
- Christe, Yves; Losowska, Hanna; Rechtl, Roland; Velmans, Tania; “Christentum - Formen und Stile”, Benedikt Taschen Verlag GmbH, 1994, ISBN 3 8228 8967 9.

D

- Dabrowski, Magdalena; "Contrasts of Form - Geometric Abstract Art 1910-1980", The Museum of Modern Art New York, 1985, ISBN 0 8707 0289 0.
- Dabrowski, Magdalena; "Kandinsky Compositions", The Museum of Modern Art New York, 1995, ISBN 0 8707 0406 0.
- Dale, John E.; "Power Plants", The Sciences, issue September/October 1994, p.28-33.
- Danto, Arthur C.; "After the End of Art - Contemporary Art and the Pale of History", Princeton University Press (Princeton, NJ), 1997, ISBN 0 6910 0299 1.
- Danto, Arthur C.; "The Abuse of Beauty - Aesthetics and the Concept of Art", Open Court (Chicago and La Salle, ILL), 2004 (orig. 2003), ISBN 0 8126 9540 2.
- Darvas, György; "Dichotomies and Trichotomies in the Eastern and Western Cultures", paper in "Katachi u Symmetry", Springer Verlag Tokyo, 1996, ISBN 4 4317 0161 3.
- Davidson, Maxwell; "George Rickey", various catalogues, Gallery Maxwell Davidson, New York.
- Davidson III, Maxwell; "George Rickey - The Early Works", Schiffer Publishing (Atglen, PA), 2004, ISBN 0 7643 1992 2.
- Davies, Chad; Hunter, J.R.; James, H.; "Counterrotating Orbits and Stability in Two- and Three-Dimensional Systems", paper in "Three-Dimensional Systems", see Kandrup.
- Davies, David; "El Greco", National Gallery Company, London, Yale University Press, 2003, ISBN 1 8570 9933 8.
- Dawkins, Richard; "The Blind Watchmaker", Penguin Books, 1988 (orig.1986), ISBN 0 1400 80562.
- Dawkins, Richard; "God's Utility Function", Scientific American issue November 1995, p.60-67.
- Debbaut, Jan, "El Lissitzky 1890-1941 - architect-schilder-fotograaf-typograaf", Stedelijk van Abbemuseum Eindhoven, 1990, ISBN 9 0701 4927 3.
- Derman, M. Ugur; "Letters in Gold - Ottoman Calligraphy from the Sakip Sabanci Collection, Istanbul", The Metropolitan Museum of Art, New York, Harry N. Abrams Inc., 1998, ISBN 0 8109 6526 7.
- Derouet, Christian; "Domela - Gouaches periode Parisienne", Editions Reflex Utrecht, Pays-Bas, 1984, ISBN 9 0632 2102 9.
- Derouet, Christian; "Kandinsky - Album de l'exposition", Centre George Pompidou, 1984, ISBN 2 8585 0266 8.
- Desai, Vishakha N.; Munroe, Alexandra; "The New Way of Tea", International Chado Culture Foundation in collaboration with Ikko Tanaka, New York, 2002.
- Deutsch, David; Lockwood, Michael; "The Quantum Physics of Time Travel - common sense may rule out such excursions - but the laws of physics do not", Scientific American, issue March 1994, p.50-56.
- Dewey, John; "Experience And Nature", Dover Publications Inc., 1958 (orig. 1929), ISBN 0 4862 0471 5.
- Dewey, John; "Art As Experience", Perigee Books, 1980 (orig. 1934), ISBN 0 3995 0025 1.
- Diehl, Gaston; "Vasarely", Gondron Verlag GmbH & Co KG, 1993, ISBN 3 8112 1039 4.
- Dobbins, James C.; "Jodo Shinshu - Shin Buddhism in Medieval Japan", Indiana University Press, 1989, ISBN 0 2533 3186 2.
- Doran, Michael: "Conversations with Cézanne", introduction by Richard Shiff, Documents of Twentieth Century Art, University of California Press, 2001, ISBN 0 5202 2519 8.
- Dube, Wolf-Dieter; "Hans Hartung - Bilder aus den Jahren 1973/74 und 1980/81", Galerie Fahnemann, 2003, ISBN 3 9808 0882 3.
- Düchting, Hajo; "Cézanne", Taschen Verlag, 1992, ISBN 3 8228 0608 0.
- Düchting, Hajo; "Robert und Sonia Delaunay - Triumph der Farbe", Benedikt Taschen Verlag, 1993, ISBN 3 8228 9629 2.
- Duff, Michael J.; "The Theory Formerly Known as Strings", Scientific American, issue February 1998, p.54-59.
- Dumoulin, Heinrich; "Zen Enlightenment - origins and meaning", Weatherhill, 7th print, 1995 (orig. "Die Erleuchtung des Zen im Buddhismus", Fischer Taschenbuch Verlag 1976), ISBN 0 8348 0141 8.
- Dupin, Jacques; "Joan Miro - Life and Work", Thames and Hudson, 1962.
- Durant, Ben; Heusch, Serge Goyensde; Maury, Jean-Pierre; Safin-Cahey, Francoise; Waedemon-Baugniet, Andre; Waedemon, Olivier; "Marcel Baugniet - Liège 1896 - Bruxelles 1995 - Dans la tourbillon des avant gardes", La Renaissance du Livre, 2001, ISBN 2 8046 0474 8.

- Eck, Caroline van; "Goethe and Alberti: Organic Unity in Nature and Architecture", The Structurist No. 35/36, 1995/1996.
- Eco, Umberto; "Art and Beauty in the Middle Ages", Yale University Press, 1986 (orig, 1959), ISBN 0 3000 3676 0.
- Eco, Umberto; "Die ästhetische Botschaft", in "Theorien der Kunst", Suhrkamp Tachenbuch Wissenschaft 1012, 1992 (1e druk 1972), (orig. "La struttura assente - introduzione alla riceraca semiologica", 1968), ISBN 3-518-2812-9.
- Eco, Umberto; "Die Grenzen der Interpretation", Carl Hanser Verlag, 1992 (orig. "I limiti dell' interpretazione", 1990), ISBN 3 4461 7120 7.
- Eco, Umberto; "Die Suche nach der vollkommenen Sprache", C.H. Beck - Europa Bauen, 1994, (orig. "La ricerca della lingua perfetta nella cultura europea", 1993), ISBN 3406 37 8889.
- Edmonds, E.A.; Candy, L.; Proceedings of the Second International Symposium "Creativity and Cognition", LUTCHI Research Centre, Department of Computer Studies, Loughborough University, 1996, ISBN 1 9007 0300 9.
- Ehrenburg, Ilja; "Und sie bewegt sich doch - Moskau/Berlin 1922", reprint LIT Verlag, 1986, ISBN 3 9067 0006 2.
- Einstein, Albert; "On the Generalized Theory of Gravitation - An account of the newly published extension of the general theory of relativity against its historical and philosophical background", reprinted in Scientific American special issue "Science in the 20th Century", 1991, p.40-45 (orig. published in Scientific American, issue April 1950).
- Eisenman, Stephen F.; Baetschmann, Oskar; Gloor, Lukas; "Ferdinand Hodler - Landscapes", translated by Danielle Nathanson, Swiss Institute for Art Research Zürich, Zürich Publishing House, 1987.
- Ekuan, Kenji; "A Prayer Design", SD Space Design Special Extra Issue No.19 "A Design Declaration - GK's 30 Year History", January 1988, Kajima Institute Publishing Co. Ltd.
- Ekuan, Kenji; "The Aesthetics of the Japanese Lunchbox", MIT Press, 2000 (orig. by Goma Shobo, Tokyo, 1980), ISBN 0 2625 5035 0.
- El-Said, Issam; Parman, Ayse; "Geometric Concepts in Islamic Art", Scorpion Publishing Ltd, 1976, ISBN 0 9059 0665 9.
- Elders, Fons; "Humanism Toward The Third Millennium II", VUB Brussels University Press, 1996, ISBN 9 0548 7100 8.
- Elders, Fons; "The Sublime and The Beautiful - On Ontology and Creative Imagination", VUB Brussels University Press, 2001, ISBN 9 0548 7244 6.
- Englert, Berthold-Georg; Scully, Marlan O.; Walther, Herbert; "The Duality in Matter and Light", Scientific American, issue December 1994, p.56-61.
- Erben, Walter; "Joan Miro - The Man and His Work 1893-1983", Taschen Verlag, 1998, ISBN 3 8228 7217 2.
- Erpel, Fritz; "Paul Cézanne - Ein Traum von Kunst - Der Maler in seinen Briefen", Henschel Verlag, 1984, ISBN 3 3620 0600 0.
- Evans, Helen C.; "Byzantium - Faith and Power (1261-1557)", The Metropolitan Museum of Art, NY, and Yale University Press (New Haven and London), 2004, ISBN 1 5883 9114 0.
- Ex, Sjarel; Hoek, Els; "Vilmos Huszar - schilder en ontwerper 1884-1960", Reflex Utrecht, 1985, ISBN 90 6322 106 1.
- Fabre, Gladys; "Tutundjian", Éditions du Regard, 1994, ISBN 2 8410 5045 9.
- Fagiola, Maurizio; "Balla", Nuovo edizione Gabriele Mazzotta, 1987, ISBN 8 8202 0762 1.
- Farmelo, Graham; "The Discovery of X-Rays", Scientific American, issue November 1995, p.68-73.
- Fath, Manfred; Brockhaus, Christoph; "Malewitsch - Mondrian, Konstruktion als Konzept - Alexander Dorner gewidmet", Wilhelm Hack Museum, Ludwigshafen, 1978 (orig, 1976).
- Feeney, Kelly; "Josef Albers: Works on Paper", Artservices International, Alexandria, Virginia, 1991, ISBN 0 8839 7100 3.

- Ferreti-Bocquillon, Marina; Distel, Anne; Leighton, John; Alyson Stein, Susan; "Signac 1863-1935", catalogue The Metropolitan Museum of Art, New York, Yale University Press, 2001, ISBN 0 8709 9999 0.
- Fesel, Galerie Karin; "Konzept: Farbe - Ausstellung und Gespräch zur Erfahrung der Farbe im Bild", Verlag Urachhaus, ISBN 3 8783 8890 X.
- Feyerabend, Paul; "Conquest of Abundance - A Tale of Abstraction versus the Richness of Being", The

University of Chicago Press, 1999, ISBN 0 2262 4533 0.
- Feynman, Richard P.; "QED - The Strange Theory of Light and Matter", Penguin Books, 1990 (orig. Princeton University Press, 1985), ISBN 0 1401 2505 1.
- Fiedeler, Frank: "Yin und Yang - Das kosmische Grundmuster in den Kulturformen Chinas", DuMont Verlag, 1993, ISBN 3 7701 2901 6.
- Fiedler, Ulrich; "Claus Goedicke", Galerie Ulrich Fiedler, Cologne, 1996.
- Flusser, Vilèm; "Ins Universum der technischen Bilder", European Photography, 1992 (4.Auflage, orig. 1985), ISBN 3 9232 8329 6.
- Flusser, Vilèm; "Angenommen - eine Szenenfolge", Immatrix Publications, 1989, ISBN 3 9261 9903 2.
- Flusser, Vilèm; "Gesten - Versuch einer Phänomenologie", Bollmann Verlag, 1991, ISBN 3 9279 011.
- Forrer, Matthi: "Hiroshige - Prints and Drawings", Royal Academy of Arts, Prestel Verlag Munich-London-New York, 2001 (orig. 1997), ISBN 3 79113 2594 9.
- Frampton, Kenneth; Quilici, Vieri; Khan-Magomedev, S.O.; "Ivan leonidov", Rizzoli New York, 1981, ISBN 0 8478 0381 3.
- Frank, Elizabeth; "Jackson Pollock", Verlag J. Bucher GmbH, 1984 (orig. in English by Cross River Press Ltd, 1983), ISBN 3 7658 0451 7.
- Franz, Erich; "Farben des Lichts - Paul Signac und der Beginn der Moderne von Matisse bis Mondrian", Edition Tertium, 1996, ISBN 3 9307 1738 7.
- Franz, Marie-Louise; "Zeit-Strömen und Stille", Kösel-Verlag GmbH & Co, 1992 (orig.1978), ISBN 3 4663 4277 5.
- Frederickson, James K.; Onstott, Tullis C.; "Microbes Deep Inside the Earth", Scientific American, issue October 1996, p.42-47.
- Friedel, Helmut; Barnett, Vivian Endicott: "Das bunte Leben - Wassily Kandinsky im Lenbachhaus", DuMont Buchverlag, 1995, ISBN 3 7701 3785 X.
- Friedel, Helmut; Hoberg, Annegret; "The Blue Rider in the Lenbachhaus, Munich", Prestel Verlag, 2000, ISBN3 7913 2216 8.
- Friedman, B.H.; "Jackson Pollock - Energy Made Visible", DaCapo Press (NY), 1995 - orig. 1972, ISBN 0 3068 0664 9.
- Fritz-Jobse, Jonneke; Burkom, Frans van; "Een Nieuwe Synthese - Geometrisch-Abstracte Kunst in Nederland 1945-1960", SDU Uitgeverij, 1988, ISBN 9 0120 5728 0.

- Gabo, Naum; "Of Divers Arts", Faber and Faber, London, 1962.
- Gadamer, Hans-Georg; "Bildkunst und Wortkunst", essay in "Was ist ein Bild?", published by Gottfried Boehm, Wilhelm Fink Verlag, 1994 (see Boehm).
- Gadamer, Hans-Georg; "Die Aktualität des Schönen - Kunst als Spiel, Symbol und Fest", Philipp Reclam Stuttgart, 1995 (first edition 1977), ISBN 3 1500 9844 0.
- Gage, John; "Colour and Culture - Practice and Meaning from Antiquity to Abstraction", Thames and Hudson, 1993, ISBN 0 5002 3654 2.
- Gamwell, Lynn; "Exploring The Invisible - Art, Science, And The Spiritual", Princeton University Press, 2002, ISBN 0 6910 8972 8.
- Gardner, Howard; "The Mind's New Science - A History of the Cognitive Revolution", Basic Books, 1987, ISBN 0 4650 4635 5.
- Gasquet, Joachim; "Joachim Gasquet's Cézanne - A Memoir with Conversations", Thames and Hudson, 1991, ISBN 0 5000 9212 5.
- Gassner, Hubertus; "Alexander Rodschenko - Konstruktion 1920 - oder die Kunst, das Leben zu organisieren", Fischer Verlag GmbH #980, 1984, ISBN 3 5962 3916 8.
- Gassner, Hubertus; Nichtigäller, Roland; "Gustav Klucis Retrospektive", Verlag Gerd Hatje, Stuttgart, 1991, ISBN 3 7757 0327 6.
- Gehrels, Neil; Fichtel, Carl E.; Fishman, Gerald J.; Kurfess, James D.; Schönfelder, Volker; "The Compton Gamma Ray Observatory", Scientific American, issue December 1993, p.38-45.
- Genz, Henning; "Nothingness - The Science of Emptiness", Perseus Publishers, 2001 (orig. "Die Entdeckung des Nichts", 1998), ISBN 0 7382 0610 5.
- Gil, In-Soo; Park, Suun-Joon; "Secret and Beauty of the Korean Tea Bowl", 1993, printed in Korea.
- Gleick, James; "Chaos - de derde wetenschappelijke revolutie", Uitgeverij Contact, 1991 (orig. 1987 "Chaos:

making a new science"), ISBN 9 0254 6941 8.
- Gleizes, Albert; "Et le Cubisme", Basilius Presse AG, Basel, 1962.
- Gleizes, Albert; Metzinger, Jean; "Du Cubisme - Cubism - über den Kubismus", R.G. Fischer Verlag, 1993 (orig. 1912), ISBN 3 8940 6728 4.
- Glover, David M.; Gonzalez, Cayetano; Raff, Jordan W.; "The Centrosome", Scientific American, issue June 1993, p.32-38.
- Goethe, J.W.; "Kleurenleer", (Nederlandse vertaling) Uitgeverij Vrij Geestesleven Zeist, 1991, ISBN 9 0603 8267 6, (orig. "Entwurf einer Farbenlehre", 1810).
- Goerner, Veit; Sommer, Caroline; Schmidt, Katharina; "Gotthard Graubner - Farblicht", Kestner Gesellschaft, Hannover, 2003.
- Goerner, Veit; "Franz Gertsch - Sylvia", Kestner Gesellschaft, Hannover, 2003.
- Gohr, Siegfried; Luyken, Gunda; "Frederick J. Kiesler - Selected Writings", Verlag Gerd Hatje (Ostfildern), 1996, ISBN 3 7757 0628 3.
- Gould, Stephen Jay; "Leonardo's Mountain of Clams and the Diet of Worms - Essays on Natural History", Vintage Books, 1999 (orig. Jonathan Cape Ltd, 1998), ISBN 0 0992 8924 5.
- Gombrich, E.H.; "The Sense of Order, A study in the psychology of decorative art", Phaidon, second edition, 1984 (orig. 1979), ISBN 0 7148 2259 0.
- Grabar, Oleg; "The Mediation of Ornament", Princeton University Press, 1992, ISBN 0 6910 4099 0.
- Graevenitz, Antje von; "Endlessness and reduction, Friedrich Kieslers 'Endless House' ", Archis Magazine, issue November 1996, p.63-80.
- Greenberg, Marvin Jay; "Euclidian and Non-Euclidian Geometries - Development and History", Third Edition, W.H. Freeman and Co, NY, 1994, ISBN 0 7167 2446 4.
- Greenberg, Clement; "Art and Culture - Critical Essays", Beacon Press (Boston), 1965 (orig. 1961), ISBN 0 8070 6681 8.
- Greene, Brian; "The Elegant Universe - Superstrings, Hidden Dimensions, and the Quest for the Ultimate Theory", Vintage Books, 1999, ISBN 0 3757 0811 1.
- Gregory, R.L.; "Eye and Brain - the psychology of seeing", World University Library, 1971 (orig. 1966).
- Grohmann, Will; "Wassily Kandinsky - Life and Work", Harry N. Abrams Inc., New York, 1958.
- Gross, Paul R.; Levitt, Norman; Lewis, Martin W.; "The Flight From Science to Reason", Annals of the New York Academy of Sciences, Volume 775, 1996, ISBN 1 5733 1003 4.
- Gsell, Paul; "Rodin on Art and Artists - conversations with Paul Gsell", Dover Publications Inc., New York, 1983, ISBN 0 4862 4487 3.
- Guderian, Dietmar; "Mathematik in der Kunst der letzten dreißig Jahre, von der magischen Zahl über das endlose Band zum Computerprogramm", Wilhelm-Hack-Museum Ludwigshafen, 1987.
- Guderian, Dietmar; "Eine Lemniskate umschreitend Äußeres und Inneres erfahren", in "Lemniskatische Prozesse", Galerie Edition Stahlberger, Weil am Rhein, 1995, Kunstverlag Gotha, ISBN 3 9311 8205 3.
- Guerrero, Pedro E.; Rower, Alexander S.C.; "Calder at Home", an Archetype Press Book - Stewart, Tabor & Chang, 1998, ISBN 1 5567 0655 3.
- Guiheux, Alain; "Kisho Kurakawa - Le metabolisme 1960-1975", Centre Georges Pompidou, 1997, ISBN 2 8585 0935 2.

H

- Haeckel, Ernst; "Die Welträtsel - Gemeinverständliche Studien über Monistische Philosophie", Verlag von Emil Stramps, 1902 (orig. 1899).
- Hachmeister, Heiner; "Mark Tobey - Werke/Oeuvres 1945-1975", Verlag Hachmeister Galerie, 1991, ISBN 3 8882 9090 2.
- Haeckel, Ernst; "Die Lebenswunder - Gemeinverständliche Studien über Biologische Philosophie, Ergänzungsband zu dem Buche über die Welträtsel", Alfred Krone Verlag, Leipzig, 1906.
- Hakeda, Yoshito S.; "Kukai: Major Works", Columbia University Press, New York, 1972, ISBN 0 2310 5933 7.
- Haldemann, Matthias; "Kandinskys Abstraktion - Die Entstehung und Transformation seines Bildkonzeptes", Wilhelm Fink Verlag, 1998, ISBN 3 7705 3517 0.
- Halley, Peter; "Collected Essays 1981-87", Bischoffberger Gallery/Sonnabend Gallery, 1991 (orig.1988), ISBN 0 9324 9968 6.
- Hamlyn, Richard; "The Invention of Clouds - How an Amateur Meteorologist Forged the Language of the Skies", Picador, 2002 (orig. 2001), ISBN 0 3303 9195 X.

H

- Hammer, Martin; Lodder, Christina; "Constructing Modernity - The Art & Career of Naum Gabo", Yale University Press, 1999, ISBN 0 3000 7688 6.
- Hammer, Martin; Lodder, Christina; "Gabo On Gabo - Texts and Interviews", Artists Bookworks, 2000, ISBN 0 9463 1111 0.
- Harrist Jr., Robert E.; Fong, Wen C.; "The Embodied Image - Chinese Calligraphy from the John B. Elliott Collection", The Art Museum, Princeton University, 1999, ISBN 0 9430 1228 7.
- Hass, Robert; "The Essential Haiku - Versions of Basho, Buson & Issha", The Ecco Press, 1994, ISBN 0 8800 1372 9.
- Heckmanns, Friedrich W.; "Erich Buchholz", Wienand Verlag, 1978, ISBN 3 8790 9088 2.
- Hedgecoe, John; Damluji, Salma Samar; "Zilij - The Art of Maroccan Ceramics", Garnett Publishing Ltd, 1992, ISBN 1 8739 3802 0.
- Held, Barbara S.; "Constructivism in Psychotherapy - Truth and Consequences", in Gross, Paul R.; Levitt, Norman; Lewis, Martin W.; "The Flight From Science to Reason", see "Gross".
- Helfenstein, Josef; "Franz Gertsch - Die Holzschnitte", Verlag Lars Müller, Kunstmuseum Bern, 1994, ISBN 3 9067 0076 3.
- Hemken, Kai-Uwe; "El Lissitzky - Revolution und Avantgarde", DuMont Taschenbücher, 1990, ISBN 3 7701 2613 0.
- Hemken, Kai-Uwe; "Morphologie des Universums - Anmerkungen zu Werken Fré Ilgens in der Galerie Lüpke Frankfurt", Art Position Magazine, 5. Jahrgang, Heft 22, 1994.
- Hemken, Kai-Uwe; Stommer, Reiner; "K.I. - Konstruktivistische Internationale Schöpferische Arbeitsgemeinschaft 1922-1927 - Utopien für eine Europäische Kultur", Verlag Gerd Hatje, ISBN 3 7757 0376 4.
- Hemken, Kai-Uwe; Edmonds, Ernest; Beckmann, Mayen; Ilgen, Fré; "Fré Ilgen - The Search", FNA Foundation for the New Arts, 2001, ISBN 9 0806 3161 2.
- Henkel, Katharina; Bohlmann, Carolin; "Garten des Lebens - Ein Wandschirm von Pierre Bonnard", Nationalgalerie Berlin, DuMont Literatur und Kunstverlag Köln, 2002, ISBN 3 8321 7017 0.
- Henkels, Herbert; Sauwen, Rik; Viatte, Germain; Seuphor, Michel; "Seuphor", Gemeentemuseum Den Haag, Mercatorfonds NV, 1971, ISBN 9 0615 3083 0.
- Henrich, Dieter; Iser, Wolfgang; "Theorien der Kunst", Suhrkamp Tachenbuch - Wissenschaft, #1012, 1992 (orig. 1984), ISBN 3 5182 8612 9.
- Herbert, Robert L.; "Seurat - Drawings and Paintings", Yale University Press, 2001, ISBN 0 3000 7131 0.
- Herrigel, Eugen; "Zen and the Art of Archery", Pantheon Books Inc., 7th printing, 1963 (first edition 1953 - orig. "Zen in der Kunst des Bogenschiessens", Otto Wilhelm Barth Verlag, Munich).
- Hess, Walter; "Das Problem der Farbe - in den Selbstzeugnissen der Maler von Cézanne bis Mondrian", Mäander Verlag Munich, 1993 (orig. 1953), ISBN 3 88219 063 9.
- Heuvel, Edward P.J. van de; Paradijs, Jan van; "X-ray Binaries", Scientific American, issue November 1993, p.38-45.
- Hill, Tom; Hill, Richard W.; "Creation's Journey - Native American Identity and Belief", Smithsonian Institution Press & National Museum of the American Indian, 1994, ISBN 1 5609 8453 8.
- Hinterreiter, Hans; "Die Kunst der reinen Form - Eine Formenlehre für moderne Künstler, Band I - Ordnung und Taufe der Elementarformen", Ediciones Ebusus, Ibiza/Amsterdam, 1978 (facsimile druk, orig.1941).
- Hirose, Takashi; "Lectures on Shin Buddhism", Higashi Honganji Publication Department, Shinshu Otani-ha Shumusho, Karasuma Shichi-jo agaru, Shimogyo, Kyoto, Japan, revised edition 1988 (orig.1980).
- Hitchcock, Henry-Russell; Johnson, Philip; "Der Internationale Stil 1932", Friedr. Vieweg & Sohn Verlag, 1985, (orig. "The International Style: Architecture since 1922", 1966), ISBN 3 5280 8770 6.
- Hoek, Els; "Theo van Doesburg - Oeuvre Katalogus", Centraal Museum Utrecht, Kröller-Müller Museum Otterlo, 2000, ISBN 9 0686 8255 5.
- Hofmann, Werner; "Caspar David Friedrich - Naturwirklichkeit und Kunstwahrheit", Verlag C.H. Beck Munich, 2000 (orig. Editions Hazan Paris, 2000), ISBN 3 4064 6475 0.
- Hofstadter, Douglas R.; "Gödel, Escher, Bach: een eeuwige gouden band", Uitgeverij Contact, 5e druk 1988, (orig. "Gödel, Escher, Bach: an eternal golden braid" Basic Books Inc, 1979), ISBN 9 0254 6637 0.
- Holt, Donald; Holt, Janet; Isaacs, Jennifer; Smith, Terry; Ryan, Judith; "Emily Kngwarreye - Paintings", Craftsman House, G+B Arts International, 1998, ISBN 9 0570 3681 9.
- Holtzmann, Harry; James, Martin S.; "The New Art - The New Life - The Collected Writings of Piet

Mondrian", Da Capo Press, 1993, ISBN 0 3068 05081.
- Holz, Hans Heinz; "Die aesthetische Gegenstand - Philosophische Theorie der bildenden Künste I", Aisthesis Verlag, 1996, ISBN 3 8952 8155 7.
- Holz, Hans Heinz; "Strukturen der Darstellung - Philosophische Theorie der bildenden Künste II", Aisthesis Verlag, 1997, ISBN 3 8952 8164 6.
- Holz, Hans Heinz; "Zerfall der Bedeutungen - Philosophische Theorie der bildenden Künste III", Aisthesis Verlag, 1997, ISBN 3 8952 8194 8.
- Hölzinger, Johannes P.; de Bruyn, Gerd; "Der öffentliche Raum - ein Projekt des Deutschen Werkbund Hessen", Deutsche Werkbund Hessen e.V., ca. 1992.
- Hölzinger, Johannes P.; "Synthese des Arts - The Combination of Art and Architecture in the Government Buildings on the Hardthöhe in Bonn", Edition Axel Menger, London, Stuttgart, 1998, ISBN 3 9325 6509 6.
- Hoog, Michel; "The Nymphéas of Claude Monet at the Musée de l'Orange", Éditions de la Réunion des Musées Nationaux, 1990, ISBN 2 7118 2092 0.
- Hoogstad, Jan; "Ruimtetijdbeweging - Prolegomena voor de architektuur", SDU, 1990, ISBN 9 0120 6547 X. (English translation: see PRO-NR.9).
- Horgan, John; "The Death of Proof", Scientific American, issue October 1993, p.74-82.
- Horgan, John; "Can Science Explain Consciousness?", Scientific American, issue July 1994, p.72-78.
- Hrushesky, William J.M.; "Timing is Everything", The Sciences, issue July/August 1994, p.32.
- Hughes, Paul; "Time Warps - Ancient Andean Textiles", Sammlung Hauser & Wirth and Paul Hughes Fine Textile Art, 1995, ISBN 0 9525 8160 4.
- Hughes, Robert; "Amish - The Art of the Quilt", Alfred A.Knopf Callaway, Esprit De Corp., 1990, ISBN 0 3945 8781 2.
- Hull, Alastair; Luczyc-Wyhowska, Jose; "Kilim - The Complete Guide", Thames & Hudson, 1993, ISBN 0 5000 1565 1.
- Husserl, Edmund; "Ideas - General Introduction to Pure Phenomenology", Collier MacMillan Publishers, 1962; (orig. "Ideen einer reinen Phänomenologie und phänomenologische Philosophie", 1913), ISBN 0 0206 5910 5.
- Hutton Galeries, Leonard; "César Domela 1900-1912, Sculptures, Reliefs, and Gouaches", Leonard Hutton Galeries New York, 2002.
- Hüttinger, Eduard; "Max Bill", ABC Verlag Zürich, 1978, ISBN 3 8550 4043 5.
- Huyler, Stephen P.; "Die Bilder Indiens", Frederking & Thales GmbH, 1994 (orig. Rizzoli Int.Publ.Inc. NY), ISBN 3 8940 5332 1.

- Iijima, Harumi; Iijima, Tahiro; Takahashi, Hideo; Shogei bunka-shinsha; Nagoya, Akira; Isazawa, Yuko; Satoh, Rumi; Togawa, Naoki, e.o.; "Heartvines: Court Calligraphy from the Heian Era", The Gotoh Museum, Tokyo, 2000.
- Ilgen, Fré; "The moment man realizes there is no reason for his existence the resulting emptiness gives serious reason for creation - PROGCY 1980-1988", Stichting PRO, 1988.
- Ilgen, Fré (AIVE); "Kleur-syllabus naar aanleiding van de lezingcyclus", AIVE Studium Generale, 1992.
- Ilgen, Fré; "Jean-Pierre Maury - Equivalent Dynamic Interaction As Concept of Being", catalogue "Jean-Pierre Maury - Recent Paintings and Soft Inks", Galerie Emile Verhaeren, Knokke, 1993.
- Ilgen, Fré; "Fré Ilgen - 'Canst Thou by Searching Describe the Universe?' Whitehead", Stichting PRO, 1993.
- Ilgen, Fré; "The Real Notion of Interactivity in Design", paper international conference "Design: Pleasure or Responsibility?", UIAH Helsinki, Finland, 1994.
- Ilgen, Fré; "Das Erweiterte Selbst - Das Objekt-Der Raum und Die Wirklichkeitswahrnehmung, über die Bedeutung des visuellen Arguments", paper Design Zentrum Stuttgart and Galerie Beatrix Wilhelm, 1994.
- Ilgen, Fré; "Extensionalism and Twistor Space: Similarities and Relations between Art and Twistor Theory", paper symposium "Creativity&Cognition 1", Loughborough University, England, published in LEONARDO magazine, Vol. 28 Nr.3, MIT Press, USA, 1995.
- Ilgen, Fré; "Gestaltung als Verbindung zwischen Denken und Handeln", paper HTL-Chur, Vortragsreihe Kunst und Architektur, 1995.
- Ilgen, Fré; "The Synchronizing Self - A Search for Harmony as a Process of Symmetry Breaking", paper in Proceedings "Katachi u Symmetry", Springer Verlag Tokyo, 1996, ISBN 4 4317 0161 3.
- Ilgen, Fré; "The Process of Self-Argumentation in the Projective Field - Design as Connection between

I

Thinking and Acting", paper international symposium "Creativity&Cognition 2", Loughborough University, England, 1996.
- Isozaki, Arata; Sato, Osamu; "Katsura - Der Kaiserpalast in Kyoto", Belser Verlag Stuttgart/Zürich, 1993 (orig. "Katsura Villa - Space and Form", 1983), ISBN 3 7630 2096 9.

J

- Jablonka, Rafael; "Philip Taaffe - Ten Paintings", Jablonka Gallery, Cologne, 2002, ISBN 3 9313 5416 1.
- Jaffé, H.L.C.; "Theo van Doesburg", Meulenhoff/Landshoff, 1983, ISBN 9 0290 8272 0.
- Jaffé, Hans L.C.; "De Stijl: 1917-1931 Visions of Utopia", Walker Art Center, ISBN 0 8965 9965 5.
- Jager, Henk de; Matthes, Hendrik G.; Schoenmakers, M.H.J.; "Het beeldende denken - Leven en werk van Matthieu Schoenmakers", Ambo Baarn, 1992, ISBN 9 0263 1151 6.
- Janaway, Christopher; "The Cambridge Companion to Schopenhauer", Cambridge University Press, 1999, ISBN 0 5216 2106 2.
- Janson, H.W.; "Wereldgeschiedenis van de kunst", translated by J.F. Kliphuis, Nederlandse Boekenclub (orig. Harry N. Abrams, Inc.), 1976.
- Jasper, Dr. Uwe Jens; "Raimer Jochims - Papierarbeiten - Malbücher - Zeichnungen 1975-1995", Hans Thoma Gesellschaft, Kunstverein Reutlingen, 1995.
- Jeanloz, Raymond; Lay, Thorne; "The Core-Mantle Boundary", Scientific American, issue May 1993, p.26-33.
- Jenny, Hans; "Kymatik - Wellen und Schwingungen mit ihrer Struktur und Dynamik", Band 2, Basilius Presse, Basler Druck- und Verlagsanstalt, Basel, 1972, ISBN 3 8556 0031 7.
- Jerome, Richard; "Animals and Magnetism", The Sciences, issue January/February 1993, p.7.
- Juda, Annely; "Kenneth and Mary Martin", Annely Juda Fine Art, 1987, ISBN 1 8702 8004 0.
- Juda, Annely and David; "Max Bill, Georges Vantongerloo - A Working Friendship", Annely Juda Fine Art, 1996, ISBN 1 8702 8057 1.
- Juda, Annely and David; "Naum Gabo", Annely Juda Fine Art, 1999, ISBN 1 8702 8075 X.
- Judd, Donald; "Complete Writings 1975-1986", Van Abbemuseum Eindhoven, 1987, ISBN 9 0701 4917 6.
- Jung, C.G.; "Der Mensch und seine Symbole", 6.Auflage, Sonderausgabe, Walter Verlag Olten, 1982 (orig. 1968), ISBN 3 5305 016.
- Jung, C.G.; "Grundwerk - Band 2 - Archetyp und Unbewußtes", Walter Verlag, 1990, ISBN 3 5304 0782 8.

K

- Kaiser, Franz-W.; Pontegnie, Anne; Todoli, Vicente; "Hartung 3x", Expressions contemporaines, Fondation Hans Hartung et Anna-Eva Bergman, 2003, ISBN 2 9091 6612 0.
- Kaminski, Marion; "Tiziano Vecellio, known as Titian 1488/1490 - 1576", Koenemann Verlagsgesellschaft GmbH, 1998, ISBN 3 8290 0257 2.
- Kandinsky, Wassily; "Concerning the Spiritual in Art", Dover Publications Inc, 1977 (orig. "Über das Geistige in der Kunst", in Engels "The Art of Spiritual Harmony", 1914), ISBN 0 4862 3411 8.
- Kandinsky, Wassily; "Point and Line to Plane", Dover Publications Inc, 1979, ISBN 0-486-23808-3, (orig. "Punkt und Linie zu Fläche", 1926).
- Kandinsky, Nina; "Kandinsky und ich - Mein Leben mit einem grossen Künstler", Knaur Nr.72226, 1999 orig. 1976), ISBN 3 4267 2226 7.
- Kandrup, Henry E.; Gottesman, Stephen T.; Ipser, James R.; "Three Dimensional Systems", Annals of the New York Academy of Sciences - Volume 751, 1995, ISBN 0 8976 6926 6.
- Karmel, Pepe; "Jackson Pollock: Interviews, Articles, and Reviews", The Museum of Modern Art, New York, Harry N. Abrams Inc., 1999, ISBN 0 8707 0037 5.
- Kassak, Ludwig; Nagy, Moholy; "Buch Neuer Künstler- 1922", reprint Verlag Lars Müller, 1991, ISBN 3 9067 0037 2.
- Kawamura, Eiko; "Das Problem von Chaos und Kosmos im Zen-Buddhismus", in "Strukturen des Chaos", Wilhelm Fink Verlag, Munich, ca 1994.
- Kedourie, Elie; "The Jewish World", Thames & Hudson, 1979, ISBN 0 5002 5066 9.
- Kemp, Gerald van der; "Une visite a Giverny", Musée Claude Monet, Giverny.
- Keiner, Marion; Kurtz, Thomas; Nadin, Mihai; "Manfred Mohr", Waser Verlag und Viviane Ehrli, 1994, ISBN 3 9080 8039 8.
- Kendall, Richard; "Monet by Himself", Chartwell Books Inc., New Jersey, 2001 (orig. 1988), ISBN 0 7858 0670 9.
- Kennedy, Brian; Dodge, Alan R.; "Monet & Japan", National Gallery of Australia, 2001, ISBN 0 6425 4135 3.

K

- Kennedy, John M.; "How the Blind Draw", Scientific American, issue January 1997, p.50-65.
- Kepes, Gyorgy; "The Nature and Art of Motion", Studio Vista London, 1965.
- Kepes, Gyorgy; "Struktur in Kunst und Wissenschaft", La Connaissance Brüssel, 1967 (uit serie "Sehen + Werten", orig. "Vision + Value" series).
- Kepes, Gyorgy; "Arts of the Environment", Vision + Value Series, Aidan Ellis, England, 1972, ISBN 0 8562 8004 6.
- Kepler Gesellschaft; "Kepler-Museum in Weil der Stadt", Kepler Gesellschaft, Weil der Stadt, 1982.
- Khan, Hazrat Inayat; "The Inner Life", Shambala, Boston and London, 1997, ISBN 1 5706 2209 4.
- Killer, Peter; Postiglione, Corey; "James Juszczyk", Waser Verlag + Viviane Ehrli, 1991, ISBN 3 9080 8031 2.
- King, Lyndel; Larsen, Susan C.; McDonnell, Patricia; "Charles Biederman", Frederick Weisman Art Museum, University of Minnesota Press, 2003, ISBN 0 8166 4385 7.
- Kirwan, James; "Beauty", Manchester University Press, 1999, ISBN 0 7190 5572 5.
- Kitagawa, Fram; Kimura, Mitsuhiro; "A 'New Century' for City and Public Art - Faret Tachikawa Art Project", Gendaikika Kushitsu Publishers, Tokyo, Japan, 1995.
- Kitagawa, Joseph; "On Understanding Japanese Religion", Princeton University Press, 1987, ISBN 0 6911 0229 5.
- Klein, Adalbert; "Japanische Keramik - Kunstwerke historischer Epochen und der Gegenwart", Hetjens Museum, Museum für Ostasiatische Kunst, Lindenmuseum, 1978.
- Klotz, Heinrich; Fischer, Volker; Gleininger-Neumann, Andrea; Schwarz, Hans-Peter; "Vision der Moderne, Das Prinzip Konstruktion", D.A.M., Prestel Verlag, 1986, ISBN 3 7913 0755 X.
- Klotz, Heinrich; "Matjuschin und die Leningrader Avantgarde", ZKM Karlsruhe, Oktogon Verlag, 1991 ISBN 3 9277 8909 7.
- Kloyber, Christian; "Wolfgang Paalen's DYN - The Complete Reprint", Springer Verlag, 2000, ISBN 3 2118 3374 9.
- König, Kaspar; "Raimer Jochims - Bilder und Vorbilder", Portikus, Frankfurt am Main, 1990, ISBN 3 9280 7100 9.
- Koninklijke Musea voor Schone Kunsten van België; "Georges Vantongerloo 1886-1965", Koninklijke Musea voor Schone Kunsten van België, 1981.
- Konishi, Masakazu; "Listening with Two Ears", Scientific American, issue April 1993, p.34-41.
- Kosinski, Dorothy; Andel, Jaroslav; "Frantisek Kupka - Die abstrakten Farben des Universums", Verlag Gerd Hatje, 1997, ISBN 3 7757 0692 5.
- Kosko, Bart; Isaku, Satoru; "Fuzzy Logic", Scientific American, issue July 1993, p.62-67.
- Koslow, Arnold; "The Changeless Order - The Physics of Space, Time and Motion", Georg Brazilier, New York, 1967.
- Kotte, Wouter; "Joegoslavisch Konstruktivisme 1921-1981", Hedendaagse Kunst Utrecht, 1983.
- Kowalska, Bozena; "Henryk Stazewski", Arkady Warsaw, 1985, ISBN 8 3213 3098 3.
- Kraetz, Otto; "Goethe und die Naturwissenschaften", Callwey Verlag München, 1998.
- Krempel, Ulrich; "ARATJARA - Art of the First Australians", DuMont Buchverlag Cologne, Kunstsammlung Nordrhein-Westfalen Düsseldorf, 1993, ISBN 3 9261 5417 9.
- Krempel, Ulrich; Elger, Dietmar; Nobis, Norbert; "Sprengel Museum Hannover: El Lissitzky 'Proun 30t' von 1920", Kulturstiftung der Länder Berlin, 2000, ISSN 0 9417 036.
- Krückmann, Peter O.; "Tiepolo in Würzburg - Der Himmel auf Erden", Band I + II, Prestel Verlag, 1996, ISBN 3 7913 1639 7.
- Krumenaker, Larry; "Rhythm Section - The pulse of planetary cycles, recorded deep in New Jersey shale", The Sciences, issue November/December 1995, p.14-17.
- Kubler, George; "The Shape of Time - Remarks on the history of things", Yale University Press, 1962, ISBN 0 3000 0144 4.
- Kugler, Walter; "Rudolf Steiner und die Anthropologie", DuMont Taschenbücher, 1991, ISBN 3 7701 2784 6.
- Kuhns, Richard; "Psychoanalytische Theorie als Kunstphilosophie", in "Theorien der Kunst", Suhrkamp Taschenbuch Wissenschaft, (orig. "Psychoanalytic Theory as a Philosophy of Art"), 1012, ISBN 3 5182 8612 9.
- Kunsthalle Tübingen; "Kandinsky - 'Die Welt klingt' - Hauptwerke aus dem Centre Georges Pompidou", DuMont, Köln, 1999, ISBN 3 7701 4991 2.
- Kunsthaus Zürich; "Walter Linck 1903-1975", 1990.
- Kunstmuseum Bern; "Franz Gertsch - Holzschnitte - Die Kunst liegt in der Natur - Wer sie herausreissen

kann der hat sie", Verlag Lars Müller, 1994, ISBN 3 9066 28 043.
- Kunstmuseum Winterthur; Koella, Dr. Rudolf; Vachtová, Dr. Ludmilla; "Dreissig Jahre Schweiz Konstruktive Kunst 1915-45", Kunstmuseum Winterthur, 1981.
- Kunstverein Grafschaft Bentheim; "Sinn Für Farbe - Franz Gertsch, Raimer Jochims, Ricardo Saro", Kunstverein Grafschaft Bentheim, Galerie Karin Fesel, Düsseldorf, 1995, ISBN 3 9268 20 5.
- Küper, Marijke; Zijl, Ida; "Gerrit Th. Rietveld - Het volledige werk", Centraal Museum Utrecht, 1992, ISBN 9 0732 8516 X.
- Kuspit, Donald; "Art as the Morale Imperative", New Art Examiner, January 1991, blz.23-25.
- Kuspit, Donald; "The Dialectic of Decadence", Stux Press, 1993, ISBN 0 9628 4180 3.
- Kuspit, Donald; "The Cult of the Avant-Garde Artist", Cambridge University Press, 1993, ISBN 0 5214 1345 1.
- Kuspit, Donald; "Signs of Psyche in Modern and Post-Modern Art", Cambridge University Press, 1995 (orig.1993), ISBN 0 5214 4611 2.
- Kuspit, Donald; Gamwell, Lynn; "Health and Happiness in 20th Century Avant-Garde Art", Cornell University Press, Binghamton University Art Museum, 1996, ISBN 0 8014 3279 0.
- Kuspit, Donald; "Idiosyncratic Identities", Cambridge University Press, 1996, ISBN 0 5215 5652 X.
- Kuspit, Donald; "Fré Ilgen - Mystical Constructions", Maxwell Davidson Gallery, 1998.
- Kuspit, Donald; "Psychostrategies of Avant-Garde Art", Cambridge University Press, 2000, ISBN 0 5214 5277 5.
- Kuspit, Donald; "The End of Art", Cambridge University Press, 2004, ISBN 0 5218 3252 7.
- Kwiat, Paul; Weinfurter, Harald; Zeilinger, Anton; "Quantum Seeing in the Dark", Scientific American, issue November 1996, p.52-58.

L

- Lacoste, Michel Conil; "Kandinsky", Bonfini Press, Naefels, Switzerland, 1979.
- Landau, Ellen G.; "Jackson Pollock", Harry N. Abrams Inc., 2000 (orig. Abradale Press, 1989), ISBN 0 8109 3702 6.
- Lane, John R.; Larsen, Susan C.; "Abstract Painting and Sculpture in America 1927-1944", Museum of Art, Carnegie Institute Pittsburgh, Harry N. Abrams Inc. Publishers, New York, 1983, ISBN 0 8803 9006 9.
- Lang, Kenneth R.; "Sun, Earth and Sky", Springer Verlag Berlin-Heidelberg New York, 1995, ISBN 3 5405 8778 0.
- Lang, Lloyd and Jennifer; "Art of the Celts", Thames and Hudson, 1992, ISBN 0 5002 0256 7.
- Lauter, Marlene; Reese, Beate; "Form Schichten - Farbstrahlen, Aspekte russischer und osteuropäischer Kunst - Eine Ausstellung aus Anlass des Jubiläums '100 Jahre Röntgenstrahlen'", Städtische Galerie Würzburg, 1995, ISBN 3 9281 5527 X.
- Laurentieu, Alexander; "Alexander Rodchenko - Spatial Constructions", Galerie Gmurzynska, Hatje - Cantz Verlag, 2000, ISBN 3 7757 1178 3.
- Lazzaro, G. di San; Lassaigne, Jacques; "Hommage to Wassily Kandinsky", special issue of the XXe siecle Review, Leon Amiel Publisher, New York, 1975, ISBN 0 8148 0634 1.
- Leclerc, Ivor; "The Nature of Physical Existence", University Press of America, 1986, ISBN 0 8191 4853 9.
- Lehr, Dr. J.J.; "De draaikolk als model voor mikro- en makrokosmos", de Erven Lehr, ISBN 9 0900 2111 6.
- Leibniz, Gottfried Wilhelm; "Metaphysische Abhandlung", (French-German) Felix Meiner Verlag, 1991 (2.Auflage, 1.Auflage 1958; orig. "Discours de Métaphysique", 1686), ISBN 3 7873 0657 9.
- Leibniz, Gottfried Wilhelm; "Monadologie" (French-German), Philipp Reclam jun. Stuttgart, 1998, ISBN 3 1500 7853 9.
- Leibniz, Gottfried Wilhelm; "Fünf Schriften zur Logik und Metaphysik", Philipp Reclam jun. Stuttgart, 1999, ISBN 3 1500 1898 6.
- Leistner, Gerhard; Rodiek, Thorsten; "Otto Freundlich - Ein Wegbereiter der abstrakten Kunst", Ostdeutsche Galerie Regensburg, 1995, ISBN 3 8918 8068 5.
- Lemoine, Serge; Contensou, Bernadette; "Domela - 65 Ans d'Abstraction", Édition Paris Musées, SAMAM, Musée de Grenoble, 1987, ISBN 9 7828 5346 0378.
- Lemoine, Serge; "Mondrian and De Stijl", Art Data, 1987, ISBN 0 9488 3504 4.
- Lemoine, Serge; "Aux origines de l'abstraction 1800-1910", Musée d'Orsay, Éditions de la Réunion des musées nationaux, 2003, ISBN 2 7118 4608 3.
- Levitas, Gloria B.; "Culture and Consciousness - Perspectives in the Social Sciences", George Braziller

New York, 1967.
- Levin, Gail; Lorenz, Marianne; "Theme & Improvisation: Kandinsky & The American Avant-Garde 1912-1950", Dayton Art Institute, a Bullfish Press Book; Little, Brown and Company (Boston, Toronto, London), 1992, ISBN 0 8212 1921 9.
- Lewis, David; "Die Maori - Die Erben Tanis", Werner Forman, Atlantis Verlag, 1988, ISBN 3 7611 0721 8.
- Lewis-Williams, David; Bannister, Anthony; "Bushmen - A changing Way of Life", Struik Publishers, 1991, ISBN 1 8682 5178 0.
- Lévi-Strauss, Claude; "Structural Anthropology", Basic Books, 1963, SBN 4 6508 2297.
- Lieber, Eduard; "Willem de Kooning - Reflections in the Studio", Harry N. Abrams Inc. Publishers, 2000, ISBN 0 8109 4560 6.
- Lindsay, Kenneth C.; Vergo, Peter; "Kandinsky - Complete Writings of Art", DaCapo Press, New York, 1994 (orig. Éditions Denoel, Paris, 1970), ISBN 0 3068 0570 7.
- Lipman, Jean; Wolfe, Ruth; "Calder's Universe", Running Press, 1989, ISBN 0 8947 1777 4.
- Lippencott, Kristin; "The Story of Time", Merrel Holberton Publishers, London, National Maritime Museum, 1999, ISBN 18589 4072 9.
- Lissitzky, El; Arp, Hans; "The Isms of Art 1914-1924", reprint Lars Müller, 1990, ISBN 3 9067 0028 3.
- Lissitzky-Küppers, Sophie; Read, Herbert; "El Lissitzky - Life-Letters - Texts", Thames and Hudson, 1992 (orig. Verlag der Kunst, Dresden, 1967), ISBN 0 5002 3090 0.
- Little, Stephen; Eichman, Shawn; "Taoism and the Arts of China", The Art Institute of Chicago, University of California Press, 2000, ISBN 0 5202 2784 0.
- Loers, Veit; "Lászlo Moholy Nagy", Verlag Gerd Hatje, 1991, ISBN 3 7757 0344 6.
- Luckiesh, Matthew; "Visual Illusions - Their Causes, Characteristics and Applications", introduction by William H. Ittelson, Dover Publications, Inc., NY, 1965 (orig. 1922).
- Lynton, Norbert; "Victor Pasmore, Paintings and Etchings 1980-92", Lund Humphries London, 1992, ISBN 0 8533 1606 6.

- Maan, Dick; van der Ree, John; "Typo-Foto/Elementaire typografie in Nederland 1920-40", Veen/Reflex, 1990, ISBN 9 0632 2157 6.
- MacNulty, W. Kirk; "Freemasonry - A Journey through Ritual and Symbol", Thames and Hudson, London, 1991, ISBN 0 5008 1037 0.
- Malin, David; "A View of the Universe", Sky Publishing Corporation and Cambridge University Press, 1995 (orig. 1993), ISBN 0 5214 4477 2.
- Martin, J.L.; Nicholson, Ben; Gabo, Naum; "Circle, international survey of Constructive Art", reprinted by Praeger Publishers (NY, Washington), 1971.
- Marzano, Stefano; "Flying over Las Vegas", EDC News Special September 1993, European Design Center, NL.
- Matheson, John; "Paul Suter", Galerie Dr. István Schlégl, Edition Franz Mäder Basel, 1992, ISBN 3 9054 8330 6.
- Matt, Daniel C.; "The Essential Kabbalah - The Heart of Jewish Mysticism", Harper San Francisco, 1994, ISBN 0 0625 1164 5.
- Mattenklott, Gert; "Karl Blossfeldt - Urformen der Kunst - Wundergarten der Natur", Schirmer/Mosel, 1994, ISBN 3 8881 4718 2.
- Maury, Jean-Pierre; Husquinet, Jean Pierre; + colleagues; "Mésures - Art International", magazine 6 issues published by group of artists around Maury/Husquinet, Belgium, 1988-1996.
- Mayer, Rudolf; Schmidt, Werner; Dittrich, Christian; "Hermann Glöckner - Die Tafels 1919-1985", Hermann Glöckner Archiv, Galerie und Verlag Beatrix Wilhelm, Stuttgart, 1992, ISBN 3 9237 1775.
- Meech, Julia; "Frank Lloyd Wright and the Art of Japan - The Architect's Other Passion", Japan Society and Harry N. Abrams Inc. Publishers, 2001, ISBN 0 8109 4563 0.
- Merkert, Jörn; Prinz, Ursula; "George Rickey in Berlin 1967-1992", Ars Nicolai, 1992, ISBN 3 9278 7320 9.
- Mertens, Phil; "Vorticism", ICSAC Cahier 8/9, edited by Andrew Wilson, ICSAC Internationaal Centrum voor Struktuuranalyse en Constructivisme, Brussel, 1988, ISSN 0 7717 636.
- Messer, Thomas M.; "Frantisek Kupka 1871-1957 A Retrospective", The Solomon R. Guggenheim Museum, New York, 1975.
- Messer, Thomas M.; "Kandinsky in Munich 1896-1914", Solomon R. Guggenheim Museum, New York, 1982, ISBN 0 8920 7030 7.

M

- Messer, Thomas M.; "Kandinsky: Russian and Bauhaus Years 1915-1933", Solomon R. Guggenheim Museum, New York, 1983, ISBN 0 8920 7044 7.
- Messer, Thomas M.; "Kandinsky in Paris 1934-1944", Solomon R. Guggenheim Museum, New York, 1985, ISBN 0 8920 7049 8.
- Metzinger, Fritz; "Albert Gleizes/Jean Metzinger - Du 'Cubisme'/On 'Cubism'/über den 'Kubismus' ", reprint, R.G. Fischer Verlag, 1993 (orig.1912), ISBN 3 8940 6728 4.
- Meurant, Georges; "Shoowa Motieven - Afrikaanse textiel van het Kuba rijk", Gemeente Krediet, 1986, ISBN 9 0506 6002 9.
- Meuris, Jacques; "Mondrian", Nouvelles Éditions Françaises, 1991, ISBN 2 7079 0027 3.
- Meyer, Esther da Costa; Wasserman, Fred; "Schoenberg, Kandinsky, and the Blue Rider", The Jewish Museum and Scala Publishers, New York, 2003, ISBN 1 8575 9312 X.
- Micha, Rene; "Helion", Flammarion, 1979.
- Miller, Arthur I.; "Imagery in Scientific Thought - Creating 20th Century Physics", MIT Press, (first edition 1984) 1987, ISBN 0 2626 3104 0.
- Miller, Arthur I.; "Insights in Genius - Imagery and Creativity in Science and Art", MIT Press, 2000, ISBN 0 2626 3199 7.
- Miller, Arthur I.; "Einstein, Picasso - Space, Time and the Beauty That Causes Havoc", Basic Books, 2001, ISBN 0 4650 1860 2.
- Milner, John; "The exhibition 5 x 5 = 25 - Its background and significance", Helikon - Van Gennep - Artists Bookworks - König, 1992, ISBN 0 9463 1106 4.
- "Mind and Brain", Scientific American special issue September 1992.
- The Minneapolis Institute of Arts; "Charles Biederman: A Retrospective", The Minneapolis Institute of Arts, 1976.
- Minor, Vernon Hyde; "Baroque & Rococo - Art & Culture", Laurence King Publishing, 1999, ISBN 1 8566 9173 X.
- Möbuss, Susanne; "Schopenhauer für Anfänger - Die Welt als Wille und Vorstellung - Eine Lese-Einführung", Deutscher Taschenbuch Verlag, 1998, ISBN 3 4233 0672 6.
- Moholy-Nagy, L.; "Vom Material zu Architektur", reprint by Florian Kupferberg, 1968 (orig. Neue Bauhausbücher, 1929), ISBN 0 1404 3339 2.
- Moortgat, Elisabeth; Hüneke, Andreas; Meier, Annette; "Der Blaue Reiter", Ausstellungsmagazin Brückemuseum, Museumspädagogischer Dienst Berlin, 1998.
- Morgan, Robert C.; "Between Modernism and Conceptual Art, A Critical Response", McFarland & Company Inc. Publishers, 1997, ISBN 0 7864 0332 2.
- Morgan, Robert C.; "The End of the Art World", Allworth Press, New York, School of Visual Arts, 1998, ISBN 1 5811 5010 5.
- Morgan, Robert C.; "Natvar Bhavsar - The Sound of Color", Sundaram Tagore Gallery, New York, 2000.
- Morgan, Robert C.; "Clement Greenberg - Last Writings", University of Minnesota Press, 2003, ISBN 0 8166 3938 8.
- Morgan, Robert C.; "Cultural Globalization and the Artist" ("Sztuka w Wieku Kultury Globalnej"), Lodz Biennale, Muzeum Artystow dia Lodz Biennale, 2003.
- Morschel, Jürgen; "Norbert Kricke", Verlag Gerd Hatje, 1976, ISBN 3 7757 0114 1.
- Motherwell, Robert; "The Documents of 20th Century Art: The Blaue Reiter Almanac, edited by Wassily Kandinsky and Franz Marc", edited by Klaus Lankheit, The Viking Press, 1974, ISBN 6 7017 355 X.
- Motherwell, Robert; "The Documents of 20th Century Art: The New Art of Color - The Writings of Robert and Sonia Delaunay", edited by Arthur A. Cohen, translated by David Shapiro and Arthur A. Cohen, The Viking Press, 1978, ISBN 0 6705 0636 2.
- Mowry, Robert D.; "World Within Worlds - The Richard Rosenblum Collection of Chinese Scholars' Rocks", Harvard University Art Museums (Cambridge, MA), 1997, ISBN 0 9167 2492 1.
- Mukerjee, Madhusree; "Trends in Theoretical Physics: Explaining Everything", Scientific American, issue January 1996, p.72-78.
- Mukerjee, Madhusree; "Profile: Albert Libchaber - Seeing the World in a Snowflake", Scientific American, issue March 1996, p.23-25.
- Müller, Lars; "Josef Müller-Brockmann Gestalter", Verlag Lars Müller, 1994, ISBN 3 9067 0039 9.
- Müller, Lars; "Vesc, Objet, Gegenstand - Berlin 1922, Il'ja Erenburg/El Lisickij", reprint Verlag Lars Müller, 1994, ISBN 3 9067 0062 3.

- Nagata, Seiji; "Hokusai - Genius of the Japanese Ukiyo-e", translated by John Bester (Tokyo, New York, London: Kodansha International, 1995), ISBN 4 7700 1928 9.
- Nagy, Dénes; Darvas, György; "ISIS-Symmetry", periodicle of ISIS Symmetry, ISSN 0 8654 824.
- Naifeh, Steven; Smith, Gregory White; "Jackson Pollock - An American Saga", Clarkson N. Potter Inc., New York, 1989, ISBN 0 5175 6084 4.
- Nakamura, Hajime; "Ways of Thinking of Eastern Peoples - India, China, Tibet, Japan", University of Hawaii Press, 1964, ISBN 0 8248 0078 8.
- Nakata, Yojiro; "The Art of Japanse Calligraphy", Weatherhill/Heibonsha, 1983 (orig. 1973), ISBN 0 8348 1013 1.
- Nakov, Andréi; "L' Avant-Garde Russe", Fernand Hazan, 1984, ISBN 2 8502 5066 10.
- Nakov, Andréi B.; "Stenberg 4-2-2-4", Annely Juda Fine Art, IDEA Books, 1975.
- Napier, Elizabeth R.; "Wassily Kandinsky 'Sounds'", Yale University Press, New Haven and London, 1981, ISBN 0 3000 2510 6.
- Nash, Steven A.; Merkert, Jörn; "Naum Gabo - Sixty Years of Constructivism", Prestel Verlag, 1987, ISBN 3 7913 0742 8.
- Nauenberg, Michael; Stroud, Carlos; Yeazell, John; "The Classical Limit of an Atom - By creating ultra large atoms, physicists hope to study how the old physics of the quantum world becomes the classical mechanics of everyday experience", Scientific American, issue June 1994, p.24-29.
- Nesme, Ribes; Baliunas, Sallie; Sokoloff, Dmitry; "The Stellar Dynamo", Scientific American, issue August 1996, p.30-36.
- Newcombe, Franc J.; Reichard, Gladys A.; "Sandpaintings of the Navajo Shooting Chant", Dover Publications Inc., 1975 (orig. published by J.J. Augustin, New York, 1937), ISBN 0 4862 3141 0.
- Newman, Teresa; "Naum Gabo - The Constructive Process", The Tate Gallery, 1976, ISBN 0 9050 0565 1.
- Nietzsche, Friedrich; "The Birth of Tragedy", translated by Shaun Whiteside, edited by Michael Tanner, Penguin Group, 1993 (orig. 1872), ISBN 0 1404 3339 2.
- Neufert, Andreas; "Wolfgang Paalen - Im Inneren des Wals", Springer Verlag, 1999, ISBN 3 2118 3304 8.
- Nishida, Kitaro; "Intuition and Reflection in Self-Consciousness", State University of New York Press, 1987 (orig. "Jikaku ni okeru chokkan to han sei", 1941), ISBN 0 8870 6370 5.
- Nishida, Kitaro; "Last Writings - Nothingness and the Religious Worldview", University of Hawaii Press, 1987 (orig. 1946), ISBN 0 8248 1554 8.
- Nishida, Kitaro; "Über das Gute", translated in German by Peter Pörtner, Insel Verlag, second edition 1990 (orig. "Zen no kenkyu", 1911; first edition Insel Verlag 1989), ISBN 3 4581 6557 6.
- Nishitani, Keiji; "Religion and Nothingness", University of California Press, Berkely, 1982, ISBN 0 5200 4946 2.
- Nitschke, Günter; "From Shinto to Ando - Studies in architectural anthropology in Japan", Academy Editions, Ernst & Sohn, ISBN 1 8549 0291 1.
- Nobis, Norbert; "El Lissitzky 1890-1941 Retrospektive", Sprengel Museum Hannover, 1988, ISBN 3 549 066 805.
- Nobis, Norbert; Pollmann, Ute; "Ella Bergmann-Michel 1895-1971", Sprengel Museum Hannover, 1990, ISBN 3 8916 9054 1.
- Nobis, Norbert; "Der Lärm der Strasse - Italienischer Futurismus 1909-1918", Sprengel Museum Hannover, Edizione Gabriele Mazzotta, Milano, 2001, ISBN 8 8202 1454 7.

- Oberhuber, Konrad; Vitali, Christoph: "Two Pioneers of Modern Art - I: Frantisek Kupka, from the Jan and Meda Mladek Collection" and "Two Pioneers of Modern Art - II: Otto Gutfreund, from the Jan and Meda Mladek Collection", Graphische Sammlung Albertina, Wien, Haus der Kunst München, Ceske Muzeum Vytvarnych Umeni, 1996, ISBN 8 0705 6053 3.
- Ogawa, T.; Miura, K.; Masunari, T.; Nagy, D.; "Katachi u Symmetry", Springer Verlag Tokyo, 1996, ISBN 4- 4317 0161 3.
- Ohashi, Ryosuke; "Kire - Das "Schöne" in Japan - Philosophisch-ästhetische Reflexionen zu Geschichte und Moderne", DuMont Verlag, 1994, ISBN 3 7701 3252 1.
- d' Orgeval, Domitille; "re-Connaitre - Felix del Marle", Musée de Grenoble, 2000, ISBN 2 7118 3804 8.
- Otto, Frei; "Lightweight Structures in Architecture and Nature", Information of the Institute for Lightweight Structures IL Nr. 32, 1983.

O

- Ouspensky, P.D.; "Tertium Organum - De derde canon van het denken - een sleutel tot de raadselen der wereld", Servire Uitgevers bv, 1990 (orig. 1912; first published in the USA in 1922), ISBN 9 0632 5391 5.
- Overduin, Hans; "Mondrian - from figuration to abstraction", Haags Gemeentemuseum and The Tokyo Shimbun, 1987.
- Overy, Paul; "Kandinsky, The Language of the Eye", Elek Books Ltd, London, 1969, SBN 2 3617 7702.
- Overy, Paul; Büller, Lenneke; Oudsten, Frank den; Mulder, Bertus; "Het Rietveld-Schröder Huis", De Haan Uitgeverij, 1988, ISBN 9 0269 4347 4.
- Overy, Paul; "De Stijl - Art.Architecture.Design", Thames and Hudson, 2000 (orig. 1991), ISBN 0 5002 0240 0.

P

- Pacquement, Alfred; "Antoine Pevsner dans les collections du Centre Georges Pompidou/Musée nationale d'art moderne", Éditions du Centre Pompidou, 2001, ISBN 2 8442 695 0.
- Page, Michael; "The Power of Ch'i - An Introduction to Chinese Mysticism and Philosophy", The Aquarian Press (Harper/Collins), 1988, ISBN 1 8553 8363 2.
- Pal, Pratapaditya; "Himmalayas - An Aesthetic Adventure", The Art Institute of Chicago, University of California Press, 2003, ISBN 0 5202 3900 8.
- Palm, Frederique van der; "Ieder zijn Domela", Museum Willem van Haren, Museum Kasteel Wychen, 2001.
- Panovsky, Erwin; "Perspective as Symbolic Form", Zone Books, New York, 1997 (orig. "Die Perspektive als 'symbolische Form' ", 1924-25), ISBN 0 9422 9953 1.
- Parry, Eugenia; "Adam Fuss", Arena Editions, 1997, ISBN 0 9657 2801 3.
- Parton, Anthony; "Mikhail Larionov and the Russian Avant-Garde", Princeton University Press, 1993, ISBN 0 6910 3603 9.
- Paturi, Felix R.; "Monumenten uit de Oertijd - Getuigen van de Prehistorie", Uitgeverij Ankh-Hermes, Deventer, 1978 (orig. "Zeugen der Vorzeit", Econ Verlag GmbH), ISBN 9 0202 5403 0.
- Peat, F. David; "Superstrings and the Theory of Everything", Abacus Books, 1992 (orig.1988), ISBN 0 7474 0583 2.
- Peat, F. David; "Synchronicity - The Bridge Between Matter and Mind", Bantam Books, 1987, ISBN 0-553-34321-1.
- Pechar, Josef; "Ceskoslovenska Architektura 1945-1977", Odeon, 1979.
- Peissi, Pierre; Giedion-Welcker, Carola; "Antoine Pevsner", Éditions du Griffon, Neuchatel, Switzerland, 1961.
- Pendorf, Jutta; "Silence, Silence, Silence - Gerhard Altenbourg - Die Sammlung Wilfried und Astrid Rugo", Lindenau Museum Altenbourg, Saarland Museum Saarbrücken, 2002, ISBN 3 8610 4048 4.
- Penrose, Roger; "The Emperor's New Mind - Concerning computers, minds, and the laws of physics", Vintage Press, 1990 (orig 1989 Oxford University Press), ISBN 0 09977 1705.
- Perre, Harold van de; "Pietro Paolo Rubens - Profeet van de moderne kunst", Elsevier, 1984, ISBN 9 0100 4571 4.
- Petersen, Ad; "De Stijl", parts 1+2, the complete reprint, Athenaeum, Amsterdam; Bert Bakker, Den Haag; Polak & Van Gennep, Amsterdam; 1968.
- Pfeiffer, Bruce Books; "Frank Lloyd Wright", Benedikt Taschen Verlag, 1991, ISBN 3 9228 9754 X.
- Pierre, Arnauld; "Frantisek Kupka - In White and Black", Facsimile Reprints of "Abstractions" 1933/48, "Four Stories of White and Black" 1926, Liverpool University Press and Artists Bookworks, 1998, ISBN 0 8532 3772 7.
- Pietzsch, Ulla und Heiner; "Leben mit Kunst - Sammlung Ulla und Heiner Pietzsch", Band I, 2000, ISBN 3 0000 7103 2.
- Pil, Eric; "Van Tongerloo Colour theories - Reactions Other Members of De Stijl Group", ICSAC-Cahier 10, ISSN 0 7717 637, 1996.
- Pommeré, Marianne Le; "The Works of Jean Gorin", Waser Verlag, 1985, ISBN 3 9080 8013 4.
- Pommer, Richard; Otto, Christian F.; "Weissenhof 1927 and the Modern Movement in Architecture", The University of Chicago Press, 1991, ISBN 0 2266 7515 7.
- Popper, Frank; "Licht-Kunst-Licht", exhibition catalogue Stedelijk Van Abbemuseum, 1966.
- Popper, Frank; "Origins and Development of Kinetic Art", translated by Stephen Bann, New York Graphic Society, 1968 (orig. Studio Vista).
- Povelikhina, Alla V.; "Organica", Galerie Gmurzynska, Cologne, 1999.
- Powell, Corey S.; "Trends in Astrophysics: In constant Cosmos", Scientific American, issue May 1993,

p.69-76.
- Powell, Corey S.; "Why So Blue?", Scientific American, issue October 1995, blz.13.
- Powell, Evor; Lewis, Mark; "Ndebele - leven tussen kleuren", New Holland Ltd, 1995, ISBN 9 0682 5159 7.
- Prather, Martha; "Alexander Calder 1898-1976", National Gallery of Art Washington, Yale University Press, 1998, ISBN 0 3000 7518 9.
- Prigogene, Ilya; Stengers, Isabelle; "Orde uit Chaos - De nieuwe dialoog tussen de mens en de natuur", Uitgeverij Bert Bakker, 1990 (orig. "Order out of Chaos", 1985), ISBN 9 0351 0959 7.
- Price, Sally & Richard; "Afro-American Arts of the Suriname Rain Forest", University of California Press, 1980, ISBN 0-520-04412-6.
- 1st PRO-Newsletter, PRO Foundation, 1986.
- 2nd en 3rd PRO-Newsletter, PRO Foundation, 1986.
- 1th PRO-Conferentie '87 Dordrecht, Dordrechts Museum, catalogue PRO Foundation, 1987.
- PRO-NR.1, magazine, PRO Foundation, 1987.
- PRO-NR.2, magazine, PRO Foundation, 1987.
- PRO-NR.3, magazine, PRO Foundation, 1988.
- 4th PRO-Newsletter, PRO Foundation, 1988.
- 2nd PRO-Conference '88 Fulda, catalogue exhibition "Null Dimension"Duitsland, PRO Foundation, Galerie "New Space", and IDEA e.V. Fulda.
- PRO-NR.4, magazine, PRO Foundation, 1988.
- PRO-NR.5, magazine, PRO Foundation, 1989.
- 5th and 6th PRO-Newsletter, PRO Foundation, 1989.
- "A New Spatiality? 4 Generations - 4 Opinions" (Kidner, Mosso, Rompza, Ilgen), catalogue Stichting PRO, 1989.
- 3rd PRO-Conference '89 Rotterdam-Vlissingen, World Trade Centre Rotterdam, Hotel Brittannia Vlissingen, catalogue Stichting PRO, 1989.
- Symposium 1989 Vlissingen Konstruktivisme-Kunst-Architektuur, catalogue PRO Foundation and Culturele Raad Vlissingen (part of 3rd PRO Conference '89), 1989.
- PRO-NR.6, PRO Foundation, 1990.
- 7e PRO-Newsletter, PRO Foundation, 1990.
- PRO-NR.7, magazine, PRO Foundation, 1990.
- PRO-NR.8, magazine, PRO Foundation, 1992.
- PRO-NR.9, "From Constructivism to Extensionalism", magazine, PRO Foundation, 1993.
- "Aspects Actuels de la Mouvance Construite Internationale", "Mésures et ses amis" (I), "Pro Verviers"(II) en "Éditions - Magazins" (III), catalogues, PRO Foundation and "Mésures - Art International" en Musée d'Art Moderne de Verviers, Verviers, België, Koninklijk Museum voor Hedendaagse Kunst/ICC Antwerpen; 1994-1995.
- 8e PRO-Newsletter, PRO Foundation, 1994.
- 9e PRO-Newsletter, PRO Foundation, 1995.
- Pullman, Bernard; "The Atom In The History of Human Thought", translated by Axel Reisinger, Oxford University Press, 1998, ISBN 0 1951 5040 6.
- Purce, Jill; "Die Spirale - Symbol der Seelenreise", Kösel-Verlag GmbH & Co, 1988 (orig. Thames and Hudson 1974), ISBN 3 4663 4186 8.
- Putterman, Seth J.; "Sonoluminescence: Sound into Light - A bubble of air can focus acoustic energy a trillion fold to produce picosecond flashes of light. The mechanism eludes complete explanation", Scientific American, issue February 1995, p.32-37.
- Pylkkänen, Paavo; "Bohm-Biederman Correspondence, David Bohm and Charles Biederman, Volume One: Creativity and Science" (London and New York: Routledge, 1999), ISBN 0 4151 6225 4.

Q

- Quispel, Prof. Dr. G.; "De Hermeneutische Gnosis in de loop der eeuwen - Beschouwingen over de invloed van een Egyptische religie op de cultuur van het Westen", Tirion, Baarn, 1992, ISBN 9 0512 1374 3.

- Rachum, Stephanie: "The Joy of Color - The Merzbacher Collection", The Israel Museum Jerusalem, DuMont, 1998, ISBN 9 6527 8218 1.
- Racine, Bruno; Pacquement, Alfred; "Frantisek Kupka - 1871-1957, Eine Retrospektive", Centre Pompidou, Kunstmuseum Liechtenstein, Hatje Cantz Verlag (Ostfildern-Ruit), 2003, ISBN 3 7757 1313 1.
- Raff, Martin C.; "Death Wish - All cells come primed for self-destruction - The challenge for medicine is to make them die on cue", The Sciences, issue July/August 1996, p.36-40.
- Railing, Patricia; "From Science to Systems of Art - On Russian Abstract Art and Language 1910-1920 and other essays", Artists Bookworks, 1989, ISBN 0 9463 11 05 6.
- Railing, Patricia; "On Suprematism - 34 Drawings - K. Malevitch", Artists Bookworks, 1990, ISBN 0 9463 1104 8.
- Railing, Patricia; "El Lissitzky About 2 Squares", reprint "More About 2 Squares", Artists Bookworks, 1990, ISBN 0 9463 1102 1.
- Railing, Patricia; "The Machine is more than a Brush - Morphology of Art and the Machine in Russian Avant-Garde Theory and Practice", The Structurist, No.35/36 "From the Mechanical to the Organic", 1995-1996.
- Railing, Patricia; "Malevich said: Art is Cognition", published in Proceedings Second International Symposium "Creativity and Cognition", see Edmonds/Candy, 1996.
- Railing, Patricia; "Mayakovski: For The Voice", box with a reprint in Russian, reprint translated in English by Peter France, "Voices of Revolution - collected essays", The British Library and Artists Bookworks, 2000, ISBN 0 7123 4669 4.
- Ramachandran, Vilayanur S.; "Blind Spots", Scientific American, issue May 1992, p.86-91.
- Ratcliff, Carter; "The Fate of a Gesture: Jackson Pollock and Postwar American Art", Farrar, Straus and Giroux (NY), 1996, ISBN 0 3741 5381 7.
- Ratcliff, Carter; "Mutability and Metaphor" (on Natvar Bhavsar), Art in America, issue December 2003, p.80-83.
- Rattemeyer, Volker; "Gotthard Graubner - Träger des Otto Ritschl Preises 2001", Museum Wiesbaden, Richter Verlag, 2001, ISBN 3 8925 8046 4.
- Read, Herbert; "Art Now - New and Enlarged Edition", Faber and Faber Ltd, 1948.
- Read, Herbert; "Kandinsky (1866-1944)", Georg Wittenborn, New York, 1959 (orig. by Faber and Faber Ltd, London).
- Read, Herbert; Martin, Leslie; "Naum Gabo - Bauten, Skulptur, Malerei, Zeichnungen, Grafik", Éditions du Griffon, Neuchatel, 1961 (orig. in English, Lund Humphries London, 1957).
- Reber, A.S.; "Woordenboek van de Psychologie", Uitgeverij Bert Bakker, 1994 (eerste druk 1989), (orig."The Penguin Dictionary of Psychology", 1985), ISBN 9 0351 1264 4.
- Reid, James; Rossi, Vincent; "Intimations of Paradise - Photographs of Christopher Burkett", West Wind Arts, 1999, ISBN 0 9670 2160 X.
- Rewald, John; "Cézanne and America - Dealers, Collectors, Artists and Critics 1891-1921", Thames and Hudson, 1989, ISBN 0 5002 3513 9.
- Riabuszyn, Aleksander; Szyskina, Iraida; "Architektura radziecka - Architektura i architekci swiata wspolczesnego", Wyclawnicto Arkady Warsaw, 1987, ISBN 8 3213 3262 5.
- Richter, Fleur; "Die Aesthetische Geometrische Körper in der Renaissance", Gerd Hatje Verlag, 1995, ISBN 3 7757 0543 0.
- Riddley, Matt; "Genome - The Autobiography of A Species in 23 Chapters", Fourth Estate, London, 1999, ISBN 1 8570 2835 X.
- Rickey, George; "Constructivism - Origins and Evolution", Georg Brazilier NY, 1967.
- Rickey, George; "A Technology of Kinetic Art", Scientific American, issue February 1993, p.50-55.
- Riese, Hans Peter; Heckmanns, Friedrich W.; "Richard Paul Lohse, Zeichnungen 1935-1985", LIT Verlag Baden, 1986, ISBN 3 9067 0005 4.
- Rietberg, Museum; "La Chine Archaque" (Collection Baur), Museum Rietberg, Zürich, 1987.
- Rilke, Rainer Maria; "Auguste Rodin", Insel Verlag, 1984 (orig. 1902), ISBN 3 4583 2466 6.
- Rilke, Rainer Maria; "Letters on Cézanne", North Point Press, New York, 2002 (orig."Briefe über Cézanne", Insel Verlag, Frankfurt, 1952), ISBN 0 8654 7639 X.
- Roberts, Laurance P.; "A Dictionary of Japanese Artists", Weatherhill Inc., 2003 (orig. 1976), ISBN 0 8348 0235 X.

R

• Roethel, Hans K.; Benjamin, Jean K.; "Kandinsky", Phaidon, 1979, ISBN 0 7148 2053 9.
• Rohatyn, Jeanne; Waxter, Dorsey; "Dorothea Rockburne - Ten Years of Astronomy Drawings 1990-2000", Lawrence Rubin - Greenberg Van Doren Fine Art, 2000, ISBN 0 9677 5730 4.
• Romain, Lothar; "Michael Bette", Edition "Libri artis", 1987, ISBN 3 8874 6196 7.
• Romain, Lothar; Salzmann, Siegfried; "Bernard Heiliger", Propylaen Verlag, 1989, ISBN 3 5490 5308 8.
• Ronte, Dieter; Jedlinski, Jaromir; "Wladyslaw Strzeminski", Kunstmuseum Bonn, 1994, ISBN 3 9297 9005 X.
• Ronte, Dieter; Smerling, Walter; Weiss, Evelyn; "China - Zeitgenössische Malerei", Kunstmuseum Bonn, DuMont Buchverlag Köln, 1996, ISBN 3 7701 3813 9.
• Ronte, Dieter; "Helmut Schober - Light-Licht", Kunstmuseum Bonn, Electa Milan, 1998, ISBN 8 8435 6439 0.
• Ronte, Dieter; Schreier, Christoph; Mizusawa, Tsutomu; Nakahara, Yusuke; Schaarschmidt-Richter, Irmgard; "Lee Ufan - Gemälde 1973 bis 2001", Kunstmuseum Bonn, 2001, ISBN 3 9297 9046 7.
• Ronte, Dieter; Adolphs, Volker; "Beat Zoderer - Der doppelte Boden ist tiefer als man denkt", Kunstmuseum Bonn, 2003 ISBN 3 9297 9056 4.
• Roshi, Eido Shimano; Vacher, Charles; "Dogen - Shobogenzo - Yui butsu yo butso shoji", Encre Marine, 1999, ISBN 2 9094 2237 2.
• Rossotti, Hazel; "Colour - Why the World Isn't Grey", Princeton University Press, 1985, ISBN 0 6910 2386 7.
• Rotzler, Willy; "Konstruktive Konzepte - Eine Geschichte der konstruktiven Kunst vom Kubismus bis heute", ABC Verlag Zürich, 1977, ISBN 3 8550 4037 0.
• Rotzler, Willy, "Paul Suter Esculturas", Veronicas Sala de Exposiciones, 1989.
• Rousseau, Robert; "Wassily Kandinsky - Retrospective", Charleroi Palais des Beaux-Arts, 1972.
• Rowell, Margit; Wye, Deborah; "The Russian Avant-Garde Book 1910-1934", Museum of Modern Art, New York, Harry N. Abrams Inc., 2002, ISBN 0 8109 6224 1.
• Rubin, William; "Frank Stella 1970-1987", The Museum of Modern Art, New York, 1988 (first edition 1987), ISBN 0 8707 0593 8.
• Rubin, William; "Painted Steel: The Late Work of David Smith", Gagosian Gallery (NY), 1998, ISBN 1 8801 5423 4.
• Russell, Bertrand; "An Essay on the Foundations of Geometry", Dover Publications, 1956 (orig. 1897).
• Russell, Bertrand; "History of Western Philosophy", Routledge, 1991 (orig.1946), ISBN 0 4150 7854 7.
• Ryosho, Hayashi; "Honen's Senchakushu - Passages on the Selection of the Nembutsu in the Original Vow (Senchaku hongan nembutsu shu)", translated and edited by Senchakushu English Tranbslation Project, a Kuroda Institute Book, University of Hawai'i Press (Honolulu) and Sogo Bukkyo Kenkyujo, Taisho University (Tokyo), 1998, ISBN 0 8248 2110 6.

S

• Sandler, Irving; "The Triumph of American Painting - A History of Abstract Expressionism", Praeger Publishers, Inc., 1970.
• Sandler, Irving; "Concepts in Construction: 1910-1980", Independent Curators Inc. New York, 1982.
• Sandler, Irving; "Art from Britain 3: Michael Kidner at-tension to the wave", Center for International Contemporary Arts, New York, 1990, ISBN 0 9623 7643 4.
• Sandler, Irving; "Mark di Suvero at Storm King Art Center", Storm King Art Center, Harry N. Abrams, Inc., 1995, ISBN 0 8109 2614 8.
• Sandler, Irving; "Natvar Bhavsar - Painting and the Reality of Color", Craftsman House G+B Arts International, 1998, ISBN 9 0570 4061 1.
• Sandler, Irving; "A Sweeper-Up After Artists - a memoir", Thames and Hudson, New York, 2003, ISBN 0 5002 3813 8.
• Saner Studen, Fondation; "Richard Paul Lohse - Die Konstruktion ist das Bild", Fondation Saner Studen + Richard Paul Lohse Stiftung, W. Gassmann AG Druck und Verlag, 1995, ISBN 9 3906 1402 37.
• Santayana, Georg; "The Sense of Beauty - Being the Outline of Aesthetic Theory", Dover Publications Inc., 1955 (orig. 1896), ISBN 0 4862 0238 0.
• Sarabianov, Dmitri V.; Adaskina, Natalia L.; "Liubov Popova", translated by Marian Schwartz, Harry N. Abrams Inc. Publishers, 1990 (orig. Philippe Sers Editeur, 1989), ISBN 0 8109 3701 8.
• Schacht, Richard; "Nietzsche", Routledge, 1996 (orig. 1983), ISBN 0 4130 9071 7.

S
•Schattscheider, Doris; "M.C. Escher - Visions of Symmetry", W.H. Freeman and Co., 1990, ISBN 0 7167 2352 0.
•Schiebinger, Londa; "The Lovers of the Plants", Scientific American, issue February 1996, p.98-103.
•Schirn Kunsthalle Frankfurt; "Die Grosse Utopie - Die Russische Avantgarde 1915-1932", Schirn Kunsthalle Frankfurt, 1992.
•Schirn Kunsthalle Frankfurt; "Eduardo Chillida - Eine Retrospektive", Schirn Kunsthalle Frankfurt, 1993.
•Schlagheck, Irma; "César Domela - Reliefs und Gouachen (1938-1987)", Galerie Sander Darmstadt, 1988.
•Schlégl, Galerie & Edition; "Nina Ossipowna Kogan - Suprematistische Werke 1920-1923", Galerie & Edition Schlégl, 1985.
•Schlégl, Galerie & Edition; "Michail Larionow Rayonistische Werke 1912-1914 und illustrierte Bücher russischer Futuristen", Galerie & Edition Schlégl, 1987.
•Schlégl, Dr. István; "Paul Suter - Eisenplastiken/Iron sculptures", Galerie & Edition Schlégl, Zürich, 1988.
•Schmidt, Werner; Holler, Wolfgang; "Gotthard Graubner - Malerei und Zeichnung", Richter Verlag Düsseldorf, 2000, ISBN 9 3380 7239.
•Schmiedt, Wieland; "Matta", Kunsthalle München, Ernst Wasmuth Verlag, 1991, ISBN 3 8030 3195 8.
•Schneede, Uwe M.; "Umberto Boccioni", Verlag Gerd Hatje, 1994, ISBN 3 7757 0449 3.
•Schneider, David; "A Spinning Crystall Ball - Seismologists discover that the inner core rotates", Scientific American, issue October 1996, p.18, 19.
•Schoenmakers, M.H.J.; "Het Beeldende Denken - leven en werk van Matthieu Schoenmakers", Stichting E.C.H.O., Ambo/Baarn, 1992, ISBN 9 0263 1151 6.
•Schopenhauer, Arthur; "Die Welt als Wille und Vorstellung", I. Teil + II. Teil, Grossherzog Wilhelm Ernst Ausgabe, Insel Verlag, 1859.
•Schreier, Christoph; "Wassily Kandinsky - Bild mit schwarzem Bogen", Insel Verlag Frankfurt am Main und Leipzig, 1991, ISBN 3 4583 3055 0 (1400).
•Schrenk, Klaus; "Gotthard Graubner - Malerei auf Papier", Staatliche Kunsthalle Karlsruhe, Richter Verlag Düsseldorf 2001, ISBN 3 9338 0740 9.
•Schroedinger, Erwin; "What is Matter?", Scientific American, special issue 1991 (orig. in Scientific American, issue September 1953), p.16-21.
•Schuffenhauer, Werner; "Ludwig Feuerbach - Philosophische Kritiken und Grundsätze (1839-1846)", UMA Verlag Wiesbaden, Verlag Phillippe Reclam, 1980, ISBN 2 0757 232.
•Schuster, Carl; Carpenter, Edmund; "Patterns That Connect - Social Symbolism in Ancient & Tribal Art", Harry N. Abrams Inc. Publishers, 1996, ISBN 0 8109 6326 4.
•Scribner III, Charles; "Peter Paul Rubens", Harry N. Abrams Inc. Publishers, 1989, ISBN 0 8109 1569 3.
•Seemann, Hellmut; "Yu-Ichi - HIN - Werke 1954 bis 1982", Publishing Trading Corporation and Schirn Kunsthalle Frankfurt, 1995.
•Seife, Charles; "Zero - The Biography of a Dangerous Idea", Penguin Books, 2000, ISBN 0 1402 9647.
•Sellenriek, Jörg; "Zirkel und Lineal - Kulturgeschichte des Konstruktiven Zeichnens", Verlag Callwey München, 1987, ISBN 3 7667 0838 4.
•Senju, Hiroshi; "Screen-Paintings for Jukoin-Betsuin, Daito kuji", 2002, ISBN 4 7630 0208 2 C0071.
•"Hiroshi Senju", Japan, 2002, ISBN 4 0969 9781 1.
•"Heart of the Paintings, Hiroshi Senju", Japan, 2003, ISBN 4 4180 3520 6.
•Seo, Audrey; Addiss, Stephen; "The Art of Twentieth Century Zen - Painting and Calligraphy by Japanese Masters", Shambala Press, Boston and London, 1998, ISBN 1 5706 2358 9.
•Serpentine Gallery; "Michael Kidner - Painting, drawing, sculpture 1959-1984".
•Seuphor, Michel; "Piet Mondrian - Life and Work", Harry N. Abrams, Inc., 1956.
•Shiff, Richard; "Cézanne and the End of Impressionism - A Study of the Theory, Technique, and Critical Evaluation of Modern Art", The University of Chicago Press, 1984, ISBN 0 2267 5305 0.
•Shimizu, Yoshiaki; Rosenfield, John M.; "Masters of Japanese Calligraphy 8th-9th Century, The Asia Society Galleries, Japan House Gallery, ISBN 0 9133 0420 4.
•Singh, Madanjeet; "Die Sonne - Das Gestirn in der Kulturgeschichte", Wasmuth/UNESCO, 1993, ISBN 380 30 30595.
•Silverman, Hugh J.; "Derrida and Deconstruction", Continental Philosophy II, Routledge, 1989, ISBN 0 4150 3094 3.
•Sivapriyananda, Swami; "Astrology and Religion in Indian Art", Abhinav Publications, 1990,

ISBN 8 1701 7231 4.
•Smith, Candida; Sandler, Irving; "The Fields of David Smith", Storm King Art Center, Thames and Hudson, 1999, ISBN 0 5000 1908 8.
•Smolik, Noemi; "Frantisek Kupka - Die Schöpfung in der bildenden Kunst", translated by Noemi Smolik, Hatje Cantz Verlag (Ostfildern-Ruit), 2001, ISBN 3 7757 0824 3.
•Smolin, Lee; "Three Roads to Quantum Gravity", Basic Books, 2001, ISBN 0 4650 7836 2.
•Sotheby; "Catalogue of Fifty Paintings by Vasily Kandinsky - The Property of the Solomon R. Guggenheim Foundation", auction catalogue 30th June 1964, Sotheby & Co, London.
•Spielmann, Heinz; "Kunst an der Seidenstrasse - Faszination Buddha", Bucerius Kunst Forum Hamburg, Hatje Cantz Verlag Ostfildern-Ruit, 2003, ISBN 3 7757 1376 X.
•Sprengel Museum; "Internationale Avantgarde 1927-1935 - Die Abstrakten Hannover", Sprengel Museum Hannover, 1987, ISBN 3 8916 9038X.
•Stachelhaus, Heiner; "Kasimir Malewitsch - Ein Tragischer Konflikt", Claassen Verlag GmbH, 1989, ISBN 3 5464 8681 1.
•Stanislawski, Ryszard; Brockhaus, Christoph; "Europa-Europa - Das Jahrhundert der Avantgarde in Mittel- und Osteuropa", Kunst- und Ausstellungshalle der Bundesrepublik Deutschland, 1994.
•Stedelijk Museum Amsterdam; "Kupka", catalogus Nr.429, 1968.
•Stedelijk Museum Amsterdam; "Kazimir Malevich 1878-1935", Stedelijk Museum Amsterdam, 1989, ISBN 9 0500 6022 6.
•Steiner, Rudolf; "J.W. Goethe - Naturwissenschaftliche Schriften", Band I, II, III, IV, V, Rudolf Steiner Verlag Dornach, 1982 (original: Band I 1883, Band II 1887, Band III 1890, Band IV 1897, Band V 1897), ISBN 3 7274 5210 2.
•Stella, Frank; "Working Space, The Charles Eliot Norton Lectures", Harvard University Press, 1986, ISBN 0 6749 5961 2.
•Stott, Carole; "Celestial Charts - Antique Maps of the Heavens", Crescent Books New York, 1991, ISBN 0 5170 5025 0.
•Straaten, Evert van; "Theo van Doesburg - schilder en architect", SDU Uitgeverij, 1988, ISBN 9 0120 6001 X.
•Strogatz, Steven H.; Stewart, Ian; "Coupled Oscillators and Biological Synchronization", Scientific American, December 1993, p.68-75.
•Strogatz, Steven H.; "SYNC - How Order Emerges from Chaos in the Universe, Nature, and Daily Life", Theia Books, Hyperion, NY, 2003, ISBN 0 7868 8721 4.
•Stryk, Lucien; Ikemoto, Takashi; "Zen Poems of China and Japan - The Crane's Bill", Grove Press, New York,1987 (orig. 1973), ISBN 0 8021 3019 4.
•Stuckey, Charles F.; "Monet - A Retrospective", Beaux Arts Éditions, Hugh Lauter Levin Associates Inc., 1985, ISBN 0 8836 3301 9.
•Stuckey, Charles F.; "Monet - Waterlilies", Hugh Lauter Levin Associates Inc., Koenemann Verlagsgesellschaft mbH, 1988. ISBN 3 8950 8057 8.
•Sugimoto, Masayoshi; Swain, David L.; "Science & Culture in Traditional Japan", Charles E. Tuttle Company, 1989, ISBN 0 8048 1614 X.
•Suzuki, D.T.; "Manual of Zen Buddhism", Grove Press Inc., New York, 10th edition, 1960 (orig. Kyoto, 1935).
•Suzuki, Daisetz T.; "Zen und die Kultur Japans", O.W. Barth Verlag, 1994 (orig. Bollingen Foundation Inc., New York, 1959), ISBN 3 5026 4600 7.
•Szymusiak, Dominique; "Herbin 1882-1960", Musée Matisse Le Cateau Cambrésis, 1994, ISBN 2 9044 2070 3.
•Szymusiak, Dominique; "Félix del Marle - la polychromie dans l'espace 1945-1952", Musée Matisse Le Cateau-Cambrésis, 1996, ISBN 2 9075 4520 5.
•Szymusiak, Dominique; "Matisse et l'Arbre", Musée Matisse Le Cateau Cambrésis, 2003, ISBN 2 85025 905 5.
•Szymusiak, Dominique; "François Morellet - quelques systèmes en hommage à Herbin", Musée Matisse Le Cateau-Cambrésis, 2003, ISBN 2 9075 4535 3.
•Szymusiak, Dominique; "Vouloir Lille 1925", Musée Matisse Le Cateau Cambrésis, 2004, ISBN 2 9075 4538 8.

- Taacke, Andreas; "Herbst der Barock - Studien zum Stilwandel", Deutscher Kunstverlag, 1998, ISBN 3 4220 6229 7.
- Taillandier, Yvon; "Monet", Südwest Verlag München.
- The Tate Gallery; "J.M.W. Turner - The "Ideas of Folkstone" Sketchbook 1845", The Tate Gallery, 1987, ISBN 0 9465 9083 4.
- The Tate Gallery; Cachin, Françoise; Cahn, Isabelle; Feilchenfeldt, Walter; Loyrette, Henri; Rishel, Joseph J.; "Cézanne", Tate Publishing, 1996, ISBN 1 85437 178 9.
- Taut, Bruno; "Ich liebe die Japanische Kultur - Kleine Schriften über Japan", Manfred Speidel, Gebr. Mann Verlag, 2003, ISBN 3 7861 2460 4.
- Tchernykhov, Jacob; "Architectural Fictions - 101 Coloured Prints - 101 Architectural Miniatures", edited by "Meshdunarodnaja Kniga" Leningrad Section, 1933.
- Terenzio, Stephanie; "The Collected Writings of Robert Motherwell", University of California Press, 1999, ISBN 0 5202 2179 6.
- Thiessen-Schneider, Gudrun; Kraft, Perdita von; "Michael Bette", Kunstverein Grafschaft Bentheim, Brandenburgische Kunstsammlungen Cottbus, 1998, ISBN 3 9228 0563 9.
- Thomas, Belinda; "Van Gogh", Artists in Focus, The Art Institute of Chicago, Harry N. Abrams Inc., 2001, ISBN 0 8109 6738 3.
- Thompson, d'Arcy Wentworth; "On Growth and Form - The Complete Revised Edition", Dover Publications, 1992 (orig. 1942), ISBN 0 4866 7135 6.
- Tschichold, Jan; "Typografische Mitteilungen - Sonderheft Elementare Typographie - Oktoberheft 1925", reprint Verlag H. Schmidt, Mainz, 1986, ISBN 3 8743 9129 9.
- Tuchman, Maurice; "The Spiritual in Art: Abstract Painting 1890-1985", Abbeville Publishers, New York, 1986, ISBN 0 8965 9-669 9.
- Tucker, Paul Hayes; Shackelford, George T.M.; Stevens, Mary Anne; "Monet in the 20th Century", Royal Academy of Art (London), Museum of Fine Arts (Boston), Yale University Press, 1998, ISBN 0 3000 7944 3.
- Turowski, Andrzej; "Konstruktywizm Polski - Proba Rekonstrukji Nurtu (1921-1934)", Polska Akademia Nauk, Institut Sztuki, Ossolineum, 1981, ISBN 8 3040 0557 3.
- Turowski, Andrzej; "Existe-t-il un Art de l'Europe de l'Est? Utopie & Idéologie", Les Éditions de la Villette, 1986, ISBN 2 9035 3912 X.
- Tyradellis, Daniel; Friedlander, Michal S.; "10 + 5 = Gott - Die Macht der Zeichen", Jüdisches Museum Berlin, DuMont Literatur und Kunst Verlag, 2004, ISBN 3 8321 7874 0.

- Uchida, Yoshiko; "We do not work alone - the thoughts of Kanjiro Kawai", Kawai Kanjiro House, Nissha Printing Company, Ltd, Kyoto, Japan.
- Unagami, Masaomi; "Wordworks for A New Millennium: Yu-Ichi", Kyoto University of Art and Design, 2000.
- Unagami, Masaomi; "Yu-Ichi, catalogue raisonné of the works 1949-1985", Volume I, II, III, limited edition (# 473), UNAC Tokyo, 1998, ISBN 4 9900 4522 X.
- Unno, Taitetsu; "The Religious Philosophy of Nishitani Keiji, Encounter with Emptiness", Asian Humanities Press, 1989, ISBN 0 8958 1871 X.

- Vachtová, Ludmilla; "Frantisek Kupka", Odeon, 1968.
- Vargish, Thomas; Mook, Delo E.; "Inside Modernism - Relativity Theory, Cubism, Narrative", Yale University, 1999, ISBN 0 3000 7613 4.
- Varnedoe, Kirk; Karmel, Pepe; "Jackson Pollock", The Museum of Modern Art, New York, Harry N. Abrams Inc., 1998, ISBN 0 8109 6193 8.
- Varnedoe, Kirk; Karmel, Pepe; "Jackson Pollock - New Approaches", The Museum of Modern Art, New York, Harry N. Abrams Inc., 1999, ISBN 0 8707 0086 3.
- Vasari, Giorgio; "The Lives of the Artists", translated by Julia Conaway Bondanella and Peter Bondanella, Oxford University Press, (orig. "Vite de' piu eccellenti architetti, pittori et scultori italiana", 1550) 1991, ISBN 0 1928 1754 X.
- Veit, Willibald; "SHO - Ausstellung zeitgenössischer japanischer Schreibkunst", Museum für Ostasiatische Kunst, The Mainichi Newspapers, The Mainichi Shodo Association, Berlin, 2000.
- Verschuur, Gerrit L.; "Hidden Attraction - The Mystery and History of Magnetism", Oxford University

Press, 1993, ISBN 0 1951 0655 5.
•Verspohl, Franz-Joachim; Ehrmann-Schindbeck, Anna-Maria; Mueller, Ulrich; "Heinrich von Kleist by Frank Stella", Verlag Buchhandlung Walther Koenig, 2001, ISBN 3 8837 5488 9.
•Verswijver, Gustaaf; "Kaiapo - Amazoni, de kunst van de lichaamsornamentiek", Koninklijk Museum voor Midden-Afrika (Tervuren), Snoeck - Ducaju & Zn Gent, 1992.
•Vivekananda, Swami; "Jnana - Yoga", Advaita Ashrama, Mayavati, Almora, 4th edition, 1930.
•Vivekananda, Swami; "The East and West", Advaita Ashrama, Mayavati, Almora, 13th edition, 1994 (orig. as series in "Udbodhan", the Bengali monthly of the Ramakrishna Order, 1899-1901), ISBN 8 1853 0186 7.
•Vöge, Peter; "The Complete Rietveld Furniture", 010 Publishers, 1993, ISBN 9 0645 0159 9.
•Volkwein, Peter; "Manfred Mohr -space-color", Museum für Konkrete Kunst Ingolstadt, 2001.
•Vollard, Ambroise; "Cézanne", translated by Harold L. van Doren, Dover Publications Inc., (orig. "Paul Cézanne: His Life and Art", 1937), 1984, ISBN 0 4862 4729 5.
•Vomm, Wolgang; "Hiroko", Städtische Galerie Villa Zanders, Bergisch Gladbach, 2001.

•Waespe, Roland; Berg, Stephen; "David Reed - You look good in blue", Verlag Moderne Kunst Nürnberg, Kunstverein St. Gallen Kunstmuseum, Kunstverein Hannover, 2001, ISBN 3 9330 9665 0.
•Waldram, Dr.J.; "Encyclopedie van de Filosofie", Tirion, 1993, ISBN 9 0512 1233 X.
•Waldrop, M. Mitchell; "Complexity - The Emerging Science at the Edge of Order and Chaos", Viking/Penguin Group, 1992, ISBN 0 6708 5045 4.
•Wallace, Robert K.; "Frank Stella's Moby-Dick, Words & Shapes", The University of Michigan Press (Ann Arbor), 2000, ISBN 0 4721 0901 4.
•Weber, Jamileh; "Jahanguir", Edition Jamileh Weber, 1996, ISBN 3 8580 9100 XA.
•Weiss, Jeffrey; "Mark Rothko", National Gallery of Art Washington, 1998, ISBN 0 8946 8229 6.
•Weiss, Peg; "Kandinsky in Munich - The Formative Jugendstil Years", Princeton University Press, 1985, ISBN 0 6910 0374 2.
•Weiss, Peg; "Kandinsky and Old Russia - The Artist as Ethnographer and Shaman", Yale University Press, 1995, ISBN 0 3000 5647 8.
•Weizsäcker, Carl Friedrich von; "Zeit und Wissen", 1992, Carl Hanser Verlag München Wien, ISBN 3 4461 6367 0.
•Wells, David; "The Penguin Dictionary of Curious and Interesting Geometry", Penguin Books, 1991, ISBN 0 1401 1813 6.
•Westgeest, Helen; "Zen in the fifties - interaction between east and west", Waanders Uitgevers Zwolle, 1996, ISBN 9 0400 9892 1.
•Whitehead, Alfred North; "Process and Reality", Free Press, 1979 (orig.1929), ISBN 0 0293 4570 7.
•Whitehead, Alfred North; "Adventures of Ideas", Free Press, 1967 (orig.1933), ISBN 0 0293 5170 7.
•Whitehead, Alfred North; "Modes of Thought", Free Press, 1966 (orig.1938), ISBN 0 0293 5210 X.
•Whitney, David; "De Kooning - A Centennial Exhibition", Gagosian Gallery (NY), 2004, ISBN 0 9623 0248 1.
•Wiesing, Lambert; "Philosophie der Wahrnehmung - Modelle und Reflexionen", Suhrkamp Taschenbuch Wissenschaft Nr.1562, 2002, ISBN 3 5182 9162 9.
•Wilson, Edward O.; "Consilience - The Unity of Knowledge", Vintage Books, 1999 (orig. 1998), ISBN 0 6797 6867 X.
•Wirth, Günther; "FormFinden Anton Stankowski", Verlag Gerd Hatje, 1991, ISBN 3 7757 0342 X.
•Wismer, Beat; "Mondrians ästhetische Utopie", LIT Verlag, 1985, ISBN 3 9070 0046.
•Wismer, Beat; "Ferdinand Hodler - Piet Mondrian - Eine Begegnung", Verlag Lars Müller, 1998, ISBN 3 9070 4478 9.
•Wismer, Beat; "Equilibre - Gleichgewicht, Aequivalenz und Harmonie in der Kunst des 20.Jahrhunderts", Verlag Lars Müller, ISBN 3 9067 0066 6, 1993.
•Wölfflin, Heinrich; "Kunstgeschichtliche Grundbegriffe - Das problem der Stilentwicklung in der neuen Kunst", 13th edition, Schwabe & Co Verlag, Basel/Stuttgart, 1963 (orig. 1915).
•Wölfflin, Heinrich; "Principles of Art History - The problem of the development of style in later art", translated by M.D. Hottinger, Dover Publications Inc., 1932.
•Worringer, Wilhelm; "Abstraction and Empathy", with introduction by Hilton Kramer, Ivan R. Dee, Inc. Publisher, 1997 (orig. "Abstraktion und Einfühlung", 1908), ISBN 1 5666 3177 7.
•Wortmann, Arthur; "Melnikov - The Muscles of Invention", Van Hezik-Fonds 90, 1990, ISBN 9 0732 6003 5.

W

- Woud, Auke van der; "Het Nieuwe Bouwen International - CIAM Housing Town Planning", Delft University Press, 1983, ISBN 9 0627 5105 9.
- Wu, John C.H.; "The Golden Age of Zen", Image Books, Double Day, 1996, ISBN 0 3854 7993 X.
- Wijers, Louwrien; "Art meets Science and Spirituality in a Changing Economy", SDU publishers, 1990, ISBN 9 0120 6619 0.
- Wylie, Charles; "Brice Marden - Work of the 1990's: Paintings, Drawings, and Prints", Dallas Museum of Art, Distributed Art Publishers, 1999, ISBN 0 9362 2725 7.
- Wijsenbeek, L.J.F.; "Piet Mondriaan", Verlag Aurel Bongers Recklinghausen, 1968.

Y

- Ytter, Harald Falck; "Aurora - The Northern Lights in Mythology, History and Science", Bell Pond Books (Hudson, NJ), (orig. Verlag Freies Geistesleben GmbH, Stuttgart), 1983, ISBN 0 8801 0468 6.

Z

- Zeidler, Birgit; "Claude Monet - Life and Work", Art in Focus, Koenemann, Cologne, 1999, ISBN 3 8290 2936 5.
- Zeki, Semir; "The Visual Image in Mind and Brain", Scientific American, issue September 1992, p.68-76.
- Zeki, Semir; "Inner Vision - An Exploration of Art and the Brain", Oxford University Press, 1999, ISBN 0 1985 0519 1.
- Zervos, Chritian; "Domela", J.M. Meulenhoff Amsterdam, 1966.
- Zhadova, Larissa A.; "Poszukiwania i eksperimenty - Z dziejow sztuki rosyjskiej i radzieckiej lat 1910-1930", Wydawnictwa Artystycne i Filmowe, Warszawa 1982, ISBN 8 3221 0211 9.
- Zhadova, Larissa Alekseevna; "Tatlin", Thames and Hudson, 1988, ISBN 0 5002 3478 7.
- Zinsser, John; "Continuous Model: The Paintings of David Row", Edition Lintel, Verlag Robert Gessler, 1997, ISBN 3 8613 6020 9.
- Zukav, Gary; "De dansende Wu-Li meesters - een overzicht van de nieuwe fysica", Uitgeverij Bert Bakker, 1991 (eerste druk 1981), (orig. "The Dancing Wu-Li Masters: An Overview of the New Physics", William Morrow and Co, 1979), ISBN 9 0351 1060 9.

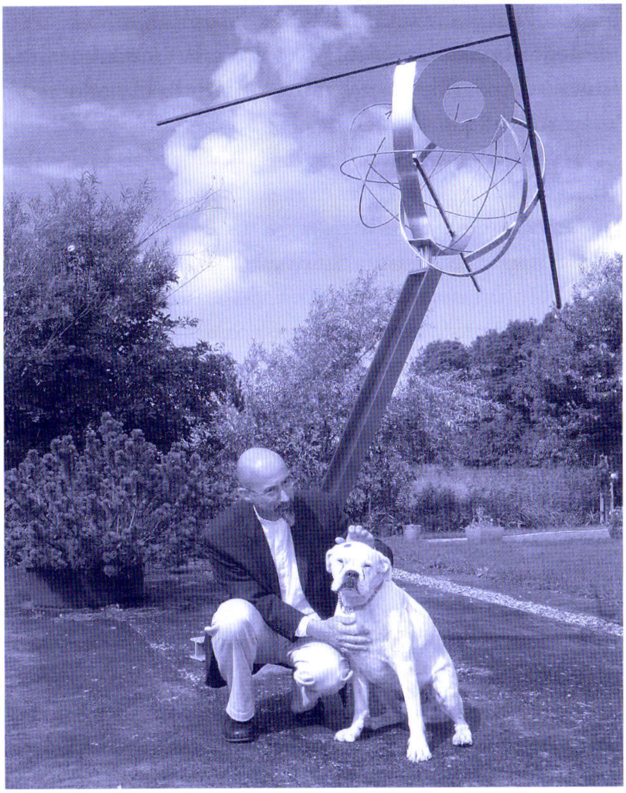

Fré Ilgen, MA, (Born 1956 in the Netherlands) studied art at the Academy of Fine Art Rotterdam. He went through surrealism and constructivism to find an idiosyncracy in his own work in a combination of geometry and gesture, both in sculptures and in paintings. He has lectured and exhibited widely in Europe, USA, Japan, Korea, and Australia. In 1986 he initiated the internationally active PRO Foundation, which originally focussed on constructive art and architecture. Since the early 1990's this non-profit organization has focussed on the analogies between art, science and philosophy. Ilgen likes to exchange the healing, tranquil climate of the Dutch country side, where he has his studios, with the hectic cultural life in New York, and other major cities in the world. He is a committed reader and is always looking for dialogue. He is also a committed collector and art lover.

www.ilgen.com/fre.htm

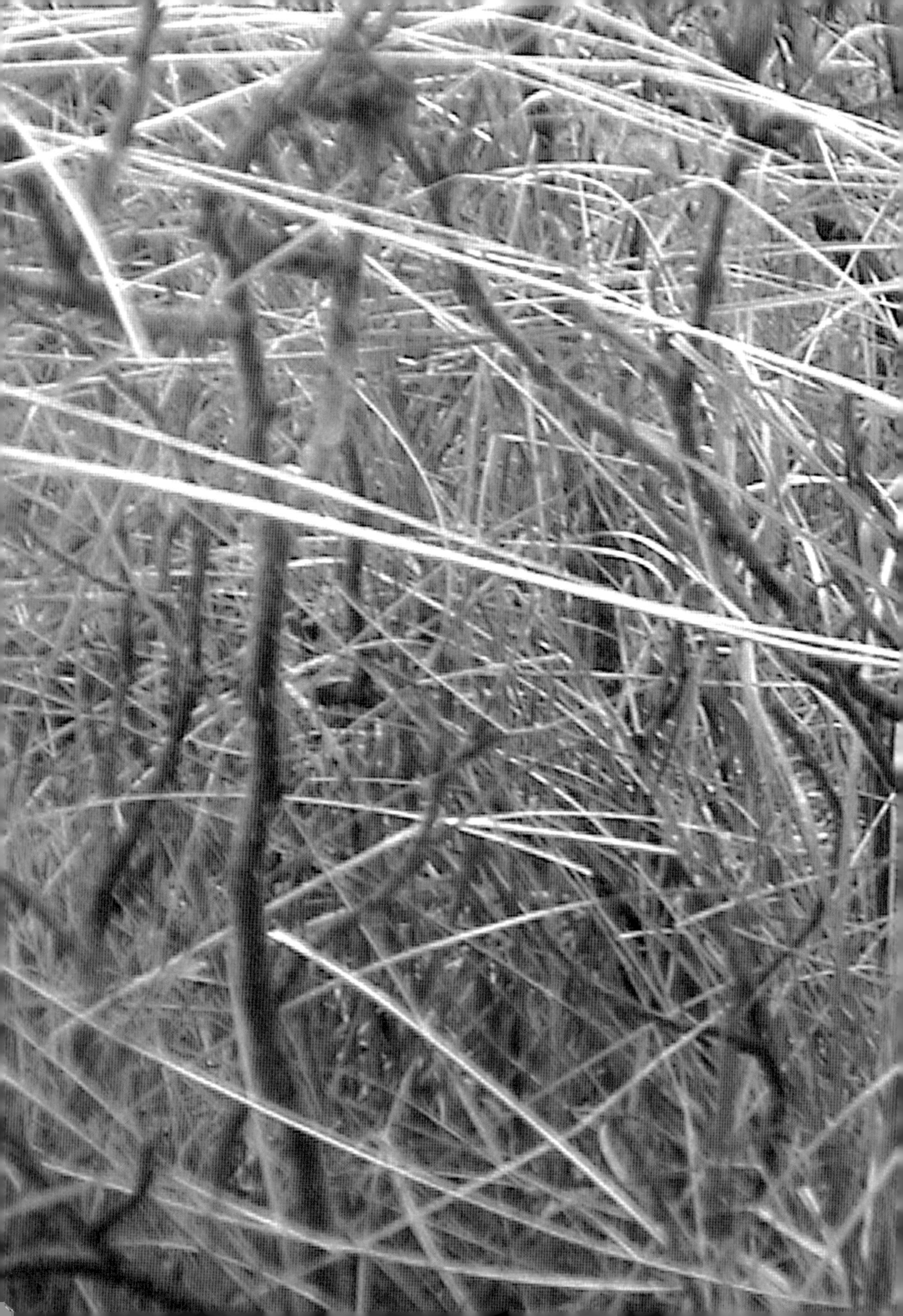

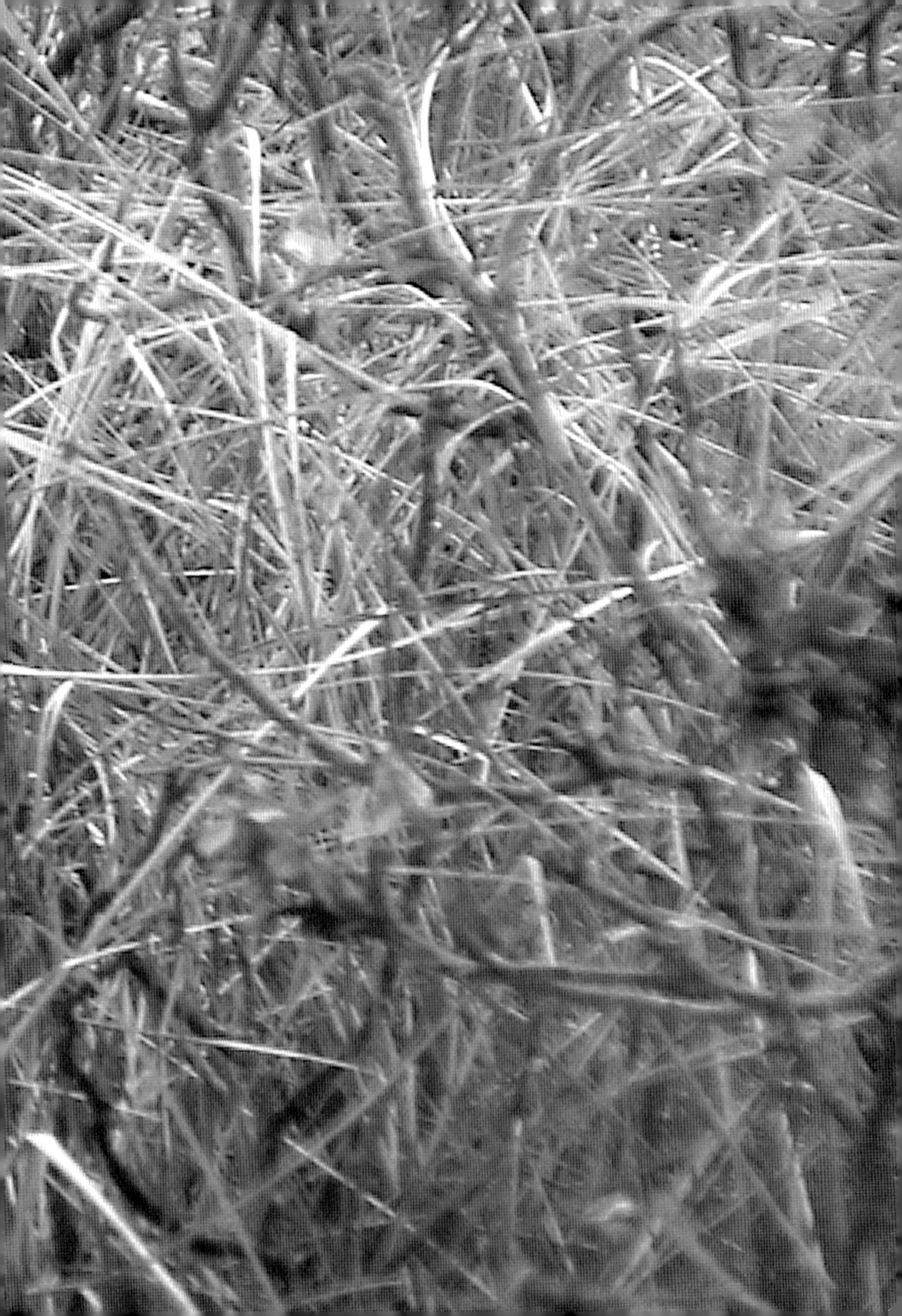